VICTIMOLOGY

LEGAL, PSYCHOLOGICAL, AND SOCIAL PERSPECTIVES

Fourth Edition

VICTIMOLOGY

LEGAL, PSYCHOLOGICAL, AND SOCIAL PERSPECTIVES

Harvey Wallace

Cliff Roberson

Boston Columbus Indianapolis New York San Francisco Upper Saddle River Amsterdam
Cape Town Dubai London Madrid Milan Munich Paris Montreal Toronto Delhi Mexico City
Sao Paulo Sydney Hong Kong Seoul Singapore Taipei Tokyo

Editorial Director: Vernon Anthony
Executive Editor: Gary Bauer
Editorial Assistant: Kevin R. Cecil
Media Project Manager: April Cleland
Director of Marketing: David Gesell
Marketing Manager: Mary Salzman
Senior Marketing Coordinator: Alicia Wozniak
Project Manager: Jessica H. Sykes
Creative Director: Jayne Conte
Cover Design: Suzanne Behnke
Cover Illustration/Photo: Corbis
Full-Service Project Management/Composition: Integra Software Services Pvt. Ltd.
Printer/Binder: Edwards Brothers/Malloy

Library of Congress Cataloging-in-Publication Data

Wallace, Harvey.
   Victimology: legal, psychological, and social perspectives / Harvey Wallace, Cliff Roberson.—Fourth edition.
      pages cm
   ISBN-13: 978-0-13-349552-2 (alk. paper)
   ISBN-10: 0-13-349552-3 (alk. paper)
   1. Victims of crimes—United States.   2. Victims of crimes—Legal status, laws, etc.—United States.
3. Criminal justice, Administration of—United States.   I. Roberson, Cliff, 1937-   II. Title.
   HV6250.3.U5W35 2015
   362.880973—dc23   2013029715

10 9 8 7 6 5 4 3 2 1

PEARSON

ISBN-10:   0-13-349552-3
ISBN-13: 978-0-13-349552-2

To Paul Harvey Wallace, coauthor, friend, and fellow Marine.
And to Elena Azaola for her tireless and dedicated work on behalf of the many
victims and to promote human rights in Latin American countries.

BRIEF CONTENTS

CONTENTS

PREFACE

The primary goal of the victims' rights movement needs to be to elevate victims' rights to the same status as the rights of the accused

—HARVEY WALLACE, 2005

NEW TO THIS EDITION

- Victimology as a discipline
- The birth of criminology
- The different approaches to victimization
- The Violence Against Women Act of 2013
- Expanded discussion on restorative justice
- Expanded discussion on the National Incident-Based Reporting System
- The consequences of grief
- Differences between ASD and PTSD
- Homeless victims
- Social media and victim services
- Vicarious/Secondary Trauma to Services Providers
- History of Amber Alerts
- How to develop a victim impact statement
- Significant partner homicides
- Sexual assault classifications
- National Child Abuse Prevention Month
- Sandusky child sex abuse and mandatory reporting
- Elder Justice Act of 2010

INTRODUCTION

Harvey Wallace was the sole author of the first edition of *Victimology*. Because of health problems when he was revising the textbook for the second edition, he asked for my assistance. We both assumed that his health problems were temporary. Little did we know that it would be one of the last projects that we would work on together. Harvey and I were friends and fellow Marines. We coauthored ten books over a sixteen-year time span. Harvey died shortly after completing the second edition. Before his death, he was teaching in the Victim Services Summer Institute presented by California State University, Fresno.

My first involvement with victim issues came in 1981 when the State Bar of Texas appointed a committee on victim issues. I was fortunate to be appointed to that committee, which was chaired by Dean John Douglas. During 1983–1984, when I served as the Director of Programs for the National College of District Attorneys, the DAs college began holding classes for career prosecutors on victim issues. For the college, victim issues were advocated by Norman S. Early, Jr., the then district attorney for the Second Judicial District in Denver, Colorado; Spencer Lawton, the then district attorney in Chatham County, Georgia (Savannah); and Michael Turpin, the then Attorney General of Oklahoma. In 1984 when I took over as Director of the Justice Center, California State University, Fresno, I authorized funds to hold a training course on victim services. The only reason that I authorized the funds was that I was being pressured to do so by Professor Steven Walker. It was easier to agree than to disagree with Stephen. Years later as a faculty member at Washburn University, I attended a conference in Kansas City on victim services. It was at this conference that the American Society of Victimology was founded and I joined as a life member. Unfortunately, the society has not been very active in recent years.

The study of victimology is in its infancy. However, the plight of victims of crime has been discussed for centuries. In our early history, victims were an integral part of the criminal process. We then moved away from that model, and the state became the representative of the victim. Finally, we are again moving toward acknowledging the rights of victims of crime. This shift has caused scholars to re-examine the victim–offender relationship in more detail.

Victimology as a discipline is an outgrowth of law, sociology, psychology, and criminology and as such has its distractors as well as its advocates. It will continue to grow and take on more substance with the passage of years. Any attempt to list those topics that are critical to the study of victimology is bound to generate controversy. Most textbooks on the market today include sections dealing with family violence issues. That may be because we have more information regarding the victim–offender interaction in these areas or because many scholars believe these are critical issues in the study of victimology. We have included a number of these same topics in this textbook.

We also drew upon Harvey Wallace's previous textbook, *Family Violence: Legal, Medical, and Social Perspectives,* published by Pearson and currently in its fifth edition, as a source of information. On the basis of comments from professors using this textbook, we have updated and changed the material when appropriate to reflect the victim's perspective.

We have also attempted to take a global perspective on the study of victimology. Chapter 1 introduces the reader to the discipline of victimology, a brief history of it and victimological theories. Chapter 2 presents an overview of the Justice System. Chapter 3 discusses the measurement of crime and its effects. The consequences of victimization are discussed in Chapter 4. Chapter 5 examines the empowerment of victims. Next, homicide victims are discussed in Chapter 6, followed by a discussion in Chapter 7 on Sexual Victimization. Intimate partner abuse, child abuse, and elder abuse are discussed in Chapters 8, 9, and 10. Chapter 11 looks at hate crimes, and in Chapter 12, special victim populations are discussed.

Chapter 13 explores tort actions. The constitutional and civil rights of victims are discussed in Chapter 14. Chapter 15 explores compensation and restitution for victims. The legal issues involved with victim impact statements are covered in Chapter 16. The final chapter examines the international aspects of victimology, and the textbook concludes with discussions on the discipline.

This is not to say that we have covered all these topics adequately. First Harvey, and now I have attempted to present an overview of some complex and controversial subjects and to supply the reader with resources in the form of references and readings that allow for more in-depth study and research of these areas. Omission of some topics, such as robbery, burglary, kidnapping, and others, does not mean that they are unimportant. Victims of these crimes would argue that they have suffered just as much as other victims. Space limitations, however, preclude discussion of every crime and its implications for victims. The crimes that are discussed, along with the broader topics such as the consequences of victimization and victims' rights, can be generalized to varying degrees to apply to all victims.

Just as we are becoming more interested in the study of family violence, so are increasingly more universities offering classes on victim issues. These classes will become more popular as students, the general public, and the various professionals who deal with victims become aware of their availability. It is a young discipline that continues to grow, and it is exciting to be present to watch that growth. Someday, maybe the victim will have as many rights as a defendant in a criminal case.

SUPPLEMENTS

To access supplementary materials online, instructors need to request an instructor access code. Go to **www.pearsonhighered.com/irc** to register for an instructor access code. Within 48 hours of registering, you will receive a confirming e-mail including an instructor access code. Once you have received your code, go to the site and log on for full instructions on downloading the materials you wish to use.

Here you will find:

- My Test
- Instructor's Manual with Test Bank
- PowerPoints

ACKNOWLEDGMENTS

On behalf of Harvey Wallace and me, I would like to express our appreciation to a number of individuals for their support, guidance, and advice during the time it has taken to complete this project. First and foremost, I would like to thank the editor, Gary Bauer, who provided support for this project. I would also like to thank Vinod Kumar, who assisted in the preparation and copyediting of the manuscript and the project manager, Allan Rayer for his assistance in creating the final product. Christine Edmunds, Anne Seymour, Ellen Alexander, Skip Sigmon, Trudy Gregorie, Janice Lord, Dan Eddy, Dean G. Kilpatrick, Jane Burnley, and other friends associated with various victim organizations provided their advice and guidance regarding a number of issues. Mario Gaboury, University of New Haven, and Steve Walker, California State University, Fresno, provided us with invaluable suggestions and corrections that helped improve this textbook. A special thanks to a friend and a tireless worker for victim rights, Stephanie Frogge , University of Texas at Austin. Thanks to the following reviewers: Brown, Kathleen, University of Pennsylvania; Muscat, Bernadette T., California State University, Fresno; Tolbert, Tracy F., California State University, Long Beach; Zimmerman, Gregory, University at Albany, SUNY. Deborah Barrett, Rowan-Cabarrus Community College; and Patrick Harvey, Slippery Rock University So many of Harvey's friends, colleagues, and students have helped me with this revision, I cannot begin to name them all. Some have been there to offer words of encouragement and support: Tom Dull, Otto Schweizer, and Arthur Wint are those good friends. Many professionals, colleagues, and academics have offered advice or suggested changes that have resulted in a better product: Thomas Underwood for his suggestions about discussing more theories and Steve Walker for his update on the history of victimology are just two of those professionals. Of special note is John Dussich, who made substantial suggestions regarding the textbook. John went through every page and updated or corrected the first edition. Most of those changes were incorporated into the second and third editions. Most important, there have been a number of students who have helped me in a variety of ways. Many graduate students, including Lindsey Fausett and Stephanie Fratto, were of great assistance in gathering various research materials for this textbook. Shiho Yamamoto, another graduate student, was also of invaluable assistance. She conducted much of the early research and was always there to assist in any manner. Finally, the many students who used this textbook in classes across the nation have contributed to its content with suggestions, questions, and comments. The nice thing about publishing with Pearson is working with the professionals such as Jessy Sykes, Gary Bauer, and Vern Anthony.

Cliff Roberson

Introduction and History of Victimology

Chapter Outline

LEARNING OBJECTIVES

After reading this chapter, you should be able to:

- Distinguish between criminology and victimology
- Discuss how laws have affected victims
- Understand social forces that have impacted on the development of victimology
- Distinguish between the various victimology theories

INTRODUCTION

Victimology in its most simple form is the study of the victim or victims of a particular offender. Victimology first emerged in the 1940s and 1950s, when several criminologists (notably Hans von Hentig, Benjamin Mendelsohn, and Henri Ellenberger) examined victim–offender interactions and stressed reciprocal influences and role reversals.[1]

Homicides in San Francisco

Coauthor Cliff Roberson in his PhD dissertation researched into the criminal homicides in San Francisco for the calendar years 1970 to 1972. In his research, he noted that there were two small convenience stores on one block in the city. One store had been robbed three times and each time an individual was murdered. The other store, which was across the street, had been robbed twice and no one had been injured in the robberies. While this is a very small sample and therefore any research conclusions would be suspect, it did raise the question of why the level of violence was much higher in one store than in the other similar store. This is the type of research that is of interest to researchers looking into the second component of victimology.

Victimology as an academic discipline is a relatively new concept in the United States. The first academic institution in the United States to offer a Bachelor of Science degree in criminology or criminal justice with a victimology option was the California State University at Fresno in the late 1990s.

The discipline of victimology can be divided into two separate components. One component deals with the injuries or harm suffered by victims, how to reduce victimization, and actions to be taken against the victimizer. This component will receive the vast majority of attention in this text. Too often when we talk about victims, we limit our discussion only to victims of crime. In this text we also include victims of other activities such as child abuse and bullying. The second and lesser known aspect of victimology deals with the victim–victimizer relationship. In this component, the victim's role in being selected as the victim is examined. Some individuals will claim that the second component is nothing but a "blaming the victim" approach. However, it is not so. The second component merely tries to understand why one person was selected over another person by the victimizer.

Victims Defined

In *Kelly v. California*, 129 S. Ct. 564 (U.S. 2008), Associate Supreme Court Justice John Paul Stevens stated:

> These two capital cases raise questions concerning the admissibility of so-called "victim impact evidence" during the penalty phase of a capital trial. The term is a misnomer in capital cases because the evidence does not describe the impact of the crime on the victim—his or her death is always an element of the offense itself. Rather, it describes the impact of the victim's death on third parties, usually members of the victim's family.

To most of us involved in victimology, the members of a murder victim's family are more than a "third party." According to Nash, the definition of "victim" is a slippery concept. Nash notes that as a matter of law, whether someone is a victim of a crime may depend, among other things, on the type and extent of injury sustained, the tenuousness of the connection of injury to the offender's conduct, and whether the victim was at fault in the criminal transaction. Nash also notes that the term "victim" is inconsistently applied in the various arenas of federal criminal law. While the definitions of "victim" found in the federal restitution and victims' rights statutes are functionally identical, the Federal Rules of Criminal Procedure define "victim" differently. It is interesting to note that the Federal Sentencing Guidelines do not define the term "victim," leaving the federal courts to sketch out the contours of its meaning.[2]

Victimology as a Discipline

Criminology is the science upon which victimology is founded. Criminology itself is a relatively new discipline, and there are those who argue that it is not a true academic discipline or science,

The Birth of Criminology

According to Adrian Raine, the scientific study of crime started one morning in November, 1871, in Italy. Cesare Lombroso, a psychiatrist and prison doctor at an asylum for the criminally insane, performed an autopsy on an infamous criminal named Giuseppe Villella. During the autopsy, Lombroso discovered an unusual indentation near the base of Villella's skull. Based on this single observation, Lombroso concluded that criminals were physically different from non-criminals.

_____

Source: Adrian Raine, *The Anatomy of Violence: The Biological Roots of Crime* (Random House, New York) 2014.

but rather a subspecialty of sociology.[3] However, there is an abundance of current literature and research to support the proposition that criminology is a science.

In 1947, Edwin H. Sutherland, an eminent criminologist, set forth the following definition:

Criminology is the body of knowledge regarding crime as a social phenomenon. It includes within its scope the process of making laws, of breaking laws.... The objective of criminology is the development of a body of general and verified principles and of other types of knowledge regarding this process of law, crime, treatment, or prevention.[4]

Criminology is the study of crime as a social phenomenon. Scholars have looked at several aspects of criminology, and several have presented definitions of victimology, which will be examined in detail later in this chapter. For purposes of clarity, however, the following definition of victimology is offered: **Victimology** is the study from the victims' perspective of the victim, the offender, and society. This definition can encompass both the research or scientific aspects of the discipline and the practical aspects of providing services to victims of crime. This combined definition allows for a wide-ranging examination of various issues affecting victims of crime.

A complete and accurate understanding of the concepts inherent in victimology can only be attained by a review of the development of law, its history, and its philosophy. Modern criminal law is the result of an evolutionary process in the development of law that has attempted to deal with deviant behavior in society.

FOCUS
Critical Dates in the History of Victimology

1750 B.C.—Code of Hammurabi adopted
1200 B.C.—Mosaic Code established
450 B.C.—Twelve Tables written
529 A.D. Roman Empire—Justinian Code drafted
1066 A.D.—Norman Conquest of England
Middle Ages—Development of common law
1215—Magna Carta signed
1787—U.S. Constitution created
1965—First victims' rights law passed
1976— NOVA established
1979—World Society of Victimology created
1985—United Nations Declaration

1996—U.S. constitutional amendment proposed
2003—American Society of Victimology established
2004—Crime Victims' Rights Act, which provides for fair treatment and opportunities for input in federal court proceedings, enacted by Congress. Office of the Victims' Rights Ombudsman was also established by the act
2004—The "Justice for All" Act was signed into law on October 30, 2004. The law includes a modified version of Senate Bill 2329, the statutory alternative to the Federal Crime Victims' Rights Amendment.
2013—The Violence Against Women Act is reenacted and is expanded to protect individuals involved in same gender relationships, in questionable immigration status, and individuals on American Indian reservations.

THE DEVELOPMENT OF LAWS

Primitive law was a system of rules used by preliterate societies to govern the tribe, clan, or other gathering of individuals. These rules or regulations represent the foundation upon which the modern legal system is built. Primitive laws usually contained three premises: (1) acts that injured others were considered private wrongs, (2) the injured party was entitled to take action against the wrongdoer, and (3) this action usually amounted to in-kind retaliation. These types of laws encouraged blood feuds and revenge as the preferred methods of making the victim whole.

As society continued to evolve, we learned the art of reading and writing. One result of this evolution was the development of written codes of conduct. An example of an early written code was the Code of Ur-Nammu, which dates back to the twenty-first century B.C. Many of these codes treated certain wrongs, such as theft or assault, as private wrongs, with the injured party being the victim.[5]

The Code of Hammurabi

The Code of Hammurabi is considered one of the first known attempts to establish a written code of conduct. King Hammurabi ruled Babylon at approximately 2000 B.C. He was the sixth king of the First Dynasty of Babylonia and ruled for nearly fifty-five years. Babylon during that period was a commercial center for most of the known and civilized world. Because Babylon's fortune lay in trade and other business ventures, the Code of Hammurabi provided a basis for order and certainty. The code established rules regarding theft, sexual relationships, and interpersonal violence, and it was intended to replace blood feuds with a system sanctioned by the state.[6]

The Code of Hammurabi had five sections:

1. A penal code listing the acts that were considered as criminal
2. A section containing instructions for judges, police officers, and witnesses
3. A section on the rights and duties of husbands, wives, and children
4. Regulations establishing wages and prices
5. An ethical code for merchants, doctors, and officials[7]

The code established certain obligations and objectives for the citizens of Babylon to follow. These included the following:

1. An assertion of the power of the state. This was the beginning of state-administered punishment. Under the code, the blood feuds that had occurred previously between private citizens were barred.
2. Protection of the weaker from the stronger. Widows were to be protected from those who might exploit them, elder parents from sons who would disown them, and lesser officials from higher ones.
3. Restoration of equity between the offender and the victim. The victim was to be made as whole as possible and in turn forgave vengeance against the offender.

Of noteworthy importance in the code was its concern for the rights of victims.[8] In reality, this code may have been the first "victims' rights statute" in history. However, it was relatively short-lived. Victims were again to be neglected in society's rush to punish the offender with the result that victims' rights would not resurface again until the mid-twentieth century.[9]

Other Early Codes and Laws

The Mosaic Code, which is based on the assumption that God entered into a contract or covenant with the tribes of Israel, had a long-lasting impact on our collective consciousness. According to legend, Moses returned from a mountaintop carrying the Ten Commandments, which were inscribed on two stone tablets. These commandments subsequently became the foundation of Judeo-Christian morality. The Mosaic Code also became the basis for many of the laws in our modern society: The prohibition against murder, perjury, and theft was present in the Mosaic Code thousands of years before the founding of the United States.[10]

Another important milestone in the development of American law was early Roman law. Roman law was derived from the Twelve Tables, which were written around 450 B.C. These laws had existed for centuries as unwritten law and applied only to the ruling patrician class of citizens. A protest by the plebeian class, who were the workers and artisans of Rome, caused commerce to come to a standstill. These workers wanted the law to apply to all citizens of Rome.[11] As a result, the laws were inscribed on twelve wooden tablets and prominently displayed in the forum for all to see and follow. These tables were a collection of basic rules relating to the conduct of family and religious and economic life.

In the middle of the first century, England was conquered by Roman legions. Roman law, customs, and language were forced on the English people during the next three centuries of Roman rule.

In 529 A.D., Emperor Justinian I codified Roman laws into a set of writings. The Justinian Code, as these writings became known, distinguished between two major types of laws: public laws and private laws. Public laws dealt with the organization and administration of the Republic. Private laws addressed issues such as contracts, possessions, and other property rights; the legal status of various persons such as slaves, husbands, and wives; and injuries to citizens. It contained elements of both our civil and criminal law and influenced Western legal theory into the Middle Ages.

Prior to the Norman Conquest of 1066, the legal system in England was very decentralized. There was little written law except for crimes against society. As a society, we had forgotten or moved away from the teaching of the Code of Hammurabi, and crimes during this period were again viewed as personal wrongs.

When an offense was committed, compensation was paid to the victim or to the victim's family. If the perpetrator failed to make payments, the victim's family could seek revenge, usually ending in a blood feud. For the most part during this period, criminal law was designed to provide equity to what was considered a private dispute.

The Norman Conquest under William the Conqueror established royal administrators who rode circuit and rendered justice. These royal judges would use local custom and rules of conduct as a guide in rendering their judgments. This system, known as **stare decisis** (Latin for the phrase "to stand by the decided law"), would have far-reaching effects on modern American criminal law.

The next major development in the history of law was the acknowledgment of the existence of common law. Early English common law forms the basis for much of our present-day legal system.[12] Common law is a traditional body of unwritten legal precedents created by court decisions throughout the Middle Ages in England. During this period, when cases were heard, judges would start their deliberations from past decisions that were as closely related as possible to the case under consideration. In the eleventh century, King Edward the Confessor proclaimed that common law was the law of the land, and subsequently court decisions were recorded and made available to lawyers who could then use them to plead their case. This concept is one of the most important aspects of today's modern American law.

Modern Codes and Laws

The Magna Carta of England and the U.S. Constitution both stand as great documents and great moments in the history of American law. The Magna Carta was signed on June 15, 1215, and was later interpreted to grant basic liberties for all British citizens. The U.S. Constitution established certain individual rights, defined the power of the federal government, and limited punishment for violation of laws.

American law combines both common law and written statutes. Statutory laws are enacted by state legislatures and Congress and are the major source of American criminal law today. These laws are usually compiled in various codes and are subject to revision by the legislatures.

An offshoot of written law, **administrative law** is made up of rules and regulations adopted by governmental agencies at the federal, state, and local levels. Many governmental agencies are invested with the power to pass regulations that prohibit certain types of conduct. Some of these regulations provide for fines rather than imprisonment of the offender.

In 1787, the U.S. Constitution was adopted. Constitutional law is another source of American criminal law. The Constitution does not define new crimes (the only crime defined in the Constitution is treason); rather it sets limits on other laws as they apply to individuals. An example of this principle is the U.S. Supreme Court ruling that flag burning, which was proscribed as criminal conduct by a state statute, is protected under the First Amendment right of freedom of expression.

SOCIAL FORCES

A number of forces in the past several decades have contributed to the development of victims' rights. The major contributing forces have been the feminist movement, the development of civil rights laws, and a growing conservatism regarding crime.[13]

The Feminist Movement

The feminist movement alerted us to centuries of discrimination and violence directed against women. By speaking out, feminists forced us to realize that women were victims not only of violent crime on the streets of cities, but also of sexual harassment within the work environment and family violence within the home. Although men may also become victims of crime and violence, the types of crimes suffered by women are distinct from those suffered by men.

Many of these crimes, although sexual in nature, are in fact nothing more than aggressive assaults that have little to do with sex. Sexual assaults are in reality a way for the perpetrator to control, dominate, and humiliate the victim.

Three works by feminist authors and researchers set the stage for the beginning of our awareness of the sexual victimization of women. Millett's *Sexual Politics,* Griffin's article "Rape: The All-American Crime," and Brownmiller's *Against Our Will* each raised our consciousness regarding the domination of women by men.[14]

Sexual Politics examines the concept of patriarchy, which Millett claims is a social and political system utilized by men to control women. She argues that patriarchy is a feature of all past and present societies and exists across cultures and socioeconomic systems today. Millett concludes that power and coercion are central features of patriarchy and are used to control women's sexuality.

Griffin's short article, "Rape, The All-American Crime," contains numerous themes. One important theme concerns the nature of the crime of rape. Griffin argues that rape is not a sexual act but rather a violent, political act. She concludes that the threat of rape is used as a method of social control and affects all women.

Brownmiller discusses the history of rape. She asserts that rape is an act used by men to maintain their dominance over women through the use of force. She expands on both Millett's and Griffin's works and concludes that the threat of rape creates a climate of fear. It is this fear that acts as a form of social control that benefits men.

Kelly, in her book *Surviving Sexual Violence,* reviewed these early feminist approaches to sexual abuse and concluded that sexual violence is based on three concepts: power, sexuality, and social control.[15]

Power in the feminist analysis is not police or political power; rather power is defined in terms of a relationship that structures the interactions between men and women. Power therefore is not a property right, but a personal force that establishes male control and dominance over women. This power is multifaceted and thus quite complex. It not only is present in interpersonal relationships but also extends to society's social structure and beliefs.

Sexuality has two aspects: First, male control of women's sexuality is a key factor in women's oppression; and second, sexuality is defined by men's experiences that legitimatize the use of force or coercion in intimate relationships. There is some conflict among feminists regarding the issue of sexuality and whether it has the same significance for women in all cultures.

Social control is the outcome of power and sexuality. The mere threat of sexual violence may result in women developing strategies for self-protection that will limit their mobility, work, or advancement. The reality of sexual violence not only impacts women in intimate and work relationships but also spills over into an environment that was previously thought safe: the campus setting. Many colleges and universities now provide "escort services" for women who attend evening classes. This measure speaks volumes for the fear that exists in all areas of our lives.

Millett, Brownmiller, Griffin, and other feminists laid the foundation that allows us to more fully understand the concept of sexual violence and women. The first concrete effort by feminist groups in the United States to help women who were victims of crime was the establishment of rape crisis centers in Berkeley, California, and Washington, D.C., in 1972. These centers have spread rapidly and are now an integral part of the criminal justice system. In 1976, the federal government established a comprehensive research program, the National Center for the Prevention and Control of Rape, within the Department of Health, Education, and Welfare (this agency is now called Health and Human Services).

The feminist movement not only attacked society's perceptions regarding victims of sexual assault but also focused its efforts on educating the public regarding domestic violence. It is important to note that at the same time battered women's shelters were being established, there was a growing awareness that victims of crime, as a class of citizens, were being treated unfairly by the criminal justice system. This awareness coincided with changes within the judicial system.

As a service provider in victim services, it is difficult to understand why anyone would hurt a young child. As we explore the various theories discussed in the text, ask yourself why a young child should suffer from violence.   © A.Drean/Fotolia.com

Development of Civil Rights Laws

During the 1960s and 1970s, a series of U.S. Supreme Court decisions established certain principles regarding the constitutional rights of individuals. These decisions were in the areas of both criminal procedure and civil rights. The Supreme Court established constitutional safeguards for those accused of crime. By interpreting the Constitution as applying to each and every individual, the court required that society afford those accused of crime certain procedural and substantive rights. These rights embraced the entire spectrum of liberties, including freedom from unreasonable search and seizures, the right to an attorney, and fundamental fairness during a criminal trial. By adopting a philosophy that individuals carried with them certain inalienable rights, the court was poised to expand this concept in the area of civil rights.

The Supreme Court acted to enforce both statutory and constitutional provisions during the 1960s and 1970s in the area of civil rights. These decisions allowed a black man to attend a previously all-white university, maintained that police officers could be held liable for use of excessive force, and required that all persons be treated equally under the law. As a result of these and other decisions, cases such as *Thurman v. City of Torrington*[16] (discussed in Chapter 14) were decided in favor of victims of family violence.

Conservatism Regarding Crime

Another factor that contributed to the awareness of the plight of victims arose as a result of a change in attitude in America. In the 1980s and 1990s, society became more conservative and concerned about crime in general. This law and order movement was a result of citizens becoming more fearful of violent crime and of many groups consequently calling for more stringent punishment of those who violate the law. In addition, the victims' rights movement was gaining momentum. Imprisoning offenders was viewed as a way of vindicating victims of crime. Victim organizations began lobbying for changes in the criminal justice system. These changes were aimed at making the system more victim-oriented. The rights of victims of family violence began to grow and expand as our society became more aware of this type of violence.

These forces brought about awareness on the plight and the dilemma of victims of crime.[17] As a result, victims began to realize that they could have an effect on sentencing in criminal cases and could pursue civil litigation to recover for damages they suffered as a result of the perpetrator's actions.

VICTIMOLOGY THEORIES

As with any new profession, many of victimology's early thinkers proposed theories or concepts that, on further study, were revealed as incorrect. However, by examining these early efforts, we can better understand the growth and present status of victimology. From its inception in the 1940s to the present day, victimology, like family violence, has been an interdisciplinary approach to violence and its effect on victims.

Mendelsohn's Theory of Victimization

Benjamin Mendelsohn was a practicing attorney. In the course of preparing a case for trial, he would conduct in-depth interviews of victims, witnesses, and bystanders.[18] He would use a questionnaire that was couched in simple language and contained more than 300 questions concerning the branches of criminology and associated sciences. The questionnaire was given to the accused and all others who had knowledge of the crime. In 1963, on the basis of these studies, Mendelsohn came to the conclusion that there was usually a strong interpersonal relationship between the offender and the victim. In an effort to clarify these relationships further, he developed a typology of victims and their contributions to the criminal act.[19] This classification ranged from the completely innocent victim to the imaginary victim. Mendelsohn classified victims into six distinct categories:

1. *The Completely Innocent Victim.* This victim may be a child or a completely unconscious person.
2. *The Victim with Minor Guilt.* This victim might be a woman who induces a miscarriage and dies as a result.
3. *The Victim Who Is as Guilty as the Offender.* Those who assist others in committing crimes fall within this classification.
4. *The Victim More Guilty Than the Offender.* These are persons who provoke others to commit a crime.
5. *The Most Guilty Victim.* This occurs when the perpetrator (victim) acts aggressively and is killed by another person who is acting in self-defense.
6. *The Imaginary Victim.* These are persons suffering from mental disorders such as paranoia who believe they are victims.

Many scholars credit Mendelsohn with coining the term *victimology*, and still others consider him the father of victimology.[20] His typology was one of the first attempts to focus on victims of crimes rather than to simply examine the perpetrator. However, Mendelsohn was only one of two early scholars who explored the relationship between victims and offenders. The other noted early researcher in victimology was Hans von Hentig.

Von Hentig's Theory of Victimization

In 1948, in an early classical text *The Criminal and His Victim*, von Hentig explored the relationship between the "doer" or criminal and the "sufferer" or victim.[21] Von Hentig also established a typology of victims.[22] This classification was based on psychological, social, and biological factors. Von Hentig established three broad classes of victims: the general classes of victims, the psychological types of victims, and the activating sufferer. His classification identified victims by examining various risk factors. The typology includes a general class of victims, the psychological class, and activating sufferer class.

The general class included the young, the female, the old, the mentally defective, and a group that consisted of minorities, immigrants, and weak individuals. The psychological class included the depressed, the lonely or heartbroken, the wanton, the acquisitive, and the tortmentor.

Von Hentig theorized that a large percentage of victims, because of their acts or behavior, were responsible for their victimization.[23] This concept has since been repudiated by modern studies that have more closely examined and defined the relationship between the victim and the offender.

Schafer's Functional Responsibility

In 1968, using von Hentig's approach, a third scholar was also instrumental in establishing another classification of victims. Stephen Schafer examined both Mendelsohn's and von Hentig's work in his text *The Victim and His Criminal* and attempted to classify victims on the basis of responsibility instead of risk factors.[24] Schafer believed that the study of the criminal–victim relationship indicated an increasing recognition that the criminal justice system must consider the dynamics of crime and treat both criminals and victims.

Schafer went on to state that "the study of criminal–victim relationships emphasizes the need to recognize the role and responsibility of the victim, who is not simply the cause of, and reason for, the criminal procedure, but has a major part to play in the search for an objective criminal justice [system] and a functional solution to the crime problem."[25] He stated that responsibility is not an isolated factor in society; rather it is an instrument of social control used at all times by all societies to maintain themselves.[26] Schafer believed responsibility was a critical issue in the problem of crime.

According to Schafer, crime was not only an individual act but also a social phenomenon. He believed that not all crimes simply "happen" to be committed, but that victims often contribute to crime by their acts of negligence, precipitate actions, or provocations. Schafer concluded that the functional role of a victim is to do nothing to prevent others from attempting to injure him and at the same time to actively prevent such attempts. In other words, this is the victim's functional responsibility.[27]

Wolfgang's Study of Homicide

From 1948 to 1952 in Philadelphia, Marvin E. Wolfgang conducted the first major study of victim precipitation.[28] He focused on homicides, studying both the victim and the offender as separate entities and as "mutual participants in the homicide."[29] Wolfgang evaluated 588 homicides and found that 26 percent (150) of all the homicides studied in Philadelphia involved situations in which the victim was a direct positive precipitator in the crime—the first to use force during the acts leading to the homicide.[30] Wolfgang's study and other theories of homicide are addressed in Chapter 6.

Karmen's Theory of Victimology

Scholars have continued to expand their scope of inquiry and explore other aspects of the victim's role in society. Karmen discusses the development of victimology and points out that those who study this relatively new discipline have three main areas of concentration:

1. Victimologists study the reasons (if any) for why or how the victim entered a dangerous situation. This approach does not attempt to fix blame on the victim; rather it examines the dynamics that resulted in the victim being in the risky situation.
2. Victimology evaluates how police, prosecutors, courts, and related agencies interact with the victim. How was the victim treated at each stage in the criminal justice system?
3. Victimologists evaluate the effectiveness of efforts to reimburse victims for their losses and meet the victim's personal and emotional needs.[31]

Karmen correctly points out that victimologists view the dynamics of the victim's role in society from a multidisciplinary perspective. There is still debate among scholars, however, regarding the correct or predominate role for the victimologist. Similar to the development and study of criminology, a number of different perspectives regarding victimology have also developed throughout the years.

OTHER THEORIES OF VICTIMOLOGY AND VICTIMIZATION

A number of more recent theories regarding victimology and victimization have emerged. Starting in the late 1970s, researchers began to examine victims and victimization from different perspectives and to also examine lifestyles and activities of potential victims. Many of the theories that developed from such research seek to examine the convergence of time, offenders, lack of guardians, and victims as the cause of victimization. Others look at society as a major factor in crime and victimization. This section briefly examines some of these newer victimology and victimization theories.

Lifestyle Theory

Hindelang and his colleagues examined exposure and guardianship as they relate to victimization. They call this theory the lifestyle approach to victimization, which argues that the likelihood of becoming a victim depends on an individual's lifestyle. In other words, various changes in everyday life and lifestyles are assumed to present a criminal opportunity by enhancing exposure and proximity of victims or targets to motivated offenders.[32]

Using the principle of homogamy, Hindelang argues that people are more likely to be victimized the more often they come into contact with groups that contain a larger share of potential offenders. For example, young persons are more likely than older persons to be victimized, since the young are more likely to come into contact with other youths who are disproportionately involved in crime or violence.

Routine Activities Approach

One of the more popular criminology theories dealing with crime trends and victimization was advanced by Cohen and Felson.[33] They argue that a "routine activities approach" should be used in analyzing crime trends and victimization. Routine activities are recurrent, prevalent activities that provide for basic population and individual needs. Routine activities may occur at home, in the workplace, or in other settings.

These researchers examined the circumstances surrounding a crime by looking at the convergence of space, time, motivated offenders, suitable victims or targets, and absence of capable guardians. Criminal violations are treated as routine activities that will occur when a set of circumstances converges. Cohen and Felson emphasized that the lack or absence of any of the three factors (offender, victim, and guardian) would probably prevent any criminal activity.

The Opportunity Model of Victimization

Cohen and several other associates later combined the lifestyle and routine activities theories to explain why income, race, and age affect the likelihood of victimization.[34] This approach examines five factors: exposure, guardianship, proximity, attractiveness of targets, and definitions of specific crimes. According to this theory, exposure and guardianship, which are aspects of the lifestyle theory, are not sufficient to establish a formal theory of victimization.

The opportunity theory links dimensions of social inequity to criminal victimization. It involves exposure to potential offenders; proximity between where victims or targets reside and where potential offenders are found; guardianship, which involves the effectiveness of persons or objects in preventing crime; target attractiveness, which is the desirability of persons or property to potential offenders; and definition of certain crimes, which establishes the difficulty in committing certain acts. For example, thefts are easier to commit than burglaries.

It is significant that Cohen does not blame persons for being victims. Rather, he and his associates approach the study of crime and victimization from the perspective that a number of factors cause crime, not just the victim.

Approaches to Victimization

It is often difficult for the reader to distinguish between the routine activities approach to victimization, the lifestyle theory, and the opportunity model of victimology. The three theories of victimization are similar and tend to build on each other. To help distinguish between the theories, a short statement on each is attached.

Routine Activities Approach

Routine activity theory is a subdivision of the crime opportunity theory. The theory focuses on situations of crimes. For example, you are more likely to be robbed or become a victim of assault on a city street than you when are in the safety of your home. For crime to be committed, three factors are needed: (1) a motivated offender, (2) a suitable target, and (3) the convergence at a time/place. The routine activity theory premise is that crime is relatively unaffected by social causes such as poverty, inequality, and unemployment.

Lifestyle Theory

Lifestyle theory focuses on crime victims rather than perpetrators. The main issue is that crime victims often become victims because of their own choices as to where to live, how to socialize, and other lifestyle-related variables.

Opportunity Model of Victimology

The opportunity model of victimization approach considers the time–space relationships in which victimization is greatest. The risk of criminal victimization is seen as largely dependent on the lifestyle and routine activities of persons that bring them and/or their property into direct contact with potential offenders in the absence of capable guardians who could potentially prevent the occurrence of a crime.

It appears that the opportunity model of victimology would apply to this situation. The victim is clearly in direct contact with her husband, who appears to be a potential abuser.   EJ White/Fotolia

Critical Victimology

Mawby and Walklate have proposed a view of victimology that they call critical victimology.[35] They define critical victimology as "an attempt to examine the wider social context in which some versions of victimology have become more dominant than others and also to understand how those versions of victimology are interwoven with questions of policy response and service delivery to victims of crime." They question why certain actions are defined as criminal and others are not. These scholars rightfully point out that many "crimes" committed by wealthy or powerful individuals or even by nations are not considered crimes. For example, genocide has occurred and is occurring in some countries, yet we do very little about it. Rape as a weapon of war has been reported in several countries. Abuse of power by those in control is very seldom mentioned as a crime in the media or other sources.

Victim Blaming

One of the most controversial areas of victimology has been and continues to be the concept known as victim blaming, victim responsibility, or victim perception. As discussed earlier in this chapter, some of the world's most prominent victimologists established classifications that included victims as a cause of criminal acts. Mendelsohn, von Hentig, Schafer, and Wolfgang all classified victims as having some form of causation in the commission of the crime.

The concept of victim perception was first used by Wolfgang in his study of homicide victims and later by Amir in one of the first studies of rape.[36] Wolfgang's interpretation dealt with situations in which the victim was a direct participator in the crime, while Amir's focused on the offender's perception of the victim's willingness to participate in the sexual act.

Wolfgang's study of homicide involved examination of homicide records in Philadelphia from 1948 to 1952. He reviewed these files and found that one out of four victims initially used force against their perpetrators. He also found that many of the victims were acquainted with the perpetrator. Amir was a student of Wolfgang, and in fact, Wolfgang wrote the introduction to Amir's text, *Patterns in Forcible Rape*. It is therefore hardly surprising that Amir would follow the same reasoning as his mentor, Wolfgang, when he analyzed the dynamics of rape.

Psychologist William Ryan has the distinction of coining the phrase "blaming the victim."[37] In his book, *Blaming the Victim*,[38] Ryan argues that the concept of victim blaming arose in the American middle class. This group of people is aware of the benefits they have and that others do not share these entitlements. This awareness creates a need to reconcile their status with others who are not as fortunate. One way to accomplish this is to accept the fact of violence and crime but blame the victim for letting it happen. This approach, argues Ryan, does not directly threaten the middle class and allows them to propose changes in society to address victimization. For example, poverty is caused under this victim-blaming approach because poor people share cultural values that make them poor and not because of any structural flaws that cause inequities in the distribution of income. The solution to poverty, according to Ryan, is to educate the poor people so that their values become more like those of the middle class.

The process of victim blaming has severe consequences for both the victim and society. For example, if the victim feels or perceives that he or she will be blamed or condemned by other members of society, the victim may not file a report of the crime. He or she may believe that the social cost of reporting the crime is too high a price to pay. Victims of certain crimes may also believe that reporting the offense may subject them to further victimization at the hands of the perpetrator. This is particularly true for crimes such as family violence, including incest, sexual assault by an acquaintance or relative, spousal abuse, and elder abuse. This failure or reluctance to report victimization is not confined to individuals. Corporations or other companies may feel pressure not to report crimes so as to avoid bad publicity and a possible drop in their stock prices. Our society suffers severe consequences when crimes are not reported, investigated, and prosecuted.

There is also a great deal of controversy surrounding the media's role in victim blaming—a debate that promises to be eternal. The media argue that they must represent the general public, and the public has a right to know all the facts surrounding any incident. Such facts may include the identity of the victim of any crime, including sexual assault. Victim advocates argue that exposing the identity of sexual assault victims increases the chances of their being revictimized. Some newspapers will not reveal the identity of sexual assault victims, while others may actually print their names or allow information to be broadcast or printed that will lead to their identification. As in so many areas of victimology, we are making progress, but we have a long way to go.

There are a number of other problems with victim blaming. First, victim blaming assumes that some victims share certain physical or psychological characteristics that cause them to be victimized. Others assume there is some sort of continuum that ranges from the totally innocent victim to the completely guilty victim.

American society is concerned with the rights of those who are accused of crimes. The first nine amendments to the U.S. Constitution focus on individual liberties and attempt to ensure that the government does not infringe upon these individual rights. However, the rights of victims of crime are not mentioned in these amendments. Kelly and Enez describe the evolution of the crime victim role as one moving from an eye-for-an-eye, in which victims were expected to deal with their perpetrator directly, to a system in which the king dispensed justice, and finally to its modern-day form in which the people of the state or federal government are the "victims," and the injured person is relegated to that of a witness.[39]

Emilio C. Viano, a prominent victimologist, has suggested that the victimization of individuals is better understood if we shift away from analyzing what they did, where they were, and how they reacted to the incident to looking at the cultural, social, and economic factors that support a view allowing for victim blaming. He argues that sexism, racism, and ageism are not always acknowledged to exist, and some would rather deny the existence of these forces and continue to blame the victim. He concludes that changing the focus of the inquiry will lead to a different understanding of what causes certain individuals or groups in society to be victimized.[40]

The movement away from victim blaming to victim protection is a relatively new process. We must continue to educate the professionals in the field as well as the general public about the dynamics of victimization to move away from this backward and harmful process of victim blaming.

VICTIM'S CONTRIBUTION TO THE CRIME

As noted in the preceding section, often a victim is blamed or seen as responsible for the crime. Many victim compensation programs either reduce or deny compensation if the victim contributed to the crime in any manner. For example, South Dakota Crime Victims' Compensation Program states: "The victim cannot contribute to the crime or the injury nor have committed a crime at the time of the incident. Claims may be reduced or denied based upon contribution/conduct." The problem with assessing the victim's contribution to the crime is that the contribution is being judged or assessed after the fact. Often, we take actions without thinking about them and later wish we had done something differently. A negligent act by a victim should not be considered as an invitation to be a crime victim.

As noted by Lynne Henderson, a determination of "relative badness" of the crime resembles the concept of comparative negligence and can produce unpredictable results. She notes that in one case, the defendant, convicted of driving under the influence and of manslaughter, received a minimal sentence for killing two drunken pedestrians, despite the arguments by the next of kin at sentencing for a harsh penalty. The sentencing judge observed that the pedestrians were "more to blame" than the driver for their deaths. Apparently, the judge did not appreciate the danger of driving under the influence.[41]

THE RISE OF THE VICTIMS' RIGHTS MOVEMENT

As the various social forces were developing, a series of events took place that began to raise the consciousness of the victims themselves regarding their impact on the criminal justice system.

The victims' movement, which gained momentum in the United States in the 1980s, continues to gain strength across the country. States continue to enact laws giving victims of crime more opportunities to participate in the criminal justice system. Therefore, those individuals who work or interact with victims need to understand the legal, psychological, and social aspects of victimology. While the victims' movement has advanced considerably since the 1980s, we still have a long way to go as noted in the following excerpt from a victims' service provider.

Currently, more than fifty academic institutions offer courses of study in victimology. In addition, some universities offer courses that examine various aspects of the victim–offender relationship. These courses are typically found in sociology, criminal justice, social work, criminology, and psychology. Victimology is a discipline that combines theoretical research with practical experience. Although there is some interaction between these two groups or approaches, there is still much to learn from the combination.

The Beginning of the Movement

During the late 1960s, victims of crime began volunteering to serve within various victim assistance programs. As these crime victims continued to speak out, states and the federal government reacted by establishing commissions to study crime and its consequences.

There were two federal responses to crime victimization during this period. One was the establishment of the National Crime Survey, which is discussed in more detail in Chapter 3. The second major action on the part of the federal government was the establishment of the Law Enforcement Assistance Administration (LEAA). This agency provided funds to law enforcement agencies for a variety of purposes including the establishment of victim–witness programs.[42] LEAA's role in fundraising is discussed in Chapter 5.

In 1974, the LEAA called a meeting in Florida of various victim advocates to discuss methods of increasing victims' rights. One consequence of this meeting was the formation of the National Organization for Victim Assistance (NOVA) in 1976. NOVA is considered one of the leading victims' rights organizations in the world.

Gains and Losses

During the late 1970s and early 1980s, the movement foundered. Lack of funding by the federal government caused many community-based victims' organizations and service providers to cease operations. In addition, within the movement, issues such as professionalism and training caused increasing divisiveness. The movement began to separate into specialized groups that focused on specific issues. Several sexual assault and domestic violence organizations, such as the National Coalition Against Sexual Assault, were established to address the specific needs of those victims.[43]

Although there was tension among various service providers because of diminishing funding and disagreement regarding specific goals, there was also progress in other areas of the victims' movement during this time period. Parents of Murdered Children (POMC) was founded by Robert and Charlotte Hullinger in 1978, and Mothers Against Drunk Driving (MADD) was founded by Candy Lightner in 1980. Both of these organizations continue to have an impact on the victims' rights and the victims' movement. In addition, Congress passed a federal Victims' Bill of Rights. By 1990, two-thirds of the states had enacted similar types of laws for protecting victims.

In what may become one of the most critical dates in the history of victims' rights, on June 25, 1996, President Clinton proposed a Victims' Rights Constitutional Amendment to the U.S. Constitution. In a speech made in the Rose Garden announcing the Victims' Rights Constitutional Amendment, President Clinton stated:

> Having carefully studied all of the alternatives, I am now convinced that the only way to fully safeguard the rights of victims in America is to amend our Constitution and guarantee these basic rights—to be told about public court proceedings and to attend them; to make a statement to the court about bail, about sentencing, about accepting a plea if the victim is present, to be told about parole hearings to attend and to speak; notice when the defendant or convict escapes or is released, restitution from the defendant, reasonable protection from the defendant and notice of these rights.[44]

The Victims' Rights Constitutional Amendment faces a long and complex process before it becomes law. It must be adopted by three-quarters of the states to become part of the Constitution. It is not something that will happen in a few weeks or months, and there are those who already claim that the proposed amendment is too detailed and should be made broader. No matter what the outcome, the simple fact that such an amendment has actually been proposed is a significant acknowledgment of the plight of victims of crime.

Increased Public Awareness

During 1982 through 1986, victims' organizations began to use the media to increase public awareness of crime victim issues. President Ronald Reagan, and Congress, responded to this heightened awareness with actions that would eventually have long-term consequences for the victims' movement. In 1982, President Reagan appointed a Task Force on Victims of Crime. This task force published a report that has since become a foundational platform for victims' rights.[45] The Office for Victims of Crime (OVC) was created in the Department of Justice to implement the task force's recommendations.

In 1984, another key event took place when Congress passed the Victims of Crime Act (VOCA).[46] This act established the OVC in the Office of Justice Programs, Department of Justice. The OVC provides grants to states for programs with direct services for victims of all crimes. VOCA also established the Crime Victims Fund to provide money to local victim assistance

Victims' Rights Constitutional Amendment

Section 1

To ensure that the victim is treated with fairness, dignity, and respect, from the occurrence of a crime of violence and other crimes as may be defined by law pursuant to section two of this article, and throughout the criminal, military, and juvenile justice process, as a matter of fundamental rights to liberty, justice and due process, the victim shall have the following rights: to be informed of and given the opportunity to be present at every proceeding in which those rights are extended to the accused or convicted offender; to be heard at any proceeding involving sentencing, including the right to object to a previously negotiated plea, or to a release from custody; to be informed of any release or escape; and to a speedy trial, a final conclusion free from unreasonable delay, full restitution from the convicted offender, reasonable measures to protect the victim from violence or intimidation by the accused or convicted offender, and notice of the victim's rights.

Section 2

The several States, with respect to a proceeding in a State forum, and the Congress with respect to a proceeding in a United States forum, shall have the power to implement further the rights established in this article by appropriate legislation.

Source: OVC, U.S. Department of Justice, Washington, D.C., 1996.

programs and state victim compensation programs. The fund receives money from federal criminal fines, penalties, and bond forfeitures. VOCA's operation is further examined in Chapter 15.

Increased Professionalism

From 1984 to the present, the victims' movement has been characterized by an increase in the professionalism of the victims' service advocates and providers. In previous times, the victims' movement was heightened by strong dynamic leaders with vision and determination. At present, the movement has expanded beyond the ability of any one person being able to influence its direction. It is now a national movement with a tremendous influence on local, state, and national politics.

Universities are expanding their victim-related courses. Various victims' organizations are offering increased training opportunities, and in 1995, the U.S. Department of Justice sponsored the first National Victim Assistance Academy in Washington, D.C. This academy was repeated in 1996 and 1997 using distance learning technology to link other universities in a joint academic effort.

The public awareness of victim issues continues to grow, and victim advocates have become an acknowledged force in modern politics. Victim services providers are realizing that their profession requires training that is multidisciplinary in nature. There is a growing awareness that to be accepted by other professionals requires continuing education, certifications, or other acknowledged credentials. This increased professionalism should translate into more sophisticated interventions and a faster rate of progress within the victims' movement.

Additional Laws

Increased professionalism also means increased knowledge and insight into the problems of victims. In 1994, Congress enacted the Violent Crime Control and Law Enforcement Act. Title IV of that law is entitled the Violence Against Women Act (VAWA). Congress mandated that various professions form partnerships and work together to respond to all forms of violence against women. The VAWA was reenacted and expanded in 2013. See the discussion on it later in this chapter.

The attorney general is required to make a report to Congress annually on the grants that are awarded under the act and ensure that research examining violence against women is encouraged. The report must include the number of grants, funds distributed, and other statistical information. In addition, the report must assess the effectiveness of any programs that are funded under VAWA.

The act provides funding for a variety of research-based studies. It also requires that federal agencies engage in research regarding violence against women. For example, the National Institute of Justice is mandated to conduct four important projects: (1) the development of a research agenda that will address violence with particular emphasis on underserved populations, (2) the assessment of establishing state databases to record the number of sexual and domestic violence incidents, (3) a study to determine how abusive partners obtain addresses of their victims, and (4) the examination with other agencies of the battered woman syndrome.[47]

Crime Victims' Rights Act of 2004

The Federal Crime Victims' Rights Act of 2004, 18 U.S.C. § 3771, provides that officers and employees of the U.S. Department of Justice shall make their best efforts to see that crime victims are notified of, and accorded, the following rights:

- The right to be reasonably protected from the accused.
- The right to reasonable, accurate, and timely notice of any public court proceeding, or any parole proceeding, involving the crime or of any release or escape of the accused.
- The right not to be excluded from any such public court proceeding, unless the court, after receiving clear and convincing evidence, determines that testimony by the victim would be materially altered if the victim heard other testimony at that proceeding
- The right to be reasonably heard at any public proceeding in the district court involving release, plea, sentencing, or any parole proceeding.
- The reasonable right to confer with the attorney for the government in the case.
- The right to full and timely restitution as provided by law.
- The right to proceedings free from unreasonable delay.
- The right to be treated with fairness and with respect for the victim's dignity and privacy.

The Federal Crime Victims' Rights Act has altered the landscape of federal criminal law. In addition, many states are following suit. For example, in May 2008, Oregon passed two constitutional amendments, affording victims legal standing to assert (rights of a party) and seek enforcement of their rights.

The 2009 case of *United States v. Okun* is an example of how the Crime Victims' Rights Act (CVRA) has altered proceedings in federal court.[48] In Okun, the government moved to permit up to 577 victims to be present at trial (eight of whom the government intended to call as witnesses at trial). The defendant opposed the motion and argued that the victim/witnesses do not qualify as victims under the CVRA because the defendant had not yet been proven guilty. The court held that this argument was "simply incorrect" because it would "eviscerate the rights given under

the CVRA to victims in any preconviction proceeding." Next, the defendant argued that the victim/witnesses should be excluded under Federal Rule of Evidence 615, which allows the court to exclude witnesses from the courtroom at the request of a party. The court disagreed, noting that the federal rules provide an exception if the potential witness is authorized by statute to be present. The court noted that the CVRA provides just such an authorization for victims of the crime being tried unless the defense makes a showing that the victim/witness's testimony would be "materially altered." Finally, the defendant argued that because of the number of victims, permitting them all to attend trial would be impractical. The court rejected this argument as well, finding it premature because there was no evidence that an unmanageable number of victims would attend the trial. The court noted that alternative means to attending trial—such as arranging for a closed-circuit television broadcast, webcast, or audio broadcast of the trial—could be considered, but that these alternate means would not be to exclude victim/witnesses based on the large number of victims.

Office of the Victims' Rights Ombudsman

The CVRA of 2004 also established the Office of the Victims' Rights Ombudsman. Accordingly, a crime victim may file a complaint against any employee of the U.S. Department of Justice who violated or failed to provide the rights established under the CVRA of 2004, 18 U.S.C. § 3771. The Department of Justice has established the Office of the Victims' Rights Ombudsman to receive and investigate complaints filed by crime victims against their employees and has implemented procedures to promote compliance with Crime Victims' Rights Obligations, 28 C.F.R. § 45.10.

A crime victim for the purposes of this act includes any person who has been directly and proximately harmed as a result of the commission of a federal offense or an offense in the District of Columbia. An employee of the Department of Justice includes any attorney, investigator, law enforcement officer, or other personnel employed by any division or office of the Department of Justice whose regular course of duties includes direct interaction with crime victims (not including a contractor).

Violence Against Women Act of 2013

In February 2013, the U.S. Congress recognized the continuing need to prevent domestic abuse and the need for a national strategy with the re-enactment of the Violence Against Women Act (VAWA) originally enacted in 1994.

According to the Congressional hearings, VAWA has improved the criminal justice response to violence against women by:

- holding rapists accountable for their crimes by strengthening federal penalties for repeat sex offenders and creating a federal "rape shield law," which is intended to prevent offenders from using victims' past sexual conduct against them during a rape trial;
- mandating that victims, no matter their income levels, are not forced to bear the expense of their own rape exams or for service of a protection order;
- keeping victims safe by requiring that a victim's protection order will be recognized and enforced in all state, tribal, and territorial jurisdictions within the United States;
- increasing rates of prosecution, conviction, and sentencing of offenders by helping communities develop dedicated law enforcement and prosecution units and domestic violence dockets;
- ensuring that police respond to crisis calls and judges understand the realities of domestic and sexual violence by training law enforcement officers, prosecutors, victim advocates, and judges; VAWA funds train over 500,000 law enforcement officers, prosecutors, judges, and other personnel every year;
- providing additional tools for protecting women in Indian country by creating a new federal habitual offender crime and authorizing warrantless arrest authority for federal law enforcement officers who determine there is probable cause when responding to domestic violence cases.

There was testimony at the Congressional hearings that VAWA has ensured that victims and their families have access to the services they need to achieve safety and rebuild their lives by:

- responding to urgent calls for help by establishing the National Domestic Violence Hotline, which has answered over 3 million calls and receives over 22,000 calls every month; 92 percent of callers report that it's their first call for help;

- improving safety and reducing recidivism by developing coordinated community responses that bring together diverse stakeholders to work together to prevent and respond to violence against women;
- focusing attention on the needs of underserved communities, including creating legal relief for battered immigrants so that abusers cannot use the victim's immigration status to prevent victims from calling the police or seeking safety, and supporting tribal governments in building their capacity to protect American Indian and Alaska Native women.

Testimony presented at the hearing indicated that since VAWA was originally passed, the following progress has been made:

- Fewer people are experiencing domestic violence.
- Between 1993 and 2010, the rate of intimate partner violence declined 67 percent.
- Between 1993 and 2007, the rate of intimate partner homicides of females decreased 35 percent and the rate of intimate partner homicides of males decreased 46 percent.
- More victims are reporting domestic and sexual violence to police, and reports to police are resulting in more arrests.
- States have reformed their laws to take violence against women more seriously.
- All states have reformed laws that previously treated date or spousal rape as a lesser crime than stranger rape.
- All states have passed laws making stalking a crime.
- All states have authorized warrantless arrests in misdemeanor domestic violence cases where the responding officer determines that probable cause exists.
- All states provide for criminal sanctions for the violation of a civil protection order.
- Many states have passed laws prohibiting polygraphing of rape victims.
- Over 35 states, the District of Columbia, and the U.S. Virgin Islands have adopted laws addressing domestic and sexual violence, and stalking in the workplace. These laws vary widely and may offer a victim time off from work to address the violence in their lives, protect victims from employment discrimination related to the violence, and/or provide unemployment insurance to survivors who must leave their jobs because of the abuse.

Summary

The history of victimology is in many ways the history of our world. As long as there has been crime, there have been victims who have suffered. Early law viewed crime as a personal act that required response by the victim or by the victim's family. The Code of Hammurabi, although harsh and violent, recognized victims as injured parties and may have been the first victims' rights law. Other codes and laws evolved throughout history to shape our modern concept of justice.

A number of social forces affected the development of victimology. The feminist movement raised our awareness of the plight of women. The civil rights movement resulted in a number of laws being passed that afforded individuals certain rights. As crime increased, our society became increasingly conservative and became more aware of the trauma suffered by victims of crime.

Theories regarding victimization have undergone a subtle but encouraging change. We have moved from the victim being the cause of the crime to studying how crime occurs and how persons are selected as victims. These newer theories include lifestyle theory, the routine activity approach, and opportunities model of victimization. It is a major accomplishment within victimology that we are developing our own theories as they relate to victimization.

The victims' rights movement began as a small group of volunteers who themselves were crime victims and who had been victimized a second time as a result of their involvement with the criminal justice system. This small group of volunteers has grown and become a powerful force in America that continues to expand and change the way we view victimology.

The CVRA of 2004 provided certain rights to victims involved with the federal criminal justice system. The act also established the Office of the Victims' Rights Ombudsman. In 2013, the Violence Against Women Act was re-enacted and expanded to protect victims in same gender relationships, victims in questionable immigration status, and victims on American Indian reservations.

Key Terms

Criminology is the study of crime as a social phenomenon.

Victimology is the study of the victim, the offender, and society.

Primitive law was a system of rules in preliterate societies.

Stare decisis means to stand by the decided law.

Administrative law is made up of rules and regulations adopted by governmental agencies at the federal, state, and local levels.

Discussion Questions

1. Explain why some authorities call the Hammurabi Code the first victims' rights law.
2. What was the most significant event in the development of law that has affected the victims' movement?
3. Is the feminist movement still important to the victims' movement? Why?
4. Compare and contrast von Hentig's and Mendelsohn's theories of victimology.
5. Why is Schafer's theory of functional responsibility important?
6. Wolfgang studied homicide; how does this relate to the study of victimology?
7. Discuss the other theories of victimology.
8. Has the victims' movement reached its full potential? Name three specific goals that the movement should strive for in the next ten years.

Suggested Readings

G. B. Vold & T. J. Bernard, *Theoretical Criminology,* 3rd ed. (Oxford University Press, New York) 1986.

Sir Henry Summer Maine, *Ancient Law,* 10th ed. (John Murray, London) 1905.

S. Schafer, *The Victim and His Criminal* (Random House, New York) 1968.

R. Masters & C. Roberson, *Inside Criminology* (Prentice-Hall, Englewood Cliffs, N.J.) 1985.

I. Drapkin & E. Viano, eds., *Victimology: A New Focus,* vol. 2 (D.C. Heath, Lexington, Mass.) 1974.

S. A. Cook, *The Laws of Moses and the Code of Hammurabi* (Adam and Charles Black, London) 1903.

S. T. Reed, *Criminal Justice,* 3rd ed. (Macmillan Publishing Company, New York) 1993.

A. Karmen, *Crime Victims: An Introduction to Victimology,* 2nd ed. (Wadsworth, Belmont, Calif.) 1995.

L. Kelly, *Surviving Sexual Violence* (University of Minnesota Press, Minneapolis, Minn.) 1988.

N. A. Weiner & M. E. Wolfgang, eds., *Pathways to Criminal Violence* (Sage, Newbury Park, Calif.) 1989.

Emilio C. Viano, *Victim/Witness Services: A Review of the Model* (GPO, Washington, D.C.) 1979.

President's Task Force on Victims of Crime (Final Report, GPO, Washington, D.C.) December 1982.

J. M. Sqazi & J. McDevitt, *Victimology: A Study of Crime Victims and Their Roles* (Prentice Hall, Englewood Cliffs, N.J.) 2002.

A. Karmen, *Crime Victims: An Introduction to Victimology* (Wadsworth Publishing, Belmont, Calif.) 2006.

L. J. Moriarty, *Controversies in Victimology* (Anderson Publishing, Cincinnati, Ohio) 2003.

Endnotes

1. "Victimology," Encyclopædia Britannica. Encyclopædia Britannica Online (April 6, 2009); available online: www.britannica.com/EBchecked/topic/1246187/victimology.
2. Andrew Nash, "Victims by Definition," 85 *Washington University Law Review*, 1419 (2008).
3. For an excellent discussion of criminology as a science, see G. B. Vold and T. J. Bernard, *Theoretical Criminology,* 3rd ed. (Oxford University Press, New York) 1986.
4. Edwin H. Sutherland, *Principles of Criminology,* 4th ed. (Lippincott, Philadelphia, Pa.) 1947.
5. Sir Henry Summer Maine, *Ancient Law,* 10th ed. (John Murray, London) 1905.
6. S. Schafer, *The Victim and His Criminal* (Random House, New York) 1968.
7. Masters & C. Roberson, *Inside Criminology* (Prentice-Hall, Englewood Cliffs, N.J.) 1985.
8. H. Gordon, *Hammurabi's Code: Quaint or Forward Looking* (Rinehart, New York) 1957.
9. G. O. Mueller & H. H. A. Cooper, "Society and the Victim: Alternative Responses," in I. Drapkin & E. Viano, eds., *Victimology: A New Focus,* vol. 2 (D. C. Heath, Lexington, Mass.) 1974, pp. 85–102.
10. S. A. Cook, *The Laws of Moses and the Code of Hammurabi* (Adam and Charles Black, London) 1903.
11. O. W. Mueller, "Tort, Crime and the Primitive," 43 *Journal of Criminal Law, Criminology, and Police Science,* 303 (1955).
12. S. T. Reed, *Criminal Justice,* 3rd ed. (Macmillan Publishing Company, New York) 1993.
13. A. Karmen, *Crime Victims: An Introduction to Victimology,* 2nd ed. (Brooks/Cole, Pacific Grove, Calif.) 1985.
14. K. Millett, *Sexual Politics* (Abacus, London) 1972; S. Griffin, "Rape: The All-American Crime," 10(3) *Ramparts,* 26–35 (1971); and S. Brownmiller, *Against Our Will: Men, Women and Rape* (Penguin Books, New York) 1975.
15. L. Kelly, *Surviving Sexual Violence* (University of Minnesota Press, Minneapolis, Minn.) 1988.
16. 595 F. Supp. 1521 (Conn. 1984).
17. G. D. Gottfredson, "The Experiences of Violent and Serious Victimization," in N. A. Weiner & M. E. Wolfgang, eds., *Pathways to Criminal Violence* (Sage, Newbury Park, Calif.) 1989, pp. 202–234.
18. B. Mendelsohn, "The Origin and Doctrine of Victimology," 3 *Excerpta Criminologica,* 239–244 (June 1963).
19. Schafer, *The Victim and His Criminal.*
20. B. Mendelsohn, "Rape in Criminology," *Giustizia Penale,* 1940.
21. Hans von Hentig, *The Criminal and His Victim* (first published by Yale University Press, New Haven, Conn. 1948 and republished by Schocken Books, New York 1979) (Hereafter *The Criminal and His Victim*).
22. Some scholars have subdivided von Hentig's original typology (probably for ease of understanding). See, for example, Doerner and Lab, *Victimology* (West Publishing, St. Paul, Minn.) 1994, where the authors list thirteen classifications. They arrive at this number by listing immigrants, minorities, and dull normals as separate categories instead of one subdivision as von Hentig did.
23. H. von Hentig, *The Criminal and His Victim* (Yale University Press, New Haven, Conn.) 1948.
24. Schafer, *The Victim and His Criminal.*
25. Ibid. at p. 5.
26. Ibid. at p. 139.
27. Ibid. at p. 152.
28. M. E. Wolfgang, *Patterns of Criminal Homicide* (University of Pennsylvania Press, Philadelphia, Pa.) 1958.
29. M. E. Wolfgang, *Analytical Categories for Research in Victimization* (Kriminologische Wegzeichen, Munich, Germany) 1967, p. 17.
30. Ibid. at pp. 24, 72.
31. Andrew Karmen, *Crime Victims, An Introduction to Victimology,* 2nd ed. (Brooks/Cole, Pacific Grove, Calif.) 1995.
32. M. Hindelang, M. Gottfredson, & J. Garofalo, *Victims of Xpersonal Crime: An Empirical Foundation for a Theory of Xpersonal Victimization* (Ballinger, Cambridge, Mass.) 1978.
33. Lawrence E. Cohen & Marcus Felson, "Social Change and Crime Rate Trends: A Routine Activity Approach," *American Sociological Review,* 588 (1979).
34. Lawrence E. Cohen, James R. Kluegel, & Kenneth C. Land, "Social Inequality and Xpredatory Criminal Victimization: An Exposition and Test of a Formal Theory," *American Sociological Review,* 505 (1981).
35. R. I. Mawby & S. Walklate, *Critical Victimology, International Perspectives* (Sage, Thousand Oaks, Calif.) 1994, p. 21.
36. M. Amir, *Patterns in Forcible Rape* (University of Chicago Press, Chicago) 1971.
37. L. W. Kennedy & V. F. Sacco, *Crime Victims in Context* (Roxbury Publishing, Los Angeles) 1998.
38. W. Ryan, *Blaming the Victim* (Vintage Books, New York) 1976.
39. R. C. Davis, A. J. Lurigio, & W. G. Skogan, eds., *Victims of Crime* 2nd ed. (Sage, Thousand Oaks, Calif.) 1997, p. 232.

40. E. C. Viano, "Victimology Today: Major Issues in Research and Public Policy," in E. C. Viano, ed., *Crime and Its Victims: International Research and Public Policy Issues* (Hemisphere, New York) 1989, pp. 3–14.

41. Lynne Henderson, "The Wrongs of Victim's Rights," 37 *Stanford Law Review*, 957 (1985).

42. Emilio C. Viano, *Victim/Witness Services: A Review of the Model* (GPO, Washington, D.C.) 1979.

43. M. Largen, "Grassroots Centers and National Task Forces: A Herstory of the Anti-Rape Movement," 32 *Aegis,* 46–52 (Autumn 1981).

44. "Remarks by the President at Announcement of Victims Constitutional Amendment," *Press Release* (The White House, Office of the Press Secretary, Washington, D.C.) June 25, 1996, p. 2.

45. *President's Task Force on Victims of Crime* (Final Report, GPO, Washington, D.C.) December 1982.

46. Victims of Crime Act of 1984, 42 U.S.C. Section 10601 (1984).

47. Jeremy Travis, "Violence Against Women: Reflections on NIJ's Research Agenda," 230 *National Institute of Justice Journal,* 21–35 (February 1996).

48. Crim. No. 3:08cr132, 2009 U.S. Dist. LEXIS 24401 (E.D. Vir. Mar. 24, 2009).

2

An Overview of the Justice System

Chapter Outline

LEARNING OBJECTIVES

After reading this chapter, you should be able to:

- Understand the principle of federalism and how it affected the structure of our court system
- Discuss how the dual system of state and federal courts functions
- Describe the characteristics of the American court system
- Discuss how the juvenile court system functions
- Understand the roles and responsibilities of each party in the criminal justice system
- Describe the various steps in the criminal justice process

- Explain the differences between the various types of pleas a defendant may enter
- Explain the basic differences between a criminal and a civil trial
- Understand the concepts of negligence and intentional torts
- Describe the various stages of a civil trial
- Discuss the phases of a juvenile dependency hearing

THE COURT SYSTEMS

Introduction

Understanding the role and functions of the various court systems in the United States provides professionals with a solid foundation for understanding the dynamics of the law. It is a complex aspect of our legal system that can be confusing and frustrating to victims when they are first exposed to it. Understanding the rationale behind its present-day structure may help victims understand more clearly the manner in which laws operate and interact.

To comprehend the role of federal and state law, it is essential to have a firm grasp of the principles of how the American justice system functions. For a victim of crime, it is the most confusing, frustrating, and complex environment to navigate. This section will provide a brief overview of the court systems in the United States.

The court systems in the United States are based on the principle of federalism. The first Congress established a federal court system, and the individual states were permitted to continue their own judicial structure. There was general agreement among our nation's founders that individual states needed to retain significant autonomy from federal control. Under this concept of federalism, the United States developed as a loose confederation of semi-independent states having their own courts, with the federal court system acting in a very limited manner. In the early history of our nation, most cases were tried in state courts. It was only later that the federal government and the federal judiciary began to exercise jurisdiction over crimes and civil matters. **Jurisdiction** in this context simply means the ability of the court to enforce laws and punish individuals who violate those laws.

As a result of this historical evolution, a dual system of state and federal courts exists today. Therefore, federal and state courts may have concurrent jurisdiction over specific crimes. For example, a person who robs a bank may be tried and convicted in state court for robbery, then tried and convicted in federal court for the federal offense of robbery of a federally chartered savings institution.

Another characteristic of the American court system is that it performs its duties with little or no supervision. A Supreme Court justice does not exercise supervision over lower court judges in the same way that a government supervisor or manager exercises control over employees. The U.S. Supreme Court and the various state supreme courts exercise supervision only in the sense that they hear appellate cases from lower courts and establish certain procedures for these courts.

A third feature of the U.S. court systems is one of specialization and occurs primarily at the state and local level. In many states, courts of limited jurisdiction hear misdemeanor cases. Other state courts of general jurisdiction try felonies. Still other courts may be designated as juvenile courts and hear only matters involving juveniles. This process also occurs in certain civil courts that hear only family law matters, probate matters, or civil cases involving damages. At the federal level, there are courts such as bankruptcy that hear only cases dealing with specific matters.

The fourth characteristic of the American court systems is its geographic organization. State and federal courts are organized into geographic areas. In many jurisdictions, these are called judicial districts and contain various levels of courts. For example, on the federal level, the U.S. Court of Appeals for the Ninth Circuit has district (trial) courts that hear matters within certain specific boundaries and an appellate court that hears all appeals from cases within that area. Several studies have been conducted regarding the differences in sentences for the same type of crime in geographically distinct courts. For example, in Iowa the average sentence for motor vehicle theft is forty-seven months, whereas the average sentence for the same offense in New York is fourteen months.[1] This and similar discrepancies may reflect different social values and attitudes within specific geographic areas.

State Court Systems

Historically, each of the thirteen original states had its own unique court structure. This independence continued after the American Revolution and resulted in widespread differences among the various states, some of which still exist today. Because each state adopted its own system of courts, the consequence was a poorly planned and confusing judicial structure. Several reform movements have attempted to streamline and modernize this system. These reforms have resulted in many of the state court systems adopting a three-tier judicial system.

Most state courts are now divided into three levels:

- Trial courts
- Appellate courts
- State supreme courts

TRIAL COURTS **Trial courts** are courts where civil and criminal cases start and finish. The trial court conducts an entire series of acts that culminate in either the defendant's release or sentencing. State trial courts can be further divided into courts of limited or special jurisdiction and courts of general jurisdiction. The nature and type of case determines which court will have jurisdiction.

Courts that only hear and decide certain limited legal issues are courts of **limited jurisdiction**. These courts hear and decide issues such as traffic tickets or set bail for criminal defendants. Typically, these courts hear certain types of minor civil or criminal cases. There are approximately 13,000 local courts in the United States. They are called county, magistrate, justice, or municipal courts. Judges in these courts may be either appointed or elected. In many jurisdictions, these are part-time positions, and the incumbent may have another job or position in addition to serving as a judge. However, simply because they handle minor civil and criminal matters does not negate the fact that these courts perform important duties. Often, the only contact the average citizen will have with the judicial system occurs at this level.

In addition, courts of limited jurisdiction may hear certain types of specialized matters, such as probate of wills and estates, divorces, child custody matters, and juvenile hearings. These types of courts may be local courts or, depending on the state, courts of general jurisdiction that are designated by statute to hear and decide specific types of cases. For example, in California a superior court is considered a court of general jurisdiction; however, certain superior courts are designated to hear only juvenile matters, thereby becoming a court of limited jurisdiction when sitting as a juvenile court.

Courts of **general jurisdiction** are granted authority to hear and decide all issues that are brought before them. These courts normally hear all major civil or criminal cases. They are also known by a variety of names, such as superior courts, circuit courts, district courts, or courts of common pleas. Because they are courts of general jurisdiction, they have authority to decide issues that occur anywhere within the state. Some larger jurisdictions such as Los Angeles or New York may have numerous courts of general jurisdiction within the city limits. These courts also hear the most serious forms of criminal matters, including death penalty cases.

Courts of general jurisdiction traditionally have the power to order individuals to do, or refrain from doing, certain acts. These courts may issue injunctions that prohibit persons from performing certain acts, or they may require individuals to do certain functions or duties. This authority is derived from the equity power that resides in courts of general jurisdiction.

In some states, like California, there is a unification movement which merges the inferior courts and the courts of general jurisdiction into one court that handles matters that were in the past handled by either the inferior courts or courts of general jurisdiction. The unification movement is an attempt by states to reduce the costs of their justice systems.

Equity is the concept that justice is administered according to fairness, as contrasted with the strict rules of law. In early English common law, such separate courts of equity were known as courts of Chancery. These early courts were not concerned with technical legal issues; rather they focused on rendering decisions or orders that were fair or equitable. In modern times, the power of these courts has been merged with courts of general jurisdiction, allowing them to rule on matters that require fairness as well as the strict application of the law. The power to issue temporary restraining orders (TROs) in intimate partner abuse cases comes from the equitable powers of the court.

Appellate jurisdiction is reserved for courts that hear appeals from both limited and general jurisdiction courts. These courts do not hold trials or hear evidence. They decide matters of law and issue formal written decisions or "opinions." There are two classes of appellate courts: intermediate, or courts of appeals and final, or supreme courts.

COURTS OF APPEALS The intermediate appellate courts are known as courts of appeals. Approximately half the states have designated intermediate appellate courts. These courts may be divided into judicial districts and will hear all appeals within their jurisdiction. They will hear and decide all issues of law that are raised on appeal in both civil and criminal cases. Because these courts deal strictly with legal or equitable issues, there is no jury to decide factual disputes. These courts accept the facts as determined by the trial courts. Intermediate appellate courts have the authority to reverse the decision of the lower courts and to send the matter back with instructions to retry the case in accordance with their opinion. They may also uphold the decision of the lower court. In either situation, the party that loses the appeal at this level may file an appeal with the next higher appellate court.

SUPREME COURTS Final appellate courts are the highest state appellate courts. They may be known as supreme courts or courts of last resort. There may be five, seven, or nine justices sitting on this court depending on the state. Final appellate courts have jurisdiction to hear and decide issues dealing with all matters decided by lower courts, including ruling on state constitutional or statutory issues. Their decision is binding on all other courts within the state. Once this court has decided an issue, the only appeal left is to file in the federal court system. There are two state court systems in which the state supreme courts do not hear criminal cases. In Oklahoma and in Texas there is a separate state criminal court of appeals that decides appeals only in criminal cases.

Juvenile Court Systems

Because of the significant increase in the importance of juvenile crime in our society, a brief overview of juvenile courts is warranted. Although there are some differences, both federal and state systems were initially founded on the concept of rehabilitating young offenders. In addition, both systems wanted to shield juveniles from public scrutiny; therefore, each contained provisions for keeping matters confidential.

The present-day American state court system of dealing with children involved in crimes began in 1899 when the state of Illinois passed the Illinois Juvenile Court Act. It was at that time that the juvenile court system as we know it today came into existence.[2] This statute separated the juvenile court system from the adult criminal system. It labeled minors who violated the law as "delinquents" rather than criminals, and required that juvenile court judges determine what "is in the best interests of the minor" in rendering their decision.

The juvenile court system is guided by five basic principles:

1. The state is the ultimate parent of all children within its jurisdiction, the doctrine of *parens patrea*.
2. Children are worth saving, and the state should utilize nonpunitive measures to do so.
3. Children should be nurtured and not stigmatized by the court process.

4. Each child is different, and justice should be tailored to meet individual needs and requirements.
5. The use of noncriminal sanctions is necessary to give primary consideration to the needs of the child.[3]

It is important to note that each state determines its own jurisdictional age of minors who are handled by its juvenile system. Most involve children who are under eighteen years of age. A few states use higher ages, up to twenty-one. Three states cover children up to fifteen years of age and adjudicate sixteen-year-olds in adult criminal courts.

Although these principles were originally adopted for delinquents or minors who committed criminal acts, they have been broadly applied to proceedings involving children who are victims of abuse.

Understanding the criminal court system is only the beginning of appreciating the complexity of the American criminal justice system. Professionals working in this area must also understand the parties involved in the criminal justice system. The different parties that comprise our system are reviewed in the following sections.

Federal Court System

Whereas state courts have their origin in historical accident and custom, federal courts were created by the U.S. Constitution. Section 1 of Article 3 established the federal court system with the words providing for "one Supreme Court, and…such inferior Courts as the Congress may from time to time ordain and establish." From this beginning, Congress has engaged in a series of acts that has resulted in today's federal court system. The Judiciary Act of 1789 created the U.S. Supreme Court and established district courts and circuit courts of appeals (later known as the U.S. Courts of Appeal). There are some federal courts, like the U.S. Court of Military Appeals, that were enacted by legislation and are considered as legislative courts and not "Article III" courts.

FEDERAL DISTRICT COURTS Federal district courts are the lowest level of the federal court system. These courts have original jurisdiction over all cases involving a violation of federal statutes. District courts handle thousands of criminal cases per year. The U.S. District Courts are the primary trial courts in the federal system. There is at least one district court in each state. These courts are defined by the geographical label of the state they are located in, for example, U.S. District Court for the Southern District of New York.

U.S. COURTS OF APPEALS The U.S. Courts of Appeals are the intermediate appellate-level courts within the federal system. These courts are also referred to as circuit courts because the federal system is divided into eleven circuits. A Twelfth U.S. Court of Appeals serves the Washington, D.C., area. These courts hear appeals from the district courts and habeas corpus appeals from state court convictions. These appeals are usually heard by panels of three appellate court judges rather than by all the judges of each circuit.

U.S. SUPREME COURT The U.S. Supreme Court is the highest court in the land. It has the capacity for judicial review of all lower court decisions, as well as state and federal statutes. By exercising this power, the Supreme Court determines what laws and lower court decisions conform to the mandates set forth in the U.S. Constitution. The concept of judicial review was first referred to by Alexander Hamilton in the *Federalist Papers*, in which he described the Supreme Court as ensuring that the will of the people will be supreme over the will of the legislature.[4] This concept was firmly and finally established in our system when the Supreme Court asserted its power of judicial review in the 1803 case of *Marbury v. Madison*.[5]

The U.S. Supreme Court and the lower federal courts have jurisdiction only in federal issues. There must be a federal issue before a federal court has jurisdiction in criminal matters. For example, if an accused is convicted in a state court for robbery, before the U.S. Supreme Court can consider his or her case, there must be a federal issue, for example, the search of his or her home violated the Fourth Amendment of the U.S. Constitution.

Although it is primarily an appellate court, the Supreme Court has original jurisdiction in the following cases: cases between the United States and a state; cases between states; cases involving foreign ambassadors, ministers, and consuls; and cases between a state and a citizen of another state or country.

The Court hears appeals from lower courts and the various state courts of last resort (generally the state supreme courts). If four justices of the U.S. Supreme Court vote to hear a case, the court will issue a **Writ of Certiorari**—an order sent to a lower court requiring the records of the case to be sent to the Supreme Court for review. The Court meets on the first Monday of October and usually remains in session until June. The Court may review any case it deems worthy but in actuality hears very few of the cases filed. Of approximately 8,000 appeals each year, the Court agrees to review fewer than 150; however, it may not issue an opinion on each case.

THE FEDERAL COURT JUVENILE SYSTEM When Congress addressed the issue of juvenile offenders, it established two alternatives for their prosecution:

- The juvenile can waive personal rights to be treated as a juvenile, or
- The juvenile can have the matter treated as a civil proceeding called *juvenile adjudication*.

If the court finds that the juvenile committed the offense, that individual faces a series of federal sanctions, including incarceration. There is a federal preference for state prosecution of juveniles, because there is no separate federal juvenile court judge or juvenile detention system. If adjudicated to be a delinquent, the juvenile is placed in a state juvenile facility. The federal government contracts with states for this service.

Until the passage of the Crime Control Act of 1990, the federal government prosecuted only juveniles who committed crimes on federal reservations, where the states had no jurisdiction. The Crime Control Act added two other categories of juveniles who fall under federal juvenile court jurisdiction: Juveniles who commit felony crimes of violence and juveniles involved in certain drug felonies. Similar to most state court systems, federal law allows for the transfer or certification of a juvenile to "adult status." This procedure allows juveniles to be tried as adults in either the state or the federal court system.

Under federal law, juveniles are those persons under twenty-one who commit a federal offense before their eighteenth birthday. A federal judge acts as the federal equivalent of the state juvenile court judge. The proceedings are confidential with no member of the public or press in attendance. Federal jurisdiction in juvenile matters is established when:

- the state does not have jurisdiction;
- the state does not have programs or services available for juveniles; or
- the offense charged is a violent felony or drug offense, and there is a substantial federal interest in the case.

A juvenile proceeding is initiated by the filing of an "information." In most cases, the U.S. attorney must file a certification stating there are grounds for federal jurisdiction. The hearing in federal court is very similar to a court trial.

THE PARTIES

Seven parties are involved in the criminal justice process: the victim, the perpetrator, the law enforcement, the prosecutor, the defense attorney, the courts, and the correctional system. Each of these parties or organizations has different goals and needs. Not all emotions or objectives are the same for all the parties. It is obvious, for example, that the prosecutor and defense attorney will have different perspectives on the outcome of the trial. Those who work in this area must be familiar with the various responsibilities of each of these parties and be able to explain their functions to those who are involved in the criminal justice system.

Victim

The victim of any crime is often the forgotten party in the criminal justice system. For many years, victims were perceived as simply another witness to the crime. The prevailing attitude was that the real victim was the "People of the State" in which the crime was committed. Families of murder victims could not obtain information regarding the case and were often ignored by over-worked and understaffed criminal justice personnel. Within the last thirty years, this attitude has begun to change as we become more aware of the needs and desires of crime victims.

Professionals dealing with crime victims should understand that they may be suffering emotional and/or physical trauma as a result of the offense.[6] Care must be taken to ensure that victims understand how the process works and what their rights are. It is also important to realize that individuals other than the original victim may have an interest in the process. These parties include the victim's family and friends, and in some situations the victim's employer. All appropriate parties should be notified of every significant event within the criminal justice process. Victim services providers must also respect and protect the victim's right to privacy if that is the victim's desire.

Victims of crime will normally have a number of questions and concerns regarding the court system and their involvement in it. One frustrating aspect of this process is that victims often perceive that the defendant has more rights and faster access to the courts than they do. Other chapters of this textbook examine in detail the rights of victims of crime during the criminal justice process.

Perpetrator

The perpetrator of a crime is guaranteed certain rights within our form of government. Many aspects of the criminal procedure process are controlled by the U.S. Constitution, specifically the Bill of Rights (the original ten amendments to the Constitution). These federal constitutional protections concerning individual rights are, for the most part, binding on state courts.[7]

These rights attach to the perpetrator early in the criminal procedure process, and violation of these rights may result in the case being dismissed. For example, if the perpetrator confesses to the crime of murder, and that confession is obtained in violation of the person's constitutional rights, it may be suppressed.[8] If the confession is the only link connecting the defendant to the crime, the case may have to be dismissed. When these types of incidents occur, it is difficult for the victim to understand why the defendant goes free when there has been a confession. If this happens, professionals working with victims must attempt to offer other alternatives such as availability of filing civil lawsuits against the perpetrator.

Law Enforcement

One law enforcement role in the criminal process is to apprehend the perpetrator.[9] Although this may seem to be a simple concept, understanding the organization and function of law enforcement agencies in the United States can be an exercise in frustration. American law enforcement activities take place on three independent levels: federal, state, and local. There is little uniformity among these entities. In addition, each of these agencies may enforce different criminal laws based on different jurisdictional authority. For example, the U.S. Customs Service may arrest individuals who violate federal laws regarding the importation of goods into the United States, the state highway patrol may be tasked with enforcing traffic laws on highways and streets, and the local police department may be engaged in tracking down a serial rapist.

To confuse the issue further, there is another emerging form of law enforcement activity in the United States whose activities are expanding. Private protective services have been defined as "those self-employed individuals and privately funded business entities and organizations providing security-related services to specific clientele for a fee...in order to protect their persons, private property, or interests from various hazards."[10] Normally these firms are employed by corporate clients to protect private interests. They act as private citizens and may make arrests for violations of crimes committed in their presence.

Prosecutor

The prosecuting attorney is a familiar individual in the criminal justice process. The office of the prosecuting attorney is known by a variety of names, including district attorney, county attorney, commonwealth attorney, and, at the federal level, the U.S. attorney. The prosecutor plays a critical role in the criminal process for a variety of reasons. That person is the go-between for law enforcement and the courts and decides what type of charges to file, whether to plea bargain a particular case, and how to present the case to the court or jury. The primary duty of the prosecutor is to promote justice, not just to prosecute.

One hotly debated issue surrounding the prosecutor's function concerns plea bargaining.[11] From a criminal justice perspective, a plea bargain serves several purposes: A defendant may receive the opportunity to plead guilty to a lesser charge that will reduce the time spent in jail or prison, or the prosecutor may have a weak case and a plea bargain may ensure that the defendant is convicted of something rather than walking free after an acquittal. Also, from the judge's perspective, a plea bargain eliminates one more case.[12] A plea bargain may also benefit a victim in several ways: A plea to a lesser offense eliminates the requirement that the victim relive the crime by testifying in court and, similar to the prosecutor's position, a plea bargain guarantees that the defendant is convicted of some crime. Conversely, many victims resent plea bargains because they believe that a jury should decide the case, and that if the perpetrator is guilty, he or she should be punished to the maximum extent allowed by the law.

Another controversial aspect of plea bargaining is that some prosecutors fail to notify the victim of their intent to reduce or dismiss some of the charges in exchange for a plea of guilty. There are victims who have found out about the plea bargain at the time the prosecutor called to inquire about the status of the case. If plea bargaining is to occur, the preferred method is to fully involve the victim in the decision-making process. If the victim is adamantly opposed to the reduction or dismissal of charges, the prosecutor should seriously consider not going forward with the plea bargain.

The prosecuting attorney is the representative of the people of the state or of the United States. This person is not the crime victim's personal attorney. This aspect of our criminal justice system is very troubling to many victims. However, a prosecutor who is sensitive to the needs and concerns of victims of crime can help reduce these concerns and many of the other traumas suffered by these individuals.

Defense Counsel

The defense counsel represents the rights and interests of the perpetrator. Unlike the prosecutor who is concerned with justice and fairness, the defense attorney's obligation as established by the American Bar Association's General Standards of Conduct is to use all available courage, devotion, and skills to protect the rights of the accused. Many defense attorneys interpret this obligation as requiring that they do everything possible to obtain an acquittal even if they know that the defendant in fact committed the offense. Unlike the prosecutor, the defense counsel, even though an officer of the court, has no duty to promote justice. The defense counsel has the primary duty to advocate for the best interests of the accused.

The Sixth Amendment to the U.S. Constitution requires that those who are accused of crimes have a right to be represented by an attorney. The Supreme Court in the landmark case of *Gideon v. Wainwright* established the principle that all defendants have a right to counsel in all felony cases even if they could not afford to hire their own attorney.[13] The court extended this concept to misdemeanor cases in *Argersinger v. Hamilin* holding that absent a waiver no person may be imprisoned for any offense, either misdemeanor or felony, unless represented by an attorney.[14]

At What Point Must the State Appoint an Indigent Defendant Counsel?

In *Rothgery v. Gillespie* County 128 S. Ct. 2578, 2008 U.S. LEXIS 5057 (2008), Justice David Souter delivered the majority opinion in which the Court held that Rothgery had been denied his right to appointed counsel at the initial hearing of the trial court.

In his opinion, Justice Souter notes that the Sixth Amendment right of the "accused" to assistance of counsel in all criminal prosecutions is limited by its terms: It does not attach until a prosecution is commenced. He states that the Court has, "for purposes of the right to counsel, pegged commencement to the initiation of adversary judicial criminal proceedings—whether by way of formal charge, preliminary hearing, indictment, information, or arraignment." He continues as follows:

[T]he rule is not "mere formalism," but recognition of the point at which "the government has committed itself to prosecute," "the adverse positions of government and defendant have solidified," and the accused "finds himself faced with the prosecutorial forces of organized society, and immersed in the intricacies of substantive and procedural criminal law."

The Court held that a criminal defendant's initial appearance before a judicial officer, where he learns the charge against him and his liberty is subject to restriction, marks the start of adversary judicial proceedings that trigger attachment of the Sixth Amendment right to counsel. The Court concluded that the county had violated Rothgery's right to appointed counsel at the initial hearing.

There are basically four types of defense counsel: public defenders, contract defense services, assigned defense counsel, and private defense counsel. Public defenders are hired and paid for by the government and are appointed to represent those persons charged with crimes who cannot afford to hire an attorney for representation. Many counties have public defender's offices that are staffed by very able, aggressive attorneys. However, there are instances when, for a variety of reasons, the public defender's office has a conflict of interest in a case. For example, this may occur if there were two defendants in one case. In this situation, the court may appoint an attorney from the contract defense services to represent one of the two defendants. Contract defense services are normally composed of a group of attorneys who have entered into an agreement with the county to represent indigent defendants for a specified amount of money.

Assigned defense counsel exists in the majority of the counties in the United States.[15] Many of these counties are small and cannot afford the cost of maintaining a public defender's office. Under the assigned defense counsel format, the court maintains a list of attorneys who are willing to be appointed to represent indigent criminal defendants. When a defendant appears in court, the judge appoints the next attorney on the list to represent the perpetrator.

Another category of defense attorney is the private defense counsel. These attorneys usually represent those defendants who are capable of paying for their services. Not only do perpetrators have a right to an attorney, the courts have held that the attorney must be competent.[16] Although the Constitution requires competent counsel who will vigorously defend the perpetrator, there is no requirement or right to have an attorney who will knowingly present perjured testimony. In *Nix v. Whiteside*, the defense attorney, upon learning that his client was going to take the stand and commit perjury, informed the client that he could not permit such testimony and if the client insisted on going forward and giving this testimony, the attorney would disclose the perjury and withdraw from the case. The perpetrator testified and did not commit perjury; however, he did file an appeal claiming ineffective counsel. The court disagreed, holding that attorneys who follow their state's rules of professional (ethical) conduct do not violate the Sixth Amendment right to counsel.[17]

Courts

Both the structure and organization of the court system were explained earlier in this chapter. Here it is only necessary to explain that the courts play a critical role in the criminal justice process. They bring an impartiality and formality to the system that provides it with balance, and hopefully justice.

Correctional System

One of the least discussed entities in the criminal justice process is the correctional system. Victims' involvement with perpetrators does not end at the conviction and sentencing phase. Many victims must appear each year and offer evidence as to why a certain perpetrator should not be released from custody. Therefore, it is necessary for any professional involved with victims to understand the role and responsibilities of the various correctional institutions.

There are two basic types of penal facilities: jails and prisons. **Jails** are operated by local agencies such as cities or counties. Jails are used for pretrial detention, holding after sentencing, and for incarceration of those persons who are not being sentenced to prison. Normally these are individuals who have been convicted of misdemeanors and will serve up to one year of imprisonment. Some jurisdictions use jail "boot camps" where the inmates undergo rigorous mental and physical training during their incarceration. **Prisons** are administrated by states or by the federal government and are reserved for the more serious offenders. There are various types of prisons that range from minimum-security institutions to those that house the most violent predators in society.

There are three types of persons involved in the corrections field: probation officers, parole officers, and correctional officers. Probation is a distinctly American institution. It began with John Augustus, who in 1841 asked a Boston judge to permit him to sponsor an offender. The court agreed to his request, and the perpetrator was sentenced to Augustus's custody instead of jail. (Augustus is considered the father of probation.) **Probation** is a conditional release of the offender after he or she has been found guilty. It is traditionally used on misdemeanor or other low-level crimes. It allows the perpetrator to remain free so long as that person meets certain conditions. Probation officers are those persons employed by the local jurisdictions to supervise these offenders. Many different forms of probation services are offered in the United States, and there is a continuing debate on which one is the most effective.

Parole is the conditional release of an inmate back into the community from a prison or other form of correctional institution. Many jurisdictions allow for the parole of offenders, which normally occurs after a board or commission has made a determination that the prisoner would benefit from early release. Victims may appear at these hearings and oppose the release of those predators. The victims are especially those who have been sexually assaulted themselves or those whose loved ones had been killed. These hearings are held every year in many jurisdictions with the result that the victim must relive the crime annually in an attempt to keep the perpetrator incarcerated.

Correctional officers are those persons who are hired to maintain security in jails or prisons. Many of these positions require only a high school education and a clean criminal background. Some states are beginning to impose more educational requirements on applicants, and several states have upgraded their training for correctional officers.

The court system and the parties involved are only a small part of the entire criminal justice system. Victim advocates must also be familiar with the criminal justice process. The next section examines the various steps in this system.

CRIMINAL JUSTICE PROCEDURES

Outline of Trial Procedure

In order that the reader may better understand the trial procedures, an outline of the general procedure in a criminal trial is included here. Depending upon the jurisdiction, there may be some slight deviation from the procedures set forth.

- Presentation of indictment or information
- Selection of jury
- Swearing in of jury (trial technically begins at this time)
- Reading of charge and plea

- Opening statement by prosecuting attorney
- Opening statement by defense (this may be waived entirely or until prosecution rests)
- Calling of first prosecution witness and administration of the oath
- Direct examination
- Cross-examination (may be waived)
- Redirect examination (may be waived)
- Recross-examination (may be waived)
- Calling of additional prosecution witnesses, administration of oath, direct examination, and other procedure as in case of first witness
- Prosecution rests
- Motion for judgment of acquittal by defense (if denied, then the following procedure)
- Opening statement by defense (if not previously given)
- Calling of first defense witness and procedure followed as in case of first prosecution witness
- Defense rests
- Rebuttal presentation by prosecution
- Closing arguments by prosecution and then by defense
- Rebuttal closing argument by prosecution
- Instructing the jury
- Deliberation
- Return of the verdict (if guilty verdict returned, then the following procedure)
- Request for new trial by defense (if denied, then the following procedure)
- Sentencing hearing
- Sentencing the defendant

A criminal proceeding involves many steps. **Adjudication** includes all the formal and informal decisions and steps within the criminal proceeding process. It is important to remember that in criminal cases, the government has the burden of proof. At each stage in the proceedings, the accused is afforded certain rights that are guaranteed by both federal and state constitutions. These constitutional protections have shaped the way in which our criminal process functions. From the first encounter to the execution of an inmate, certain constitutional protections mandate that law enforcement officers and those representing the government carry out their duties in certain ways. These constitutional mandates have resulted in a complex series of hearings and/or actions that must occur during any criminal proceeding. The examination of this process starts with the first formal court activity; that is, those pretrial activities associated with bringing an accused into the system.

Pretrial Activities

Pretrial activities include a variety of acts, including the arrest, the booking, and the filing of a complaint. An **arrest** is taking a suspect into custody in a manner prescribed by law. An arrest usually occurs in one of two ways: When a warrant of arrest has been issued by a magistrate or when an officer has probable cause to believe that the suspect has committed a crime. Arrest usually involves transporting the suspect to jail so that charges regarding the offense can be filed. In misdemeanor or infraction cases, instead of taking the suspect to jail, the officer may simply issue a citation to the suspect. A **citation** is an order to appear before a judge at a later time. An example of a citation is a traffic ticket issued by an officer to a person who violates the vehicle code laws.

When the officer transports the offender to the local police station, the booking process begins. **Booking** involves entering the suspect's name, offense, and other information into the police records. The suspect is also fingerprinted and photographed at this time. The suspect is usually allowed to make a phone call during this process. For certain types of offenses, a bail schedule is established and made available at the police department. If the suspect can pay the amount listed on the bail schedule, he or she is freed and ordered to report to a judge at a predetermined time. In more serious cases, the suspect is taken before a judge for a bail hearing. This type of hearing is discussed in more detail later in this chapter.

In many jurisdictions, pretrial activities include filing a complaint by the local prosecutor's office. However, prior to filing the complaint, the prosecutor reviews the facts of the case and decides what charge to file. This process takes place with both felonies and misdemeanors.

First Appearance

Once the suspect is in custody, the suspect (who is now called the defendant) must be brought before a judge without unnecessary delay. In *County of Riverside v. McLaughlin,* the Supreme Court held that defendants must be brought before a judge within forty-eight hours.[18] The court further held that weekends and holidays could not be excluded from the forty-eight-hour rule, and in some cases delays of less than two days may still be considered unreasonable.

At this first hearing, the defendant is informed of the charges and of his or her right to counsel. If the defendant is indigent, the judge begins the process of appointing an attorney for him or her. It is during this first appearance that bail is set.

Historically, the right to bail was considered so important that the drafters of the U.S. Constitution included it in the Bill of Rights. The Eighth Amendment states that excessive bail shall not be required; however, this does not mean that all defendants have a right to bail for all crimes. The right to bail requires that the judge consider the defendant's individualized circumstances in setting bail.[19] These factors include the nature and circumstances of the offense, the weight of evidence against the defendant, the financial ability of the defendant to pay the bail, and the character of the defendant.

In recent years, the defendant's dangerousness has also come under scrutiny in establishing bail. Preventive detention allows the court to deny bail based on a finding that the defendant may commit further crimes if released. The most elaborate preventive detention scheme in existence is found in the Federal Bail Reform Act of 1984, which makes the safety of any other person, or the community, a relevant consideration in setting bail.[20] This aspect of bail is especially important in family violence situations, and every effort must be made by professionals who work in this field to gather all pertinent information and forward it to the prosecutor in a timely manner so that it can be presented to the judge during the bail hearing.

Preliminary Hearing or Grand Jury Hearing

In felony cases, the next step is the preliminary hearing or grand jury hearing. The preliminary hearing is similar to the first appearance in that it occurs before a judge of a lower or municipal court. The purpose of the preliminary hearing is for the judge to make an impartial determination of whether there is probable cause to believe that a crime has been committed and that the defendant committed it. The defendant is present during this hearing and is represented by counsel who has the right to cross-examine any witnesses who are called to testify by the prosecutor. At the end of the presentation of evidence, the judge must determine if there is sufficient evidence to "bind over" or forward the case to the superior court for further proceedings and/or trial.

The grand jury hearing is conducted in secret. The grand jurors are citizens selected to serve for one year. They decide by majority vote whether to issue an indictment. The prosecuting attorney presents the evidence, and neither the defendant nor the defendant's attorney is present. If the grand jury finds there is sufficient evidence, it files a "true bill" with the superior or district court. A true bill is an indictment charging the defendant with the crime or crimes.

The Constitution does not require that states use a grand jury.[21] In about one-half of the states, a grand jury indictment is used for at least some of the felony cases. Grand juries are used in federal courts and in those states that mandate the use of grand juries. In many states, if the prosecutor has a sensitive case such as one dealing with a young child who has been molested, that prosecutor may decide to use a grand jury even if not mandated to do so by state statute. If a grand jury indictment is not used, the preliminary hearing is held, and any information is filed by the prosecutor with the trial court. Similar to an indictment, the information sets forth all charges against the defendant.

Arraignment

Once the indictment or information is filed, the defendant is brought before the court and *arraigned*. In this hearing, the charges are formally read and the defendant is asked to enter a plea. This is not a trial, and other than reading the charges, the court does not examine any of the evidence against the defendant at this time.

It is during this hearing that the defendant may enter one of three basic pleas: guilty, not guilty, or nolo contendere. In a guilty plea, the defendant admits to committing the offenses charged. If the defendant is entering a guilty plea, the court will normally inquire if he or she understands the nature and consequences of the plea and if the plea is being entered voluntarily. Many courts will read all the consequences of a plea into the record to prevent appeals by the defendant at a later time.

A not-guilty plea requires that the matter be set for trial and mandates that the prosecutor prove every element of the crimes charged and prove that the defendant committed the crime. Once the defendant enters a not-guilty plea, the judge will then inform him of his right to a court or jury trial and set the case for further proceedings. Another form of not-guilty plea that may be entered at the arraignment is not guilty by reason of insanity. This type of plea is used when the defense attorney has reason to believe that her client may not be responsible for his actions as a result of a mental disorder or disease.

Nolo contendere pleas literally mean "no contest." The defendant is not contesting the charges. In essence, it is a guilty plea and carries the same criminal sanctions as a guilty plea, but significantly for victims, it cannot be used in any subsequent civil action to establish liability against the defendant.

Jury Selection

The right to a jury trial is one of our most fundamental constitutional guarantees. The use of twelve jurors in criminal cases is common, but not constitutionally mandated. It is more an historical tradition than a legal requirement. In *Williams v. Florida*, the U.S. Supreme Court held that the individual states may decide how many jurors should hear a noncapital criminal case, and as long as the number is large enough to ensure a cross-section of the community, it will be considered constitutionally sound.[22]

Prospective jurors are selected based on the various states' legislative schemes. Many states use a combination of property tax roles, Department of Motor Vehicles listings, and voter registration records. When these jurors report for duty, a panel is sent to the courtroom for further selection. Twelve jurors are initially called to take their seats in the jury box, and the voir dire examination of prospective jurors begins. **Voir dire** means to "seek the truth." While this process may vary by jurisdiction, it normally involves the judge questioning jurors about details in their past or about present beliefs that might uncover possible bias or prejudice. Once the judge has finished with the questioning, the defense attorney and the prosecutor each have an opportunity to question jurors. Either side may challenge a juror for cause, meaning that the juror has disclosed something that will not allow him or her to be fair during the trial. Once all the challenges for cause are finished, each side may use what is called peremptory challenges to remove other prospective jurors from the panel. A **peremptory challenge** does not require an explanation and is used by either side to excuse a prospective juror without stating the reason for the dismissal. There are a limited number of peremptory challenges available, and once they are exhausted, or the prosecutor or defense attorney is satisfied with the panel, the remaining jurors will sit as the jury.

Opening Statement

The opening stat...

bout the detailed
table of contents
ning statements
e of the opening
g statements are
roduced during
ense may make
ning statement

e dealing with
ll be called to
dant commit-

r the defense
witness again
e prosecution
who watched
witnesses for
ge, the pros-

efense does
to the jury
n which the
n the event
cribed.
pportunity
back and
lence, the

secution
right to a
al cases.
made the
believe
y in the
ered by
history
orneys.

are the
selects
verdict

CRJ 246 FEMA Extra Credit – Human Trafficking

- Complete the FEMA training IS-1150: DHS Human Trafficking Awareness for FEMA Employees https://training.fema.gov/is/courseoverview.aspx?code=IS-1150
  - This training is approximately 30 minutes long
  - You must complete the entire course to receive credit
- Complete the final exam, after completing the training, with a score of 75% or higher
  - You will be required to register for a SID (Student Identification Number) at https://cdp.dhs.gov/femasid (or follow the link when you click to take the final exam). Keep your SID for future FEMA courses
  - You will have to enter your personal information, so use a secure computer
- **Print and turn in a copy of your completion certificate for IS-1150 by the start of class on 12/05/18** (do not email it to me)
  - The certificate must be dated **11/28 – 12/04/18** (if you previously completed this training, you must completed it again to receive credit)
  - Note - keep all copies of any FEMA courses you complete for the future courses and employment
- Worth 1 point
- This will NOT be accepted late

regarding whether the defendant is guilty of the crimes charged. In the event the jury cannot reach a verdict, it informs the judge. This is called a "hung jury," and the judge may declare a mistrial. If the jury reaches a verdict, it notifies the judge and all parties to reassemble in the courtroom. The judge's clerk reads the verdict. If found not guilty, the defendant is free to go. In the event the defendant is found guilty of all or some of the charges, the next step in the criminal process begins.

Sentencing

A review of our history demonstrates that various views and beliefs regarding punishment have evolved over time.[23] At one point in ancient Rome, punishment was viewed as a right of the victim's family. Eventually, we began to accept the concept of the sovereign as the dispenser of justice and punishment.

The four basic purposes for sentencing are deterrence, rehabilitation, retribution, and incapacitation. **Deterrence** involves the concept that criminal sanctions, such as imprisonment, deter the public and convince them that they should not commit crimes. **Rehabilitation** focuses on reducing the offender's criminal propensities by counseling, therapy, and vocational training while incarcerated. **Retribution** is based on the biblical theme of "an eye for an eye, a tooth for a tooth." K. G. Armstrong has argued that retribution is not based on vengeance but rather is the lawful act of the state to protect its members from further injury.[24] Another theory regarding retribution involves the concept of "just desserts." This rationale for punishment is based on Von Hirsh's classic work, *Doing Justice*, in which he argues that those who commit crimes deserve to be punished.[25] **Incapacitation** removes offenders from society by keeping them incarcerated. The "Three Strikes and You're Out" law is an example of incapacitation of offenders.

Before imposing a sentence, the court usually receives a presentence report. This report is generally prepared by the probation department and normally begins with a recitation of the crime. It then presents the prosecution's version of the case followed by the defendant's version. It may present information about the background of the offender, including the parents and siblings, marital history, education, health, financial condition, and previous employment. The report also includes the nature and extent of previous criminal activities and discusses the victim's desires and needs. It makes a recommendation regarding what the probation department considers to be the most appropriate sentence for this particular defendant.

Once the presentencing report is complete, the defendant is returned to court for sentencing. At this time, the prosecution has an opportunity to argue for whatever sentence it feels is appropriate. The defense can also present any evidence it chooses to convince the judge to sentence the offender according to its desires. In many jurisdictions, victims have a right to appear and tell the judge of their own wishes and how the crime has impacted on their lives. This victim impact statement is addressed in more detail later in this textbook.

CIVIL COURT PROCEEDINGS AND VICTIMS

The preceding sections discussed various aspects of the criminal justice system and its effect on victims. This section briefly explores the second aspect of the legal system to impact victims: the civil law system. A criminal action punishes a person for committing a public wrong, whereas a civil action punishes a person for committing a private wrong or injury.[26] Civil law includes all actions that are not deemed criminal in nature.[27] Understanding the civil law system is important to those studying victimology, because many victims of crime turn to civil law in an effort to obtain redress for injuries not compensated by the criminal law system.[28]

Victims file civil actions against their perpetrators for various reasons. One reason may be that they do not believe they received appropriate satisfaction as a result of any criminal proceedings. The defendant may have been acquitted or convicted of a lesser charge than the victim believes is proper. Victims may also feel mistreated by the criminal justice system and have a desire to be in control of the proceedings instead of being treated as merely a witness in a case.

They may also want to receive more compensation for injuries than is available in the criminal justice system.

Civil law includes a wide variety of subjects, including the following:

- *Torts:* Injury that does not involve a contract
- *Contracts:* Violation of an agreement
- *Property:* Disputes relating to real or personal property
- *Estates:* Issues relating to inheritance and probate
- *Family:* Issues regarding marriage, children, and divorce
- *Civil rights:* Injury to another in violation of certain statutory rights

Some of these common legal concepts that affect victims are examined in more detail in other chapters. When a victim suffers a civil injury, it is necessary to begin the civil process. This process starts with an examination of whether the courts have jurisdiction over the parties and the cause of action. The next section examines the concept of jurisdiction.

Jurisdiction

Jurisdiction is the ability of a court to hear and decide issues of law and fact. If a court does not have jurisdiction, it is without the power to act. Courts must have jurisdiction over both the parties and the subject matter of the complaint.[29]

Jurisdiction over the parties or personal jurisdiction requires that the court be able to bring the party before it. Personal jurisdiction is of two types: in personam and in rem. **In personam** personal jurisdiction refers to the court's powers to bind the parties to the court's judgment. **In rem** personal jurisdiction is one that involves property that is located in the state where the court is located, and in which the parties have their dispute. Jurisdiction of the person is normally obtained by serving upon the individual a copy of the complaint. This process is discussed later in this section.

Jurisdiction of the subject matter requires that the court have authority to hear and decide the issue of law involved in the dispute. For example, some courts require that a minimum level of damages be requested before the matter can be heard in their court.[30] Other courts hear only certain types of matters and cannot rule on any issues. For example, probate courts cannot hear family law issues and vice versa.

Due process is a constitutional mandate that requires fairness in judicial proceedings. Occasionally one raises a question as to whether a person or organization that does not live or is headquartered in a state can be forced to appear in that state and defend a lawsuit that has been filed there. The doctrine of due process may prevent the out-of-state defendant from having to appear and defend lawsuits unless the defendant has some sort of minimum contacts in the state. This doctrine is based on the concept that it would be unfair to require a person or business to travel to a state and defend a lawsuit where that defendant has had no other contact with that state. In the leading case of *International Shoe Co. v. State of Washington,* the U.S. Supreme Court held that certain activities engaged in by a corporation in a state will allow it to be sued in that state.[31] These activities must involve some minimum contacts in the forum state of such character that being forced to defend a suit in that state would not offend traditional notions of fair play and substantial justice.

The concept of venue is closely associated with jurisdiction but is a separate and distinct aspect of civil litigation. Lawsuits must be filed in the proper location. Venue statutes determine the geographic districts in which the case can be heard. Once the question of jurisdiction and venue is determined, the plaintiff can evaluate the possibility of filing a complaint for damages.

Filing a Complaint

Filing a complaint is the first concrete step in the civil process. Unlike the criminal law process in which the prosecutor determines the nature and type of charges to file, the victim and the victim's attorney have complete control over the causes of action that are filed against the perpetrator.

In addition, as mentioned previously, the victim as the plaintiff has control over the location where the complaint is filed. Figure 2.1 is an example of a civil complaint.

A **complaint** is a written document, called a *pleading*, that contains three essential components: (1) It establishes the subject matter jurisdiction, (2) it sets forth facts constituting various causes of action, and (3) it asks for certain types of relief (see Figure 2.1). Causes of action are legal theories that, if proved, entitle the plaintiff to recover for any injuries suffered. Many victims will allege alternative, and sometimes conflicting, causes of actions in the complaint and after discovery dismiss those that cannot be proved.

A variety of relief is available in civil proceedings. The first and most common form of relief is monetary damage. Monetary damages may be either compensatory or punitive in nature. **Compensatory damages** are awarded to plaintiffs to make them whole financially for any injuries they suffered as a result of the defendant's actions. **Punitive damages** are awarded to punish the defendant and to send a message to other similarly situated persons that if they commit the same or similar type of action they could face a similar fate.

Other forms of relief available in civil courts are *injunctions*, or orders that prohibit a person from doing certain acts. This form of relief is possible because of the courts' equity power.

FIGURE 2.1 Sample Complaint

UNITED STATES DISTRICT COURT FOR THE CENTRAL DISTRICT OF CALIFORNIA

Judy Jones

v. _____   No. _____

Dan Defendant   Civil Action

COMPLAINT

Plaintiff Judy Jones complains against Dan Defendant as follows:

1. Jurisdiction in this case is based on diversity of citizenship and the amount in controversy. Plaintiff is a citizen of the State of California and defendant is a citizen of the State of Oregon. The amount in controversy exceeds, exclusive of interests and costs, the sum of One hundred thousand ($100,000) dollars.
2. On September 30, 2014, at approximately 10:00 P.M., plaintiff Judy Jones (Jones) was standing near the intersection of First Street and Thomas Road in Fresno, California. Defendant Dan Defendant (Defendant) was driving a vehicle eastbound on Thomas Road at that intersection.
3. Defendant intentionally fired a handgun at Jones, which resulted in a bullet entering Jones's left arm.
4. As a direct and proximate result of Defendant's actions, Jones suffered injuries to her arm and shoulder and other body parts, received other physical injuries, suffered physical and mental pain and suffering, and incurred medical expenses and lost future income.

WHEREFORE, plaintiff Judy Jones demands judgment against defendant Dan Defendant for the sum of $1,000,000 with interest and costs.

Dated:

_____

John Smith

Attorney for Plaintiff

This power authorizes the court to issue orders for preventing injustice or wrongs from occurring. This power resides with the court, and juries do not decide issues of equity.

These orders are issued by judges after they receive evidence regarding the facts surrounding the necessity for the issuance of an injunction. A specific form of injunction, the temporary restraining order (TRO) or protective order, is used in domestic violence or stalking cases and is discussed in more detail in Chapter 14, which examines constitutional and civil rights of victims.

The complaint is filed in a court that has jurisdiction over the parties and the subject matter. For example, a case dealing with the commission of intentional torts on federal land would be filed in federal court, because only that court has jurisdiction. The same acts if committed elsewhere would be filed in state court.

The complaint lists the parties and is known by the name of the plaintiff and the defendant. For example, if Laura Leonard was suing John Jones for striking her, the lawsuit would be entitled *Leonard v. Jones.* After identifying the parties and stating that the court has jurisdiction, the complaint sets forth the various causes of actions and asks for relief. This relief is contained in what is known as the *prayer*. The prayer sometimes asks for a specific amount of money or may include language stating "damages according to proof." This allows the plaintiff extra time to fully assess the nature and extent of any damages.

The complaint is usually filed by the plaintiff's attorney. All courts require parties filing a lawsuit to pay a filing fee. Depending on the jurisdiction, this can range from a nominal fee in small claims courts to several hundreds of dollars in superior or district courts. Once the complaint is filed, the defendant must be served with a copy. Normally, the plaintiff pays the county to serve the complaint using deputy sheriffs. Sometimes, private process servers are used to serve defendants that are hard to contact or who are evading service of the complaint. There are several other methods of serving the defendant, including using registered mail, posting a copy of the complaint on the defendant's property, or publishing the complaint in a newspaper. It is not necessary that the defendant have actual notice of the complaint so long as the method of service is likely to provide notice.[32] Once the defendant is served with a copy of the complaint or has received notice of the lawsuit, a response is required within certain number of days, or a default judgment may be entered for the plaintiff. A default judgment is an order granting the plaintiff the relief asked for in the complaint. Because of the drastic nature of default judgments, most defendants respond to complaints.

Filing a Response

Once the defendant is served with a copy of the complaint, there are a number of alternative responses available. The defendant may file any of the following responses: an answer with or without affirmative defenses, a demurrer, a motion to strike, or a cross-complaint or counter-claim. Each response has a definite purpose and is commonly used in many civil cases.

ANSWER The defendant may file a response that is known as an **answer**, which is a response to the complaint, and may admit or deny the allegations. Answers are pleadings and may contain detailed responses or be a general denial of everything contained in the complaint. An answer, like the complaint, is filed with the court and served on the plaintiff.

AFFIRMATIVE DEFENSES The defendant may assert **affirmative defenses**, which are certain defenses that, if proved, negate any legal responsibility for the injuries suffered by the plaintiff. Affirmative defenses include such common theories as accord and satisfaction, assumption of the risk, contributory negligence, duress, estoppel, fraud, illegality, laches, license, statute of frauds, statute of limitations, and any other matter constituting an avoidance. The affirmative defenses are usually listed at the end of the answer before the prayer.

DEMURRER A **demurrer** is a response that in essence admits all the allegations of the complaint as true but goes on to state that even if they are true the plaintiff has not pled any theories that would allow for recovery of damages.[33] The demurrer is filed instead of the answer, because if the court grants the demurrer, the case is over. Most courts allow the plaintiff to amend the complaint to overcome the defects raised in the demurrer.

MOTION TO STRIKE A motion to strike is a response that requests the court to strike out certain language in the complaint. Motions to strike are often used in conjunction with demurrers in an attempt to get the case dismissed.

CROSS-COMPLAINT OR COUNTERCLAIM If the defendant answers the complaint but claims that another party caused the plaintiff's injuries, the defendant may file a lawsuit against that party at the time the answer is filed. This lawsuit, which is made a part of the original action, is known as a cross-complaint or counterclaim. The defendant may also file a cross-complaint or counterclaim against the plaintiff alleging that the plaintiff injured the defendant.

Once the initial pleadings have been filed, the lawsuit moves into the pretrial stage. In some jurisdictions, this occurs very quickly because of a court procedure known as fast tracking of civil cases. In other jurisdictions, the case can take several years before anything further occurs.

Pretrial Activities

Pretrial activities include a wide range of legal maneuvers designed to clarify the issues and/or reach settlement regarding liability. Much of the criticism aimed at the legal profession has centered around some of the activities that occur during this stage of a civil lawsuit.[34] Pretrial activities include filing motions, discovery, and settlement conferences.

MOTIONS There are a number of motions that may be filed during the pretrial stage of a civil case. The most important motion is called a *summary judgment*. This motion can be used to dismiss the entire case or strike portions of the complaint. A summary judgment motion is a pleading that alleges there is no triable issue of fact established by the pleadings or discovery, and therefore the undisputed portions of the case should be dismissed. If these portions are essential to the plaintiff's case, this motion may result in the dismissal of the entire complaint.

For instance, if the plaintiff is alleging that he was battered by the defendant and during discovery it is established that the plaintiff and the defendant both agree that the incident occurred during a sporting event, the defendant could file a summary judgment motion that would be granted by the court. The court would hold that when one is injured during a sporting event or game, no cause of action for battery is available because the law presumes the injured party consented to the actions of the other person while they were on the playing field. Conversely, if the plaintiff alleges that the defendant struck him after the game was over and the defendant contends the injury occurred during the game, there is a triable issue of fact for the jury to decide (when and how the injury occurred), and the summary judgment motion will not be granted.

DISCOVERY The discovery process in civil lawsuits can be both time consuming and expensive. *Discovery* is the legal term that includes a number of devices that allow each party to learn the facts and theories that the other side is claiming will allow them to prevail. Both the plaintiff and defendant engage in discovery during the pretrial period. In fact, a television drama showing a civil attorney being surprised during trial is a myth and has little basis in modern courtroom procedures. It is more the exception than the rule that surprises occur in civil cases. By the time a case goes to trial, attorneys representing each side know exactly what each witness will testify and what the theories of recovery or defense are.

There are a number of discovery techniques used in civil cases. The more complex cases use all, or most, of these discovery tools. They include depositions, interrogatories, and requests for production of documents. Each of these discovery techniques has specific goals and purposes.

Depositions. **Depositions** are formal, out-of-court procedures in which one party questions others regarding the facts surrounding the case. The questioning occurs under oath and is recorded by a court reporter. Either the plaintiff or the defendant may conduct a deposition, and both parties are usually deposed by the other. Witnesses, experts, and other persons that may have information regarding the lawsuit may be deposed. The rules of evidence are relaxed during depositions, and the parties are allowed to ask questions that may lead to other information. Once a party has given its deposition, if they change the statement during the trial, the deposition may be introduced to impeach the party's credibility.[35]

Interrogatories. **Interrogatories** are written inquiries to the other side asking specific questions. Interrogatories may ask for a party to state the theory behind a cause of action and all the facts supporting that theory. Interrogatories may also ask parties to admit or deny certain specific issues.

Production of Documents. In many cases, one party will ask the other to produce all the records surrounding the occurrence that is the basis for the lawsuit. Some defendants are reluctant to produce these records absent a court order. A motion to produce can be enforced by the court, and if the party fails to bring or send all the records to the other party, a court may order sanctions.

CONFERENCES Once the discovery phase of the civil action is complete, many jurisdictions require the parties to meet and discuss the possibility of settling the case or narrowing the issues.[36] This conference may result in the parties entering into agreements or stipulations about issues that are not in conflict such as the date of events, who took which pictures, and other items that move the trial along without undue time being spent on mundane matters.

Often, the parties will enter into serious settlement discussions at these pretrial conferences.[37] After the discovery phase ends, the attorneys representing each side and the settlement judge have a fairly accurate idea of how the trial is going to go and what the probable outcome will be. The judge, as a disinterested third party, may facilitate these discussions by separating the parties and by talking to each one individually. The judge may make recommendations regarding the value of the case and discuss the credibility of certain witnesses. Some judges will move back and forth between the two parties, communicating offers and counter-offers until the parties agree to settle. Many attorneys believe a good settlement judge can dispose of most, if not all, civil lawsuits. In the event the case cannot be settled, the next phase is the trial.

Trial

The trial of a civil case is conducted in much the same manner as a criminal case. The jury selection, including the voir dire, is very similar to a criminal case. Opening statements are conducted with the plaintiff's attorney going first, followed by the defendant's attorney. The plaintiff's attorney presents that side's evidence, and then the defendant presents evidence if desired. Closing arguments and rebuttal follow the same pattern as a criminal case; the jury receives its instructions and then retires to deliberate.

However, there are some significant differences between a criminal trial and a civil trial. These differences include constitutional issues, the burden of proof, and the number of jurors who must agree on a verdict. The Fifth Amendment prohibition against self-incrimination does not apply, and therefore the plaintiff may call the defendant to the stand to testify during the plaintiff's case-in-chief. Civil cases only require a preponderance of the evidence, whereas criminal cases require proof beyond a reasonable doubt. Finally, in civil cases, only nine of twelve jurors must agree for a verdict to be reached. In criminal cases, the great majority of states require a unanimous verdict.

Verdict

Unlike a criminal case in which the jury renders a verdict of guilty or not guilty, civil cases may require juries to evaluate complex facts and legal theories. Some cases require juries to apportion fault among the parties. For example, juries may be asked to determine if the plaintiff contributed to his or her own injuries. In these cases, the jury may return a verdict finding the defendant 80 percent at fault and the plaintiff 20 percent at fault. If the jury determined that the plaintiff suffered injuries in the amount of $100,000, the award based on this division of fault would then be reduced by 20 percent, leaving the plaintiff with a final award of damages in the amount of $80,000.

In complex civil cases, judges may use what is known as a special verdict form. Instead of simply ruling for either the plaintiff or the defendant, the jury is given a series of questions regarding factual issues. On the basis of its response, the judge determines the outcome of the case.

Judgment

There is no sentence in a civil case. If the jury finds for the defendant, the case is over. However, if the jury returns a verdict for the plaintiff, the court must enter a judgment. Once a judgment is recorded, the plaintiff can request the sheriff or marshal to execute the judgment and seize and sell most of the defendant's real and personal property to pay the amount listed in the judgment. However, many persons are judgment-proof in that they have very little if any assets that can be used to pay the judgment. Others, such as O. J. Simpson, have assets such as pensions that cannot be attached. When this situation occurs, plaintiffs must look at other options for recovery. These alternatives are discussed in more detail in the sections dealing with victims' rights.

JUVENILE COURT DEPENDENCY PROCEDURES

An earlier section discussed juvenile courts and those minors classified as either delinquents or status offenders. This section discusses dependent children, as these proceedings are normally considered civil rather than criminal in nature. Dependent children are defined as those children who are in need of state intervention because of abuse or neglect by their caretakers.

Although the procedure is basically the same for delinquents and dependent minors, the juvenile court process dealing with children who are victims of abuse or neglect is of particular importance to professionals who work in the criminal justice field. This process is normally initiated by filing a petition with the court. A petition is a formal pleading that alleges that the parents or custodians endangered the health or welfare of the child. The petition may allege neglect or physical, emotional, or sexual abuse of the child, and it gives the juvenile court the authority to act.

Detention Hearing

Once the petition is filed, many jurisdictions hold a show cause or detention hearing. This hearing is usually conducted within twenty-four to forty-eight hours after filing the petition or the emergency removal of the child. The **detention hearing** requires child protective services or police to produce evidence justifying the emergency removal of the child or to present evidence that would allow the court to order the removal of the child if the child is still in the custody of the parents. The parents may also admit or deny the allegations contained in the petition at this hearing.

If they admit the allegations, the court orders child protective services to conduct an investigation to determine where the child should be placed as a result of the admissions by the parents. If the parents deny the allegations, the court sets a date for an adjudicatory or jurisdictional hearing. Pending this hearing, the court may order the child temporarily placed in a living arrangement outside the home.

Adjudicatory or Jurisdictional Hearing

An **adjudicatory or jurisdictional hearing** is used to determine if there is sufficient evidence to determine that the allegations in the petition are true. At the conclusion of this hearing, the court will render its decision. If the petition is upheld, the court sets a date for a dispositional hearing. If the petition is not upheld, the child is returned to the parents and the case is dismissed.

During the adjudicatory hearing, the state presents evidence to support its claim that the child has been abused. This may take the form of having the child testify to the incident, or experts employed by the state may render their opinion regarding the facts surrounding the case. The state is represented by a juvenile prosecutor, state's advocate, county counsel, or other governmental attorney. The parents have a right to cross-examine witnesses and present any evidence they desire in rebuttal to the state's evidence. At the end of the hearing, both parties may present arguments in favor of their position. The burden of proof to uphold the petition is the same as for a civil case. In civil trials, the plaintiff has the burden of proving the case by a preponderance of the evidence. This is normally defined as slightly more than 50 percent. A criminal case requires proof beyond a reasonable doubt. This is not proof beyond all doubt, because all things are subject to some doubt, but it is proof beyond a reasonable doubt to a moral certainty that all the material facts did occur.

In juvenile dependency cases, to remove the child from the custody of the parents, some jurisdictions require proof by clear and convincing evidence. This is more than a preponderance of the evidence but less than beyond a reasonable doubt.[38]

The Dispositional Hearing

Once the adjudicatory or jurisdictional hearing is concluded, the next hearing to occur is the **dispositional hearing**. This hearing is to determine where the child should be placed. The court will decide whether the child should be immediately returned to the parents or placed in an out-of-home environment for a specific time. The guiding principle in this hearing is "the best interests of the child." If the court orders the child placed outside the home, it may schedule periodic reviews to determine if or when the child will be reunited with the parents. Typically, a specific plan regarding placement is established and monitored.

From the beginning of the intervention process until the final dispositional hearing and beyond, every party in the action has certain rights. The parents and the child each have distinct rights that must be observed and protected. These rights include the following:

- Notice
- An opportunity to be heard and to present evidence
- The right to confront and cross-examine witnesses
- Effective representation by an attorney

In a dependency hearing, the rights of a child include appointing an attorney who will speak on behalf of the child. This attorney must represent what is believed to be in the best interests of the child regardless of what Child Protective Services (CPS) or the parents' advocate believes is appropriate. In some jurisdictions, this is a government-funded attorney; in others, it is a private attorney appointed by the court to represent the child. Depending on the case, the attorney may side with the parents and argue for return of the child to their care, or the attorney may take the position that it is in the best interests of the child to be removed from the custody of the parents. Even if the child is removed temporarily from the custody of the parents, the child has a right to reunification efforts after a reasonable time.

Many jurisdictions additionally engage court-appointed special advocates (CASAs), or similarly trained (typically nonattorney) individuals. The role of these child advocates is to present to the court an independent analysis of what is best for the child. This is particularly important; as the child's legal representative, the court-appointed lawyer must forward the child's wishes when an objective view would be to the contrary. For example, the lawyer may decide to vigorously advocate a juvenile's wish to return home, when an independent child advocate may determine that this is not actually in the child's best interest.

During dependency hearings, parents have a right to notice of the hearing, an opportunity to be present at that hearing, and to be represented by an attorney. They may present any evidence they desire to rebut the charges. If the child is removed from their custody, they have the right in most jurisdictions to a reunification plan that will allow them to regain custody of the child once they have finished treatment or counseling.

Juvenile courts that hear dependency cases oftentimes face a conflict: protection of the child versus the trauma of removing a child from the parents. Courts will normally err on the side of removing the child if there is any substantial evidence to support the allegations that the child is in danger. The juvenile court dependency process is a civil action that must always stay focused on the best interests of the child.

RESTORATIVE JUSTICE

Introduction

More and more researchers are suggesting an alternative to the traditional criminal sanctions imposed on perpetrators by the state. These scholars are examining the concept of restorative justice as a new vision for dealing with both offenders and victims.[39] The topic of restorative justice is included in a discussion of the civil justice system, because it is more similar to that philosophy than the current philosophy of criminal sanctions.

Some believe that the United States is the most punitive nation in the Western world and that this country outstrips all other nations in prison-building programs. A common refrain in almost all elections is that one's opponent is too soft on crime. Therefore, American politicians must be tough on crime to get elected. This political stance has resulted in harsher criminal sanctions in an effort to stop or deter future criminal activity.

The general public is frightened of crime and its consequences. The media feed this fear by showing drive-by shootings and all the grisly details on television daily. Americans are demanding a stop to this violence. At the same time, the public is demanding that victims of crime be included in the prosecution process. Society is not only interested in including victims in the process, but it also wants to make them whole emotionally and financially. This section deals with some methods of making victims whole financially by using the civil justice system. Restorative justice is also a method of healing victims.

Restorative justice promotes maximum involvement of the victim, the offender, and the community in the justice process and presents a clear alternative to sanctions based on retribution and punishment.[40] Restorative justice is based on three principles: (1) All parties (offender, victim, and the community) should be included in the response to crime; (2) government and local communities' actions should complement each other; and (3) accountability is based on the offender's understanding of the harm that has been inflicted.

The restorative justice philosophy gives meaning to sanctions such as restitution and community service. Without an understanding of the restorative justice philosophy, these sanctions appear to be simply bureaucratic and punitive in nature. Restorative justice also links different programs such as restitution, community services, and victim–offender mediation together with the goal of accomplishing its mission.

Function of a Restorative Justice Program

There are three roles in any restorative justice program: accountability, competency, and community protection. No single role or principle is more important than another. Each role is intertwined with the others in an effort to present a balanced approach to justice.[41]

The accountability role or principle holds that when a crime occurs, a debt incurs and justice requires that every effort be made by the offender to restore any losses suffered by the victim. Accountability requires that offenders become aware of the harmful consequences of their action and make every effort to make amends to the victim and the community. The competency development role or principle requires that offenders leave the criminal justice system more capable of participation in society than when they entered the system. Competency involves work experience, active learning, and opportunities for offenders to develop productive skills. The community protection role or principle holds that the public has a right to a safe environment and the criminal justice system should use a progressive response system to ensure offender control in the community. Community-based control and surveillance can channel the offender's energy into productive activities during nonschool or nonworking hours.

Restorative justice programs focus on repairing the harm inflicted on the victim and the community using a process of negotiation, mediation, victim empowerment, and reparation. Restorative justice believes that victims are central to the process of resolving a crime and offers direct involvement of the participants in the process. One common strategy used in restorative justice programs is victim–offender mediation.

Victim–Offender Mediation

Victim–offender mediation (VOM) has its roots in the Victim–Offender Reconciliation Program (VORP) started in Canada in the mid-1970s.[42] The purposes of the original VORP project were to provide an alternative method of dealing with crime, to allow the victim and offender to mutually agree on restitution, to use third parties to facilitate reconciliation, and to resolve the conflict caused by crime.[43]

Increasing numbers of crime victims are choosing to meet face-to-face with their perpetrator. In these meetings, the victim can let the offender know how the crime affected his or her life and possibly receive from the offender answers to lingering questions the victim may have. In addition, this form of mediation allows the victim to be directly involved in holding offenders accountable for the harm they caused.

There are more than 300 VOM programs in various communities across the United States.[44] These programs are different from the traditional mediation program in that there is no "dispute" for the parties to resolve. One of the parties in VOM is an offender, and guilt has already been established. These programs focus on dialogue with emphasis on the victim's needs, offender accountability, and some restoration of losses. Victims who meet with their offenders appear to be more satisfied with the justice system response to their cases than do victims of similar crimes who go through the traditional court process. The four most common offenses referred to VOM in order of frequency are vandalism, minor assaults, theft, and burglary. Almost half (45 percent) of the VOM programs work exclusively with juvenile offenders. The satisfaction with VOM appears to be high, and it should be evaluated as an alternative to the traditional sanctions imposed by courts.

Summary

Understanding the criminal justice system is a critical aspect in the study of victimology. Many people are victimized or feel victimized for a second time when they become involved in the judicial process. Long delays, complex procedures, and technical arguments by both prosecutors and defense attorneys can lead to a renewed feeling of helplessness on the part of a victim who only wants to see justice carried out.

The American criminal court system is a combination of historical accident and thoughtful planning by our founding fathers. Criminal courts function at both the federal and state levels. The nature of the crime may determine where the offender is prosecuted.

Concern regarding the increasing role of juveniles in the commission of crime has led to a renewed interest in the juvenile justice system. This system operates out of the general public's view most of the time because of the fundamental principle of confidentiality. This concept was instituted to protect the identity of the juvenile offender and thereby avoid stigmatizing the offender as a criminal. It was believed that this would assist in the juvenile's rehabilitation; however, this concept has recently come under a great deal of criticism.

Each party in the criminal justice system has a distinct role to play, which makes it adversarial in nature. Understanding the roles and responsibilities of each party is a necessary aspect of the duties of any victim services provider.

In many instances, criminal justice procedures are based on constitutional protections set forth in the Bill of Rights and in other amendments to the Constitution. The process can be very confusing to the victim, who often must navigate it alone. Because conviction of crime may result in restricting the freedom of the accused, the criminal is afforded a number of rights. These rights may cause the victims of crime much frustration and anger.

It is important to remember that the criminal justice system is only a small part of the entire spectrum of victimology; however, this process is critically important to any victim. Professionals in this area must maintain the proper perspective when dealing with all parties involved in the criminal justice system.

The civil system is an important aspect of the study of victimology. Often, victims do not feel that they received justice in the criminal justice system. Victims become plaintiffs and engage in civil lawsuits for a variety of reasons. These victims turn to the civil system in an effort to obtain redress for injuries suffered that could not be addressed in the criminal justice process. They may also believe that the defendant did not receive just punishment in the criminal justice system. Civil lawsuits allow victims to control the proceedings—something they are denied in criminal actions. They hire their own attorney and have the right to participate in all phases of the lawsuit. They sit at the counsel table during the trial, and they can direct the proceedings by ordering or by asking their attorney to carry out certain acts in certain ways.

The juvenile justice system provides civil remedies for children who are abused or neglected. The system is based on the premise of doing whatever is in the best interest of the child. The dependency process is very powerful, and children can be removed from the care and custody of their parents if the court finds they are in danger.

The civil law process is complex, time consuming, and expensive. It can also be frustrating to victims of crime. Professionals must exercise care before advising any victim to pursue civil remedies. The consequences and benefits of filing a civil lawsuit should be fully explained, and victims must make this decision with their head, not with their emotions.

More victims are turning to the use of restorative justice programs in an effort to deal with the consequences of crime. For the most part, these programs deal with nonviolent crimes. These programs appear to fulfill a need for some victims.

Key Terms

Adjudication includes all the formal and informal decisions and steps within the criminal proceeding process.

Adjudicatory or jurisdictional hearing is used to determine if there is sufficient evidence to determine that the allegations in the petition are true.

Affirmative defenses are certain defenses that, if proved, negate any legal responsibility for the injuries suffered by the plaintiff.

Answer is a response to the complaint and may admit or deny the allegations.

Arrest is taking a suspect into custody in a manner prescribed by law.

Booking involves entering the suspect's name, offense, and other information into the police records.

Citation is an order to appear before a judge at a later time.

Compensatory damages are awarded to the plaintiff to make them whole financially for any injuries they suffered as a result of the defendant's actions.

Complaint is a written document, called a *pleading*, that contains three essential components: (1) It establishes the subject matter jurisdiction, (2) it sets forth facts constituting various causes of action, and (3) it asks for certain types of relief.

Correctional officers are those persons who are hired to maintain security in jails or prisons.

Demurrer is a response that in essence admits all the allegations of the complaint as true but goes on to state that even if they are true, the plaintiff has not pled any theories that would allow for recovery of damages.

Depositions are formal, out-of-court procedures in which one party questions others regarding the facts surrounding the case.

Detention hearing requires child protective services or police to produce evidence justifying the emergency removal of the child or to present evidence that would allow the court to order the removal of the child if the child is still in the custody of the parents.

Deterrence involves the concept that criminal sanctions, such as imprisonment, deter the public and convince them that they should not commit crimes.

Dispositional hearing is to determine where the child should be placed.

Due process is a constitutional mandate that requires fairness in judicial proceedings.

Equity is the concept that justice is administered according to fairness, as contrasted with the strict rules of law.

General jurisdiction courts are granted authority to hear and decide all issues that are brought before them.

In personam jurisdiction refers to the court's powers to bind the parties to the court's judgment.

In rem jurisdiction is one that involves property that is located in the state where the court is located and in which the parties have their dispute.

Incapacitation removes offenders from society by keeping them incarcerated.

Interrogatories are written inquiries to the other side asking specific questions.

Jails are operated by local agencies such as cities or counties. Jails are used for pretrial detention, holding after sentencing, and incarceration of those persons who are not being sentenced to prison.

Jurisdiction means the ability of the court to enforce laws and punish individuals who violate those laws. Jurisdiction is also the ability of a court to hear and decide issues of law and fact.

Limited jurisdiction courts are those that hear and decide only certain limited legal issues.

Nolo contendere pleas literally mean "no contest." The defendant is not contesting the charges. In essence, it is a guilty plea and carries the same criminal sanctions as a guilty plea, but significantly for victims, it cannot be used in any subsequent civil action to establish liability against the defendant.

Parole is the conditional release of an inmate back into the community from a prison or other form of correctional institution.

Peremptory challenge does not require explanation and is used by either side to excuse a prospective juror without stating the reason for the dismissal.

Prisons are administrated by states or by the federal government and are for the more serious offenders.

Probation is a conditional release of the offender after having been found guilty. It is traditionally used on misdemeanor or other low-level crimes. It allows the perpetrator to remain free so long as that person meets certain conditions.

Punitive damages are awarded to punish the defendant and to send a message to other similarly situated persons that if they commit the same or similar type of action, they could face a similar fate.

Rehabilitation focuses on reducing the offender's criminal propensities by counseling, therapy, and vocational training while the criminal is incarcerated.

Retribution is based on the biblical theme of "an eye for an eye, a tooth for a tooth."

Trial courts are courts where criminal cases start and finish.

Voir dire means to "seek the truth." While this process may vary by jurisdiction, it normally involves questioning jurors about details in their past or about present beliefs that might uncover possible bias or prejudice.

Writ of certiorari is an order sent to a lower court requiring the records of the case to be sent to the Supreme Court for review.

Discussion Questions

1. Why is it important for victim services providers to understand the criminal justice system? Doesn't anyone who watches television already have a basic understanding of how courts work?
2. Should we continue to have separate state and federal courts? Wouldn't one unified court system make more sense and be more efficient?
3. Should we treat juveniles as adults once they commit a violent crime? What crimes would apply, and how old would the minor have to be in order to be tried as an adult?
4. Should the victim have the same constitutional rights as the defendant?
5. Should victims have the right to veto any proposed plea bargain? Why? Why not?
6. Should all child sex abuse cases go to the grand jury?
7. Which justification for punishment is the most popular in today's climate of violent crime? Is it the most effective use of our resources?
8. List all the reasons victims may desire to sue perpetrators. Which reason is the most important?
9. Why should victim services providers understand the civil justice system?
10. Compare and contrast the criminal justice procedures and the civil justice procedures. List those areas that empower victims.
11. Why are juvenile court dependency procedures important for victims to understand?
12. If you could change one thing about the civil justice system that would help victims, what would it be?

Suggested Readings

American Bar Association, *Law and the Courts: A Handbook about United States Law and Court Procedures* (American Bar Association, Chicago) 1987.

H. J. Berman & W. R. Greiner, *The Nature and Functions of Law*, 4th ed. (Foundation Press, Mineola, N.Y.) 1980.

R. Grutman & B. Thomas, *Lawyers and Thieves* (Simon and Schuster, New York) 1990.

G. C. Hazard Jr. & M. Taruffo, *American Civil Procedure: An Introduction* (Yale University Press, New Haven, Conn.) 1993.

M. S. Umbreit, *Victim Meets Offender: The Impact of Restorative Justice and Mediation* (Willow Tree Press, Inc., Monsey, N.Y.) 1994.

R. Cranston, *How Law Works: The Machinery and Impact of Civil Justice* (Oxford University Press, New York) 2006.

L. Territo, J. B. Halsted, & M. L. Bromley, *Crime and Justice in America: A Human Perspective* (West Publishing Company, St. Paul, Minn.) 1992.

L. Siegal & T. Senna, *Juvenile Justice* (West Publishing Company, St. Paul, Minn.) 1994.

D. W. Neubauer, *America's Courts and the Criminal Justice System*, 7th ed. (Centage, Belmont, Calif.) 2007.

F. Adler, *Criminology and the Criminal Justice System*, 6th ed. (McGraw-Hill, Columbus, Ohio) 2006.

C. Roberson, H. Wallace, & G. Stuckey, *Procedures in the Justice System*, 10th ed. (Pearson, Columbus, OH.) 2013

Endnotes

1. Robert Pursley, *Introduction to Criminal Justice*, 6th ed. (MacMillan Publishing Company, New York) 1994.

2. S. Fox, *Modern Juvenile Justice: Cases and Materials* (West Publishing Company, St. Paul, Minn.) 1972.

3. R. Cadwell, "The Juvenile Court: Its Development and Some Major Problems." *Juvenile Delinquency: A Book of Readings* (John Wiley & Sons, New York) 1996, p. 358.

4. *The Supreme Court of the United States* (Government Printing Office, Washington, D.C.)

5. 1 Cranch 137 (1803).

6. M. Randall & L. Haskell, "Sexual Violence in Women's Lives," 1(1) *Violence against Women*, 6 (1995).

7. The Fifth Amendment's right to grand jury indictment and the Eight Amendment's right regarding excessive bail have not been applied to the states. See *Hurtado v. California*, 110 U.S. 516 (1884).

8. If the confession was obtained by coercion, it may not be admitted, even for impeachment purposes. See *Mincey v. Arizona*, 437 U.S. 385 (1978).

9. H. Wallace, C. Roberson, & C. Steckler, *Fundamentals of Police Administration* (Prentice Hall, Englewood Cliffs, N.J.) 1994.

10. *Private Security: Report of the Task Force on Private Security* (U.S. Government Printing Office, Washington, D.C.) 1976, p. 4.

11. See H. Wallace & C. Roberson, *Principles of Criminal Law*, 4th ed. (Allyn-Bacon, Boston) 2008.

12. See P. W. Lewis & K.D. Peoples, *The Supreme Court and the Criminal Process* (W.B. Saunders, Philadelphia, Pa.) 1978, pp. 974–975.

13. 372 U.S. 335 (1963).

14. 407 U.S. 25 (1972). See also *Scott v. Illinois*, 440 U.S. 367 (1979), where the U.S. Supreme Court held that the right to counsel only applies when imprisonment is actually imposed rather than merely authorized by statute.

15. Bureau of Justice Statistics Bulletin, *Criminal Defense Systems* (U.S. Department of Justice, Washington, D.C.) August 1984, p. 6.

16. *Strickland v. Washington*, 466 U.S. 668 (1984).

17. 475 U.S. 157 (1986).

18. 500 U.S. 44 (1991).

19. *Stack v. Boyle*, 342 U.S. 1 (1951).

20. 18 U.S.C. Section 3141 et seq. (1984).

21. *Hurtado v. California*, 110 U.S. 516 (1884).

22. 399 U.S. 78 (1970). However, in *Ballew v. Georgia*, 435 U.S. 223 (1978), the court held that a five-person jury was a violation of the Fifth Amendment. More recently, a statute authorizing a vote of five of six jurors was struck down in *Burch v. Louisiana*, 441 U.S. 130 (1970).

23. For more information on the various aspects of sentencing, see H. Wallace & C. Roberson, *Principles of Criminal Law*.

24. K. G. Armstrong, "The Retributionist Hits Back," 70 *Mind*, 471 (1969).

25. Andrew von Hirsh, *Doing Justice* (Hill and Wang, New York) 1976.

26. See *Leatherman v. Tarrant County Narcotics Intelligence & Coordination Unit*, 113 S. Ct. 1160 (1993).

27. Linda S. Mullenix, "The Influence of History on Procedure: Volumes of Logic, Scant Pages of History," 50 *Ohio Law Journal*, 803 (1989).

28. F. Carrington & G. Nicholson, "Victims' Rights: An Idea Whose Time Has Come—Five Years Later: The Maturing of an Idea," 17 *Pepperdine Law Review*, 1 (1987).

29. Lawrence W. Moore, "Federal Jurisdiction and Procedure," 41 *Loyola Law Review*, 469 (Fall 1995).

30. See *DeAguilar v. Boeing Co.*, 47 F.3d 1404 (5th Cir. 1995) for a discussion regarding the amount in controversy requirement in federal courts.

31. 326 U.S. 310 (1945). More recently, the U.S. Supreme Court has narrowed the scope of such contacts. See *Asahi Metal*

Industry Co. v. Superior Court, 480 U.S. 102 (1987), where the court held that merely placing a product in the stream of commerce is not an act that will subject a party to the forum state jurisdiction. Minimum contacts require some action directed toward the forum state.

32. H. J. Berman & W. R. Greiner, *The Nature and Functions of Law,* 4th ed. (Foundation Press, Mineola, N.Y.) 1980.

33. Mark D. Robins, "The Resurgence and Limits of the Demurrer," 27 *Suffolk University Law Review,* 637 (Fall 1993).

34. R. Grutman & B. Thomas, *Lawyers and Thieves* (Simon and Schuster, New York) 1990.

35. Kevin A. Moore, "Simple Answers to Common Problems During Depositions," 68 *Florida Bar Journal,* 111 (June 1994).

36. G. C. Hazard Jr. & M. Taruffo, *American Civil Procedure: An Introduction* (Yale University Press, New Haven, Conn.) 1993.

37. William L. Adams, "Let's Make a Deal: Effective Utilization of Judicial Settlements in State and Federal Courts," 72 *Oregon Law Review,* 427 (Summer 1993).

38. D. V. Otterson, "Dependency and Termination Proceedings in California—Standards of Proof," 30 *Hastings Law Journal,* 1815–1845 (1979).

39. M. S. Umbreit, *Victim Meets Offender: The Impact of Restorative Justice and Mediation* (Willow Tree Press, Inc., Monsey, New York) 1994, hereinafter cited as *Victim Meets Offender.*

40. Paul McCold, "Restorative Justice: The Role of the Community," paper presented at the Academy of Criminal Justice Sciences Annual Conferences, Boston, Mass. (March 1995).

41. G. Bazemore and M. S. Umbreit, *Balanced and Restorative Justice* (Office of Justice Programs, Washington, D.C.) October 1994.

42. Umbreit, *Victim Meets Offender,* 1994.

43. S. P. Hughes & A. L. Schneider, *Victim–Offender Mediation in the Juvenile Justice System* (Office of Justice Program, Washington, D.C.) September 1990.

44. "The Restorative Justice and Mediation Collections: Executive Summary," *OVC Bulletin* (U.S. Department of Justice, Washington, D.C.) July 2000.

3

Measurement of Crime and Its Effects

Chapter Outline

LEARNING OBJECTIVES

After reading this chapter, you should be able to:

- Explain the differences between the various types of official reports
- Distinguish between the other types of reports that provide information regarding the commission of crimes
- Understand the advantages and disadvantages of each of the various mechanisms that are used to measure crime
- Explain the limitations of statistical reports of criminal activities
- Discuss the advantages of the National Incident-Based Reporting System over the Uniform Crime Reports

OFFICIAL REPORTS

There are many different types of official reports, which are compiled by private or public agencies in the form of statistical data. These provide a much-needed resource for further research into the extent of crime and victimization. Those most commonly relied on are reports by local law enforcement agencies, the Uniform Crime Reports (UCR), the National Incident-Based Reporting System (NIBRS), and the National Crime Victimization Surveys (NCVS).

Uniform Crime Reports

During the 1920s, the International Association of Chiefs of Police (IACP) formed the Commission on Uniform Crime Reports to develop a uniform system of reporting criminal statistics. The committee evaluated various crimes based on their seriousness, frequency of occurrence, commonality across the nation, and likelihood of being reported to the police. In 1929, the committee finished its study and recommended a plan for crime reporting that became the foundation of the UCR program.

Seven crimes were chosen to serve as an index for determining fluctuations in the overall rate of crime. These seven offenses became known as the "crime index" and included the following crimes: murder and manslaughter, forcible rape, robbery, aggravated assault, burglary, larceny-theft, and motor vehicle theft. In 1979, Congress mandated that an eighth crime, arson, be added to the index. During the study phase of the project, members recognized that differences in state criminal codes would cause the same act to be reported in various methods and categories. To avoid this problem, they made no distinction between felony and misdemeanor crimes and established a standardized set of definitions to allow law enforcement agencies to submit data without regard for local statutes.

In 1930, Congress enacted federal law that authorized the attorney general to gather crime information.[1] The attorney general designated the FBI as the national clearinghouse for all data, and since that time data based on this system have been obtained from the nation's law enforcement agencies.

The **Uniform Crime Reports (UCR)** program is a nationwide statistical computation involving more than 1,800 city, county, and state law enforcement agencies that voluntarily provide data on reported crimes. During 2012, law enforcement agencies in the UCR program represented approximately 95 percent of the total population of the United States. The program is administered by the FBI, which issues assessments on the nature and type of crime. The program's primary objective is to generate a set of reliable criminal statistics for use in law enforcement administration, operation, and management.[2]

The FBI is tasked with administering the UCR program and issues periodic reports addressing the nature and type of crime in the United States. Although the UCR's primary objective is the issuance of reliable statistics for use by law enforcement agencies, it has also become an important social indicator of deviance in our society.

The UCR prepares an annual crime index. This index is composed of selected offenses used to gauge changes in the overall rate of crime reported to law enforcement agencies. The crime index is composed of those specific crimes that have been previously discussed. Therefore, the index is a combination of violent and property crimes. For example, approximately 15 percent of the index offenses are violent crimes and 85 percent are property crimes.

The UCR is an annual report that includes the number of crimes reported by citizens to local police departments and the number of arrests made by law enforcement agencies in a given year. This information is of somewhat limited value, because the data are based on instances of violence that are classified as criminal and are reported to the local law enforcement agencies. Many serious acts of violence are not reported to the police and therefore do not become part of the UCR.

A number of factors influence the reporting or nonreporting of crimes to local law enforcement. The Bureau of Justice Statistics reports that the most common reason victims give for reporting crimes to the police is to prevent further crimes from being committed against them by the same offender.[3] For both household crimes and other theft-related crimes, the most common reason given by victims in reporting the offenses is to assist in the recovery of the property.

Violent crimes are the most likely to be reported to the police. Household crimes are the next highest reported form of crime. Personal thefts are the least likely crimes to be reported to the police.

The most common reason given for not reporting violent crimes to the police is that the crime was considered by the victim to be a private or personal matter. The second most common reason for not reporting violent crimes is that the offender was unsuccessful in his attempt to commit the crime. The most common reason for not reporting household crime or other theft-related crime is that the object was recovered.

Victims gave different reasons for not reporting crimes to the police when the offender was a stranger instead of an acquaintance. They gave the following reasons for not reporting:

- The offender was unsuccessful.
- The victim considered the police inefficient.
- The victim felt the police did not want to be bothered.
- It was not important enough to the victim to report the crime.

Victims of crimes committed by acquaintances gave the following reasons for not reporting:

- The victim considered the crime a private or personal matter.
- The victim had reported the crime to another official.

The Hate Crime Statistics Act was passed by Congress in 1990 and mandates that a database of crimes motivated by religion, ethnic, racial, or sexual orientation be collected. On January 1, 1991, the UCR program distributed guidelines for reporting hate crimes, and the first report was published in 1992. Participation in reporting hate crimes continues to grow, and as of 2012, approximately 14,545 law enforcement agencies were reporting hate crime data.

With the exception of the hate crime category as noted, the UCR remained virtually unchanged for fifty years. Eventually, various law enforcement agencies began to call for an evaluation and redesign of the program. Because the UCR only lists crimes that are reported to it, this presents a serious problem as not all police agencies report crimes to the FBI and the Department of Justice. Because the UCRs rely on law enforcement agencies to voluntarily report crimes, there is the possibility of underreporting by some agencies based on political reasons.[4] The UCR generally provides only tabular summaries of crime and does not provide crime analysts with more meaningful information. In addition, the method of counting crimes causes problems. For example, only the most serious crime is reported. If a person is robbed and his car stolen, police agencies are instructed to report only the robbery. Finally, some crimes, such as white-collar crime, are excluded from the UCR system. After many years of study, the FBI began to institute various modifications to the UCR program. These changes established a more effective crime reporting system, the NIBRS. The transition from the USRs to the NIBRS has been slow and has taken many years. For example, as will be discussed later, the NIBRS system was approved in 1988 and as of 2013 has yet to be fully implemented.

National Incident-Based Reporting System

National Incident-Based Reporting System (NIBRS) is an incident-based reporting system in which agencies collect data on each single crime occurrence. NIBRS data come from local, state, and federal automated records' systems. An agency can build a system to suit its own needs,

UCRs

The Uniform Crime Reporting (UCR) Program has been the starting place for seeking information on crime in the nation. The program was started in 1929 by the International Association of Chiefs of Police. The reports were designed to meet the need for reliable uniform crime statistics for the nation. In 1930, the FBI was tasked with collecting, publishing, and archiving those statistics.

Today there are three annual publications; Crime in the United States, Law Enforcement Officers Killed and Assaulted, and Hate Crime Statistics. These are produced from data received from over 18,000 city, university/college, county, state, tribal, and federal law enforcement agencies voluntarily participating in the program. The crime data are submitted either through a state UCR Program or directly to the FBI's UCR Program.

In addition to these reports, information is available on the Law Enforcement Officers Killed and Assaulted (LEOKA) Program and the Hate Crime Statistics Program, as well as the traditional Summary Reporting System (SRS) and the NIBRS. Also available are frequently asked questions about the UCR Program.

including any collection/storage of information required for administration and operations, as well as to report data required by the NIBRS to the UCR Program.

The NIBRS collects data on each single incident and arrest within 22 offense categories made up of 46 specific crimes called Group A offenses. For each of the offenses coming to the attention of law enforcement, specified types of facts about each crime are reported. In addition to the Group A offenses, there are 11 Group B offense categories for which only arrest data are reported.

The NIBRS was designed to replace the UCRs. As the UCR data evolved, and law enforcement expanded its capabilities to supply crime information. In the late 1970s, the law enforcement community called for a thorough evaluation of the UCR Program to recommend an expanded and enhanced data collection system to meet the needs of law enforcement in the twenty-first century. The State of South Carolina's Law Enforcement Division was the first entity to use the proposed system to determine its workability. At a national UCR conference in 1988, the new system was approved.

The benefits of participating in the NIBRS are as follows:

- The NIBRS can furnish information on nearly every major criminal justice issue facing law enforcement today, including terrorism, white collar crime, weapons offenses, missing children where criminality is involved, drug/narcotics offenses, drug involvement in all offenses, hate crimes, spousal abuse, abuse of the elderly, child abuse, domestic violence, juvenile crime/gangs, parental abduction, organized crime, pornography/child pornography, driving under the influence, and alcohol-related offenses.
- Using the NIBRS, legislators, municipal planners/administrators, academicians, sociologists, and the public will have access to more comprehensive crime information than the UCR reporting can provide.
- The NIBRS produces more detailed, accurate, and meaningful data than the traditional UCR reporting. Armed with such information, law enforcement can better make a case to acquire the resources needed to fight crime.
- The NIBRS enables agencies to find similarities in crime-fighting problems so that agencies can work together to develop solutions or discover strategies for addressing the issues.
- Full participation in the NIBRS provides statistics to enable a law enforcement agency to provide a full accounting of the status of public safety within the jurisdiction to the police commissioner, police chief, sheriff, or director.

Many of the general concepts for collecting, scoring, and reporting UCR data in the *Uniform Crime Reporting (UCR) Handbook* (2004) remain applicable in the NIBRS. For example, the jurisdictional rules for collecting data from the city, county, state, tribal, and federal law enforcement agencies and the conditions under which a state UCR Program must operate remain the same. The *UCR Handbook*, NIBRS Edition (1992), provides a comprehensive look at NIBRS and combines the old requirements retained from the traditional UCR Program with the new NIBRS requirements.

The NIBRS has much more detail in its reporting system than the traditional summary reporting system used in the UCRs. In the NIBRS, agencies collect offense information on 46 crimes known as Group A offenses; in the UCRs, agencies collect offense information on eight crimes known as Part I offenses. In the NIBRS, an updated definition of rape includes both male and female victims; in the UCRs, only females can be reported as rape victims. In addition, the UCRs do not differentiate between attempted and completed offenses. The NIBRS does.

In the UCR reporting system, the "Hierarchy Rule" governs multiple offense reporting. If more than one crime was committed by the same person or group of persons and the time and space intervals separating the crimes were insignificant, then the crime highest in the hierarchy is the only offense reported. The NIBRS does not use the Hierarchy Rule. Accordingly, if more than one crime was committed by the same person or group of persons and the time and space intervals were insignificant, all of the crimes are reported as offenses within the same incident.

The UCR Summary reporting system has two crime categories: Crimes Against Persons (e.g., murder, rape, and aggravated assault) and Crimes Against Property (e.g., robbery, burglary, and larceny-theft). In the NIBRS, a third crime category was added, Crimes Against Society, to represent society's prohibitions against certain types of activities (e.g., drug or narcotic offenses).

The NIBRS collects information about crimes committed using a computer; the UCR system does not. The NIBRS collects more comprehensive data about drug offenses than the UCR system.

The following offense categories, known as Group A offenses, are those for which extensive crime data are collected in the NIBRS.

1. Arson
2. Assault Offenses—Aggravated Assault, Simple Assault, Intimidation
3. Bribery
4. Burglary/Breaking and Entering
5. Counterfeiting/Forgery
6. Destruction/Damage/Vandalism of Property
7. Drug/Narcotic Offenses—Drug/Narcotic Violations, Drug Equipment Violations
8. Embezzlement
9. Extortion/Blackmail
10. Fraud Offenses—False Pretenses/Swindle/Confidence Game, Credit Card/Automatic Teller Machine Fraud, Impersonation, Welfare Fraud, Wire Fraud
11. Gambling Offenses—Betting/Wagering, Operating/Promoting/Assisting Gambling, Gambling Equipment Violations, Sports Tampering
12. Homicide Offenses—Murder and Nonnegligent Manslaughter, Negligent Manslaughter, Justifiable Homicide
13. Kidnapping/Abduction
14. Larceny/Theft Offenses—Pocket-picking, Purse-snatching, Shoplifting, Theft from Building, Theft from Coin-Operated Machine or Device, Theft from Motor Vehicle, Theft of Motor Vehicle Parts or Accessories, All Other Larceny
15. Motor Vehicle Theft
16. Pornography/Obscene Material
17. Prostitution Offenses—Prostitution, Assisting or Promoting Prostitution
18. Robbery
19. Sex Offenses, Forcible—Forcible Rape, Forcible Sodomy, Sexual Assault with an Object, Forcible Fondling
20. Sex Offenses, Nonforcible—Incest, Statutory Rape
21. Stolen Property Offenses (Receiving, etc.)
22. Weapon Law Violations

There are eleven additional offenses, known as Group B offenses, for which only arrest data are reported.

1. Bad Checks
2. Curfew/Loitering/Vagrancy Violations
3. Disorderly Conduct
4. Driving Under the Influence
5. Drunkenness
6. Family Offenses, Nonviolent
7. Liquor Law Violations
8. Peeping Tom
9. Runaway (as of 2011, the FBI no longer collects data on runaways.)
10. Trespass of Real Property
11. All Other Offenses

The Bureau of Justice Statistics conducted a study comparing the differences in reporting between the UCR and the NIBRS and found the average differences between the two reports to be small—less than 2 percent.

Agencies and state UCR Programs are constantly developing, testing, or implementing the NIBRS. As of June 2012, 32 states have been certified to report NIBRS to the FBI, and three additional states and the District of Columbia have individual agencies submitting NIBRS data. Fifteen states are only submitting incident-based data, covering 100 percent of their state law enforcement agencies. Approximately 29 percent of the population is covered by NIBRS reporting, representing 27 percent of the nation's reported crime and 43 percent of law enforcement agencies. Seven additional states, two individual agencies and four federal agencies are currently in the testing phase, while NIBRS is still in the developmental stage in seven states or territories. According to the FBI, currently six states have no formalized plan to report incident-based data.[5]

National Crime Victimization Survey

The **National Crime Victimization Survey (NCVS)** is a nationwide sample of interviews of citizens regarding victimization. It attempts to correct the problems of nonreporting inherent in the UCR. The report was originally entitled the National Crime Survey (NCS) but was renamed to more clearly reflect its emphasis on the measurement of victimizations experienced by citizens. The NCVS began in 1973 and collects detailed information about certain criminal offenses, both attempted and completed, that concern the general public and law enforcement. These offenses include the frequency and nature of rape, robbery, assault, household burglary, personal and household theft, and motor vehicle theft.[6] The NCVS does not measure homicide or commercial crime.

A single crime may have more than one victim; for example, a bank robbery may involve several bank tellers. Victimization, the basic measure of the occurrence of crime, is a specific criminal act because it affects a specific victim. The number of victimizations, however, is determined by the number of victims of each specific criminal act.

NCVS is an annual survey of citizens that is collected by the U.S. Bureau of Census in cooperation with the Bureau of Justice Statistics of the U.S. Department of Justice. Census Bureau personnel conduct interviews with all household members over the age of twelve. These households stay in the sample for three years and are interviewed every six months. The total sample size of this survey is approximately 66,000 households with 101,000 individuals.[7]

The NCVS provides data regarding the victims of crime, including age, sex, race, ethnicity, marital status, income, and educational level, as well as information about the offender. Questions covering the victim's experience with the justice system, details regarding any self-protective measures used by the victims, and possible substance abuse by offenders are included in the survey. There are periodic supplemental questionnaires that address specific issues such as school crime.

However, the NCVS suffers from problems that mitigate its validity, such as respondents underreporting or overreporting crimes. The NCVS is based on an extensive scientific sample of American households. Therefore, every crime measure presented in the NCVS report is an estimate based on results of the sample. Because it is only an estimate, it will have a sampling variation or margin of error associated with each sample. In addition, it is only an estimate of criminal activity and does not mean that the crime actually occurred.

Each method of collecting data on violence presents a different perspective and has its own validity problems. What is certain is that violence occurs on all social and economic levels in our nation. Its toll on victims is severe and long lasting. No matter which statistic or sample one uses, all agree further research is necessary. Other researchers have gathered data regarding specific forms of violence.

The NCVS as noted earlier began in 1972, was redesigned, and the new methodology was systematically field tested and introduced, starting in 1989. The first annual results from the redesigned survey were published for 1993. Criticism of the earlier survey's capacity to gather information about certain crimes, including sexual assaults and domestic violence, prompted numerous improvements. Improved survey methodology enhanced the ability of people being interviewed to recall events. Public attitudes toward victims have changed, permitting more direct questioning about sexual assaults. Victims are now reporting more types of crime incidents to the survey's interviewers. Previously undetected victimizations are being captured. For example, the survey changes have substantially increased the number of rapes and aggravated and simple assaults reported to interviewers. For the first time, other victimizations, such as non-rape sexual assault and unwanted or coerced sexual contact that involve a threat or attempt to harm, are also being measured.

One limitation of the NCVS is that it does not capture homeless individuals or those living in institutional settings, such as prisons and detention centers. The NCVS also does not capture the experiences of a person who has left a household to escape violence (shelters or group homes). Furthermore, the NCVS does not count homicides (as the victim is unavailable).

Interest in community policing continues to grow. Although the controversy around the effectiveness of community policing still exists, most law enforcement officials express a desire to implement all or portions of a community policing program in their jurisdiction. This approach recognizes the importance of involving the community in addressing the crime problem.

The program points out that we continue as a nation to become more culturally diverse. Law enforcement officials acknowledge this trend in a variety of ways. Sheriffs and police chiefs state that they are aware of the need to respond to culturally diverse populations in the wake of changing national demographics.

These findings will assist policymakers in establishing research priorities for the near future. Professionals in the field have the same concerns that researchers and citizens display—the need for an end to violence in our society. These official reports provide insight into the problem, but they do not offer any concrete solutions.

A Comparison of the Uniform Crime Reports and the National Crime Victimization Survey

The U.S. Department of Justice administers both the UCR and the NCVS. These programs provide valuable information about various aspects of the United States' crime problems. The UCR and its replacement the NIBRS serve different purposes and use different methods to measure crime from the NCVS. Because of the different approaches, the information the three reports produce provides a comprehensive picture of the crime problem in the United States.

The NCVS was designed to complement the UCR, and each program therefore has similarities. Both programs examine rape, robbery, assault, burglary, theft, and motor vehicle theft. Rape, robbery, theft, and motor vehicle theft are defined in the same way in both programs. However, the UCR only measures rape against women, while the NCVS measures rape against both sexes.

The UCR's primary mission is to produce a reliable set of criminal justice statistics for law enforcement administration, operation, and management. The NCVS was established to provide previously unreported data about crime, victims, and offenders. The UCR measures crime reported to law enforcement agencies, while the NCVS includes both reported crime and unreported crime.

The programs define some crimes differently. For example, the UCR defines burglary as the unlawful entry or attempted entry of a structure to commit a felony or theft. The NCVS does not want victims to try to determine the intent of the offenders, so it defines burglary as the entry or attempted entry of residence by a person who had no right to be there.

For certain property crimes, the UCR measures these crimes per capita (number of crimes per 100,000 persons), while the NCVS measures these crime per household (number of crimes per 1,000 households). Because the number of households may not grow at the same rate as the total population, any growth or decline in these crimes may not be similar.[8]

National Assessment Program

The National Institute of Justice conducts the **National Assessment Program (NAP)** survey approximately every three years, which seeks to determine the needs and problems of state and local criminal justice agencies. Although not technically a measurement of crime, it identifies the day-to-day issues affecting professionals in the criminal justice system. It therefore provides a valuable insight into concerns that are raised by the professionals whose job it is to fight crime.

The NAP survey contacts more than 2,500 directors of criminal justice agencies, including police chiefs and sheriffs, prosecutors, judges, probation and parole agency directors, commissioners of corrections, state court administrators, prison wardens, and other criminal justice professionals. The samples covered all fifty states and the District of Columbia. Both urban (populations greater than 250,000) and rural (populations of 50,000 to 250,000) counties were included in the survey. Respondents were asked a variety of questions dealing with workload problems, staffing, and operations and procedures.

The results of the survey indicate a great concern about the impact that violence, drugs, firearms, and troubled youth are having on society and an overburdened criminal justice system. Overall, the survey indicates that cases involving violence caused problems with agencies'

Uniform Crime Reports (UCR) and the National Crime Survey (NCS) Are the Main Sources of National Crime Statistics

How do UCR and NCS compare?

	Uniform Crime Reports	National Crime Survey
Offenses measured	Homicide Rape Robbery (personal and commercial) Assault (aggravated) Burglary (commercial and household) Larceny (commercial and household) Motor vehicle theft Arson	Rape Robbery (personal) Assault (aggravated and simple) Household burglary Larceny (personal and household) Motor vehicle theft
Scope	Crimes reported to the police in most jurisdictions; considerable flexibility in developing small-area data	Crimes both reported and not reported to police; all data are available for a few large geographic areas
Collection method	Police department reports to FBI or to centralized State agencies that then report to FBI	Survey interviews; periodically measures the total number of crimes committed by asking a national sample of 49,000 households, encompassing 101,000 persons aged twelve and over about their experiences as victims of crime during a specified period.
Kinds of information	In addition to offense courts, provides information on crime clearances, persons arrested, persons charged, law enforcement officers killed and assaulted, and characteristics of homicide victims	Provides details about victims (such as age, race, sex, education, income, and whether the victim and offender were related to each other) and about crimes (such as time and place of occurrence, whether or not reported to police, use of weapons, occurrence of injury, and economic consequences)
Sponsor	Department of Justice Federal Bureau of Investigation	Department of Justice Bureau of Justice Statistics

Source: Report to the Nation on Crime and Justice, 2nd ed., Bureau of Justice Statistics, U.S. Department of Justice, Washington, D.C., March 1988, p.11.

workloads. Police chiefs and sheriffs indicated that domestic violence was primary among crimes of violence, causing them increased workload problems. Prosecutors ranked child abuse and domestic violence as significantly increasing their workload.[9] In the opinion of police chiefs and sheriffs, programs that prevent young people from obtaining guns are one of their greatest needs. In essence, it appears that law enforcement views the problem of juvenile crime in large part as a result of firearms.

OTHER REPORTS

National Family Violence Surveys

Two of the most comprehensive studies of family violence were carried out by Murray Straus and Richard J. Gelles in 1975 and 1985.[10] Both surveys involved interviews with a nationally representative sample of 2,143 respondents in 1975 and 6,014 respondents in 1985. The results of these landmark surveys continue to provide information and data for study in the area of family violence. They are continually cited as authorities in numerous texts, articles, and research projects.

In both surveys, violence was defined as an act carried out with the intention, or perceived intention, of causing physical pain or injury to another person. Acts of violence that had a high probability of causing injury were included even if injury did not occur as a result. Violence was measured by using the Conflict Tactics Scale (CTS). This tool was developed at the University of New Hampshire in 1971 and is still used in many studies of family violence. The CTS measures three variables: (1) use of rational discussion and agreement, (2) use of verbal and nonverbal expressions of hostility, and (3) use of physical force or violence. Respondents were asked how many times during the last year they used certain responses that fell within one of the three classifications when they had a disagreement or were angry with family members.

Both studies were judged to be reliable because of the sampling procedure, the large number of respondents, and the validity of the CTS as a measuring instrument. The studies surveyed families from all fifty states and assessed several different relationships: parent to child, child to parent, wife to husband, husband to wife, and sibling interactions. Interviews were conducted by trained investigators and lasted approximately one hour in the 1975 study and thirty minutes in the 1985 survey.

A comparison of the results of these studies indicated that physical child abuse declined from 1975 to 1985. Straus points out that there are several explanations for such a result. First is the increased awareness of child abuse from 1975 to 1985. During that ten-year period, child abuse became a common media topic. This knowledge, on the part of the respondents, may have lessened the likelihood of their reporting such acts of violence. Second, different data collection techniques were used in the two surveys: The 1975 data were obtained via the telephone, and the 1985 results were collected by means of personal interviews. Finally, there may have actually been a decline in child abuse incidents from 1975 to 1985. Even if the last explanation is correct, as Straus points out, this still translates into the fact that one of every thirty-three children, three to seven years old and living with their parents, are victims of child abuse.

Self-Reports of Crime

Researchers have used self-reports of crime to determine the extent of crime and deviance. Generally, the self-report studies involve using confidential questionnaires that invite the respondents to record voluntarily whether or not they have committed any of the offences listed. The data can then be compared with official conviction rates to discover which types of offenders are most likely to be convicted. Self-report studies indicate that criminal acts are spread throughout the population, and that the official difference between male and female, or working and middle class, rates of criminality are far smaller than the official statistics would suggest. In addition, generally self-report studies identify more offenders than the official crime statistics and different types of offenders. These research methods have thus brought into question many of the conventional explanations of crime, which have been based on official police records.

Some problems of self-report studies include the reliability of the answers, the fact that respondents may have a tendency to exaggerate and they generally do not include middle-class crime. Often, researchers are not able to gain access to certain categories of offenders, and most self-report studies have involved a captive audience of school-age students or prisoners.

Other Sources of Data on Violence

Clinical studies are another source of information regarding violence. These studies are carried out by practitioners in the field—medical professionals, psychiatrists, psychologists, and counselors—all of whom use samples gathered from actual cases of family violence. These researchers collect information from hospitals, clinics, and therapy sessions. Clinical studies normally have small sample sizes, and therefore caution must be used when drawing any conclusions. However, these studies provide valuable data on the nature of abuse and assist in evaluating the different types of interventions utilized in family violence as well as pointing out areas for further research.

Women are not the only victims of violent crime. Researchers and professionals have attempted to study violent crime from a variety of perspectives, including both the offender's and the victim's. In 1989, Weiner conducted a review of the major research dealing with individual violent crime.[11] He reviewed more than forty major studies conducted by scholars between 1978 and 1987. He concluded that the further an offender advances into the sequence of violent crime, the greater the risk that the offender will continue his violent behavior.[12]

There are also other violent acts that have only recently become criminalized. Stalking is the crime of the nineties.[13] It is a newly emerging area of criminal law that is being studied by several experts in the field of human behavior. Zona and his associates are using the files of the Threat Management Unit of the Los Angeles Police Department in an effort to study stalkers.[14] Meloy has published several articles and textbooks that examine the nature and extent of stalkers and violence.

Other Types of Crime Research

Violent crime receives most of the publicity in our society; however, it is only one of many crimes suffered by citizens. Property crime, fraud, and white-collar crime take a tremendous toll on their victims. There are a number of reasons for this lack of attention regarding nonviolent crime: the victims' movement initially focused on serious violent crime, a lack of understanding regarding the psychological and financial consequences of property or economic crimes, and a traditional underreporting of the nature and extent of this type of crime.

Sutherland's classic definition of white-collar crime is one way of viewing this offense. He defined white-collar crime as an offense committed by a person of respectability and high social status in the course of his occupation.[15] The FBI, on the other hand, defines white-collar crimes as those illegal acts characterized by deceit, concealment, violation of trust, and nondependence on the application or threat of physical force or violence. They are committed to obtain money, property, or services; or to avoid the payment or loss of money, property, or services; or to secure personal or business advantage.[16] Both of these definitions deal with economic crimes, or crimes that have the gathering of assets from the victim as their objective.

Several prominent researchers have called for more information about economic crime.[17] Understanding the nature and extent of economic crime is necessary if we are to attempt to respond to its consequences. One of the most common forms of economic crime is fraud. A nationwide survey of fraud revealed that a sizable portion of the adult population in the United States is affected.[18] Fraud was defined as a deliberate intent, targeted against individuals, to deceive for the purpose of illegal financial gain.[19] Included in this definition were various forms of telemarketing frauds, frauds involving consumer goods and services, deceptive financial advice, and insurance scams.

The survey used a random sample of the adult population of the United States. The respondents were asked about twenty-one types of fraud plus a catch-all category and were asked if they had ever been victimized or if an attempt had been made to victimize them. Fraud crosses all sociological barriers, and victimization occurs in all ages, genders, races, or incomes.

More than half of those surveyed indicated that they experienced victimization, or an attempted victimization at some time in their past. Approximately one in every three respondents were potential victims of fraud within the year preceding the survey. The attempt to defraud these victims was successful 50 percent of the time.

Economic crime is a serious form of victimization that is often overlooked by those tasked with, or interested in, studying the effects of crime on individuals. The consequences of fraud will be addressed in more detail later in this textbook. At this stage, it is important to acknowledge that there are other forms of victimization than violence-related crimes.

Summary

It is important in the study of any discipline to know how to measure the variables that affect that discipline. Because of a number of factors, which are discussed in more detail later in this textbook, the measurement of crime can never be completely accurate.

Official reports are those measurements of crime conducted by federal agencies. The most well-known official report is the UCR. This report, prepared annually by the FBI, acts as a barometer of our society. Because of several inherent shortcomings in the UCR, the NCVS was developed. This survey relies on self-reporting in an attempt to determine a more accurate accounting of the nature and extent of crimes in our society.

Other reports include the National Family Violence Survey and a variety of other sources of information regarding acts of violence. Researchers are paying significant attention to economic crimes and their effects on victims. Recent studies indicate that economic crimes, such as fraud, are widespread and occur at all socioeconomic levels within our society.

We continue to modify our measurement tools in the hope of perfecting a valid and true method of measuring crime. Understanding the nature and extent of criminal victimization is only the beginning in understanding the process of victimization itself. However, it is a critical phase in the study of victimology and one that all professionals in the field should understand.

Key Terms

National Crime Victimization Survey (NCVS) is a nationwide sample of interviews of citizens regarding victimization.

National Assessment Program (NAP) seeks to determine the needs and problems of state and local criminal justice agencies.

National Incident-Based Reporting System (NIBRS) is an incident-based reporting system used by law enforcement agencies in the United States for collecting and reporting data on crimes. Local, state and federal agencies generate NIBRS data from their records management systems.

Uniform Crime Reports (UCR) program is a nationwide statistical computation involving more than 1,600 cities, counties, and state law enforcement agencies that voluntarily provide data on reported crimes.

Discussion Questions

1. Explain the problems in using the UCR. If you were in charge of preparing it, what changes would you suggest to make it more reliable?
2. How would you improve the NCVS?
3. How does the NAP information benefit victim services professionals?

4. The National Family Violence Surveys were conducted over ten years ago. Why are data from the surveys still important?
5. Compare and contrast the other types of crime research. Can you think of another method to collect information about crime and victims?

Suggested Readings

M. A. Straus, R. J. Gelles, & S. K. Steinmetz, *Behind Closed Doors: Violence in the American Family* (Anchor/Doubleday, New York) 1980.

M. A. Straus, "Is Violence Toward Children Increasing? A Comparison of the 1975 and 1985 National Survey Rates," in R. J. Gelles, ed., *Family Violence* (Sage, Newbury Park, Calif.) 1987.

D. G. Kilpatrick, C. N. Edmunds, & A. K. Seymour, *Rape in America: A Report to the Nation* (National Victim Center, Arlington, Va.) 1992.

D. E. H. Russell, *Sexual Exploitation* (Sage, Beverly Hills, Calif.) 1984.

N. A. Weiner and M. E. Wolfgang, eds. *Violent Crime, Violent Criminals* (Sage, Newbury Park, Calif.) 1989.

E. H. Sutherland, *White Collar Crime, The Uncut Version* (Yale University Press, New Haven, Conn.) 1983.

Report of the Attorney General, *National Practices for the Investigation and Prosecution of White Collar Crime* (U.S. Department of Justice, Office of the Attorney General, Washington, D.C.) 1990.

G. Geis & Ezra Stotland, *White Collar Crime: Theory and Research* (Sage, Newbury Park, Calif.) 1980.

Endnotes

1. 28 USC 534 (1930).
2. "Crime in the United States, 2011," *Uniform Crime Reports* (Superintendent of Documents, Washington, D.C.) 2012.
3. Bureau of Justice Statistics, *Criminal Victimization in the United States, 1992* (U.S. Department of Justice, Washington, D.C.) 1994, p. 100.
4. M. E. Milakovich & Kurt Weis, "Politics and the Measure of Success in the War on Crime," 21 *Crime and Delinquency,* 1–10 (January 1975).
5. Bureau of Justice Statistics NIBRS Web site at http://www.jrsainfo.org/ibrrc/background-status/nibrs_states.shtml (April 15, 2013).
6. The UCR states that the NCVS started in 1973. See "Crime in the United States, 1994," *Uniform Crime Reports* (Superintendent of Documents, Washington, D.C.) 1994.
7. The UCR presents a different estimate of households than the NCVS. See Crime in the United States, 1994, *Uniform Crime Reports* (Superintendent of Documents, Washington, D.C.) 1994.
8. Michael R. Rand and Callie M. Rennison, "True Crime Stories? Accounting for Differences in Our National Crime Indicators," 15(1) *Chance,* 47 (2002).
9. Tom McEwen, "National Assessment Program: 1994 Survey Results," *Research in Brief,* National Institute of Justice (May 1995), p. 2.
10. See M. A. Straus, R. J. Gelles, & S. K. Steinmetz, *Behind Closed Doors: Violence in the American Family* (Anchor/Doubleday, New York 1980) for an in-depth discussion of the 1975 survey; and M. A. Straus, "Is Violence Toward Children Increasing? A Comparison of the 1975 and 1985 National Survey Rates," in R. J. Gelles, ed., *Family Violence* (Sage, Newbury Park, Calif. 1987) for an analysis of the 1985 survey.
11. N. A. Weiner, "Violent Criminal Careers and 'Violent Career Criminals,'" in N. A. Weiner and M. E. Wolfgang, eds., *Violent Crime, Violent Criminals* (Sage, Newbury Park, Calif.) 1989.
12. Ibid. at p. 127.
13. See for example, H. Wallace, "Stalkers, the Constitution's and Victims' Remedies," 10(1) *Criminal Justice,* 16–19 (Spring 1995).
14. Michael A. Zona, et al., "A Comparative Study of Erotomonic and Obsessional Subjects in a Forensic Sample," 38 *Journal of Forensic Science,* 894 (July 1993).
15. E. H. Sutherland, *White Collar Crime, the Uncut Version* (Yale University Press, New Haven, Conn.) 1983.
16. Report of the Attorney General, *National Practices for the Investigation and Prosecution of White Collar Crime* (U.S. Department of Justice, Office of the Attorney General, Washington, D.C.) 1990.
17. G. Geis & Ezra Stotland, *White Collar Crime: Theory and Research* (Sage, Newbury Park, Calif.) 1980.
18. Much of the material presented in this section dealing with fraud comes from Richard Titus, Fred Heinzelmann, & John M. Boyle, "The Anatomy of Fraud: Report of a Nationwide Survey," Research in Action, 229 *National Institute of Justice Journal,* 28 (August 1995).
19. Ibid.

The Consequences of Victimization

Chapter Outline

LEARNING OBJECTIVES

After reading this chapter, you should be able to:

- Explain the types of physical injuries suffered by victims
- Understand from a nonmedical perspective the extent and nature of the various physical injuries inflicted on victims of crime
- Discuss the three stages of crisis
- List the effects on victims suffering from posttraumatic stress disorder
- Explain the symptoms of acute stress disorder
- Distinguish between posttraumatic stress disorder and long-term crisis reaction
- Understand the other types of mental consequences suffered by victims
- Explain the financial consequences of crime victimization
- Explain the general stages of grief
- Understand the HIV/AIDS disease
- Explain how the HIV/AIDS disease impacts victims of crime
- Distinguish between the various victim populations that are impacted by the HIV/AIDS disease

PHYSICAL CONSEQUENCES

One obvious consequence of victimization is the physical injuries suffered by victims. These injuries are easy to observe and treat. They are also the ones we are most knowledgeable about, because majority of us know someone who has suffered a broken arm, leg, or other injury.

Types of Injuries

There are four general classifications of physical injuries inflicted on victims during the commission of a crime. These physical traumas include immediate injuries that heal leaving no trace, injuries that leave visible scars, unknown long-term physical injuries, and long-term catastrophic injuries. Figure 4.1 indicates the rate at which victims are subjective to being a victim of a violent crime resulting in physical consequences.

Immediate injuries include bruises, contusions, cuts, and broken bones. These injuries generally heal quickly and are not perceived as serious by most people. In fact, many of us have suffered these same types of injuries due to accidents or mishaps. However, some victims face more serious consequences as a result of immediate injuries. An older person who suffers a broken hip during a purse snatch may have significant complications during the healing process that could lead to death. A person with diabetes suffering from a stab wound may take two to three times as long to heal as another person.

Injuries that leave visible scars include those that result in facial scars; loss of teeth; loss of fingers or toes; scars on the neck, arms, or legs; and loss of mobility due to incomplete healing. The injuries are not considered catastrophic in nature but can cause changes in life activities. For example, facial scarring may result in a model being unable to pursue her career.

Unknown long-term physical injuries can include a potential exposure to human immunodeficiency virus (HIV) and acquired immunodeficiency syndrome (AIDS). These types of diseases can result in loss of life or a complete change in life activities. Other sexually transmitted diseases (STDs) may occur as a result of a sexual attack, including but not limited to gonorrhea, syphilis, and the herpes simplex viruses.

Long-term catastrophic injuries include those that restrict a victim's physical movements. For example, a person struck by a drunk driver may become a paraplegic or may lose an arm or a leg. These severe injuries often result in family members having to alter their lifestyles to care for the victim, while others may result in a reduction in the life span of the victim, change in identity, and change in the quality of life.

Medical Aspects

The types of physical injuries suffered by victims of crime cover the entire spectrum of trauma, from simple bruises to deadly gunshot wounds to the head. Although victim services providers

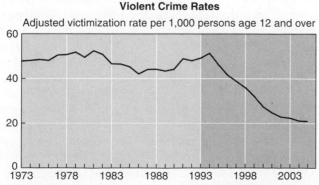

FIGURE 4.1   Violent Crime Rates for Victims 12 Years Old.   *Source:* Bureau of Justice Statistics, Criminal Victimization, 2005

IN FOCUS

The following crime clock statistics for 2011 is based on the FBI's UCRs. According to the crime clock statistics, there was on average, a violent crime committed in the United States every 20.2 seconds.

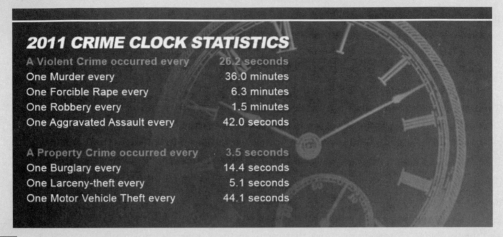

2011 CRIME CLOCK STATISTICS

A Violent Crime occurred every	26.2 seconds
One Murder every	36.0 minutes
One Forcible Rape every	6.3 minutes
One Robbery every	1.5 minutes
One Aggravated Assault every	42.0 seconds
A Property Crime occurred every	3.5 seconds
One Burglary every	14.4 seconds
One Larceny-theft every	5.1 seconds
One Motor Vehicle Theft every	44.1 seconds

Source: FBI website: http://www.fbi.gov/about-us/cjis/ucr/crime-in-the.u.s/2011/crime-in-the.u.s.-2011/offenses-known-to-law-enforcement/standard-links/national-data. Accessed on April 19, 2013.

are not expected to be physicians, they should have a basic understanding of the various types of injuries that victims may suffer. The next section briefly examines the medical aspects of some of the more common traumatic injuries.[1]

GUNSHOT WOUNDS   The U.S. civilian population is the most heavily armed in history.[2] More than 850,000 civilians have been killed by bullets in this century.[3] The science of ballistics is complex, but a few basic rules will assist in understanding the nature of injuries that result from gunshot wounds. The magnitude of the injury is proportional to the amount of kinetic energy impacted by the bullet striking the victim. This kinetic energy is determined by a variety of factors, including the distance between the assailant and the victim, the muzzle velocity, and the various characteristics of the bullet. At medium velocity, the missile has an explosive impact and creates a temporary passage in the tissue along its course. Bone and tissue may be fractured and torn without being directly struck by the missile. High-velocity missiles cause additional damage, including the possibility of fragmentation, which causes additional multiple trajectories and injuries. Medical personnel are interested in obtaining information regarding the type of weapon used, the distance from the assailant when the victim was shot, the suspected number of shots, the blood lost at the scene, and any type of fluids administered before arrival at the hospital.

Shotgun wounds present special types of problems. The shotgun was designed to strike a small, fast-moving target at close range. Because of the design of the pebbles inside the round, the shotgun is not an effective weapon at long range. However, when used at close range, a shotgun is extremely lethal. Shotgun wounds have been classified into three groups: according to the range, the pattern of the pellets, and the depth of penetration. Type I wounds involve long range (greater than seven yards) and basically result in a penetration of subcutaneous tissue and deep fascia only. Type II wounds involve medium range (between three and four yards) and may create a large number of perforated wounds. Type III wounds involve short or point-blank range (less than three yards) and involve a massive destruction of tissue. Type III wounds are lethal in nature, carrying a mortality rate of 39 to 65 percent.

STAB WOUNDS Knives are not the only instrument used in stabbings. Ice picks, pens, coat hangers, screwdrivers, broken bottles, and other sharp objects have all been used as weapons by assailants. Stab wounds usually result in lacerations or punctures. These injuries may be only a minor inconvenience or they may be life threatening, depending on the location and depth of the wound. Frequently, more than one stab wound is sustained in a violent incident. Medical personnel are interested in obtaining information regarding the type and size of the weapon, the estimated blood loss at the scene of the crime, the time of injury, and whether the victim had ingested any drugs or alcohol.

BURNS Burns are one of the most painful and devastating types of physical injuries. They are classified into superficial (first degree), partial thickness (second degree), and full thickness (third degree) according to the depth of the burned area. First-degree burns involve the epidermis tissue and may exhibit red or pink skin accompanied by hyperesthesia and tingling. The more common causes of first-degree burns are sunburn and brief contact with hot liquids. Second-degree burns involve the epidermis and dermis tissues and may exhibit red or mottled skin with blisters, considerable swelling, wet surfaces, pain, and sensitivity to cold air. The most frequent causes include scalds and flash flames. Third-degree burns involve the dermis or deeper tissues and may exhibit a pale white or charred appearance with a dry surface, exposed body fat, and systemic symptoms that include shock, hematuria, and hemolysis. The most common causes include fire, contact with hot objects, and electrical and chemical burns.

The severity of burns is based on both the extent and type of burn. The American Burn Association classifies burns as major, moderate, or minor in nature. Major burns include second-degree burns over more than 25 percent of an adult's body and 20 percent of a child's body; third-degree burns involving 10 percent of the body surface; all burns involving hands, eyes, face, ears, and feet; and all inhalation injuries and burns complicated by other injuries. Moderate burns include second-degree burns over 15 to 25 percent of an adult's body and 10 to 20 percent of a child's body and all third-degree burns of 2 to 10 percent not involving eyes, ears, face, hands, or feet. Minor burns include second-degree burns over less than 15 percent of an adult's body and less than 10 percent of a child's body and third-degree burns of 2 percent or less not involving eyes, ears, face, hands, or feet.

TRAUMA TO THE HEAD A significant portion of all emergency department work involves the care of people suffering from trauma to the head. Vehicle accidents, including drunk driving incidents, account for a significant percentage of this form of injury. Other criminal acts such as muggings and batteries also constitute another important cause of head trauma. Often, people who sustain head injuries receive other associated major traumatic injuries at the same time.

One effect of trauma to the head may be the inducement of a coma. Coma may be the result of a subdural hematoma, epidural hematoma, traumatic intracerebral hemorrhage, contusion, or concussion. Defining a coma is difficult; but for the purposes here, it is an altered state that exists in a person manifesting inappropriate responses to external stimuli and who maintains eye closure throughout the stimuli.

The victim's ability to relate the course of events leading to the injury may be compromised by injury, alcohol, drugs, hysteria, or any number of factors. Medical personnel will want to know if the victim was struck on the head by the assailant and what type of object was used. Police and firefighters will be questioned about whether the victim was awake on their arrival, and any changes in consciousness between the incident and arrival at the emergency room should be noted.

OTHER MEDICAL CONCERNS In addition to the different types of physical injuries suffered by victims of violent crime, victims of sexual assault endure a specific trauma that results in specialized medical issues. Rape victims will undergo a particular type of examination intended to assist in the prosecution of the perpetrator. In the recent past, these medical examinations were conducted by hospital staff with little or no specialized training regarding the effects of rape on the victim. In addition, there were times when a male police officer remained in the examination room to conduct questioning of the victim during the examination. Fortunately, there has been progression in the medical treatment of sexual assault victims; and in many jurisdictions, rape crisis counselors are available and present during this examination. They have been trained to provide support to the victim during this and other phases of the criminal justice process.

The rape victim should discuss the issue of pregnancy with hospital staff. If she was pregnant prior to the assault, the possible effects on the fetus should be discussed. If she was not pregnant, the possibility that the assailant impregnated her should be evaluated. The victim should discuss all aspects of this issue at the earliest possible time with the medical staff at the hospital or with her own physician.

The possibility of contracting an STD must be evaluated. Many of these diseases can be successfully avoided if treated immediately after the assault; however, many STDs will not show up during the physical examination, so rape victims should be tested several weeks following the attack. It is therefore critical that victims discuss this possibility with medical personnel.

With the threat of AIDS and HIV so much a part of our lives today, the possibility of contracting the disease is perhaps one of the most frightening aspects of sexual assaults. HIV causes AIDS. AIDS is a disease that attacks the body's immune system, rendering the person vulnerable to infections and diseases, and ultimately results in death. A victim may contract HIV in various ways. Victims should be tested immediately for HIV and request appropriate periodic follow-up testing. HIV/AIDS victimization is discussed in more detail later in the chapter.

MENTAL CONSEQUENCES

Crisis

Eric Lindemann is considered by many scholars to be a leading pioneer in the study of the effects of crisis on the mental health or emotional well-being of humans.[4] Lindemann offered both a new understanding of the dynamics of crisis and a systematic approach to treating those suffering from it.[5] His study dealing with the grieving process of the survivors in the Coconut Grove fire in Boston in 1942 has become the foundation on which much of the knowledge concerning the grief process has been built. Lindemann believed that acute grief was a natural and necessary reaction to significant loss. Another scholar, Gerald Caplin, extended Lindemann's theories to include all human reactions to traumatic events and not only the grieving process as a result of loss.[6]

Individuals react differently to different situations, and what may be a crisis to one person may only be a minor annoyance to another. As a result, the term *crisis* has many valid meanings. In medicine, *crisis* has one meaning, whereas in psychiatry the term is used in a different context. A number of scholars have defined the term *crisis*. Rather than adopting a sociological, medical, psychological, or legal definition of the term, it will be viewed from the perspective of a victim's reaction to crime. **Crisis** is therefore defined as a specific set of temporary circumstances that results in a state of upset and disequilibrium, characterized by an individual's inability to cope with a particular situation using customary methods of problem solving.[7]

Although some authorities may differ regarding the number of steps in the crisis reaction, one common analysis describes this process as involving three stages: impact, recoil, and reorganization.

THE IMPACT STAGE The impact phase occurs immediately after the crime. Victims feel as if they are in shock. Some victims cannot eat or sleep; others may express disbelief that the crime actually occurred. Statements such as "I can't believe this happened to me!" are common during this stage. Many victims feel exposed and vulnerable or express feelings of helplessness.

The impact phase may last for several hours to several days after the crime and is often punctuated by episodes of severe mood swings. One moment the victim may appear to be in control and the next moment exhibits disorganized and uncontrolled emotions. A crime victim is especially vulnerable at this time and susceptible to the influence of others. What may appear to be innocent statements offered by friends may be interpreted by the victim as blame for being the victim.

THE RECOIL STAGE During the recoil phase, victims attempt to accept or adapt to the crime and begin to reintegrate their personalities. Victims commonly experience a variety of emotions including guilt, fear, anger, self-pity, and sadness. Some victims struggle to accept the painful feelings caused by the crime; at other times, they deny experiencing any of these feelings at all. Caplin explained this process as involving victims who need opportunities to rest from wrestling with their situation, but who must eventually awake and return to consideration of the problem.[8] In essence, after trying to cope with their feelings regarding the crime, victims become emotionally exhausted and put these feelings aside so that they can rest, recover, and begin the healing process. Later, they are able to examine their feelings regarding the crime with renewed emotional resources.

Many victims are in denial during this phase. This emotional detachment can be an extension of the shock of the impact phase. Such detachment allows victims to develop a gradual immunity to the feelings that would overwhelm them if they faced them all at once. Victims may believe that they must seal off any feelings to get on with their lives. Some victims defend against any feeling during this phase by engaging themselves in work or other projects. Other victims accomplish the same objective by becoming almost obsessional with the criminal justice system—learning about the procedures, criminal laws, parties, and so forth.

It is during this phase that victims begin to deal with their feelings about the crime. Some victims will re-examine every detail of the crime in their minds. They may want to talk about it endlessly; others will dream about the crime. As victims confront the reality of the criminal act, they may re-experience the fear. Some victims only allow themselves to feel the full intensity of emotions after the immediate threat of the crime has passed. This feeling of fear can be immobilizing. Victims must verbalize their fears and other intense emotions associated with the criminal act to begin the healing process. With time, most of the traumatic impact associated with these feelings will lessen.

Another common feeling during the recoil stage is anger toward the criminal. Victims may experience rage but be unable to vent this feeling. Some victims may spend hours thinking about revenge, especially those who have suffered from a violent attack. Victims must understand that the desire for revenge is natural and a normal part of the healing process. Many victims want to construct a reason for their victimization. These victims search for the answer to the question, "Why me?"

THE REORGANIZATION STAGE After a period of time, the recoil stage gives way to the reorganization stage. The victim moves toward a more balanced state as feelings of fear and rage diminish in intensity, and he or she has energy left over to confront life's daily activities. The victim becomes more normalized as the need to deny the victimization lessens. Victims are gradually able to put their experiences in perspective and commit their energies to the task of living in the present.

Victims will never forget the experience and, as indicated earlier, they will respond in a variety of ways. This discussion has focused on one reaction to victimization. Other victims may experience different feelings. Acute stress disorder (ASD) is another reaction that victims of crime may experience.

Acute Stress Disorder

Acute stress disorder is acute stress that is experienced in the immediate aftermath of a traumatic event. This is a newly categorized disorder that was first listed in the *Diagnostic and Statistical Manual of Mental Disorders*, 4th edition (*DSM-IV*) in 1994.[9] The characteristics of ASD are the development of anxiety, dissociative symptoms, and other manifestations that occur within one month after exposure to the traumatic event. To receive a diagnosis of ASD, the victim must have experienced, witnessed, or been confronted with an event that involved actual or threatened death, serious injury, or a threat to the physical safety of the victim or others. In addition, the victim's response to such a condition must involve intense fear, helplessness, or horror. This diagnosis requires that the victim experience three of five posttraumatic stress disorder (PTSD) dissociative symptoms during or immediately after the traumatic incident. These symptoms must persist for at least two days but last no more than thirty days. The dissociative symptoms are derealization, depersonalization, dissociative amnesia, subjective sense of numbing, and reduction in awareness of surroundings. In the event these symptoms last longer than thirty days, the victim may be suffering from PTSD.

Posttraumatic Stress Disorder

PTSD was first identified when some Vietnam veterans began experiencing flashbacks of events that occurred during combat. **Posttraumatic stress disorder** is defined as the development of characteristic symptoms following a psychologically distressing event that is outside the range of usual human experience.[10] Traumatic events include, but are not limited to, military combat, violent personal assault (including rape, child sexual abuse, and child physical abuse), terrorist attack, torture, incarceration as a prisoner of war, natural or man-made disasters, severe automobile accidents, being kidnapped or taken hostage, or being diagnosed with a life-threatening illness. The characteristic symptoms require that the person experience, witness, or be confronted with an event or events that involve actual or threatened death or serious injury, or a threat to the physical integrity of self or others, and that the person's response involves intense fear, helplessness, or horror. The symptoms that the victim may experience include re-experiencing the traumatic event, avoidance of stimuli associated with the event, numbing of general responsiveness, and increased agitation.[11]

Victims of any type of crime can experience PTSD. However, several scholars have researched the effect of rape on victims.[12] Victims of rape have reported or been diagnosed as suffering from PTSD. Rothbaum's study found that 94 percent of rape victims displayed classic symptoms of PTSD one week after the assault. This figure dropped to 47 percent twelve weeks after the incident.[13] Kilpatrick and his colleagues' study *Rape in America* reported that 11 percent of all women who were raped still suffer from PTSD, and the authors estimated that 1.3 million women in the United States are currently suffering from PTSD as a result of a rape or multiple rapes.[14]

What is the difference between ASD and PTSD?

Readers often have difficulty distinguishing between ASD and PTSD. The following two paragraphs define each. Note there are many similarities between the two. The biggest difference is that ASD short term whereas PSTD is long term.

Acute Stress Disorder (ASD) is a psychiatric diagnosis that was introduced into the DSM-IV in 1994. The current diagnostic criteria for ASD are similar to the criteria for PTSD, although the criteria for ASD contain a greater emphasis on dissociative symptoms and the diagnosis can only be given within the first month after a traumatic event. The inclusion of ASD in the DSM-IV was not accompanied by extensive research, and some debate exists regarding whether the diagnostic criteria accurately reflect pathological reactions to trauma that occur within the first month after a trauma. However, even though debate exists about the empirical basis of the diagnosis, it has been found to be highly predictive of subsequent PTSD.

Post-traumatic stress disorder (PTSD) is an anxiety disorder that some people get after seeing or living through a dangerous event. When in danger, it's natural to feel afraid. This fear triggers many split-second changes in the body to prepare to defend against the danger or to avoid it. This "fight-or-flight" response is a healthy reaction meant to protect a person from harm. But in PTSD, this reaction is changed or damaged. People who have PTSD may feel stressed or frightened even when they're no longer in danger.

Source: R. A. Bryant & A. G. Harvey (2000). *Acute Stress Disorder: A handbook of theory, assessment, and treatment.* Washington, D.C.: American Psychological Association and the National Health Institute web site, http://www.nimh.nih.gov/health/publications/post-traumatic-stress-disorder-ptsd/what-is-post-traumatic-stress-disorder-or-ptsd.shtml. Accessed on May 1, 2013

Long-Term Crisis Reaction

Long-term crisis reaction is the name of a condition identified by the National Organization for Victim Assistance (NOVA). As discussed in Chapter 1, NOVA is considered one of the early leaders in the victims' rights movement. Organization members have responded to a number of crises throughout the world. Professionals from NOVA working with crisis victims have observed this reaction on a number of occasions. **Long-term crisis reaction** is a condition that occurs when victims do not suffer from PTSD, but may re-experience feelings of the crisis reaction when certain events trigger the recollection of the trauma in their lives.[15] The trigger event may be a number of situations, including the anniversaries of the crisis, birthdays, or holidays of loved ones lost during the trauma; significant life events such as marriages, divorces, births, and graduations; media events that broadcast similar types of incidents; and involvement in the criminal justice system.

The intensity and frequency of long-term crisis reactions usually diminish with the passage of time. As the victim develops coping mechanisms to deal with the trauma, these resources may lessen the victim's reaction to triggering events. The victim must learn to continue to function despite these reactions.

Other Mental Disorders

Victims of crime may suffer a wide variety of mental disorders as a result of their victimization. They are going through a process of attempting to regain their mental equilibrium that is off center as a result of the traumatic event. Following is a brief discussion of two common mental problems faced by victims of crime.

DEPRESSION Depression is described as a major depressive episode lasting at least two weeks, during which there is either a depressed mood or the loss of interest or pleasure in nearly all activities. Possible symptoms include changes in appetite or weight, sleep, and psychomotor activity; decreased energy; feelings of worthlessness or guilt; difficulty thinking, concentrating, or making decisions; or recurrent thoughts of death or suicide. The victim experiences clinically significant distress or impairment in social, occupational, or other important areas of functioning.

SUBSTANCE ABUSE The essential feature of substance abuse is a maladaptive pattern of substance use leading to significant adverse consequences related to the repeated use of substances. Normally, these substances are drugs or alcohol. The victim may suffer repeated failure in fulfilling major role obligations, repeated use of substances in situations in which they are physically dangerous, legal problems related to the use of the substance, and social and interpersonal problems.

Other Effects

Different victims of the same crime suffer different reactions to that crime, and conversely, victims of different crimes may suffer similar reactions. There is no "clear bright line" that professionals can look to and determine which symptoms victims will suffer. However, researchers have attempted to establish general categories of problems suffered by victims of certain crimes. In Susman and Vittert's text *Building a Solution: A Practical Guide for Establishing Crime Victim Service Agencies*, they listed certain crimes and typical reactions.[16] Although individual crime victims' reactions will vary depending on a number of factors, Table 4.1 summarizes these findings.

With the passage of time and other intervention techniques, the mental and emotional consequences associated with the trauma of a criminal act may lessen or be alleviated, but the victim may never be the same person as before the crime. In addition to the mental effects victims endure as a result of the crime, they also suffer fiscal consequences.

TABLE 4.1   Victim Reactions to Various Crimes

Burglary	Robbery	Assault	Sexual Assault
Home is no longer a safe haven	Fear of walking alone on the streets	Anger and/or bitterness	Embarrassment
Reluctant to leave home	Relief at survival	Realization of mortality	Difficulty in describing the incident
Reluctant to stay home	Realization of mortality	Physical injury	Concern about STD/ pregnancy
Express lots of "I shoulds"	Frustration at loss of personal effects	Medical bills	Bills for the medical examination
Heavy financial loss	Fear of intimidation	Time loss from work	Fear of telling family members
Sorrow at loss of sentimental items	For commercial robberies, fear of loss of job	Fear of reprisals	Fear the neighbors will find out
Disgust with destruction that occurred during the burglary		If assailant is a family member, feelings of betrayal	Fear of media publicity
Realization of isolation		If a result of a traffic incident, fear of driving	Recurring nightmares, changes in sleeping patterns, loss of appetite
Frustration with police who don't investigate thoroughly		If a result of jealousy, feeling of vulnerability	Decision to prosecute
Expense of securing home		For male victims, shame at losing a "fight"	Fear that they will have to testify about prior sexual history
			Bitterness against the offender
			Sexual dysfunction

Battered Women	Homicide-Survivor Victims	Child Victims	Older Victims
Decision to stay	Acceptance of death	Parents' reaction	Fear of crime
Decision to leave	Funeral arrangements	Signs of emotional distress	Acute financial loss
Financial worries	Financial problems when breadwinner is killed	Guilt	Change in lifestyle
Decision to prosecute	Delayed emotional reaction	Parents' unconcern	Loneliness
Desire counseling for batterer and/or themselves	Reaction of children	Difficulty in describing incident	Family reactions
For separated couples, visitation offers opportunities for further attacks	Need for information on the criminal case	Fears about testifying	Reluctance to get involved in the criminal justice system
Isolation	Media publicity	Incest—decision about family's future	
Helplessness	Feelings of powerlessness in the criminal justice system	Incest—mixed reaction by mother	
Psychological dependence	Ordeal during trial	Reaction of other children	
Fear of recurrence	Loneliness	Fear of intimidation	
Feeling of personal failure	Can't stop ruminating		
Reaction of other children	Desire for revenge		

Traumatic Incident Stress

The previous sections dealt with the mental consequences to the victims of crimes or natural disasters. This section focuses on the mental consequences to those who respond to various types of victimization. Traumatic incident stress may occur during or after exposure to such traumas as catastrophic events (earthquake, fire), severely injured children or adults, dead bodies or body parts, or the loss of colleagues. Emergency response personnel, as well as untrained volunteers and others who find themselves in a "helping" role during a crisis, may experience physical, cognitive, emotional, or behavioral symptoms (or a combination of these symptoms) that result from their involvement with victims of crime or natural disasters. The Centers for Disease Control and Prevention and the National Institute for Occupational Safety and Health have established a list of actions that emergency response team members can take if they believe they are being unduly affected at the scene of crime or disaster.

Vicarious/Secondary Trauma to Service Providers

In addition to victims, service providers frequently suffer vicarious/secondary trauma reaction similar to many of the trauma effects discussed in this section. Care should be taken to ensure that they are provided assistance should they experience any of the symptoms.

The likelihood of crisis reaction of service providers increases when they are exhausted. These on-site responders must pace themselves, because the rescue or recovery efforts may continue for days or weeks. Workers need to take frequent rest breaks, because many operations take place in extremely dangerous environments. Coworkers should watch out for each other. Responders should ensure that they maintain a normal schedule and eat, drink liquids, and sleep as much as possible. Whenever possible, they should take breaks away from the scene of the crime or disaster.

Once the responders return to their regular duty station or home, they should continue to adjust to the experience. They need to reconnect with their community. They should avoid making any major life decisions immediately after returning from their response to a mass victimization. The responder's family may also be affected by the experience. Each family member needs patience, understanding, and the opportunity to communicate his or her emotions and concerns.[17]

NEGATIVE SOCIAL CONSEQUENCES

As noted by Lynne Henderson, victims frequently encounter social isolation and an invalidation of their efforts to come to terms with their experiences, while at the same time confront the existential isolation presented by the reality of death.[18] Henderson contends that experiencing a violent crime—confronting one's own death—powerfully reminds the individual that he or she is alone. Although others may commiserate or empathize, they cannot negate the reality of the event. According to Henderson, the inability of friends and relatives of victims to confront the issues raised by victimization—either by "blaming the victim," minimizing the event, or by withdrawing from the victim's distress—may deprive the victim of the reassurance of relationship to others. Many times we tell the victims what they should feel or think, or we blame the victims for their plight and expect them to return to their "old selves" quickly to protect themselves from perceived threats to their own sense of invulnerability. Henderson notes that even if members of the victim's family or community are initially responsive and supportive, tolerance for a victim's feelings of loss, anger, fear, or meaninglessness is likely to wane long before the victim has time to begin to integrate the experience.

FINANCIAL CONSEQUENCES

About 12 percent of total mental health costs is spent on crime victims.[19] In 1996, the National Institute of Justice released *Victim Costs and Consequences: A New Look*, an in-depth study of the costs of victimization. The report was updated in 2001.[20] This study, as updated, raised serious questions regarding previous estimates of the costs of crime. Unfortunately, as of the date this text was published, the study has not been updated since 2001.[21] Using the data from the Bureau of Justice Statistics and including "quality of life" or intangible losses, this study concludes that the cost of crime is higher than previously suggested. The following sections examine the results of this study.

Introduction

It is fairly easy to establish the tangible costs of crime. These costs include a number of fairly easy-to-measure items such as medical care, police services, and other items that have a specific monetary value. However, it is not as easy to value the loss of "quality of life" or intangible losses suffered by victims of crime. How much is a murder victim's life worth? What is the cost for the pain and suffering experienced by a rape victim? In addition, costs associated with society's response to crime are difficult, if not impossible, to measure. Table 4.2 lists the major tangible and intangible costs of crime to victims, as well as society's costs associated with crime.

As Table 4.2 indicates, society's response to crime includes a variety of items that are not normally considered when discussing costs of crime. Measuring our actions and resulting costs based on our fear of crime is difficult. On the other hand, measuring items such as alarms for cars and homes, which are typical of the precautionary expenditures associated with protecting ourselves from criminal activity, is relatively easy. In addition, everyone understands the costs associated with running the criminal justice system and keeping offenders incarcerated. Thus, it can be observed that society's response to crime includes both tangible and intangible costs. The Cost of Crime to Victims column also includes tangible and intangible losses suffered as a result of criminal acts. These costs include tangible items such as medical and mental health treatment costs. The intangible costs include quality of life and loss of companionship. Table 4.3 examines both tangible and intangible costs of crime.

Table 4.3 indicates that costs of crime show tangible and intangible losses, which generally exceed all tangible losses combined. By multiplying the costs of crime by the annual crime incidence, you can obtain the aggregate figures. The tangible losses amounted to approximately $115 billion each year, and the intangible losses were more than three times that amount at an approximately annual cost of $400 billion. The next section examines the tangible costs of victimization.

TABLE 4.2 Major Costs Associated with Crime	
Cost of Crime to Victims	**Cost of Society's Response to Crime**
Direct property losses	Precautionary expenditures
Medical and mental health care	Fear of crime
Victim services	Criminal justice system
Lost workdays	Victim service organizations and volunteer time
Lost school days	Other noncriminal programs
Lost housework	Incarcerated offender costs
Pain and suffering/quality of life	Overdeterrence costs
Loss of affection/enjoyment	Justice costs
Death	
Legal costs associated with tort claims	
Second-generation costs	

Source: From *Victim Costs and Consequences: A New Look* (U.S. Department of Justice) 1996, p. 11.

TABLE 4.3 Tangible and Intangible Costs of Crime

- The direct costs of child abuse and neglect in the United States total more than $27 billion annually. When factoring in indirect costs, the annual cost rises to approximately $100 billion.
- The average monetary value of property stolen during a robbery is approximately $1,350.
- The average loss from the misuse of a victim's personal information is about $5,000.
- Telemarketing fraud has estimated losses to U.S. elderly exceeding $500 million per year.
- Many school districts report losses in excess of $250,000 because of school closings and costs of bomb search squads.

Sources: Crime in the United States 2011, U.S. Department of Justice, Washington D.C., October 2012, Identity Theft Survey Report , Federal Trade Commission, Washington D.C. September 2003; Total Estimated Cost of Child Abuse and Neglect, Prevent Child Abuse America, Chicago, 2001; Bomb Threats in Schools, U.S. Department of Justice, Washington D.C. February 2005.

Tangible Losses

Personal crime costs taxpayers, businesses, and victims approximately $115 billion per year in medical costs, lost earnings, and public programs related to victim assistance. These tangible losses do not account for the full impact of crime on victims, because they ignore pain and suffering and the reduced quality of life that many victims suffer as a result of a crime. These costs are estimated at $450 billion annually. Violent crime, including drunk driving and arson, accounts for $426 billion of this total and property crime costs $24 billion.

The following figures put these sums into perspective to help clarify the true magnitude of the costs of crime to victims:

- Violent crime and its resulting injuries account for 3 percent of all U.S. medical spending.
- Violent crime results in wage losses equal to 1 percent of all American earnings.
- Violent crime causes 10 to 20 percent of mental health expenditures in the United States.
- Personal crime reduces the average American's quality of life by 1.8 percent.

Victims usually suffer three types of losses: (1) out-of-pocket expenses such as medical costs and property loss, (2) reduced productivity at work because of sick days, attending trial, and so forth, and (3) nonmonetary losses such as pain and suffering and loss of quality of life. Some of these losses are easily quantified, but even the intangible losses may be valued in dollars. Tangible losses include property damage and loss, medical care, mental health care, police and fire services, victim services, and productivity. Each of these losses is explained in the following paragraphs.

Property damage and loss includes the value of the property damaged during the crime, or property taken and not recovered. It also includes insurance claims administration costs that arise as a result of compensating the victim under an insurance policy.

Medical care includes payments for hospital and physician care, emergency medical transportation, rehabilitation, prescriptions, allied health services, medical devices, and related insurance claims processing costs. Managed care systems are changing health care payments and are not reflected in these costs. More study is necessary in this area as medical costs adapt to changing circumstances.

Mental health care provides funding for services to crime victims by psychiatrists, psychologists, social workers, and counselors. This cost has been one of the least researched areas in crime victimization.

Police and fire services cover initial police and fire responses and follow-up investigations. The costs of other components of the criminal justice system are not included in this element. Generally speaking, police and fire costs are a relatively small portion of the cost of crime, averaging $225 per case.

Victim services costs include victim service agencies and child protective service agencies as well as foster care for maltreated children removed from their homes.

Productivity costs include lost wages, fringe benefits, housework, and lost school days suffered by victims and their families. This category includes lost productivity of coworkers and supervisors recruiting and training victims who are disabled as a result of a crime. It also includes processing costs for insurance claims and legal expenses associated with recovering productivity from drunk drivers and their insurers.

Intangible Losses

Intangible losses are hard to quantify; however, scholars have begun to place monetary values on certain aspects of a victim's quality of life. Researchers such as Ted R. Miller and others have divided intangible losses into two categories: fatal and nonfatal injuries. The monetary value for fatalities is based on the amount people routinely spend to reduce their risk of death. For example, this amount would include the cost of smoke detectors, alarm systems, and bars on house windows.

The intangible value for nonfatal injuries was established by analyzing jury verdicts for pain, suffering, fear, and loss of quality of life. As discussed in other chapters of this text, violent perpetrators rarely have sufficient funds to pay these awards, but third-party codefendants such as insurance companies or businesses that were negligent can be held liable for injuries to the victim.

M. P. Armour reviewed studies of the impact of victimization on survivors of homicide.[22] The studies included family and friends of homicide victims. Armour found that the survivors experienced a variety of mental health problems: PTSD, nightmares, fear, anger, survivor guilt, and other bereavement conditions that seriously impacted their social and personal functioning.

There is no doubt that attempting to establish a monetary value on intangible aspects of victimization is a relatively recent development in the field of victimology. For example, in 1994 a Bureau of Justice Statistics publication, *The Costs of Crime to the Victim*, specifically did not examine the intangible costs of crime.[23] Because this is a new aspect of victimization, it will continue to be controversial. However, we cannot truly appreciate the consequences of crime and victimization until we begin to accept the reality of intangible costs to victims and their families. This is an area of victimology that will continue to generate more study and debate in the future.

Grief

Victims frequently suffer grief as the result of their loss. Grief is also frequently suffered by law enforcement and mental health professionals who observe or are involved in assisting victims. Grief is difficult to define. It generally occurs when a person experiences a significant loss. Grief has no set patterns. In addition, the length and severity of each grief experience varies. Reactions and responses to a grief experience may include a feeling of shock and or numbness. Often, grief is followed by disbelief—"It can't be real." "How can this occur?" Frequently, the person suffering a grief experience will be confused and will try to make sense of it—"Why has this happened to me?" Anger and feeling deserted are frequent experiences. The person often feels that nobody seems to care or yearns for life to return to normal again.

To help understand the phenomena, we can examine some of the common stages that a person experiences during the grief process. The stages are general and not all may be experienced by everyone undergoing a grief experience.

SHOCK AND DENIAL The first stage is generally the reaction when a person learns of the loss. Often the person denies the reality of the loss at some level as an effort to avoid the pain. Shock provides emotional protection from being overwhelmed all at once. This may last for weeks.

Pain and Guilt

As the shock wears off, it is replaced with the suffering of pain. Most counselors contend that it is important to experience the pain and not hide it, avoid it, or escape from it with alcohol or drugs. The person may have guilty feelings or remorse over things he or she did or didn't do to prevent the loss.

ANGER Frequently the feeling of frustration gives way to anger, and the person may lash out and lay unwarranted blame for the death on someone else.

DEPRESSION, REFLECTION, AND LONELINESS When the person's friends think that he or she should be getting on with life, a long period of sad reflection often overtakes the person. It is during this time that the person finally realizes the true magnitude of the loss, and it depresses the person. Frequently the person will go into isolation and focus on memories of the past. He or she may sense feelings of emptiness or despair.

START OF RECOVERY Eventually the person starts to adjust to life without the dear one and life becomes a little calmer and more organized. The physical symptoms lessen, and depression begins to lift slightly.

RECONSTRUCTION As the person becomes more functional, his or her mind starts working again. The person starts seeking realistic solutions to problems posed by life without the help of a loved one. The individual will start to work on practical and financial problems and reconstructs him- or herself.

ACCEPTANCE Finally the individual learns to accept and deal with the reality of the situation. Acceptance does not necessarily mean instant happiness. Given the pain and turmoil the person may have experienced, he or she may never return to the carefree, untroubled person that existed before the event.

General Tips on Responding to Victims

Responders often feel uneasy when dealing with victims. In addition, the victims feel helpless, vulnerable, and frightened. As a general rule, the first responder needs to help the victim feel safe. The Office for Victims of Crime, U.S. Department of Justice recommends the following general responses:[24]

- Introduce yourself to the victim and briefly explain your role and duties.
- Reassure the victim of their safety and of your concern for them.
- Ask the victims to tell you what happened.
- Offer to contact a family member or close friend.
- Be mindful of the victims' privacy.
- Ask simple easy to understand questions.
- Ask victims about any special needs.
- Provide a safety net before leaving victims.
- Give victims in writing your name and contact information.

- Do not cut short or interrupt victims' expressions of their emotions.
- Observe and note victims' body language including their posture, facial expressions, tone of voice, gestures, eye contact or lack thereof, and general appearance.
- Assure victims that their emotional reactions are not unusual.
- Counter any self-blame by the victims.
- Encourage the victims to tell the whole story.
- Ask open-ended questions, for example, "Can you tell me what happened?"
- Show that you are listening and are concerned.
- Repeat or rephrase what you think you heard, for example, "Let's see if I understand you correctly, did you say…?
- Explain to the victims what comes next.
- Ask victims if they have any questions.

While the experience of grief is normal and painful, the person's reactions may vary. Remember that a person experiencing grief needs support. If grief is not recognized and acknowledged, it can fester and have a detrimental effect on a person's health and well-being.

COSTS OF FRAUD CRIMES

When we think of the consequences of victimization, we typically focus on violent crime and do not automatically consider the consequences of fraud crimes such as white-collar crime. This form of crime encompasses a wide variety of criminal offenses. Some of them make the front-page headlines, while others are a statistic on police blotter records. This section examines some of the more common white-collar crimes and their costs to the victims and society in general.

One of the better-known forms of fraud is software piracy. Software piracy is a continuing problem that involves illegal copies of software. According to the National White Collar Crime Center, a trade group that represents the world's major software manufacturers, global losses for software piracy total almost $50 billion a year.[25]

Distress Situation Fraud

A new category of victimization involves distress situation fraud. This type of fraud targets individuals who are in a distress situation, such as victims of a natural disaster or victims in economic crisis. A typical distress situation fraud involved Norma Lopez and her husband. In 2007, Mrs. Lopez and her husband were on the verge of losing their home in El Paso, Texas, when Mrs. Lopez received a flier from a Florida company, offering help for a fee to homeowners facing possible foreclosure. At that time, she and her husband were five months behind the mortgage payments and on the verge of having their home auctioned off. Mrs. Lopez filled out the forms the Florida company asked for and paid them about $1,400. They never did anything for her and her husband.[26]

Mrs. Lopez is one of a growing number of people across the country that have fallen victim to mortgage modification scams, according to federal officials. Federal officials in April 2009 announced a broad crackdown on such companies. The scammers charge upfront fees of $1,000 to $3,000 for help with loan modifications that rarely occur. The frauds often involve companies with official-sounding names that are designed to make borrowers think they are using the 2009 federal government efforts to modify or refinance 7 million to 9 million mortgages. Since the economic downturn in 2008, homeowners have flooded state attorneys general, including in Texas, with complaints about for-profit loan modification consultants. While some are legitimate, authorities say most are con artists.

In view of disasters such as the tsunami that struck Indonesia in December 2004 and hurricanes Katrina and Ike, which devastated the north-central Gulf Coast of the United States in August 2005 and September 2008, respectively, it is important to understand the costs generated by disaster fraud. Disaster fraud is any activity the purpose of which is to defraud individuals or the government after a natural or man-made catastrophe. The total amount of disaster fraud costs is difficult to determine. Following a disaster, most relief agencies focus on providing victims with various forms of relief. However, property and casualty insurance fraud costs Americans an estimated $20 billion each year. For example, it estimated that the average household may pay as much as $200 to $300 extra in insurance premiums annually as a result of insurance fraud.[27]

White-Collar Crime

White-collar crime is generally a form of fraud, because it is an act of deliberate deception for unlawful gain. The term *white-collar crime* was coined in 1939 by Professor Edwin Sutherland during his speech to the American Sociological Society. He used the term to describe "a crime committed by a person of respectability and high social status in the course of his occupation."[28]

The key element of white-collar crime is that it is committed by an offender in the course of his or her occupation. It is estimated that a great deal of white-collar crime is undetected, or if detected, it is not reported. While the use of deception and fraud is not new, today's con artists are more savvy and sophisticated than ever, engineering everything from slick online scams to complex stock and health care frauds.

Bernard Lawrence Madoff, an American businessman and former nonexecutive chairman of the NASDAQ stock exchange, was convicted of operating a scheme that was probably the largest investor fraud ever committed by a single person. On March 12, 2009, he pled guilty to an eleven-count criminal complaint, admitting to defrauding thousands of investors. Federal prosecutors estimated client losses, which included fabricated gains, of almost $65 billion. His victims included many famous people. Several individuals whose life savings were lost committed suicide.[29]

Most white-collar crimes are difficult to prosecute, because the offenders use sophisticated means to conceal their crimes, and generally their activities involve a series of complex transactions. White-collar offenses include antitrust violations, computer and Internet fraud, credit card fraud, phone and telemarketing fraud, bankruptcy fraud, health care fraud, environmental law violations, insurance fraud, mail fraud, government fraud, tax evasion, financial fraud, securities fraud, insider trading, bribery, kickbacks, counterfeiting, public corruption, money laundering, embezzlement, economic espionage, and trade secret theft.[30] According to the FBI, white-collar crime is estimated to cost the United States more than $300 billion annually. Often, the government charges and prosecutes both individuals and corporations for white-collar crimes. Defenses available to non-white-collar defendants in criminal court are also available to those accused of white-collar crimes. A common defense used by white-collar offenders is the defense of entrapment. This was the case in *United States v. Williams*, 705 F.2d 603 (2nd Cir. 1983), one of the cases arising from "Operation Abscam" in which Senator Harrison Williams attempted unsuccessfully to argue that the government induced him into accepting a bribe.

The Commerce Clause of the U.S. Constitution gives the federal government the authority to regulate white-collar crime, and a number of federal agencies, including the FBI, the Internal Revenue Service, the Secret Service, U.S. Customs, the Environmental Protection Agency, and the Securities and Exchange Commission, are involved in the enforcement of federal white-collar crime legislation. Also, most states employ their own state agencies to enforce state white-collar crime laws at the state level.

Organized Crime

According to recent FBI reports, organized crime is not just the Italian and Sicilian Mafioso of the television and the silver screen. The FBI contends that in recent years, the face of organized crime has changed, and the threat is broader and more complex than ever. Today, organized crime includes Russian mobsters who fled to the United States in the wake of the Soviet Union's collapse; groups from African countries like Nigeria that engage in drug trafficking and financial scams; Chinese tongs, Japanese Boryokudan, and other Asian crime rings; and enterprises based in Eastern European nations like Hungary and Romania. All of these groups have a presence in the United States or are targeting our citizens from afar—using the Internet and other technologies of our global age. More and more, they are literally becoming partners in crime, realizing they have more to gain from cooperating than competing.[31]

The impact of organized crime is not easily measured, but according to the FBI it is significant. Organized crime rings manipulate and monopolize financial markets, traditional institutions such as labor unions, and legitimate industries such as construction and trash hauling. They bring drugs into cities and raise the level of violence in communities by buying off corrupt officials and using graft, extortion, intimidation, and murder to maintain their operations. Their underground businesses—including prostitution and human trafficking—sow misery nationally and globally. They also con individuals out of millions of dollars each year through various stock frauds and financial scams. The economic impact alone is staggering; it is estimated that global organized crime reaps illegal profits of around $1 trillion per year.[32]

Identity Theft

Identity theft is rapidly becoming a crime of immeasurable proportions that is causing untold injury to thousands of Americans each year. It occurs when a person knowingly transfers or uses, without legal authority, the identification documentation of another person with the intent to commit, aid, or abet any unlawful activity that constitutes a felony.[33]

According to a Federal Trade Commission report on the impact of identity theft, victims have the following experiences:[34]

- Victims spent considerable time in resolving problems caused by the theft. Ten percent of the victims reported spending 100 hours or more resolving problems. The top 5 percent reported spending at least 1,200 hours.
- Almost one-quarter of all victims were able to resolve any problems experienced as a result of identity theft within one day of discovering that their personal information had been misused. This refers to the amount of time that passed from when they discovered the crime to when their problems were resolved, not to the number of hours spent resolving their problems.
- Thirty-seven percent of victims reported experiencing problems other than out-of-pocket expenses or the expenditure of time resolving issues as a result of having their personal information misused.
- The problems victims reported include, among other things, being harassed by collection agents, being denied new credit, being unable to use existing credit cards, being unable to obtain loans, having their utilities cut off, being subject to a criminal investigation or civil suit, being arrested, and having difficulties obtaining or accessing bank accounts.

The Consumer Sentinel database, which is maintained by the Federal Trade Commission, estimates that approximately 13 percent of all identity theft victims reported out-of-pocket expenses totaling $12.9 million. The average amount of out-of-pocket expenses reported per victim was $1,173. These costs were tangible costs and did not include intangible costs of the nature discussed earlier in this chapter. Approximately 17 percent reported dollar amounts totaling $98,253,576, or an average $6,767 per victim, stolen from their financial institutions by criminals using identity theft.[35]

Another costly form of white-collar crime is telemarketing fraud. It involves solicitations or campaigns to entice the purchase of goods or services or to entice charitable contributions through false representations in which telemarketing, via the mails, telephones, and the Internet, is an integral part of the effort. Many consumers do not report telemarketing fraud to law enforcement agencies as they are personal or property crime victimizations. Shame, embarrassment, disbelief, or simple unawareness that a crime has been committed may influence the nonreporting of these crimes. Congress has estimated that American consumers lose $40 billion each year to telemarketing fraud.[36]

White-collar crime continues to drain our society's resources and to impact each individual victim. While we have made progress in responding to and preventing this form of victimization, much work remains to be done. We are seeing more public awareness campaigns in the media, and such victimization appears to be losing the stigma it once carried. This change in viewing victims of white-collar crime will allow them to come forward and report such crime with the result that we as a society may better respond to their needs.

FOCUS

Have You Been Contacted?

A well-known scam involves an unsolicited e-mail stating that a West African national has an unclaimed or unreported fortune in that country. The message then reports that the recipient of the e-mail was chosen as a trusted agent to help get money out of the country. All the recipient needs to do is provide bank account details. The recipient is promised a share of the fortune but is usually swindled out of large sums of money withdrawn from his or her account.

HIV/AIDS VICTIMS

HIV/AIDS was the black plague of the nineties. It causes normally rational professionals to become emotional at the thought that they may have been exposed to AIDS. We are still learning the consequences of this disease; however, two facts remain constant—persons with AIDS die because of the infection, and at present there is no known cure. It is therefore critical that professionals in victim services understand how to respond to victims who have been exposed to this disease.

Medical and Psychological Aspects of HIV/AIDS

AIDS is the acronym for the medical term *acquired immune deficiency syndrome.* The "acquired" portion of the term means that the condition is not a birth defect but is acquired from another person after birth. "Immune deficiency" means that the immune system is repeatedly attacked by infections and diseases until it becomes so weak that it cannot perform its job. "Syndrome" means that a series of signs or symptoms occur together and characterize this particular abnormality. The term *AIDS* is to be used only when the person has become seriously ill and has fulfilled the Centers for Disease Control and Prevention's (CDC's) criteria for a formal diagnosis of AIDS. Otherwise, the more correct description "HIV positive" should be used to describe persons who have the HIV disease or infection.[37]

HIV stands for *human immunodeficiency virus,* which overcomes and destroys the body's natural immune system. As the immune system deteriorates, the person's body is unable to protect itself from infections and diseases. The person dies from a disease or infection. The person does not die from AIDS or HIV; rather death results from one or more of the infections that overcome the person's weakened immune system.

There are two primary types of HIV: HIV-1 is the most common and deadly, and HIV-2 acts in the same way as HIV-1 but reproduces more slowly. Almost all infected persons in the United States suffer from HIV-1. Once a person is infected with HIV, there is no known cure. The progression of the disease can be slowed with medication, but it cannot be stopped. Most cases result in death; however, some persons, known as "nonprogressive long-term survivors," have the virus, but it does not destroy their immune system and they do not become sick and die from the disease. Researchers continue to study these individuals in an attempt to learn why the virus affects them differently than it does the majority of the infected population.[38]

HIV has various phases, running the spectrum from wellness to illness.[39] Normally, the virus replicates itself in the lymph glands and then begins to dump copious amounts of itself into the bloodstream, thus setting the stage for progression of the disease. There are five phases in the HIV infection.

> **Phase 1.** Asymptomatic incubation period, which lasts from four to six weeks. Phase 1 is often called the window period, because the infected person has HIV present and replicating in the blood but generally has no detectable symptoms. This is a dangerous period, because infected persons have no idea that they are contagious. At some point during this phase, the first antibody is produced, and the infected person converts from HIV negative to HIV positive. This conversion is called the *seroconversion.*

> **Phase 2.** Acute primary infection, which lasts from one to two weeks. During phase 2, the person experiences some symptoms of early infection but may not recognize the cause of the symptoms. For example, the person may attribute aches, pains, and swollen glands to the flu. The infected person has sufficient antibodies in his or her system to detect the HIV virus during this phase.

> **Phase 3.** Asymptomatic phase, which lasts from three to fifteen years. This phase is characterized by seemingly good health while HIV continues to replicate in the blood and certain tissues and begins slowly to erode the body's immune system. The length of this phase varies among people depending on a number of factors, including the person's overall general health, self-care, and medical treatment received.

Phase 4. Symptomatic phase with persistent, generalized lymphadenopathy, which lasts from one to three years. Serious symptoms signal the beginning of phase 4. Infections that a healthy person would fight off will make an HIV-positive person ill. The symptoms for this phase include fever, night sweats, diarrhea, enlargement of the lymph glands, weight loss, oral lesions, fatigue, rashes, and cognitive slowing.

Phase 5. AIDS case, which lasts from one to three years. This condition meets the CDC's criteria for the definition of AIDS. As the person approaches death (end-stage AIDS), it is common to have multiple symptoms. The person dies as a result of infections and disease.[40]

HIV is not transmitted by animals or insects or by using swimming pools or hot tubs. It cannot be transmitted after contact with an infected person's clothes or use of the same toilet seat, eating utensils, drinking glasses, or telephone. There has never been a case in which HIV was transmitted by kissing or CPR. For HIV to be passed from one person to another, there must be an infected party, an uninfected party, and a route of entry to get particles of the virus from the donor to the recipient. HIV has been found in blood, semen, saliva, serum, urine, tears, breast milk, vaginal secretions, lung fluid, and cerebrospinal fluid. However, its presence in those fluids does not mean it is transmissible via those fluids. The three most common routes of HIV transmission are sexual transmission, blood-to-blood transmission, and mother-to-child transmission.

Most cases of HIV transmission occur as a result of sexual activities. Anal intercourse carries the highest risk of transmission because the fragile tissues of the anus and rectum may tear as a result of the friction of intercourse. Vaginal intercourse is also a high-risk practice with an infected person. Oral sex with a man or woman, although lower in risk than anal or vaginal intercourse, may also transmit the virus. Because of the violent nature of most sex crimes, there is a great concern that victims may be exposed to HIV.

Blood-to-blood transmission can also occur in a variety of ways. Using infected needles can transmit the disease. This method of transmission is common among drug users and is of concern to health workers who may receive needle sticks during their work with patients. The virus may be transmitted when contaminated blood or body fluids come into contact with open wounds. This is an area of concern in domestic violence cases when one party may get infected blood into an open wound of another person.

Mother-to-child transmission occurs when the virus is transmitted to the fetus of a pregnant woman. This is the most common form of pediatric transmission. A newborn may also become infected as a result of breast-feeding from an HIV-positive mother.

AIDS and HIV present social, psychological, and medical problems. AIDS has changed our view of public health and has affected how we judge others. People with HIV respond like all others in a crisis situation. Learning that one has HIV is a severe stressor because of almost certain result—death. Service providers must understand that there is no right or wrong way to respond to this life-threatening disease.

When individuals learn they are infected with HIV, they may react with a wide range of emotions similar to those experienced by victims of crime. The trauma of victimization is discussed in detail in Chapter 3. Once they have passed through these emotions, they must face the physical, social, and psychological aspects of living and dying with this disease. As death becomes more imminent, AIDS victims begin to plan for their death. This process becomes difficult and sometimes impossible because they may be coping with HIV-related dementia.

HIV-induced dementia is judged to be the direct pathophysiological consequence of the HIV disease. The major features of this type of dementia are forgetfulness, slowness, poor concentration, and difficulties with problem solving. The infected person may exhibit apathy and social withdrawal and occasionally experience delirium, delusions, or hallucinations.[41]

Victim services providers must remember that AIDS is a medical disease that has additional social and psychological aspects. Because some victims of crime may become infected by the virus, professionals must be knowledgeable regarding the disease and be prepared to address sensitive issues. The next section will examine some of these issues.

Victim Services Issues

Since society acknowledged the existence and impact of HIV, victim services providers have attempted to deal with its impact on the victims they serve. Most victim services providers focused solely on victims of rape. However, with the passage of time and expansion of knowledge regarding the disease, victim services providers now must understand how HIV affects victims of child sexual abuse and other violent crimes. Service providers must also be ready to deal with persons who are infected with the disease and who are victimized. In addition, they must respond to family members, friends, and colleagues of these victims who bring their own concerns, biases, and feelings to their interactions with victim services providers.

HIV/AIDS is a medical condition, and therefore a person's HIV status is considered confidential information. Victim services providers must always remember that they may not disseminate the medical status of a victim suffering from this disease without his or her express permission. Victim services providers must be able to explain the consequences to victims of disclosing or not disclosing their condition to others.

Creating a safe and open environment in which a victim, family member, friend, or colleague will feel secure enough in raising the HIV/AIDS issue is a critical first step in responding to these victims' special needs. In a safe environment, victims receive a message that they are with someone who has some knowledge of the disease and is open to discussing it. Victims must be reassured that the professional is not sitting in judgment of them or their lifestyle.

Displaying AIDS awareness posters in the office may assist in establishing this open environment. Posters can be obtained from local AIDS service organizations, county health departments, and the CDC. Information regarding the disease should be made available in brochures. Many victims have found lists of local AIDS service organizations to be very helpful.[42]

Raising the issue of HIV/AIDS with a victim who may be at risk is one of the most difficult tasks undertaken by a victim services provider. This topic may be made easier by the open and safe office environment. Victims may not want to discuss this topic for a variety of reasons: They may not realize that they are at risk; they may understand that they are at risk but be fearful of discussing the risk with anyone; or they may already know they are infected and decide not to disclose that fact.

Victim assistance professionals should take the time to review the victim's risk of infection and motivation for being tested. They should explain the testing process, including the various test results. They may need to consider a collaborative response to a victim's inquiry by using a local AIDS service provider. Victim services providers should never deliver the victim's HIV/AIDS test results. This would possibly introduce an uncomfortable aspect to the existing relationship because the victim professional may become a constant reminder of the moment the positive results were delivered to the victim.[43]

One controversial issue in the criminal justice field today involves involuntary testing of offenders. In recent years, several states have passed laws that give victims of sexual assault access to information about the HIV status of their offender.[44] These laws apply to those arrested, convicted, or who have pled guilty to crimes involving sexual penetration or other exposure to an offender's bodily fluids. At the federal level, sexual assault victims can request an order requiring the HIV testing of the defendant if the court finds there is probable cause to believe that the defendant committed the offense, that the victim has received appropriate counseling, and that the information is necessary for the health of the victim.

If the offender is positive, it does not mean that the victim will have contracted the virus, but simply learning of the offender's status may cause the victim unnecessary emotional upheaval. The victim must also be tested to be absolutely sure that the virus was or was not transmitted. Other professionals fear that imposing mandatory testing on offenders will lead to mandatory testing of other groups or professions. This continues to be a hotly debated topic.[45] The practicum that follows lists distinct classes of persons in our society. Discuss the advantages and disadvantages of mandatory testing of these persons.

If we adopt mandatory testing of offenders and other groups for the HIV/AIDS disease, isn't it also reasonable to test those groups for additional diseases, such as all other sexually transmitted diseases?

Professionals in this field normally work with persons who have already experienced the trauma of victimization. Most victim assistance providers do not encounter a person who has a life-threatening illness such as HIV/AIDS. When they work with these victims, it is with the knowledge that the victim will likely die as a result of this disease. It is therefore critical that everyone in the criminal justice system understand the effect on victims of HIV/AIDS.

Specific Victim Populations

Victim services providers must not only understand the HIV/AIDS disease but also be able to relate to specific victim populations who might be exposed to the disease. This section focuses on those victims for whom HIV/AIDS is a concern. The victim populations include victims of rape, child abuse victims, family violence victims, and HIV-positive persons who are victimized.

VICTIMS OF RAPE Even as enlightened as we like to think our society is about crime and victimization, victims of rape are still reluctant to report such assaults. Although many victims have experienced difficulty disclosing their rape to their significant partners, the additional factor of possible exposure to HIV may make disclosure even more difficult. The grieving process that normally occurs after a rape may now be extended and deepened because of the added fear regarding HIV.[46] These issues will continue to confront victim services providers as they work with victims of rape until we find a cure for the HIV/AIDS disease.[47]

CHILD VICTIMS The CDC reports that there were 6,209 pediatric cases of AIDS in the United States as of the end of 1994. Children who are sexually assaulted are considered to be at higher risk than adult victims of sexual assault. This increased risk is based on two factors: (1) Child victims may be repeatedly assaulted over a long period of time by the same perpetrator, and (2) children are at a greater risk of injury during penetration, and as a result there is a higher likelihood of transmission of the virus during the sexual act.

Victim services providers must assist parents in making informed decisions regarding how much information to give to a young child who has been sexually assaulted by an HIV-positive perpetrator. The victim services provider should work closely with the AIDS service provider regarding counseling and other support techniques for both the child and the parents.[48]

FAMILY VIOLENCE VICTIMS Family violence occurs every day from the mansions of Brentwood to the slums of New York. This type of violence crosses all ethnic, social, and sexual boundaries. Some family violence victims are forced to participate in drug usage with the abuser and his friends. In addition, the abuser may be using drugs or engaging in sexual acts with multiple partners that exposes him to the disease. He can then pass the virus along to his partner during

PRACTICUM
Who Should Undergo Mandatory Testing for HIV/AIDS?

Sexual predators	Professional athletes
Physicians, dentists, nurses	Law enforcement personnel
Members of the military	All persons above the age of fifteen

"consensual" sexual relations. The victim's request for use of a condom or other device may be met with violence by the abuser.

Shelters for battered women have traditionally been places of sanctuary for these victims. The spread of HIV/AIDS disease has added another complication to the heavy burden carried by these shelters. Victim services providers must ensure that staff working in the shelters understand the medical and legal aspects of the disease so as not to traumatize further those residents who are HIV positive.

HIV-POSITIVE PERSONS WHO ARE VICTIMIZED Persons who are HIV positive are no different from the rest of society as it relates to becoming a victim of a violent crime. What is different is that some persons have been victimized merely because of their real or perceived HIV status. Other HIV-positive victims must decide if they are going to disclose their status to authorities when reporting crimes of violence.

HIV-related violence covers a wide spectrum of acts from simple verbal abuse, to harassment, to job discrimination and actual physical attacks. The person's appearance may suggest that he or she is at risk of carrying HIV. Certain groups, such as homosexuals, drug users, and those wearing AIDS support ribbons and other symbols, have suffered HIV-related violence.

A person who is living with HIV must expend a great deal of energy on day-to-day survival, including taking medications, attending medical appointments and treatment sessions, and going to support groups. Suffering criminal victimization with its attendant responsibilities of reporting the crime, interviewing with law enforcement officers, attending court, and facing the perpetrator can add a tremendous amount of stress to the victim's life. This increased stress can dramatically impact the victim's health. For this and other reasons, HIV-positive victims may decide not to pursue reporting victimization. Still others may report, but as the burdens of appearing in court increase, they may opt to drop the charges. Victim services providers must be aware of the dynamics of this form of victimization and respond accordingly by supporting the victim.

Summary

We have known for centuries that victims of crime suffer from specific types of physical injuries as a result of their victimization. These are for the most part easy to recognize and treat. The broken arm or jaw may be repaired, and hopefully the victim will regain full use of such physical faculties.

More recently, society has acknowledged that victims of crime may also suffer a wide variety of mental problems as a consequence of their victimization, including ASD, PTSD, long-term crisis reaction, or other mental disorders. These reactions do not mean that the victims are insane or crazy. Rather, these are normal reactions to an abnormal event. Victim services providers and professionals who deal with victims must understand these dynamics in order to work with and assist victims of crimes.

Traumatic incident stress may be a consequence that victim services providers suffer as a result of rendering aid and support to victims of crime. In the past, we have focused on the consequences of victimization from the perspective of the victim and the victim's family. We must continue our research and study in this area. However, we must also be mindful of the consequences suffered by victim services providers and ensure that we care for the caretakers.

In addition to the physical and mental injuries, victims experience financial consequences of most crimes. Determining the amount of money taken from a robbery victim is relatively easy; however, it is harder to place a value on the intangible costs suffered by that victim. Recent studies have begun to address this long-overlooked aspect of crime victimization. The consequences of crime are multifaceted and, like a stone dropped in a calm pool of water, move out in ever-widening circles affecting victims, their families, and society as a whole. Professionals in the field must understand all the consequences of victimization to be able to function effectively.

Key Terms

Crisis is a specific set of temporary circumstances that result in a state of upset and disequilibrium, characterized by an individual's inability to cope with a particular situation using customary methods of problem solving.

Acute stress disorder is acute stress experienced in the immediate aftermath of a traumatic event.

Posttraumatic stress disorder is the development of characteristic symptoms following a psychologically

distressing event that is outside the range of usual human experience.

HIV stands for *human immunodeficiency virus,* which overcomes and destroys the body's natural immune system.

Long-term crisis reaction is a condition that occurs when victims do not suffer from PTSD but may re-experience feelings of the crisis reaction when certain events trigger the recollection of the trauma in their lives.

Discussion Questions

1. What are the four stages of physical injury? How do they differ from each other?
2. Describe the various types of physical injuries that victims may suffer.
3. List and discuss the three stages of crisis. In your opinion, which stage is the most critical for the victim? Justify your answer.
4. What is ASD? How is it different from a crisis reaction?
5. Explain the symptoms of PTSD.
6. Define long-term crisis reaction and explain a trigger event.
7. Compare and contrast PTSD with long-term crisis reaction.
8. List other mental effects of crime on victims. Which one, in your opinion, is the most serious? Justify your answer.
9. Should persons who commit disaster fraud be sentenced more severely than those who steal from a single victim? Why? Why not?
10. Should victims who are HIV positive be treated any differently than other victims? Why?
11. Should a person suffering from HIV/AIDS be required to disclose that fact to family members? to sexual partners? to workplace associates? to friends?
12. Should there be stiffer criminal penalties for perpetrators who commit crimes when HIV positive? What if they were unaware of their infection?

Suggested Readings

Albert J. Reiss Jr. & Jeffery A. Roth, eds., *Understanding and Preventing Violence* (National Academy Press, Washington, D.C.) 1993.

Albert R. Roberts, ed., *Crisis Intervention and Time-Limited Cognitive Treatment* (Sage, Thousand Oaks, Calif.) 1995.

R. B. Ruback & M. P. Thompson, *Social and Psychological Consequences of Violent Victimization* (Sage, Newbury Park, Calif.) 2001.

C. P. Wing, *Crisis Intervention as Psychotherapy* (Oxford, New York) 1978.

C. Roberson, *Investigating Identity Thefts* (Kaplan Publishing, New York) 2008.

Gerald Caplin, *Principles of Preventive Psychiatry* (Basic Books, New York) 1964.

Morton Bard & Dawn Sangrey, *The Crime Victim's Book,* 2nd ed. (Brunner/Mazel, New York) 1986.

Endnotes

1. Much of this information was gathered from interviewing members of the Fresno Valley Medical Center emergency room staff.
2. J. D. Wright, "The Demography of Gun Control," *The Nation,* 241 (September 20, 1976).
3. L. Adelson, "The Gun and the Sanctity of Human Life: or the Bullet as a Pathogen," *The Phasos,* 15 (Summer 1980).
4. Albert R. Roberts & Sophia F. Dziegielewski, "Foundation Skills and Applications of Crisis Intervention and Cognitive Therapy," in Albert R. Roberts, ed., *Crisis Intervention and Time-Limited Cognitive Treatment* (Sage, Thousand Oaks, Calif.) 1995.
5. E. Lindemann, "Symptomatology and Management of Acute Grief," 101 *American Journal of Psychiatry,* 141–148 (1944).

6. C. P. Wing, *Crisis Intervention as Psychotherapy* (Oxford, New York) 1978 and Gerald Caplin, *Principles of Preventive Psychiatry* (Basic Books, New York) 1964.

7. See Albert R. Roberts, *Crisis Intervention Handbook: Assessment, Treatment and Research* (Wadsworth, Belmont, Calif.) 1990; and Morton Bard & Dawn Sangrey *The Crime Victim's Book*, 2nd ed. (Brunner/Mazel, New York) 1986.

8. Caplin, *Principles of Psychiatry*, p. 46.

9. *Diagnostic and Statistical Manual of Mental Disorders,* 4th ed. (American Psychiatric Association, Washington, D.C.) 1994.

10. Ibid., pp. 427–429.

11. Ibid.

12. For an excellent discussion of the effects of rape on victims, see Bruce Taylor, "The Role of Significant Others in a Rape Victim's Recovery: People Who Are More Likely to Be Harmful Than Helpful," paper presented at the 1996 ACJS Annual Meeting, Las Vegas, Nevada, March 1996.

13. B. O. Rothbaum, E. B. Foa, T. Murdock, D. S. Riggs, & W. Walsh, "A Prospective Examination of Post-Traumatic Stress Disorder in Rape Victims," 5 *Journal of Traumatic Stress*, 455–475 (1992).

14. D. G. Kilpatrick, C. N. Edmunds, & A. K. Seymour, *Rape in America: A Report to the Nation* (National Victim Center, Arlington, Va.) 1992.

15. Marlene A. Young, "Crisis Response Teams in the Aftermath of Disasters," in Albert R. Roberts, ed., *Crisis Intervention and Time-Limited Cognitive Treatment* (Sage, Thousand Oaks, Calif.) 1995.

16. Jarjorie Susman & Carol Holt Vittert, *Building a Solution: A Practical Guide for Establishing Crime Victim Service Agencies* (National Council of Jewish Women, St. Louis Section) 1980.

17. Adapted from "Traumatic Incident Stress: Information for Emergency Response Workers," Centers for Disease Control and Prevention and the National Institute for Occupational Safety and Health (2005); available online: www.cdc.gov/niosh.

18. Lynne Henderson, "The Wrongs of Victim's Rights," 37 *Stanford Law Review*, 937–956 (April 1985).

19. Mark Cohen and Ted Miller, "The Cost of Mental Health Care for Victims of Crime," 13(1) *Journal of Interpersonal Violence*, 93–110 (1998).

20. Ted R. Miller, Mark A. Cohen, & Brian Wiersema, *Victim Costs and Consequences: A New Look*, National Institute of Justice (U.S. Department of Justice, Washington, D.C.) February 1996. This section is adapted from the material presented in this study.

21. Alfonso E. Lenhardt, "The Economics of Prevention: Reducing Costs and Crime," *The Police Chief*, 4–8 (April 2013).

22. M. P. Armour, "Experiences of Co-victims of Homicide: Implications for Research and Practice," 3 *Trauma, Violence, and Abuse*, 109–124 (2002).

23. Patsy A. Klaus, "The Cost of Crime to Victims," *Crime Data Brief* (Bureau of Justice Statistics, Washington, D.C.) February 1994.

24. U.S. Department of Justice, *First Response to Victims of Crime: A Guidebook for Law Enforcement Officers* (July 2010); available online: http://www.ojp.gov accessed on April 24, 2013, pp. 2–4.

25. Business Software Alliance (BSA), "Faces of Internet Piracy"; available online: www.bsa.org (April 13, 2009).

26. As reported by the El Paso, *Times Newspaper*, April 6, 2009, p. A-1.

27. Shawn Hutton, *Disaster Fraud* (National White Collar Crime Center, Glen Allen, Va.) September 2002; available online: www.nw3c.org.

28. Edwin Sutherland, *White Collar Crime* (Dryden Press, Hinsdale, Ill.) 1949.

29. "The Madoff Case: A Timeline," *The Wall Street Journal*, A-1 (March 6, 2009).

30. Legal Information Institute, "White Collar Crime: An Overview," (Cornell University Law School) 2009; available online: http://topics.law.cornell.edu/wex/White-collar_crime (April 14, 2009).

31. FBI "Report on Organized Crime"; available online: http://www.fbi.gov/hq/cid/orgcrime/aboutcs.htm (April 14, 2009).

32. Ibid.

33. The Identity Theft and Assumption Deterrence Act of 1998 (amending 18 U.S.C. Section 1028).

34. Federal Trade Commission—Identity Theft Survey Report (2007).

35. Ryan Brown & John Kane, *Identity Theft* (National White Collar Crime Center, Glen Allen, Va.) September 2002; available online: www.nw3c.org.

36. Kathryn Malbon, *Telemarketing Fraud* (National White Collar Crime Center, Glen Allen, Va.) February 2003; available online: www.nw3c.org.

37. *HIV/AIDS and Victim Services,* pp. II-1–II-2.

38. *HIV/AIDS and Victim Services,* pp. II-3–II-4.

39. *HIV/AIDS and Victim Services,* p. II-5.

40. *HIV/AIDS and Victim Services,* pp. II-5–II-8.

41. *HIV/AIDS and Victim Services,* pp. II-30–II-32.

42. *HIV/AIDS and Victim Services,* p. III-3.

43. *HIV/AIDS and Victim Services,* p. III-5.

44. See for example, Florida Code Section 960.003 (1) (1994).

45. *HIV/AIDS and Victim Services,* p. III-18.

46. *HIV/AIDS and Victim Services,* p. IV-7.

47. *HIV/AIDS and Victim Services,* pp. IV-21–IV-30.

48. *HIV/AIDS and Victim Services,* pp. IV-31–IV-33.

5

Victim Advocacy

Chapter Outline

LEARNING OBJECTIVES

After reading this chapter, you should be able to:

- Explain how social media may be used in victims' issues
- Distinguish between the different types of public media and their objectives
- Explain the legislative process and how special interests affect the drafting of laws
- Understand how to draft a speech
- Make a presentation in public
- Understand the use of volunteers in victim services programs
- Understand the role of fundraising in victim services programs

INTRODUCTION

One common feeling experienced by victims of crime when they become involved in the criminal justice system is helplessness. Many victims want and need to do more than simply testify in a criminal trial regarding the facts of the incident. Victim services providers can assist victims in this endeavor by providing them with advice regarding the different ways that they may become involved in the system. In addition, professionals in this field need to understand how they can work within the system to make it more responsive to the needs of the victim.

     According to the National Center for Victims of Crime, victim advocates are professionals trained to support victims of crime[1]. According to the center, advocates' duties include: offering victims information, providing emotional support, and helping finding resources and filling out paperwork. Frequently they accompany victims to court hearings. Advocates may also contact organizations, such as criminal justice or social service agencies, to get help or information for victims. Many advocates staff crisis hotlines, run support groups, or provide in-person counseling. Victim advocates may also be called victim service providers, victim/witness coordinators, or victim/witness specialists.

Advocates work in many different locations. Some serve in the criminal justice system (in police stations, prosecutor's offices, courts, probation or parole departments, or prisons). They may also be part of private nonprofit organizations such as sexual assault crisis centers or domestic violence programs. Some advocates are paid staff, and others are volunteers. Many advocates have academic degrees that prepare them to work with victims. They may have studied social work, criminal justice, education, or psychology. Advocates often receive significant additional training on the specific knowledge and skills they need on the job. This chapter will focus on those aspects of advocacy that concern using the media, public speaking, and getting people involved in victims' services.

SOCIAL MEDIA

Since the publication of the first edition of *Victimology*, technological advancements and social media, along with the coming of smart phones and the applications that permit us to access social media virtually anywhere, have increased our ability to communicate with large numbers of people. The use of such technologies are widespread and makes it easy for information to be disseminated quickly and efficiently, while at the same time allowing the sender or recipient of such information to remain anonymous if they so choose.

"Facebook," "MySpace," "Twitter," "LinkedIn," and "You Tube" reach millions of people and have the ability to unite groups of people over a shared cause, whether it is finding a missing child or putting pressure on members of Congress to re-enact the Violence Against Women Act. A status update, tweet, video, or blog can reach people in a matter of minutes; friends, family, and strangers alike. These sites increase the ways that people can raise awareness about a cause, issue, or idea, and also invite other people to join them. For example in 2013, when the U.S. Congress was considering whether or not to renew the Violence Against Women Act, victim agencies successfully used social media to put pressure on the representatives to pass this act.

Due to the number of people that these sites can reach, many missing children's parents and victim organizations are using them to gain support for their causes and disseminate information as well. Agencies actively using social media for presenting victims' issues include Canadian organizations such as the Missing Children's Society of Canada, Child Find, Victims of Violence Centre for Missing Children, Kids Help Phone, and the Canadian Resource Centre for Victims of Crime. These organizations not only have their own Web pages, but can also be found on Facebook, Twitter, and other social media sites. The organizations post relevant information on their news feeds, accounts, or threads which help keep people updated about current issues, controversies, missing children's information, resources, legislation, as well as a host of other important information.

Consider Amber Alert, which has traditionally relied on television and radio to inform the public of an abducted child that is in imminent danger, is now also on Facebook and is able to reach thousands of more people via their "app." In the case of Amber Alerts, smart phone users can download the appropriate app and receive alerts as soon as they are released in specific areas, allowing them to carry the information on their phone where ever they go. In addition to the app for Amber Alert, location-based apps, which are essentially a GPS system for your phone, are also now being used to locate missing children for whom an Amber Alert has not been issued.

Amber Alert Web site

In April 2013, the State of New York announced an updated Amber Alert system that sends alerts to wireless devices in the area where the alert has been issued.

The U.S. Department of Justice operates the Amber Alert Program, which is a voluntary partnership between law-enforcement agencies, broadcasters, transportation agencies, and the telephone industry, to activate an urgent bulletin in the most serious child-abduction cases. The goal of an Amber Alert is to instantly galvanize the entire community to assist in the search for and the safe recovery of the child.

The Amber Alert program was named for Amber Hagerman, a nine-year-old who was abducted and murdered in 1996. Amber was abducted while riding her bicycle in Arlington, Texas. A neighbor who witnessed the abduction called the police, and Amber's brother, Ricky, went home to tell his mother and grandparents what happened. Richard Hagerman and Amber's mother, Donna Whitson, called the news media and the FBI. The Whitsons and their neighbors began searching for Amber. Four days after the abduction, a man walking his dog found Amber's body in a storm drainage ditch. Her killer was never found, causing her homicide to remain unsolved. Her parents soon established People Against Sex Offenders (P.A.S.O.). They collected signatures hoping to force the Texas Legislature into passing more stringent laws to protect children.

In July 1996, Richard Hagerman attended a media symposium in Arlington. Although Richard had remarks prepared, on the day of the event the organizers asked Bruce Seybert to speak instead. In his twenty-minute speech, Seybert spoke about efforts that local police could take quickly to help find missing children and how the media could facilitate those efforts. A reporter from radio station KRLD approached the Dallas police chief shortly afterward with Seybert's ideas. This launched the Amber Alert.

For the next two years, alerts were sent manually to participating radio stations. In 1998, the Child Alert Foundation created the first fully automated Alert Notification System (ANS) to notify surrounding communities when a child was reported missing or abducted. Alerts, as originally requested, were sent not only to radio stations but also to television stations, surrounding law enforcement agencies, newspapers, and local support organizations. These alerts were sent all at once via pagers, faxes, e-mails, and cell phones with the information immediately posted on the Internet for the general public to view.

In October 2001, the National Center for Missing and Exploited Children launched a campaign to have Amber Alert systems established nationwide. By 2005, all fifty states had operational programs and today the program operates in a seamless capacity across state and jurisdictional boundaries.

Amber Alerts are spread via commercial radio stations, Internet radio, satellite radio, television stations, and cable TV by the Emergency Alert System and NOAA Weather Radio. There were some alternate regional alert names used, such as in Georgia, "Levi's Call" (named after Levi Frady); in Hawaii, "Maile Amber Alert" (after Maile Gilbert); and Arkansas, "Morgan Nick Amber Alert" (in memory of Morgan Chauntel Nick).

In order to launch an Amber Alert, police authorities need to meet the following four criteria simultaneously and with no exceptions:

1. The missing person is a child under the age of 18.
2. The police have reason to believe that the missing child has been abducted.
3. The police have reason to believe that the physical safety or the life of the child is in serious danger.
4. The police have information that may help locate the child, the suspect, and/or the suspect's vehicle.

Sources: http://online.wsj.com/article/AP48312122bba140198 7239c04ace7e30f.html. Accessed on April 25, 2013. "Senate approves national child abduction alert legislation", USA Today, September 10, 2002, page 01. Tomas Mainelli, (November 21, 2002), "AOL Puts AMBER Alert Service Online", PC World, p. 12. U.S. Department of Justice "Guidance on Criteria for Issuing AMBER Alerts (PDF)" Washing-ton, DC: U.S. Department of Justice. April 2004.

PUBLIC MEDIA

The public media have the ability to bring crime directly into our living rooms. It is therefore critical for victim services providers to understand how the media work and how to effectively communicate with them. The media can help or hinder the victim's recovery and subsequent attitude toward life. It is therefore important that professionals develop a working relationship with the media to help bridge the gap between the media and victims.

Many victims, police officers, and criminal justice professionals view news reporters with distrust.[2] Just as the police have a mission to accomplish, so do the media. The Constitution of the United States prohibits federal and state governments from passing any law that abridges the

FOCUS
Office of Crime Victims Advocacy

State of Washington

The Office of Crime Victims Advocacy (OCVA) was established in 1990 by the State of Washington. The office serves as a voice within government for the needs of crime victims in Washington State. Its functions include:

- Advocating on behalf of victims obtaining needed services and resources.
- Administering grant funds for community programs working with crime victims.
- Assisting communities in planning and implementing services for crime victims.
- Advising local and state government agencies of practices, policies, and priorities which impact crime victims.

The stated mission of the Office of Crime Victims Advocacy is to identify the opportunities and resources victims need in order to recover and to facilitate the availability of those resources and opportunities in communities statewide. In addition, the OCVA assists crime victims in accessing needed services and resources. It serves as an ombudsman for crime victims who are dissatisfied with the response they received in the aftermath of a crime. OCVA also provides individual case consultation to service providers and victim advocates regarding clients. OCVA administers grant funds in all communities throughout Washington State. Grant funds are provided by the legislature or the federal government to coordinate and enhance services designed to benefit crime victims.

freedom of the press. The media call this "the people's right to know." The media's attempts to inform the public occasionally conflict with a law enforcement agency's desire to keep certain information confidential. Only by understanding the media and their roles in society can victims deal effectively with the media to present their side of the story.

Relations with the Media

Understanding the media must begin with a clarification of the different types of media. The victim services provider must understand that there are certain basic fundamental principles that apply to the media in general. In addition, there are distinct rules, goals, and standards that pertain to each different type of communication system.

There are three basic types of public media with which criminal justice agencies interact: newspapers, radio, and television.

NEWSPAPERS Newspapers usually provide more in-depth coverage than the electronic media. They have the ability to print charts and graphs using statistics that allow the reader to place the current story in visual perspective. In addition, many newspapers are interested in the human aspect of the story. Newspapers may run a major story, coupled with a sidebar story that touches on another aspect of the main story. A **sidebar** story is usually an article that is placed in a column next to the main article. Many newspapers assign a reporter full time as either the police or court reporter. This reporter will know the officers, the language of the streets, and the law nearly as well as any police officer.

Different types of newspapers exist, and victim services providers need to know about the ones in their area. Some publishers print a daily newspaper and others go to press only once a week. Knowing the type of newspaper assists in understanding the time constraints or deadlines that the reporter faces. Most often when dealing with dailies, the reporter must have the information right away, whereas weeklies usually allow several days before the item must be turned in to the editor. In addition to local or regional newspapers, news or wire services such as United Press International (UPI) and Associated Press (AP) provide up-to-date coverage of local, state, national, and international events that are sent across the nation and the world on a news line.

RADIO A radio broadcast carries only the voice of the speaker, so the news broadcaster must paint a verbal picture of the situation for the listeners. Because radio reporters do not capture the scene with live pictures, many of the interviews with the victim or a victim services provider are conducted over the telephone.

There are a variety of radio formats, and anyone who has driven in a car and "surfed" the channels can vouch for many types of programs broadcast on the radio at any given moment. They include rock music, easy listening, classical, ethnic, educational, religious, all news, and talk shows. Each of these programs appeals to different audiences.

Many radio stations have hourly newscasts, and they can therefore update the public more effectively than can daily newspapers or nightly newscasts. In this day of visual media, an effective victim services provider should not overlook the radio as an additional source by which the public may be informed of the activities of their program.

TELEVISION Television is the most familiar medium. It brings the action directly into our living room as it occurs. Many of us have watched hostage scenes and riots as they are happening from the comfort of our easy chairs.

There are basically three forms of television: networks, independents, and cable companies. Network television includes the major corporations, such as the American Broadcasting Corporation (ABC), National Broadcasting Corporation (NBC), and the Turner Broadcasting System. Independent stations may contract with the networks for some of their shows or they may buy programs that are syndicated by private companies. Cable television combines both national and independent broadcasts and many times provides a news channel for local activities or community programming.

Television by its very nature is visual. A simple news release does not satisfy the television director, who wants and needs pictures and action: a uniformed officer speaking, a suspect being placed in a patrol vehicle, the front of a shot-up building. These graphic scenes are what television is searching for on a daily basis. In addition, television news is short and to the point. Normally, a story on the evening news is twenty to thirty seconds long. No matter how long the television reporter interviews a victim or other service provider, the final broadcast usually will run no longer than one minute.

Understanding the distinctions between the different types of media allows victims and professionals to deal with them in an effective manner. It is also important that victims understand how law enforcement agencies respond to requests for information from the media.

Some criminal justice agencies have codified the rules for these contacts by distributing a standard operating procedure (SOP) on media relations. This procedure has several advantages. First, it assures the media and the administrator of the agency that there is uniformity in dealing with the press. Second, it establishes procedures that both parties can follow. If media representatives are consulted when the document is being drafted, they will be more understanding of its purpose and will follow the procedures more readily. Last, the SOP informs the officer on the street how to respond to an unexpected contact with a news reporter. Understanding the process that law enforcement agencies use to release information will allow a victim services provider to interact more effectively with both the criminal justice agency and the media.

Using a public affairs officer (PAO) is more common in law enforcement agencies.[3] A PAO is the department's official point of contact with the media. There are several approaches to utilize a PAO. One approach is to make the PAO the official spokesperson for the department. All interviews are conducted by this person. While this approach may provide continuity, it is not the most effective method of dealing with either the public or the media. Any top-level administrator should be able to conduct a live interview with the media if he or she has above-average communications skills. A second approach is to establish the position as an official assignment and rotate officers through it based on their experience, intelligence, and abilities. This alternative allows the public and the media to "talk" to a sworn officer. The disadvantage to this approach is that depending on the length of the assignment, the media will have to readjust to a new officer with every rotation.

Victim services providers should become acquainted with the department's PAO. This affords them the opportunity to hold joint press releases in which both law enforcement officials and the victim's representative may present their views to the public.

Occasionally, members of the media will report information regarding private aspects of the victim's life. Some of this information is a matter of public record, whereas other sources of data may have been obtained through leaks from criminal justice agencies that have access to what is normally viewed as confidential information. News reporters are ethically bound not to reveal the identity of their sources. Just as police officers refuse to reveal the names of their confidential reliable informants, so do news reporters carefully guard the identity of their sources. Some states have "shield" laws that prevent a news reporter from being held in contempt of court for refusing to comply with a court order to reveal the name of a source. In addition, there have been numerous incidents of reporters going to jail rather than giving up the identity of their sources.

Victim services providers should accept that there may be leaks to the media concerning information that the victim wishes to remain confidential. By doing so, the effective victim services provider can attempt to work out a relationship with the press to minimize the impact of such a leak. One technique is to appeal to the integrity of the reporter and inform the reporter of the consequences of releasing the story. It is fruitless to get angry at the reporter or the unnamed source. Human nature being what it is, leaks will continue for as long as there is a reporter who is willing to listen.

Members of the media are also concerned about the plight of victims of crime. Organizations such as Criminal Justice Journalists have published procedures that inform reporters about various aspects of crime and the justice system. These procedures include valuable information regarding crime victimization.[4] Criminal Justice Journalists reports that crime and justice are the major subjects of American news coverage and that police and crime news rank third in the amount of space newspapers devote to it. The number one topic is politics and government, and the number two topic is sports. Crime news is even more prominent on television. It has been the number one subject of news coverage for the last five years, accounting for about one-fourth of all stories aired.

Journalists are responsible for providing readers, viewers, and listeners an accurate picture of crime, but they must also offer that view in context. Doing so may mean allowing the victim to comment on the consequences of the crime and how it has affected him or her as well as his or her family.

The Michigan State University School of Journalism offers the Victims and the Media Program, which educates journalists about various victim issues.[5] In "Tips on Interviewing Victims," Bonnie Bucqueroux, coordinator of the program, sets forth the following information about victims:

1. *Aim for the truth* Many journalists try to make some stories fit a preconceived idea of what has happened. It is important to accurately report what really happened, not some idealized or sensationalized version that the journalist has in his or her mind.
2. *Denial* Understand that victims may engage in denial, and journalists must be sensitive to the perils of pushing a person to accept what has happened before he or she is ready to do so.
3. *Anger* Many victims feel anger, which may sustain them and may also motivate them to work in the victims' movement to improve it or to make a difference.
4. *Bargaining* Some victims may engage in "bargaining" behavior: for example, a victim may promise that if her child is returned, she will devote her life to the church.
5. *Depression* Many victims may feel depression and appear exhausted and detached, but it is a mistake for a reporter to confuse this behavior with lack of caring.

While these symptoms and reactions are common knowledge to victim advocates, many journalists are unaware of them, and it may assist in the interviewing process if they are informed of some of the more basic reactions that victims of crime may suffer.

Bucqueroux sets forth the following guidelines for journalists to use when interviewing victims of crime:

1. Do your research before you interview the victim. Previous stories may have been inaccurate. Do not put yourself in the situation of having to interrupt a victim to get the spelling of a name.
2. Be empathic. It is respectful to acknowledge the victim's loss, but do not use phrases that might be hurtful.
3. Focus on active listening. Give the victim a chance to tell the story in his or her own way.
4. Be prepared for tears. The honest expression of grief deserves respect and not exploitation.
5. Understand the victim's guilt. Many victims blame themselves even if the blame is not justified. Be careful not to include statements by victims that indicate it was their fault. Such statements in print may have repercussions in any subsequent civil or criminal case.
6. Think twice about touching. Seeing someone in pain leads many of us to want to comfort that person with a hug or touch. You can offer nonverbal support by body gestures, but touching can be misinterpreted.
7. Consider allowing an advance reading. If possible, allow the victim to read the entire story before it is published. This is a controversial guideline among journalists.

Victim services professionals may find it helpful to inform journalists of these guidelines, provide a copy of them, or refer the journalists to the Victims and the Media Program Web site. Working with reporters instead of working against them can, in some instances, benefit the victim.

We as a society are becoming more sensitive to suicide. The Centers for Disease Control and Prevention, along with several other government and nonprofit agencies, published a study on reporting suicides.[6] It offers tips and techniques for the media to use when interviewing surviving relatives and friends of the deceased. It raises concerns and recommends the use of certain language in reporting suicides in print and on television and radio.

Victim services providers must be aware of these and other techniques to assist the victim when dealing with media. While the great majority of journalists are ethical and concerned about the accuracy and effect of their story on victims, others tend toward sensationalism, and victim services providers must make independent judgments on how to approach each journalist to ensure that their victims are not revictimized.

Effective media relations should include occasional conferences between the victim services provider and the news director of television and radio stations and the editor or publisher of the newspaper. Periodic conferences allow each party to understand the others' points of view. This relationship is especially helpful when adverse or derogatory information is disseminated about the victim. Media representatives should always attempt to contact the victim or the victim's representative for that side of the story before it is run. In the event the reporter "neglects" to reach the victim, the victim services provider should call the editor to arrange a follow-up story giving the victim's position.

Establishing an ongoing relationship with the media is a necessary function of any victim services provider. It must always be based on trust and mutual respect. Once such a relationship has been created, it will be of great benefit to all victims.

Preparing for and Conducting the Interview

Understanding the goal of the media assists the victim services provider and the victim in preparing for and conducting an interview. Most people talk with friends and colleagues on a daily basis, and although this is a form of communication, there is a distinct difference between this type of interaction and being interviewed by the local television station. This section examines some techniques that can facilitate a victim services provider's ability to effectively communicate in public situations. The first few times a victim services provider participates in a media interview can be frightening. When a person begins to speak and the newspaper reporter

Victims of Violence Web site	

Victims of Violence Web site is a Canadian government registered charitable organization. It was started in 1984. The mission of Victims of Violence includes:

- Providing long-term support and guidance to victims of violent crime and their families and aiding families of missing children in the search for their loved ones;

- Conducting research on issues affecting victims of violent crime and acting as a resource center;
- Providing information on these topics for victims and the community; to governments, news media, and the community—a victim's perspective on issues affecting victims of violent crime; and
- Generally promoting public safety and the protection of society.

begins to take notes, or the radio or television reporter thrusts a microphone in the provider's face, it can be an overpowering experience.

Preparation before the interview can help relieve some of the anxiety. Being knowledgeable about the facts of the incident and the agency's position can enhance the communication. If photo opportunities are available, the media should know about them. One should never, never lie or distort the truth. The victim services provider's credibility is on the line.

Once the professional has reviewed the facts and has had preliminary discussions with the media, the actual interview takes place. By this time, it may seem anticlimactic. The services provider should remember to speak clearly in everyday language and avoid the use of jargon.

If the victim services provider is anxious about talking to a reporter because her picture will be on the nightly news, which is seen by thousands of citizens, she should remember that this is a one-on-one conversation. The cameraperson only records what is being said between the professional and the reporter. On occasion, a victim services provider is called on to give an interview "live" instead of having it taped, edited, and replayed at a later time. The person should approach this situation in the same manner as with a taped interview. She must be professional and must clearly communicate with the reporter, not the unseen public.

Relations with the media have traditionally been tense. By understanding their purpose and working conditions and by trying to assist them when possible, a victim services provider may become an effective spokesperson for the victim.

LEGISLATION

One emotional issue within the victims' rights movement is the passage of the Victims' Rights Constitutional Amendment. As indicated in Chapter 1, NOVA and other victims' rights organizations have made this a priority on their agendas. In the meantime, a number of other state and federal laws can be revoked, amended, or passed that will assist victims. The purpose of this section is to provide a brief summary of legislative efforts and lobbying activities in which victims and their advocates can engage. These efforts can be very satisfying and empowering to victims, or they can be very frustrating, causing victims to feel like they have been victimized one more time.

The Legislative Process[7]

Victim advocates must understand how the legislature works and what is possible from a political perspective. That a proposed law may solve a problem from the victim's perspective does not mean it will be acceptable to other interest groups. We only have to turn on the evening news to hear about political gridlock at both the state and national levels to understand how politics affect our daily lives.

One of the first decisions that must be made when attempting to obtain passage of a victims' rights bill is choosing an author. The role of the author, or sponsor, is critical to the successful passage of the bill. The author must be committed to the proposed legislation. The legislator should have a record of supporting other victims' issues. In addition, the potential author should not be so controversial that he or she alienates other legislative members. If the author is the chairperson of a key committee or serves in other leadership positions within the legislature, this position assists in moving the bill through the process. The reality of modern-day politics is that victim advocates will deal with the elected official's staff more often than with the actual author. It is therefore important to maintain a cordial working relationship with these staffers. Many times, these staff persons will assist in identifying other cosponsors for the bill. Although obtaining an author or sponsor is critical, the addition of cosponsors, especially from both parties, indicates widespread support for any proposed legislation and dramatically improves the chances that it will become law.

The legislature has established the committee process to screen the thousands of bills that are introduced each year. A proposed bill or act is subject to review by a policy committee, and if the bill involves appropriation of funds, it must also be reviewed by a fiscal committee. A major portion of the committee's time is spent holding hearings on the proposed legislation. Private citizens, victims organizations, and other special interest groups may appear and testify at these hearings. The following are four key committees with which victim advocates must be familiar:

Rules Committee: **Rules committees** act as housekeepers or gatekeepers and control the assignment of bills to other committees. A rules committee will normally assign bills to certain standing committees. It is an extremely powerful and important group.

Appropriations Committee: An **appropriations committee** may be known by a variety of names, including *ways and means committee* or simply *finance committee.* Any bill requiring the expenditure of state funds will normally require a vote by this committee.

Standing Committee: **Standing committees** (also known as *policy committees*) consist of a group of legislators who hear testimony from interested parties. Each standing committee is responsible for a specific policy area such as criminal justice, education, or health and welfare. This committee may either pass the bill or kill it.

Select Committee: A **select committee** functions much like a standing committee except that it reports or makes recommendations to a standing committee. Sometimes, bills are so complex that they need specialized hearing and select committees to serve this purpose. The select committee may propose passage of the legislation, offer amendments to the bill, or recommend that it be defeated.

Once a bill reaches a committee, victims and their advocates may testify on behalf of their bill. This is one of the most exciting aspects of the U.S. legislative process, and some would consider it to be democracy in action. It is important to coordinate the efforts of everyone who will be testifying in support of the bill. This allows for a united front to be presented to the committee members.

Individual citizens, including victims, have a right to testify at committee hearings. Many law enforcement professionals believe that the dramatic testimony from a stalking victim in front of a standing committee was a critical ingredient in the passage of the California's stalking law, which was the first one of its kind in the nation.[8] In addition, a representative from a state or local victims organization, or coalition, should offer testimony. Whoever is selected to make the presentation should be eloquent, capable of quick thinking, and knowledgeable not only about the pending bill but also about victims' rights legislation in general.

Victim advocates should always check with the bill's sponsor prior to testifying. The author may want certain points emphasized or explained in more detail. The sponsor may want other committee members contacted before the hearing. In many jurisdictions, decisions regarding particular bills are made before the actual hearing.

The testimony should be clear and succinct. A rambling, disjointed, or boring presentation can go a long way toward killing the bill in committee. Testimony should never be read by those who are making their presentations. It should simply be discussed with the committee in a conversational tone as one would address another person. The victim services provider should know the names and districts of each committee member, and if asked a question should try to

FOCUS

How a Bill Becomes a Law

A citizen, organization, special interest group, or elected official proposes potential legislation.
↓
A legislator authors the bill, often a simple, nonlegal statement of the concept.
↓
The legislative counsel drafts the bill.
↓
The drafted bill is returned to the legislator.
↓
The bill goes to the legislative desk where it is introduced, assigned a bill number, and "read" for the first time.
↓
The bill is printed.
↓
The bill is sent to the rules committee where it is assigned to a standing committee.
↓
After a certain number of days, the bill is heard in that committee.
↓
The committee acts upon the bill in one of three ways: It may pass the bill "as is," it may amend the bill, or it may hold the bill in committee. The latter course of action effectively kills the bill.
↓
If the bill involves the expenditure of state funds, it is sent to an appropriations committee.
↓
The bill is then sent to the legislative floor for a second reading.
↓
Bills that survive the second reading are again sent to the legislative floor for a third and final reading.
↓
Bills are then forwarded to the governor for signature.
↓
After signed by the governor, the bill becomes a law.

respond to that member by name and explain how the bill affects that member's district. Victims who testify should not focus on their victimization; rather they should emphasize their concern as a victim who is representing all other similarly situated actual or potential victims.

The victim advocate should write the presentation and give a copy to each member of the committee. The written document should be clear, concise, and error free. It should be double-spaced with large (inch and one-half inch) margins. The advocate's name, the committee's name, bill number, and date should be on the upper corner of each page.

None of these suggestions ensure passage of a bill. The legislative process is complex, confusing, and at times defies logic. Because of the number of special interests that compete for a legislator's time, victim advocates must understand the principles involved in lobbying. The next section addresses this highly controversial activity.

Advocacy

Advocating for victims in the legislative arena can take many forms. One of the most common forms of advocacy is lobbying. The purpose of **lobbying** is to inform, educate, and persuade elected officials to support certain legislative goals. Lobbyists can be individuals, local groups, national corporations, or coalitions of any of these entities.

Today, political action committees, the high cost of running for re-election, high-powered lobbyists, and long-term planning have turned lobbying into a professional business. There are a number of firms located in most state capitals and in Washington, D.C., whose sole income is derived from lobbying elected officials. In some of these firms, former elected officials now represent business interests and are not reluctant to call in favors rendered during their tenure in office. However, not all lobbying involves the trading of favors or the purchasing of lunches. Many organizations and individuals strive to influence by the use of information only. They rely on their expertise and reputations to carry the day with elected officials.

The Internal Revenue Service monitors nonprofit organizations to ensure that they comply with all legal requirements. An effective program should carefully observe any restraints imposed by the Internal Revenue Service regarding activities by nonprofit organizations. If lobbying becomes a substantial part of the organization's activities, it stands the chance of losing its nonprofit status.

Victim advocacy is more effective if a large number of paid or volunteer individuals work to support the legislative efforts. The following is a short list of activities that can be delegated to citizens who support this work:

SELECTION OF A BILL MANAGER The bill manager tracks the bill and coordinates all the activities involved in presenting testimony at hearings. This person will be able to answer any questions regarding the status of the bill.

COORDINATOR OF SUPPORT LETTERS This coordinator gathers supporters from both organizations and individuals and assists them in writing letters of support for the legislation to the appropriate elected official. These letters should be more than simple form postcards. They should indicate the organization and person and why they are supporting the bill.

COORDINATOR OF TELEPHONE CALLS The coordinator of phone calls can be the same person who is coordinating support letters because the purpose is the same. Persons should call the elected officials and inform them of their names, organizations, and the fact that they are supporting the bill. They will not talk directly to the legislator, but their calls will be noted by the staff member handling the bill.

PRESS LIAISON The press liaison is in charge of drafting press releases regarding the proposed bill and attempts to get media coverage of its progress and its impact on the field. Sometimes, calling a press conference with the sponsor of the bill, victims, their organizations, and other community leaders will create an impact on undecided legislators.

It is obvious that there are no clear guidelines in the area of lobbying. It is also important to remember that other organizations may be advocating against the proposed legislation. A small organization may combine the just-mentioned functions into one volunteer position, whereas a national organization may have paid staffers working on each activity. It is important to remember the long-range goal of serving victims and not to get discouraged by defeats.

PUBLIC SPEAKING

Most victim services providers will be called on to make presentations to the general public. It may be an informal presentation, perhaps a Neighborhood Watch meeting, or a formal presentation to the city council. Many people suffer from stage fright when speaking to groups. As with any other skill, practice makes perfect. This is not to say all of us will become dynamic and forceful speakers. Some people are better than others at appearing and communicating in public. However, by mastering certain basic and simple procedures, any victim services provider can make a creditable presentation.

Preparing for the Speech

Some of the most outgoing professionals become quivering masses of insecurity at the thought of facing a group of citizens and explaining the victim's perspective on crime. Although we may talk to other people all the time, we do so on an individual basis, not in front of a collective body. Even though public speaking can be viewed as simply talking to more than one person, the rules of communication change when we move into a group setting. Feedback may be delayed or never received, or there may be physical barriers such as a nonworking microphone that prevent those in the back of the room from hearing adequately. Add to this the typical worry of making a mistake or looking unprofessional makes many people dread speaking in public.

Drafting the Speech

Having to stand and present a speech to a room full of people can be an intimidating experience, and writing a speech can be an agonizing task for many victim services providers. However, a speech should be prepared differently than a term paper or an agency position paper. The following are some simple rules for speech writing:

1. *Prepare an outline of the topics to be discussed* Start with the main objective or theme. The first thing to write is what the audience should be motivated to do as a result of the speech. Keep this objective in mind while writing the rest of the speech.
2. *Draft an outline of the main points of discussion* There should only be three or four major items on the list. If the list looks like a laundry list, consider combining some items or reconsider the desired goals of the speech.
3. *Revise the outline several times* Then begin to add additional information to the main points. Think about each new piece of information. Does it explain the main point?
4. *Remember, we write differently than we speak* Practice the speech by speaking it out loud. Based upon several rehearsals, the presentation may require revision.
5. *Prepare an outline and deliver the speech based on the outline* Know the subject matter well enough beforehand to be able to refer only to the outline instead of the typewritten speech. The delivery will be more natural.
6. *When writing a speech, start at the middle or the end* The most difficult part of a speech is the opening. This should be done last.

Once the speech is written, the next step is delivery. The following section briefly examines some simple principles that can make public presentations more professional for victim services providers.

Some Do's and Don'ts of Public Speaking

There are as many rules to effective public speaking as there are dynamic speakers.[9] No one approach will work for all persons. However, there are several simple methods that are easily mastered that will allow most professionals to make a clear and meaningful presentation. The following are some rules that will assist you, as a victim services provider, in making oral presentations.

1. *Understand the topic of the speech* What does the group expect to hear? If they want to be informed about the concept of restitution, do not deliver a speech regarding sentencing and victim impact statements.
2. *Know the audience and direct the speech to their interests and knowledge level* Nothing is more boring than a speech full of technical jargon that the audience does not understand. Talk on their level, and the reward will be an interested audience.
3. *Humor is excellent, but it can backfire* If you are comfortable, humor can break the ice and relax the audience for the speech. However, a long, drawn-out joke that does not go over with the audience leaves a bad taste with everyone.
4. *Always be on time and dress appropriately* Common courtesy requires that you do not keep the audience waiting for your arrival. Know the exact starting time and show up a few minutes early.
5. *Do not read the speech verbatim* We have all sat through public speeches where the speaker droned on and on reading from prepared notes.
6. *Understand how long the speech is to last, and stay within that time limit* Even if the audience is cooperative, do not prolong the speech. Remember, the group may have other business, and if you are that good, they will ask you to return.

7. ***When possible, use visual aids to assist in making your points*** Nothing makes points as well as visual aids. Businesses have known this for years. We in the public sector should take the hint and use visual aids when possible.

8. ***Rehearse as often as possible*** Rehearse, rehearse, rehearse, especially during the beginning of your public speaking career.

9. ***Ask for honest feedback from the person who requested the speech*** Do not simply say, "How was I?" This will lead to the standard response, "You were great." Politely press the person to offer comments on ways to make the presentation better the next time. It is amazing that, once encouraged to give feedback, many people will provide helpful suggestions on how to make a presentation more effective.

Public speaking is really more of an art than a science, but by following these rules any victim advocate can become a better public speaker. Addressing a group of citizens or elected officials requires certain techniques. These techniques can only become more refined with practice. With the passage of time and more frequent speaking experience, you may find yourself actually enjoying this aspect of victim advocacy.

FUNDRAISING

Introduction

In this age of tightening governmental budgets, professionals in the area of victim services must be knowledgeable regarding fundraising techniques and opportunities. Some victim assistance programs are fortunate to receive a steady supply of funds that allows them to properly administer their programs. However, most victim services organizations must always be on the lookout for additional funding sources. Fundraising is more an art than a science, but any professional who works with victims should have a basic understanding of how the process works, and its pitfalls.

Many victim-related programs were originally funded by the Law Enforcement Assistance Administration. From 1974 to 1981, Congress authorized spending of funds on a variety of law enforcement-related activities. Victim assistance was included under this definition, and as a result many prosecutors' offices established such programs. In 1981, Congress ended funding for these activities and many victim assistance programs were subsequently downsized or abolished. From 1981 to 1984, victim assistance programs had to rely on other sources of funding. In 1982, President Reagan's Task Force on Victims of Crimes made a series of recommendations addressing a variety of crime victim issues. One recommendation was the passage of a federal law addressing the plight of crime victims. In 1984, Congress passed the Victims of Crime Act (VOCA), which established a federal Crime Victims Fund. This fund received federal criminal fines, penalty assessments, and forfeited bail, which is used to fund local victim assistance programs and state compensation programs. The original fund was capped at $100 million, but in 1992 the cap was removed. VOCA helps pass these funds to each state, which in turn provides financial assistance to a number of victim programs. As a condition of receiving these funds, each state is required to certify that it is giving priority in funding to local programs that are assisting victims of spousal abuse, sexual assault, or child abuse.

Types of Fundraisers

Although VOCA funds may provide assistance to some organizations, there are a number of other victims' groups that do not receive VOCA funding. These groups must look elsewhere for funding. There are a number of methods used to raise funds for local victims' programs. The most common fundraising activities include government and private grants and local fundraising events.

Grants are cash donations, by either the federal or state government or private foundations, for specific projects. Unfortunately, on an average less than 2 percent of all foundation grants are for criminal justice projects including victim-related programs. Taken as a whole, the nation's foundations have not gotten the word that the public considers crime a major issue.[10] Federal and state grants are normally a one-time source of funding for very specific projects. However, these governmental grants have decreased dramatically since the 1970s.

The federal government continues to award grants each year. Some of the more common grants are awarded for research, others study "best practices" in the field, and still others provide funding to train professionals who serve in the field. A number of different governmental agencies and departments award grants. These grants vary from year to year and from agency to agency. The first step for obtaining a grant is to find out which state or federal department is awarding it. The local library is an excellent place to start the search for government funds. Victim services providers should not overlook their local elected officials. Many state and congressional staff persons have information regarding the availability of government grants. Finally, victim services providers should make contact with the local university. Many universities have offices that specialize in obtaining grants, and some offer extension classes to the public on how to write a grant proposal. These universities are not only a source of information, but also they may lead to contacts that will result in joint grant writing endeavors, involving faculty members and victim services providers.

Grants are handed out selectively. Most grants are very competitive, and therefore victim services providers should be prepared for a series of rejections when they first attempt to obtain grants. Grant writing is a time-consuming and very technical process.

In the event that there are insufficient funds available in state or federal government for a specific program, victim services providers should consider private corporation or foundation grants. These funding opportunities are even more limited than federal grants, but they should not be overlooked. The same sources that provided information regarding federal grants can be contacted about private grants or awards.

There are disadvantages to government or private grants or awards. A victim services provider should not automatically apply for every grant that is available. Often, grants contain hidden costs. They may require local objectives to be re-evaluated and/or reprioritized, or impose burdensome paperwork. Some grants require matching funds that take money from other programs, and some grants build in expectations for ongoing future activities. All grants should be evaluated for any strings that are attached as well as the long-term commitments for the continued funding of the project. If possible, grants should be used for individual, one-time projects, rather than ongoing projects. Finally, those grants that require an extraordinary amount of funds in the form of matching dollars should be critically evaluated.

The final method to obtain funding involves local fundraising events. These events can be as varied as the mind of the organizer. They are not guaranteed to turn a profit, and many times they take a great deal of volunteer and staff time to organize and execute. Typical fundraisers include dinners, banquets, auctions, house or garden tours, and sporting events. If the first fundraiser is a success, organizers should consider making it an annual event. In addition, victim services providers should always consider asking local businesses to cosponsor these events. Their support may include monetary donations and many times will add visibility to the event.

Victim services providers must be knowledgeable regarding the various types of fundraising. With our constantly changing economic situation, no source of funding is ever 100 percent safe. Victim services providers should consider having a variety of funding mechanisms available to them so that they can more effectively service their clients.

Summary

The media are not an enemy to be attacked or avoided. Certain issues require that victims be involved with the media. These might include an appeal to a kidnapper to release a victim, an assistance call to search areas where a child was last seen, or a statement to stir up public opinion regarding the release of an offender back into the community. The efficient victim services provider will become familiar with the different types of media and their specific needs.

All victim services providers need to understand the legislative process, its complexities, and its strengths and weaknesses to understand the process by which the laws that affect victims are drafted, amended, and passed.

Public speaking, like any other skill, requires practice and the knowledge that speeches are most effective when tailored to the different types of audiences. An effective victim services provider can enhance a program by knowing how to present that information to members of the community.

Fundraising is a necessary activity of most victim programs. Various types of funds are available to these programs; however, the competition for this money is fierce. Often, the best way to become proficient in this area is to work with people who already have established a successful track record of raising money. By watching and by learning their techniques, victim services providers can adapt those techniques to their individual programs.

Key Terms

Appropriations committee may be known by a variety of names including *ways and means committee* or simply *finance committee.*

Grants are cash donations, by either the federal or state government or private foundations, for specific projects.

Lobbying is to inform, educate, and persuade elected officials to support certain legislative goals.

Rules committees act as housekeepers or gatekeepers and control the assignment of bills to other committees.

Select committee functions much like standing committees except that it reports or makes recommendations to a standing committee.

Standing committees (also known as *policy committees*) consist of a group of legislators who hear testimony from interested parties. Each standing committee is responsible for a specific policy area such as criminal justice, education, or health and welfare.

Sidebar story is usually an article placed in a column next to the main article.

Discussion Questions

1. Is there any occasion that you can think of when a victim services provider should become a "source" for a news reporter?
2. What is the most important hearing in the legislative process?
3. Should victim advocates compromise on amendments to their bills? What if failure to compromise means that the bill will be killed in a committee?
4. What is the most difficult aspect of public speaking?
5. What makes one speaker more dynamic than another? List specific characteristics that you believe are essential to effective public speaking.
6. How would you secure a steady form of money for a victims' program?

Suggested Readings

H. Wallace & C. Roberson, *Written and Interpersonal Communication Methods for Law Enforcement*, 5th ed. (Pearson) 2011.

B. Wurman, *Information Anxiety* (Bantam Books, New York) 1990.

Endnotes

1. National Center for Victims of Crime website, http://www.victimsofcrime.org accessed on April 25, 2013
2. Some of this mistrust is based on law enforcement's perception of how the media report crime; see Steven M. Chermak, "Body Count News: How Crime Is Presented in the News Media," 11(4) *Justice Quarterly,* 561 (December 1994).
3. See Craig A. Sullivan, "Police Public Relations," *Law and Order,* 94 (October 1993), for a discussion of how one agency interacts with the media.
4. See for example, Ted Gest, *Covering Crime and Justice*; available online: www.justicejournalism.org/crimeguide/intro.html.

5. Bonnie Bucqueroux, "Tips on Interviewing Victims: The Anniversary Story," University of Michigan School of Journalism, Victims and the Media Program (no date); available online: http://victims.jrn.msu.edu/public/articles/anniv.html.

6. *Reporting on Suicide: Recommendations for the Media,* Centers of Disease Control and Prevention et al.; available online: www.afsp.org/education/recommendations/5/1.htm.

7. The material in this section and the diagram are based on the author's discussions with leaders of several victims' rights organizations that monitor legislation in California. The actual format and process may differ slightly in other jurisdictions.

8. Presentation by Lt. John Lane, LAPD Threat Management Unit (Threat Assessment Conference, Los Angeles, Calif.) July 1995.

9. For an excellent discussion of public speaking, see Steven N. Bowman, "The Practical Local Government Manager," *Public Administration,* 22–23 (December 1991).

10. See Ordway P. Burden, "Big-Game Hunting: Foundations' CJ Bucks Are a Rare Quarry," *Law Enforcement News,* 9 (April 30, 1991).

Homicide Victims

Chapter Outline

LEARNING OBJECTIVES

After reading this chapter, you should be able to:

- Recognize the survivors of homicide victims
- Describe the extent of homicide in the United States
- Describe the typical homicide victim
- Understand the different types of homicide
- Understand the dynamics involved in the death of a family member
- Explain the mental and emotional consequences suffered by homicide survivors
- Understand how death notification adds to the trauma suffered by homicide victims

INTRODUCTION

Criminal acts take many forms and shapes. However, one particular crime has a drastic and long-lasting impact on society. Homicide not only affects the immediate victim whose life is cut short but also has a lifelong impact on the victim's family and friends. Tens of thousands of survivors of homicide victims suffer shock, grief, and an overwhelming sense of helplessness at the loss of a loved one, friend, or acquaintance. **Survivors of homicide victims** are those individuals who had special ties of kinship with the person murdered and who were thus victimized not only by the loss of someone close to them but also by the horrific circumstances of that untimely death.[1]

Nature and Extent of the Problem

On an average, in the United States homicide is the second leading cause of death for infants. Homicide with a firearm is the second leading cause of death for persons between the ages of 10 and 24, the third leading cause for persons between ages 25 and 34, and the fourth leading cause for persons between ages 5 and 9 or between ages 35 and 44. For persons between ages 45 and 64, homicide with a firearm is the seventh leading cause of death.

Homicide with a firearm or by any means is not among the top ten causes of death for persons aged 65 or older, whereas there were at least two forms of homicide among the top ten causes of death for all persons under age 44.

The FBI defines **murder** as the willful (nonnegligent) killing of one human being by another. This definition does not include deaths caused by negligence, suicide, or accident, nor does it include justifiable homicide or attempted homicides. Generally, there are about 14 to 15 thousand reported murder victims each year. Males constituted about 78 percent of the victims. Of murder victims for whom race is known, about 50 percent are black, 47 percent are white, and the remaining victims are of other races. The situation of single victim/single offender generally accounts for 48 percent of all murders for which the Uniform Crime Report (UCR) Program receive supplementary data. Concerning single victim/single offender incidents in which the age of the offender is known, about 94 percent of the victims are killed by adults (persons eighteen years of age or older). Of single victim/single offender incidents, about 92 percent of black victims are murdered by black offenders, and 83 percent of white victims are murdered by white offenders. Among the single victim/single offender incidents, about 90 percent of female victims were killed by male offenders. For murders in which the offender's gender was known, about 90 percent were males. These statistics are yearly averages. For a current breakdown of the percentages for the last reported year, visit the FBI Web site.

Homicide is of interest to researchers not only because of its severity but also because many professionals believe it is a fairly accurate indicator of violent crime in general. Victimologists study it because of the severe impact it has on the survivors.

Among murder offenders for whom race was known, about 54 percent were black, 44 percent were white, and 2 percent were other races. Of the homicides for which the type of weapon was specified, about 73 percent of the offenses involved the use of firearms. Handguns comprised about 88 percent of the firearms specified.

Among female victims for whom their relationships with their offenders were known, about 33 percent were murdered by their husbands or boyfriends. Of the known circumstances surrounding homicides, about 42 percent of the victims were murdered during arguments (including romantic triangles) and about 23 percent were killed in conjunction with a felony (the victim was slain while being raped, robbed, etc.). Circumstances were unknown for about 37 percent of reported homicides.

Theories, Types, and Characteristics of Homicide

As indicated in Chapter 1, Wolfgang conducted the first major study of victim precipitation.[2] He focused on homicides and studied both the victim and the offender as separate entities and as "mutual participants in the homicide."[3] Wolfgang found that 26 percent of all homicides studied in Philadelphia involved situations in which the victim was the first to use force during the acts leading to the homicide.[4]

Wolfgang identified several factors that he associated with victim participation in homicides: (1) The victim and the perpetrator usually had some sort of prior relationship—spouse, family members, or close acquaintances; (2) the events leading up to the homicide started as a small disagreement that escalated into a burst of anger that resulted in a killing; and (3) alcohol was used or consumed by many of the victims prior to the incident.[5]

Significant partner homicide involves the killing of one's significant partner. This definition does not require that the parties be cohabitating at the time of the killing. In this section, when the phrase "spousal homicides" are used, we are referring to situations where the individuals are legally married in their state of residence. The problem with studying spousal partner homicides is that it excludes those relationships involving same-gender partners in states that do not recognize their status and mixed-gender couple living together. So keep in mind that when referring to spousal homicides, there are significant gaps in the data involving partner homicides. Segall and Wilson conducted an eight-year study involving spousal homicides and established certain

FOCUS
Murderers

Do You Know a Killer When You See One?

Wouldn't life be simpler and safer if all murderers resembled large, ugly, and deformed Neanderthals? Unfortunately, this is not the case even though our fears may conjure up such images. In reality, a murderer may be a middle-aged man who is a Boy Scout leader and church congregation president. Such was the lifestyle of the infamous "BTK" serial killer, Dennis Rader. BTK stands for Bind, Torture, and Kill, which is what Rader did to his ten victims over a thirty-year period before he was caught in 2005 and sentenced to ten consecutive life terms. Kansas, where the crimes occurred, did not have the death penalty during the time of Rader's killings.

Statistical facts drawn from arrest records indicate the following regarding murderers:

Age:	50% were 25 to 49 years old
Sex:	88% males
	12% females
Race:	46% white
Relationship:	50% acquaintance
	17% family
	20% stranger
	12% unknown
Weapon preferred:	64% firearm

Source: H. Snyder, T. Finnegan, Y. Wan, & W. Kang, "Easy Access to the FBI's Supplementary Homicide Reports: 1980–2000," available online: http://ojjdp.ncjrs.org/ojstatbb/ezashr/asp/profile.asp accessed on 2002.

characteristics associated with these types of cases.[6] Most of the homicides in his study occurred in major urban locations and involved single-victim–offender killings. Spousal homicide victims tended to be older than other homicide victims. Spousal homicide victims were typically female in contrast to male victims in most other homicides. In a classic study of family violence, David Finkelhor established characteristics that can lead to spousal homicide.[7] According to Finkelhor, the presence of these characteristics in family violence situations can also lead to homicide. These factors include power differentials between the parties, perceived powerlessness on the part of the abused, and ambiguity regarding acceptable discipline and punishment.

One type of homicide that is most difficult to understand is **parricide**, which is the killing of one's parents. The trials of the Menendez brothers brought the specter of children killing their parents into our living rooms via television. Statistics indicate that about 2 percent of all murder victims in the United States were killed by their children.[8] Parricide usually does not occur as a result of a single episode; rather it is a manifestation of a culmination of unresolved conflicts.

Heide researched adolescents who killed their parents and found certain characteristics to be present in these events.[9] There was a history of family violence, the adolescent's attempt to get help or escape from the situation failed, the children experienced isolation, and the family situation became increasingly desperate immediately prior to the killings. The youths felt helpless in coping with their stressful situations and ultimately experienced a loss of control. Most of the murderers had no prior criminal history; however, they did have easy access to guns. Recognizing and intervening in family violence situations may prevent parricide, a particularly devastating form of murder.

Considered particularly violent are mass murderers, and until the relatively recent emergence and research into serial killers, they were considered society's most dangerous of predators. **Mass murderers** are those who kill several people at one time in the same location. One of the most famous mass murderers is James O. Huberty, who is believed to have committed the worst one-day massacre in the United States. Huberty was an unemployed security guard who told his friends that he would kill others if he could not find a job and support his family. On July 18, 1984, he walked into a McDonald's restaurant in San Ysidro, California, and opened fire, killing twenty-one persons and wounding another twenty. In 1989, a deranged welder named Patrick Edward Purdy entered the school yard of Cleveland Elementary School in Stockton,

California, armed with an AK-47 assault rifle and began a killing rampage that ended with five dead children and thirty wounded victims. The Stockton School Yard Massacre is another chilling example of mass murder. When studying mass murders think of Timothy McVeigh, the Oklahoma City bomber who killed 168 people and injured over 800. In 2013, Adam Lanza killed 26 people, mostly young school students in Newtown, Connecticut. Also, at the 2012 Boston Marathon, two brothers in an attempt to kill numerous people killed three people and injured about 160.

A variation on the mass murderer is the spree murderer. A **spree killer** kills several persons at two or more locations with very little, if any, time break between the killings. Some experts would call the former Eagle Scout leader and college honor student Charles Whitman a spree killer. In 1966, Whitman murdered his wife and mother, and then armed with a variety of weapons and ammunition, climbed to the top of a tower at the University of Texas. Whitman continued his killing spree, and as a result sixteen persons died and another thirty were wounded before the police shot and killed him. He subsequently became known as the Texas Tower Killer. Prior to the killing spree, Charles Whitman served a tour of duty in the U.S. Marine. While in the marines, he was court-martialed for assault on a fellow marine. During his court-martial, a psychiatrist testified that he had examined Whitman and concluded that Whitman was a non-violent person.

One of the most deadly and fearsome murderers is the serial killer. With the chilling film *The Silence of the Lambs,* our collective consciousness was raised to acknowledge that killers similar to Hannibal "the Cannibal" Lecter exist and, indeed, may have sat next to us on a bus, train, or plane. In 2013, a television serial, *Hannibal*, was developed based on the Hannibal Lecter character. The serial killer is the night stalker of murders. Although debate continues over a comprehensive definition, most authorities agree that a **serial murderer** is one who kills several persons over a period of time that can range from weeks to years.[10]

One of the best-known and notorious serial murderers is Jack the Ripper, who killed several women in London over a period of time during the 1800s. He was never caught and the crimes were never solved, although speculation continues as to his identity, and theories and articles are still written about his grievous acts. Other well-known serial murderers are the Green River Killer, who is believed to have killed more than fifty female hitchhikers, transients, and prostitutes near the Seattle area; the "Witch," Sarah Aldrete, who sacrificed victims to provide an aura of protection for members of a Mexican drug smuggling ring; Dorothea Puente, who poisoned renters at her boardinghouse and then cashed their social security checks; and the infamous Hillside Stranglers Angelo Buono and Kenneth Bianchi in Los Angeles.

In 2005, the BTK Killer saga was a topic of morbid discussion across the nation. Dennis Rader, who called himself the BTK Killer, admitted to killing ten people over a thirty-year period. Rader was a former Cub Scout leader, regular church member, and local ordinance enforcement officer in Wichita, Kansas. His killing spree started in 1974 and stopped in the late 1970s. He would send letters to the media naming himself the BTK Killer and asking how many more he had to kill before he received national notice. He also included clues to his identity in several letters. In 1979, he stopped communicating and remained silent for twenty years. Then he sent another letter discussing an unsolved 1986 killing. On the basis of DNA evidence, the police arrested Rader in 2005.

In an effort to understand crime and criminals, researchers create typologies or classifications based on certain characteristics. By studying these characteristics, scholars, researchers, law enforcement officials, and others hope to understand why particular individuals commit certain types of crimes. Several noteworthy typologies of serial murderers have been developed. Holmes and DeBurger identified four types of serial killers:[11]

Visionary type: These serial killers murder in response to commands or directions from a voice or vision. Many of these killers suffer from some form of psychosis.

Mission-oriented type: These serial killers believe their mission or goal in life is to rid society of certain types of people, such as prostitutes.

Hedonistic type: These serial killers are perhaps the most chilling of the lot in that they seek thrills during the murder. Many of these killers become sexually involved with their victims either prior to or after killing them. They may also engage in sexual mutilation of their victims.

Power/control-oriented type: These serial killers seek power over their victims. They report enjoyment from watching their victims plead, beg, and cower before them.

Eric Hickey has conducted several studies on serial killers and is considered a nationally recognized expert in this area. In an early work, he classified serial killers into three distinct groups based on mobility:[12]

Traveling serial killers: These serial killers often travel to different locations seeking victims to kill.

Local serial killers: This type of serial killer stays in one area and conducts crimes in this location.

Serial killers who never leave their home or place of employment: These serial killers lure their victims into their residence or place of employment, and the killing takes place within these areas.

The study of serial killers continues today, and more typologies are certain to emerge as knowledge of the psychology of these killers and profiling techniques become more sophisticated. Those professionals who study this type of behavior admit that there is both a repulsion and attraction inherent in their research; however, the suffering of the survivors of these types of homicides must not be allowed to recede into the background.

Although these crimes are committed by only a marginal percentage of society, the number of their victims is not insignificant. Hickey pointed out that thirty-four female and sixty-nine male serial killers were responsible for a minimum of 1,483 and a maximum of 2,161 deaths![13] The toll in human tragedy and the resulting trauma perpetrated on the survivors requires extraordinary skill and compassion on the part of today's victim services providers.

Drinking, Driving, and Homicide

Many vehicular homicides happen as a result of a person drinking and then getting behind the wheel of a car. This behavior used to be called "drunk driving," and although most people still use this term as a shorthand way of describing a behavior, it is not considered a legal term. A person does not have to be drunk to be convicted under most "driving under the influence" laws. These laws simply require that the driver's ability to operate a motor vehicle be impaired. In fact, many statutes define "under the influence" in a variety of ways. One example states that the defendant is under the influence if it can be proved that the alcohol, or alcohol and drugs, have affected the nervous system, brain, or muscles to the degree so as to impair, to an appreciable degree, the ability to operate a motor vehicle in a manner like that of an ordinary, prudent, and cautious person in full possession of his faculties using reasonable care and under like circumstances.

In 1983, in an effort to address drinking and driving, some states began raising the minimum drinking age to twenty-one. All states now have twenty-one as the minimum age that a person can drink. In addition, a majority of the states adopted laws that require administrative sanctions for all persons who, when asked, refuse to take a test measuring the presence and concentration of alcohol. Many of these states now permit the law enforcement officer on the scene to immediately confiscate the driver's license of a person arrested for driving under the influence (DUI) who refuses such tests.[14]

In November 1979, five-month-old Laura Lamb was riding in a car seat next to her mother as they drove to the store. They were hit head-on by a drunk driver going in excess of 120 miles per hour. The perpetrator had no driver's license, no insurance, and thirty-seven previous traffic violations, including three prior drunk driving arrests. Laura became one of America's youngest quadriplegics.

In May 1980, thirteen-year-old Cari Lightner was walking to a church carnival with her friend when she was hit and killed by a man who had been out of jail for only two days for another hit-and-run drunk driving crash.

As a result of these incidents, in 1980 Mothers Against Drunk Driving (MADD) was formed. Since then, thousands of volunteers and other victims have joined this organization in its fight against death on the highway. MADD has become one of the most notable victim organizations in the nation with chapters in every state.

Unfortunately, despite increased penalties at the state and federal level, the death on our roadways continues. According to the National Highway Traffic Safety Administration, about 17,000 people are killed in alcohol-related crashes yearly: that is almost one death every half hour. These alcohol-related fatalities constituted approximately about 40 percent of the total traffic deaths each year.

Blood alcohol level is a legal and medical term that is expressed in milligrams of alcohol per milliliters of blood. This level has been translated into the ability or fitness to operate a motor vehicle based on several broad categories, or zones of impairment. Tables 6.1 and 6.2 indicate the blood alcohol level of an individual who has consumed an alcoholic beverage. The data in Table 6.1 are based on weight and amount of alcohol consumed; Table 6.2 indicates the effects on the individual based upon the blood alcohol level.

Some states have enacted presumptions that shift the burden of proving this element. If the driver of the vehicle has tested for a certain blood alcohol level, and it can be shown that this level existed during the operation of the vehicle, the offender must prove that he was not under the influence. This level varies from state to state, but many statutes establish the range with the 0.08 to 0.10 blood alcohol level as a presumptive indication that the defendant was under the influence of alcohol and/or drugs at the time of the operation of the motor vehicle.

Homicide in any form has a devastating effect. Family members, friends, and others within the community are left in a state of shock as a result. The next section briefly examines the impact of homicide on the survivors.

TABLE 6.1 Blood Alcohol Level and Impairment

Two Drinks	Four Drinks			Six Drinks			Eight Drinks			Ten Drinks		
Hours Spent Drinking (hours)	Body Weight			Body Weight			Body Weight			Body Weight		
	120	150	180	120	150	180	120	150	180	120	150	180
1	0.05	0.04	0.03	0.11	0.09	0.07	0.16	0.13	0.11	0.21	0.17	0.14
2	0.02	0.01	—	0.08	0.05	0.04	0.14	0.10	0.08	0.20	0.15	0.12
3	—	—	—	0.06	0.04	0.02	0.12	0.08	0.06	0.18	0.13	0.10
4	—	—	—	0.05	0.02	0.01	0.11	0.07	0.04	0.17	0.12	0.09

TABLE 6.2	Blood Alcohol Level and Behavioral Effects
Present Blood Alcohol Level	**Behavioral Effects**
0.02	Pleasant feelings, including a sense of warmth and well-being
0.04	Relaxed, energetic, and happy; flushed skin and slight impairment of motor skills
0.06	Lightheadness, giddiness, lowered inhibitions, impaired of judgment
0.08	Definite muscle coordination impairment, slowed reaction time, heavy pulse and slow breathing; numbness in cheeks, lips, and extremities may occur
0.10	Clear deterioration of coordination and reaction time, staggering and slurring of speech, judgment and memory further affected
0.20	Increased depression of motor and sensory skills, pronounced slurred speech, double vision, difficulty in standing and walking
0.30	Stuporous and confused; individuals may lose consciousness
0.40	Unconscious; skin is sweaty and clammy; circulation and respiration are depressed
0.50	Near death or dead

RESPONDING TO SPECIAL NEEDS

Family Relationships

Grief, sorrow, and emotional pain are the hallmarks of suffering experienced by the homicide victim's surviving relatives, friends, and acquaintances. The level of grief that is experienced can generally be measured by the intensity of the relationship that existed between the survivor and the victim before death. The following section will briefly examine several relationships within a family unit and how those relationships are affected by the homicide of one of its members.

The murder of a child is one of the least expected incidents in life.[15] In the normal order of things, parents expect to die before their children. Parents serve as protectors, healers, and givers of life. These duties or obligations can, in turn, promote a sense of guilt in the parents of a murdered child, even if the child was an adult when the murder occurred.

This is, in part, due to the amount of time parents invest in planning for their child's future. They want their child to accomplish more and hopefully transcend their own circumstances. Many parents link their own immortality to their child, hoping and believing that they themselves will continue to live on in some form, even after their own death. Therefore, the grief suffered over the loss of a child is increased by the perception of the loss of the parents' own immortality.

Today, many families are intermixed, or "blended," with stepparents and stepchildren as a result of second or even third marriages. Because many stepparents love their stepchildren as much as their own natural children, they may also suffer guilt at the loss of the child, and their grief should not be ignored by victim services providers.

Also, parents must not only deal with their own sorrow or grief but also at the same time attempt to comfort any other siblings and/or relatives who are feeling the pain of loss. Some parents may idealize the deceased child, bestowing on the victim qualities that are longed for rather than real, thereby magnifying the grief.

The murder of a significant partner affects the surviving partner in a variety of ways. The reaction to the death of a partner depends on the nature and quality of the relationship prior to the homicide. If there was discord, anger, or bitterness in the partnership, the survivor may feel intense guilt at not trying harder to make the relationship better while the deceased was alive. If the relationship was a loving, close, supportive one, the loss may be overwhelming to the survivor.

The age of the surviving partner also plays a critical role in the grief process. In some instances, older survivors do not recover as quickly and easily as their younger counterparts. They may be displaced from their home either because they can no longer care for themselves alone or because their financial situation has changed as the result of the loss of one income or pension. The surviving partner, no matter what age, may also experience feelings of anger and bitterness at being left with responsibilities he or she now has to face alone. These responsibilities may include raising children as a single parent, attempting to make ends meet financially, or caring for relatives of the deceased partner.

The murder of a parent may leave young children worrying about their own life and stability.[16] They may see the death as a form of desertion by the parent. They may also blame the parent and question why the parent did not fight back. Children will certainly feel an overwhelming sense of loss and abandonment that can affect them for the rest of their lives. Older children may feel guilty, because they did not pay enough attention to their parent prior to the murder, or they may blame themselves if the parent–child relationship was strained prior to death.

Murder of a sibling may leave the other brothers and sisters neglected by the professional caregivers. Many agencies concentrate on assisting the parents of murdered children and occasionally overlook the fact that the other children are suffering as a result of the loss of a cherished brother or sister. Siblings may also experience extreme guilt that they are left alive and their brother or sister is dead. They may experience anger at the parents' preoccupation with the dead sibling. They may feel vulnerable and experience anxiety at being left alone. They may wonder if they also will be murdered.

If the siblings are young, this may be their first encounter with death and they may not understand why their brother or sister will not be coming home. In addition, the victim may also have been the surviving siblings' best friend, playmate, and confidant. This loss can leave them feeling isolated and alone and increase their sense of sorrow and grief.

Although many families share emotional responses to the death of a family member and appear to be mutually supportive of one another, victim services providers must be aware of the special needs of each one of them and respond accordingly. The loss of a loved one is traumatic and long lasting. In the event that the perpetrator was a family member, the grief and suffering endured by the survivors can be immeasurable.

Mental and Emotional Responses

Chapter 4 examined the consequences of victimization; however, homicide by its very nature is a unique type of crime that presents special needs and responses. Parents of Murdered Children, Inc., has examined a number of mental and emotional problem areas for survivors of homicide.[17]

There are *unexpected financial consequences*. Funeral, medical expenses, and psychiatric care for family members are all unanticipated expenses. These are serious consequences that contribute to the continuing distress that survivors of homicide suffer.

As discussed in previous chapters, *the criminal justice system* adds to the stress suffered by survivors of homicide. These survivors must learn to cope with body bags, crime scene pictures, autopsies, and other stressors inherent in a homicide trial. One of the most comforting acts a victim services provider can do in assisting the survivor of a homicide is obtain information from the participants within the criminal justice system regarding the facts surrounding the killing.

Survivors of homicide often report that there is *an impact on their ability to function at their job or work*. Motivation may be altered, and what was considered important at work before the homicide is no longer viewed as critical. Some survivors may experience emotional outbreaks of crying or shouting during work, and having to apologize for these outbreaks at a later time contributes to their stress. Other survivors use work as an excuse or an escape to avoid working through their grief.

It is not uncommon for marriages to break up when a child of that marriage is murdered. Each partner grieves and may blame the other for the loss. They may also find it painful to be with their partner because of the memories evoked by that person. Some parents are unable to help each other, because their grief is so terrible that they cannot help themselves.

Children within the family of survivors of homicide also are affected by the killing. Children who actually witness the murder suffer a special mental and emotional upheaval, discussed in more detail later in this section. However, children who do not witness the murder are also impacted. If the murdered victim was a child, the other children in the family may be ignored by the parents as they attempt to deal with their own grief. The children sense the parents' suffering and simply withdraw into themselves. In addition, children suffer the same psychological reactions as other survivors of homicide.

Many survivors report that their *religious faith has been weakened* as a result of homicide. Some express anger and frustration or question their deity regarding the reason for the death of their loved one. Others seek answers from unorthodox sources such as spiritual advisors and those who claim to talk to the dead.

Homicide survivors are often subjected to the *scrutiny of an insensitive press.* The quest for news may cause members of the media to televise a survivor's anguish on the evening news. Survivors may be subjected to views of the crime scene or other painful memories during the homicide trial as the press attempts to re-create the killing for its audience.

Finally, survivors of homicide may be *revictimized by professionals within the criminal justice system.* Many survivors report that some professionals do not fully understand the impact of a death by homicide on the remaining members of the family. This is an area that victim services providers can contribute to by continuing to educate professionals regarding the effect of crime on victims.

As indicated, children who witness homicide suffer a terrible experience.[18] Many of them suffer posttraumatic stress disorder. Children who witness killings must many times perform other tasks associated with homicides such as calling 9-1-1, trying to assist the dying victim, telling police what occurred, and testifying in court. These additional tasks can present intense conflicts or dilemmas for children. They may blame themselves for not protecting the victim or not responding to the killing in other more acceptable ways. Depending on the age of the child and the circumstances surrounding the homicide, witnessing a murder can have long-range serious mental health consequences for the child.

In some situations, a child who could also have been killed is spared for no apparent reason. This can create both terror and extraordinary guilt. Any witnesses, but especially children, may be afraid that the killer will retaliate against them at another time. This is especially true if a child witnesses a continuing history of spousal abuse against the mother that finally ends in her death. The child may then endow the perpetrator with imagined superhuman powers and feel extremely threatened that the offender will return to kill him or her.

Survivors of sudden death sometimes have unusual experiences. MADD is only one organization studying this phenomenon.[19] Mystical experiences, as they are known, can take a variety of forms both before and after death. These experiences include premonitions of death; visitations from loved ones at the time of death or shortly following; unusual dreams or nighttime visitations; or the presence of the loved one sensed through sound, smell, touch, or taste.

Professionals who work with survivors of homicide victims should not discount these experiences. When the issue of mystical experiences is raised in support groups around the country, more than half of those in attendance indicate that they have experienced some sort of unusual episode. The vast majority of those surveyed indicate that the experience was both positive and concrete.[20] These were not ghostly sightings; rather they involved explicit, physical incidents with the loved one. Mystical experiences occur across all socioeconomic, race, and gender lines. Because mystical experiences appear to be common and comforting to survivors of homicide victims, it is important to normalize the experience and allow the survivors the opportunity to express their feelings.

Notification

One of the most traumatic moments in a survivor's life is receiving notification of his or her loved one's death.[21] The notification by itself is a devastating event, but it can become even more traumatic if it is carried out in an insensitive manner.[22] Some authorities believe that death notification should be given by a uniformed officer because that person is generally perceived by most citizens as an authority figure. However, some communities are training crisis intervention workers. They are usually members of the local victim assistance staff. These persons accompany the officer on the notification call. This procedure allows for a notification team that can work together to ease the pain of the survivor.

Whoever makes the notification call should have as much information regarding the death as possible. The team should be able to tell the survivor what happened, when it occurred, how the victim died, and the source used to identify the victim. The notification team should never, if at all possible, make a death notification by telephone. The team should never take personal items with them on the call—these items will only add to the suffering of the victim. However, at a later time, the victim services provider should offer to retrieve and return all property of the deceased.

When making a call, the notification team should ask to enter the home and indicate that they have important medical information but would rather talk inside the house. Once inside the home, the team should ensure that they are talking to the appropriate relative. If a child has been murdered, the team should ask to speak to both parents at the same time if at all possible. A team member should ask the survivors to take a seat and then sit down next to them. The message should be clear, direct, and simple. For example, the team may tell the parents, "I have some very bad news for you. Your son, John, was shot during an armed robbery, he died immediately." They should not use terms such as "expired" or "passed on," as they can confuse the message and leave room for doubt or false hope.

Members of the notification team should not be shocked by a variety of responses their news might elicit from the survivors. The survivors may cry, faint, laugh, or simply withdraw. The notification team should attempt to focus on the immediate needs of the survivors and help them get in touch with close relatives or friends if they want assistance. As indicated elsewhere in this chapter, one of the most important aspects of the notification process is furnishing all available information to the survivors. This simple detail may alleviate some of the suffering and allow them to understand exactly how and why the death occurred. This process is one of the hardest duties a victim services provider will have to perform. Notification is not something that gets easier with the passage of time, but it can provide survivors with the information they need to begin the healing process.

Summary

Homicide forever affects the lives of the survivors. It is a serious crime that has long-term effects for anyone close to the victim, including family, friends, neighbors, and possibly even the community where the victim lived.

There are a number of different types of homicide, including, but not limited to, spousal homicide, mass murder, serial murder, and vehicular homicide. Any murder represents a special problem for the victim services provider who becomes involved. These individuals should be as knowledgeable as possible regarding the different types of homicide and their effects on the survivors.

Murder affects the whole family. When a child is murdered, the effect on the parents and remaining siblings can be devastating. Professionals should ensure that in their desire to provide assistance to the parents, they do not overlook the siblings or other family members who may also be suffering shock, despair, and tremendous loss.

Just as professionals should take the lead in training law enforcement agencies regarding cultural sensitivity, so should they ensure that death notification procedures do not traumatize the survivor. Law enforcement personnel should consider including victim services providers on all notification calls. This allows for immediate contact with the survivor and provides the professional with the opportunity to coordinate details and activities with the survivor from the very beginning of the process. This technique may help some survivors begin the grieving process.

Key Terms

Survivors of homicide victims are those individuals who had special ties of kinship with the person murdered and who were, thereafter, victimized not only by the loss of someone close to them but also by the horrific circumstances of that untimely death.

Murder is the willful (nonnegligent) killing of one human being by another.

Significant partnership is use to describe couples living together either married or unmarried as a family unit without regard to the genders of the partners.

Parricide is the killings of one's parent.

Mass murderers are those who kill several people at one time in the same location.

Spree killer kills several persons at two or more locations with very little if any time break between the killings.

Serial murderer is one who kills several persons over a period of time that can range from weeks to years.

Discussion Questions

1. Is homicide on the rise in your community? What can your local elected officials do to solve this problem?
2. What type of homicide is the most dangerous? Justify your answer from a law enforcement perspective, a victim services provider's perspective, and a prosecutor's point of view.
3. Who suffers the most when a family member is killed? Parents, children, siblings, or others?
4. How would you notify parents that their child has been murdered? Would the notification process be any different if the child was the perpetrator in a crime and was killed by the intended victim during a shootout?

Suggested Readings

M. E. Wolfgang, *Patterns of Criminal Homicide* (University of Pennsylvania Press, Philadelphia, Penn.) 1958.

A. Y. Wilson, ed., *Homicide: The Victim-Offender Connection* (Anderson, Cincinnati, Ohio) 1993.

D. Finkelhor, R. J. Gelles, G. T. Hotaling, & M. A. Strauss, eds., *The Dark Side of Families: Current Family Violence Research* (Sage, Beverly Hills, Calif.) 1983.

Eric W. Hickey, *Serial Murderers and Their Victims,* 3rd ed. (Wadsworth, Belmont, Calif.) 2002.

R. M. Holmes & J. DeBurger, *Serial Murder* (Sage, Newbury Park, Calif.) 1988.

T. A. Rando, *Parental Loss of a Child* (Research Press Company, Champaign, Ill.) 1986.

E. Furmann, *A Child's Parent Dies* (Yale University Press, New Haven, Conn.) 1974.

Lula M. Redmond, *Surviving When Someone You Love Was Murdered* (Consultation and Education Services, Inc., Clearwater, Fla.) 1989.

R. J. Meadows, *Understanding Violence and Victimization*, 4th ed. (Prentice Hall, Englewood Cliffs, N. J.) 2004.

Endnotes

1. "Survivors of Homicide Victims," 2/3 *NOVA Network Information Bulletin,* 1 (Washington, D.C.), October 1985.
2. M. E. Wolfgang, *Patterns of Criminal Homicide* (University of Pennsylvania Press, Philadelphia, Penn.) 1958.
3. M. E. Wolfgang, *Analytical Categories for Research in Victimization* (Kriminologische Wegzeichen, Munich, Germany) 1967, p. 17.
4. Ibid., pp. 24, 72.
5. Wolfgang, *Patterns in Homicide*, p. 265.
6. W. Segall & A. Y. Wilson, "Who Is at Greatest Risk in Homicides? A Comparison of Victimization Rates by Geographic Region," in A. Y. Wilson, ed., *Homicide: The Victim-Offender Connection* (Anderson, Cincinnati, Ohio) 1993.
7. D. Finkelhor, R. J. Gelles, G. T. Hotaling, & M. A. Strauss, eds., *The Dark Side of Families: Current Family Violence Research* (Sage, Beverly Hills. Calif.) 1983.
8. J. M. Dawson & P. A. Langan, *Murder in Families,* Bureau of Justice Statistics (Department of Justice, Washington, D.C.) 1994.
9. Kathleen Heide, "Adolescent Parricide Offenders: Synthesis, Illustration and Future Directions," in A. Y. Wilson, ed., *Homicide: The Victim-Offender Connection* (Anderson, Cincinnati, Ohio) 1993.

10. See Eric W. Hickey, *Serial Murderers and Their Victims* (Brooks/Cole Publishing Company, Pacific Grove, Calif.) 1991, p. 8.

11. R. M. Holmes & J. DeBurger, *Serial Murder* (Sage, Newbury Park, Calif.) 1988, pp. 55–60.

12. E. Hickey, "The Female Serial Murder," 2 *Journal of Police and Criminal Psychology,* 72–81 (October 1986).

13. Hickey, *Serial Murderers and Their Victims,* pp. 18–19.

14. Robyn L. Cohen, "Drunk Driving," Bureau of Justice Statistics (U.S. Department of Justice, Washington, D.C.) September 1992.

15. T. A. Rando, *Parental Loss of a Child* (Research Press Company, Champaign, Ill.) 1986.

16. E. Furmann, *A Child's Parent Dies* (Yale University Press, New Haven, Conn.) 1974.

17. "Additional Problems of Survivors of a Homicide," *Report on Families of Homicide Victims Project* (Parents of Murdered Children, Inc., Victim Service Agency, New York) 1989.

18. This section is based on information provided by the Family Bereavement Center, 1441 St. Antoine Street, Detroit, Mich.

19. Stephanie Frogge, "Mystical Experiences." Paper presented at 1995 NOVA Conference, Maui, Hawaii (August 1995).

20. Ibid.

21. For an excellent in-depth discussion of this process, see "Survivors of Homicide Victims," 2(3) *NOVA Network Information Bulletin* (October 1985).

22. Lula M. Redmond, *Surviving When Someone You Love Was Murdered* (Consultation and Education Services, Inc., Clearwater, Fla.) 1989.

Sexual Victimization

Chapter Outline

LEARNING OBJECTIVES

After reading this chapter, you should be able to:

- Understand the various theories regarding sexual violence
- Distinguish between the various types of rape typologies
- Explain the classifications of sexual aggressors
- Explain the historical resistance to acknowledging the existence of acquaintance and marital rape
- Recognize a hostile working environment

SEXUAL ASSAULT

Definition

Exactly what do the terms *rape, marital rape, acquaintance rape,* and *sexual violence* mean? Should we define sexual violence strictly from a legal perspective, a medical view, a psychological view, or a combination of these views? Each discipline has valid reasons for defining sexual violence in a certain manner. Sexual victimization can mean several things—verbal coercion to have sex with an intimate partner, rape by a stranger, a woman or man fondled in a bar, or forced intercourse when a woman is too intoxicated to consent or object.

The use of aggression and violence against women and men has existed since the beginning of recorded history. Sexual violence against a person has traditionally been viewed as stranger rape—a violent, forceful sexual assault on a victim. Only recently have we recognized other forms of sexual violence. We now acknowledge that spouses or partners may be raped, and "acquaintance rape" has become a common term in our vocabulary. In addition, there are other forms of sexual violence that are more subtle but just as damaging—sexual harassment and sexual discrimination are still rampant in the United States. To define sexual violence by any one of these acts is to do injustice to the whole concept that the two genders are equal. A legal definition of sexual violence focuses on certain conduct that is prohibited and strictly defined. A medical definition views sexual violence as injury to the body. A psychological evaluation of sexual violence examines the effect on the mind and emotions of the victim. Each of these approaches has certain strengths and weaknesses.

Sexual violence can take the form of a single act or a long and protracted series of incidents. It can also involve aggression and/or discrimination against a person because of his or her gender. For purposes of this discussion, **sexual violence** is any intentional act or omission that results in physical, emotional, or financial injury in a sexual context to a woman or man. The phrase "financial injury" is included to cover sexual harassment situations in which employees have been terminated from employment for refusing to engage in sexual acts with their supervisors or coworkers. In most cases, sexual violence does not include the termination of a romantic relationship. If however, the relationship terminates in violence, under certain circumstances it may be considered sexual violence. The ritual of courting, dating, and marriage in America commonly results in one person being hurt or heartbroken when the relationship terminates. Although this may not be appropriate, it does not rise to the level of sexual violence. Although some may argue that this definition is too comprehensive, too narrow, it would need to exclude certain types of acts that result in harm to an individual.

Theories of Sexual Violence

As with other forms of violence, a number of theories regarding violent sexual aggression exist, but the exact cause of sexual violence is undetermined. No single factor can be highlighted as the cause of rape or other forms of sexual violence. Just as there are many forms of sexual violence, so are there a multitude of theories on the cause or causes of sexual aggression toward individuals. Some of the more common theories on the causes include sexual motivation, socialization, machismo, biological factors, psychological forces, and our culture of violence.

SEXUAL MOTIVATION Most current research dismisses the sexual motivation theory of sexual violence. It is not viewed as a sexual act, rather as an act of violence, aggression, and power by the aggressor.

SOCIALIZATION The socialization concept holds that in our society youths are taught to be aggressive, forceful, tough, and a winner in any sport or activity. This socialization creates aggressors and can spill over into the sexual areas where individuals are taught to sexually conquer as many persons as possible. This aggressive attitude encourages, if not gives consent, for individuals to engage in sexual violence.[1]

MACHOISM The machoism theory holds that individuals who believe in machism will be more aggressive than other individuals. Machoism is a set of beliefs that includes a view of individuals as objects simply to be added to a numerical list of sexual conquests. These conquests may include the act of rape or other forms of sexual violence.[2]

BIOLOGICAL FACTORS The view of biological factors argues that rape or other forms of sexual violence is a male instinctive reaction, which is a drive to perpetuate the species. Symons believes that men still have a genetic holdover that impels them to have sex with as many women as possible, and he argues that rape is closely linked to sexuality and violence.[3]

FOCUS
Some Common Facts About Sexual Violence

- Most rapes and other acts of sexual violence are not reported to the police.
- About 18 percent of young women experience sexual victimization.
- A smaller number of young men experience sexual victimization.
- A National Institute of Justice study indicated that the annual sexual victimization rate is about 35 per 1,000.
- Sexual violence may occur in any type of relationship, but most perpetrators of sexual assault are known to their victims. Among victims ages 18 to 29, about two-thirds had a prior relationship with the offender. The Bureau of Justice Statistics (BJS) reports indicate that six in ten rape or sexual assault victims said that they were assaulted by an intimate partner, relative, friend, or acquaintance. A study of sexual victimization of college women indicates that nine out of ten victims know the person who sexually victimized them. One research project found that 32 percent of victims surveyed were victims of sexual coercion by a spouse or by an intimate partner in their lifetime.
- Women are more likely to be victims of sexual violence than are men. The National Violence Against Women (NVAW) Survey sampled 8,000 women and 8,000 men

and found that 1 in 6 women (17 percent) and 1 in 33 men (3 percent) reported experiencing an attempted or completed rape at some time in their lives.
- Women are significantly more likely than men to be injured during an assault. In one NIJ-funded study, 31.5 percent of female rape victims, compared with 16.1 percent of male rape victims, reported being injured during their most recent rape.
- Sexual violence may begin early in life. Researchers also found that among female rape victims surveyed, more than half (54 percent) were younger than age 18; 32.4 percent were ages 12–17; and 21.6 percent were younger than age 12 at time of victimization.
- Early abuse is a risk factor for later victimization. Although child sexual abuse before age 13 is not by itself a risk factor, many victims who were victimized before turning 12 and then again as adolescents (ages 13–17) were at much greater risk of both types of victimization as adults than other individuals.

Sources: Rape, Abuse, & Incest Network web site, http://www.rainn.org accessed May 2, 2013; National Center for the Victims of Crime web site, http://www.victimsofcrime.org/ accessed on May 2, 2013; and Florida Council against Sexual Violence web site, http://www.fcasv.org/ accessed on May 2, 2013.

PSYCHOLOGICAL FORCES The theory of psychological forces holds that individuals rape or commit other acts of sexual violence because they suffer from some sort of personality disorder or mental illness. Studies have attempted to define the dynamics of convicted sex offenders and determine exactly what type of people rape and what mental condition causes them to commit violent sexual acts.

CULTURE OF VIOLENCE The culture of violence theory states that our society is a violent environment, which encourages some individuals to use violence to obtain sex. The use of violence and aggression is expected, and these individuals view their victims as legitimate targets of sexual aggression. These individuals believe that certain individuals want to be dominated and overpowered by an aggressive person.[4]

Rape Typologies

Although there are many causes of rape and sexual violence, past studies have failed to define clearly or predict who will rape. Researchers have now developed different typologies of rapists in an effort to streamline and to define this type of personality. One authority states that there are more than fifty different types of rapists.[5]

Groth and his associates conducted a study in Massachusetts of 133 convicted rapists and 92 victims. This classic study, *Rape: Power, Anger and Sexuality*, established that issues of power, anger, and sexuality are important concepts in understanding the various types of rape. In addition, this was one of the first research efforts to recognize that rape is a crime of violence and not a sexual act.[6] Groth and his associates classified rape types into two major categories: power and anger.

Power rapes involve the offender seeking power and control over his victim by use of force or threats. The sexual assault is evidence of conquest and domination. The perpetrator will plan and fantasize about the rape believing that the victim will respond to his advances after initially resisting. Power rapes may be further classified as power-assertive rapes or power-reassurance rapes. The power-assertive rapist views the assault as an expression of his virility, mastery, and dominance. The power-reassurance rapist, on the other hand, commits rape to resolve doubts about his masculinity and sexual adequacy.

Anger rapes involve the expression of anger, rage, contempt, or hatred toward the victim. The objective of this type of rapist is to vent his rage on the victim and to retaliate for rejections or perceived wrongs he has suffered in the past by other women. Anger rapes may be categorized as anger-retaliation or anger-excitation rapes. In anger-retaliation rapes, the rape is an expression of hostility and rage toward women. Anger-excitation rape occurs as a result of the offender's desire to obtain pleasure, thrills, and arousal secondary to the suffering of the victim during the assault.

Two years after their initial publication, Groth and Birnbaum established a more refined version of the original typology. In *Men Who Rape,* they established three categories of rapists and determined three types of rape offenses: anger rapes, power rapes, and sadism rapes.[7]

The anger and power rapes are very similar to those in the earlier study, and the sadistic rapist is obsessed with ritual during the rape. He may tie up his victim, torture her, or humiliate her and may become intensely excited during the act. This type of rape is very traumatic, and Groth found that victims of this type of rape needed long-term psychiatric counseling.

Sexual violence will continue to be researched, and perhaps one day rapists will be identified by a series of tests or events. However, until that time, sexual violence continues to be a serious problem that must be evaluated and treated.

Sexual Aggression Classifications

Building on Groth's work, two later researchers Prentky and Knight researched sexual aggressors. Sexual aggression typically reflects a chronic pattern of maladaptive behaviors. Those factors considered to be most importantly related to rape were researched by Prentky and Knight.[8] The researchers determined that in most cases certain factors were present. The factors include:

- Impaired heterosexual relationships with peers.
- Relative lack of empathy.
- Poorly controlled and improperly expressed anger.
- Cognitive distortions, particularly around women and sexuality.
- Sexual fantasy that includes thoughts and images of coercion, force, and deviant or paraphilic acts.
- A highly impulsive lifestyle that often includes antisocial elements.

While all of these factors may be present in varying degrees, typically several of the factors predominate in a particular offender. When factors are sufficiently robust to differentiate among rapists, they may serve as the basis for classification.

Knight and Prentky used the following dimensions in classifying sexual aggressors:

- **Expressive Aggression** Nature, amount, and quality of expressed aggression in all known instances of sexually aggressive behavior.
- **Pervasive Anger** Indicating the presence of global, undifferentiated anger in the life of the offender, as reflected by a history of nonsexual assaults, fighting, and verbal aggression directed at men as well as women.
- **Juvenile and Adult Unsocialized Behavior** Conduct disordered, delinquent, and impulsive antisocial behavior.
- **Social Competence** As reflected by stability and quality of interpersonal relationships with peers, and stability and level of vocational achievement.

- **Sexualization**   As evidenced by high sexual drive, sexual preoccupation, strong and frequent sexual urges, evidence of compulsivity in sexual assaults, and evidence of paraphilias.
- **Sadism**   Evidence that pain, fear, or discomfort increases sexual arousal, preoccupation with sadistic fantasies, ritualization of violence, and symbolic expressions of sadistic fantasy.

Prentky and Knight classified sexual aggressors based on the previous listed dimensions into nine major classifications:

- Type 1 (Opportunistic, High Social Competence)
- Type 2 (Opportunistic, Low Social Competence)
- Type 3 (Pervasive Anger)
- Type 4 (Overt Sadism)
- Type 5 (Muted Sadism)
- Type 6 (Sexualized, High Social Competence)
- Type 7 (Sexualized, Low Social Competence)
- Type 8 (Vindictive, Low Social Competence)
- Type 9 (Vindictive, High Social Competence)

According to the researchers, the sexual offenses of the two Opportunistic subtypes (Types 1 and 2) are impulsive, unplanned, predatory crimes, controlled more by situational factors and immediately antecedent events than by any long-standing, recurrent rape fantasy.

The sexual assaults of the Pervasive Anger type (Type 3) are driven by undifferentiated anger. These offenders are, in effect, "angry at the world." They are as likely to assault men as women. Their anger is not sexualized, and there is no evidence of protracted rape fantasy. The two Sadistic subtypes (Types 4 and 5) evidence poor differentiation between sexual and aggressive drives, and long-standing, frequent occurrence of sexually aggressive and violent fantasies. The two non-sadistic, sexual types (Types 6 and 7) evidence frequent sexual and sexually coercive fantasy that is devoid of the synergistic connection between sex and aggression that characterizes the sadistic types. The fantasies and offense-related behaviors of these non-sadistic, sexual types are hypothesized to reflect an amalgam of sexual preoccupation, distorted attitudes about women and sexuality, and feelings of inadequacy.

The Vindictive types harbor (Types 8 and 9) focal anger at women. Their attitudes and behavior reflect this exclusive misogynistic focus. The sexual assaults by these rapists are marked by statements and behaviors that are intended to defile, demean, and humiliate the victims, as well as to physically injure.

Extent of the Problem

How many victims are raped or sexually assaulted each year? Exactly what is involved in the act of sexual violence? Is sexual assault the same as rape? Should we determine if a person has been sexually assaulted or raped once in a lifetime or just attempt to determine how many victimizations occur each year? These are legitimate questions that surface when the study and research of sexual violence is undertaken. Determining the exact nature and extent of sexual violence is a complex and difficult process.

One major problem in the area of sexual violence is the lack of agreement among scholars, researchers, and professionals on definitions and research methodology. Depending on which article, paper, or textbook one reads, the estimates regarding the incidence of rape will vary. This disparity has caused problems and confusion within the professional community ever since the study of sexual violence began. There are a number of reasons for the different figures and definitions within this area of violence. The following is a summary of some of the more common problems encountered when this phenomenon is studied.

DEFINITIONAL ISSUES   Some scholars use the term *rape*, others use *sexual assault*, and still others define each of the foregoing terms differently. For example, one researcher may define rape as vaginal intercourse accomplished by use of force or fear, whereas other researchers may define rape as vaginal, oral, or rectal intercourse accomplished by force or fear. The simple addition of two terms changes the entire results of any study. The more modern studies or definitions include both genders as victims of rape or sexual assault.

PROFESSIONAL ISSUES Various professionals approach rape from different perspectives. Attorneys view rape in a certain legalistic way, physicians treat it as a medical problem, and psychologists approach it from a mental health point of view.

GATHERING OF INFORMATION Problems in the screening techniques, formation of questions, context of questioning, and issues of confidentiality all impact the validity and type of response that the researcher will receive.[9]

Koss compiled many of the various studies on rape, and her work illustrates the different approaches various researchers have used when attempting to determine the incidence of sexual violence against women in America.[10]

One study was conducted by the National Victims Center entitled *Rape in America: A Report to the Nation,* and it caused an uproar across America when it was released in April 1992.[11] The National Victims Center relied on a comprehensive study entitled "The National Women's Study" to gather their information. This report was based on a national sample of 4,008 women who were interviewed regarding their experience with rape. The report indicated that rape occurred at a much higher incidence than previously accepted. In looking at this report in 2013, it appears that only women victims were considered and the figures would have been much higher under the present definition of rape or sexual assault which includes victims of both genders.

Sexual violence is a serious and continuing problem in the United States and around the world. As Kilpatrick's report indicates, rape is one of the most underreported crimes in the United States. It is estimated that less than 40 percent of sexual assaults are reported to law enforcement.[12]

Two out of every 1,000 children were confirmed as having been victims of sexual assault. The authors have concluded that the rate of victimization is much higher than what figures confirm. Approximately 9 percent of all high school students reported that they had been raped. Among college students, approximately 25 percent report being attacked or actually being raped. Finally, more than 300,000 women and 90,000 men generally report that they had been raped each year. About one in six women will report experiencing an attempted or completed rape some time during their lives.[13]

The crime data indicate that rape and sexual assault in America are more common than previously thought, and rape is only one form of sexual violence that is perpetrated against a victim. Sexual violence can happen to any person, at any time and in any place. No one is completely secure from this type of assault. The following sections examine different aspects of this form of sexual violence.

STRANGER RAPE OR SEXUAL ASSAULT

There are still myths regarding the crime of rape or sexual assault. Some of these myths hold that individuals really want to be raped, that they like rough sex, and when they dress in a certain manner they are asking for sex. These myths apply to stranger, marital, or acquaintance rape situations.

Definitions

"Carnal knowledge of a female" was one of the first terms used to connote sexual violence. It was defined as *penile-vaginal penetration.*[14] *Black's Law Dictionary* defines carnal knowledge as "coitus; copulation; the act of a man having sexual bodily connections with a woman; sexual intercourse."[15]

Traditional penal codes reflected this bias and misunderstanding of the crime of rape. Criminal codes are enacted by each state, and the federal government set forth various definitions of crime. This has resulted in a patchwork of different definitions applied to basically the same act. In an effort to establish uniformity within the area of criminal law, a distinguished group of scholars and attorneys worked together for several years in drafting a Model Penal Code (MPC). The purpose of this code was to set forth the most reasoned thinking on various crimes and encourage states to adopt these definitions of the various crimes, so uniformity would be established throughout the United States. The MPC defines rape as follows:

A male who has sexual intercourse with a female, not his wife, is guilty of rape if:

a. he compels her to submit by force or by threat of imminent death, serious bodily injury, extreme pain or kidnapping to be inflicted upon anyone, or
b. he has substantially impaired her power to appraise or control her conduct by administrating or employing without her knowledge drugs, intoxicants or other means for the purpose of preventing resistance, or
c. the female is unconscious, or
d. the female is less than ten years old. Rape is a felony of the second degree unless (i) in the course thereof the actor inflicts serious bodily injury upon anyone, or (ii) the victim was not a voluntary social companion of the actor upon the occasion of the crime and had not previously permitted him sexual liberties, in which case the offense is a felony of the first degree.[16]

The drafters of the MPC were not purposefully discriminating against women. However, it is clear that the MPC perpetuated the bias of the times. A reading of the MPC reveals several flaws: the statute is gender biased, does not punish acquaintance rape as seriously as stranger rape, and does not provide for marital rape. The MPC only prohibits men from raping women. It makes no provision for female rape of a man. Second, although it allows that an acquaintance might rape his companion, this form of rape is not as serious as stranger rape; therefore, it will not be punished as harshly. Finally, it would not be a crime for a husband to rape his wife under the code. Some states adopted the provisions of the code, and others have modernized their criminal statutes relating to the crime of rape. Many statutes now define the crime of **rape** as "an unlawful act of sexual intercourse with another person against that person's will by force, fear, or trick."[17]

These statutes are gender neutral: either a man or a woman may commit the crime. Second, the very definition allows for the charging and prosecution of marital rape. Finally, a person may be prosecuted for acquaintance rape under this statute. The only area that is not covered by these statutes is insertion of an object into the vagina during the assault.

Some authorities define rape as the penetration by a penis or by other object into the mouth, vagina, or anal openings by force or by fear.[18] There is a small but growing movement among the states to adopt this more modern definition of rape. Part of the rationale for the expanded definition is that rape is not a sexual crime; rather it is a violent assault on the victim, and any type of forced penetration should be punished. This definition attempts to punish all forms of sexual assault. In addition, it attempts to provide uniformity in an area where each state has adopted differing statutes regarding sexual violence. Other authorities suggest doing away with the term *rape* and using instead *sexual assault* or *sexual battery* and prohibiting oral, vaginal, or anal penetration by force or by fear.[19] Someday we may move toward a more comprehensive definition of this type of sexual violence, but at present the great majority of statutes define rape in a manner similar to that discussed here. This definition in turn triggers reporting requirements by professionals in certain instances. Therefore, the definition set forth here is used for purposes of clarity and conformity with existing statutes. It should not give the impression that forcible anal intercourse or oral copulation is not a crime in most states. Under most statutes, these are considered separate offenses distinct from the crime of rape.

Legal Aspects

Rape carries with it certain physical, mental, and legal consequences. Many times during a rape, the offender will perform or attempt to perform a variety of acts, including vaginal, oral, and anal sex. As mentioned, each of these acts is considered a separate and distinct crime.

The crime of rape requires penetration of the penis into the vagina. The offense is complete on the slightest entry into the victim; therefore, it is possible for a woman to be raped and still retain her hymen. There is no requirement that the offender ejaculate for the crime to be complete.

As indicated, rape may be committed by force, fear, or trick. Forcible rape involves the offender using brute force to overpower the victim. He may use his fists or a foreign object, or other objects to strike the victim prior to raping her. The second situation occurs when the offender threatens the victim, and she submits out of fear for her safety. This type of rape may not leave any physical scars, torn clothing, or other signs of physical violence. The third type of rape occurs when the offender tricks the victim. This is a broad category that includes sex with incompetents, as well as the use of drugs and alcohol to render the victim incapable of consenting.

The *New York Times* conducted an informal survey of rape crisis centers and concluded that more rapists are wearing condoms.[20] Rapists are not wearing condoms out of concern for the victim, but they are wearing them to avoid receiving AIDS from the victim and to hinder prosecution. Condoms make the job of the prosecutor harder, because there is no access to semen from which DNA samples might be obtained. The use of condoms by rapists reinforces the theory that the crime is a planned act of violence rather than an impulsive act.

Once the crime is complete and if the victim reports the offense to the authorities, the criminal justice system begins its slow and methodological prosecution of the offender. The rape victim will have to testify in open court about the incident. As late as the early 1960s, rape victims were treated as the criminals in sexual assault cases, and defense attorneys were allowed to ask questions regarding their previous sexual experiences. There were a variety of theories that allowed for admission of this type of "evidence." Two of the more common theories involved the victim's reputation: (1) Because she had intercourse with other persons, she was therefore likely to have consented during this act. (2) Because of the proof that she was a person of loose morals, she was therefore willing to have sex with anyone, including this defendant. These antiquated and biased rules are no longer accepted in our judicial system. All fifty states and the federal government have adopted **rape shield laws**, which are statutes that prohibit the defendant or his attorney from questioning the rape victim regarding her previous sexual history or introducing any other evidence concerning her past sexual practices.[21]

Victim Selection

As with so many other aspects of sexual assault, we do not know why certain rapists select certain victims. This is one of the many subjects in this area that needs further research. One study attempted to answer this question by interviewing convicted sexual predators. Stevens used other convicted felons to conduct a survey of sixty-one sexual offenders incarcerated in a maximum security prison.[22] He trained thirteen incarcerated violent offenders enrolled in his class at a maximum security prison as student interviewers. They conducted interviews with convicted sexual predators, which resulted in sixty-one valid interviews.

The average respondent was thirty-two years old and had served seven years in prison at the time of the interview. The average rapist had attended eighth grade and was employed in a menial type of job before his arrest. The subjects averaged 3.4 prior adult arrests. Fifty-six percent of the sample was black, 42 percent white, and 2 percent Hispanic.

The author cautions against accepting the word of criminals. However, the data show some interesting results: The most common characteristic for selecting victims was that the victims were perceived as "easy prey," meaning that the victims were thought to be vulnerable. In other words, either these predators selected victims who they thought could or would not resist an attack, or an opportunity presented itself that allowed them to attack the victim.

One common defense in rape cases is that the victim consented. This is especially true in fear or trick rapes, when the victim suffers no outward physical injuries.

In Texas, a rape trial caught the attention of the nation. The victim was single and lived alone. One evening after she returned from a friend's party, she looked up and saw the defendant with a knife in his hand; he had entered through a sliding glass door. He approached her and demanded sex. The victim, fearing for her life, consented and asked the offender to wear a condom, which she supplied. The defendant was later arrested and tried for the crime of rape. He claimed the act was consensual in nature and pointed to the victim supplying him with a condom as proof of his assertion. One grand jury refused to indict the offender because the victim asked the offender to use a condom. The case was then presented to a second grand jury which did indict the offender. The jury did not buy his story, and he was convicted of rape and received a forty-year sentence to prison.

Some of the predators viewed young women as easy prey. One predator talked about attacking sixty or seventy victims by scouting financial districts and by looking for middle-class workingwomen. Still other predators found that female shoppers were easy prey. They identified them by their demeanor. One predator stated, "If she's not watching what's happening all around her, then [she] doesn't know how to handle herself, how to use the things around her to hurt me, or get me caught." Finally, other predators wait for situations to develop in which the victim puts herself in a vulnerable position. For example, one predator attacked a woman in the parking lot by threatening to harm her young child unless she cooperated.

Stranger rape is a violent physical assault on women; however, it is not the most common form of sexual assault. Recent studies have indicated that more women are raped by persons they know than by strangers. The next section examines this form of sexual violence—acquaintance rape.

ACQUAINTANCE RAPE

Introduction

Intimate sexual violence includes marital and acquaintance rape. These forms of assault are not isolated incidents that occur to only a few women. *Rape in America* reported that only 22 percent of all women raped were sexually assaulted by someone they had never seen before or did not know![23] Nine percent of all victims were raped by their husbands or ex-husbands, 10 percent by boyfriends or ex-boyfriends, and 21 percent by other nonrelatives such as friends or neighbors. The remaining percentages were composed of fathers or stepfathers, other relatives, and a "not sure" category of 3 percent. This report indicates that approximately 683,000 women were raped in a one-year period. Using the figures provided in this report, it means in one year 61,470 women were raped by their husband or by ex-husband, 68,300 women were raped by their boyfriend or by ex-boyfriend, and 143,430 women were raped by other known acquaintances.

The Focus box on when it is rape illustrates forms of sexual violence faced by women on a daily basis. Some men and defense attorneys would argue that situations 1 and 3 were clearly not rape and that a man should not be responsible for getting inside the mind of his date. Depending on what further facts are added, situation 1 may have involved the use of force and therefore qualify as a sexual assault and rape. Situation 2 is clearly a rape by trick situation in which the victim was unable to give consent. Situation 3 may be classified as rape, because many authorities argue that when a woman says "no," the advances by the man must stop. Others will argue that it may be rape depending on the victim's state of mind.

Sexual violence in dating relationships is not a new topic to social scientists and other professionals. As early as 1957, Kanin studied college students' sexual aggression. He found that more than half of all college women (50 to 60 percent) reported being offended by sexual aggression, whereas only 20 to 30 percent of college men admitted to such aggressive

FOCUS
When Is It Rape?

1. A couple attending college decides to break up. They have been intimate for three years, engaging in oral, anal, and vaginal sexual activities. One week after they separate, the man arrives at the woman's apartment intoxicated and states they are going to have sex. The woman insists the relationship is over; however, the male gets angry, punches the wall, and demands sex. The woman knows he will not hit her and is therefore not frightened for her own safety, but she gives in and they engage in sexual relations.

2. On a third date, the man double-shots his date's drinks. She is not an experienced drinker and passes out while they are engaged in heavy petting. The man proceeds to have intercourse with her.

3. A couple has been dating for three weeks. They both have had several drinks and are intoxicated. They engage in heavy petting and the woman responds physically, but says "Please darling, no." The man continues his sexual advances and the woman continues to respond physically, but also continues to say "no." They finally engage in intercourse.

Are any of these examples acquaintance rape? Why? Who is responsible in these situations? Are both parties at fault?

behavior.[24] This indicates a serious lack of empathy on the part of male college students as to what is appropriate behavior. Whereas a majority of the women found the acts aggressive, only 20 to 30 percent of the men found them to meet their definition of sexual aggression. Other researchers have confirmed these percentages and come to the conclusion that the double standard still exists in America.[25] This attitude in turn leads to situations in which date rape can and does occur.

One of the most controversial rape studies was conducted by Mary Koss, who was then a professor at Kent State University. Koss was contacted by *Ms.* Magazine and commissioned to conduct a national rape survey. Koss and her associates interviewed more than 3,000 women nationwide. They concluded that 15.4 percent of the respondents had been raped, and 12.1 percent were victims of attempted rape—a total of 27.5 percent of respondents had been victims of sexual assault. This percentage led to the "one-in-four" victims of rape slogan. Koss's study became one of the most widely cited articles on rape. It also became, and still is, one of the most controversial articles on rape.[26]

Another study of acquaintance rape was conducted by the Bureau of Justice Statistics.[27] The authors utilized the National College Women Sexual Victimization Study, which had a sample of 4,446 women who were attending a two- or four-year college or university. The study found 2.8 percent of the sample had experienced a completed rape or attempted rape. This equaled 27.7 rapes per 1,000 female students during the academic year. This statistic would place the numbers at only one in thirty-six college women. However, the authors point out that these statistics are misleading, because the data are for only 6.91 months instead of for a full year. This limited time frame may lead to the conclusion that nearly 5 percent of college women are victimized in any given calendar year (2.8 + 2.8 = 5.6), and since a college education now typically lasts five years, the percentage of rapes or attempted rapes in colleges and universities could be as high as 20 to 25 percent. The "one-in-four" figure again appears as a statistic.

Although sexual aggression in dating relationships has been studied for over thirty years, Americans still have problems in accepting the concept of rape by a person known to the victim. There are still individuals who want to believe that rape is committed in some dark alley by a sadistic monster and only "nice girls" who resist and whose resistance was overcome by physical force can be raped.

In assessing sexual violence during dating or courtship, Lloyd explained that sexual violence in a dating relationship does not necessarily lead to the breakup of the relationship.[28] Many victims reported that the relationship continued for some time after the violence. Lloyd also explained that violence in a dating situation occurs in a context of control by the aggressor.

Stranger rape at one time was thought to be the most common form of sexual violence. However, we now understand that intimate violence is more frequent than suspected. One survey reported that on a midwestern campus, 100 percent of all rapists knew their victims.[29]

Definition

Similar to marital rape, date or acquaintance rape situations are covered by the general definition of rape as set forth in the previous section. However, for purposes of explaining this special type of sexual violence, **acquaintance rape** is defined as the unlawful sexual intercourse accomplished by force or by fear with a person known to the victim who is not related by blood or by marriage.

The following actual cases[30] illustrate the continuing problems faced by victims of acquaintance rape:

- A young woman reports to the police that she was kidnapped and raped by a former boyfriend. He had beaten her in the past, leading to his arrest on at least one occasion. The prosecutor resists bringing rape charges because of the victim's prior relationship with her assailant and offers the man a plea to reduced charges—a misdemeanor assault for which the attacker receives a six-month sentence and eighteen months' probation. Less than a year later, the attacker brutally rapes and almost kills another woman.
- A group of young men meets a woman in a bar at night; they surreptitiously slip a tablet of LSD in her drink before leaving the bar with her. At the home of one of the young men, they slip her four more doses of LSD. The woman is then repeatedly raped with objects as the group cheers and takes pictures, which are destroyed later. One assailant stops the attack when someone suggests raping the woman with a statue of Christ. Three of the attackers are given immunity for providing statements helpful to the prosecution. One defendant pleads to evidence tampering and delivery of illegal drugs; he serves three months of an eight-month sentence in jail, with eight years' probation. None of the defendants are convicted of sexual assault.
- A woman ends her engagement with a man. Several weeks later, he goes to her house and they get into an argument in his car. She tells the police that he dragged her into the back seat of the car and raped her. After the attack, she goes to the hospital and files a police report. The prosecutor in the case accepts the defendant's plea to "unlawful restraint"—a fourth-degree felony with a two-year sentence—saying, "It's not like she didn't have sex with him before." The attacker serves six months and one day in jail.

Acquaintance rape will continue to be a serious problem in America as long as we socialize men to view women as inferior members of society who really want to be chased, conquered, and dominated. We must learn to view women as equals in interpersonal, social, and professional relationships.

MARITAL RAPE

An article in the *Journal of the American Medical Association* discussed the various forms of family violence with a subsequent recommendation that the American Medical Association undertake a campaign to sensitize its members to marital rape.[31] The recommendation includes training and dissemination of protocols on identifying and treating victims of marital rape. As discussed, the medical community is slowly becoming aware of the need to respond to intimate sexual violence. Although there is more awareness now of marital and acquaintance rape primarily because of the media, many people, including professionals in the legal field, have difficulty with the concept that a spouse can be accused and convicted of raping his or her partner or that a date who "consented" the evening before can raise the specter of rape the next day. Although the perception is slowly changing, there still remain those who believe sex is a matter of right in marriage or other intimate relationships.

Yllo cited several disturbing trends in marital rape.[32] She reported data from recent studies indicated that approximately 10 to 14 percent of wives were forced by their husbands to have sex against their will. She further illustrated that because of the sexual nature of marriage, marital rape has not been regarded as a serious form of assault. Finally, Yllo stated that many rape crisis shelters and battered women's shelters often feel that marital rape is the responsibility of some other organization.

Other studies indicate that marital rape accounts for approximately 25 percent of all rapes. Studies dealing with battered spouses indicate that between one-third and one-half of battered spouses are raped by their partners at least once. One study reported that while spouses of all ages were raped by their partners, almost two-thirds of the spouses were first raped by their partners when they were under the age of 25. Finally, spouses who were raped by their partners are likely to be raped repeatedly—often twenty times or more during the marriage or relationship.[33]

Historical Perspective

For centuries, our society has believed that a man is entitled to sex with his wife. A man could not be charged or convicted of raping his wife in eighteenth-century England. Wives were considered chattel and clearly subordinate to the husband.[34] Fathers had a property right or interest in their daughter's virginity and husbands in their wives' fidelity. The rape of an unmarried woman destroyed her value as a suitable bride and sexual mate. The rape of a married woman was an infringement on the property rights of and a disgrace of her husband.

The marital exemption for rape can be traced to Sir Matthew Hale, a seventeenth-century English jurist. Hale was the chief justice of King's Bench from 1671 to 1675. A book based on his writing was published after his death in 1736.[35] Geis, in his review of early English common law, indicated that Sir Matthew Hale's statement helped establish a precedent for spousal immunity from rape when he held: "But the husband cannot be guilty of rape committed by himself upon his lawful wife, for by their mutual matrimonial consent and contract the wife hath given up herself in this kind unto the husband which she cannot retract."[36]

Blackstone, the great English legal scholar, helped to perpetuate this reasoning. He stated that the legal existence of a woman is suspended during marriage, or at the very least incorporated into that of her husband. Blackstone's argument served to continue the legal fiction of unity of the person on marriage. Therefore, a wife was deemed to have irrevocably consented to sex when and where her husband wished.[37] This philosophy continued in England and elsewhere almost to modern times. R. E. Martin pointed out that Winston Churchill's mother could not refuse her husband's sexual advances even though he was suffering from incurable syphilis.[38]

The feminist movement in the 1970s sought to change the laws to allow for charges to be brought against a husband who raped his wife. It was not an easy victory. State- and congressional-elected officials made such comments as: "But if you can't rape your wife, who can you rape?" and "[T]he Bible doesn't give the state permission anywhere in the Book for the state to be in your bedroom…."[39] Unbelievable as it may seem now, there was a great deal of resistance to passage of any laws that would delete spousal immunity from the books and thus allow a wife to charge her husband with rape. Through the efforts of several dedicated groups and individuals, laws began to be amended to define marital rape as a specific crime.

As mentioned, many rape statutes now allow for the prosecution of a spouse who rapes the other partner. Therefore, there is no separate legal definition of marital rape. However, for purposes of explaining and distinguishing this form of sexual violence from stranger rape, **marital rape** is defined as unlawful sexual intercourse with a spouse or ex-spouse against his or her will by means of force or fear.

Finkelhor and Yllo conducted extensive research in the area of marital rape and classified marital rape into three categories: force-only rapes, battering rapes, and obsessive rapes. A force-only rape occurs when one partner attempts to gain control over the type and frequency of sexual activity within the marriage. Finkelhor and Yllo compare this type of rape with Groth and Birnbaum's power rape. A battering rape involves a spouse attempting to humiliate and degrade his or her partner. This type of marital rape is similar to Groth and Birnbaum's anger rapes. The last type of marital rape is the obsessive rape and involves sexual sadism, fetishes, and forcible anal intercourse. This type of rape is similar to Groth and Birnbaum's sadistic rape.[40]

Factors Contributing to Marital Rape

Just as there are a number of theories as to why spousal abuse and stranger rape occur, so are there a variety of theories dealing with factors that encourage or promote marital rape. Previous chapters have discussed factors that increase the risk of family violence, including child physical and sexual abuse, spousal abuse, and marital rape. The following discussion focuses on factors and forces within our society that specifically encourage or contribute to marital rape. These factors include our historical perspective toward the family, spousal immunity, economics, and our culture's preoccupation with violence.

HISTORICAL PERSPECTIVE TOWARD THE FAMILY For generations, the family has been viewed as the last stronghold of absolute privacy. What happened in the wedding bed was believed to be no one else's business. This concept of family privacy has caused delays and problems in researching issues such as marital rape. In addition, women were raised with the belief that they had to "submit" to their husbands' sexual advances. Only recently have we begun to study the dynamics within the family bedroom, and many women now understand that they do not owe sex on demand to their spouse.

SPOUSAL IMMUNITY As mentioned, early common law established the proposition that a husband could not be accused of raping his wife. Rape of a stranger was considered a violent and unspeakable act; however, rape of a wife was unknown. The wife was considered to be part of the husband, and therefore he was immune from charges of rape brought by his spouse. Only recently have spouses been able to bring charges of rape against their husbands.

ECONOMICS Similar to other causes of family violence, economics and dependency play a role in promoting marital rape. In some marriages, both spouses are aware of the wife's economic dependency. Some men argue that they provide the paycheck, so the wife must take care of the home. This "taking care of the home" includes, in the man's mind, sex on demand—any kind of sex.

PREOCCUPATION WITH VIOLENCE Violence and its effect on families have already been discussed in detail earlier in this textbook. Because some films, books, and television programs devalue women, it is easier for men to utilize violence as an acceptable form of sexual expression.

Although none of these factors may be the single or sole cause for marital rape, they contribute along with other factors to a general climate of violence in America that promotes sexual violence against women.

STALKING

Stalking may be defined as a knowing, purposeful course of conduct directed at a particular person that can cause a reasonable person to believe that she or he or a member of her or his family is in danger of physical injury or death.[41] Stalking may involve a celebrity, a complete stranger, or an individual who is related to the stalker by marriage or by other intimate or casual relationship. Stalking may happen to a person who forms a relationship with the stalker or is found by the stalker on the Internet or other electronic or print media.

Cyberstalking involves sending e-mails or hacking into e-mails or other personal accounts while pursuing the victim on the Internet. Cyberstalking has become more prevalent as our society increasingly relies on the use of computers and the Internet. In many ways, cyberstalking and identity theft are the new crimes of the twenty-first century. Some cyberstalkers may obtain the victim's personal data using the Internet and then attempt to destroy their credit or cause other harm. For instance, in a West Coast university, an ex-boyfriend accessed the university's registration Web site and disenrolled his former girlfriend from all of her classes without her knowledge or consent. This was a clear attempt on his part to injure or hurt his former girlfriend.

Stalking is composed of six elements that must be met before an act or a series of acts can be classified as stalking:

1. The stalker must have knowledge that the acts undertaken by him or her will place the victim in fear of injury.
2. The acts must be conducted in a purposeful or conscious manner that a reasonable person would believe will cause the victim fear.
3. The perpetrator must engage in more than a single act in order to be classified as a stalker.
4. A stalking crime is judged by a reasonable person standard, not by what the victim may feel. In other words, it is judged by what a reasonable person would think or feel if the reasonable person was in the particular situation that the victim has experienced.
5. The conduct by the perpetrator must consist of acts that would cause the victim to fear injury or death as a result of the perpetrator's actions.
6. The actions of the perpetrator must be directed at the victim or his or her immediate family, including spouses, children, or parents. Many stalkers may also attack the victim's pet as a way of intimidating or threatening the victim.

The four most common types of stalking behaviors are (1) *erotomania*, (2) *love obsessional*, (3) *simple obsessional*, and (4) *false victimization syndrome*.[42] The erotomaniac stalker has a delusional disorder. Often, the victim is a person, such as a public figure or celebrity, who does not know the stalker. The stalker believes that the victim would love him or her back if not for external influences. These individuals do not accept any opposing evidence or suggestions and remain delusional for a long period of time.

The characteristics of love obsessional stalkers are similar to the ones of erotomanic stalkers. The main difference between the erotomanic stalker and the love obsessional stalker is that

FOCUS

Like domestic violence, stalking is a crime of power and control. Stalking is conservatively defined as "a course of conduct directed at a specific person that involves repeated (two or more occasions) visual or physical proximity, nonconsensual communication, or verbal, written, or implied threats, or a combination thereof, that would cause a reasonable person fear."

Statistics on Stalking

According to the National Intimate Partner and Sexual Violence Survey (NISVS), 1 in 6 women and 1 in 19 men have been stalked during their lifetime. For both female and male victims, stalking was often committed by people they knew or with whom they had a relationship. Two-thirds of the female victims of stalking (66.2 percent) reported

stalking by a current or former intimate partner and nearly one-quarter (24.0 percent) reported stalking by an acquaintance. About 1 in 8 female victims (13.2 percent) reported stalking by a stranger.

Sources: National Institute of Justice website on Stalking, http://www.nij.gov/topics/crime/stalking/welcome.htm accessed on May 9, 2012.; Black, M.C., K.C. Basile, M.J. Breiding, S.G. Smith, M.L. Walters, M.T. Merrick, J. Chen, and M.R. Stevens, "The National Intimate Partner and Sexual Violence Survey (NISVS): 2010 Summary Report," Atlanta, GA: National Center for Injury Prevention and Control, Centers for Disease Control and Prevention, 2011; and Department of Justice. "Cyberstalking: A New Challenge for Law Enforcement and Industry: A Report From the Attorney General to the Vice President." Washington, DC: U.S. Department of Justice, 1999, NCJ 179575.

Cyberstalking

Stalking can be carried out in person or via electronic mechanisms (phone, fax, GPS, cameras, computer spyware, or the Internet). Cyberstalking—the use of technology to stalk victims—shares some characteristics with real-life stalking. It involves the pursuit, harassment, or contact of others in an unsolicited fashion initially via the Internet and e-mail. Cyberstalking can intensify in chat rooms where stalkers systematically flood their target's inbox with obscene, hateful, or threatening messages and images. A cyberstalker may further assume the identity of his or her victim by posting information (fictitious or not) and soliciting responses from the cybercommunity. Cyberstalkers may use information acquired online to further intimidate, harass, and threaten their victim via courier mail, phone calls, and physically appearing at a residence or work place.

Although cyberstalking does not involve physical contact with a victim, it is still a serious crime. The increasing ubiquity of the Internet and the ease with which it allows others unusual access to personal information, have made this form of stalking ever more accessible. Potential stalkers may find it easier to stalk via a remote device such as the Internet rather than to confront an actual person. Conduct that falls short of the legal definition of stalking may in fact be a precursor to stalking and must be taken seriously. As part of the Violence Against Women Reauthorization Act of 2005, Congress extended the Federal interstate stalking statute to include cyberstalking (18 U.S.C. §2261 A).

Source: National Institute of Justice web site on Stalking: http://www.nij.gov/topics/crime/stalking/welcome.htm accessed on May 9, 2012 and Department of Justice. "Cyberstalking: A New Challenge for Law Enforcement and Industry: A Report From the Attorney General to the Vice President." Washington, DC: U.S. Department of Justice, 1999, NCJ 179575.

the latter has a primary psychiatric diagnosis. The love obsessional stalker often engages in activities such as writing, telephone calling, or other activities to contact the victim so that the victim will acknowledge the existence of the stalker.

Simple obsessional stalkers have been involved in a prior relationship with the victim. This relationship could be a former spouse, cohabitant, boyfriend/girlfriend, employer/employee, or neighbor. This type of stalking occurs after the relationship has ended or when the stalker perceives that the victim has mistreated him or her. The simple obsessional stalker attempts to solve the problem or seek revenge by stalking the victim.

False victimization syndrome is the fourth classification of stalking. It occurs when a victim believes that he or she is being stalked but in fact there is no stalking. This is the rarest classification of stalking. Although it is not truly stalking, it is included for the purpose of comparison and understanding the stalking process.

Responses to stalking vary, but one of the most common responses is the use of protective or restraining orders, which are court orders directing the perpetrator to stay away from and have no contact with the victim. The National Stalker and Domestic Violence Reduction Act established a database of all civil restraining orders in the National Crime Information Center database in an effort to facilitate the use of one state's restraining order in another state.

There is a continuing controversy over the effectiveness of restraining orders. In *Castle Rock vs. Gonzales*, the U.S. Supreme Court refused to allow a domestic violence victim to sue Castle Rock Police Department for failure to enforce a restraining order against her former husband.[43] The husband kidnapped the children, murdered them, and was eventually killed by the police. The mother filed a civil action against the city, but the Supreme Court held that the victim's due process rights had not been violated because there was no personal entitlement to police protection despite the existence of a restraining order.

SEXUAL HARASSMENT

The title of this section was purposely chosen. Sexual harassment is the overall umbrella under which specific forms of sexual violence take place. Although it is true that men have been targets of sexual harassment, most victims are women. Because sexual harassment is a form of violence against women, it is included in this chapter to allow for comparison between sexual violence within the family and sexual violence in the workplace. Only by understanding the full spectrum of sexual violence can we begin to respond appropriately to it.

We have faced discrimination in America since its founding. Lincoln began the process of doing away with discrimination when he freed the slaves, and for decades our courts have held that one citizen should not discriminate against another simply because of skin color. However, that battle still goes on in coffee shops that refuse to serve people of color, banks that decline to make home loans to persons living in certain locations, and many service-related businesses such as automobile dealers who simply ignore persons of different races. Discrimination against women simply because of their sex is one bias that is also reaching our collective consciousness. One offensive form of this discrimination is sexual harassment. Employment-based sexual harassment is dehumanizing, and it changes the focus of employment from the woman's work performance to her sex. In addition, it degrades women by reinforcing their traditionally inferior role in the workplace. The following sections will provide a brief overview of sexual harassment.

Introduction

Sexual harassment is a widespread phenomenon. One of the first work-related surveys of 9,000 women found that nine out of ten women reported instances of sexual harassment.[44] Probably the most comprehensive survey of sexual harassment ever done was conducted by the U.S. Merit System Protection Board in 1980. The board surveyed 23,000 federal employees and stated that 42 percent of all women reported being the subject of some form of sexual harassment.[45]

Demands for sexual favors in exchange for continuing employment have long been a common abuse of personal power in the workplace. The clandestine squeeze on the factory floor, the stolen kiss in the copy room, or the lewd suggestion regarding sex has been commonplace in American businesses for years. Until recently, the victim of such sexual violence had two choices: agree or lose her job. In addition, she was led to believe that the activities that she found offensive were in reality a common practice in the workplace. There was no legal recourse for victims of sexual harassment until the 1980s.

In 1964, we began the long process of outlawing all forms of discrimination. Congress passed Title VII of the Civil Rights Act of 1964, which prohibited employment discrimination based on race, color, religion, sex, pregnancy, or national origin.[46] Title VII states:

It shall be an unlawful employment practice for an employer—

1. to fail or refuse to hire or to discharge any individual, or otherwise to discriminate against any individual with respect to his compensation, terms, conditions, or privileges of employment, because of such individual's race, color, religion, sex, or national origin; or
2. to limit, segregate, or classify his employees or applicants for employment in any way which would deprive or tend to deprive any individual of employment opportunities or otherwise adversely affect his status as an employee, because of such individual's race, color, religion, sex, or national origin.[47]

Even though the language of the statute was clear, women continued to be exposed to discrimination because they were pregnant at the time or might become pregnant in the future. This continuing discrimination caused Congress to pass the Pregnancy Discrimination Act of 1978, which prohibited discrimination based on pregnancy, childbirth, or other related medical conditions.[48]

Many scholars believe the Civil Rights Act of 1964 was the basis for the current prohibition against sexual harassment. However, Congress never directly addressed that issue when it passed the act. In fact, sex was added as a prohibited classification in a last-minute attempt by opponents to block passage of the legislation.[49] Rather, courts and administrative agencies have used the Civil Rights Act as the foundation on which to base their rulings regarding sexual harassment.[50]

Definitions

There are a number of definitions of sexual harassment. From a traditional perspective, sexual harassment is a demand that a subordinate, usually a woman, grant sexual favors to retain a job benefit.[51] A more encompassing definition defines **sexual harassment** as the imposition of any unwanted condition on any person's employment because of that person's sex. Under this definition, harassment includes jokes, direct taunting, disruption of work, vandalism or destruction of property, and physical attacks.[52] Sexual harassment occurs in a wide variety of forms, including rape, pressure for sexual favors, sexual touching, suggestive looks or gestures, sexual joking or teasing, and the display of unwanted sexual material.

Sexual harassment may occur in either of two forms: quid pro quo harassment or hostile environment harassment. These are not mutually exclusive situations. Many times, they will overlap, and both forms may be present in the workplace.

Quid pro quo harassment occurs when an agent or supervisor of the employer uses his position to induce a female employee to grant him sexual favors. The exchange of continued employment or job benefits for sex suggests the name quid pro quo. The essence of a quid pro quo harassment is that the victim must choose between suffering economic disadvantage or enduring sexual advances.[53]

Hostile environment harassment occurs when unwelcome conduct of a sexual nature creates a hostile working environment. The conduct usually involves a series of incidents rather than a single episode of harassment. The essence of a hostile working environment form of harassment is that an individual is forced to work in an environment that, although it does not cause direct economic detriment, results in psychological or emotional harm or humiliation.

Barnes v. Costle established the principle that sex-based assignments or sexual advances in which the employer enforces the demand by threat of discharge or other adverse economic consequences violate Title VII of the Civil Rights Act.[54] In *Barnes,* the plaintiff alleged that she was hired as an administrative assistant to the director of the agency's equal employment opportunity division at the Environmental Protection Agency. Shortly after commencing employment, the director solicited her to join him after hours at social functions and stated that if she cooperated with him in a sexual affair her employment status would be enhanced. She refused these advances and her position was abolished. The appellate court held that such actions were a clear violation of Title VII of the Civil Rights Act.

In 1980, the Equal Employment Opportunity Commission (EEOC) adopted regulations in the form of guidelines that prohibited discrimination based on sex. These guidelines specifically state that an individual's response to unwelcome conduct of a sexual nature may not be made on the basis of any adverse employment decision.[55] Although the EEOC guidelines are not binding, they have been held to constitute a body of experience and informed judgments to which courts and litigants may properly resort to guidance.[56]

It was not until 1986 that a case concerning sexual harassment based on a hostile working environment was decided. In *Meritor Savings Bank v. Vinson,* the U.S. Supreme Court held that a working environment that is hostile to women may violate Title VII of the Civil Rights Act even without any question of economic detriment. In *Meritor,* the victim was hired by the bank as a teller and eventually advanced to the position of assistant branch manager. She alleged that a supervisor subjected her to sexual harassment for over four years. This harassment included sexual intercourse, fondling her in front of other employees, exposing himself to her, and even following her into the ladies' restroom. The Supreme Court upheld the victim's claim of sexual harassment based on the theory that the actions of the aggressor established a hostile working environment.

In 1993, the Supreme Court again addressed the issue of sexual harassment when it decided *Harris v. Forklift Systems, Inc.*[57] The Court extended its ruling in *Meritor* to include conduct that does not actually cause psychological injury. In *Harris,* the Court held that Title VII is violated when a workplace is permeated with unwelcome discriminatory intimidation, ridicule, and insult that are so severe or pervasive as to alter the conditions of the victim's employment. In essence, the court held that sexual harassment can occur if the environment can reasonably be perceived as hostile or abusive. The Supreme Court acknowledged that there is no clear line that determines whether a working environment is hostile but noted that some factors can be examined as part of the circumstances of any case. These factors include frequency of the discriminatory conduct, severity of that conduct, whether it is physically threatening or humiliating or a mere offensive utterance, and whether it unreasonably interferes with an employee's work performance.

Tangri, Burt, and Johnson established three models or types of sexual harassment: the natural/biological model, the organizational model, and the sociocultural model.[58] Using data from the initial Merit Systems Protection Board 1980 survey, they partially tested these models.

The *natural/biological model* assumes that sexual behavior in the workplace is an extension of human sexuality. It is assumed that men and women possess strong sex drives, but the man whose sex drive is stronger takes the role of the aggressor. From this perspective, sexual harassment is not discriminatory in nature; it is simply the result of natural biological mating urges. This model presupposes that all sexual advances are mutual in nature and part of a courtship or mating behavior. We now understand that all advances are not in fact part of a courtship, and therefore this model fails to explain sexual harassment.

The *organizational model* is a result of the workplace environment, which provides opportunities for sexual aggression. From this perspective, sexual harassment becomes an issue of power, not sex. This power is derived from the formal roles in an organizational context. For this model to be valid, only those women in positions of low hierarchical power would be targets of sexual harassment. Women have been harassed in a variety of positions, some of which were considered high on the organizational scheme. Therefore, this model does not adequately explain sexual harassment.

The *sociocultural model* views sexual harassment as reflecting the more dominant position of men in our culture in which they are the source of economic and political power. This model suggests that sexual harassment is the result of a patriarchal power system in which men rule the society. From this perspective, sexual harassment is based on the personal power of gender, in which men are dominant. Power is an important factor in sexual harassment. The male aggressor may control advancement, benefits, and even continued employment.

Sexual harassment does not exist only in the workplace. It has been called one of the best-kept secrets on college campuses, and some feminists are concerned that certain professors have used their position of power to obtain sexual favors from students. Dziech and Weiner list the following actions they consider inappropriate behavior by professors:

- *Staring, Leering, Ogling* These behaviors may be surreptitious or obvious. Professors, who by the very nature of their occupation, must look at and/or observe students should not cross over the boundaries of reason.
- *Frequently Commenting on Personal Appearance of the Student* In an academic setting, professors should refrain from discussing apparel and physical characteristics of students.
- *Touching out of Context* Touching of students should be minimal and only to the extent necessary to carry out certain types of instruction.
- *Excessively Flattering and Praising the Student* This behavior, with others listed here, is especially seductive to students with low self-esteem or high expectations. By convincing the student that she is exceptional, the professor gains psychological access to her.

Many would hesitate to consider the circumstances depicted in the photo as sexual violence. But consider the situation where the female worker needs this job to support her family, to her the unwanted sexual touching is very offensive and degrading. (Lisa S./Shutterstock)

- *Injecting a "Male versus Female" Tone into Discussions with the Student* This type of disparaging remark about women and their abilities is a clear signal of a bias or negative perception on the part of the professor.
- *Persistently Emphasizing Sexuality in All Contexts* Pervasive emphasis on sex inside or outside the classroom is inappropriate.[59]

This discussion should not be construed to label every professor as a potential sexual harasser. However, even in academia, the controversy about professor–student relationships continues to be debated. In April 1993, the University of Virginia Faculty Senate was considering a policy that would prohibit faculty members from dating students. Representatives of the American Civil Liberties Union (ACLU) questioned the appropriateness of the actions, stating that the university might be infringing on privacy and associational rights of teachers. The ACLU instead recommended that the university beef up its sexual harassment codes. The University Faculty Senate proceeded to approve the no-dating policy. Many universities have sexual harassment codes, and some are beginning to adopt a no-dating policy between students and faculty members. The relationship between students and faculty members is one of power. When a professor uses his position to extract sexual favors from a student, this becomes a serious quid pro quo form of sexual harassment.

Simply having agencies and courts establish procedures and processes to handle sexual harassment cases does not eliminate this behavior. The perception of women must be changed, and they should be viewed as equals instead of sex objects. Only when women are approached as partners and equals will sexual harassment stop.

Summary

Sexual violence is a complex and far-ranging topic. The study of sexual violence has been and will continue to be hindered by a lack of agreement among the different professions on terminology and research methodology. All professionals agree that sexual violence continues to be a serious problem in the United States. Studies have indicated that women are more at risk from someone they know than from a stranger lurking in the darkness. Also, the consequences of any type of sexual violence are severe and in many instances long lasting. We really should begin to think about a "war on rape" in addition to the "war on drugs."

We are slowly advancing in our perception of rape victims. No longer can only "nice" girls be raped. We have accepted that rape is a violent physical assault that has very little if anything to do with sexual gratification. Our legislatures have passed rape shield laws that now provide some protection to the victims of rape. These laws bar questions to the victim that require her to explain her previous sexual experiences to the judge and jury. As long as men rape women, lawyers will raise consent as a defense. However, as we become more educated as a nation, that rationalization will stop bearing credibility.

Sexual harassment continues to be a form of sexual violence in the United States and will continue as long as men view women as sexual trophies or playthings instead of equals. Only by continuing our education of society can we hope to put an end to this form of sexual violence.

Key Terms

Sexual violence is any intentional act or omission that results in physical, emotional, or financial injury to a person.

Rape is an unlawful act of sexual intercourse with a person against her or his will by force, fear, or trick.

Rape shield laws are statutes that prohibit the defendant or his attorney from questioning the rape victim regarding her previous sexual history or introducing any other evidence concerning her past sexual practices.

Acquaintance rape is unlawful sexual intercourse accomplished by force or by fear with a person known to the victim who is not related by blood or by marriage.

Marital rape is unlawful sexual intercourse with a spouse or ex-spouse against her or his will by means of force or fear.

Sexual harassment is the imposition of any unwanted condition on any person's employment because of her or his sex.

Discussion Questions

1. Why is it so hard to define sexual violence?
2. In your opinion, what is the most acceptable theory on the cause of sexual violence? Justify your answer.
3. Should the definition of rape include more than sexual intercourse? Why? Why not?
4. Is victim selection an important issue in studying sexual violence? Isn't this a form of blaming the victim?
5. Should we call rape between nonstrangers "acquaintance rape"? Does that terminology degrade the crime into something less than what it is?
6. Should there be a requirement for independent evidence to support a charge of marital rape? Why? Why not?

Suggested Readings

D. J. Graney & B. A. Arrigo, *The Power Serial Rapist: A Criminology-Victimology Typology of Female Victim Selection* (Charles C Thomas Publisher Ltd., Springfield, Ill.) 2004.

A. P. Giardina, E. Datner, J. Asher, B. W. Giradin, D. K. Faugno, & M. J. Spencer, *Sexual Assault Victimization Across the Life Span: A Comprehensive Clinical Guide and Color Atlas for Professionals Who Deal with Sexual Assault* (G. W. Medical Publishing, St. Louis, Mo.) 2003.

L. F. Alarid & P. Cromwell, eds., *In Her Own Words: Women Offenders' Views on Crime and Victimization* (Roxbury Publishing, Los Angeles) 2005.

T. K. Logan, R. Walker, C. E. Jordan, & C. G. Leukefeld, *Women and Victimization: Contributing Factors, Interventions and Implications* (American Psychological Association, Washington, D.C.) 2005.

Enforcement of Protective Orders (U.S. Department of Justice, Office for Victims of Crime, Washington, D.C.) 2002.

P. Phillips, *Marx and Engels on Law and Laws* (Barnes and Noble, Totowa, N.J.) 1980.

K. Millett, *Sexual Politics* (Abacus, London) 1972.

S. Brownmiller, *Against Our Will: Men, Women and Rape* (Penguin Books, New York) 1975.

L. Kelly, *Surviving Sexual Violence* (University of Minnesota Press, Minneapolis) 1988.

D. E. H. Russell, *Sexual Exploitation* (Sage, Beverly Hills, Calif.) 1884.

D. Russell, *The Politics of Rape* (Stein and Day, New York) 1975.

D. Symons, *The Evolution of Human Sexuality* (Oxford University Press, Oxford) 1979.

C. McCaghy, *Deviant Behavior: Crime, Conflict, and Interest Groups* (MacMillan, New York) 1976.

A. N. Groth & J. Birnbaum, *Men Who Rape* (Plenum Press, New York) 1979.

H. Wallace & C. Roberson, *Principles of Criminal Law,* 4th ed. (Pearson, Columbus, Ohio) 2007.

R. E. Martin, *The Life of Lady Randolph Churchill* (New York American Library, New York) 1969.

D. Finkelhor & K. Yllo, *License to Rape* (Holt, Rinehart & Winston, New York) 1985.

B. Lindemann & D. D. Kadue, *Sexual Harassment in Employment Law* (Bureau of National Affairs, Washington, D.C.) 1992.

A. M. Jaggar & P. S. Rothenberg, eds., *Feminist Frameworks,* 3rd ed. (McGraw-Hill, New York) 1993.

Endnotes

1. D. Russell, *The Politics of Rape* (Stein and Day, New York) 1975.

2. D. Mosher & R. Anderson, "Macho Personality, Sexual Aggression and Reactions to Guided Imagery of Realistic Rape," 20 *Journal of Research in Personality,* 77–94 (1987).

3. D. Symons, *The Evolution of Human Sexuality* (Oxford University Press, Oxford) 1979.

4. C. McCaghy, *Deviant Behavior, Crime, Conflict and Interest Groups* (MacMillan, New York) 1976.

5. J. Rabkin, "Epidemiology of Forcible Rape," 49(4) *American Journal of Orthopsychiatry,* 634–647 (1979).

6. A. N. Groth, A. W. Burgess, & L. L. Holmstrom, "Rape: Power, Anger, and Sexuality," 134(11) *American Journal of Psychiatry,* 1239 (November 1977).

7. A. N. Groth & J. Birnbaum, *Men Who Rape* (Plenum Press, New York) 1979.

8. Marita P. McCabe, & Michelle, Wauchope "Behavioral characteristics of men accused of rape: evidence for different types of rapists." *Archives of Sexual Behavior* (April 1, 2005); and R. A. Prentky, & R. A. Knight, "Identifying Critical Dimensions for Discriminating Among Rapists." 59 *Journal of Consulting and Clinical Psychology,* 643–661 (1991).

9. For an excellent in-depth discussion of these issues, see M. P. Koss, "Detecting the Scope of Rape," 8(2) *Journal of Interpersonal Violence,* 198–222 (June 1993).

10. Koss, "Detecting the Scope of Rape," 200–203 (June 1993).

11. Personal communication with Christine N. Edmunds, co-author and project director, National Victims Center, Washington, D.C.

12. Bureau of Justice statistics, *Criminal Victimizations 2002* (U.S. Department of Justice, Washington, D.C.) 2003.

13. National Center for Injury Prevention and Control, *Sexual Violence: Fact Sheet* (Centers for Disease Control and Prevention, Atlanta, Ga.) December 30, 2005.

14. L. B. Bienen, "Rape III—National Developments in Rape Reform Legislation," 6 *Women's Rights Law Reporter,* 171–213 (1981).

15. H. C. Black, *Black's Law Dictionary* (West Publishing Co., St. Paul, Minn.) 1990, p. 213.

16. Model Penal Code Section 213.1 (American Law Institute, Chicago) 1985.

17. H. Wallace & C. Roberson, *Principles of Criminal Law* 4th ed. (Allyn & Bacon, Boston) 2008.

18. D. G. Kilpatrick, C. L. Best, B. E. Saunders, & L. J. Veronen, "Rape in Marriage and in Dating Relationships: How Bad Is It for Mental Health?" 528 *Annals of the New York Academy of Sciences,* 335–344 (1988).

19. Koss, "Detecting the Scope of Rape," 198 (June 1993).

20. Craig Wolff, "Rapists Increasingly Using Condoms," *The Fresno Bee,* A-7 (August 22, 1994).

21. See *Michigan v. Lucas,* 111 S. Ct. 1743 (1991), where the United States Supreme Court upheld the constitutionality of these statutes. See also *Vermont Statute,* Title 13, Chapter 72, Section 3255 (3)(A)(B) for an example of a rape shield law.

22. Dennis J. Stevens, "Predatory Rapist and Victim Selection Techniques," 31 *The Social Science Journal,* 421 (1994).

23. D. G. Kilpatrick, C. N. Edmunds, & A. K. Seymour, *Rape in America: A Report to the Nation* (National Victim Center, Arlington, Va.) 1992.

24. E. Kanin, "Male Aggression in Dating–Courtship Relationships" 63 *American Journal of Sociology,* 197–204 (1957).

25. Mary P. Koss & Sarah L. Cook, "Date and Acquaintance Rape Are Significant Problems for Women," in Richard J. Gelles & Donileen R. Loseke, eds., *Current Controversies on Family Violence* (Sage, Newbury Park, Calif.) 1993.

26. Christina Sommers, "Researching the 'Rape Culture' of America," LeadershipU; available online: www.lead-eru.com/real/ri9502/sommers.html. A recent review of Internet blogs finds continuing dialogue and debate on Koss's methodology and findings (Archive for the "Mary Koss controversy," www.amptoons.com).

27. Bonnie Fisher, Francis Cullen, and Michael Turner, *The Sexual Victimization of College Women* (Bureau of Justice Statistics, U.S. Department of Justice, Washington, D.C.) December 2000.

28. Sally A. Lloyd, "Physical and Sexual Violence during Dating/Courtship," in Richard J. Gelles, ed., *Vision 2010: Families & Violence, Abuse, & Neglect* (National Council on Family Relations, Minneapolis) 1995.

29. T. Meyer, "Date Rape: A Serious Campus Problem That Few Talk About," *Chronicle of Higher Education,* A15 (December 5, 1990).

30. *The Response to Rape: Detours on the Road to Equal Justice* (Majority Staff of the Senate Judiciary Committee), May 1993, pp. 18–19.

31. Council of Scientific Affairs, "Violence against Women," *Journal of the American Medical Association,* 3/84 (267/23) (June 17, 1992).

32. Kersti Yllo, "Marital Rape," in Richard J. Gelles, ed., *Vision 2010: Families & Violence, Abuse, & Neglect* (National Council on Family Relations, Minneapolis) 1995.

33. Raquel K. Bergen, *Marital Rape,* VAWnet, National Resource Center on Domestic Violence (March 1999).

34. See Comment, "Abolishing the Marital Exemption to Rape: A Statutory Proposal," *University of Illinois Law Review.* 201 (1983).

35. M. Hale, *The History of the Pleas of the Crown* (E. & R. Nutt & R. Gosling, London) 1736. The first American edition of the book, *Pleas of the Crown,* was published in 1874. See Comment, "Sexual Assault: The Case for Removing the Spousal Exemption from Texas Law," 38 *Baylor Law Review,* 1941 (1986).

36. G. Geis, "Rape and Marriage: Historical and Cross-Cultural Considerations," Paper presented at the annual meeting of the American Sociological Association, New York (1980).

See also M. Hale, *The History of the Pleas of the Crown* (E. & R. Nutt & R. Gosling, London) 1736, p. 629.

37. L. D. Waggoner, "New Mexico Joins the Twentieth Century: The Repeal of the Marital Rape Exemption," 22 *New Mexico Law Review,* 551 (1992).
38. R. E. Martin, *The Life of Lady Randolph Churchill* (New York American Library, New York) 1969.
39. J. Schulman, "The Marital Rape Exemption in the Criminal Law," 13(6) *Clearinghouse Review* (1980).
40. D. Finkelhor & K. Yllo, *License to Rape* (Holt, Rinehart & Winston, New York) 1985.
41. See H. Wallace, *Family Violence: Legal, Medical, and Social Perspectives*, 4th ed. (Allyn & Bacon, Boston, Mass.) 2005.
42. M. A. Zona, K. K. Sharma, & J. Lane, "A Comparative Study of Erotomanic and Obsessional Subjects in a Forensic Sample," 38 *Journal of Forensic Science,* 894 (July 1993).
43. 545 U.S. 748 (2005).
44. Safran, "What Men Do to Women on the Job: A Shocking Look at Sexual Harassment," *Redbook*, 149 (November 1976). Redbook received more than 9,000 responses to their questionnaire regarding sexual harassment.
45. "Sexual Harassment in the Federal Workplace—Is It a Problem?" (Merit System Protection Board 1981); see also W. Pollack, "Sexual Harassment: Women's Experience vs. Legal Definitions," 13 *Harvard Women's Law Journal,* 35 (Spring 1990) for a discussion of this and other surveys.
46. 42 U.S.C. 2000e to 2000e-17 (1964).
47. 42 U.S.C. 2000e-2(a) (1982).
48. 42 U.S.C. 2000e(k) (1982).
49. *Wilson v. Southwest Airlines Co.,* 517 F. Supp. 292 at 297 fn. 12 (N.D. Tex. 1981).
50. *Meritor Saving's Bank v. Vinson,* 106 S.Ct. 2399, 2404 (1986).
51. B. Lindemann & D. D. Kadue, *Sexual Harassment in Employment Law* (Bureau of National Affairs, Washington, D.C.) 1992.
52. See note, "The Dehumanizing Puzzle of Sexual Harassment: A Survey of the Law Concerning Harassment of Women in the Workplace," 24 *Washburn Law Journal,* 574 (1985).
53. See *Barnes v. Costle,* 561 F.2d 983 (D.C. Cir. 1977).
54. 561 F.2d 983 (D.C. Cir. 1977).
55. 29 C.F.R. ss 1604.11(a).
56. *Meritor Saving's Bank v. Vinson,* 106 S.Ct. 2399 (1986).
57. 114 S.Ct. 367 (1993).
58. S. Tangri, M. Burt, & L. Johnson, "Sexual Harassment at Work: Three Explanatory Models," 38 *Journal of Social Issues,* 33–54 (1982).
59. B. W. Dziech & L. Weiner, "The Lecherous Professor," in A. M. Jaggar and P. S. Rothenberg, eds., *Feminist Frameworks*, 3rd ed. (McGraw-Hill, New York) 1993, pp. 323–327.

Intimate Partner Abuse

Chapter Outline

LEARNING OBJECTIVES

After reading this chapter, you should be able to:

- Explain why victims stay in abusive relationships
- Distinguish between the cycle theory of violence and the battered woman syndrome
- Define and give examples of the Stockholm syndrome
- Understand the various theories of intimate partner abuse
- Explain the advantages and disadvantages of mandatory arrest policies for those who assault their intimate partners

INTRODUCTION TO INTIMATE PARTNER ABUSE

Historically called "domestic violence or spouse abuse," "intimate partner violence" describes physical, sexual, or psychological harm by a current or former intimate partner or spouse. Intimate partner abuse or violence (IPA) is when one person in a relationship purposely hurts another person physically or emotionally. IPA is also called domestic violence because it is often caused by a husband, ex-husband, boyfriend, or ex-boyfriend. Women also can be abusers. IPA includes:

- Physical abuse like hitting, shoving, kicking, biting, or throwing things
- Emotional abuse like yelling, controlling what the other partner does, or threatening to cause serious problems for the victim
- Sexual abuse like one partner forcing the other partner to do something sexual that the partner doesn't want to do

IPA can occur among heterosexual or same-sex couples. Violence by an intimate partner is linked to both immediate and long-term health, social consequences, and economic consequences. Factors at all levels—individual, relationship, community, and societal—contribute to intimate partner violence. Preventing intimate partner violence requires reaching a clear understanding of those factors; coordinating resources; and fostering and initiating change in individuals, families, and society.

There is probably no more misunderstood form of violence than intimate partner abuse. Gelles has published a series of *Domestic Violence Factoids,* which are statements or sound bites used by various individuals or agencies when discussing family violence.[1] Gelles explained that many of these statements have taken on a life of their own and are presumed to be true or accurate. In many instances, this "truth" is based on misinterpretation or faulty analysis of research. The following are some of these factoids and Gelles's response:

Domestic violence is the leading cause of injury to women between the ages of fifteen and forty-four in the United States—more than car accidents, muggings, and rapes combined.

> Gelles explained that as good a sound bite as this statement is, it is simply not true. The actual research that this statement is based on was a small survey of only one emergency room, and the authors of the study stated that domestic violence may be a more common cause of emergency room visits than car accidents, muggings, and rapes.

The March of Dimes reported that battering during pregnancy was the leading cause of birth defects and infamortality.

> Gelles responded that the March of Dimes knows of no such study.

Nationally, 50 percent of all homeless women and children are on the streets because of violence in the home.

> Gelles stated that this factoid can be attributed to a U.S. Senator, but there is no actual published scientific research supporting this figure.

There are nearly three times as many animal shelters in the United States as there are shelters for battered women and their children.

> Gelles indicated that although this is another great sound bite, there is no verified count of either type of shelter.

As this discussion indicates, there is still a great deal of misinformation and controversy surrounding intimate partner abuse. These factoids should not be interpreted to mean that intimate partner abuse is not a serious and deadly problem. It is. However, to understand this form of violence, we must base our knowledge on facts or theories that are accepted within the various professions that deal with intimate partner abuse, not on sound bites.

Definition

There is no clear, single definition of intimate partner abuse. Different authorities include different acts within their definition, and some authorities have established levels of intimate partner abuse. They categorize intimate

An argument between partners can rapidly escalate into violence. Both partners need to temper their language and feelings (Tomalu/Fotolia)

partner abuse into two forms of violence. The lesser forms include yelling and throwing things, and the more severe forms include striking and hitting.

As the practicum below indicates, there are shades of grey in any situation, and reasonable people may disagree as to what constitutes intimate partner abuse. For purposes of this chapter, **intimate partner abuse** is defined as any intentional act or series of acts that cause injury to the spouse or intimate partner. These acts may be physical, emotional, or sexual. Partner is gender neutral, and therefore the abuse may occur to a man or woman. The term includes those who are married, cohabitating, or any partners involved in a serious relationship. It also encompasses individuals who are separated and living apart from their former partners. Although there is some disagreement regarding the exact definition of intimate partner abuse, all scholars and authorities agree it exists. The next section will examine the extent of this form of domestic violence.

Extent of the Problem

Depending on whose study is reviewed, the extent of intimate partner abuse varies. In their landmark study of 8,145 families, Straus and Gelles estimated that just over 16 percent, or one in six American couples, experienced an incident of physical assault each year. Projecting that number to the 54 million couples in America in that year leads to a startling figure of approximately 8.7 million couples who were involved in intimate partner abuse.[2] Other scholars point out that 20 percent of all women who go to emergency rooms for treatment have been battered.[3] These authorities cite figures that pertain to physical violence. As the definition here indicates, intimate partner abuse also includes psychological and sexual abuse. When a woman is emotionally abused, she may not go to an emergency room or even report the acts because she may believe that she deserved the treatment and therefore it is not abuse. "After all, he didn't hit me" is a common refrain in some intimate partner abuse cases.

Although it is true that the definition of intimate partner abuse is gender neutral and in fact men can be battered by women, most of the victims of intimate partner abuse are women. In 1977, Steinmetz presented a paper entitled "The Battered Husband Syndrome." This presentation was the basis for an article dealing with husbands who are battered.[4] Steinmetz's research, which was widely publicized in the media, claimed that men were abused at a far greater rate than

FOCUS
Types of Intimate Partner Violence

The Centers for Disease Control and Prevention (CDC) defines the main types of intimate partner violence:

Physical violence is the intentional use of physical force (e.g., shoving, choking, shaking, slapping, punching, burning, or use of a weapon, restraints, or one's size and strength against another person) with the potential for causing death, disability, injury, or physical harm.

Sexual violence can be divided into three categories: (1) the use of physical force to compel a person to engage in a sexual act unwillingly, whether or not the act is completed; (2) an attempted or completed sexual act involving a person who, because of illness, disability, or the influence of alcohol or other drugs, or because of intimidation or pressure, is unable to understand the nature or condition of the act, decline participation, or communicate unwillingness to engage in the act; and (3) abusive sexual contact.

Threats of physical or sexual violence communicate the intent to cause death, disability, injury, or physical harm through the use of words, gestures, or weapons.

Psychological/emotional violence traumatizes the victim by acts, threats of acts, or coercive tactics (e.g., humiliating the victim, controlling what the victim can and cannot do, withholding information, isolating the victim from friends and family, denying access to money or other basic resources). In most cases, emotional violence has been preceded by acts or threats of physical or sexual violence.

Source: Office of Justice Programs, U.S. Department of Justice; available online: http://nij.gov/topics/crime/intimate-partner-violence/welcome.htm (May 9, 2013)

PRACTICUM

Intimate Partner Abuse

Which of the following, in your opinion, would be considered intimate partner abuse?

- A man is upset at his girlfriend, who is late for a date. He calls her lazy and irresponsible.
- During a date, the man takes his date's arm and steers her to an exit, commenting that she is stupid for not seeing that this is the fastest way to leave the theater.
- A couple living together while attending college get into a yelling match, with each of them calling the other names.
- The same couple's argument escalates, and the woman throws a textbook at her male friend. It misses and strikes the television.
- During a heated argument, the man grabs the woman's arms and shakes her.

- A husband yells at his wife and calls her an obscenity after she overdraws the bank account, causing him to bounce a check.
- The husband does not allow his wife access to any funds after she bounced three checks and almost caused him to lose his job at the bank.
- The wife is tired and wants to sleep, but the husband forces her to engage in sex.
- The wife does not enjoy anal sex, stating that it hurts her, but the husband forces her to engage in it at least once a month.
- The husband completely controls the couple's financial resources and requires the wife to justify her spending before he will give her any money.
- The husband does not allow his wife to have any friends excepts the ones that he chooses for her. (Office of Justice Programs, U.S. Department of Justice).

previously believed. Steinmetz went even further and claimed that wives abused their husbands more often and more severely than vice versa. This claim was attacked by feminists, professionals, and scholars. In 1988, Steinmetz and Lucca published a follow-up article, discussing husband battering in more detail.[5] In this article, they continued to assert that husbands are battered and concluded that all forms of violence must be prevented by placing greater emphasis on changing the attitudes and values of a society that glorifies violence.

One result of Steinmetz's position is the acknowledgment that both parties in an abusive relationship need to be evaluated. Some studies indicate that there are higher levels of female aggression by women toward their spouses than previously thought.[6] However, the type and severity of aggression is different than that experienced by women. As Campbell explained, most authorities agree that the detrimental effects of abuse affect women disproportionately.[7] Furthermore, Campbell stated that gender inequity is a significant risk factor in battering.

Although it may be true that some men are abused by women in an intimate relationship, it appears that the majority of all domestic abuse is inflicted by men. The National Institute of Justice and the CDC undertook a comprehensive survey to determine the nature and extent of intimate partner abuse. They contacted 8,000 women and 8,000 men via telephone. The results of this survey support previous samples that indicate that intimate partner abuse is a serious and ongoing phenomenon. This survey, entitled the National Violence Against Women Survey, indicated that approximately 8 percent of all the female respondents had been raped by their intimate partner at some time in their lives. Using the U.S. Census population, this translates into over eight million women who have been raped by an intimate partner during their lives. The survey also found that 22.1 percent of all female respondents had been physically assaulted by their intimate partner at some time during their lives.[8]

A 2012 report on nonfatal intimate partner violence among U.S. households from 1993 to 2010 was made by Shannan M. Catalano. She studied intimate partner violence including rape, sexual assault, robbery, aggravated assault, and simple assault by a current or former spouse, boyfriend, or girlfriend. She conclude that

- From 1994 to 2010, the overall rate of intimate partner violence in the United States declined by 64 percent, from 9.8 victimizations per 1,000 persons age 12 or older to 3.6 per 1,000.

National Domestic Violence Fatality Review Initiative

To find out the specific laws and executive orders that are applicable to your home state, visit the National Domestic Violence Fatality Review Initiative Web site. For example, the Web site under state statutes and under the State of New Jersey lists the New Jersey Statute 52:27D-43.17a, "Definitions relative to domestic violence." The NJ statute establishes a Domestic Violence Fatality and Near Fatality Review Board. The statute also defines "domestic violence-related fatality" as a death which arises as a result of one or more acts of domestic violence as defined in the act.

The National Domestic Violence Fatality Review Initiative (NDVFRI) was established to provide technical assistance for the reviewing of domestic violence-related deaths with the underlying objectives of preventing them in the future, preserving the safety of battered women, and holding accountable both the perpetrators of domestic violence and the multiple agencies and organizations that come into contact with the parties.

THE CRIMINAL JUSTICE RESPONSE TO INTIMATE PARTNER ABUSE

Introduction

There are excellent textbooks and research material that discuss police and domestic violence.[34] This material provides an in-depth scholarly examination of the causes, effects, and police responses in this area. The purpose of this section is to acquaint readers with an overview of policing of spousal assault cases. This will allow them to have an understanding of some of the existing controversies in this highly debated area of domestic violence.

The term *spousal assault* is used to distinguish this form of family violence from intimate partner abuse. From a legal perspective, the term *spousal assault* is inaccurate. As will be discussed later in this chapter, in a majority of states an assault does not involve any physical injury to the victim. However, to be consistent with other professionals and writers in the field of family violence, **spousal assault** is used and defined as the act of intentionally inflicting physical injury on the spouse or other person who is cohabiting with the abuser. It is distinct and yet a part of intimate partner abuse in that all the dynamics that cause intimate partner abuse may be present in spousal assault. However, this form of assault may occur without the existence of the other forms of abuse, such as emotional or psychological injury, that typically accompany intimate partner abuse.

Similar to many other areas of domestic violence, police response to spousal assault is still being researched and studied. As with so much of domestic violence and other criminal acts, we simply do not have the answers to the problem. Scholars such as Cynthia Bowman would even argue that we do not yet even understand what questions to ask.[35]

If spousal assault were like any other crime, the police response would be fairly simple: investigate, arrest, charge, and cooperate with the district attorney in the prosecution of the perpetrator. Unfortunately, spousal assault involves certain factors that make it unique. These factors are explored in detail in this chapter. These forces all interact to cause law enforcement agencies to respond differently to spousal assault than they do to robberies, rapes, and other crimes of violence.

As the Thurman case described in the Focus box "Two Cases of Indifference" illustrates, spousal assault can have serious consequences for both the victim and any professionals who are involved with either the abuser or the victim. However, we are slowly beginning to acknowledge that spousal assault is one of the crimes society has ignored. Part of the reason for society's reaction to this form of domestic violence is the perceived difficulty in responding to physical assaults between adult family members. Another factor is our inability to classify those who assault their spouses into any identifiable category. Finally, as with other forms of family violence, we cannot with any certainty predict who will be the aggressor or victim in the area of spousal assault.

Thurman v. City of Torrington, 595 F. Supp. 1521 (Conn. 1984)[36]

Starting in October 1982 and continuing until June 1983, Tracey Thurman repeatedly contacted the Torrington Police Department in Connecticut, begging for protection from her estranged husband, Buck. Tracey signed several sworn complaints against Buck; however, the police department considered the incidents a family matter and did not respond to them in the same manner as they did to "stranger assaults."

On the day of the final beating, Buck stabbed Tracey repeatedly. A police officer arrived and asked Buck for the knife but did not arrest or restrain him in any manner. Buck gave the officer the knife and then proceeded to stomp on Tracey's head in front of the officer. He then went inside the house and returned with their son and cursed and kicked Tracey in the head. This series of blows left her partially paralyzed. Other officers arrived, and they did not arrest Buck until he tried to assault Tracey as she lay on the ambulance stretcher.

Tracey filed suit in federal court against the City of Torrington, its police department, and all twenty-four officers that she had contacted over the years about Buck's assaultive acts. She alleged that the police department and its officers had been negligent in responding to her and, further, that they had violated her constitutional rights to equal protection under the law by treating her differently than they would do to other persons who were assaulted by strangers.

The jury awarded Tracey $2.3 million in damages. Although the city's insurance company paid the judgment, it indicated that it might not pay any future awards of any police department that refused or failed to educate their officers about domestic violence.[37]

Castle Rock v. Gonzales, 125 U.S. 417 (2005)

In 1999, the Castle Rock Police Department refused to enforce a protective order that Jessica Gonzales had obtained against her husband, Simon, as part of a divorce decree. The order allowed for visitation on alternate weekends. One late afternoon, Mr. Gonzales kidnapped all three of the children while they were playing outside. Mrs. Gonzales contacted the Castle Rock Police Department to enforce her protective order; however, the agency took no action.

At 3:30 the next morning, Mr. Gonzales appeared at the police station and opened fire and was killed by the officers. Upon examining the truck he had arrived in, the officers discovered the dead bodies of all three of the children.

Mrs. Gonzales sued the town of Castle Rock, alleging the police had failed to enforce her protective order as mandated by state law and had therefore violated her due process rights. The U.S. Supreme Court, in a surprise decision, held that Mrs. Gonzales's due process rights had not been violated, since she had not had personal entitlement requiring the police to enforce the protective order.

Factors Affecting Police Response

Law enforcement's acknowledgment and response to spousal assault have been slow in coming. Even today, there are police officers who would rather not get involved in a "family matter." This should not be surprising in that the battering of women has existed for thousands of years. As indicated in Chapter 7, women were considered chattel, and it was perfectly proper to "discipline" spouses as long as there was no permanent injury inflicted upon the wife.[38] There is clear evidence that numerous early laws accorded men's rights and power over women.[39] The privacy that families enjoyed behind the closed doors of the home continued into modern times.

The *Journal of Marriage and the Family* did not even discuss spousal assault until 1971.[40] Slowly, however, scientific data emerged that indicated criminal violence occurred behind those closed doors. By the mid-1970s, numerous other studies began to elevate intimate partner abuse to the status of a national social problem.

Feminist groups, scholars, and others raised a hue and cry regarding this form of criminal conduct. Between 1975 and 1980, forty-four states passed some sort of legislation on domestic violence. Despite the existence of laws regarding intimate partner abuse, studies have indicated that police have been reluctant to enforce violations of this type of criminal conduct.[41]

No single factor has resulted in this hesitation or reluctance to enforce the laws in the area of spousal assault. Scholars have examined this phenomenon in detail and have noted a series of influences that affected police agencies' enforcement of spousal assault. These factors include call screening, beliefs regarding financial hardship on the family in the event of an arrest, the family argument theory, the classification of spousal assault as a misdemeanor, the victim's preference not to arrest, and perceived danger to the police in domestic violence situations.

Numerous police departments engage in **call screening**, which is downgrading by the law enforcement agency of the priority assigned to domestic violence calls for service. Call screening results in a slower response time by the police officer than for other calls of the same or similar seriousness. This dynamic allows the abuser to beat the victim and leave the scene of the crime before the arrival of the officers. In addition, the failure of police to respond in a timely manner may increase the power of the abuser over the victim and lead the victim to believe that she is truly alone and helpless.

Police officers were and are reluctant to arrest the abuser in the mistaken belief that an arrest would pose a financial hardship on the family. An **arrest** is the taking of a person into custody in the manner prescribed by law. In addition, many law enforcement officers believe that arrest is a futile act in view of the lack of prosecution and lenient sentences imposed (if at all) by the courts.

Many officers would arrest only if, in their opinion, the injury to the victim was severe. This is clearly not the law; however, it illustrates the thinking and reluctance of police to intervene in a "family argument."[42]

Until recently, another factor affecting the decision to arrest was the statutory limits on arrests for certain types of crimes. Traditionally, criminal violations are divided into two major classifications: felonies and misdemeanors. In the United States, this distinction is spelled out by statute or by state constitution.[43] A **felony** is considered the most serious type of crime and is usually punished by imprisonment in state prison. Many statutes provide that all other crimes are misdemeanors. A **misdemeanor** is considered less serious and is punished by incarceration in local jails not to exceed one year. Normally, police may arrest persons who have committed felonies based on reasonable grounds or probable cause. **Probable cause** is that set of facts that would lead a reasonable person to believe that a crime has been committed by the suspect. This felony arrest may occur even if the officers did not personally witness the offense. Misdemeanor arrests, on the other hand, require the officers to witness the crime. If they did not see the offense committed, they could request the victim to make a citizen's arrest, and then on behalf of the citizen they would take the perpetrator into custody.

This distinction in the nature and classification of crimes had a direct impact on the ability of police officers to make arrests for domestic violence assaults. Many domestic violence disputes involve a battery. Most statutes define a **battery** as the unlawful application of force on a person by another.[44] Battery is the unlawful touching of another, whereas assault is the act of placing another in fear and does not require any physical touching of the other person.[45] Absent serious injury, many state laws define battery as a misdemeanor. The victim's preference not to file charges also affects the police officer's decision not to arrest the offender. Several studies have indicated that many times victims of spousal assault did not want the police to make an arrest.[46] This resulted in the officers admonishing the offender and leaving the scene of the crime.

Many police officers perceive family disputes as potentially dangerous situations in which both parties, the abuser and the victim, may turn on the officer. Although there are conflicting studies as to whether family disputes are in fact more dangerous to police officers, the fact that many officers believe this to be the case can result in a delay in responding to these types of calls for service.[47] This perception may cause officers to delay in responding to spousal assault calls until they have a backup unit.

In the last several years, many states have passed mandatory arrest statutes that require the officer to arrest the suspect. These laws allow police to make arrests for misdemeanors that are not committed in their presence. The passage of these laws and their effectiveness is a subject of debate within the field of criminal justice. The following section discusses the factors that resulted in the passage of these statutes.

Arrest of Abusers

In recent years, victims of family violence have turned to the courts in an attempt to require law enforcement departments to provide effective intervention and protection against spousal assault. Increasingly, courts have begun to listen and rule in their favor both on constitutional and tort grounds. However, lawsuits and personal liability did not result in the amendment of various state statutes mandating arrest of abusers. This development started in 1984 with a federally funded experiment in Minneapolis.

The Minneapolis Domestic Violence Experiment

In the area of policing and domestic violence, there is probably no more controversial study than the Minneapolis Domestic Violence Experiment dealing with the effect of arrest on those who batter their spouses. The dean of policing and domestic violence, Lawrence Sherman, was the architect of the Minneapolis Domestic Violence Experiment. This study was the first controlled evaluation of the effect of arrest on individuals who commit assaultive types of crimes against their spouses.[48]

The Police Foundation and the Minneapolis Police Department joined forces to conduct a controlled experiment to test the effectiveness of arrest on prevention or deterrence of domestic violence. Funded in part by the National Institute of Justice, the Minneapolis Domestic Violence Experiment utilized a lottery system of three possible actions by police when dealing with domestic violence.

Police officers responding to a domestic disturbance were required to utilize one of the following options:

1. Arrest with at least one night incarceration
2. Send the offender away from the scene of the disturbance or arrest him if he refused to leave
3. Give the couple some form of advice, including mediation

The officers were not allowed to select which of these options would be used, rather they carried a pad of forms that listed the available options. When they encountered a situation that met the experiment's criteria, they were required to utilize the option listed on the top form.

The experiment involved only misdemeanor batteries in which both the victim and the suspect were present when the officers arrived at the scene of the disturbance. Cases involving serious threats or danger to the victim were excluded, as were situations in which the victim demanded the officers arrest the suspect.

After the officers finished their assignment, they turned in a brief report to the researchers for follow-up. The research staff utilized two measures to determine the amount of repeated violence by the offenders: official police reports and victim interviews. Official police reports were monitored to determine if the suspect committed another similar offense within a specified time period. In addition, the research staff contacted the listed victims and conducted a detailed interview with subsequent interviews for a period of twenty-four weeks after the initial offense.

The experiment produced a sample of 314 cases that met all the criteria. The results indicated that the arrest option produced the lowest percentage of repeated violence of all the alternatives. Official police reports revealed that 10 percent of the arrested suspects committed a subsequent offense, 24 percent of those suspects who were sent from the home repeated acts of violence against their spouse, and 19 percent of the suspects who were advised by the officers committed another offense. Interviews with victims produced even more dramatic percentages: 19 percent of the arrest suspects, 33 percent of those suspects sent from the home, and 37 percent of those advised by the officers committed another offense.

On the basis of the results of the study, Sherman and his colleagues made three recommendations. The first and probably the least controversial recommendation was to change existing laws to allow the police to make warrantless arrests for misdemeanor spousal assaults that are not committed in their presence. The second recommendation was read to suggest that mandatory arrest was the preferred option in most cases of domestic violence. The final recommendation suggested that additional experiments be conducted in other cities to validate the results of the Minneapolis study.

The Minneapolis Domestic Violence Experiment acted as a change agent within the criminal justice system. Armed with its results, advocates of mandatory arrest and other sanctions were able to find support in various state legislatures for long overdue reform of criminal statutes dealing with domestic violence. Eleven states adopted legislation that authorized warrantless arrest in misdemeanor domestic violence cases, and another sixteen states enacted mandatory arrest laws in family violence situations.[49]

Prior to the experiment, only 10 percent of police departments serving cities more than 100,000 in population encouraged their officers to make arrests in domestic violence situations. Within five years of the announcement of the results of the experiment, 84 percent of all major police departments in the United States had adopted a policy that stated arrest was the preferred option in domestic violence situations.[50]

The Minneapolis experiment was hailed as a breakthrough study of domestic violence and criticized by a number of prominent scholars as inadequate and flawed.[51] In retrospect, it may not matter whether the results of the study were accurate; its greatest contribution may be that it generated an incredible amount of debate within academia and the law enforcement profession regarding how we should respond to domestic violence.

Other Replications

One direct result of the Minneapolis experiment was the funding of additional replications by the National Institute of Justice. Five additional studies were undertaken in the following locations: Metro-Dade (Miami), Colorado Springs, Milwaukee, Omaha, and Charlotte. What was consistent about these additional studies was the finding of inconsistency in the deterrent effect of arrest.

The Metro-Dade Experiment established two major categories with two subgroups under each of these categories. The two major subdivisions were those suspects who were arrested and those who were not arrested. Each of these groups was further divided into subgroups that did or did not receive follow-up counseling by specially trained police officers.[52] The Metro-Dade Experiment clearly supports the theory that arrest is a deterrent to future domestic violence.

The Colorado Springs Experiment employed four options in its replication: (1) arrest and issuance of a restraining order, (2) counseling for the offender and issuance of a restraining order, (3) issuance of a restraining order, and (4) restoring order at the scene of the crime without arrest or use of a restraining order. The Colorado Springs experiment supports the hypothesis that arrest in some situations does in fact act as a deterrent to future violence.[53]

The Milwaukee experiment was carried out in a city that in May 1986 had adopted a citywide policy of mandatory arrest for domestic violence cases.[54] However, the study did not involve arrests of all offenders, rather it utilized three options: full arrest, short arrest, or warning. The full arrest involved taking the suspect into custody pursuant to existing policy and allowing him bail in the amount of $250. The short arrest required officers to arrest the suspect but allowed him to be released on his own recognizance, preferably within two hours after arrest. The warning option utilized a standard warning of arrest if the officers had to return to the location at any time during the same day.

The results were obtained by a review of police records and by follow-up interviews with the victims. The researchers found that there was a clear initial deterrent effect in both the full arrest and short arrest situations as compared with the warning-only option. However, this deterrence did not last, and there appeared to be no long-term difference between the arrest options and warning option.

The original Minneapolis Domestic Violence Experiment and these three replications may lead one to conclude that arrest does in fact deter either short-term or long-term spousal assault.

Unfortunately, the Omaha and Charlotte replications came to the opposite conclusion. These studies were conducted in the same manner as the other replications and indicated that arrest does not deter future violence.

The Omaha experiment randomly assigned eligible police calls regarding domestic violence into three categories when both the suspect and the victim were present.[55] These classifications were arrest, separation, or mediation. In those cases in which the suspect had already left the scene of the crime when the police arrived, the police randomly assigned him to a warrant or no warrant group.

The police relied on five conditions when making their determination of whether to include the suspect within the experiment: (1) the existence of probable cause to arrest for misdemeanor assault, (2) a clearly identifiable victim and suspect, (3) both the victim and suspect were adults, (4) the victim and the suspect must have cohabitated some time during the year preceding the assault, and (5) neither party had an outstanding arrest warrant. Although the Omaha experiment excluded felony domestic violence cases, a majority of the calls for service involved physical injuries to the victim.

The results of the experiment were measured in two ways: review of police reports and victim interviews. Contrary to the Minneapolis experiment, the Omaha study concluded that arrest of a suspect at the scene of the domestic assault did not have any greater deterrent effect than the other two options.[56] However, the issuance of a warrant for an offender who was absent from the scene of the crime at the time the officers arrived did appear to extend significantly the time frame in which the victim was free from further violence in comparison with those situations in which the police simply informed the victim that she had the right to obtain a warrant for the suspect.

The Charlotte experiment tested three distinct alternatives to domestic violence.[57] Police responses included advising the couple, issuing a citation to the offender, or arresting the offender. Excluded from the study were situations in which the victim insisted on the arrest of the suspect, the suspect threatened or assaulted the officer, or the officer believed that the victim was in imminent danger. Similar to the other replications, the Charlotte experiment evaluated the effect of these alternatives using only two methods: police reports and victim interviews. The results indicated no significant difference in the deterrent effect of advising, citing, or arresting the offender.

In 2001, the National Institute of Justice and the CDC conducted a scientific evaluation of the results of the 1984 Minneapolis Domestic Violence Experiment and its five replications.[58] Because of the inconsistent and conditional findings of the previous studies, scholars and policymakers re-evaluated the deterrent effect of arrest using an approach that was more statistically sound. The study pooled incidents from the five replications, computed comparable independent and outcome measures from common dates intentionally embedded in each experiment, and standardized the experimental design and statistical models.

This method of re-evaluating the data produced the following significant results:

- Arresting batterers was consistently related to reducing subsequent aggression against female partners.
- The research found no relationship between arresting the perpetrator and an increased risk of subsequent aggression against the female partner.

This study re-examined the Minneapolis replications and found evidence of a consistent and direct, though modest, deterrent effect of arrest on aggression by males against their female partners. This effect existed for the first several days after the incident regardless of the length of incarceration and lasted up to one year after the incident. The research also pointed out that a minority of perpetrators continued their violence regardless of the intervention that occurred.

As a result of these studies and other factors, many police departments have adopted policies that encourage or mandate the arrest of a spouse abuser. To ensure the effectiveness of these policies, some police departments have created special domestic violence units, trained personnel on the dynamics of intimate partner abuse, and created sophisticated tracking and monitoring communication systems.[59]

Is Male Perpetrated Intimate Partner Violence More Underreported than Female Violence?

Clifton R. Emery attempted to answer this question in his research project. He started out with two hypotheses about under-reporting in intimate partner violence data. The first hypothesis was that significant amounts of under-reporting of intimate partner violence occur due to stigma. The second examined the empirical evidence behind the contention that equal rates of intimate partner violence perpetration among men and women occur through a combination of heterogeneity in type of intimate partner violence and missing data. He used domestic violence data obtained from Chicago Neighborhoods. His conclusion was that there was strong support for establishing general under-reporting of domestic violence but only weak support for concluding that there was greater under-reporting of male violence.

Source: Clifton R. Emery, "Examining an Extension of Johnson's Hypothesis: Is Male Perpetrated Intimate Partner Violence More Underreported than Female Violence?" Journal of Family Violence, Volume 25, Issue 2, pp 173–181.

For arrest to be an effective domestic violence intervention policy, there must be a coordinated and integrated response to the problem on the part of the criminal justice system. If police, prosecutors, judges, and probation and parole agencies all respond appropriately and the victims feel that the system is committed to protecting them and their children, we will have taken a major step forward in responding to this type of violence.[60]

Summary

Although intimate partner abuse has been intensely researched in the past years, it is still one of the most commonly misunderstood issues within family violence. Our society has placed women in inferior and subordinate positions throughout history, and even today some segments of our society continue to treat them as property rather than partners. These beliefs contribute to the interpersonal dynamics that result in violence against women. The nature and extent of intimate partner abuse is staggering. Current figures indicate that women today are being brutalized at alarming numbers.

One common question asked by both professionals and laypersons is, "Why does the victim stay in such a relationship?" It is clear today that there are a number of dynamics that occur in a battering relationship. These dynamics many times bind victims to their abusers more tightly than if they were handcuffed to them.

There are numerous theories to explain why men batter women. In fact, there are so many theories that entire textbooks are devoted to explaining them. Yet no one theory is accepted by all scholars, practitioners, or professionals in the field as the theory that explains intimate partner abuse. Even though no one theory prevails, professionals should be aware of the more common and well-known studies of intimate partner abuse. They include studies of social stress, power, dependency, alcohol, pregnancy, and marriage.

The criminal justice system is still searching for ways to respond to intimate partner abuse. As a result of a number of factors, there are mandatory arrest policies in effect in a number of jurisdictions. This may stop the immediate battering but will not solve the problem. We must continue to search for ways to prevent this type of abuse. Only by stopping it before it occurs can we grow as a nation and society.

Key Terms

Intimate partner abuse is any intentional act or series of acts that cause injury to the spouse or partner. These acts may be physical, emotional, or sexual. "Spouse or partner is gender neutral, and therefore the abuse may occur to a man or a woman. The term includes those who are married, cohabiting, or involved in a partner relationship. It also encompasses individuals who are separated and living apart from their former spouse or former partner.

Cycle theory of violence sets forth the dynamics of battering in intimate partner abuse.

Battered woman syndrome theorizes that victims of intimate partner abuse gradually become immobilized by fear and believe that they have no other options. As a result, these women stay in the abusive relationships and cope the best they can. The battered woman syndrome involves one who has been, on at least two occasions, the victim of physical, sexual, or serious psychological abuse by a man with whom she has an intimate relationship. It is a pattern of psychological symptoms that develop after somebody has lived in a battering relationship.

Stockholm syndrome is a phenomenon that occurs when persons who are held as hostages, captives, or prisoners of war begin to identify with their captors.

Traumatic bonding theory explains why battered women stay in abusive relationships. This theory holds that when a woman finally leaves an abusive partner, her immediate fears begin to diminish and her hidden attachment to her abuser begins to manifest itself. Emotionally drained and vulnerable, she becomes susceptible to her partner's loving contrite pressure to return. As her fears lessen and the needs previously provided by her partner increase, she may decide to give him another chance.

Power is the ability to impose one's will on another and make life decisions.

Marital dependency is a multifaceted concept that involves economic, emotional, and societal forces that result in a woman being dependent on her spouse for support.

Spousal assault is used and defined as the act of intentionally inflicting physical injury on the spouse or other person who is cohabitating with the abuser.

Call screening is downgrading by the law enforcement agency of the priority assigned to domestic violence calls for service.

Arrest is the taking of a person into custody in the manner presented by law.

Felony is considered the most serious type of crime and is usually punished by imprisonment in state prison.

Misdemeanor is considered less serious and is punished by incarceration in local jails not to exceed one year.

Probable cause is that set of facts that would lead a reasonable person to believe that a crime has been committed by the suspect.

Battery is the unlawful application of force on one person by another.

Discussion Questions

1. Can you narrow the definition of intimate partner abuse? What would you exclude and why?
2. Do we really know the extent of spouse abuse? Why is it important to know how many spouses are abused?
3. Which of the theories regarding the dynamics of battering do you believe is the major reason why spouses stay with their abuser? Justify your answer.
4. Isn't Dutton's theory of traumatic bonding just another form of the battered woman syndrome? Why? Why not?
5. Which of the theories regarding spouse abuse do you believe is the major reason why one spouse abuses the other?
6. What can we do to improve the criminal justice system's treatment of abused spouses?

Suggested Readings

D. A. Hines & K. Malley-Morrison, *Family Violence in the United States: Defining, Understanding, and Combating Abuse* (Sage, Newbury Park, Calif.) 2004.

K. Little, *Family Violence: An Intervention Model for Dental Professionals* (U.S. Department of Justice, Office of Victims of Crime, Washington, D.C.) 2004.

M. A. Straus & R. J. Gelles, *Physical Violence in American Families* (Transaction Publishers, New Brunswick, N.J.) 1990.

V. B. Hasselt, R. L. Morrison, A. S. Bellack & W. Frazier, eds., *Handbook of Family Violence* (Plenum, New York) 1988.

R. J. Gelles, ed., *Vision 2010* (National Council on Family Relations, Minneapolis) 1995.

R. T. Ammerman & M. Hersen, eds., *Case Studies in Family Violence* (Plenum, New York) 1991.

L. E. Walker, *The Battered Woman* (Harper & Row, New York) 1979.

L. E. Walker, *The Battered Woman Syndrome* (Springer, New York) 1984.

D. J. Sonkin, ed., *Domestic Violence on Trial* (Springer, New York) 1982.

M. D. Pagelow, *Family Violence* (Praeger, New York) 1984.

D. G. Dutton, *The Domestic Assault of Women* (UBC Press, Vancouver, B.C.) 1995.

E. S. Buzawa & C. G. Buzawa, eds., *Domestic Violence: The Changing Criminal Justice Response* (Auburn House, Westport, Conn.) 1992.

A. M. Jaggar & P. S. Rothenberg, eds., *Feminist Frameworks*, 3rd ed. (McGraw-Hill, New York) 1993.

L. W. Sherman, *Policing Domestic Violence* (The Free Press, New York) 1992.

F. G. Bolton & S. R. Bolton, *Working with Violent Families* (Sage, Newbury Park, Calif.) 1987.

W. R. LaFave & A. W. Scott Jr., *Criminal Law,* 2nd ed. (West Publishing Co., St. Paul, Minn.) 1986.

R. M. Perkins & R. N. Boyce, *Criminal Law,* 3rd ed. (Foundation Press, Inc., New York) 1982.

M. Steinman, ed., *Women Battering: Policy Responses* (Anderson Publishing Co., Cincinnati, Ohio) 1991.

Endnotes

1. R. J. Gelles, *Domestic Violence Factoids,* www.umn.edu/mincava/factoid.htm (file created October 16, 1995).

2. M. A. Straus & R. J. Gelles, *Physical Violence in American Families* (Transaction Publishers, New Brunswick, N.J.) 1990, pp. 96–98.

3. E. Stark & A. Flitcraft, "Violence among Intimates: An Epidemiological Review," in V. B. Hasselt, R. L. Morrison, A. S. Bellack, & W. Frazier, eds., *Handbook of Family Violence* (Plenum, New York) 1988, pp. 292–317.

4. Suzanne Steinmetz, "The Battered Husband Syndrome," 2 (3/4) *Victimology,* 499–509 (1978).

5. S. K. Steinmetz & J. S. Lucca, "Husband Battering," in V. B. Van Hasselt, R. L. Morrison, A. S. Bellack, & M. Hersen, eds., *Handbook of Family Violence* (Plenum, New York) 1988, pp. 233–246.

6. K. D. O'Leary, J. Barling, I. Arias, A. Rosenbaum, J. Malone, & A. Tyree, "Prevalence and Stability of Physical Aggression between Spouses: A Longitudinal Analysis," 57 *Journal of Consulting and Clinical Psychology,* 263–268 (1989).

7. Jacquelyn Campbell, "Violence Toward Women: Homicide and Battering," in Richard J. Gelles, ed., *Vision 2010* (National Council on Family Relations, Minneapolis) 1995.

8. *Costs of Intimate Partner Violence against Women in the United States* (Department of Health and Human Services, Centers for Disease Control and Prevention, Atlanta, Ga.) March 2003.

9. E. W. Gondolf & E. R. Fisher, "Wife Battering," in R. T. Ammerman & M. Hersen, eds., *Case Studies in Family Violence* (Plenum, New York) 1991, pp. 273–274.

10. L. E. Walker, *The Battered Women* (Harper & Row, New York) 1979.

11. L. E. Walker, *The Battered Woman Syndrome* (Springer, New York) 1984.

12. See *People v. Humphrey,* 96 *Daily Journal D.A.R.* 10609 at 10612 where the California Supreme Court addressed this issue.

13. M. A. Douglas, "The Battered Women Syndrome," in D. J. Sonkin ed., *Domestic Violence on Trial* (Springer, New York) 1982.

14. M. D. Pagelow, *Family Violence* (Praeger, New York) 1984, p. 308.

15. G. NiCarthy, *Getting Free: A Handbook for Women in Abusive Relationships* (Seal Press, New York) 1986, pp. 117–118.

16. D. G. Dutton & S. L. Painter, "Traumatic Bonding: The Development of Emotional Attachments in Battered Women and Other Relationships of Intermittent Abuse," 6 *Victimology,* 139 (1981).

17. D. G. Dutton, *The Domestic Assault of Women* (UBC Press, Vancouver, B.C.) 1995.

18. Ibid. at p. 190.

19. Ibid. at p. 191.

20. Demie Kurz, "Battering and the Criminal Justice System: A Feminist View," in Eve S. Buzawa & Carl G. Buzawa, eds., *Domestic Violence: The Changing Criminal Justice Response* (Auburn House, Westport, Conn.) 1992.

21. See K. Newman, "Middle-Class Women in Trouble," in A. M. Jaggar & P. S. Rothenberg, eds., *Feminist Frameworks,* 3rd ed. (McGraw-Hill, New York) 1993, pp. 319–323.

22. M. Roy, "A Current Study of 150 Cases," in M. Roy, ed., *A Psychological Study of Domestic Violence* (Van Nostrand Reinhold, New York) 1977.

23. D. S. Kalmuss & M. A. Straus, "Wife's Marital Dependency and Wife Abuse," in M. A. Straus & R. J. Gelles, eds., *Physical Violence in American Families* (Transaction Publishers, New Brunswick, N.J.) 1990, pp. 379–380.

24. K. J. Sher, "Subjective Effects of Alcohol: The Influence of Setting and Individual Differences in Alcohol Expectancies," 46 *Journal of Studies on Alcohol,* 137–146 (1985).

25. D. H. Coleman & M. A. Straus, "Alcohol Abuse and Family Violence," in E. Gottheil, K. A. Druley, T. E. Skoloda, & H. M. Waxman, eds., *Alcohol, Drug Abuse and Aggression* (Charles C Thomas, Springfield, Ill.) 1983, pp. 104–124.

26. D. C. McClelland, W. N. Davis, R. Kalin, & E. Wanner, *The Drinking Man* (Free Press, New York) 1972.

27. K. Pernanem, "Theoretical Aspects of the Relationship between Alcohol Use and Crime," *Drinking and Crime: Perspectives on the Relationships between Alcohol Consumption and Criminal Behavior,* J. J. Collins Jr., ed. (Guilford Press, New York) 1981.

28. A. Helton, "Battering during Pregnancy," 86 *American Journal of Nursing,* 910–913 (1986).

29. R. J. Gelles, "Violence and Pregnancy: Are Pregnant Women at Greater Risk of Abuse?" in M. A. Straus & R. J. Gelles, eds., *Physical Violence in American Families* (Transaction Publishers, New Brunswick, N.J.) 1990, p. 282.

30. M. A. Straus & R. J. Gelles, "How Violent Are American Families? Estimates from the National Family Violence Survey and Other Studies," in G. T. Hotaling, D. Finkelhor, John T. Kirkpatrick, & M. A. Straus, eds., *New Directions in Family Violence Research* (Sage, Beverly Hills, Calif.) 1988.

31. J. E. Sets & M. A. Straus, "The Marriage License: A Comparison of Assaults in Dating, Cohabiting, and Married Couples," in M. A. Straus & R. J. Gelles, eds., *Physical*

Violence in American Families (Transaction Publishers, New Brunswick, N.J.) 1990, pp. 227–244. Published earlier in 4 *Journal of Family Violence,* 161–180 (1989).

32. J. E. Stets & M. A. Pirog-Good, "Violence in Dating Relationships," 50 *Social Psychology Quarterly,* 237–246 (1987).

33. See Sets & Straus, "The Marriage License: A Comparison of Assaults in Dating, Cohabiting, and Married Couples," 1990, pp. 227–244.

34. See for example, Lawrence W. Sherman, *Policing Domestic Violence* (The Free Press, New York) 1992; Frank G. Bolton & Susan R. Bolton, *Working with Violent Families* (Sage, Newbury Park, Calif.) 1987; and Eve S. Buzawa & Carl G. Buzawa, eds., *Domestic Violence, The Changing Criminal Justice Response* (Auburn House, Westport, Conn.) 1992.

35. See Cynthia Grant Bowman, "The Arrest Experiments: A Feminist Critique," 83 *Journal of Criminal Law and Criminology,* 201–208 (1992), in which Bowman argues that current research in the area of spousal assault is flawed because it is usually conducted from the abuser's perspective, ignores feminist thinking, and does not consider various social factors.

36. The judgment was later reduced to $1.9 million.

37. M. Buddy & K. Taylor, "Please, Somebody Help Me," *20/20 News* (January 23, 1986).

38. Lisa A. Frisch, "Research That Succeeds, Policies That Fail," 83 *Journal of Criminal Law and Criminology,* 209 (1992).

39. For an excellent discussion of these laws, see Arnold Binder & James Meeker, "The Development of Social Attitudes Toward Spousal Abuse," in Eve S. Buzawa & Carl G. Buzawa, eds., *Domestic Violence, The Changing Criminal Justice Response* (Auburn House, Westport, Conn.) 1992.

40. John E. O'Brien, "Women Abuse: Facts Replacing Myths," 33 *Journal of Marriage and the Family,* 362–398 (1971).

41. Edna Erez, "Intimacy, Violence and the Police," 39 *Human Relations,* 265–281 (1986).

42. Eve S. Buzawa & Carl G. Buzawa, *Domestic Violence, The Criminal Justice Response* (Sage, Newbury Park, Calif.) 1990, p. 44.

43. Wayne R. LaFave & Austin W. Scott Jr., *Criminal Law,* 2nd ed. (West Publishing Co., St. Paul, Minn.) 1986, p. 30.

44. Rollin M. Perkins & Ronald N. Boyce, *Criminal Law,* 3rd ed. (Foundation Press, Inc., New York) 1982, p. 152.

45. LaFave & Scott *Criminal Law,* 1986, p. 684.

46. See Donald Black, *The Manners and Customs of Police* (Academic Press, New York) 1980, p. 189.

47. For an excellent discussion of this area, see Sherman, *Policing Domestic Violence,* pp. 30–31.

48. Lawrence W. Sherman & Richard A. Berk, "The Specific Deterrent Effects of Arrest for Domestic Assault," 49 *American Sociological Review,* 261 (1984).

49. Jacob R. Clark, "The Minneapolis Study: Policy Gets Made Despite Cautions," *Law Enforcement News,* 9 (March 31, 1993).

50. J. David Hirschel & Ira Hutchinson, "Police-Preferred Arrest Policies," in Michael Steinman, ed., *Women Battering: Policy Responses* (Anderson Publishing Co., Cincinnati) 1991, p. 59.

51. See Delbert S. Elliot, "Criminal Justice Procedures in Family Violence Crimes," in Lloyd Ohlin & Michael Tonry, eds., *Family Violence* (University of Chicago Press, Chicago) 1989, p. 458, which cites the study as a landmark study on the effectiveness of alternative police responses to family violence and compares that position with Richard Lempert, "Humility is a Virtue," 23 *Law & Society Review,* 146 (1989), which argues that the experiment lacked a scientific basis.

52. Antony Pate, Edwin E. Hamilton, & Annan Sampson, *Metro-Dade Spouse Abuse Replication Project, Draft Final Report* (National Institute of Justice, Washington, D.C.) 1991.

53. Richard A. Berk, Alec Campbell, Ruth Klap, & Bruce Western, "A Bayesian Analysis of the Colorado Springs Spouse Abuse Experiment," 83 *Journal of Criminal Law and Criminology,* 170 (1992).

54. Lawrence W. Sherman, Janell D. Schmidt, Dennis P. Rogan, Douglas A. Smith, Patrick R. Gartin, Ellen G. Cohn, Dean J. Collins, & Anthony R. Bacich, "The Variable Effects of Arrest on Criminal Careers: The Milwaukee Domestic Violence Experiment," 83 *Journal of Criminal Law and Criminology,* 137 (1992).

55. Franklyn W. Dunford, David Huizinga, & Delbert S. Elliot, "The Omaha Domestic Violence Police Experiment," *Final Report to the National Institute of Justice* (National Institute of Justice, Washington, D.C.) 1989.

56. Ibid. at p. 34.

57. J. David Hirchel, Ira W. Hutchinson III, Charles W. Dean, Joseph J. Kelly, & Carolyn E. Pesackis, "Charlotte Spouse Assault Replication Project." *Final Report to the National Institute of Justice* (National Institute of Justice, Washington, D.C.) 1991.

58. This section is adapted from C. D. Maxwell, J. H. Garner, and J. A. Fagan, *The Effects of Arrest on Intimate Partner Violence: New Evidence from the Spouse Assault Replication Program* (National Institute of Justice, Washington, D.C.) June 2001.

59. *Grants to Encourage Arrest Policies* (Office of Justice Programs, Washington, D.C.) 1996.

60. B. J. Hart, "Coordinated Community Approaches to Domestic Violence," presented at the Strategic Planning Workshop on Violence Against Women, sponsored by the National Institute of Justice in Washington, D.C., March 31, 1995.

Child Abuse

Chapter Outline

LEARNING OBJECTIVES

After reading this chapter, you should be able to:

- Distinguish between the different types of physical child abuse
- Recognize when poor parenting becomes child neglect
- Understand the dynamics involved in child sexual abuse
- Distinguish between the different theories regarding child abuse
- Explain some excuses used by parents to justify the acts of aggression between siblings
- Understand the controversies surrounding the topic of ritualistic child abuse

TYPES OF CHILD ABUSE

Physical Child Abuse

Is a parent unfit or considered abusive if, while bathing his one-year-old daughter, his daughter slips from his grasp and hits her head against the faucet causing a cut over her eye that requires two stitches? Is this child abuse? Although some might blame the father for not being alert to that possibility, others would not classify him as a child abuser.

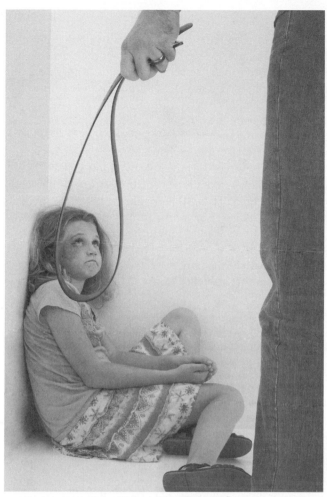

While most people would not associate spanking a child with child abuse, in the scene above it appears that excessive force is being used, which is clearly child abuse. (Jaime Dumplass/Fotolia)

Accidents happen. They are a part of growing up, and painful as they may be to the parent and the child, they are part of a normal, healthy relationship. Thus, not all injuries sustained by children can be classified as child abuse. If not all injuries are child abuse and parents have a right to inflict corporal punishment on children as a form of discipline, how do we draw the line and define physical injuries to children?

Numerous authorities have defined child abuse. Part of the problem in this area has been the continued struggle to agree on what the term *child abuse* means. Van Hasselt, Pagelow, Gelles, and other scholars in the field have excellent discussions and definitions of this condition.[1] For purposes of this textbook and ease of understanding, we have accepted the following definition: **Physical child abuse** may be defined as any act that results in a nonaccidental physical injury by a person who has care, custody, or control of a child.

There are two key aspects to this definition—the act is intentional or willful and the act resulted in a physical injury. An accidental injury does not qualify as child abuse. In the previous example, an accidental slip in a bathtub would not qualify as child abuse even if the child received an injury that required several stitches. Child abuse as discussed in this chapter is manifested by physical injury that can be proved or documented. Simply yelling at the child is not physical child abuse within the meaning of this definition; nor is spanking the child on the hand or the buttocks if those acts do not result in a physical injury. Although it is true that any form of spanking causes injury in the form of pain and some trauma to the child, unless the force is sufficient to leave marks, most medical and legal authorities will not classify these acts as child abuse. This lack of a clear definition is part of the problem of physical child abuse. The next section addresses the issue of child neglect—an area that is even more emotional and hard to define.

PRACTICUM

When Is It Child Abuse?

Situation 1: A three-year-old boy is running around the supermarket, knocking down cans of food and does not stop when his grandmother asks him to. The grandmother takes the child by the arm and the child starts yelling, "You're hurting me!" Assume there is no physical injury to the child. Is it child abuse? What if the child is just acting out?

Situation 2: The father leaves the four-year-old child in the fenced-in backyard with the family pet, a collie. The child hits the dog, who bites her arm. Assume there is no history of aggression on the part of the dog. Is it child abuse?

Situation 3: A mother is babysitting the next-door neighbor's five-year-old girl. She has a six-year-old boy. She decides to give them a bath together. The boy keeps touching the girl's genital area. Is it child abuse?

Situation 4: An older brother decides to tease his younger sister. When their parents are gone, he holds her down and tickles her until she cries. Is it child abuse?

Situation 5: In 2012, a football coach at a Minnesota college was charged with child pornography. The coach turned in his school-issued cell phone to have it repaired. School officials found videos of his naked children on his phone. After the school officials reported this to the police, he was charged with child pornography. Does having pictures of your children on your cell phone constitute child pornography? [Note: In November 2012, a trial judge cleared him ruling that short videos of his children acting silly after a bath were not child pornography and was not illegal.]

Child Neglect

In the past twenty years, numerous textbooks, articles, and studies have dealt with the subject of neglect. The literature runs the gamut from examining assessment techniques of neglect[2] to listing the different forms of this abuse.[3] Except for rare instances, child neglect does not receive the public attention that child sexual and physical abuse generates. Part of the reason for this lack of emphasis may lie in the definition and nature of child neglect.

Child neglect is the negligent treatment or maltreatment of a child by a parent or caretaker under circumstances indicating harm or threatened harm to the child's health or welfare. Although this appears at first glance to be a simple and straightforward statement, it covers a wide range of activities or omissions that affect the physical and emotional well-being of a child. At what point does mere inattention or lack of knowledge translate itself into child neglect? This definition would require an act or omission that results in harm or threatens to cause harm to the child's health or welfare. This act or omission may be physical or psychological. A strict interpretation of this definition would require that parents or caretakers guard their children like prisoners. However, this is unrealistic because children are mobile. They get into drawers, cabinets, and every corner in the house and yard. Therefore, as Figure 9.1 illustrates, we are dealing with a continuum that stretches from momentary inattention to gross inaction.

Somewhere on the line in Figure 9.1, acceptable parenting ends and child neglect begins. Although no specific place on this line establishes child neglect, it is a common form of child abuse. The next section addresses another aspect of child abuse—sexual abuse of children.

Child Sexual Abuse

Child sexual abuse is sexual exploitation or sexual activities with children under circumstances, which indicate that the child's health or welfare is harmed or threatened.[4] This definition includes inappropriate sexual activities between children and adults. The inappropriate behavior may be between family members or between a stranger and the victim.

Intrafamilial sexual abuse includes incest and refers to any type of exploitative sexual contact occurring between relatives. **Extrafamilial sexual abuse** refers to exploitative sexual contact with perpetrators who may be known to the child (neighbors, babysitters, live-in partners) or unknown to the child.[5]

One major problem with this definition is the requirement that the child be harmed. From a legal perspective, harm to the victim is not an element of the crime of child sexual abuse. If certain physical acts occur, the crime is complete. In criminal proceedings, it is not necessary to prove that the perpetrator intended to harm or actually harmed the child. However, this definition is useful in exploring the consequences of child sexual abuse, and retaining the requirement of an injury to the child will allow for such a discussion.

The following acts are examples of child sexual abuse: exposing one's sexual organs to the child, voyeurism, touching the sex organs of the child, mutual or self-masturbation with the child, oral sex, intercourse, and anal sex. In addition, allowing the child to view or participate in pornographic or obscene movies is considered child abuse.

Child sexual abuse may be distinguished from rape in that the perpetrator may use a variety of "techniques" to achieve the objective of sexual gratification. Rape normally involves sexual acts as the result of force or fear. Child abuse offenders may also use force or fear; however,

Momentary inattention _____ Gross action or inaction

FIGURE 9.1   Child Neglect Continuum

they also employ other pressures or influences to accomplish their goal. These actions include manipulation of the child (psychologically isolating the child from other loved ones), coercion (using adult authority or power on the child), force (restraining the child), and threats or fear (informing the child if he tells, no one will love him).[6]

EXTENT OF THE PROBLEM

Physical Child Abuse

The physical battering of children is not a new phenomenon. 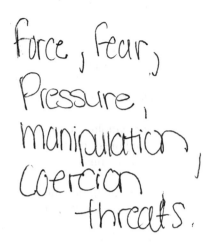 the hands of their parents and caretakers since the beginning o the birth of Moses, the pharaoh ordered the death of all male c infanticide on a large scale when Jesus was born.

Early history records the practice of burying infants aliv bridges.[7] Excavations of Canaanite dwellings have uncovered j tion of buildings.[8] Although officially outlawed, this practice Europe, and children were found buried in the foundations of

Plato (428–348 B.C.) and Aristotle (348–322 B.C.) both with birth defects. Children with birth defects, female infants, were killed as a matter of course several hundred years before law of the Twelve Tables prohibited raising a child with a defe were examined by a local council of elders, who had the power to throw those children considered unfit into a canyon.[9]

force, fear, pressure, manipulation, coercion, threats.

Infanticide was not the only form of abuse practiced by early civilizations. During the Middle Ages, families would often mutilate or sever limbs from children so as to make them more effective beggars. The histories of the European school system are filled with records detailing beatings and abuse by teachers inflicted on their young charges.

The industrial revolution was characterized by repeated maltreatment of children. Young children were forced to work long hours under inhumane conditions in factories or other heavy industries. Many were beaten, shackled, or starved to force them to work harder at their tasks.

In 1874, an eight-year-old child named Mary Ellen Wilson was discovered by a social worker to have been beaten and starved by her adoptive parents. The worker referred the case to the New York Police Department, which refused to take any action because there were no laws on the books that addressed the abuse of children by their parents or caretakers. In an effort to save the child, the city filed charges against the caretakers utilizing a statute that prevented cruelty to animals. The adoptive mother was sentenced to one year in jail, and the resulting publicity surrounding Mary Ellen's plight led to the formation of the Society for the Prevention of Cruelty to Children in 1875.

From this beginning, we have expanded our concern and care for abused children. Every state has laws preventing the physical abuse of children. The phenomenon of child abuse has generated many studies. One commonly cited study was conducted by the American Association for Protecting Children.

Some researchers take the position that there is no method of obtaining reliable data in this field.[10] Even the federal government has failed to establish standards for reporting child abuse. The FBI's Uniform Crime Reports (UCR) is the accepted method of reporting crimes on a nationwide basis. The UCR publishes crime statistics reported by law enforcement agencies. However, it provides no specific information on crimes against children. With the exception of murder, the UCR does not list the victim's age. The National Center on Child Abuse and Neglect (NCCAN), a division within the U.S. Department of Health and Human Services, has commissioned studies to provide a national estimate of the incidence of child maltreatment.

Many authorities believe that the number of reported cases of child abuse is only the tip of the iceberg. This is particularly true for those children between the ages of twelve and nineteen. This age group is far less likely than younger victims to report crimes, especially when the offender is not a stranger.[11] Part of the problem with determining the magnitude of physical child abuse may have something to do with the definition itself.

By defining the characteristics or hallmarks of physical child abuse differently, the research data can also differ significantly. Researchers select their sample populations based on criteria that differ from scholar to scholar and study to study. Some social scientists view physical child abuse in the context of determining whether the child is "at risk," whereas those working in the criminal justice field emphasize physical evidence. This multifaceted approach to understanding physical child abuse presents both problems and opportunities for growth. As mentioned earlier, the problem is reaching consensus on the definition of physical child abuse and how we respond to it. The opportunities for growth are based on the premise that professionals can and should learn from each other. The social worker may learn the difficulties in proving certain types of abuse, while at the same time teaching the prosecuting attorney to accept the seriousness of a situation that might not otherwise be apparent from a legal perspective.

Child Neglect

Some scholars have stated that child neglect is the most common form of maltreatment. According to Green, the reported cases of neglect in New York outnumbered those of physical abuse by eleven to one.[12] The U.S. Department of Health and Human Services (HHS) reported that more than 900,000 children are abused and/or neglected each year. Historically, children below one year have the highest rate of victimization—at 25 percent per 1,000 children. Of the children victimized each year, about 40 percent are neglected, and physical abuse is a major contributor to child fatalities. Child neglect is an important topic all professionals should understand. Neglect is less obvious than physical or sexual abuse, and it may continue for years without any outsider even being aware that the child they see daily is a victim. Neglect has many faces, forms, and appearances. There are serious cases in which a child's life is threatened and more mundane acts when the child is simply neglected on a daily basis.

Child Sexual Abuse

The American people have a widespread interest in child sexual abuse; however, the true magnitude of this problem is difficult to establish. There is a general agreement among both scholars and professionals in the field that the incidence of child sexual abuse reporting is understated.[13] Estimates on the number of child sexual abuses vary from source to source. According to a fact sheet distributed by the American Academy of Child and Adolescent Psychiatry, child sexual abuse is reported up to 80,000 times a year, but the number of unreported instances is far greater because the children are afraid to tell anyone what has happened, and the legal procedure for validating an episode is difficult. The problem should be identified, the abuse stopped, and the child should receive professional help. The long-term emotional and psychological damage of sexual abuse can be devastating to the child.

Rape in America, which was published by the National Victims Center, indicates that sexual violence occurs at a much higher rate than previously expected.[14] This study was discussed in more detail in Chapter 7 dealing with sexual violence, but it illustrates that sexual violence is still a major problem in America. On the basis of this study, the National Victims Center estimates at least 12.1 million women in the United States have been subjected to sexual violence as children or adults.

Although the figures may vary from study to study regarding the types and incidents of child sexual abuse, there is some agreement among researchers that the classification of offenders shown in Table 9.1 is a valid estimate.[15]

TABLE 9.1 Classification of Offenders	
Stranger as the offender	Approximately 8–10 percent
Family member as the offender	Approximately 47 percent
Acquaintance as the offender	Approximately 40 percent

The true extent of child victimization is unknown; however, simply discussing this subject raises our awareness and makes it more likely that we will acknowledge its existence. Professionals must not only be aware that it occurs, they should also have a basic understanding of some of the more common theories dealing with causation of child abuse. The next section examines one popular theory in this area, the intergenerational cycle of violence.

Child Fatality Review Teams

Despite a growing awareness of child abuse, we continue to experience child fatalities. Deaths of children due to illness or accidents can be, for the most part, easily identified; however, it is much harder to track deaths that result from physical assault or neglect. Many researchers believe that deaths due to abuse and neglect are underreported, since some of these deaths are labeled as accidents. In addition, many states differ on the definition of key terms such as *child homicide*, *child abuse*, and *child neglect*.

In response to various concerns regarding child fatalities, a number of organizations and jurisdictions have formed child fatality review teams composed of a variety of professionals from different backgrounds who review child fatalities. The team members vary among jurisdictions, but usually include a medical examiner, a pediatrician, a representative from the district attorney's office, law enforcement and child protective services members, and other professionals as appropriate.

The teams integrate the separate disciplines with specific roles and mandates to ensure that services do not overlap or conflict. Teams also gather statistics to determine whether or not patterns exist that increase the likelihood of child fatalities and serious injuries within the community. There are generally two types of reviews: prospective and periodic. Prospective reviews usually occur within seventy-two hours of the death and are designed to assist the death investigation and delivery of services. Period reviews are designed to evaluate and discuss all deaths within a designated time frame.[16]

INTERGENERATIONAL TRANSMISSION OF VIOLENCE

Some scholars would argue that the most effective method of stopping child abuse is to break the intergenerational transmission of violence. The intergenerational transmission of violence theory is discussed as a distinct and separate aspect of child abuse. Simply separating it from the other theories should not imply that this is the definitive answer to why people commit aggressive acts; rather it is singled out for examination because professionals and laypersons constantly refer to it as a scientifically accepted fact. As with other causes or theories of family violence, there is no way to prove or disprove the intergenerational transmission of violence theory. However, because of the widespread acceptance of this theory, it is necessary to explore fully both the premises on which it is founded and the criticisms directed to it.

The intergenerational transmission of violence concept has generated continuing controversy among researchers for several decades. Scholars have attempted to determine whether violent tendencies can be inherited from the family of origin as a result of observing it or being a victim. Other scholars have attempted to explain criminal behavior by reference to this cycle.[17]

Definitions

Previously, the term used to describe the process involved in this concept was *cycle of violence;* however, this theory is now considered as the "intergenerational transmission of violence theory." The **intergenerational transmission of violence theory** asserts that violent behavior is learned within the family and bequeathed from one generation to the next. This theory holds that children who are victims of child abuse or who witness violent aggression by one spouse against the other will grow up and react to their children or spouses in the same manner. The childhood survivor of a violent family develops a predisposition toward violence in his or her own family. Thus, so this theory holds, we have a never-ending chain of violence that is passed from one generation to the next. There have been numerous studies on the intergenerational transmission of violence, and the results of these studies will be discussed later in this section.

Intergenerational Transmission of Violence and Family Violence

The sources for most studies of the intergenerational transmission of violence theory are case studies, clinical interviews, self-reporting, and agency records. One widely cited study in support of the intergenerational transmission of violence theory is Steele and Pollock's research, which appeared in Helfer and Kempe's *The Battered Child Syndrome*.[18] Their study involved sixty parents who were referred to them as a result of their children being treated for child abuse. Steele and Pollock gathered data by testing and by interviewing the parents. The parents stated that as children they had experienced intense, pervasive, and continuous demands from their own parents. Lost within the conclusions of the study was the fact that some parents were physically abused and others were not. The researchers had cautioned against drawing too many inferences from their research; however, their study is constantly cited as evidence supporting the intergenerational transmission of violence theory.

Straus conducted an extensive study by interviewing 1,146 families with children.[19] The results of the study indicated an 18 percent rate of generational transmission of violence. The results of this study may have been low because the researchers limited the definition of abuse to physical acts that occurred during adolescence. As discussed in Chapter 3, child abuse is more likely to occur at a younger age with a gradual tapering off in incidents as the child reaches the teenage years.

Hunter and Kilstrom interviewed 282 parents of newborn infants.[20] These researchers followed the parents and determined that the intergenerational transmission of violence was 18 percent. However, 82 percent of the parents who were abused as children did not abuse their offspring. Those parents appeared to be able to break the intergenerational transmission of violence because of social support, healthy children, and a more supportive relationship with one of their own parents. Hunter and Kilstrom's study is suspect because it examined only infants who had been admitted to an intensive care nursery. In addition, there was no extended follow-up of the families or their children.

England and Jacobvitz concluded a major study of 160 single-parent mothers.[21] Each mother had at least one child under the age of five. The sample was divided into three groups: severe physical child abuse, including being struck by objects or burned; borderline child abuse, including weekly spankings; and finally, those children who were being raised by another caretaker. The researchers found a 70 percent intergenerational transmission of violence for those mothers who had suffered severe abuse as a child.

Cappell and Heiner analyzed 888 childrearing families and measured the incidence of aggression in the respondent's families.[22] The presence or absence of aggression was classified into family member relationships: husband to wife aggression, wife to husband aggression, and respondent to child aggression. These researchers found that women who witnessed or experienced violence as children were more likely to discipline their own children aggressively. Perhaps more important, these scholars suggested that children who are raised in a violent family learn or inherit vulnerability. Cappell and Heiner theorize that this intergenerational transmission of vulnerability causes men and women to provoke violence, accept violence as normal, and select aggressive partners. These scholars rightfully explain that this research is limited, because the same group was composed only of intact couples.

Intergenerational Transmission of Violence and Aggression

Dodge and his associates examined the effect of the intergenerational transmission of violence on development of aggressive tendencies in children.[23] They studied a representative sample of 309 four-year-olds in kindergarten. This research was multisite in nature, with children being selected from Nashville and Knoxville, Tennessee, as well as Bloomington, Indiana. The researchers interviewed the mothers, evaluated the children, and received responses regarding the children's behavior from school personnel, peer ratings, and direct observation.

They found that children who had been physically abused were more aggressive toward other children than those who had not been harmed.[24] The teacher-rated aggression index for abused children was 93 percent higher than for nonabused children. The researchers also found that abused children were less able to process information and solve interpersonal problems. Although the authors accurately point out several caveats to their study, it does demonstrate the harm inflicted on children by abuse.

This harm may translate into future acts of aggression that take the form of crime against society. One comprehensive study in this area of child abuse and delinquency was undertaken by Widom.[25] She followed 1,575 cases from childhood through young adulthood. The study compared arrest records of two groups:

- One group was composed of 908 children with documented histories of abuse or neglect.
- The control group was composed of 667 children with no reported incidents of child abuse.

These groups were tracked through official records over the next fifteen to twenty years. The children were eleven years old or younger at the time of the abuse; therefore, an inherent weakness in the Straus research was avoided. The study classified abuse into three distinct areas: physical, sexual, and neglect cases. Court and probation records were the source of data for the initial acts of abuse, and subsequent arrest data were obtained from federal, state, and local law enforcement agencies.

The study found that children who had been abused were more likely to commit crimes as juveniles and adults than the control group. Furthermore, these children were arrested more often for violent crime (11 percent) than the nonabused children (8 percent). Those children who were physically abused were more likely to be arrested for a violent crime. Interestingly, this study pointed out that the next biggest arrest rate for violent crimes was for those children who had been neglected.

As this discussion illustrates, the intergenerational transmission of violence theory continues to dominate the literature. This and other theories of family violence will continue to be researched in an attempt to find the cause of family violence, predict its occurrence, and search for a cure.

OTHER THEORIES REGARDING CHILD ABUSE

Theories of Physical Child Abuse

Rather than attempting to describe all acceptable theories of the causes of child abuse, this section will set forth one model that encompasses several theories. Cynthia Crosson Tower established a series of categories that grouped several theories into three distinct models: (1) the psychopathological model, (2) the interactional model, and (3) the environmental–sociological–cultural model.[26]

The **psychopathological model** stresses the characteristics of the abuser as the primary cause of abuse. The abuser's personality predisposes the abuser to injure the child. This model includes three separate approaches to child abuse: (1) the psychodynamic model, (2) the mental illness model, and (3) the character-trait model.

The psychodynamic model is based on the work of C. Henry Kempe and Ray Helfer. This model theorized that a lack of bonding between the parent and child is an important factor in child abuse. This theory assumes that the abuser was part of a cycle of parental inadequacy. These individuals are unable to bond with children, and when a crisis occurs they respond with abusive acts. This model also assumes that the abuser will engage in role reversal. In other words, the parents expect the child to nurture them instead of vice versa.

The mental illness model sets forth the proposition that the parent's mental illness is the primary cause of child abuse. This is an easy theory for laypersons to accept, because it is easy to believe that anyone who would repeatedly beat or torture a child must be crazy. B. Justice and R. Justice suggested this model as a viable category.[27] Although some scholars have found abusive parents to be mentally disturbed, many others argue that abusive parents do not fit any existing psychiatric classification. For example, Kempe found that fewer than 5 percent were psychotic.

The character-trait model focuses on specific traits of abusers without regard to how they acquired these traits. Scholars such as Merrill and Delsordo have categorized abusive parents by specific traits that cause child abuse.[28] Merrill's study included such traits as hostility, rigidity, passivity, dependence, and competitiveness. Delsordo's categorization of abusive parent's traits included mental illness, frustration and irresponsibility, and severe disciplinarian and misplaced abuse.

The **interactional model** views child abuse as a result of a dysfunctional system. This category of abuse focuses on the following factors in child abuse: (1) the role of the child, (2) chance events, and (3) the family structure.

The role of the child and the perceptions of the parent toward that child are viewed as a cause of child abuse by some scholars. Martin suggests that abuse not only requires a certain type of adult, but also that certain acts of the child trigger the abuse. If the parent has certain expectations that the child does not meet, abuse may occur.[29]

"Chance events" is the somewhat inaccurate name given to events that prevent the parent from bonding with the child. This lack of attachment is viewed as a predisposition toward child abuse. Lynch suggests that difficulties in pregnancy, labor, or delivery can have a bearing on the attachment of the mother to the child.[30]

The family structure model theorizes that child abuse is a result of a dysfunctional family. The adult members of the family blame the child for their own shortcomings, and this leads to abuse.

The **environmental–sociological–cultural model** views child abuse as a result of stresses in society that are the primary causes of abuse. This category of abuse includes the following causes of child abuse: (1) the environmental stress model, (2) the social learning model, (3) the social psychological model, and (4) the psychosocial systems model.

The environmental stress model accepts the proposition that factors such as lack of education, poverty, unemployment, or occupational stress result in child abuse. As these outside forces build, the parent or caretaker is unable to cope and reacts by hitting or injuring the child.

The social learning model emphasizes the inadequacy of the parenting skills of abusive parents. These parents never learned appropriate responses to childrearing, and therefore their lack of skill leads to frustration. This frustration in turn causes abusive behavior.

The social psychological model assumes stress results from a number of social and psychological factors, including marital disputes, unemployment, or too many or unwanted children. These factors induce stress that causes the individual to react to the child in an abusive manner.

The psychosocial systems model stresses that abuse results from interactions within the family. The family as a system is out of balance and incapable of caring for the child. The child becomes the target for family members' frustration, and abuse is the result.

As this discussion indicates, several theories attempt to explain who the abusers are and why they abuse children. Although no authority can point to one single cause of child abuse, it is clear that it continues to occur. The causes of physical child abuse are multifaceted; therefore, it is necessary to review who are the victims or recipients of this violence to attempt to understand this phenomenon more fully.

Theories of Child Neglect

Are poor children neglected and rich kids well-cared for? Unfortunately, a substantial number of people in society equate poverty with neglect, but simply being poor does not make a neglectful parent. There are children who live at the edge of poverty or below the poverty level and are loved and nurtured. On the other hand, there are children who live in $1 million homes but are neglected or psychologically abused on a daily basis. The causes of neglect are varied and wide-ranging.

Polansky and his colleagues in their classic textbook, *Damaged Parents: An Anatomy of Child Neglect,* established three major causes of neglect: (1) economic causes, (2) ecological causes, and (3) personalistic causes.[31] The **economic theory** suggests that neglect is caused by stress as a result of living in poverty. The **ecological theory** views the family behavior and neglect as a result of social causes. The **personalistic theory** attributes child neglect to individual personality characteristics of the caretakers.

Numerous studies have indicated that poverty is an important factor in the parents' ability to care for their children, and the question must be asked, "Does poverty cause neglect, or is poverty the result of the parents' inability to function?"[32]

Some scholars have indicated that families who neglect their children live in an environment that is unfriendly and characterized by low morale and hopelessness.[33] As indicated, the issue is whether environment causes neglect or whether the environment is a characteristic of the parents' inability to function.

The more reasoned approach seems to be that of the personalistic theory. In this approach, neglect is viewed as being caused by complex maladaptive interactions and/or lack of essential caretaking behaviors that are influenced by the level of parental skill, knowledge deficits, and other stress factors.[34] The following is a list of some important characteristics of parents or caretakers who neglect their children:[35]

Inability to plan: These parents lack the ability to establish goals, objectives, and direction. These parents may have low frustration levels and little ability to delay gratification.

Lack of knowledge: Parents have little or no knowledge about children's needs, housekeeping skills, cooking, and so on.

Lack of judgment: Parents may leave a young child alone and unsupervised.

Lack of motivation: Parents lack energy, have little desire to learn, and have no other standard of comparison. These parents are apathetic or ineffective in that they are withdrawn and feel that nothing is worth doing. (H. B. Cantwell, "Child Neglect," in The Battered Child, C. H. Kempe and R. E. Helfer, eds. University of Chicago Press, Chicago, 1980, pp. 183–197).

There are other models that profile personalities of neglectful parents or caretakers, and no one study or theory has gained universal acceptance. The next section examines an even more controversial subject—the reason why perpetrators molest young children.

Theories of Child Sexual Abuse

Numerous studies indicate that child abusers do not fit any stereotype. The common lay perception that all abusers are ugly old men who prey on children is simply not true, but researchers have attempted to find a common thread or factor that connects all child abusers. They have examined the degree of violence, the age of the victim, the age and education of the offender, preoffense social and occupational adjustment, alcohol abuse, physiological responses of offenders, and aggression. Conti reviewed the literature in this area and described the following factors that were considered important when evaluating characteristics of abusers:[36]

1. Measurement of sexual arousal is essential to discriminate between various categories of sexual offenders.
2. The role of sexual fantasies with children is important due to its connection to deviant sexuality. Fantasies about children coupled with masturbation during these fantasies serve as a form of rehearsal for contact with the victims.
3. The types of rationalizations used by adult offenders who have sexual relations with children commonly take the form of statements or thoughts to the effect: "A child who doesn't resist really wants to have sex," or "Having sex with a child is the best way to teach her about sex," or "You become closer to the child when you share sex with him," and so on.

In addition to the various forms of psychopathology present in child abuse, Finkelhor established four factors involved in sexual abuse.[37] He called this theory the **four preconditions model of sexual abuse,** which establishes preconditions that create a personal and social context for expressing sexually abusive behaviors: (1) motivation to abuse sexually, (2) overcoming internal inhibitors, (3) factors predisposing to overcome external inhibitors, and (4) factors predisposing to overcome the child's resistance.

Precondition I: Motivation to Abuse Sexually. The motivation to abuse a child sexually includes emotional congruence, sexual arousal, and blockage. Emotional congruence involves satisfying an emotional need by relating to the child in a sexual manner. Sexual arousal occurs when the child becomes the source of sexual gratification. Blockage occurs when other alternative forms of sexual satisfaction are not present, not available, or less satisfying. The motivation to abuse a child is based on individual as well as sociological grounds. Individual explanations include the need for power and control, unconscious re-enactment of a previous childhood trauma, and biological abnormality. Sociological reasons include the male-oriented society that demands male dominance, child pornography, and erotic portrayal of children in the media.

Precondition II: Overcoming Internal Inhibitors. The perpetrator must overcome internal controls that would prevent him from sexually abusing the victim. Some of these controls are overcome by use of alcohol or drugs, existing psychosis, inability of the offender to identify with the needs of the victim, weak criminal sanctions against offenders, and child pornography.

Precondition III: Factors Predisposing to Overcome External Inhibitors. These conditions are outside the control of the perpetrator. These factors include social situations such as the type and amount of supervision a child receives, lack of a parental figure who is close to or protective of the victim, and unusual sleeping or living arrangements. In addition, the lack of social support for mothers, barriers to equality, and erosion of the family's social networks contribute to the ability of the offender to overcome external inhibitors.

Precondition IV: Factors Predisposing to Overcome the Child's Resistance. These factors concern the victim's ability to resist the sexual advances. The child may be emotionally insecure, deprived, or lacking in sexual experience or knowledge. The victim may feel powerless, or a situation of trust exists between the offender and the victim.

There is no distinct or clear answer as to why adults sexually abuse children. The offender may commit these acts for a variety of reasons. Both psychological forces and social structure enter into this complex mesh of forces to allow individuals to engage in sexual activities with young victims.

We traditionally think of the abuser as a man and the victim as a girl. However, studies indicate that boys may be the victims of sexual abuse at a higher rate than previously thought. One study in San Jose, California, indicates a rise in the reported incidents of sexual abuse of boys.[38]

Boys who are victims of abuse may not report the acts or incidents for several reasons. First, boys may not want to be viewed as victims or "sissies" or be perceived as weak. Second, boys normally do not have to account for their movements and are given greater degrees of freedom and less protection through supervision, and therefore parents may not notice unusual behavior that may indicate sexual abuse. And third, our stereotypes lead us to look for abuse with girls, not with boys.[39]

The high-risk years for child sexual abuse range from between four and nine years old.[40] At the former age, children are naive and sexually curious, and by the time they reach the age of nine, their loyalty, desire to please, and trust of adults are traits manipulated by offenders to accomplish their goal of molestation. Generally, sexual abuse is terminated by the time the child reaches fourteen. This termination occurs because the victim may threaten the offender with disclosure or engage in activities, such as running away, that would lead authorities to suspect abuse.[41]

Contrary to popular belief, the actual physical attractiveness of the female child has little if anything to do with whether the child is a victim of molestation. In addition, the seductiveness of the female child is now discounted as a contributing factor in sexual abuse situations. Although we may be able to dispel certain stereotypes about female victims, there needs to be more research on the issue of male victims. Two scholars have isolated at least one factor that may identify why certain male children are molested. Finkelhor and Porter suggested that the less assertive boys are more likely to be victims of sexual abuse.[42]

Children are at a higher risk of sexual abuse if they are socially isolated, left alone, and unsupervised. If the mother is absent from the home for long periods, because of either work or other commitment, the child is more likely to be abused. Some authorities theorize that the presence of a stepfather in the home adds to the risk of sexual abuse.[43] These factors establish situations in which the child becomes vulnerable to the perpetrator.

We are still researching and learning about the characteristics of those who abuse, and why certain children are chosen for abuse over others. Misconceptions and stereotypes have contributed to the confusion in this very important area. We do not have all the answers on why and who is involved in child sexual abuse, but we are making progress.

There are normally two situations or factual patterns that occur in child sexual abuse: One is a sudden, violent assault by a stranger and involves the use of force or fear, and the other involves sexual activities by a perpetrator known to the child. The former is the classic sexual assault of the victim, which is discussed in detail in Chapter 7. This section discusses those situations in which the offender knows or is related to the victim. As with most relationships, child sexual abuse requires interaction between the perpetrator and the victim. There is often a progression of acts that lead to the sexual encounter. Tower established five stages or phases of child sexual abuse: the engagement phase, the sexual interaction phase, the secrecy phase, the disclosure phase, and the suppression phase.[44]

The engagement phase involves the perpetrator gaining access to the victim. This access may occur as a result of a living arrangement, a trip, babysitting, or any other situation in which the offender has an opportunity to discuss sex with the child without supervision of any other adult. The adult may offer rationalizations or attempt to convince the victim that sex is proper. Comments such as "This is how daddies teach their daughters about sex" and "You will make me and your mommy happy by doing this" are examples of verbal communications that occur during this stage. The perpetrator may engage in what appears to be "accidents" to see how the child responds. Acts such as walking in while the child is bathing or allowing the child to see the adult nude or view the offender's genitals are examples of these types of actions. If the child reacts negatively to these tentative approaches, some offenders will back off and try another approach.

The sexual interaction phase involves actual sexual contact. This may range from viewing the child nude or having the child observe the adult without clothes, fondling the child and vice versa, oral sex, or sexual penetration. Groth established two categories of sexual contacts: pressured sex and forced sex.[45]

Pressured sex involves the perpetrator attempting to convince the child to engage in sexual activity. This is accomplished by bribing or rewarding the child with attention, praise, or material goods. If the child refuses the advances, the perpetrator may resort to force to achieve sexual contact. Forced sex involves the threat of harm or use of force to complete the act. The perpetrator may use his position of authority as an adult to obtain compliance from the child. Other offenders will carry out the act in the traditional sexual assault form of rape.

The secrecy phase involves the perpetrator convincing the child to remain silent about the acts. This allows the offender to continue with sexual relations over an extended period of time. The adult may threaten, blackmail, or bribe the child to remain silent. The most common tactic is intimidation.[46] Statements such as "If they found out, your daddy would have to leave you and your mommy" are common forms of threats that may occur during this stage of sexual exploitation.

The disclosure phase may occur relatively soon after the act or at a later time when the victim is an adult. The disclosure may occur accidentally when the participants are observed in the act of sex, or when the child visits a physician and is diagnosed as the victim of sexual

NOW, THEREFORE, I, BARACK OBAMA, President of the United States of America, by virtue of the authority vested in me by the Constitution and the laws of the United States, do hereby proclaim April 2013 as National Child Abuse Prevention Month. I call upon all Americans to observe this month with programs and activities that help prevent child abuse and provide for children's physical, emotional, and developmental needs. The President on March 29, 2013 declared April 2013 as child abuse prevention month. May we make this a continuing effort? (ulegundo/Fotolia)

SANDUSKY CHILD SEX ABUSE SCANDAL RAISED QUESTIONS REGARDING
State Mandatory Reporting Requirements

The investigations that resulted in the 2012 trial of former Penn State University Assistant Football Coach Jerry Sandusky raised some serious questions about state sexual abuse reporting requirements. According to the investigative reports, numerous individuals at Penn State University suspected the assistant coach of child sexual abuse but failed to report their suspicions to the police.

After the case made the media, many states reviewed their reporting requirements of the statutes and expanded the mandatory reporting requirements. Presently, while in some states the reporting requirements apply only to professionals like doctors and teachers, in 18 states the mandatory reporting requirements apply to all adults.

There is a conflict of opinion among experts as to whether increasing the number of mandatory reporters will make the pubic more vigilant or does it merely add more work to an overloaded child welfare system? Critics of the mandatory reporting statutes claim that such laws force child welfare workers to investigate an endless flow of inconsequential complaints. It is often stated by these critics that we do not have problem with underreporting, the public already overreports.

Prior to the breaking of the news on the Sandusky case, the State of New Jersey hotline for child sexual abuse received about 400 calls a day. In the months after the case

was in the media, the number of calls increased to about 750 per day. In Pennsylvania, the number of child abuse reports more than doubled after the case went public. Other states faced similar increases.

While as of July 2012 eighteen states required all adults to report suspected child sexual abuse, other states vary as to which professionals are included in the mandatory reporting requirements. The list includes teachers, school nurses, doctors, day care workers, coaches, and camp counselors.

One of the problems is that many of the state mandatory reporting statutes have no specific sanctions for those who failed to comply with the laws. And others have penalties that are rarely enforced unless the case is particularly heinous or deadly.

An interesting question that will only be decided by time is whether or not the state university will be held liable and be required to pay damages to the victims based on the failure of certain university personnel to report suspected child abuse by the assistant coach?

Source: "Sandusky Child sex abuse scandal raises questions about state laws." *Christian Science Monitor* Web site at www.csmonitor .com accessed on July 12, 2012.

abuse. Intentional disclosure involves the child informing someone of the actions of the perpetrator. Many victims of sexual abuse do not disclose its existence until they are adults and out of the reach, authority, or power of the offender. Occasionally, adult women will disclose the activity, because they are afraid the perpetrator may be molesting a younger brother or sister.

The suppression phase occurs after the disclosure or discovery of the abuse and involves caretakers attempting to force the child to recant the accusations of abuse. If the molester is a father figure or sole support for family, pressure may be brought on the child to keep quiet. Some families will promise the child that it will not happen again. Other techniques involve telling the child that a loved one will go to prison if the child continues to tell others of the molestation. The purpose of these activities is to get the child to recant so that no action will be taken by the authorities.

This discussion has focused on the progression of sexual abuse. In these situations, the offender is usually known to the victim. These activities may occur with a relative or a caretaker who is associated with the family. Child sexual abuse is a serious form of victimization that has long-lasting consequences for the victim. However, there are other forms of child abuse that also have long-term consequences for the victims. The next section addresses some of these special types of child abuse.

SPECIAL TYPES OF CHILD ABUSE

Sibling Abuse

Sibling abuse is probably the most common form of family violence in the United States. Gelles and Cornell stated this fact in another manner when they wrote that the most commonly victimized family members are siblings.[47] If sibling abuse is in fact the most common form of family violence, why is there such a reluctance on the part of society and professionals to discuss it? There are very few textbooks devoted exclusively to this topic. Most academic articles dealing with child abuse may include as an afterthought a discussion of sibling abuse. Two areas of sibling abuse that are being examined in some detail are incest and the abuse of a sibling by parents.

There are a variety of reasons for this lack of discussion regarding sibling abuse. We consider sibling aggression to be a normal part of growing up. As the following Focus box indicates, we have all heard excuses for sibling aggression. They are common refrains in families with more than one child. As a society, we tend to minimize sibling aggression. Yet early studies in New York and Philadelphia indicated that 3 percent of all homicides committed in those cities were committed by siblings against siblings.[48] In another classic study of sibling abuse, Steinmetz found that parents did not consider their children's physical aggression toward siblings as abuse. They would even talk with friends, neighbors, and relatives about the aggression—viewing it as an inevitable part of siblings growing up.[49]

When a young child tapes her teddy bear's mouth closed, is that an indication of child abuse or that something is wrong? (Pixel & Creation/Fotolia)

No one has accurate figures on the nature, type, or extent of sibling abuse. However, most authorities agree that it is the most common form of family violence. The popular media first addressed this issue in 1979 with a report in *U.S. News & World Report* that stated 138,000 children aged three to seventeen had used a weapon on a sibling within the last year.[50] In a 1980 study, Straus, Gelles, and Steinmetz reported that 82 percent of parents of children surveyed considered sibling violence to be the most common form of intrafamily violence.[51] In another early

How many of the following excuses have you heard used to justify one sibling's acts toward another?

Don't worry about it, it's just normal sibling rivalry.

They were just playing doctor.

Kids will be kids.

He really didn't mean to hurt his sister; he loves her.

It's only normal childhood curiosity.

Kids are always calling each other names.

I told him not to hit her again.

They will grow out of it.

study, Steinmetz (1981) found that a clear majority of children used physical violence to resolve conflict with their siblings.[52]

In 1988, Pagelow presented the findings of her study of 1,025 college students at 3 university campuses in southern California at the annual meeting of the Pacific Sociological Association. Pagelow's survey revealed that almost half of the siblings living at home at the age of twelve were either aggressors or victims of violent acts of kicking and punching. Ten percent said their siblings beat them, and 4 percent stated that their siblings had threatened them with a gun or knife or used a gun or knife against them.

In 1992, Carson and Daane presented the results of their study of 3,357 students in an Indiana school district at the annual meeting of the American Sociological Association. Seventy-four percent of the students approved of hitting their sibling if they were reacting to being hit first. Forty-three percent approved of striking their sibling if that sibling broke the stereo. Thirty-eight percent believed it was appropriate to hit their sibling if that sibling made fun of the aggressor in front of friends. Almost one-quarter of all students surveyed approved of hitting their sibling if there was an argument and the other sibling did not listen to reason.

These and other studies indicate that sibling abuse is a common form of family violence. Its existence can no longer be denied; however, we are still studying its nature, causation, and extent. As with many other forms of family violence, there is no one single definition of sibling abuse.

The question then must be, "Do we really need a separate definition of sibling abuse, or would other definitions within this textbook cover most if not all of the situations that arise in which children commit acts of violence toward their siblings?" Earlier in this chapter, *physical child abuse* was defined as any act that results in a nonaccidental physical injury by a person who has care, custody, or control of a child. Many acts of sibling abuse occur when the older or more powerful sibling has care or control over the victim. However, there are acts of sibling abuse that occur within the home when parents are present but unaware of the acts of the abusing sibling. Therefore, the definition of physical child abuse does not cover all situations that might arise in sibling abuse. Although it is possible to draft a broad definition of child abuse that would cover acts of sibling abuse, by defining it as a separate and distinct form of child abuse, its importance in any study of family violence is highlighted.

Sibling abuse is any form of physical, mental, or sexual abuse inflicted by one child in a family unit upon another. This definition covers the various types of abuse that will be discussed later. In addition, it does not require that the children be related by birth. There are situations in which children from different marriages end up in the same household. Finally, the definition uses the term *child*. This term requires further explanation. There are reported incidents of one sibling abusing the other after they have reached the age of eighteen. However, it appears that the vast majority of abuse occurs when the victim and/or the abuser are under the age of adulthood. Therefore, **child** is defined as a person under the age of legal majority. This age is typically stated to be eighteen. It should be clear that this definition does not include abuse of different children within the same family by an adult member of the household.

Child Sexual Abuse Accommodation Syndrome (CSAAS)

Excerpts from the two following court cases discuss the concept of child sexual abuse accommodation syndrome.

Excerpts from *People v. Michael Luis Grant*
2012 WL 1437453 (Cal.App. 6 Dist. 2012)

At trial, R. testified that she loves defendant and wants to continue being married to him. R. testified that she had lied to the police and that she also told her daughter M. and her sister I. to lie to the police. R. testified that she was angry and upset after learning that defendant was seeing Lisa Duncan, and expressed her feelings to M. while I. was present. R. wanted defendant to "get in trouble" and wanted him "away from Lisa." She testified that she "made" the girls "believe that it happened." According to R., defendant would wrestle and tickle the girls and nothing improper occurred. However, she told the girls that defendant was doing "nasty things" to them and putting his "'private part...on your private part.'" She further told I. to tell their mother.

R. testified that she later felt "bad" about "making the girls believe that [defendant] molested them" when she heard "something about" defendant facing a twenty-five–year–to–life sentence. The first time that R. disclosed that she had influenced the girls was during the meeting in defense counsel's office. She was scared of her mother learning that she had put the girls up to this.

R. testified that she talked to defendant frequently while he was in jail. It was common for him to call her two to four times a day, and they would talk for the entire time allowed. R. paid for all of defendant's calls to her. At trial, she admitted that she lied on jail visitation logs by writing down the name of defendant's cellmate when in fact she was visiting defendant.

R.'s cousin testified that she talked "quite a bit" with R. and that, after defendant was arrested, she talked to R. almost every day. R. initially told her cousin that she believed the girls. R. also told her cousin about an incident involving defendant. R. had left the two girls with defendant at a condominium. When R. returned, she walked into a room and saw defendant behind I., who was bent over. When defendant saw R. walk into the room, he "jumped off I. and adjusted his penis."

Carl Lewis, a private investigator and retired police officer, testified as an expert on CSAAS. Lewis did not know defendant or the specific charges in the case, and had not been told about the specific facts of the case. Lewis testified about the five categories of CSAAS: secrecy, helplessness, entrapment and accommodation, delayed conflicted unconvincing disclosure, and retraction. Lewis cautioned that the categories are not present in every case of abuse, and that CSAAS is not a tool for discerning whether a child is telling the truth about being abused. He explained that CSAAS is "background information" and is "intended to dispel some commonly held myths about child sexual abuse as an occurrence and child sexual abuse victims in particular."

Jenny August Adler, volunteer and counseling coordinator at the YWCA of Silicon Valley Rape Crisis Center, testified as an expert in "coping behaviors of victims and intimate partner and family battering and its effects." She did not read any reports or listen to any tapes in defendant's case, and she did not know anything about the facts of the case.

Adler explained that there is a "cycle of violence" in a "domestic abuse relationship." The relationship starts with a "hearts and flowers" stage where both parties put their best foot forward. Tension builds in the relationship, leading to an explosion and the display of some type of violence. The abuser will often apologize and make promises, leading to the hearts and flowers stage again.

In domestic abuse relationships, one partner continuously has more power and control in all the different areas of the relationship, whereas in most relationships, the partners have power and control in different areas, such as finances and the social calendar, but ultimately there is equality. Power and control may be taken away from a partner in different ways, including through physical or verbal abuse. This power dynamic may occur in a dating relationship and may occur between family members.

Jealousy is part of many domestic abuse relationships and may be used as an excuse to monitor or isolate the victim from others. The victim may also be jealous of the abuser, "because of insecurity created by the power and control difference." Victims often have very low self-esteem because of the abuse, and "frequently they feel like they aren't worth anything unless they are with the abuser."

It is very common for domestic violence victims who report violence within the family to later deny it, downplay it, or lie for the abuser. Statistics reflect that a victim leaves an abusive relationship seven times before the victim is able to really disconnect from that relationship. In the cycle of abuse, when the victim is reconciling with the abuser, very often they're going back into that hearts and flowers stage and the victim does not want to look at the abuse that the victim previously experienced. There may also be a lack of support for the victim and the charges of abuse when those in the victim's social circle know the abuser but are unaware of the abuser's negative side or controlling side.

In a domestic violence relationship, coping strategies include "learned helplessness," which refers to a person who has experienced ongoing abuse, is unsuccessful in getting away from the abuse, and stops trying to get away...

At trial, Lewis testified about the five categories of CSAAS. First, secrecy "describes the fact that sexual abuse of a child occurs almost exclusively when the offender is alone or somehow isolated with the child." Second, helplessness describes a child's feelings as the child is unable to stop the abuse by an adult. Third, entrapment and accommodation refers to a child "trapped by the circumstances of sexual abuse but accommodat[ing] that circumstance by a variety of means," such as acting as if nothing is wrong or engaging in anti-social behavior. Fourth, delayed conflicted unconvincing disclosure describes the fact that there is usually a delay between the time the child suffers the abuse and when it is disclosed, the child experiences internal conflict in determining whether to disclose, and the disclosure is "usually done at a time or in a manner that makes the child seem unconvincing," such as when the child is being punished. Fifth, retraction may occur as the disclosure results in a "great deal of chaos and attention" to the child and the family, such as by child protective services, law enforcement, the criminal justice system, and the medical field, and the child feels "very uncomfortable" from all the attention.

As we explained, the trial judge instructs the jury that an expert's testimony about CSAAS "is not evidence that the defendant committed any of the crimes charged against him," and that the jury "may consider this evidence only in deciding whether or not the victim's conduct was not inconsistent with the conduct of someone who has been molested, and in evaluating the believability of the victim's testimony."

In this case, Lewis readily acknowledged the limits of CSAAS and did not offer an opinion about the specifics of defendant's case. Lewis testified that CSAAS is "not a tool for discerning whether a child is telling the truth" about being abused. He further admitted that CSAAS is "not a diagnosis" and that, for example, a child might retract a claim of abuse because there actually had been no abuse. Lewis explained that CSAAS is simply "background information" and is "intended to dispel some commonly held myths." He

also testified that he did not know defendant and had not been told about the specific facts of the case. Lewis's testimony concerning CSAAS was accordingly general and not directed to a particular child in this case. Defendant's own expert witness, Dr. Abbott, similarly testified that CSAAS is not a "diagnostic tool" and "cannot be used to diagnose whether a child has been sexually abused or not." We believe that this testimony by both experts in the case eliminated any risk that the jury might misuse or misapply the CSAAS evidence. (People v. Michael Luis Grant 2012 WL 1437453 (Cal.App. 6 Dist. 2012)).

Excerpts from *People v. James Edmond Daly* 2009 WL 757337 (Cal.App. 6 Dist.)

Dr. Anthony Urquiza testified as an expert in the area of child sexual abuse. He described the components of the child sexual abuse accommodation syndrome as secrecy, helplessness, entrapment and accommodation, delayed and unconvincing disclosure, and retraction. Dr. Rahn Minagawa, a psychologist who has worked extensively in the field of child sexual abuse, testified that the child sexual abuse accommodation syndrome was "intended specifically for clinical use" and "was never intended to be used in a forensic arena."

He agreed with Dr. Urquiza that "anywhere between 2 to possibly 8 percent of allegations about sexual abuse from children or adolescents was false." He said, "Fictitious allegations appear to occur in two populations .... One is coached children in custody disputes. And the second, adolescents who make up convincing reports out of boredom, infatuation or in an effort to retaliate." (People v. James Edmond Daly 2009 WL 757337 (Cal.App. 6 Dist.)).

Munchausen Syndrome by Proxy

One type of child abuse has recently become a topic of discussion.[53] **Munchausen syndrome by proxy** is defined as a psychiatric disorder, whereby individuals intentionally produce physical symptoms of illness in their children. It is still being researched but has surfaced as a diagnosis in a number of cases.[54]

The term *Munchausen syndrome* was coined by Richard Asher in 1951 to describe patients who fabricated histories of illness. These individuals described complex medical histories and often displayed symptoms of the alleged disease. These fabrications invariably led to complex medical interventions and hospitalizations. Asher named this disorder after Baron von Munchausen. Hieronymous Karl Fredrich von Munchausen was an eighteenth-century German baron and mercenary officer in the Russian cavalry. The baron was famous for dramatizing his "amazing" adventures. Some might describe him as a world-class teller of tall tales.

There is some debate as to who first used the term *Munchausen syndrome by proxy*. Money used it in 1976 to describe four children who were so severely abused that they were dwarfed.[55] However, in 1977 Meadow also used the term to describe the more commonly accepted definition of this form of abuse. Meadow examined two children who were being poisoned by a parent. The parent knew what was happening but encouraged the medical professionals to search for a diagnosis. This diagnostic process was painful and dangerous to the children.[56]

Megan's Laws

A series of highly publicized violent sex offenses committed on unsuspecting victims by newly released sex offenders heightened the general public's awareness of this type of offender. One of the most famous cases concerned a recently released sex offender who raped and murdered seven-year-old Megan Kanka in 1994. Her family became one of the guiding forces behind the adoption of the sex offender notification law in New Jersey. The movement by victims and their families to prevent these types of offenders from committing new crimes gained momentum. As a result of these forces, by August 1995, forty-three states had adopted laws requiring offenders to register with a department or law enforcement agency. The 1994 Violent Crime Control and Law Enforcement Act may result in the enactment of registration laws by all states because failure to do so may result in loss of funding from the federal government. By 2000, all states had adopted laws requiring notification to individuals and organizations.

The existing notification statutes vary in their scope and level of detail. However, four models have emerged that typify existing laws:

1. An agency is identified as determining the level of risk posed by the offender and then implements the notification plan on the basis of that level of risk. Frequently, the notification plan has three levels or requirements, depending on the offender risk:
   - The first level may involve notification of only selected organizations.
   - The second level adds community residents.
   - The third level includes the media.
2. Some state statutes stipulate which type of offender is subject to notification and what notification methods to use. Under this model, a state agency may carry out the notification but plays no role in how notification will be implemented.
3. The offenders must do the actual notification, although they may be supervised by a criminal justice agency.
4. The burden is on the community organizations and individuals to take the initiative to request information about whether a sex offender is living in their community.

Source: Harvey Wallace & Cliff Roberson, *Family Violence*, 7th ed., Columbus, OH: Pearson.

The warning signs of the disorder include repeated hospitalizations and medical evaluations without definitive diagnosis; inappropriate symptoms and/or medical signs that are inconsistent; signs and symptoms that disappear when away from the parent; a parent who welcomes medical tests of the child, even if they are painful; increased parental uneasiness as the child recovers; and a parent who is less concerned with the child's health and more concerned about spending time with hospital staff.[57]

Today, professionals in the field have come to the conclusion that Munchausen syndrome by proxy is of continuing concern. Some authorities predict that 10 percent of these child victims will die at the hands of their parents.[58] Professionals in the field must recognize this form of child victimization and respond accordingly.

Ritual Abuse

On a daily basis, we are beginning to hear tales of horror and disgust involving children being victimized in so-called satanic cults. Adults who were victims are coming forward and shedding light on this new form of family violence. Just as we were slow in accepting the fact that fathers were molesting their young daughters, so are we as a society hesitant to believe that many of the described practices of ritualistic abuse occur. Child abuse, neglect, and sexual molestation are difficult to accept, but satanic ritualistic abuse not only causes harm to our children, but it also strikes a cord in our collective consciousness as to the evil that is perpetrated by our species. It is for these reasons that we must examine this controversial and highly emotional issue.

Professionals are only now beginning to treat survivors of ritualistic abuse. However, controversy rages as to the validity of many of the claims made by these survivors and to the extent of their abuse. Other scholarly works in the field are silent or only briefly touch on this new issue.[59] Even though this is a relatively new form of family violence and we are still researching its causes and consequences, it is included in this textbook for purposes of familiarizing students with the general nature and types of ritualistic abuse.

The 1960s and 1970s were decades of rebellion in the United States. The Age of Aquarius was upon us. The concept of mind-expanding drugs gained widespread acceptance. During this period of change, it was popular to question authority and beliefs. The advent of birth control, the first stirrings of the women's movement, and the breakdown of traditional roles all combined to force change in America. Magic, free love, and drugs were accepted tenets in our life.

During this period, Anton LaVey established the Church of Satan and drafted *The Satanic Bible*. Although he was denounced as a fraud by some, LaVey had a far greater impact than most people were willing to admit.[60]

In the late 1980s, tales began to surface of massive sexual abuse at daycare centers. Americans were angered and repulsed by allegations of ritualistic child abuse allegedly perpetrated on scores of preschool children by Peggy McMartin Buckey and her son, Raymond Buckey, at the Virginia McMartin Preschool in Manhattan Beach, California. Several children testified that they had been subjected to satanic rituals, including animal sacrifices and sexual abuse inside churches. After one of the longest and most expensive trials in the United States, all the defendants were acquitted. The defendants were found not guilty. Most scholars feel that the reports of abuse were either false or without foundations. The role that the media played has been widely criticized. It appears that the media treatment of the investigation was probably based on the desire of the media to generate commercial revenues. A review of the case and surrounding issues is a learning experience in ethics of investigation and what not to do when investigating claims of child sexual abuse. Many scholars believe that the McMartin case publicity also resulted in more religious fanaticism.

Because of the media coverage, many day care centers were forced to close their doors after insurance companies dramatically raised liability insurance rates. Early publicity surrounding the McMartin investigation also spawned a rash of charges against day care providers elsewhere, many of which proved to be unsubstantiated.

One of the positive things that resulted from the investigation was the need to refrain from using leading questions and the need to use professional techniques in questioning children. As one expert noted, young children are vulnerable to "suggestive questioning," in which the interviewer coaches a child into saying things that incriminate the accused person.

The nature and extent of allegations of sexual abuse of children in day care settings in recent years is a controversial subject among clinicians. Cases of sexual abuse in day care often involve

Excerpts from the California case of *People v. Michael Luis Grant* 2012 WL 1437453 (Cal. App. 6 Dist. 2012)

The appellate judge restated a witness's testimony as follows: Dr. Abbott testified that open-ended questions are better for eliciting information from children. Research shows that "yes" or "no" questions tend to lead to more errors with respect to the information that is provided because children tend to simply answer "yes" or "no" rather than providing more detailed information. Moreover, to the extent the "yes" or "no" question contains false information, "it increases the probability of a child assenting to false or misleading information that may be contained in the question."

In addition, children are generally more susceptible to coaching or leading questions coming from adults than from other children. Even if the information conflicts with the child's recollection of the event, the child will "often acquiesce to what the adult says because [children] put so much trust in what adults think and what adults say." The child may then incorporate that false or misleading information into the child's memory of the events. Repeating the same question to a child also raises an issue. "Typically when children are asked the same question more than once in an interview, there is a tendency for them to interpret the repeat question as their answer being wrong to the earlier question." Thus the information provided by the child to the repeat question may be inaccurate. False information may also be provided by a child due to "negative stereotyping." If the interviewer or another person related to the child provides negative information about the suspect, "children will often elaborate on their recall of the event with false information consistent with the negative stereotype that's being presented about the suspect."

California case of People v. Michael Luis Grant 2012 WL 1437453 (Cal. App. 6 Dist. 2012).

numerous factors that differ from what clinicians are typically confronted with in cases of intra-familial sexual abuse. These factors include the young age of the child victims, the involvement of multiple victims and multiple perpetrators, women as perpetrators, use of extreme threats, and in some cases ritualistic activities.[61]

Ritualistic child abuse in day care centers is a particularly disturbing type of reported day care center abuse. Children who have been ritualistically abused describe participation in group ceremonies; use of chants and songs; adults dressed in costumes and masks; threats with super-natural powers often involving Satan or demons; the sacrifice of animals; the ingestion of blood, feces, and urine; and murders.[62]

The definition of *ritualistic child abuse* is still evolving. One of the most cited definitions was established by the Los Angeles County Commission for Women. This commission set forth the following definition of **ritual abuse:**

> A brutal form of abuse of children consisting of physical, sexual, and psychological abuse, and involving the use of rituals. Ritual does not necessarily mean satanic. However, most survivors state that they were ritually abused as part of satanic worship for the purpose of indoctrinating them into satanic beliefs and practices. Ritual abuse rarely consists of a single episode. It usually involves repeated abuse over an extended period of time.[63]

As the definition states, ritualistic child abuse does not have to involve religion. However, most of the survivors claim that the ritualistic abuse was definitely tied to satanic worship. All rituals are not evil. The word *ritual* is defined simply as the established form for a ceremony, a system of rites, and any formal and customarily repeated act or series of acts.[64] It is only when ritual is combined with abuse that we as a society can intervene. We have established that ritualistic child abuse involves long-term repeated abuse of the most severe form. These abuses may be inflicted and believed justified because of certain tenets held by the cult or organization.

It would be easy to explain satanism as the creation of a deranged mind. Doing so would permit us to dismiss it as something out of the ordinary so that it does not bear thinking about, except in a curious nonanalytical way. But this approach does not allow for a complete under-standing of this form of family violence. Although historians still dispute the historic nature and extent of satanism and many present-day scholars continue to discount stories of ritualistic child abuse, the fact remains that more people are coming forward and claiming to be victims of this type of abuse. It is therefore imperative that professionals in the field have a general understanding of ritualistic abuse.

Who Reports Child Abuse?

For 2010, three-fifths of reports of alleged child abuse and neglect were made by professionals. The term "professional" means that the person had contact with the alleged child maltreatment victim as part of the report source's job. This term includes teachers, police officers, lawyers, and social services staff. "Other" and unknown report sources submitted 13.7 percent of reports. The remaining reports were made by nonprofessionals, including friends, neighbors, and relatives:

- The three largest percentages of report sources were from such professionals as teachers (16.4 percent), law enforcement and legal personnel (16.7 percent), and social services staff (11.5 percent).

- Anonymous sources (9.0 percent), other relatives (7.0 percent), parents (6.8 percent), and friends and neighbors (4.4 percent), accounted for nearly all of the nonprofessional reporters.

Source: U.S. Department of Health & Human Services, Administration for Children and Families, Administration on Children, Youth and Families Children's Bureau (2012) "Child Maltreatment Report." available at their Web site http://www.acf.hhs.gov/programs/cb/stats_research/index.htm#can. And Harvey Wallace & Cliff Roberson, (2013) Family Violence, 7th ed. Columbus, OH:Pearson.

Summary

At this stage in the development of our society, we cannot prevent all forms of child abuse, so we must be alert to its existence and understand some of the more common theories on how and why it occurs. We have won half the battle if we are aware that child abuse occurs in all segments of our society. On the other hand, we must be willing to accept reasonable explanations of injuries. Children are active human beings—as such they will trip, fall, and run into objects. Our goal is to be able to distinguish between a normal injury and a non-accidental one. This ability may save a child's life.

In many instances, there is no clear line between simply poor parenting and neglect. Each situation must be evaluated on its own merits, and professionals must look at the totality of the circumstances in determining whether the child is a victim of neglect. The causes of neglect are varied and do not simply rest on the assumption that poverty is the cause. The rich and famous can, and do, subject their children to acts that are clearly child neglect.

Child sexual abuse is one of the most emotional areas of family violence. It is a crime that occurs in secret and may last only moments or for years. Even the definition of child sexual abuse is shrouded in controversy. Although we cannot explain why it occurs, some scholars have established certain theories or characteristics regarding child sexual abuse.

Unlike other forms of child abuse, sexual molestation may not leave scars that are visible to other persons. Sexual abuse in children takes many forms. Scholars have established certain steps or a progression in the nonviolent sexual abuse of children. These include a gradual increase in sexual activity culminating in intercourse.

The consequences of child sexual abuse are traumatic and long lasting, and various scholars have attempted to study the ramification of this type of child maltreatment. Although disagreement exists among these authorities, all agree that it is a serious problem that must be studied and hopefully a solution found to ease the pain of the survivors of sexual abuse.

The victimization of children is an emotional and complex topic. Not only are children kidnapped, raped, and killed by strangers, sometimes they face a worse fate in their own homes. Understanding the types, extent, and theories surrounding child abuse will benefit any professional who works in the criminal justice field.

Key Terms

Physical child abuse may be defined as any act that results in a nonaccidental physical injury by a person who has care, custody, or control of a child.

Child neglect is the negligent treatment or maltreatment of a child by a parent or caretaker under circumstances that indicate harm or threatened harm to the child's health or welfare.

Child sexual abuse is sexual exploitation or sexual activities with children under circumstances that indicate that the child's health or welfare is harmed or threatened.

Intrafamilial sexual abuse includes incest and refers to any type of exploitative sexual contact that occurs between relatives.

Extrafamilial sexual abuse refers to exploitative sexual contact with perpetrators who may be known to the child (neighbors, babysitters, live-in partners) or unknown to the child.

Intergenerational* transmission *of violence theory asserts that violent behavior is learned within the family and bequeathed from one generation to the next.

Psychopathological model stresses the characteristics of the abuser as the primary cause of abuse. The abuser's personality predisposes the abuser to injure the child.

Interactional model views child abuse as a result of a dysfunctional system.

Environmental–sociological–cultural model views child abuse as a result of stresses in society that are the primary causes of abuse.

Economic theory suggests that neglect is caused by stress as a result of living in poverty.

Ecological theory views the family behavior and neglect as a result of social causes.

Personalistic theory attributes child neglect to individual personality characteristics of the caretakers.

Four preconditions model of sexual abuse establishes preconditions that create a personal and social context for expressing sexually abusive behaviors.

Sibling abuse is any form of physical, mental, or sexual abuse inflicted by one child in a family unit upon another.

Child is defined as a person under the age of legal majority. This age is typically stated to be eighteen.

Munchausen syndrome by proxy is a psychiatric disorder whereby individuals intentionally produce physical symptoms of illness in their children.

Ritual abuse is a brutal form of abuse of children consisting of physical, sexual, and psychological abuse, and involving the use of rituals. Ritual does not necessarily mean satanic. However, most survivors state that they were ritually abused as part of satanic worship for the purpose of indoctrinating them into satanic beliefs and practices. Ritual abuse rarely consists of a single episode. It usually involves repeated abuse over an extended period of time.

Discussion Questions

1. If a child is injured and the physician is uncertain of whether the injury is physical child abuse, should the physician alert the police? Why? Why not? Would it make any difference if the physician knew the parents and had been to their home for a social event?
2. What is the most serious form of physical child abuse? Why?
3. If a child has been seriously injured by his mother, should that child ever be returned to the mother's care? Why?
4. Should convicted child abusers be required to inform all social partners of their crimes? What if the criminal is dating someone who has small children and she asks him to watch her children while she goes to work for the day?
5. On the basis of your reading, what is the single most important cause of neglect? Why?
6. On the basis of your reading of this chapter, can you provide a more comprehensive definition of child sexual abuse? What about a more specific definition?
7. If you were a professional working in an environment that includes young children and you observed a child exhibiting symptoms that led you to suspect child sexual abuse, what would you do?
8. Should we punish or treat child molesters? Because some would argue that you can never cure a pedophile, does this mean that we should lock the offender up forever?

Suggested Readings

Vincent B. Van Hasselt et al., eds., *Handbook of Family Violence* (Plenum Press, New York) 1988.
R. T. Ammerman & M. Hersen, *Assessment of Family Violence* (John Wiley & Sons, New York) 1992.
R. Helfer & C. H. Kempe, eds., *The Battered Child,* 2nd ed. (University of Chicago Press, Chicago) 1974.
G. Gerber, C. Ross, & E. Zigler, eds., *Child Abuse: An Agenda for Action* (Oxford University Press, New York) 1980.
R. Ammerman & M. Hersen, eds., *Case Studies in Family Violence* (Plenum Press, New York) 1991.
D. Cicchetti & V. Carlson, eds., *Child Maltreatment* (Cambridge University Press, Cambridge, Mass.) 1989.
J. L. Mullings, J. W. Marquart, & D. J. Hartley, eds., *The Victimization of Children* (Hawthorn Press, New York) 2003.
L. A. Fontes, *Child Abuse and Culture: Working with Diverse Families* (The Guilford Press, New York) 2005.
Child Physical and Sexual Abuse: Guidelines for Treatment (National Crime Victims Research Center and Center for Sexual Assault and Traumatic Stress, Charleston, S.C.) 2004.

T. P. Doyle, A. W. R. Sipe, & P. J. Wall, *Sex, Priests, and Secret Codes: The Catholic Church's 2000-Year Paper Trail of Sexual Abuse* (Bonus Books, Los Angeles, Calif.) 2006.
J. E. B. Myers, *Meyers on Evidence in Child, Domestic and Elder Abuse* (Aspen Publishers, New York) 2005.
D. Finkelhor, *Child Sexual Abuse: New Theories and Research* (Free Press, New York) 1984.
D. G. Kilpatrick, C. N. Edmonds, & A.K. Seymour, *Rape in America: A Report to the Nation* (National Victims Center, Arlington, Va.) 1992.
Cynthia Crosson Tower, *Understanding Child Abuse and Neglect,* 2nd ed. (Allyn & Bacon, Boston) 1993.
N. Polansky, M. Chambers, E. Buttenwieser, & D. Williams, *Damaged Parents: An Anatomy of Child Neglect* (University of Chicago Press, Chicago) 1981.
M. A. Straus, R. J. Gelles, & S. K. Steinmetz, *Behind Closed Doors: Violence in the American Family* (Doubleday, New York) 1980.
D. K. Sakheim & S. E. Devine, *Out of Darkness* (Lexington Books, New York) 1992.

Endnotes

1. See, for example, Vincent B. Van Hasselt et al., eds., *Handbook of Family Violence* (Plenum Press, New York) 1988.
2. R. T. Ammerman & M. Hersen, *Assessment of Family Violence* (John Wiley & Sons, New York) 1992.
3. J. Meyers, *Evidence in Child Abuse and Neglect,* 2nd ed. (John Wiley & Sons, New York) 1992.
4. This is a shortened version of the definition contained in the Child Abuse Prevention and Treatment Act of 1974, which is one of the most widely adopted statutes defining child sexual abuse.
5. D. A. Wolfe, V. V. Wolfe, & C. L. Best, "Child Victims of Sexual Assault," in V. B. Van Hasselt, R. L. Morrison,

A. S. Bellack, & M. Hersen, eds., *Handbook of Family Violence* (Plenum Press, New York) 1988.

6. J. R. Conte, "Victims of Child Sexual Abuse," in R. T. Ammerman & M. Hersen, eds., *Treatment of Family Violence* (John Wiley & Sons, New York) 1990, pp. 64–65.

7. S. Radbill, "A History of Child Abuse and Infanticide," in R. Helfer & C. H. Kempe, eds., *The Battered Child,* 2nd ed. (University of Chicago Press, Chicago) 1974.

8. C. F. Potter, "Infanticides," in M. Leach, ed., *Dictionary of Folklore, Mythology and Legend,* vol. 1 (Funk & Wagnalls, New York) 1949.

9. N. C. Sorel, *Ever Since Eve: Personal Reflections on Childbirth* (Oxford University Press, New York) 1984.

10. R. Uviler, "Save Them from Their Saviors: The Constitutional Rights in the Family," in G. Gerber, C. Ross, & E. Zigler, eds., *Child Abuse: An Agenda for Action* (Oxford University Press, New York) 1980, pp. 147–155.

11. U.S. Department of Justice, Bureau of Justice Statistics, *Criminal Victimization in the United States, 1987* (Government Printing Office, Washington, D.C.) 1989, Table 4.

12. Arthur H. Green, "Child Neglect," in R. Ammerman & M. Hersen, eds., *Case Studies in Family Violence* (Plenum Press, New York) 1991, p. 135.

13. C. R. Hartman & A. W. Burgess, "Sexual Abuse in Children: Causes and Consequences," in D. Cicchetti & V. Carlson, eds., *Child Maltreatment* (Cambridge University Press, Cambridge, Mass.) 1989, p. 98–99.

14. D. G. Kilpatrick, C. N. Edmonds, & A. K. Seymour, *Rape in America: A Report to the Nation* (National Victims Center, Arlington, Va.) 1992.

15. Hartman & Burgess, "Sexual Abuse of Children," pp. 98–99.

16. Lauren Perrotto, "Prospective vs. Retrospective in Child Fatality Review," Unified Response, Inter-Agency Council on Child Abuse and Neglect Associates (Winter 2004), El Monte, Calif.

17. L. J. Siegal, *Criminology,* 3rd ed. (West Publishing Co., St. Paul, Minn.) 1989, p. 188.

18. B. Steele & V. Pollock, "A Psychiatric Study of Parents Who Abuse Infants and Small Children," in R. Helfer & C. H. Kempe, eds., *The Battered Child Syndrome* (University of Chicago Press, Chicago) 1968. It is interesting to note that later editions of this classic book on child abuse do not contain the article. For example, see the 4th edition published in 1987.

19. M. A. Straus, "Family Patterns in a Nationally Representative Sample," 3 *International Journal of Child Abuse and Neglect,* 23 (1979).

20. R. Hunter & N. Kilstrom, "Breaking the Cycle in Abusive Families," 136 *American Journal of Psychiatry,* 1320 (1979).

21. B. England & D. Jacobvitz, "Intergenerational Continuity of Parental Abuse: Causes and Consequences." Paper presented at the Conference on Biosocial Perspectives in Abuse and Neglect, York, Maine (1984).

22. C. Cappell & R. B. Heiner, "The Intergenerational Transmission of Family Aggression," 5(2) *Journal of Family Violence,* 135 (1990).

23. K. A. Dodge, J. E. Bates, & G. S. Pettit, "Mechanisms in the Cycle of Violence," 250 *Science,* 1678 (December 1990).

24. Ibid. at p. 1681.

25. C. S. Widom, "The Cycle of Violence," *Research in Brief, National Institute of Justice* (U.S. Department of Justice, Washington, D.C.) October 1992.

26. Cynthia Crosson Tower, *Understanding Child Abuse and Neglect,* 2nd ed. (Allyn & Bacon, Boston) 1993.

27. B. Justice & R. Justice, *The Abusing Family* (Human Services Press, New York) 1976, p. 37.

28. See J. D. Delsordo, "Protective Casework for Abused Children," 10 *Children,* 213–218 (1963).

29. H. P. Martin, ed., *The Abused Child* (Ballinger, Cambridge, Mass.) 1976.

30. M. Lynch, "Risk Factors in the Child: A Study of Abused Children and Their Siblings," in H. P. Martin, ed., *The Abused Child* (Ballinger, Cambridge, Mass.) 1976, pp. 43–56.

31. N. Polansky, M. Chambers, E. Buttenwieser, & D. Williams, *Damaged Parents: An Anatomy of Child Neglect* (University of Chicago Press, Chicago) 1981, p. 21.

32. See L. Young, *Wednesday's Children* (McGraw-Hill, New York) 1964; and S. N. Katz, *When Parents Fail* (Beacon Press, Boston) 1971.

33. I. Wolock & B. Horowitz, "Child Maltreatment and Maternal Deprivation among AFDC Families," 53 *Social Service Review,* 175–184 (1979).

34. D. J. Hansen & V. M. MacMillan, "Behavioral Assessment of Child Abuse and Neglectful Families: Recent Development and Current Issues," 14 *Behavior Modification,* 225–278 (1990).

35. H. B. Cantwell, "Child Neglect," in C. H. Kempe and R. E. Helfer, eds., *The Battered Child,* (University of Chicago Press, Chicago) 1980, pp. 183–197.

36. See J. Conti, "The Effects of Sexual Abuse on Children: A Critique and Suggestions for Future Research," 10 *Victimology: An International Journal,* 110–130 (1985); and J. Conti, I. Berliner, & J. Schurman, "The Impact of Sexual Abuse on Children: Final Report," Available from the authors at the University of Chicago, 969 E. 60th Street, Chicago, Ill. 60637.

37. D. Finkelhor, *Child Sexual Abuse: New Theories and Research* (Free Press, New York) 1984.

38. E. Porter, *Treating the Young Male Victims of Sexual Assault* (Safer Society Press, Syracuse, N.Y.) 1986.

39. A. N. Groth, *Men Who Rape* (Plenum Press, New York) 1979.

40. D. J. Gelinas, "The Persisting Negative Effects of Incest," 46 *Psychiatry,* 312–322 (1983).

41. C. A. Courtios, "Studying and Counseling Women with Past Incest Experience," 5 *Victimology: An International Journal,* 322–334 (1980).

42. D. Finkelhor, *Child Sexual Abuse.* See note #51 (1984) and E. Porter, *Treating the Young Male Victim of Sexual Assault.* See note #45 (1986).

43. D. Finkelhor, *Child Sexual Abuse* (Free Press, New York) 1984.

44. Tower, *Understanding Child Abuse and Neglect*, 1993.

45. Groth, *Men Who Rape*, 1979.

46. E. D. Farber, J. Showers, C. F. Johnson, J. A. Joseph, & L. Oshins, "The Sexual Abuse of Children: A Comparison of Male and Female Victims," 13 *Journal of Clinical Child Psychology*, 294–297 (1984).

47. Richard J. Gelles & Claire Pedrick Cornell, *Intimate Violence in Families*, 2nd ed. (Sage, Newbury Park, Calif.) 1990, p. 85.

48. See M. Bard, "The Study and Modification of Intrafamily Violence," in J. L. Singer, ed., *The Control of Aggression and Violence* (Academic Press, New York) 1971 for study of homicides in Philadelphia; M. Wolfgang, *Patterns in Criminal Homicide* (John Wiley, New York) 1958 for the study of homicides in New York.

49. S. K. Steinmetz, *The Cycle of Violence: Assertive, Aggressive, and Abusive Family Interaction* (Praeger, New York) 1971.

50. "Battered Families: A Growing Nightmare," *U.S. News & World Report*, 60–61 (January 15, 1979).

51. M. A. Straus, R. J. Gelles, & S. K. Steinmetz, *Behind Closed Doors: Violence in the American Family* (Doubleday, New York) 1980.

52. S. K. Steinmetz, "A Cross-Cultural Comparison of Sibling Violence," 2(3/4) *International Journal of Family Psychiatry*, 337–351 (1981).

53. See for example, David D. P. Jones, "The Syndrome of Munchausen by Proxy," 18 *Child Abuse and Neglect*, 769 (1994).

54. E. J. Kudsk & J. A. Nolan, "Munchausen Syndrome by Proxy: The Case for Adult Victims," paper presented at the annual meeting of Academy of Criminal Justice Sciences, Boston (March 1995).

55. J. Money, "Munchausen's Syndrome by Proxy: Update," 11(4) *Journal of Pediatric Psychology*, 583 (November 1986) discussing an earlier article that appeared in the *Bulletin of the American Academy of Psychiatry and the Law in 1976*.

56. R. Meadow, "Munchausen Syndrome by Proxy: The Hinterland of Child Abuse," 2 *The Lancet*, 351 (1977).

57. S. J. Boros & L. C. Brubaker, "Munchausen Syndrome by Proxy," *FBI Law Enforcement Bulletin*, 16 (June 1992).

58. Ibid. at p. 20.

59. See D. Cicchetti & Vicki Carlson, eds., *Child Maltreatment* (Cambridge University Press, Cambridge, Mass.) 1989; Tower, *Understanding Child Abuse and Neglect*, 1993; Ammerman & Hersen, *Assessment of Family Violence* 1992, which do not discuss ritual abuse; and compare C. C. Kent, "Ritual Abuse," in R. T. Ammerman & M. Hersen, eds., *Case Studies in Family Violence* (Plenum Press, New York) 1991; and D. K. Sakheim & S. E. Devine, *Out of Darkness* (Lexington Books, New York) 1992, which covers the entire realm of ritualistic abuse.

60. C. Raschke, *Painted Black: Satanic Crime in America*, p. 123.

61. For an excellent discussion of this area, see S. J. Kelly, R. Brant & J. Waterman, "Sexual Abuse of Children in Day Care Centers," 17 *Child Abuse & Neglect*, 71–89 (1993).

62. Ibid.

63. *Ritual Abuse: Definitions, Glossary, the Use of Mind Control* (Ritual Abuse Task Force, Los Angeles County Commission for Women, Calif.) September 15, 1989.

64. *Webster's Ninth New Collegiate Dictionary* (Merriam-Webster Inc., Springfield, Mass.) 1987, p. 1018.

Elder Victims

Chapter Outline

LEARNING OBJECTIVES

After reading this chapter, you should be able to:

- Discuss the nature and extent of elder abuse in the United States
- Define issues that affect the validity of examining the problem of elder abuse
- Explain the different causation theories of elder abuse
- Describe the various types of criminal victimizations and their impact on elders

ELDER ABUSE

Although we became aware of certain forms of family violence in the 1960s and 1970s, it was not until the 1980s that the plight of elder victims entered our national consciousness as a problem that must be dealt with. One of the first studies dealing with elder abuse was published in 1979. Block and Sinnott entitled their work *The Battered Elder Syndrome: An Exploratory Study*. They contacted twenty-four agencies in Maryland and surveyed 427 professionals and 443 elders. They found twenty-six cases of elder abuse. Unfortunately, the study went no further, but it was the first step in the long process of recognizing that elders can be victims of family violence.[1] By 1988, the research examining elder abuse consisted of more than 200 research papers.[2] Today, that number continues to expand rapidly. Although several problems exist in the study of elder abuse, defining the term itself and determining its extent are two of the most controversial and difficult issues to resolve.

Extent of the Problem

How pervasive is elder abuse? Domestic elder abuse, like other forms of family violence, occurs behind closed doors in the privacy of the home. One significant study of elder abuse published by Pillemer and Finkelhor involved 2,020 Boston elders who were sixty-five and older and living on their own or with their families. This research found a rate of thirty-two abused elders per thousand. The results of this survey would translate into more than one million abused elders in the United States in one year.[3]

Estimates on the nature, type, and prevalence of elder abuse continue to vary widely. One congressional committee estimated that 1.5 million cases of elder abuse occur each year.[4] More shocking is the fact that known numbers of elder abuse has steadily increased since 1980.[5] Callahan claims that between 4 and 10 percent of all elders suffer abuse.[6] Other researchers believe the figure is higher, contending that only one in six incidents of elder abuse is ever reported to the authorities.[7]

The National Committee for the Prevention of Elder Abuse and the National Adult Protective Services Association released a survey of *Abuse of Adults Age 60+*.[8] The findings show an alarming 19.7 percent increase in the total number of reported cases of elder and vulnerable adult abuse and neglect cases. About 52 percent of the perpetrators of abuse were female. The most common relationship of the victims to the perpetrators was parent–adult child.

Controversy continues regarding who is the abused and who is the abuser—is it the children who abuse the parents? Or the elder's wife? Or the husband? This confusion is further illustrated by the fact that some authorities believe victims are primarily women over the age of seventy-five,[9] whereas others believe that the wife is the one who perpetrates the abuse.[10] Other scholars argue that adult children inflict abuse on their parents. The Boston survey indicated that elders were abused more by their spouses than by their children. This result is somewhat skewed once

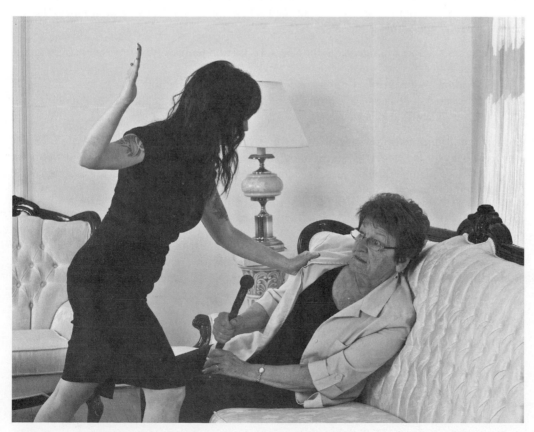

A daughter abusing her elderly mother is not an uncommon occurrence.
(© O Driscoll Imaging/Shutterstock)

FOCUS

What Should *I* Do if I Suspect Elder Abuse?

Report Your Concerns.
Remember: Most cases of elder abuse go undetected. Don't assume that someone has already reported a suspicious situation.

To report suspected abuse in the community, contact your local Adult Protective Services agency. For state reporting numbers, visit the NCEA Web site or call the *Eldercare Locator* at **1-800-677-1116.**

If you or someone you know is in a life-threatening situation or immediate danger, contact 911 or the local police or sheriff's department.

To report suspected abuse in a nursing home or other long-term care facility, contact your state-specific agency. To find your local listing, visit the Long-Term Care Ombudsman Web site.

---

it is understood that elders live with spouses more than adult children, and therefore the chance is greater of being abused by a spouse than by an adult child. Although both men and women may be victims of elder abuse, the abuse inflicted by husbands is more severe than that inflicted by wives. More research is necessary to determine the extent and nature of elder abuse, but the central issue is that abuse is likely to be inflicted by the people with whom the elder is living.

There is a continuing failure to report and act on this form of abuse, and two major factors that may contribute to this failure are:

1. There is a failure to understand the size, severity, and nature of the problem because of the conflicting definitions of elder abuse.
2. The number of controlled studies and the case reporting methods that are used in most of the research in this area have produced difficulties in estimating the true extent of the various acts of abuse and neglect.[11]

In addition, methodology and sampling procedures differ from study to study. Some research focus on the elderly population, other studies examine agency records, and still other investigations poll professionals. As a result, there are no definitive figures that are accepted by all scholars and researchers.

Definition

The term *elder abuse* was first used during congressional hearings in the late 1970s. The House Select Committee on Aging, chaired by Representative Claude Pepper (the Pepper Commission), examined the mistreatment of the elderly and introduced the term *elder abuse* to the nation.[12] However, coining a term does not always clearly define the parameters for the scholars and professionals trying to do the research.

Some scholars, when examining elder abuse, have included persons under the age of sixty in their research, whereas others simply include everyone who is over the age of sixty regardless of the circumstances.[13] Well-respected authorities defined elder abuse as occurring only between those who share a residence with the victim, and in other studies out-of-home caretakers were included.[14] The debate, confusion, and inability to agree on any acceptable conceptual framework from which to study elder abuse continue to cause problems in this area.

In an effort to clarify this confusion, some authorities attempted to develop a list of definitions involving abuse of the elderly by establishing typologies. Unfortunately, these typologies lacked uniformity and resulted in more confusion. Hudson and Johnson pointed out that

FOCUS

Common Types of Elder Abuse Recognized by the National Center on Elder Abuse

Physical abuse: Use of force to threaten or physically injure a vulnerable elder

Emotional abuse: Verbal attacks, threats, rejection, isolation, or belittling acts that cause or could cause mental anguish, pain, or distress to a senior

Sexual abuse: Sexual contact that is forced, tricked, threatened, or otherwise coerced upon a vulnerable elder, including anyone who is unable to grant consent

Exploitation: Theft, fraud, misuse, or neglect of authority, and use of undue influence as a lever to gain control over an older person's money or property

Neglect: A caregiver's failure or refusal to provide for a vulnerable elder's safety, physical, or emotional needs

Abandonment: Desertion of a frail or vulnerable elder by anyone with a duty of care

Self-neglect: An inability to understand the consequences of one's own actions or inaction, which leads to, or may lead to, harm or endangerment

some typologies differed considerably in defining neglect, whereas others classified withholding of personal care as physical abuse and/or psychological abuse.[15] As a result of this continuing confusion, other researchers began to attempt to frame the definition of elder abuse from a conceptional perspective. For example, some scholars placed the issue of elder abuse within the broad category of inadequate care.[16] However, the same problems that were faced in trying to establish an acceptable typology were present in the effort to conceptualize the whole issue.[17]

Several prominent scholars, including Wolf, Pillemer, and Godkin, subsequently distilled these various definitions down to a multifaceted definition that classified elder abuse into five areas:

1. *Physical abuse* includes the infliction of physical pain or injury, physical coercion, sexual molestation, or physical restraint.
2. *Psychological abuse* includes the infliction of mental anguish.
3. *Material abuse* includes the illegal or improper exploitation and/or use of funds or resources.
4. *Active neglect* includes the refusal or failure to undertake a caretaking obligation.
5. *Passive neglect* includes the refusal or failure to fulfill a caretaking obligation.[18] (See R. S. Wolf & K. A. Pillemer, Helping Elderly Victims: The Reality of Elder Abuse (Columbia University Press, New York) 1989; M. A. Godkin, R. S. Wolf & K. A. Pillemer, "A Case-Comparison Analysis of Elder Abuse and Neglect," 28(3) International Journal of Aging and Human Development, 207–225 (1989)).

This discussion clearly illustrates the difficulty in attempting to define the term *elder abuse* and helps to explain the continuing scholarly debate and controversy. On the basis of this confusion and conflict, a simple, clear definition of elder abuse may not be possible. However, for purposes of consistency with other definitions contained in this textbook, **elder abuse** is defined as conduct that results in the physical, psychological, or material harm, or

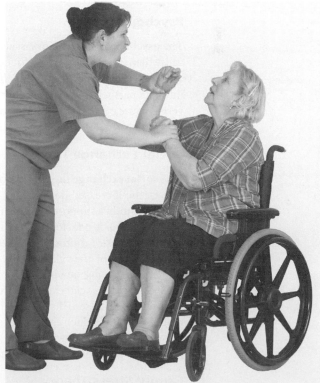

Abuse of the elderly by health care professionals is not unusual.
(© Sylvie Bouchard/Fotolia)

neglect or injury to an elder. This definition applies both to domestic and institutional abuse. **Material** in the context of elder abuse refers to the exploitation or use of resources. An **elder** is a person sixty-five years or older. The initial age determination of sixty-five years is based on common acceptance of that age by most authorities, scholars, and professionals.[19] This age group may be further subdivided into those between sixty-five and seventy-five who are called the young-old and those above seventy-five who are referred to as the old-old.[20]

Elder abuse can occur in a domestic or institutional setting. Pillemer and Moore explained that despite two decades of state and federal regulation of nursing homes, abuse of the elderly still occurs on a regular basis.[21] The focus of this section will be on the domestic abuse aspect of this form of violence, as more research has been done in this area. However, abuse of the elderly in nursing homes and long-term care institutions is a fact of modern life and should not be forgotten or overlooked when considering the overall plight of the elderly in our society.

THEORIES OF ELDER ABUSE

Authorities may disagree as to the exact cause of elder abuse, but they generally agree that it is similar to other forms of family violence and that it crosses all social and economic lines. Most researchers agree that elder abuse is not an isolated event; rather it is a repetitive pattern of acts by the abuser toward the victim.

Intergenerational Transmission of Violence Theory

The intergenerational transmission of violence theory or cycle of violence theory was discussed in detail in Chapter 9. Galbraith argues that it has proven ineffective in predicting elder abuse.[22] Wolf and Pillemer also point out that those who abuse elders do not necessarily grow up in families characterized by violence.[23]

Psychopathology

The **psychopathology theory** is based on the premise that abusers suffer from mental disorders that cause them to be violent. Wolf found a high prevalence of mental illness among elder abusers.[24] This approach seems to have greater validity in explaining elder abuse than in explaining either child or intimate partner abuse. Researchers have found psychopathology present in cases of physical and verbal abuse of elders.[25] Other scholars indicate that a number of abusers have had previous hospitalizations for serious psychiatric disorders, such as schizophrenia and other psychoses.[26]

Social Exchange Theory

One **social exchange theory** assumes that dependency in relationships contributes to elder abuse; that is, the increased dependency of the victim on the abuser results in acts of violence. Other research studies support this theory.[27] The abuser's financial dependency on the victim also has been found to be a factor in a number of studies of elder abuse.[28]

The loss of mutual resources between the elder and the caretaker also contributes to the deterioration of the relationship. This results in the caretaker perceiving the relationship as unfair, with a subsequent increase in hostility toward the elder.[29]

A second social exchange theory assumes that the dependency of the abuser on the elder victim causes abuse. This concept focuses on adult children becoming dependent on the elder for material rewards, such as housing and finances. Because these children perceive themselves to be as weak as and less powerful than the elder, abusing the elder is a way to equalize the balance of power and gain control over the relationship.[30]

Family Stress Theory

The family stress theory is one of the most widely accepted theories of elder abuse.[31] The **family stress theory** is based on the premise that providing care for an elder induces stress within the family. This stress may take many forms, including economic hardship, loss of sleep, intrusions into normal family privacy routines, and other activities that may cause the caregiver to feel resentment toward the elder. Adult children may have to give up economic security to provide care for an aged parent or other close relative. In addition, the physical toll of caring for an elderly ill person can sometimes overwhelm the adult child, which results in a loss of control and subsequent abuse.[32] However, even this theory is subject to controversy. Phillips suggests that stress levels may not be as important a factor in causing elder abuse as previously believed.[33]

Neutralization Theory

The **neutralization theory** was originally developed by Sykes and Matza to explain juvenile delinquency in our society.[34] This theory views the delinquent as being affected by the norms and values of a larger social system rather than by a counterculture. This concept holds that delinquents show guilt and shame for their antisocial behavior.[35] To commit criminal or antisocial acts, persons develop techniques of neutralization. These techniques are rationalizations or justifications for their behavior. Matza established five techniques that allow individuals to justify their acts:

1. *Denial of responsibility* The person may claim that something else, such as alcohol, made him commit the criminal act.
2. *Denial of injury* Juveniles may believe that even though they violated the law, no one was really hurt. For example, theft of an automobile is okay because the owner's insurance company will replace it with a new model anyway.
3. *Denial of victim* Delinquents may claim that the victim had it coming, and therefore their acts were justified under the circumstances.
4. *Condemnation of the condemners* Juveniles may shift the blame to others, calling them corrupt or incompetent.
5. *Appeal to higher loyalty* Some offenders claim that they violated the law to satisfy a higher authority or goal.

FOCUS
Triads

Community Involvement in Fighting Elder Victimization

The concept that emphasizes community cooperation in combating elder victimization is succeeding in a number of areas throughout the nation. This innovative concept is the triad program.

Triads are formed when the local police and sheriff's department agree to work cooperatively with senior citizens to prevent the victimization of the elderly in the community. The three groups share ideas and resources to provide programs and training for vulnerable and often fearful elderly citizens.

A triad program usually begins when a police chief, a sheriff, or a leader in the senior citizen community contacts the other two essential participants to discuss a combined effort. Although each entity may already have programs in place to reduce the victimization rate among the elderly, the three-way involvement of triads adds strength, resources, and greater credibility.

Most triads include representatives from agencies that serve older persons, such as the Agency on Aging, senior centers, and Adult Protective Services. Law enforcement leaders then invite seniors and those working with them to serve on an advisory council, often called Seniors and Lawmen Together (SALT).

Some triads establish programs to prevent elder abuse through education and to address the plight of seniors in personal care homes. For example, in Columbus, Georgia, the plight of some seniors in such facilities came to the attention of a very active SALT council. Learning that older residents were suffering from abuse and neglect, the SALT council devised a strategy to investigate specific situations.

To begin, the council enlisted the assistance of the sheriff's office and the police and health departments. Through these agencies, a search warrant of the homes was obtained, proper lodging and care was arranged for those seniors living in unhealthy and unsafe conditions, and a plan for more careful monitoring of such homes was initiated.

The essence of the triad program is cooperation. This program allows the service providers—law enforcement—to work together with the consumers—senior citizens. Through positive programs that affect safety and quality of life, mutual respect and appreciation evolve between the law enforcement community and citizens.

Source: From Betsy Cantrell, "Triad, Reducing Criminal Victimization of the Elderly," *FBI Law Enforcement Bulletin,* 19–23 (February 1994).

Tomita has applied the neutralization theory to elder abuse and suggests that, although it cannot be used to establish a direct cause, it may be viewed as reasons employed by abusers to justify their acts.[36] She examines each technique of neutralization and explains how it is used by the perpetrators to justify their abuse of elders.

1. *Denial of responsibility* In these situations, the abuser claims that the mistreatment was caused by forces beyond his control, such as poverty, bad parents, and so on.
2. *Denial of injury* The abuser rationalizes that the injury was not really that serious, because the victim did not have to go to the emergency room. In material abuse situations, the abuser justifies her actions by stating that the parent can afford to give away property or assets.
3. *Denial of the victim* Abusers may state that the victim does not need help, that he/she is only attempting to gain attention. For example, the abuser may refuse to dress the victim, claiming the victim feigns disability because he/she wants attention, when in reality, the victim cannot dress himself/herself.
4. *Condemnation of the condemners* In these situations, the abuser condemns protective services or other agencies for interfering with the family.
5. *Appeal to higher loyalty* The abuser may believe he/she must act in a certain way to satisfy his spouse. (S. K. Tomita, "The Denial of Elder Mistreatment by Victims and Abusers: The Application of Neutralization Theory," 5(3) Violence and Victims, 171 (1990)).

As this discussion illustrates, several theories attempt to explain why people abuse the elderly. Just as with other causes of family violence, no single theory is universally accepted by all scholars. Continued research is needed in this area to determine if a cause can be established.

ELDER VICTIMIZATION[37]

Even with programs such as triads, the incidence of elder victimization continues to escalate in our society. This section will examine a few of the more common crimes committed against elders. Not only are elders preyed upon by family members because of their frail condition, they are also prime targets for certain kinds of criminals who seek easy targets.

Sexual Assault

For many elderly women who were raised during a time when sexual matters were never discussed publicly, becoming a victim of a sexual assault can be a traumatic experience that the elder is not able to process. In adults age 60 and older, about 1 percent report sexual mistreatment each year. Of those who were sexually abused, about 16 percent reported to police and about 53 percent said they were sexually mistreated by a family member.

Some elders are still surrounded with embarrassment about sexual activity and have never discussed it even with their children. To these elders, the thought of having to discuss sexual acts in public is unthinkable. Many older victims believe it is the worst form of lost dignity. They may experience shame in discussing the case or participating in a medical examination with law enforcement officers present. They may have been required to perform sexual acts that they have never participated in before, which only add to the humiliation.

Elderly rape victims often sustain injuries different from those experienced by younger victims. Vaginal linings are not as elastic as those of younger women because of hormonal changes. This may cause increased sexual trauma, including infections, bruising, and tears that never fully heal. More alarmingly, many elders have brittle bones, such as the pelvis and hips that can be more easily broken or crushed by the weight of the rapist.

Intervention with the elderly is critical and may afford the victims some choices they may not have otherwise had. For example, victim assistance professionals can offer to work with the victim on a relocation plan if that is her desire and she has the financial ability to move from the place of the attack. If the elder agrees, the victim services provider can work with family members to help educate them about the special needs of the victim as a result of the crime. If there is no family, close contact should be maintained with the victim to help increase her feelings of self-worth.

Other Violent Crimes

Elder victims are the least likely to be physically injured during the commission of a violent crime. In a study of elder abuse and mortality, those who reported elder abuse had a mortality rate 2.3 times higher than those who did not report abuse.[38] However, if they are injured, these injuries tend to be more serious because of their frailty and aging bodies. Bones become more brittle with advanced age and break more easily than those of a twenty-year-old. One study points out that when elders are physically injured during a violent crime, they are twice as likely as any other age group to be seriously injured and require hospitalization.[39] However, the elderly as a whole are significantly less likely than younger age groups to become victims of most types of crime, including violent crime.[40] This may be because they are not as mobile and therefore do not go out in public as much as their younger counterparts and therefore are not as easily approached or victimized.

Most homicide victims over the age of sixty-five were killed during the commission of another felony and were more likely to be killed by a stranger. The elderly are also less likely to protect themselves during the incident and may suffer injuries that younger victims would avoid. A purse snatcher may cause a younger victim to stumble and regain her stability, whereas the same incident may cause an elderly victim to fall and break her hip.

Fraud

The elderly are targeted for crimes involving finances more than any other victim population. Of those who reported crimes to the Federal Trade Commission, 14 percent of fraud complaints and 13 percent of identity theft complaints were made by people ages 60 and older.[41] Although elderly victims may not sustain any physical injury as a result of this type of crime, the psychological impact can be devastating. The loss of one's entire life savings can create severe and debilitating depression. Many victims blame themselves for the loss and because of this can suffer additional health problems related to depression such as loss of appetite, decreased interest level, increased withdrawal, and diminished sleep. Some victims feel ashamed that they did not recognize the "con" and become reluctant to report the crime, because they think family members will blame them for mismanagement of their funds and seek to terminate their financial independence.

A majority of the elderly live on fixed incomes, and the impact of a financial crime can be devastating to them. They may lose their life savings and even their homes. This may result in the loss of their independence, which many elderly people value more than money itself.

FOCUS
Financial Abuse of the Elderly

Financial vulnerability is a by-product of aging. The elderly are often forced to live on fixed incomes, which fails to reflect rising costs of living. When inflation is taken into account, some estimate that as many as 40 percent of the elderly do not have enough income.

The financial impact of being a victim of burglary, assault, or robbery can be devastating. The larceny of $100 may mean that an individual goes without food, or medication, or even forfeits his/her apartment because of lack of rent. For example, when one senior's purse was stolen, she lost $100. Her heat and lights were cut off because she could not to pay her utility bills. She remained without heat and lived in candlelight for three additional months because of the extra charges she had to pay to reconnect the utilities.

Burglaries and vandalism cause untold damage and require repair and replacement. Another elderly couple's home and furniture were destroyed by the vandalism that accompanied a burglary of their home. They could not afford to clean or repair it. They were forced to move from the house in which they had lived for thirty-five years. They ended up living in an apartment far from their friends and their neighbors.

FOCUS
National Center on Elder Abuse (Title II)

The National Center on Elder Abuse (NCEA) was established by Section 202(d) of the Older Americans Act of 1965, as amended. The Center was established in 1988 as a national elder abuse resource center. In 1992, NCEA was granted a permanent home as part of the U.S. Department of Health and Human Services by amendments made to Title II of the Older Americans Act (OAA). The NCEA serves as a national resource center dedicated to the prevention of elder mistreatment, and operates as a multidisciplinary consortium of collaborators with expertise in elder abuse, neglect, and exploitation.

The NCEA provides relevant information, materials, and support to enhance state and local efforts to prevent and address elder mistreatment. NCEA disseminates information to professionals and the public, and it provides technical assistance and training to states and to community-based organizations. The NCEA makes available news and resources; collaborates on research; provides consultation, education, and training; identifies and provides information about promising practices and interventions; answers inquiries and requests for information; operates a listserve forum for professionals; and advises on program and policy development. NCEA also facilitates the exchange of strategies for uncovering and prosecuting fraud and scams targeted at seniors.

Victim services providers can provide the elderly and their families with information on the victim's right to file civil actions against the perpetrator. The elderly may need help in rearranging their finances as a result of the loss. The courts should be asked to allow for an expiated payment schedule on any restitution plan. The elderly victim may need the funds now, not three or five years from now.

Burglary

For many of the elderly, the home becomes the center of their world as they gradually lose friends and their own mobility. They retire from jobs, family members begin to die, and outside activities decrease due to increasing physical or mental limitations. This imposed isolation explains, in part, why a majority of the elderly are victimized near or in their homes.

The loss of certain possessions, especially those that have sentimental value, can have a great impact on an older person. The loss of other material items such as televisions can further restrict an elder's outside contact with the world. Many victims may want to relocate after a burglary but may not have the financial ability to do so. Once their home has been invaded, they may never feel safe again.

Victim services providers should work with other organizations in the community to assist elderly victims. The local law enforcement agency may provide advice and assistance in evaluating the elder's home to determine if other points of entry should be made more secure. Neighborhood Watch participants should be alerted to the fact that their neighbor was victimized and to increase their vigilance of any suspicious activity that might involve the perpetrator returning to an "easy target." In addition, every Agency on Aging operates an information and referral line that can refer the elderly to a variety of services.

COMBATING ELDER ABUSE IN THE FUTURE

The number of people over sixty-five years in the United States is growing as baby boomers transition into the age bracket of sixty-five and older. According to a study by the American Society of Pain Educators, "Where people age 65 and older represent 12 percent of the overall population today, they will represent 18 percent in 2025." By the year 2045, seventy-nine million people in the United States will constitute 21 percent of the nation's population over the age of sixty-five (American Society of Pain Educators, *ASPE Membership*). The United States will soon have more elderly people in hospitals, nursing homes, and private homes than ever before.

There was a lot of media attention when the federal Health Care Reform Act of 2010 was enacted. Included in amendments to the act were some significant legislation focusing on elder abuse. The amendments included the Elderly Justice Act, the Nursing Home Transparency and Improvement Act, and the Patient Safety and Abuse Prevention Act.

FOCUS

Elder Justice Act and the Nursing Home Transparency and Improvement Act

The federal health care reform bill of 2010 included the elder justice act, the nursing home transparency and improvement act, the patient safety and abuse prevention act, the class act and provisions designed to improve the ability of people to get needed long-term care services at home. The federal elder justice act for the first time coordinates efforts to prevent elder abuse on a federal level. It also

- Established an elder justice coordinating council to make recommendations to the secretary of health and human services on the coordination of activities of federal, state, local and private agencies, and entities relating to elder abuse, neglect, and exploitation.
- Established a twenty-seven-member advisory board on elder abuse, neglect, and exploitation.
- Adult protective services (aps) funding which provided for the first-time dedicated funding for adult protective services.
- Provided for establishment and support of elder abuse neglect and exploitation forensic centers to develop forensic expertise regarding and provide services relating to elder abuse, neglect, and exploitation.
- Provided grants to support the long-term care ombudsman program and training programs for national organizations and state long-term care ombudsman programs.
- Authorized grants to enhance long-term care staffing through training and recruitment and incentives for individuals seeking or maintaining employment in long-term care, either in a facility or a community-based long-term care entity.
- Requires the immediate reporting to law enforcement of crimes in a long-term care facility and establishes civil monetary penalties for failure to report.
- Provides for penalties for long-term care facilities that retaliate against an employee for filing a complaint against or reporting a long-term care facility that violates reporting requirements.
- Established a nationwide program for national and state background checks on direct patient access employees of long-term care facilities, and provides $160 million in funding.

Nursing Home Transparency and Improvement Act

The nursing home transparency provisions were the first comprehensive improvements in nursing home quality since 1987. When fully implemented, the law will provide consumers a substantial amount of new information about individual facilities.

Key provisions of the act include the following:

- Public disclosure of nursing home owners, operators, and other entities and individuals that provide management, financing, and services to nursing homes.
- Establishment of internal procedures by nursing homes ("compliance and ethics programs") to reduce civil and criminal violations and improve quality assurance.
- Electronic collection of staffing data from payroll records and other verifiable sources and public reporting of hours per resident day of care, turnover, and retention rates.
- Improved public information on nursing home compare, including staffing data for each facility that includes hours of care per resident day, turnover, and retention rates; links to facilities survey reports and plans of correction on state Web sites; summaries of complaints against facilities, including number, type, severity and outcome; a standardized complaint form; and adjudicated criminal violations by facilities and their employees inside the facility, including civil monetary penalties levied against the facility, its employees, contractors, and other agents.
- Establishment of a consumer rights information page on nursing home compare, including services available from the long-term care ombudsman.
- A review of nursing home compare's accuracy, clarity, timeliness, and comprehensiveness and modifications of the site based on the review.
- A government accountability office study of the five-star quality rating system.
- Improved timeliness of survey information made available to the public.
- A requirement for nursing homes to make surveys and complaint investigations for three years available on request and to post a notice that they are available.
- A requirement that states maintain a Web site with information on all nursing homes in the state, including survey reports, complaint investigation reports, plans of correction, and other information that the state or Centers for Medicare or Medicaid services (CMS) considers useful.
- A statutory requirement for a special focus facility program.
- Establishment of a methodology for categorization and public reporting of facilities' expenditures, regardless of source of payment, for direct care (including nursing, therapy, and medical services); indirect care (including housekeeping and dietary services); capital assets; and administrative services.
- Improved complaint handling, including a voluntary standardized form for filing complaints with the survey

(continued)

agency and ombudsman; and protection of residents' legal representatives and other responsible parties from retaliation when they complain about quality of care.

- Escrowing of civil monetary penalties after an independent informal dispute resolution process and pending resolution of further appeals.
- Sixty-day advance notification of facility closure and authorization to continue medicaid payments pending relocation of all residents.
- Dementia care and abuse prevention in nurse aide training programs.
- Demonstration projects to identify best practices in culture change and information technology.
- Demonstration program to develop, test, and implement federal oversight of interstate and large intrastate chains. (Chains apply to participate in the demonstrations.)

Patient Safety and Abuse Prevention Act

The legislation created a national program of criminal background checks on employees of long-term care providers who have access to residents of facilities or people receiving care in their own homes.

Home and Community-Based Services Act

This legislation

- Creates a state medicaid option to provide community-based attendant services and supports for people who meet their state's nursing home eligibility standards.
- Gives states the option to provide home and community-based services through a state plan amendment, rather than a waiver. Requires the plan to be statewide; prohibits caps on the number served; and enables targeting of individuals with specific conditions. Creates incentives for states to move medicaid beneficiaries out of nursing homes into home and community-based services. Extends the Money Follows the Person program for six years.
- Extends spousal impoverishment protections to spouses of medicaid beneficiaries receiving home and community-based services.
- Eliminated medicare "Part d" cost-sharing requirements for people who are receiving long-term care under a home and community-based waiver.
- Provided for grants and demonstration programs to train workers in geriatrics and long-term care.

Summary

Elder abuse has become still another form of violence in our society. Authorities cannot agree on a definition, and as a result the outcome of different studies varies widely regarding the nature, cause, and extent of this type of violence. Elder abuse, like other forms of family violence, is not an isolated event; rather it is a pattern of behavior that increases both in intensity and frequency over time. The rich, poor, college educated, and uneducated suffer from elder abuse. The dynamics and etiology of this type of abuse are still being theorized, with some theories holding more promise than others. Continued research is of paramount importance if we are to understand and intervene in this type of behavior.

It is a grim fate that awaits our maturing population: That after years of productivity and work, seniors face the prospect of being beaten and shamed by other members of our society. As a society, we owe it to ourselves and those who will come after us to actively pursue detection and prevention of this form of violence.

Key Terms

Elder abuse is defined as conduct that results in the physical, psychological, or material harm or neglect or injury to an elder.

Material in the context of elder abuse refers to the exploitation or use of resources.

Elder is a person sixty-five years or older. Some federal programs use age 60 or older as the guide.

Psychopathology theory of elder abuse is based on the premise that abusers suffer from mental disorders that cause them to be violent.

Social exchange theory of elder abuse assumes that dependency in relationships contributes to elder abuse.

Family stress theory regarding elder abuse is based on the premise that providing care for an elder induces stress within the family.

Neutralization theory was originally developed by Sykes and Matza to explain juvenile delinquency in our society. This theory views the delinquent as being affected by the norms and values of a larger social system rather than by a counterculture.

Discussion Questions

1. Is elder abuse more or less serious than child abuse? Why?
2. Do you agree with the definition of elder abuse contained in the textbook? Draft another definition that you believe is more appropriate, and justify your answer.
3. Which of the theories discussing elder abuse do you favor? Why?
4. What is the most serious type of crime that an elder can experience? Why?
5. What is more important in your mind for an elderly victim—independence or security from further victimization? Why?
6. What efforts were included in the 2010 Health Care Reform Act in an attempt to reduce elderly abuse?

Suggested Readings

R. B. Wallace, ed., *Elder Mistreatment: Abuse, Neglect, and Exploitation in an Aging America* (National Academies Press, Washington, D.C.) 2003.

B. Brandl, C. B. Dyer, & C. J. Heiser, *Elder Abuse Detection and Intervention: A Collaborative Approach* (Springer Publishing Co., New York) 2006.

M. J. Mellor & P. J. Brownell, eds., *Elder Abuse and Mistreatment: Policy, Practice, and Research* (Haworth Social Work, Binghamton, N.Y.) 2005.

E. Podnieks, ed., *Elder Abuse: Selected Papers from the Prague World Congress on Family Violence* (Haworth Press, Binghamton, N.Y.) 2005.

L. Curtis, *Partnering with Faith Communities to Provide Elder Fraud Prevention, Intervention, and Victim Services* (U.S. Department of Justice, Office for Victims of Crime, Washington, D.C.) 2005.

L. A. Stiegel, *Elder Abuse Fatality Review Teams* (U.S. Department of Justice, Office of Victims of Crime, Washington, D.C.) 2005.

B. Schlesinger & R. Schlesinger, eds., *Abuse of the Elderly: Issues and Annotated Bibliography* (University of Toronto Press, Toronto) 1988.

Peter Decalmer & Frank Glendenning, eds., *The Mistreatment of Elder People* (Sage, London, England) 1993.

V. B. Van Hasselt, et al., eds., *Handbook of Family Violence* (Plenum Press, New York) 1988.

R. S. Wolf & K. A. Pillemer, *Helping Elderly Victims: The Reality of Elder Abuse* (Columbia University Press, New York) 1989.

R. Filenson & S. R. Ingman, eds., *Elder Abuse: Practice and Policy* (Human Sciences Press, New York) 1989.

R. T. Ammerman & M. Hersen, eds., *Assessment of Family Violence: A Clinical and Legal Sourcebook* (John Wiley & Sons, Inc., New York) 1992.

M. R. Block & J. D. Sinnott, eds., *The Battered Elder Syndrome: An Exploratory Study* (University of Maryland Center on Aging, College Park, Md.) 1979.

Endnotes

1. M. R. Block & J. D. Sinnott, "The Battered Elder Syndrome: An Exploratory Study" (Center on Aging, University of Maryland) 1979.
2. B. Schlesinger & R. Schlesinger, eds., *Abuse of the Elderly: Issues and Annotated Bibliography* (University of Toronto Press, Toronto) 1988.
3. K. A. Pillemer & D. Finkelhor, "The Prevalence of Elder Abuse: A Random Sample Survey," 28(1) *The Gerontologist,* 51 (1988).
4. U.S. House of Representative, Select Committee on Aging, "Elder Abuse: Curbing a National Epidemic" (Hearings) (Washington, D.C. GPO) December 10, 1990.
5. Ibid.
6. J. J. Callahan, "Elder Abuse: Some Questions for Policymakers," 28 *The Gerontologist,* 453–458 (1988).
7. J. I. Kosberg, "Preventing Elder Abuse: Identification of High Risk Factors Prior to Placement Decision," 28 *The Gerontologist,* 43–50 (1988).
8. Joanne M. Otto, *Abuse of Adults Age 60+* (National Committee for the Prevention of Elder Abuse and the National Adult Protective Services Association, Boulder, Colo.) February 2006.
9. U.S. House of Representatives, Select Committee on Aging, "Elder Abuse: A Decade of Shame and Inaction" (Hearings) (Washington, D.C. GPO) May 1, 1990.
10. Pillemer & Finkelhor, "The Prevalence of Elder Abuse: A Random Sample Survey," 1988.
11. Peter Decalmer & Frank Glendenning, eds., *The Mistreatment of Elder People* (Sage, London, England) 1993, p. 35.
12. "Elder Abuse," 1 (17) *Infolink* (National Victims Center, Washington, D.C.) 1992.
13. Karl Pillemer & J. J. Suitor, "Elder Abuse," in V. B. Van Hasselt et al., eds., *Handbook of Family Violence* (Plenum Press, New York) 1988.
14. Compare Block & Sinnott, "The Battered Elder Syndrome: An Exploratory Study," 1979 with S. Steinmetz & D. J. Amsden, "Dependent Elders, Family Stress and Abuse," in T. H. Brubaker, ed., *Family Relationships in Later Life* (Sage, Beverly Hills, Calif.) 1983.

15. M. F. Hudson & T. F. Johnson, "Elder Abuse and Neglect: A Review of the Literature," in C. Eisdorfer et al., eds., 6 *Annual Review of Gerontology and Geriatrics* (Springer, New York) 1986.

16. T. A. O'Malley, H. C. O'Malley, D. E. Everitt, & D. Sarson, "Categories of Family-Mediated Abuse and Neglect of Elderly Persons," 32(5) *Journal of the American Geriatrics Society,* 362–369 (1984).

17. Ibid.

18. See R. S. Wolf & K. A. Pillemer, *Helping Elderly Victims: The Reality of Elder Abuse* (Columbia University Press, New York) 1989; M. A. Godkin, R. S. Wolf & K. A. Pillemer, "A Case-Comparison Analysis of Elder Abuse and Neglect," 28(3) *International Journal of Aging and Human Development,* 207–225 (1989).

19. R. Bachman, "Elderly Victim," *Special Report, Bureau of Justice Statistics* (U.S. Department of Justice, Washington, D.C.) 1992.

20. M. D. Pagelow, *Family Violence* (Praeger, New York) 1984, p. 359.

21. K. A. Pillemer & D. W. Moore, "Abuse of Patients in Nursing Homes: Findings from a Survey of Staff," 29(3) *The Gerontologist,* 314 (1989).

22. M. W. Galbraith, "A Critical Examination of the Definitional, Methodological and Theoretical Problems of Elder Abuse," in R. Filenson & S. R. Ingman, eds., *Elder Abuse: Practice and Policy* (Human Sciences Press, New York) 1989, pp. 35–42.

23. Wolf & Pillemer, *Helping Elderly Victims: The Reality of Elder Abuse,* 1989.

24. R. S. Wolf, C. Strugnell, & M. Godkin, *Preliminary Findings from Three Model Projects on Elder Abuse* (University of Massachusetts Medical Center, Worcester, Mass.) 1982.

25. T. Hickey & R. L. Douglas, "Mistreatment of the Elderly in the Domestic Setting: An Exploratory Study," 71 *American Journal of Public Health,* 500–517 (1981).

26. R. S. Beckman & R. D. Adelman, "Elder Abuse and Neglect," in R. T. Ammerman & M. Hersen, eds., *Assessment of Family Violence: A Clinical and Legal Sourcebook* (John Wiley & Sons, Inc., New York) 1992, p. 238.

27. J. L. Davison, "Elder Abuse," in M. R. Block & J. D. Sinnott, eds., *The Battered Elder Syndrome: An Exploratory Study* (University of Maryland Center on Aging, College Park, Md.) 1979, pp. 49–55.

28. R. S. Wolf, M. Godkin, & K. A. Pillemer, *Elder Abuse and Neglect: Report from the Model Projects* (University of Massachusetts Medical Center, University Center on Aging, Worchester, Mass.) 1984.

29. S. K. Steinmetz, *Duty Bound: Elder Abuse and Family Care* (Sage Publications, Newbury Park, Calif.) 1988.

30. G. J. Anetzberger, *The Etiology of Elder Abuse by Adult Offspring* (Charles C Thomas, Springfield Park, Ill.) 1987.

31. Steinmetz, *Duty Bound: Elder Abuse and Family Care,* 1988.

32. R. J. Gelles, "An Exchange/Social Control Theory," in D. Finkelhor, G. Hotaling, R. J. Gelles, & M. A. Straus, eds., *The Dark Side of Families: Current Family Violence Research* (Sage, Beverly Hills, Calif.) 1983.

33. L. Phillips, "Theoretical Explanations of Elder Abuse: Competing Hypotheses and Unresolved Issues," in K. Pillemer & R. Wolf, eds., *Elder Abuse: Conflict in the Family* (Auburn House Publishing Co., Dover, Mass.) 1986.

34. G. M. Sykes & D. Matza, "Techniques of Neutralization: A Theory of Delinquency," 22 *American Sociological Review,* 664–670 (1978).

35. J. F. Short Jr. & Fred Strodtbeck, *Group Process and Gang Delinquency* (University of Chicago Press, Chicago) 1965.

36. S. K. Tomita, "The Denial of Elder Mistreatment by Victims and Abusers: The Application of Neutralization Theory," 5(3) *Violence and Victims,* 171 (1990).

37. This section has been adapted from Ellen Alexander, "Elderly Victims of Crime," *National Victim Assistance Academy Text* (Office for Victims of Crime, Washington, D.C.) 1996, which was funded by a federal grant.

38. XinQi Dong et al., "Elder Self-Neglect and Abuse and Mortality Risk in a Community-Dwelling Population," 302(5) *Journal of American Medical Association* (2009); available online http://jama.ama-assn.org/content/302/5/517 (accessed May 10, 2013).

39. *Elder Victimization* (Bureau of Justice Statistics, Washington, D.C.) 1987.

40. *Highlights from 20 Years of Surveying Crime Victims, 1973–1992* (Bureau of Justice Statistics).

41. Federal Trade Commission, *Consumer Fraud and Identity Theft Complaint Data January—December 2012* (GPO, Washington, D.C.) 2013, p. 13; available online http://www.ftc.gov/sentinel/reports/sentinel-annual-reports/sentinel-cy2012.pdf (accessed May 10, 2013).

11

Hate Crimes

Chapter Outline

Hate Crimes
Introduction
Legal Aspects of Hate Crimes
Identifying Bias Crimes
Typology of Offenders
Hate Crime Legislation
Homeless Hate Crime Victims

Cultural Awareness
Introduction
Cultural Awareness Training

Cultural Awareness Case Study
Summary
Key Terms
Discussion Questions
Suggested Readings
Endnotes

LEARNING OBJECTIVES

After reading this chapter, you should be able to:

• Explain why it is important to understand different cultures

• List the elements of an effective cultural diversity program

• List the indicators of bias crimes

• Explain the different types of bias crime offenders

To understand hate crimes fully, victim services providers must be sensitive to cultural issues. Each victim of a crime needs to be treated as an individual. However, some victims face more difficult tasks than others, necessitating a more comprehensive approach from the service provider. This difficulty may arise because of the nature of the crime; that is, a murder victim's family will suffer more trauma than the victim of a car theft. Other victims face difficult times because they are from special populations that are different from the established cultures in our country. This difference may be based on skin color, sex, religious beliefs, sexual orientation, or a number of other factors that make people culturally different. This textbook cannot possibly address all the issues facing the victims who are members of special groups. Its purpose is to examine selected special victim populations and to suggest specific methods professionals should use when responding to crimes committed against them. One of the characteristics of hate crimes is the use of extreme brutality.

FOCUS
Hate Crimes in America

- In Greeley, Colorado, Angie Zapata was killed two weeks before her nineteenth birthday. She was beaten to death with a fire extinguisher. Her apparent killer, Allen Andrade, told the police that he killed her because he discovered that biologically she was a man after they had met on the Internet and had a sexual encounter. He told the police that he killed "it." Andrade was convicted of first-degree murder. According to a national gay rights group, the trial was the first known trial in the United States in which a hate-crime statute has been used to prosecute the killing of a transgender person. The accused was quoted as stating: "It is not like I went up to a schoolteacher and shot her in the head or killed a straight law-abiding citizen." At the time, Colorado is one of eleven states that have hate crime laws that cover gender identity.[1]

  In Mississippi, a sixty-one-year-old African-American Sunday school teacher was hit and killed by an eighteen-year-old white driver. The teen told the Sheriff deputies he thought he hit a deer but the driver's two passengers said he steered straight for the teacher. One passenger said he could see that the victim was black.

  In Los Angeles, prosecutors used civil rights statutes against a Latino gang leader who had targeted African-Americans. The gang leader was sentenced to nearly twenty years in prison after pleading guilty not just for breaking racketeering laws, but also for violating the civil rights of African-Americans who lived in the area around where he operated.

- As of 2013, 14 states and Washington, DC, had hate-crime statutes that included crimes against individuals because of their transgender status. Hate crime legislation also has not stopped the endemic violence against transgender people. Just weeks after the President signed the Matthew Shepard and James Byrd Hate Crimes Prevention Act of 2009, the country's first gender identity and sexual orientation inclusive hate crimes bill, two young people of color were murdered, one in Maryland, the other in Puerto Rico. In the wake of both the Act and the killings, two anti-violence organizations, the Audre Lorde Project in New York and Communities United Against Violence in San Francisco, issued a statement pointing out that the bill provides no funding or resources to actually prevent violence.

Sources: Truth-Out Web site at http://truth-out.org/news/item/3320:antitransgender-violence-how-hatecrime-laws-have-failed, accessed on May 10, 2013; and Transgender Law and Policy Web site at http://www.transgenderlaw.org/hatecrimelaws/index.htm, accessed on May 10, 2013.

HATE CRIMES

Introduction

Hate violence has a long history in the United States. However, some sources suggest that it has increased in the recent past.[2] Accurately measuring the number of hate crimes that are committed is extremely difficult even though the Hate Crime Statistics Act of 1990 requires them to be reported. Factors that contribute to the lack of meaningful statistics in this area include: The lack of training by law enforcement causes many officers to fail to recognize incidents of racial violence, and there is natural reluctance on the part of many victims of hate crimes to report such incidents to law enforcement agencies.[3] Acts of racial violence reflect a racial prejudice or interpersonal hostility that is based on the view that different cultures do not merit treatment as equals or that they deserve blame for various problems within society. Many minority cultures are viewed in a certain manner.[4] These stereotypes are race-based generalizations about a person's behavior or character that are typically not substantiated in scientific data. This stereotyping may act as a trigger to violence in different cultures. Stereotyping does not cause violence; however, physical violence is easier to perform on a dehumanized victim. Attackers may believe that the minority is "invading their turf." This may occur when a minority family moves into a traditional neighborhood and has not had any previous experience with that particular culture. Attackers may also claim that minority cultures are taking jobs that rightfully belong to "real" Americans. These and other rationalizations deny minority cultures status as accepted citizens. Persons of color and certain religious groups have traditionally been the target of hate crimes. These groups have been victimized both on national and international scales. They continue to be victimized today. For example, in New York about 30 percent of all bias incidents are committed against African-Americans, and another 30 percent are perpetrated against people of Jewish descent. In Los Angeles, the majority of racial incidents were against African-Americans, and more than 90 percent of religiously motivated incidents were against people of Jewish descent.[5] The arson of African-American churches is but another example of the continuing victimization of persons of color.[6]

Disabled persons are also victims of hate or bias crimes. As the number of disabled persons in our nation has increased, so too has the number of hate crimes and abuse against them. Some perpetrators seek out disabled victims because their disability makes them "easy prey" for this type of offender. An example is a developmentally disabled woman with the intellectual ability of a seven-year-old child who may be sexually assaulted by a caretaker. A **disabled person** is defined by the Americans with Disabilities Act as one who has a physical or mental impairment that substantially limits one or more of the major life activities of that individual, or has a record of such impairment, or is regarded as having such an impairment. Major life activities include walking, seeing, hearing, speaking, breathing, learning, and working.

Antigay and antilesbian violence became a national issue with the murders of San Francisco mayor George Moscone and city supervisor Harvey Milk in 1978. Their deaths became symbols of both the strength of the homosexual community and the hostility that is directed at them. Women also have been the subject of hate and bias crimes. They continue to be targets of violence because of their gender. Many states include gender as a classification within their hate crime statutes. Crimes against women, including sexual assault and spousal abuse, are discussed in Chapter 7. The next section examines the conflict between the First Amendment of the U.S. Constitution, which protects freedom of expression, and prosecuting hate or bias crimes.

Legal Aspects of Hate Crimes

Prosecuting a perpetrator for violation of a hate crime raises several emotional and constitutional issues. The First Amendment prohibits the federal government and the states from enacting any law that unduly regulates a person's freedom of expression.[7] However, from the founding of our nation, the Supreme Court has held that such freedom of expression is not unlimited. There are situations in which conduct or other activities, although expressing beliefs or thoughts, are outside the scope of First Amendment protection.

Hate crimes deal with both the expression of beliefs and action. The expression of beliefs reflects hatred or loathing toward a certain group, and the action is criminal in nature. Thus, crafting a criminal statute that regulates hate crimes is no easy task. In 1992, the Supreme Court struck down a local hate crime ordinance in St. Paul, Minnesota, that criminalized the use of hate symbols, such as the burning of a cross, on the grounds that it violated an individual's right to freedom of expression.[8]

On June 11, 1993, in *Wisconsin v. Mitchell,* the U.S. Supreme Court unanimously upheld the constitutionality of Wisconsin's hate crime statute, which increased penalties for crimes motivated by hate or by bias.[9] Todd Mitchell was a nineteen-year-old black man, who was outraged over a scene in the film *Mississippi Burning* that depicted a young black child being attacked by a white racist. Upon seeing a fourteen-year-old white boy, Mitchell asked his companions if they wanted to "get that white boy." They attacked the white boy, leaving the victim comatose for four days with possible brain damage. Mitchell was convicted for aggravated battery, and the sentence was doubled from two to four years after it was proved he had intentionally selected his victim based on race. Mitchell challenged the constitutionality of the hate crime enhancement statute, claiming that it violated the First Amendment guarantee of freedom of expression.

The U.S. Supreme Court upheld the statute, stating bias or hate crimes were valid for three main reasons:

1. While the government cannot punish an individual's abstract beliefs, it can punish a vast array of depraved motives for crime, including selecting a crime victim based on race, religion, color, disability, sexual orientation, national origin, or ancestry.

2. Hate crimes do not punish thoughts; rather they address the greater individual and societal harms caused by bias-related offenses in that they are more likely to provoke retaliatory crimes, inflict distinct emotional harms on their victims, and incite community unrest.
3. Hate crime penalty enhancement laws do not punish people because they express their views. (The U.S. Supreme Court).

As indicated, laws prohibiting certain conduct will be considered constitutionally valid. Nonthreatening bigoted expression is still protected as long as it does not evolve into bias-motivated action. When such beliefs are the basis for hate or bias crimes, professionals in the field should be able to identify them. The next sections discuss factors that may indicate that the offense was a hate crime.

Identifying Bias Crimes

To identify hate or bias crimes, we must first define these offenses. In this textbook, hate crime and bias crime are used interchangeably. Finn and McNeil define hate crimes as "words or actions designed to intimidate an individual because of his or her race, religion, national origin or sexual [preference]."[10] In the Hate Crimes Statistics Act of 1990, **bias crimes** are those offenses that are motivated by hatred against a victim based on race, religion, sexual orientation, ethnicity, or national origin.[11] Many states have also adopted hate crime statutes that prohibit the same or a similar type of conduct. As indicated, hate or bias crimes are not new; what is new is that we are beginning to recognize these crimes and respond to them.

Recognizing bias crimes involves an evaluation of a number of factors. There is no generally accepted foolproof list of indicators that indicates that the offense is motivated by bias or by hate of a particular group. However, the Office for Victims of Crime has identified seven general categories that should be examined when evaluating criminal acts.[12] These factors include cultural differences, written or oral comments, use of symbols, representation of organized hate groups, prior hate crimes, victim–witness perceptions, and lack of other motive. Depending on the situation, one of these factors standing by itself may strongly indicate that the offense may be classified as a bias or hate crime. Conversely, several of these indicators may not present conclusive evidence that the crime was motivated by hate or by bias. Each case should be evaluated on its own merits.

RACIAL, ETHNIC, GENDER, AND CULTURAL DIFFERENCES Is the victim of a different culture than the offender? Investigators may not be able to establish this fact from the victim. They may have to look for other indicators that point to any cultural differences between the victim and the offender. These other factors include the cultural diversity of a number of locations, including the place of attack, the victim's home, or the workplace. Inquiry should be made as to whether the victim was engaged in activities that represent or promote a group, such as a gay rights march. Did the incident occur on a date that has a special significance to certain cultures, such as Martin Luther King's birthday? Even if the victim is not a member of any recognized cultural or ethnic minority, that person may have supported such a group and the attack may be in reprisal for that activity. Finally, questions must be asked as to whether there is a history of violence between the victim's culture and any other group.

WRITTEN OR ORAL COMMENTS OR GESTURES Inquiry should be made as to whether the attackers made any comments or gestures before, during, or immediately after the attack. These comments may refer to the victim's race, sexual orientation, or gender. Likewise, the attackers may make certain gestures indicating their own affiliation with another group.

DRAWINGS, MARKINGS, SYMBOLS, AND GRAFFITI Care should be taken to look for any drawings or symbols that may indicate membership in a group. These may be on the victim's house, place of work, house of worship, or where the attack occurred.

REPRESENTATIONS OF ORGANIZED HATE GROUPS Sometimes hate groups will call members of the media and take credit for a bombing, burning, or other act of violence. They may also leave their trademark at the scene of the crime. For example, a burning cross may be found outside the victim's home.

PREVIOUS EXISTENCE OF BIAS OR HATE CRIME INCIDENTS Did the incident occur in a location where previous hate crime has occurred? If there have been a series of crimes involving victims of the same culture, or the incidents occurred in the same location that is frequented by members of a specific culture, those facts may indicate that the crimes are motivated by hate or by bias. Interview the victims to determine if they have received previous harassing mail or phone calls based on their affiliation or membership in a group.

VICTIM–WITNESS PERCEPTION Victims should be questioned to determine if they perceive the crime as motivated by bias. This may not always be accurate, but the victims' input in this area is always critical.

LACK OF OTHER MOTIVES If there is no other motive for the incident and the victim is a member of minority culture, the fact that it may be motivated by bias or by hatred of that group should always be considered.

As indicated, the presence or absence of these factors does not establish the existence of a hate-related crime. In fact, there are several caveats that must be exercised when evaluating these crimes. These caveats might appropriately be called false-positive factors. These factors include the following:

Requirement for a Case-by-Case Assessment. Each crime must be evaluated on its own merits. The existence or nonexistence of bias or hate as the motivation for the offense must be evaluated in light of all facts and circumstances surrounding the crime.

Misleading Facts. Care must be taken not to rush to judgment in what appears to be a hate crime. There may be other facts that negate this first impression. For example, the victim may tell the officers that the perpetrator used a racial epithet during the assault. Further investigation may reveal that the victim and the offender were both of the same race or culture.

Feigned Facts and Hoaxes. Some offenders may leave hate symbols in an effort to give the false impression that the offense was motivated by bias or by hatred when in fact it was simply an ordinary crime. Other perpetrators may leave symbols or signs of certain groups as a hoax or to mislead investigators.

On occasion, determining whether the offense is really a hate crime may be difficult. Even if police officers cannot prove that the offense was a hate crime, the victim may believe that hate or bias was in fact the motivation. The effect of such crime on victims is unique and in many cases more devastating than other crimes because of the psychological impact on the victim.[13]

The victim must live with the realization that the crime was not a random act of violence; rather, the victim was targeted or selected for victimization based on beliefs, race, culture, religion, or sexual preference. Bias crimes are "message crimes" that send a message of terror to the victim because the victim is different from the majority of other Americans. Some victims of bias crimes may not have any community support systems within their communities. They may have recently arrived in the United States and may not have developed a support base within the general community or their specific culture. Other victims may fear discovery of their status and therefore decline to report suspected hate crimes. This aspect of victimization is especially true for closeted gays and lesbians, undocumented aliens, and those who suffer from other disabilities such as HIV/AIDS infection.

Bias crimes also impact the victim's immediate community and culture. Such crimes increase tension with the minority community and raise the specter of retaliation by members of that community. As a result of these factors, bias or hate crimes pose special problems for victim services providers.

Typology of Offenders

Understanding more about those who commit hate crimes allows victim services providers to help the victim understand some of the dynamics involved in this type of crime. Although research is still being developed in this area, Levin and McDevitt have established three categories of offenders: thrill-seeking offenders, reactive offenders, and mission offenders.[14]

The thrill-seeking offenders are generally groups of teenagers who are not otherwise associated with any other formal hate group. They engage in these acts for a variety of reasons, including an attempt to gain a psychological or social thrill or rush, a desire to be accepted by others, or to be able to brag about the act at a later time. Almost any member of a minority group may be a target of these groups. They generally operate outside of their own area or neighborhood and actively look for targets and opportunity. Because these attacks are random and usually fail to follow any pattern, it is often difficult to identify the perpetrators of these types of hate crimes.

The reactive offenders have a sense of entitlement concerning their rights or lifestyle that does not extend to the victim. They usually do not belong to any organized hate group but may associate with one to mitigate a perceived threat to their way of life. When a victim acts in such a manner as to cause these offenders to feel that their lifestyle is threatened, they may react with violence. They will commit hate crimes to send a message to the victim and/or the victim's community that will cause the victim to stop whatever action is threatening the perpetrator's rights or lifestyle. These crimes normally occur within the offender's own community, school, or place of work. Examples of these types of hate crimes include burning crosses at a minority's new home in a predominately white neighborhood, beating a minority who takes a job in a traditionally white occupation, and other acts of violence directed at maintaining the status quo.

The mission-oriented offenders may suffer from a mental illness, including psychosis. They may experience hallucinations, withdrawal, and impaired ability to reason. These offenders may believe they have received instructions from a higher deity to rid the world of this "evil." They typically have a sense of urgency about their objectives and believe that they must act before it is too late. The victim is usually a member of a group that is targeted for elimination. These perpetrators will look for victims in the victim's own neighborhood. An example of this type of offender was Marc Lepine, who killed fourteen women at the University of Montreal, stating that he hated all feminists.

Sapp and his associates developed a typology of hate offenders based on their ideology.[15] They believed that ideology is used by hate groups to serve as a symbolic set of ideas that provides the group with a perceived social legitimacy. Ideology is a way of thinking used by a group to express its beliefs and social values. Sapp classified hate groups into three basic categories: Christian conservatism based on the identity movement, white racial supremacy, and patriotism and survival.

Christian conservatism based on the identity movement uses passages in scripture identifying certain groups as superior to others and the notion that a nation, rather than being a geographic, political, or economic entity, is a culture grouped according to bloodlines and shared history. Racial identity thus becomes the basis for national identity.

These groups may adopt a postmillennial view that holds that the second coming of Christ cannot happen until Christians purge the Earth of sin and establish the Holy Land.[16] As Gale points out, this is potentially a blueprint for genocide in that it allows these groups to cleanse the Holy Land of "sinners." Therefore, mass murder of inferiors and those who oppose the groups and their churches is mandated.[17]

White racial supremacy groups also include racial purity proponents. Racial purity is concerned with the purity of the Aryan race or God's children. Refugees, illegal aliens, legal immigrants, Jews, blacks, Hispanics, Asians, and non-Christians are all considered a threat to white racial purity theorists. The Ku Klux Klan is an example of a white supremacy group. Its founding fathers stated that its purpose was the maintenance of the supremacy of the white race in the republic because that race is superior to all other races.[18]

FOCUS

What Is Racism?

In 1937, Ruth Benedict penned a definition of racism that is still valid today. "Racism is the dogma that one ethnic group is condemned by nature to congenital inferiority and another group is destined to congenital superiority. It is the dogma that the hope of civilization depends upon eliminating some races and keeping others pure. It is the dogma that one race has carried progress with it throughout human history and can alone ensure future progress....[R]acism is essentially a pretentious way of saying that 'I belong....For such a conviction, in the most gratifying formula that has ever been discovered, for neither my own unworthiness nor the accusations of others can ever dislodge me from my position....' It avoids all embarrassing claims by 'inferior' groups about their own achievements and ethical standards."

Source: Ruth Benedict, "Race: Science and Politics," in Jacques Baryan, ed., *Race: A Study in Modern Superstition* (MacMillan, New York), 1937, pp. 153–154.

Patriotism and survival groups have recently come to the attention of the general public because of the incidents in Idaho and Montana involving various members of militia groups. These groups offer an attractive ideology to some conservative groups in America. They point out the economic troubles, including unemployment, and blame these problems on refugees and other nonwhite groups. They argue that special interests control the government and decry the moral bankruptcy of our leaders.

These groups blame lax courts for encouraging criminals. They target the media because they believe the media glorify criminals and are responsible for the total breakdown of morals in America. Some of these groups use quotes from the Constitution as a basis for their beliefs and argue that they are no longer subject to the laws of the United States.

Bias and hate crimes do not simply happen, they are motivated by a variety of feelings, beliefs, and emotions. The result is intimidation of the individual as well as the community. Victim services providers must understand these crimes and their impact to assist these victims properly.

Hate Crime Legislation

FEDERAL HATE CRIMES LEGISLATION The Criminal Code of the United States Federal Government treats bias-motivated crimes as specific offenses. The first federal hate crimes legislation, 18 USC 245, was adopted in 1968. It gave federal authorities jurisdiction to investigate and punish crimes motivated by bias toward a person's race, religion, or national origin and because of a person's participation in one of six federally protected activities.

The federal statute requires federal prosecutors to demonstrate that a hate crime was committed both because of bias and because of the victim's participation in a federally protected activity. The legislation limits the scope for federal prosecutions of hate crimes. Accordingly, most hate crime prosecutions are undertaken under state laws. Often federal prosecutors have been unable to charge bias crime suspects at the federal level because of this statutory requirement. In other cases, prosecutions on federal charges failed because of the double requirements that crimes were both motivated by bias and intended to obstruct the victim's exercise of federally protected activities.

Other federal laws concerning hate crimes include the Church Arson Prevention Act of 1996, which prohibits intentional desecration or damage to religious property as well as interference with the enjoyment of any person's exercise of religious beliefs, and the Fair Housing Act of 1968, which prohibits housing-related violence on the basis of race, color, religion, sex, handicap, familial status, or national origin, including such crimes as cross burnings, arson, fire bombings, vandalism to property, written and oral threats, and assaults on persons attempting to exercise their fair housing rights. In 2009, the federal government enacted the Matthew Shepard and James Byrd Jr. Hate Crimes Prevention Act which added transgender as a protected class.

The Hate Crimes Statistics Act enacted in 1990 mandated the attorney general to acquire data and publish an annual report on crimes committed based on prejudice of "race, religion, sexual orientation, or ethnicity." The Violent Crime Control and Law Enforcement Act was enacted into law in 1994. On the basis of this legislation, enhanced sentencing for hate crimes is permitted. After a person is found guilty of a violent crime, a judge may increase his/her sentence if the judge determines that it was motivated by "hate." For purposes of this law, "hate crime" is defined as: "A crime in which the defendant intentionally selects a victim, or in the case of a property crime, the property that is the object of the crime, because of the actual or perceived race, color, religion, national origin, ethnicity, gender, disability, or sexual orientation of any person."

The federal hate crime legislation has many critics. For example, one critic called the 2009 Act "another nail in the coffin of the First Amendment." Another critic stated that "All violent crimes are hate crimes, and all crime victims deserve equal justice." To many individuals the hate crime legislation is a grave threat to the First Amendment because it provides special penalties based on what people think, feel, or believe and it violates free speech or free exercise of religion rights that are protected by the constitutional law. One noted scholar testified before a Congressional subcommittee substantially as follows: "It is fundamentally unjust for the government to treat some crime victims more favorably than others, just because they are homosexual or transsexual. This bill is an unnecessary federal intrusion into state law-enforcement authority, and it is an unwise step toward silencing religious and moral viewpoints." Many contend that hate crime laws criminalize behavior that already is criminal. They raise the uncomfortable question of whether people should be penalized for what they think, and are not just redundant but more difficult to prove.

To counter those arguments, the supporters of hate crime laws content that the power of hate crimes to terrorize an entire category of people cannot be ignored. Hate crimes are criminal acts that send a message far beyond the initial victim. Because of the rationale behind hate crimes, when a person's race, religion, disability, ethnic origin, or sexual orientation is a motivator for an attack, the crime is a warning to all individuals in that category or class. And everyone in that category lives in fear not knowing if they might be the next one attacked.

There is also controversy over which classes or categories of people should be protected by hate crime legislation. In Manchester, Great Britain for example, attacks and abuse aimed at punk rockers, heavy metal fans, Goths and other subcultures are recognized as hate crimes. In Manchester, victims of crime who feel they have been targeted because of their distinctive clothing, hairstyle, and even musical tastes receive special support from the police.

STATE HATE CRIME LEGISLATION Forty-five states and the District of Columbia have adopted some form of penalty-enhancement hate crime statute, many based on an Anti-Defamation League model hate crime law, which increases the sentence if the crime was motivated by the victim's actual or perceived personal characteristics. Under this type of law, the prosecutor needs to prove two things:

1. that the perpetrator committed the crime and
2. that the perpetrator's motivation was because of the victim's race, religion, or some other personal characteristic.

Homeless Hate Crime Victims

A hate crime, as defined by the FBI in the report by the National Coalition for the Homeless, is a "criminal offense committed against a person, property or society that is motivated, in whole or in part, by the offender's bias." Presently in most states, the homeless are not listed as a protected class under federal law, so crimes against the homeless are not listed as hate crimes. Several states have enacted or are considering expanding the statutory definition of hate crimes to include the homeless as a protected class.

FOCUS
Hate Crime Based on Perceived Religion

In 2013, a woman was arrested for pushing a man to his death in front of an oncoming subway train in Queens, New York. The woman allegedly pushed the victim because he was Hindu and the woman grouped Hindus with Muslims and resented both groups because of the September 11 attack on the World Trade Center in New York.

Clearly, religious hatred and ethnic bias played a part in her killing the victim and the woman was also clearly suffering from serious mental illness. The question presented to the prosecutor was whether he or she should consider the offender's actions a hate crime to draw attention to the often infectious and dangerous consequences of discrimination in our society. But charging her with a hate crime under the penal code makes the case more difficult to prove.

The argument for charging her under the state homicide rather than just under the hate crime legislation include the fact that there are two justifications for enhanced sentencing under hate crime laws in America, including the hate crime laws on the books in New York State. The first is deterrence—that the existence of hate crime statutes will dissuade potential perpetrators from acting on their bias with violence. But if tough sentencing were generally an effective deterrent to crime, we would expect that states with the death penalty (the strongest deterrent of all, supporters say) have lower crime rates than states without the death penalty. In fact, the opposite is true—states that do not have the death penalty

have had consistently lower homicide rates for the past twenty years compared with states that do have the death penalty.

Similarly, in the case of "three strikes" laws imposing harsh minimum sentences for repeat offenders, research has found that the enhanced sentencing laws have no deterrent effect on crime. Furthermore, enhanced sentencing means longer prison terms that tend to increase rates of recidivism after release. So enhanced sentencing may drive up rates of crime instead of making us safer.

The other justification for imposing harsher penalties under hate crime laws is largely symbolic, sending a message to offenders and the public that we as a society will not tolerate discrimination whether based on gender, sexual orientation, race, or religious creed. This is a collective, concrete way to show that we sympathize with the victims of such crimes and stand against hatred and bias.

If you were a member of the religious groups Hindus or Muslims, would you feel safer if the prosecutor charged her with a hate crime or treated the crime as a standard homicide?

Question

If you were the prosecutor how would you charge the offender?

Note: The Queen's prosecutor charged her with a hate crime.

The National Coalition for the Homeless recorded 1,289 incidents of what it characterizes as hate crimes against the homeless in a thirteen year period ending in 2013. These crimes were committed by people who were not homeless themselves. In 2011, there were 105 attacks that resulted in 32 deaths, and the study found that violent acts are becoming more lethal over time. Nonfatal attacks include rape and beatings. Many violent acts against homeless populations go unreported, so the true number of incidents is likely to be much higher. The majority of those committing these crimes are between the ages of 13 and 24 and are poor and uneducated. They also often appear to be heavily influenced by these games and videos.[19]

MAJOR CONCERNS REGARDING HATE CRIMES LEGISLATION

- It violates the concept of equal protection under the law by granting more government protection to certain classes of people.
- It is an overreach of federal power—allowing federal government intervention into local and state affairs.
- It paves the way to religious persecution through "hate speech," in particular for Christians and other faith groups who hold traditional beliefs on homosexuality.

CULTURAL AWARENESS

The United States has traditionally been a melting pot of different peoples who have come to its shores and taken their unique place in our society. We pride ourselves on our diversity and multiculturalism. However, the other side of this coin reflects a darker side to our relationship with these groups.

Clashes between ethnic and racial minority groups and other more established cultures in the United States have escalated over the last ten to twenty years. In addition, new refugees, recent immigrants, and other minority groups are prime targets for certain types of perpetrators. These victims face an almost overwhelming task when attempting to pursue redress in the criminal or civil justice system. Victim services providers need to be aware of these issues when dealing with these victims.

Introduction

Simply saying to those who work in the criminal justice system that a victim comes from a different culture and is different from the rest of us does not automatically guarantee sympathetic treatment and/or an understanding response to that victim's special needs. Stereotyping must be guarded against, and relying on third-hand information when responding to the needs of minority victims should be avoided. Different cultures may not be as homogeneous as they appear on the surface, and care should be taken to not attribute characteristics to special populations based on conversations or interactions with one member of the group. The person being interviewed may be advocating personal beliefs that may not represent the feelings of other members of that particular culture. It is essential that professionals working in the criminal justice profession be both culturally sensitive and careful to validate their information if possible.

Cultural awareness can be defined as the understanding an individual has regarding different cultures. The term *culture* includes different races, religions, genders, ages, physical disabilities, and gay or lesbian issues. Therefore, cultural awareness encompasses a wide range of issues, any of which may confront those working within this field. The next section will provide some guidelines for professionals to use when evaluating cultural awareness programs or setting up such training programs.

Cultural Awareness Training

The Practicum indicates how important cultural awareness or sensitivity training is within the criminal justice system. This is an emerging area to which victim services providers can contribute greatly and in which they should take the lead. They should become knowledgeable regarding

PRACTICUM
Cultures and Misunderstanding[20]

The Officer's Perspective

A Nigerian cab driver runs a red light. An officer pulls him over in the next block, stopping the patrol car at least three car lengths behind the cab. Before the officer can exit his patrol car, the cabbie gets out of his vehicle and approaches the officer. Talking rapidly in a high-pitched voice and making wild gestures, the cab driver appears to be out of control.

The officer steps from his vehicle and yells for the cab driver to stop, but the cabbie continues to advance until he is about two feet from him. The cab driver does not make eye contact and appears to be talking to the ground. Finally, the officer arrests the cabbie for disorderly conduct and resisting arrest.

The Cab Driver's Perspective

Although most Americans know to remain in their cars, the Nigerian exited his cab to show his respect by not troubling the officer to leave his own vehicle. The Nigerian ignores the command to stop advancing on the officer because in his eyes he is not even close to the officer. The social distance for conversation in Nigeria is much closer for conversations than in the United States. For Nigerians, it may be less than fifteen inches, whereas two feet represents a comfortable conversation zone for Americans.

Anglo-Americans expect eye contact during conversation; the lack of it usually signifies deception, rudeness, defiance, or a means to end a conversation. In Nigeria, however, people often show respect and humility by averting their eyes. The Nigerian believes he is sending a message of respect by averting his eyes and by talking to the ground.

1. Is either party at fault in this encounter?
2. Is the officer responsible for understanding other cultures? Is the cabbie responsible for conforming to the standards of the country in which he is working?
3. List ways to avoid such situations.

different cultures within their community and be prepared to conduct training sessions regarding the customs and traditions of those cultures and their responses to crime and the criminal justice system.

They have an opportunity to provide a valuable service to future victims by ensuring that those in the criminal justice system respond appropriately to members of different cultures. Occasionally, law enforcement agencies will contact victim services providers and ask that they provide cultural awareness or sensitivity training to members of their organization. Unfortunately, this request for training occurs after an incident involving a minority victim has resulted in adverse publicity being directed toward the department. The victim services providers should use this request as an opportunity to "train the trainers" regarding what is an appropriate cultural awareness training program.

No single technique or program will work for all agencies. Professionals may find themselves adapting programs or training techniques to fit specific situations. There are a number of different techniques that may be used to train professionals in the area of cultural awareness.

St. George lists a variety of factors that trainers should consider when conducting cultural awareness training.[21] These factors include multidimensional learning from several perspectives, learning that is relevant and structured to meet specific needs, that is behavior-based so that students express their feelings by actions, empathetic to the feelings and concerns of community minority members, practical in nature, and allows for controversy and provides follow-up support.

Shusta and his associates recommended a multifaceted cultural awareness training program.[22] They suggested that the trainer should use a variety of training aids and techniques to accomplish the objective of teaching cultural awareness. These techniques include the following strategies:

Lectures. Lectures should be interspersed between other activities and include local demographics. This information may be obtained from city and county departments, housing authorities, state and federal census data, and community-based organizations. Lectures should introduce students to culture-specific information about the various subcultures within a community.

Role-playing. Role-playing should include communication skills. Role-playing is intended to create a realistic environment in which the participants may interact and be trained to respond in an appropriate manner.

Simulations. The purpose of simulations is to allow the participants to identify their own feelings and thereby achieve a better understanding of others. A number of commercial simulation packages specifically designed for cultural awareness programs are on the market.

Work Groups or Presentations. The work group or presentation aspect of a cultural awareness program allows the participants to discuss various issues. Small groups are a useful technique that allows participants to express their feelings more freely than if they were in a large group.

Critical Incidents or Case Studies. In critical incidents or case studies, participants are asked to bring in news stories of actual conflict expressing hate or bias based on ethnicity, gender, or sexual orientation. An experienced facilitator interjects comments and asks questions to the students regarding their reactions to the incidents. Students discuss how they would have responded to the situation and how they can avoid similar situations in the future.

Local Culture Video Profiles and Cross-Cultural Films. Local agencies or universities might cooperate in producing a video that examines local cultural groups. Students might be assigned to write the script, direct, or even act in the video. In this day of inexpensive camcorders, videos are relatively easy to make and show. Students learn by researching local information for the production.

Experiential Assignments. Students are assigned to spend time in a minority community or work environment. They return to class and explain their reactions and feelings based on their experience.

Interactive Computer Video. Probably the most innovative tool available to trainers is the interactive computer video. Students use computers and computer disks (CDs) to move through interactive sessions dealing with cultural issues. Students cannot progress from one stage until they have successfully completed all tasks at prior steps. (Robert M. Shusta, Deena R. Levine, Philip R. Harris, & Herbert Z. Wong, Multicultural Law Enforcement (Prentice Hall, Englewood Cliffs, N.J.) 1995).

As indicated, many scholars advocate cultural awareness training as a continual process. An example of one successful cultural awareness project is the federally funded Head Start program. This program teaches parenting skills to families, provides medical and social services to children, and prepares them for school. Congress has established a series of performance standards for Head Start programs.[23] Some of these performance standards are excellent examples of continuing cultural awareness training. Although these standards obviously apply to a preschool classroom setting, they are easy to modify to make them relevant to a variety of situations. Samples of Head Start performance standards are listed here:

45 Code of Federal Regulations 1304.2-2 Education Services and Objectives and Performance Standards
 (c) The education services component of the plan shall provide for a program which is individualized to meet the special needs of children from various populations by:
 (1) Having a curriculum which is relevant and reflective of the needs of the population served.

This standard can be accomplished by including in each classroom materials and activities that reflect the cultural background of the children. Examples of materials include books, records, posters, maps, dolls, and clothing. Activities may include celebrating cultural events and holidays; serving food related to other cultures; and enjoying stories, music, and games representative of children's background.

 (2) Having staff and program resources reflective of the racial and ethnic population of the children in the program.

This standard may be accomplished by having an adult present who speaks the primary language of the children and who is knowledgeable about their heritage. This adult may be a teacher or aide, other member of the center staff, a parent or family member, or a volunteer.

 (3) Including parents in the curriculum development and having them serve as resource persons. (The Code of Federal Regulations).

Parents can be valuable resources in planning which activities reflect the children's heritage. Teachers may request suggestions from parents on ways to integrate cultural activities into the program. For example, parents may wish to plan holiday celebrations; prepare foods unique to various cultures; recommend books, records, or other materials for the classroom; act as classroom volunteers; or suggest games, songs, and art projects that reflect cultural customs.

As this discussion indicates, there is no easy answer to the problem of dealing with minority populations. Feelings, perceptions, and past experiences all enter into our reactions to those who are different from us. Unfortunately, some members of our society do more than simply feel uncomfortable around members of other cultures or other minority groups. As indicated in the

Focus box at the beginning of this chapter, some groups engage in acts of violence directed at special populations.

CULTURAL AWARENESS CASE STUDY

You live in a medium-sized community with a wide range of cultures and subcultures. These groups include people from South America and the Far East. During the last several months, there have been reports of the use of excessive force on the part of law enforcement officers when they encountered these minorities. The minority groups have responded by picketing city hall and by threatening recall campaigns against the local elected officials.

You are the local victim–witness coordinator and have spoken at a variety of meetings regarding cultural awareness and its impact on and importance to victims. The chief of police has asked you to assist his department in the establishment of a cultural awareness program. You understand that for such a program to be successful, it must be continuing and multifaceted. Reread the Head Start performance standards listed in this chapter. Revise them so that they could apply to a local law enforcement agency instead of a school setting. For example, instead of a parent providing suggestions, you may want to substitute a leader of a minority group.

Summary

Cultural awareness is more than a series of "politically correct" sayings and posters that hang in an office. Victim services providers are in unique positions to serve both the victims and the criminal justice agencies within the system. They can act as advocates for the victims and as cultural awareness trainers to law enforcement agencies.

Hate or bias crimes continue to happen in this country. Victim services providers must be aware of the dynamics involved in these crimes from both the offender's perspective and the victim's position. The commission of a hate crime not only affects the individual victim, it also impacts the victim's entire community. A message of terror is sent to these victims, their families, and their communities. Service providers must be able to offer advice, guidance, and support to these special victims.

Key Terms

Cultural awareness is the understanding that an individual has regarding different cultures.

Disabled person is defined by the Americans with Disabilities Act as one who has a physical or mental impairment that substantially limits one or more of the major life activities of that individual, or that person has a record of such impairment, or that person is regarded as having such an impairment.

Bias crimes are those offenses that are motivated by hatred and directed against a victim based on race, religion, sexual orientation, ethnicity, or national origin.

Discussion Questions

1. List the various cultures that exist in your city. Explain how they are different from the mainstream population of your area. What do you know of the history and culture of these populations?
2. What is the most important aspect of a cultural awareness program?
3. Save your local newspaper for one week and list all the incidents involving hate crimes. How do these crimes compare with the material listed in the book? Discuss each crime using the criteria set forth in the book.
4. Are there any other groups that you can identify that might be subject to hate crimes?
5. Should membership in organizations that espouse hate doctrine be a crime? Why? Why not?

Suggested Readings

Robert M. Shusta, Deena R. Levine, Philip R. Harris, & Herbert Z. Wong, *Multicultural Law Enforcement* (Prentice Hall, Englewood Cliffs, N.J.) 1995.

Marlene A. Young, *Victim Assistance Frontiers and Fundamentals* (Kendall/Hunt Publishing, Dubuque, Iowa) 1993.

Robert J. Kelly, ed., *Bias Crimes: American Law Enforcement and Legal Responses* (Office of the International Criminal Justice Administration, Reading, Berkshire, United Kingdom) 1993.

National Bias Crimes Training for Law Enforcement and Victim Assistance Professionals, Office for Victims of Crime (U.S. Department of Justice, Washington, D.C.) January 1995.

M. Welch, *Scapegoats of September 11th: Hate Crimes and State Crimes in the War on Terror* (Rutgers Press, New York) 2006.

P. Connors, ed., *Hate Crimes (Current Controversies)* (Greenhaven Press, Chicago) 2006.

H. A. Lim, *Race, Bigotry, and Violence: Understanding the Impact of Hate Crimes on Asian Americans* (ProQuest, Ann Arbor, Mich.) 2006.

R. D. King, *When Law and Society Disagree: Group Threat, Legacies of the Past, and the Organizational Context of Hate Crime Law Enforcement* (ProQuest, Ann Arbor, Mich.) 2006.

Endnotes

1. As reported by the *New York Times*, Friday April 17, 2009, p. A15.
2. "1990 Audit of Anti-Semitic Incidents," Anti-Defamation League of B'nai B'rith, New York (1991).
3. For example, it was not until January 1995 that the Office for Victims of Crime published a *National Bias Crimes Training Manual for Law Enforcement and Victim Assistance Professionals* (U.S. Department of Justice, Washington, D.C.) 1995.
4. Harry H. L. Kitano, "Asian-Americans: The Chinese, Japanese, Koreans, Philipinos and Southeast Asians," 454 *Annals American Academy of Political & Social Science,* 125 (1981).
5. R. J. Kelly, ed., *Bias Crimes: American Law Enforcement and Legal Responses* (Office of the International Criminal Justice Administration, Reading, Berkshire, United Kingdom) 1993.
6. But see Fred Bayles, "Church Arsons Not All Linked to Racism," Associated Press, *Fresno Bee*, A-1 (July 5, 1996), where the reporter points out that after reviewing six years of federal, state, and local data, the Associated Press found arsons increasing, but with only random links to racism. Of the seventy-three African-American church arsons since 1995, fewer than twenty cases had clear links to racism. On the whole, the Associated Press reported that church arsons increased across the nation.
7. See Edwin J. Delattre & Daniel L. Schofield, "Combating Bigotry in Law Enforcement," *FBI Law Enforcement Bulletin*, 27 (June 1966).
8. *R.A.V. v. City of St. Paul,* 112 S. Ct. 2538 (1992).
9. 113 S. Ct. 2194 (1993).
10. Peter Finn & Taylor McNeil, *The Response of the Criminal Justice System to Bias Crimes: An Exploratory Review* (Abt Associates, Inc., Washington, D.C.) 1987.
11. U.S. Public Law 101–275 (1990).
12. *National Bias Crimes Training for Law Enforcement and Victim Assistance Professionals,* Office for Victims of Crime (U.S. Department of Justice, Washington, D.C.) January 1995.
13. Marlene A. Young, *Victim Assistance Frontiers and Fundamentals* (Kendall/Hunt Publishing, Dubuque, Iowa) 1993.
14. Jack Levin & Jack McDevitt, *The Rising Tide of Bigotry and Bloodshed* (Plenum, New York) 1993.
15. Allen D. Sapp, Richard N. Holden, & Michael E. Wiggins, "Value and Belief Systems of Right-Wing Extremists," in Robert J. Kelly, ed., *Bias Crimes: American Law Enforcement and Legal Responses* (Office of the International Criminal Justice Administration, Reading, Berkshire, U.K.) 1993.
16. Normal Geiser, *Moody Monthly,* 129–131 (October 1985).
17. William Gale, *Racial and National Identity* (pamphlet) (Ministry of Christ Church, Glendale, Calif.) undated.
18. William P. Randel, *The Ku Klux Klan: A Century of Infamy* (Chilton Books, New York) 1965, pp. 15–16.
19. Thomas Betar, "Hate Crimes Against the Homeless Remain a Problem," *Desert News* (Salt Lake City) (May 6, 2013), p. A-1.
20. Adapted from Gary Weaver, "Law Enforcement in a Culturally Diverse Society," *FBI Law Enforcement Bulletin,* 1 (September 1992).
21. Joyce St. George, "Sensitivity Training Needs Rethinking," 7(347) *Law Enforcement News*, 8–12 (November 30, 1991).
22. Robert M. Shusta, Deena R. Levine, Philip R. Harris, & Herbert Z. Wong, *Multicultural Law Enforcement* (Prentice Hall, Englewood Cliffs, N.J.) 1995.
23. 45 Code of Federal Regulations 1304 et. seq. (1992).

12

Special Victim Populations

Chapter Outline

Victims with Disabilities
    Introduction
    Legal Issues
    Types of Victimization
    Emerging Issues
Prisoners as Victims
Abuse of Students
    Introduction
    Causation and Theories
    Bullying

    Fighting
    Gangs
    Sexual Assault
    Homicide in Schools
        Summary
        Key Terms
        Discussion Questions
        Suggested Readings
        Endnotes

LEARNING OBJECTIVES

After reading this chapter, you should be able to:

- Discuss the victimization of persons with disabilities
- Explain why prisoners are a protected class
- Discuss issues relating to abuse of school children
- Understand the bullying problems in schools
- Discuss the legislation designed to protect school children

VICTIMS WITH DISABILITIES

Introduction

Victims with disabilities have the same rights as any other victim; however, they remain one of the largest categories of victims to be neglected by our criminal justice system.[1] This is because they are not afforded the same type of access, legitimacy, or respect as other victims. For example, as the Practicum "Disability and Crime" illustrates, some material in the criminal justice system is in several languages, but very few agencies may have information in Braille. This section will provide victim services providers with an overview of some of the problems faced by persons with disabilities.

    Crimes against persons with developmental and other severe disabilities are a problem similar to other forms of violence.[2] Some research indicates that the level of violence against children and adults with developmental and other severe disabilities is as much as five times higher than against the general public, that such crimes are reported at a much lower rate, and that there are indications of lower rates of prosecution and conviction.[3]

One of the first issues confronting victim services providers is how to respond to victims of crimes who also have a disability.[4] Each type of disability may require a different response on the part of the victim services provider. For example, a victim with a hearing impairment has different needs than a victim with sight impairment. However, certain rules apply to all crime victims who are disabled.

- Look directly at the victim when speaking. Deliberately averting your eyes is impolite and can be uncomfortable.
- Feel free to ask a victim with disabilities how you should act or communicate most effectively if you have any doubts about correctness in the situation.
- Address and speak directly to the person with disabilities, even if the person is accompanied or assisted by a third-party nondisabled person.
- Feel free to offer physical assistance to a person with disabilities, such as offering your arm if the need arises, but do not assume the person will need it or accept it.
- Ask a victim with disabilities about any personal needs that will require special services or arrangements, and then attempt to make arrangements to meet those needs.
- Do not stare or avoid looking at a visible disability or deformity or express sympathy to the victim with disabilities.
- Do not tell the victim with disabilities you admire his or her courage or determination for living with the disability. The person with disabilities doesn't want to be thought of as a hero.
- Do not avoid humorous situations that occur as a result of a disability. Take your cue from the victim.[5] (Adapted from the Draft Report, Criminal Justice Task Force for Persons with Developmental Disabilities, Victim of Crime Section (Office of Criminal Justice Planning, Sacramento, Calif.) October 1, 1996, p. 1).

These suggestions should be used as guidelines when working with persons with disabilities. Victim service professionals must understand that the person with disabilities, like all other victims, is an individual and must be approached and interacted with as a separate and distinct individual. For years, people with disabilities tolerated discrimination and hardship as a result of society's reaction to their disability. Congress finally addressed this issue when it enacted the Civil Rights Act of 1964 and the Americans with Disabilities Act (ADA) of 1990.

PRACTICUM
Disability and Crime

It was late in the evening when John was returning home from the local convenience store with a carton of milk and some other groceries. It was cold and rainy, and John was hurrying as fast as he could to reach his apartment, when two persons grabbed him from behind and pulled him into an alley.

They took his wallet, trashed his bag of groceries, and proceeded to kick him in the ribs, legs, and head. Several other people walked by the attack but did nothing to render assistance. The perpetrators fled only when they heard a police siren. John gave a report to the police and was informed by the investigating officer of his right to contact the local victim–witness office. Several days later, John went downtown to that office. He had to ride ten stories in a crowded elevator and was late for the scheduled appointment. Once inside the office, he was asked to have a seat and waited approximately thirty minutes before he finally was interviewed regarding his victimization. After the interview with a victim services provider, John wanted to take some of the information home so he could study his rights as a victim more closely. Unfortunately the office did not have any pamphlets in his language—John was blind.

1. What are the issues faced by a victim services provider in this situation?
2. What problems did John encounter? How would you attempt to solve those problems? Assume you do not have any additional funds in your agency.

Legal Issues

There are approximately 43 million Americans with one or more disabilities. These disabilities may be mental, physical, or both. They may be congenital (occurring at birth) or adventitious (occurring after birth). As indicated earlier in this chapter, a **person with disabilities** is one who has a physical or mental impairment that substantially limits one or more of the major life activities of that individual, or has a record of such impairment, or is regarded as having such an impairment. This definition is founded on the language contained in the ADA of 1990. This is one of the most comprehensive pieces of civil rights legislation passed by Congress since the Civil Rights Act of 1964. The ADA was enacted by Congress to protect the employment and accessibility rights of persons suffering from disabilities. Any agency receiving any type of governmental funding (federal, state, or local) must comply with the provisions contained in the ADA.

Some authorities state that persons with developmental and other severe disabilities represent approximately 10 percent of the population of our country (1.8 percent developmental disabilities, 5 percent adult onset brain impairment, 2.8 percent severe major mental disorders). As many as 30 percent to 40 percent of all families may have loved ones or close friends with developmental or other severe disabilities. These numbers may increase as our population ages. Fifteen percent of Americans over the age of fifty-five have cognitive disabilities, and 25 percent of those over the age of seventy-five suffer from this form of disability.[6]

Disabilities covered by the law include physical and mental impairments. Physical disabilities include physiological disorders or conditions, disfigurement, or loss of use of any part of the body. Specific examples include cerebral palsy, epilepsy, multiple sclerosis, AIDS/HIV infections, cancer, heart disease, and diabetes. Mental impairments include any mental or psychological disorder, such as mental retardation, organic brain syndrome, emotional or mental illness, and specific learning disorders.

Victim services providers must anticipate serving victims with disabilities. They must work with local governmental agencies and be prepared to provide a wide variety of services to those persons with disabilities in need of their help. They should become familiar with the ADA and be spokespeople for victims with disabilities within the criminal justice system.

Types of Victimization

Persons with disabilities can be victimized in the same way as other persons; however, their response to crime is different from other victims. Crimes against persons with disabilities are underreported for a number of reasons: There may be communication and mobility barriers; the person with disabilities may be unable to report the crime because of a mental or developmental reason, or the person may be dependant on others to do so; and finally, some reporting agencies fail to record the fact that the victim was disabled.[7]

One researcher reported that 60 percent of all persons who have mental disabilities become victims of crime sometime during their life, and 60 percent of all women with hearing impairment will be victims of sexual assault.[8] Another source indicates that many people with disabilities do not receive any form of sex education, and some of them are socialized to obey others without question. Consequently, they do not complain or report acts of sexual maltreatment.[9] Individuals with disabilities in institutions are twice as likely as those in the community to be abused.[10]

Although the data are extremely limited, there is reason to believe that substantial numbers of persons with disabilities are victims of domestic abuse. These studies also indicate that women with hearing impairment have a high probability of becoming victims of domestic violence.[11] For years, professionals have acknowledged that there is a higher risk of child abuse if the child is suffering from a disability.[12]

Emerging Issues

The realization that victims with disabilities present unique challenges to those in the criminal justice system is just being acknowledged at local, state, and federal jurisdictions.

California has assembled a task force to study these issues, and this group has formulated a series of recommendations regarding the treatment of crime victims with disabilities.[13] These recommendations still need further study and revision, but they represent an important first step in this newly emerging area of victimization of the disabled. The following is a brief summary of these recommendations.

THE LEGAL PROCESS Each service provider should have a criminal justice coordinator. Knowledgeable service professionals and disability advocates should be available to assist the police, prosecutors, and courts. Each developmental disabilities regional center and other primary care or case management service agencies should have a twenty-four-hour phone number to respond to requests for information on an emergency basis. Criminal justice organizations should have specialized staff for cases involving persons with disabilities. This will allow for the gathering of information and building of expertise by those in the system. It will also provide a single point of contact for service organizations. There should be sentence enhancements when persons with disabilities are victims. This protects those who cannot protect themselves. Regular and relatively comprehensive training on victims with disabilities should occur for police, prosecutors, judges, defense attorneys, probation officers, victim–witness officers, and others in the criminal justice system.

Reporting laws should be amended to require mandatory reporting of possible crimes against victims with disabilities. Persons who deal with victims with disabilities on a regular basis should receive training in recognizing criminal acts against these victims and how to report them. Multidisciplinary teams, including victims with disabilities, should be formed in all local jurisdictions. These teams should meet on a regular basis to address various problems encountered by victims with disabilities. These teams should review sudden, unexpected deaths or major traumatic injuries to these victims when the death or injury occurs in an institution, residential, or other service facility.

VICTIM SUPPORT Each community should develop multidisciplinary teams to provide victim support cooperatively. Each team should include, as a minimum, victim services providers, sexual assault advocates, and service providers who work with the persons with disabilities. All case management agencies should have a designated staff person to serve as an advocate for victims with disabilities. There should be a coordinated public relations campaign to encourage victims with disabilities to report all crimes committed against them.

RISK REDUCTION AND PREVENTION Curriculums and required training for residential programs, vocational training, day programs, recreational programs, and special education should be modified to include personal safety training skills for persons with disabilities. This training should include self-defense skills, individual rights, assertiveness training, social skills, and training about the criminal justice system. All education and service plans for clients with disabilities should include a personal safety plan as a component. Crime prevention should involve the client, service providers, family, and friends. Special training should be conducted for family members on how to overcome isolation, facilitate attachments, support family relationships, and increase and improve communication skills of the client and family members. Safer living environments are necessary to prevent victimization of the persons with disabilities. The more connected and integrated these persons are with their community, the lower the risk of victimization. Steps should be taken to break down the traditional barriers that exist between the persons with disabilities and the community. Adult protective service agencies should have adequate resources to investigate reported abuse of these victims.

INSTITUTIONAL ABUSE There is a critical need to improve standards for screening and hiring of staff in institutions that serve the persons with disabilities. Staff training in institutions needs to be improved and updated. Use of the "buddy system" for mentoring new and problem employees should be implemented. Advocacy systems that are independent of any institutional provider should be created and supported. Ombudsperson programs need to be expanded to address these concerns. Administrators and professional staff must be actively present in all institutions to monitor and supervise staff and the clients. Management staff must be held accountable for abuse that occurs in their institutions and yet must also be encouraged to report such abuse. They must look beyond individual cases and accept the moral and professional responsibility to care for these individuals.

PRISONERS AS VICTIMS

We have known for a number of years that inmates who are incarcerated may be victimized. It seems that we just have not cared enough to seriously address the issue of prisoners as victims. There are many forms of inmate victimization; however, this section focuses on sexual violence perpetrated by one inmate on another. One estimate places the number of inmates who have been sexually assaulted over the past twenty years in excess of one million.[14] Various efforts to address this form of violence and victimization have not solved this immense social problem.

The U.S. Supreme Court, in *Farmer v. Brennan*, held there was no legitimate penological purpose that is served by allowing rape to occur within prisons.[15] Furthermore, the court held that inmates who are raped as a result of deliberate indifference by prison officials suffered cruel and unusual punishment within the meaning of the Eighth Amendment of the U.S. Constitution. Unfortunately, this ruling that established possible liability for prison officials has done little to stop prison rape.

New inmates are more vulnerable to prison rape than are recidivists who have prior imprisonment experiences and knowledge. The latter group of inmates has learned of safety zones, such as gang membership and religious group affiliations that insulate them from sexual violence. New inmates do not know of these zones and are judged vulnerable by sexual predators. This vulnerability may show up in the way a new inmate walks, his speed in finding acquaintances, and his actions in the dining hall. The characteristics of prison rapists are somewhat unclear, but several patterns are beginning to emerge. The perpetrators are younger and frequently larger or stronger than their victims and generally are more assertive and more at home in the prison environment. Typically, many of them have been convicted of crimes of a more violent nature than the crimes of their victims.[16]

With a national jail and prison population of two million, the United States likely exposes tens of thousands of male inmates to rape and consequently to HIV/AIDS and other STDs. The release of inmates from jails and prisons transforms the consequences of male rape from a correctional matter into a public health crisis. Inmates experience stigmatization as well as physical and mental trauma by other inmates and staff. Civil rights litigation on behalf of the victims rarely succeeds, and damage awards in successful litigation are usually small.[17]

The Prison Rape Elimination Act (PREA) of 2003 established a zero tolerance for rape and sexual assault in prisons. The law requires several actions by the Department of Justice, including collection of statistics, establishment of a review panel, and training.

One interim finding regarding sexual activities in prison is that it takes many forms: (1) the traditional sex assault incident with use of force or fear, (2) services for services (sex for protection), and (3) services for property (sex for cigarettes or commissary items). Some of these activities are considered as equal and consensual; however, others involve force and fear or emotional- and incentive-driven pressure.[18]

In one survey, there were more than 5,500 allegations of sexual violence. Prison systems reported 42 percent of all allegations, local or private juvenile facilities 23 percent, local jails 21 percent, and state juvenile system 11 percent. Sexual violence in confinement situations includes nonconsensual sexual acts, abusive sexual acts, staff sexual misconduct, and staff sexual harassment. Nonconsensual sexual acts include contact of any person without his or her consent and involve rape, sodomy, or oral copulation. Abusive sexual contacts encompass contact of any

FOCUS
Prison Rape Elimination Act (PREA)

Under the Prison Rape Elimination Act, governors need to certify that their states are in compliance with the PREA to qualify for certain federal funds. The Act passed by Congress in 2003 also restricts the placement of youth in adult jails and prisons. The U.S. Department of Justice regulations state: "as a matter of policy, the Department supports strong limitations on the confinement of adults with juveniles."

The regulations further ban the housing of youth in the general adult population, prohibit contact between youth and adults in common areas, ensure youth are constantly supervised by staff; and limit the use of isolation, which causes or exacerbates mental health problems for youth.

Research has established that youth are not safe in adult jails and prisons and are at the greatest risk of sexual victimization. According to Bureau of Justice Statistics, youth under the age of 18 represented 21 percent of all substantiated victims of inmate-on-inmate sexual violence in jails in 2005—disproportionately high since only 1 percent of jail inmates are juveniles. The National Prison Rape Elimination Commission found that "more than any other group of incarcerated persons, youth incarcerated with adults are probably at the highest risk for sexual abuse."

person who is unable or unwilling to consent, including intentional touching directly or through clothing of the genitalia, anus, groin, breast, inner thigh, or buttocks. Staff sexual misconduct is any sexual act directed at an inmate by an employee, volunteer, or agency representative. Staff sexual harassment involves repeated verbal comments of a sexual nature to an inmate by a staff person.[19]

Allegations involving inmate sexual violence at local and state agencies are usually investigated by outside authorities. However, investigations of staff sexual misconduct were left to prison authorities in 43 percent of the cases. Less than 20 percent of all the inmate allegations of nonconsensual sexual acts were substantiated or found to have occurred. In juvenile facilities, approximately 33 percent of alleged nonconsensual sexual acts were substantiated. Males comprised 90 percent of the victims and perpetrators in nonconsensual sexual acts in prison.

There still exists a difference in definitions regarding the sexual activity of inmates. Some institutions lack effective reporting mechanisms, while others do not have uniform procedures for recording allegations.[20]

The PREA is a substantial step forward in addressing sexual violence within U.S. prisons. Future surveys and information will assist us in understanding this complex and often misunderstood form of sexual violence.

ABUSE OF STUDENTS

Introduction

In Chapter 9, the abuse of children was examined. In this section we will examine a special population of children—students. The violence that occurs in our schools was forefront on December 14, 2012, when Adam Lanza, a twenty year-old, fatally shot twenty children and six adult staff members in a mass murder at Sandy Hook Elementary School in the village of Sandy Hook in Newtown, Connecticut. Before driving to the school that morning, Lanza had shot and killed his mother Nancy at their Newtown home. As first responders arrived, he committed suicide by shooting himself in the head. On that December morning, Sandy Hook Elementary School had 456 children enrolled in kindergarten through fourth grade. According to school authorities, the school's security protocol had recently been upgraded, requiring visitors to be individually admitted after visual and identification review by video monitor. The doors to the school were locked at 9:30 A.M. each day after morning arrivals. Newtown is located in Fairfield County, Connecticut, about 60 miles outside New York City. Violent crime had been rare in the town of 28,000 residents; there was only one homicide in the town in the ten years prior to the school shooting.[21]

School violence is an emotional and controversial topic in our society. Violence can include bullying behavior, fighting, sexual misconduct, gang activity, and various forms of homicide. This section will briefly examine causes and theories relating to violence in our schools, discuss bullying behavior, study fighting on school grounds and elsewhere, look at sexual misconduct on campus, talk about gangs within schools, and finally highlight homicide within schools.

Causation and Theories

A number of theories have been proposed to explain the cause of violence in our schools. For the most part, they are the same theories that address violence in our society: social learning theory, exchange theory, and violence in the media theory, to name a few.

Most criminologists and victimologists have known for years that delinquency occurs most often in the company of peers. This phenomenon has been labeled *group offending* or *co-offending*.

The Social Learning Theory. The primary theme of the social learning theory is that delinquency is learned through peer group interactions. One of the most prominent social theorists was Edwin Sutherland, who developed a theory that attempted to explain how group relations impact a person's attitudes and behaviors. When applied to youths, this theory assumes that juvenile delinquency is learned from others during the course of their social interaction. Sutherland's famous theory is called the theory of differential association. It covers criminal acts from traditional street crimes to white-collar crime and juvenile delinquency.

The Exchange Theory. This theory is based on the premise that people act according to a system of rewards or punishments. The exchange theory, as applied to bullying behavior, is based on a determination of costs and rewards.[22] One expert in the area of family violence states, "To put it simply, people [become bullies] because they can."[23] Individuals resort to violence to obtain psychic or material goals as long as what they achieve is outweighed by the cost of aggression.

Violence in the Media. Violence is an everyday part of our existence. For the most part, our society glamorizes violence. The boxer, football player, and actor are examples of media heroes who are sought after by men and women alike. Video games and their graphic depiction of violence also may desensitize people to the effects of violence and promote an attitude that rewards aggressive behavior in our society.[24]

Two students at an elite prep school are bullying a third student.
(© michaeljung / Fotolia)

Bullying

This section discusses the different aspects of bullying. As with many other aspects of victimology, there are conflicting views on what constitutes bullying.

As the situations in the Practicum indicate, many dynamics occur in a school setting. Some may be explained as simple, adolescent behavior, and others are clearly acts of bullying and even criminal in nature. Now let's examine some definitions of bullying.

Definition: There is no single accepted definition of bullying. Some researchers attempt to define bullying by classifying actors as the aggressor or the victim. Other academics define bullying as a set of behaviors. One of the classic definitions of bullying was purposed by Olweus, who defined it from the victim's perspective: "Bullying behavior occurs when a victim is exposed, repeatedly and over time, to negative actions on the part of one or more persons."[25]

Scope: Bullying may be the most common form of school violence. Worldwide estimates range from 10 percent of secondary students to 27 percent of middle school students. In addition, some researchers report that an astonishing 75 percent of school-aged children report having been bullied at least one time in their lives. It appears that bullying is on the rise. Just as important, some authorities are suggesting that there is a positive relationship between bullying and more serious forms of violence.

Types: The definition of bullying given above is a very broad and inclusive definition. It typically involves an imbalance of power. It covers teasing, taunting (including name calling and labeling), shoving, stealing, extortion, and a variety of violent acts imposed on a person by one or more others who have more power. This power may be physical size, aggressive behavior, or simply numbers of actors in relation to the victim. Many authorities consider failure to include the victim in school activities such as sports as a form of bullying. However, it may be that such behavior has less to do with bullying and more to do with perceived athletic ability or popularity. No matter what the reason is, the person who is the last to be selected or who is not even considered is going to suffer hurt and sometimes humiliation.

Reactions: As a society, we have become increasingly concerned with bullying. The media have conducted extensive investigations and published a wide variety of newspaper

PRACTICUM
Who Is the Bully?

Which of the following situations do you consider to be acts bullying.

1. Several male students surround a new seventh-grade student and demand that he not cross a certain area of the lawn, stating that the walkway is only for ninth graders. They inform him that they are ninth graders and will be watching to make sure he doesn't walk on that area of the lawn.

2. One female approaches another, grabs her purse, and throws it in the trash stating that she is the only one on campus who can carry that type of purse.

3. Several friends have a disagreement about a girl whom they all like, and decide not to speak to Sam Student, who is dating her. They further agree to ignore him whenever he approaches the group and not to include him in any after-school activities.

4. Several students wait in the restroom and demand money from each student for the privilege of using that restroom.

5. The class is dividing itself into two soccer teams, and no one wants to pick a new student who is very clumsy.

articles and television specials regarding bullying. Some academic researchers have proposed various programs that aim to reduce or eliminate bullying on campuses. Others have listed actions to be taken by the victim if bullying behavior occurs. Numerous publications that deal with bullying behavior are available for teachers and students. For example, *At-Risk Resources* offers more than 142 books, DVDs, games, and other items that focus on bullying.[26]

We have not solved the problem of bullying. It has existed for years and will likely continue for the immediate future. What is hopeful is that now, for the first time, we are acknowledging it and conducting research to find its causes and how to respond to its victims.

Fighting

Clearly, as the previous discussion indicates, when there is an imbalance of power that leads to aggression, the resulting acts may be defined as bullying behavior. However, when the aggression leads to a physical fight and takes on the character of mutual combat, it becomes a distinct form of violence. Therefore, for purposes of this discussion, *fighting* may be defined as the physical attack of one person by another or others. Fighting goes beyond the shoving, threatening, and taunting typical of bullying. It is physically violent behavior provoked sometimes by bullying, sometimes by personal differences, sometimes by gang disputes, and sometimes by causes that are not easily identified.

Stopping Bullying should be an ongoing campaign.
(© kikkerdirk / Fotolia)

Fighting on school grounds may be spontaneous or may be planned. Sometimes, the actual combat is delayed until after school when the combatants meet at a preselected place to settle their differences. Fighting may escalate from the use of fists and feet to knives, other weapons, and even guns.

Gangs

Despite our concern over gangs, there is not a widely accepted definition of a "gang." Nor is there any agreement when a group of delinquents becomes a gang. In the 1920s, Frederic Thrasher set forth one of the earliest definitions of a gang. He stated that a gang is an interstitial group originally formed spontaneously and then integrated through conflict. It is characterized by face-to-face interaction, milling, movement through space as a unit, conflict, and planning.[27] There are a number of other definitions of gangs, including that of Decker and Van Winkle, which characterizes gangs as an age-graded peer group that exhibits some permanence, engages in criminal activity, and has some symbolic representation of membership.[28]

In 1987, in response to nationwide concern, the U.S. Department of Justice established a program to study and respond to the gang problem in the United States. Called the National Youth Gang Suppression and Intervention, the project identified five strategies that were considered as promising practices:

1. Mobilizing community leaders to respond to gang-involved and at-risk youth
2. Using outreach workers to engage gang members
3. Providing social, economic, and educational opportunities for gang members
4. Conducting gang-suppression activities
5. Help community agencies better address gang problems[29]

Gangs continue to exist on our streets, in our prisons, and within our schools. Some schools have gone so far as to prohibit the wearing of certain apparel or colors because these items might indicate gang membership. Gangs will continue to be a problem within our society for the immediate future.

Sexual Assault

Acquaintance rape was discussed in Chapter 7. It is one of the biggest problems our campuses are facing today, from middle schools to college campuses.

How do we turn this tide of sexual violence in our schools? We have college classes that deal with family violence. We have women's studies programs or departments that focus on empowering women. Many college campuses have women's resource centers that provide a wide range of support for female students. However, most of these programs do not go far enough. Just as we educate our youth about the history of our country and the form of our government, so should we educate them about sexual violence. Someday, we will have classes in our middle schools and high schools that teach our students about the dynamics of sexual violence, how to prevent it, and what to do when it occurs.

Legislation on School Sexual Abuse

State laws pertaining to sexual abuse in schools vary widely—from the legal age of consensual sex to the definition of the crime. All states have child abuse legislation, but some make it a distinct crime with harsher penalties if educators or others in a position of authority abuse their trust. Some states also require schools to report to the state licensing agency when a teacher is convicted of a crime or resigns amid allegations of abuse, so their licenses can be reviewed or revoked.

A Maryland state statue is typical of most states. The Maryland statute requires criminal background checks for employees at public schools, private schools, and parochial schools and prohibitions against individuals who use their positions of authority by having sexual contact with students. The statute, however, does not cover part-time employees, coaches, or tutors or offenders whose victims attend a different school. The violation is not a felony. Maryland does require school officials to report to state education department when an employee is dismissed or resigns after notice of allegations of misconduct. A somewhat similar statute is the one in Washington, D.C., which requires a criminal background check for public school employees, but not private and parochial schools. It is a felony in Washington, D.C. for a person in "a significant relationship" with a minor to engage in a sexual act with that minor. The District does not require schools to report educators who resign amid abuse allegations. Only criminal convictions are reported.

Homicide in Schools

Homicide was discussed in Chapter 6. This section examines it from the perspective of violence within the school. Less than 1 percent of all homicides among school-aged children occur on or near school grounds. However, nearly two-thirds of school associated deaths were those of students, approximately one-tenth were teachers or other staff members, and one-quarter were the community members. Eighty percent of school homicide or suicide victims were male. Finally, 28 percent of the deaths occurred inside school buildings, while 36 percent occurred outdoors, and 35 percent occurred off campus.[30]

The Center for Disease Control and Prevention (CDC) conducted a number of studies regarding school violence and produced an excellent report dealing with the myths and realities of youth violence.[31] These misconceptions need to receive wide dissemination so that we can focus on the real causes and reasons for youth violence.

Myth 1: The epidemic of violent behavior of the early 1990s is over, and young people are much safer today.

Fact: While some reports indicate significant reductions, self-reports by youths reveal that some violent behavior remains high.

Myth 2: Most future offenders can be identified in early childhood.

Fact: Exhibiting uncontrolled behavior as a young child does not predetermine violence in adolescence. The majority of young people who were violent during their adolescence were not out of control in early childhood.

Myth 3: African-American and Hispanic youths are more likely than other ethnic groups to get involved in violence.

Fact: Race and ethnicity have little bearing on the overall proportion of racial and ethnic groups that engage in nonfatal violent behavior.

Myth 4: A new breed of young superpredators threatens the United States.

Fact: There is no scientific evidence to document the claim of increased seriousness or callousness.

Myth 5: Getting tough with juvenile offenders by trying them in adult criminal courts reduces the likelihood that they will commit more crimes.

Fact: Youths transferred to adult criminal court have significantly higher rates of reoffending and a greater likelihood of committing other felonies than do youths who remain in the juvenile justice system.

These are just some of the myths that exist about youth violence. They show the need for continued research in this critical phase of school violence. Homicide within schools or on school grounds carries a special sort of sorrow. We have witnessed individual students shoot teachers and other students. Some of these acts appear spontaneous, and others have involved careful planning. Just as we are responding to bullying, so must we prevent rather than react to homicide within our schools. There is hope for the future and for our children.

In a few pages, I have attempted to cover a series of topics that could occupy all of our attention for an entire Congressional session. Simply because I presented an overview does not mean that these are easily solved problems. We must, as Mad Eye Moody—a character in the Harry Potter series—stated, "Maintain constant vigilance." We must continue our crusade to protect our future both on and off the school grounds.

Summary

This chapter is a general overview of a serious issue within the criminal justice system. Special population victimization continues and in some instances is on the increase. Because the United States is becoming more diverse with the passage of each year, victim services providers need to become very aware and sensitive to the needs of these special victims. More important, they need to act as the spokespeople for these victims to individuals and agencies within the criminal justice system.

Victims with disabilities are only one of the many special populations that exist in the United States. However, their victimization carries special problems and issues that must be addressed by those within the criminal justice system. Because of their status, these victims may not report crimes. In addition, they may be victimized a second time during the criminal justice process. Victim professionals must be aware of these potential problems when dealing with these special populations.

Key Terms

Person with disabilities is an individual who has a physical or mental impairment that substantially limits one or more major life activities of that individual, or has a record of such impairment, or is regarded as having such an impairment.

Discussion Questions

1. Why are handicapped individuals specially subject to abuse?
2. Explain how you would work with a victim with sight impairment, a victim with hearing impairment, and a victim confined to a wheelchair. What problems or issues do you see that they will face in the criminal justice system?
3. Should teachers be armed to prevent homicides in schools?
4. Why is it necessary to prevent bullying in schools?
5. What type of relationship may a teacher have legally with a student?

Suggested Readings

Jack Levin & Jack McDevitt, *The Rising Tide of Bigotry and Bloodshed* (Plenum, New York) 1993.

William P. Randel, *The Ku Klux Klan: A Century of Infamy* (Chilton Books, New York) 1965.

J. Boswell, *Christianity, Social Tolerance, and Homosexuality* (University of Chicago Press, Chicago) 1980.

Kerry Lobel, ed., *Naming the Violence: Speaking Out about Lesbian Battering* (The Seal Press, Seattle, Wa.) 1986.

M. J. Elias & J. E. Zins, eds., *Bullying, Peer Harassment, and Victimization in the Schools: The Next Generation of Prevention* (Haworth Press, Binghamton, N.Y.) 2004.

D. Finkelhor, T. P. Cross, & E. N. Cantor, *How the Justice System Responds to Juvenile Victims: A Comprehensive Model* (U.S. Department of Justice, Office of Justice Programs, Washington, D.C.) 2005.

Reporting School Violence (U.S. Department of Justice, Office for Victims of Crime, Washington, D.C.) 2002.

Endnotes

1. Much of the material in this section has been adapted from *Focus on the Future: A Systems Approach to Prosecution and Victim Assistance,* sponsored by a grant from the Office for Victims of Crimes (U.S. Department of Justice, Washington, D.C.) (National Victims Center, Arlington, Va.) 1992.
2. Kathi Wolfe, "Bashing the Disabled: The New Hate Crime," 9(11) *The Progressive,* 24 (November 1995).
3. This paragraph was adapted from the *Draft Report, Criminal Justice Task Force for Persons with Developmental Disabilities, Victim of Crime Section* (Office of Criminal Justice Planning, Sacramento, Calif.) October 1, 1996, p. 1 [hereinafter referred to as *Task Force for Persons with Developmental Disabilities*].
4. L. Merkin & M. J. Smith, "A Community-Based Model Providing Services for the Deaf and Deaf–Blind Victims of Sexual Assault and Domestic Violence," 13(2) *Sexuality and Disability,* 97–106 (1995).
5. "Eight Do's and Don'ts in Working with Disabled Victims of Crime," *Focus on the Future: A Systems Approach to Prosecution and Victim Assistance* (National Victims Center, sponsored by a grant from the Office for Victims of Crimes, U.S. Department of Justice, Washington, D.C.) 1992, p. C-13.
6. Adapted from *Task Force for Persons with Developmental Disabilities,* p. 1.
7. Cheryl G. Tyiska, "Responding to Disabled Victims of Crime," 8(12) *NOVA Network Information Bulletin* (NOVA, Washington, D.C.) 1990, p. 10.
8. George Marshall Worthington, "Sexual Exploitation and Abuse of People with Disabilities," 7(2) *Response to Violence in the Family and Sexual Assault,* 43 (1984).
9. *Sexual Exploitation of Handicapped Students: Teachers Training Manual* (Seattle Rape Relief Disabilities Project, Seattle, Wash.) 1981.
10. Cathy McPherson, "Bringing Redress to Abused Disabled Persons," 8(12) *NOVA Network Information Bulletin,* 14 (NOVA, Washington, D.C., 1990).
11. Louise Melling, "Wife Abuse in the Deaf Community," 7(1) *Response to Violence in the Family and Sexual Assault,* 12 (1984).
12. Denise Aiello & Lee Capkin, "Services for Disabled Victims: Elements and Standards," 7(5) *Response to Violence in the Family and Sexual Assault,* 14 (1984).
13. Adapted from *Task Force for Persons with Developmental Disabilities,* pp. 11–22.

14. Stephen P. Teret, "New Hope for Victims of Prison Sexual Assault," 31(4) *Journal of Law, Medicine & Ethics,* 602 (Winter 2003).

15. 511 U.S. 825 (1994).

16. No Escape: Male Rape in U.S. Prisons: Summary and Recommendations, Human Rights Watch (2001); available online: www.hrw.org/reports/2001/prison/report1.html.

17. James E. Robertson, "Rape among Incarcerated Men: Sex, Coercion and STDs," 17 *Aids Patient Care and STDs,* 423 (2003).

18. Morris L. Thigpen & Larry Solomon, *Annual Report to Congress, Prison Rape Elimination Act (PREA)* (National Institute of Corrections, Washington, D.C.) September 2004.

19. Allen J. Beck & Timothy A. Hughes, *Sexual Violence Reported by Correctional Authorities, 2004,* Bureau of Justice Statistics (Department of Justice, Washington, D.C.) July 2005.

20. Ibid. at pp. 4–5.

21. Richard Esposito, Candice Smith, & Christina Ng, "20 Children Died in Newtown, Conn., School Massacre," *ABC News* (Associated Press, December 14, 2012), retrieved December 14, 2012; "Connecticut School Victims were Shot Multiple Times," *CNN,* retrieved December 16, 2012; and Becky Bratu, "Connecticut School Shooting is Second Worst in US history," *NBC News* (December 14, 2012), retrieved December 16, 2012.

22. P. M. Blau, *Exchange and Power in Social Life* (Wiley and Sons, New York) 1964.

23. R. J. Gelles, *Family Violence,* 2nd ed. (Sage, Newbury Park, Calif.) 1987, p. 17.

24. See for example, K. Polk's "Male to Male Homicide: Scenarios of Masculine Violence," paper presented at the annual meeting of the American Society of Criminology, San Francisco, November 18–23, 1991.

25. D. Olweus, "Bullies on the Playground: The Role of Victimization," in C. H. Hart, ed., *Children on Playgrounds: Research Perspectives and Applications* (State University of New York Press, Albany, N.Y.) 1993, p. 9.

26. *At-Risk Resources* (The Bureau of At-Risk Youth, Hawthorne, N.Y.) 2006.

27. F. Thrasher, *A Study of 1,313 Gangs in Chicago* (University of Chicago Press, Chicago) 1927.

28. S. Decker and B. Van Winkle, *Life in a Gang: Family, Friends, and Violence* (Cambridge University Press, New York) 1988.

29. Spergel, *The Youth Gang Problem: A Community Approach* (Oxford university Press, New York) 1995.

30. *School Violence Injury Fact Book,* Centers for Disease Control and Prevention; available online: www.cdc.gov (April 21, 2006).

31. *Youth Violence: A Report of the Surgeon General: The Public Health Approach*, Centers for Disease Control and Prevention; available online: wwwmentalhealth.samhsa.gov (April 21, 2006).

Negligence and Intentional Torts

Chapter Outline

LEARNING OBJECTIVES

After reading this chapter, you should be able to:

- Compare and contrast negligence and intentional torts
- Explain the difference between torts and criminal acts
- Distinguish between the torts of assault and of battery
- Explain why the tort of mental distress is important to victims
- Understand the various defenses to negligence and intentional torts

INTRODUCTION

This chapter deals with negligence and the intentional torts of wrongful death, assault, battery, false imprisonment, and intentional infliction of mental distress. The great majority of all victim-related issues occurs in the area of tort law, and therefore it is important to understand the basic rules that apply to an action based on tort.

A tort may be based on negligence or on intentional acts. *Negligence* is a complex legal concept that under certain circumstances holds persons liable for acting, or failing to act, in a certain manner. Many persons, including victims of crime, have been injured because of the negligence of another party.

Many other issues relating to victims arise because of an intentional act of another. Intentional torts include wrongful death, assault, battery, false imprisonment, and intentional infliction of mental distress. Each of these torts requires the perpetrator to act with a certain state of mind or intent. The intent required for these types of injuries requires that the tortfeasor intend to cause some physical or mental effect on another person. There is no requirement that the tortfeasor intend to harm the victim. The intent to harm is irrelevant as long as the tortfeasor intended the act.[1] The law also calls a tortfeasor's actions intentional even if he did not desire a certain type of occurrence but knew with substantial certainty that it would occur as a result of his actions.

In the majority of intentional torts, a certain doctrine applies. The doctrine of **transferred intent** holds that so long as the tortfeasor had the necessary intent to act in a certain manner toward one person, he will be held liable for torts committed against any other person who happens to be injured. Many states incorporate this doctrine into their criminal codes that establish criminal liability.[2]

The significance of proving intent relates to the award of damages. If the jury finds that the tortfeasor acted intentionally, the jury may award nominal damages even if no injury occurred to the plaintiff. **Nominal damages** are token damages, for example, $1.00. Although this may seem insignificant, many jurisdictions also allow the prevailing party to recover attorneys' fees. In this case, the award of token damages may allow the victim to recover attorneys' fees and the costs of the suit. An intentional tort victim may also recover punitive damages if the jury finds that the defendant's acts were outrageous or malicious. As discussed later in this chapter, punitive damages are to punish the tortfeasor.

Each of these torts has a "companion" criminal act. Although there are differences between the criminal and civil acts, they are similar in many ways. Table 13.1 compares some of the more common criminal acts with their companion civil tort.

One significant difference between a criminal case and a civil case is the amount of evidence necessary to prove the case. Normally the criminal process will have been completed prior to the civil trial. If the defendant is found guilty in the criminal action, this fact may be presented in the subsequent civil action to prove culpability. Even if the perpetrator is found not guilty in the criminal case, the victim still has the right to pursue a civil cause of action because of the difference in the burden of proof between the two types of proceedings. In criminal cases, the government must prove the case beyond a reasonable doubt, whereas in civil cases the plaintiff need only present a preponderance of the evidence. Table 13.2 illustrates the difference between the two levels of proof.

The difference in the burden of proof is important because unlike criminal proceedings, there is no double jeopardy bar to filing a civil action after an acquittal in the criminal case.

TABLE 13.1 A Comparison of Torts and Crimes

Intentional Torts	Crimes
Wrongful Death	Murder
	Involuntary manslaughter
	Voluntary manslaughter
	Negligent manslaughter
Assault	Assault or stalking
Battery	Battery or any sexual crime such as rape, sodomy, or oral copulation
False Imprisonment	False imprisonment
Mental Distress	Stalking

TABLE 13.2	Standards of Proof

Possible Amount of Proof

0.. 100%

Beyond a Reasonable Doubt

0... 90–95%

Preponderance of the Evidence

0.................................... 51%

In criminal cases, the double jeopardy clause of the Fifth Amendment prevents the state from refiling the criminal charges if the defendant is acquitted.[3] This prohibition, however, does not apply to the filing of civil cases. Therefore, even if the defendant is acquitted in a criminal action, a civil intentional tort action may be filed. This is exactly what happened in the O. J. Simpson saga. After Mr. Simpson was acquitted of the double murder of his ex-wife, Nicole Brown Simpson, and her friend Ronald Goldman, both families of the victims filed civil actions against O. J. Simpson. Both families prevailed in the civil action when the jury found Mr. Simpson liable for the wrongful death of Nicole and Ronald.

Victims file civil actions against their perpetrators for a variety of reasons. They may believe that they did not receive appropriate satisfaction as a result of any criminal proceedings. The defendant may have been acquitted or convicted of a lesser charge than the victim believes is proper. Victims may also feel mistreated by the criminal justice system and have a desire to be in control of the proceedings instead of merely being a witness. Many victims may also want to receive more compensation for injuries than is available in the criminal justice system.

NEGLIGENCE

Introduction

Often we hear others refer to the fact that someone was negligent. The lay or common meaning of the term *negligent* simply means someone was careless or slipshod in performing some act. The term *negligence* in tort law is a far more complex and confusing concept. The legal definition of **negligence** comprises several components, including a duty, a breach of that duty, proximate

FOCUS
The O.J. Simpson Case

Although the O.J. Simpson murder trial occurred almost two decades ago, it provides a good example of the differences between a criminal case and a civil case. O.J. was a star running back at the University of Southern California and late in the National Football League with the Buffalo Bills. He won the Heisman Trophy at Southern California and was elected to the Pro Football Hall of Fame in 1985.

In 1989, Simpson pleaded no contest to a domestic violence charge and was separated from his wife, Nicole Brown Simpson, to whom he was paying child support. They divorced in 1992. In 1995, he was acquitted by a jury in a California State criminal court of the 1994 murder of his ex-wife Nicole and her friend Ronald Goldman after a lengthy and internationally publicized criminal trial, the *People v. Simpson*. After the acquittal he was sued in civil court by the Goldman and Brown families for the wrongful death of Ronald and Nicole. In 1997, a civil court awarded a judgment against Simpson for their wrongful deaths; as of 2013, he has paid little of the $33.5 million penalty assessed by the civil court judgment.

In 2008, he was found guilty of robbery in a Nevada criminal trial and sentenced to thirty-three years' imprisonment, with a minimum of nine years without parole. As of 2013, he was serving his sentence at the Lovelock Correctional Center in Lovelock, Nevada.

cause, and actual injury. Under the concept of negligence, the injured party must show that the tortfeasor had a legal duty that required him to conduct himself according to certain standards, so as to avoid harming others. The plaintiff must also prove that the defendant breached or failed to conform his conduct to that standard. Once these two elements have been established, there must be proof that they were the proximate cause or causal link between the defendant's acts and the injury suffered by the plaintiff. Finally, there must be proof of actual damages as distinguished from intentional torts that allow for recovery of nominal damages even without proof of actual injury.

Elements of Negligence

The definition of negligence contains several distinct elements. Each must be proved before the injured party can recover damages. The problem with negligence is that there are many gray areas in each element. For ease of understanding, only basic concepts are discussed in this textbook.

The injured party must prove that the defendant owed a legal duty to avoid unreasonable risk to others. Courts utilize a balancing test to determine if the defendant's conduct exposed the victim to unreasonable harm. The test is simply whether a reasonable person would have recognized the risk of harm and sought to avoid it.[4]

In applying this test, courts often examine the situation using an objective test. Juries are asked to view the defendant's conduct from a reasonable person's point of view. If a reasonable person of ordinary prudence in the defendant's position would have avoided harming the victim, the defendant is found negligent if the actions injured the plaintiff.

The defendant must fail to conform his conduct to the legal duty. This duty to others many times is determined by the relationship between the defendant and the victim. Some relationships impose a higher standard of care or duty on the defendant than others.

The victim must also show a close causal relationship between the defendant's acts and the injury. This is known as the *proximate* or *legal cause* of the injury. This is the one area of negligence that gives lawyers, judges, and juries the most problems. For example, suppose two drivers are intoxicated and run into each other. Who is at fault? Suppose one driver had two drinks and the other driver had ten drinks? The short answer is that the law will presume that each driver will be held to be a proximate or legal cause of the accident. Therefore, if the defendant has "caused" the injury to the victim, the law may hold him liable. However, the issue is further complicated by another concept that deals with foreseeability of harm.

Foreseeability is viewing harm as a set of dominoes. When the defendant acts in certain ways, his actions cause other effects similar to pushing over one domino in a line. The public policy question is how far down that line of toppling dominoes will the courts look in holding the defendant accountable. The generally accepted rule is that if the injuries were a direct result of the defendant's action, the defendant will be held liable even if the injuries were not the kind one would normally expect as a result of the act.[5] This position is based on several rationales, including that many serious cases arise from single acts of negligence that are caused by large corporations, government, or utilities. These entities are able to bear the burden of compensating the victim who had no reason to guard against that particular loss.

Finally, the victim must suffer actual damage or injury. The extent of the victim's injury may not be easy to determine. This aspect of negligence may require the services of expert witnesses to explain how the victim was injured, the extent of those injuries, and how long they will last.

Victims may not be aware of the true extent of their injuries. Care should be taken when advising victims to settle with insurance companies immediately after an incident. There are some injuries that do not show up right away, and most settlement agreements prevent the victim from asking for additional money for other injuries that are discovered after the settlement. Many states allow victims of negligence up to one year before they lose their right to sue. Victims should be advised to consult their own insurance company as well as an attorney and have a thorough medical examination before signing any settlement.

WRONGFUL DEATH

Wrongful death actions may be brought based on negligence, strict liability, or intentional acts by the defendant. They are discussed in this chapter because many wrongful death causes of action arise from criminal acts that are based on homicide statutes. When a perpetrator kills the victim, her or his family must cope with the loss. In addition, the family may have been deprived of the economic support that the victim would have contributed over her or his lifetime.

The Parties

In common law, when a person died, his or her right to recover for any injuries was extinguished upon death. This rule also applied to decedent's heirs so that they were precluded from recovering damages they suffered as a result of the loss of a loved one. Every state has modified this common law rule by adopting survival statutes and wrongful death statutes.

   Survival statutes modify the common law rule by allowing the decedent's claim for personal injuries to be brought by his or her heirs. Many of these states also allow the filing and maintenance of a personal injury action against the defendant's estate if he or she dies before the filing of the civil case. Most states have special **wrongful death statutes**, which allow a defined group of individuals to recover the loss it sustained as a result of the victim's death. The parties that may sue under these wrongful death statutes are the decedent's spouse, children, and parents. Because wrongful death actions are based on statutorily created rights, courts are reluctant to expand the scope of these remedies. Thus, live-in lovers who are not legally married may be denied recovery.[6]

Elements of Damage

Certain types of damages are unique to wrongful death cases and include loss of companionship, sexual intercourse, and moral guidance of the decedent. Some states also allow for grief or other mental suffering of the survivors as an element of damages.

   When a child is murdered and a civil action is brought by the child's parents, it is sometimes hard to establish pecuniary loss on the part of the parents, because it is generally agreed that the cost of raising and educating a child is more than any earning the child could be expected to contribute to her or his parents. However, many courts are now allowing damages for loss of companionship of the child.

   A very emotional issue that sometimes arises in wrongful death cases involves the doctrine of unjust enrichment. This common law rule prohibits persons—in wrongful death cases it would be the perpetrator—from profiting from their own wrongdoing. The doctrine of unjust enrichment is implemented by court decisions that are founded upon *Salyer's Rules or Statutes*. These are statutes that prohibit a murderer from profiting from his or her illegal acts. There are numerous court decisions that prevent intrafamilial killers from gaining an economic advantage because of their actions. For example, in one famous case, a husband murdered his wife and then filed to become the administrator of her estate. As the administrator, he would have been entitled to fees for his services to the estate. The court rejected his claim because he had been convicted of her murder.[7]

ASSAULT AND BATTERY

Assault and battery are common intentional torts. Many laypersons confuse assault with battery and vice versa. It is not uncommon for an assault and battery to occur during the commission of a crime. However, it must be understood that although they are discussed together for purposes of comparison, they are distinct and separate intentional torts. You may have an assault without a battery, and you may also have a battery without an assault.

Defined

The tort of **assault** has been defined as the intentional causing of an apprehension or offensive contact.[8] The defendant has committed the tort of assault when he has caused the victim to believe that she will be subjected to harmful or offensive contact. The interest that is being protected is the victim's freedom from apprehension of wrongful contact. Assault can therefore occur even if no actual contact occurs between the defendant and the victim.

The tort of **battery** has been defined as the intentional infliction of harmful or offensive bodily contact.[9] The tort of battery includes touching or contact that causes injury to the victim as well as any bodily contact that is considered offensive. The standard used to determine if the contact is offensive is whether an ordinary person would have been offended by the contact.

Fear versus Contact

As the previous definitions indicate, the key distinction between an assault and battery is whether the victim experienced fear or was touched in a harmful or offensive manner by the defendant. Some states argue whether words alone may constitute an assault. The states requiring more than words mandate that the words be accompanied by some overt act that adds to the threatening character of the words. Other states and the *Restatement of Torts* indicate that there may be situations in which words by themselves without any overt act are sufficient to constitute the tort of assault.[10] This distinction between threats and overt acts was also a dilemma faced by law enforcement agencies who responded to threats made by perpetrators prior to the adopting of the stalking laws. Most criminal assault statutes required that the defendant have the present ability to inflict injury upon the victim. Stalking statutes allow law enforcement to take action based on a threat to harm the victim in the future.[11]

Because the tort of assault protects the peace of mind of the victims, they must be aware of the threat. The victim needs only to experience apprehension. Apprehension is not necessarily the same emotion as fear. In other words, the victim only need be concerned rather than scared. The threat must be directed at the victim and not a third person. If a family member is threatened, the victim may experience apprehension or even fear but cannot recover based on the traditional tort of assault. As will be discussed later, the modern tort of infliction of mental distress would apply in these types of situations.

Unlike assault, the tort of battery may be committed even if the victim is unaware of the contact at the time it occurs. For example, the perpetrator may slip something in the victim's drink, causing him/her to pass out. The perpetrator then engages in sexual intercourse with the victim. The crime of rape and the tort of battery have both occurred even though at the time of the contact the victim was unconscious.

FALSE IMPRISONMENT

Defined

The tort of **false imprisonment** is defined as the intentional infliction of a confinement. The victim must show that the perpetrator intended to confine him/her. He or she must be confined within definite physical boundaries. Simply blocking the victim's path or preventing him or her from entering a particular place does not meet the requirement of this tort. However, if the victim initially consents to the confinement, there is no tort. If the perpetrator is under a duty to release the victim and fails to do so, the tort has been committed. For example, a victim may meet the perpetrator at a bar and agree to a ride home with him or her. There is no false imprisonment during the ride to the victim's home. Once they arrive at the victim's home and the perpetrator refuses to allow the victim to leave the car unless the victim has sex with him or her, the tort of false imprisonment occurs. This is true even though the victim agreed to ride in the perpetrator's car.

The Confinement Requirement

The essence of the confinement requirement is that the victim is held within certain limits, not simply prevented from entering certain places. Thus, preventing the victim from entering a store is not false imprisonment, whereas holding the victim in an office within that store would be such a tort. Confining the victim to a locked room clearly meets the definition of this tort. However, there are other instances of more subtle acts that will give rise to the tort of false imprisonment. If the perpetrator threatens the victim with force if he or she tries to escape from an unlocked building and the perpetrator has the apparent ability to carry out the threat, the tort of false imprisonment is complete. Unlike assault, the tort of false imprisonment may occur if the perpetrator threatens harm to family members if the victim does not remain in a particular room or tries to escape.[12] The threat or duress that confines the victim must be of imminent harm. Threats of future harm are not sufficient. The tort of false imprisonment usually does not occur in a vacuum. Perpetrators usually commit other torts such as assault and battery in connection with the false imprisonment. Victim services providers should always be aware that several intentional torts may arise from one crime. For example, the offense of kidnapping may give rise to the intentional torts of assault, battery, false imprisonment, and mental distress.

MENTAL DISTRESS

The intentional tort of infliction of mental distress is a relatively new tort. An increasing number of jurisdictions are recognizing that victims suffer mental problems as a result of criminal or other intentional acts, and these jurisdictions are allowing the victims to sue for damages alleging infliction of mental or emotional distress. The tort of **mental distress** has been defined as the intentional or reckless infliction, by extreme or outrageous conduct, of severe emotional or mental distress. This tort does not require any physical harm or injury to the victim.

Intent Requirement

Unlike the majority of other intentional torts, the doctrine of transferred intent does not generally apply to the infliction of emotional distress. The most common reason given for precluding the application of this doctrine is that it would open the floodgates of litigation by unrelated parties. Professor Prosser points out that if the doctrine of transferred intent were allowed in emotional distress cases, millions of Americans who witnessed President Reagan being shot on television would be able to sue John Hinckley for infliction of emotional distress.[13]

The courts have fashioned one important exception in this area that deals with family members who witness the defendant injure or harm another family member. However, this exception is quite narrow and requires that the defendant know of the plaintiff's presence so that the infliction of mental distress is a reasonable consequence of the defendant's actions toward the other family member. For example, in a California case, the plaintiff watched the defendant beat up her father, and as a result of observing the beating she suffered severe emotional distress. The court held that because there was no allegation or proof that the defendant knew of her presence nor that he intended to cause her emotional distress, her claim was invalid and the case dismissed.[14] However, the *Restatement of Torts* would liberalize this position and allow for recovery by victims who witness injury to others even if they are not related so long as the victim suffers physical illness as a result of the incident.[15]

Conduct Requirement

For the victims to recover damages, they must show that the defendant's conduct was extreme and outrageous. The defendant is not liable for insults or hurt feelings. The *Restatement of Torts* points out that certain conduct does not meet the standard of outrageous. Nonqualifying conduct includes "mere insults, indignities, threats, annoyances, petty oppressions, or other trivialities."[16] The test that is normally applied requires that the conduct be so outrageous in character and so extreme as to go beyond all possible bounds of decency and be regarded as atrocious and utterly intolerable in a civilized society.[17] Once the victims show that the defendant's conduct was extreme and outrageous, they must also prove that they suffered severe emotional distress. Most jurisdictions require as a minimum that victims show that as a result of the defendant's conduct they sought and received medical treatment.

DEFENSES TO INTENTIONAL TORTS

Simply establishing that the perpetrator injured the victim does not end the inquiry. Just as there are defenses that persons accused of crimes may raise in criminal actions, so are there the same or similar defenses that may be asserted in civil actions. This is especially true if there was no criminal case filed or it was dismissed on a technicality and no conviction or plea entered. If that is the case, then many of the defenses that would have been raised in the criminal case will most likely be used by the perpetrator in the civil case in an attempt to escape liability.

Self-Defense

Just as criminal law recognizes the privilege of self-defense, so does civil law. The rules regarding the use of self-defense are substantially the same in both situations. In understanding self-defense, it is important to distinguish between deadly and nondeadly force. A person is justified in using deadly force only to protect oneself or others from what the person reasonably believes is imminent, unlawful deadly force.

The concept of self-defense includes the components of proportionality and necessity. *Proportionality* mandates that the force used in self-defense not be out of proportion to the force necessary to protect the person from the threatened harm. Necessity requires that a person use force only to prevent imminent, unlawful deadly force. Therefore, a person is normally not authorized in using deadly force to combat threats of future harm.

This is the dilemma faced by many battered spouses. There have been numerous cases and articles dealing with situations in which battered spouses have killed their abusing partners.[18] The victims may have attacked and killed the abuser defending themselves from a physical assault, or in some cases they may be threatened with harm in the future such as when the perpetrator awakes or returns home. In some cases, the victim has responded with force as the abuser enters the home or while the victim is sleeping or passed out. The abused spouses believe in their own minds that they will be killed or seriously injured. Victims have no doubt regarding the offender's ability to carry out any threats, because they have experienced the perpetrator's violent behavior in the past.

When a spouse kills another under a subjective opinion that they face death or danger, several jurisdictions have called this an "imperfect" form of self-defense. The courts are divided in this area, with some courts authorizing the use of deadly force and others claiming the use of force improper with the result that the abused spouse faces criminal charges for homicide.[19] This imperfect self-defense is what the Menendez brothers used in their high-profile murder trial in which they were accused of murdering their mother and father. The brothers alleged that their father was going to kill them when they threatened to expose the fact that he had sexually molested them for years. The jury rejected this defense and found the brothers guilty of homicide.

The general rule is that the nonaggressor or original victim does not have a duty to retreat before using deadly force to defend oneself. However, the aggressor may not normally use deadly force in self-defense of his or her actions. Most states deny the defense to those who initiate the fight. However, if the aggressor starts the fight, then clearly tries to retreat, deadly force may be used if the retreat is unsuccessful.

Defense of Others

A person is authorized in using force to defend another from imminent attack. The defender is justified in using the same amount or type of force in defending others as in self-defense. Some early cases required the defender to be related to the one being attacked, but modern cases have done away with this requirement, and a person can now use force to defend a stranger.

Defense of Property

There is a right to use force to defend both real and personal property. The property owner can only use as much force as is reasonable to protect the property. There is authority for the position that the owner must first make a verbal demand that the perpetrator stop before using force, unless it appears that the harm is imminent or that the request to stop is useless. Although a property owner may use reasonable force to defend his or her property, he or she may not use deadly force to protect the property, nor can the person use any force to reclaim property not in possession. The law does not favor self-help. A person may also not use mechanical devices such as spring guns in defending the home from theft or trespass. Spring guns are triggered to go off when a perpetrator enters the premises. In a widely discussed case, the defendant owned an unoccupied boarded-up farmhouse that had been broken into and vandalized a number of times. The defendant placed a shotgun in a bedroom and rigged it so that when a person entered the bedroom, the gun would discharge. The plaintiff entered the house to steal some jars he thought were antiques. When he entered the bedroom, the gun discharged, striking him in the leg. In the civil trial that followed, the plaintiff (intruder) was awarded damages for his injuries, and the property owner's claim of defense of property was denied. On appeal, the court stated that a property owner may not use deadly force to defend his property against a trespasser, unless the latter is committing a felony of violence or endangering human life by his act. Furthermore, what a property owner may not do directly, he also may not do indirectly by a spring gun or by other mechanical device.[20]

Consent

If the victim gives consent, the defendant will not be liable for any injuries. The defense of consent is frequently used in sexual assault cases. The perpetrator will claim that the victim consented to the sexual acts, and if there are physical injuries, the offender will attempt to dismiss them stating that the victim enjoyed or asked for rough sex. A number of sexual assault cases involve situations in which consent is an issue. These areas include lack of capacity to consent, exceeding the scope of consent, and duress causing consent.

Lack of Capacity to Consent. This situation occurs when for a variety of reasons the victim, as a matter of law, is unable to give consent. Young children are incapable of consenting to sexual acts. For example, a defendant would never raise the issue of consent when the victim of his sexual advances was five years old. Adults with developmental disabilities may also be incapable of consenting to sexual acts. Persons who are unconscious because of excessive drinking or the use of drugs cannot give consent. Thus, the male college student who engages in sexual acts with his date who has passed out cannot raise the defense of consent.

Exceeding the Scope of Consent. If the victim gives actual consent to certain acts, the offender will not be able to raise the defense of consent if he goes substantially beyond the scope of that consent. In these situations, the perpetrator argues that the victim consented to having sex, and the victim states that she may have consented to certain acts, such as kissing and petting, but not sexual intercourse. Because there may be no physical evidence to support the victim's position, it becomes an issue of credibility in which the victim gives one statement, and the perpetrator claims the events occurred in a different manner.

Duress Causing Consent. Recently in Texas, a woman was in her home alone at night and a stranger entered through a window. The intruder stated he was going to have sex with her. The women fearing that she might get AIDS asked that he wear a condom during the act. She placed the condom on his penis, and they engaged in sexual intercourse. Immediately after the perpetrator fled the scene, the women called the police and they arrested the offender. He claimed consent arguing that she had invited the acts by urging him to wear a condom. One Texas grand jury refused to indict the defendant for rape; however, a second grand jury did indict him.

Another situation involves the defendant threatening the victim with a weapon and causing her to comply with his demands for sex. In this situation, there may not be any physical evidence that supports the victim's claim of rape, but clearly such a fact pattern meets all the elements of the crime of rape and the torts of assault and battery.

Necessity

The defense of necessity is based on a balancing of the evil that faces a person. For example, a person trapped on a hill during a snowstorm may have a choice of breaking into a cabin or freezing to death. The person understands that he is committing a crime (of burglary or trespass) by breaking into the cabin, but he also realizes that to stay out in the unprotected environment will result in his death. Although the person may have committed a criminal offense in breaking into the cabin, the defense of necessity will allow him to escape punishment. A person cannot raise this defense if the threatened harm will occur sometime in the future. In other words, a person cannot simply enter a store and take food claiming that a snowstorm is coming and he needs food to exist.

Two types of emergencies justify a person in harming another's property: cases of public necessity and cases of private necessity. When the person injures another's property in order to prevent harm to a substantial number of persons or to himself, the defense is based on public necessity. When the person is protecting only his own interest or the interest of a few citizens, the defense is based on private necessity. Public necessity defenses normally arise when the interference or damage to the lands of another is necessary or appears to be necessary to prevent a disaster to the community or a substantial number of persons within the community.[21] Private necessity defenses arise when a person injures private property to protect his property or the person or property of a third party if there is no other way to prevent the harm.[22]

Authority of Law

Acts committed by persons under authority of law are generally considered a valid defense. For example, a law enforcement officer who executes a valid warrant and uses proper procedures in doing so has a defense against a lawsuit based on the tort of false imprisonment by the person arrested. When an officer makes an arrest based on an arrest warrant that is valid on its face and uses proper procedures in making the arrest, the officer will have a valid defense even if it is later shown that the arrest warrant was invalid. Arrests without a warrant are complex and confusing. An officer or private citizen may make an arrest for a felony or misdemeanor committed in her presence. Officers may also make a warrantless arrest for a felony not committed in their presence if they have reasonable cause to believe that the defendant committed it. Officers are privileged even if it later turns out that no crime was committed or that they arrested the wrong person so long as their beliefs were reasonable at the time of the arrest. Private citizens will lose their immunity if no felony was committed; however, like the officer they will still retain the immunity even if they arrested the wrong person if their beliefs were reasonable.

Summary

A significant number of victims file civil lawsuits against the perpetrators who injure them during the commission of a crime. Victims file these actions for a variety of reasons. As a result, victim services providers must be familiar with civil causes of actions that allow victims to recover for their injuries. Negligence is a complex legal doctrine that holds parties liable for injuries suffered as a result of a breach of duty owed to the victim.

In addition, a number of other torts correspond to the more common criminal offenses. These civil actions include the intentional torts of wrongful death, assault, battery, false imprisonment, and mental distress. In addition, victim advocates must be familiar with the basic rules regarding liability of joint tortfeasors, issues surrounding the common defenses to these torts, the various types of intent necessary to commit these torts, and the different levels of proof in a criminal and civil case.

The intentional tort of wrongful death is one of the most emotional torts victim services providers must handle. The primary victim of this crime is dead, and the remaining victim must deal with grief regarding the loss of a loved one as well as the complexities of pursuing a civil lawsuit. Victim services providers must understand who can recover and be prepared to discuss issues regarding damages that may be available to the remaining family victims.

There are a number of defenses to intentional torts. Many of these civil defenses are the same ones that will be raised in any criminal action. In many homicides, for example, the defendant will claim to have been provoked by the deceased and was simply acting in self-defense. Understanding the various defenses to intentional torts is an important aspect of this area of victims' rights.

Key Terms

Transferred intent holds that so long as the tortfeasor had the necessary intent to act in a certain manner toward one person, that person will be held liable for torts committed against any other person who happens to be injured.

Nominal damages are token damages, for example, $1.00.

Negligence comprises several components, including a duty, a breach of that duty, proximate cause, and actual injury.

Survival statutes modify the common law rule by allowing the decedent's claim for personal injuries to be brought by his heirs.

Wrongful death statutes allow a defined group of individuals to recover the loss it sustained as a result

of the victim's death. The parties that may sue under these wrongful death statutes are the decedent's spouse, children, and parents.

Assault is the intentional causing of an apprehension or offensive contact.

Battery is the intentional infliction of harmful or offensive bodily contact.

False imprisonment is the intentional infliction of a confinement.

Mental distress is the intentional or reckless infliction, by extreme or outrageous conduct, of severe emotional or mental distress.

Discussion Questions

1. Can we obtain insurance that covers us in the event of a negligent act on our part? If we didn't have insurance, would we be more careful in our actions?
2. What is the most important element in the tort of negligence? Why is it more critical than the other elements?
3. Other than wrongful death, what is the most serious intentional tort? Justify your answer.
4. Should people be held liable for acts of others? Why? Why not?
5. Should we have a "no-fault" tort system and pay those who are injured instead of arguing over who is at fault and which defense may apply? Would such a system save us money?
6. Which is the most important defense to the intentional torts? Why?

Suggested Reading

J. W. Wade, J. W. Prosser, & V. E. Schwartz, *Cases and Materials on Torts,* 5th ed. (West Publishing Co., St. Paul, Minn.) 1984 w/1988 Supp.

Endnotes

1. *Vosburg v. Putney,* 50 N.W. 403 (Wis. 1891).
2. See H. Wallace & C. Roberson, *Principles of Criminal Law,* 5th ed. (Pearson, Columbus, Ohio) 2012.
3. The double jeopardy clause applies to state and federal actions. *Benton v. Maryland,* 395 U.S. 784 (1969).
4. *U.S. v. Carroll Towing Co.,* 159 F2d 169 (2nd Cir. 1947).
5. See the classic case of *In Re Polemis,* 3 K.B. 560 (Eng. 1921) for a full discussion of this concept.
6. See *Steed v. Imperial Airlines,* 524 P.2d 801 (Cal. 1974), where the court held that a stepchild was not an heir under the wrongful death statute and therefore could not recover damages even though the child suffered loses of economic support and moral guidance.
7. *Brown v. Blue,* 724 S.W. 2d 400 (Tex. App. 1986).
8. See *Restatement Second of Torts,* Section 21, American Law Institute (1995).
9. See *Restatement Second of Torts,* Section 13, American Law Institute (1995).
10. See *Restatement Second of Torts,* Section 31, American Law Institute (1995).
11. H. Wallace, "A Prosecutors Guide to Stalking," *The Prosecutor,* 26 (January/February 1995).
12. See *Restatement Second of Torts,* Section 40A, American Law Institute (1995).
13. J. W. Wade, W. L. Prosser, & V. E. Schwartz, *Cases and Materials on Torts,* 5th ed. (West Publishing Co., St. Paul, Minn.) 1984 w/1988 Supp, p. 64.
14. *Taylor v. Vallelunga,* 339 P.2d 910 (Cal. App. 1959).
15. See *Restatement Second of Torts,* Section 40A, American Law Institute (1995).
16. See *Restatement Second of Torts,* Section 46, American Law Institute (1995).
17. See *Restatement Second of Torts,* Section 46 Comment d, American Law Institute (1995).
18. See H. Wallace, "The Battered Women Syndrome: Self-defence and Duress as Mandatory Defences?" *The Police Journal,* 133 (April June 1994). (Note title uses English spelling.)
19. H. Wallace, *Family Violence: Legal, Medical and Social Perspectives* (Allyn & Bacon, Boston) 1996.
20. *Katko v. Briney,* 183 N.W. 2d 657 (Iowa 1971).
21. For a case dealing with public necessity by public officials, see *Surocco v. Geary,* 3 Cal. 69 (1853); and for a case dealing with public necessity by a private person, see *Harrison v. Wisdom,* 54 Tenn. 99 (1872).
22. See *Ploof v. Putnam,* 71 A. 188 (Vt. 1908) for a discussion of the defense of private necessity.

14

Constitutional and Civil Rights of Victims

Chapter Outline

Section 1983 Actions
Introduction
Requirement of State Action
Scope of Liability

Section 1983 Theories of Liability
Denial of Equal Protection
Failure to Act

Violence Against Women Act
Background
Gender-Based Civil Rights

Injunctions
Background and Use of Restraining Orders
Advantages and Disadvantages

Defenses
Absolute Immunity
Qualified Immunity
Summary
Key Terms
Discussion Questions
Suggested Readings
Endnotes

LEARNING OBJECTIVES

After reading this chapter, you should be able to:

- Distinguish between the various theories upon which liability may be imposed on tortfeasors

- Explain the history and significance of 42 U.S.C. Section 1983

- Discuss the ramifications of the Violence Against Women Act and how it affects the field of victimology

- Understand the use of injunctions

- Distinguish between absolute and qualified immunity

Up to this point, the textbook dealt with situations in which victims have been injured by individuals acting alone or in concert with other perpetrators. In these situations, victims turn to those employed by the criminal justice system to assist them in punishing these persons. However, occasionally there are instances when those who work in the criminal justice system harm or contribute to the harm suffered by persons. These offenders may face criminal penalties as well as civil damages. In addition to pursuing recovery based on theories of negligence and/or intentional torts, the law provides victims with an additional set of rights that should always be considered when evaluating alternatives dealing with monetary recovery or other efforts to make these victims whole.

SECTION 1983 ACTIONS

Introduction

It must be stressed that the great majority of those who work in the criminal justice system are honest, caring professionals. However, there are those who intentionally or negligently injure citizens. When those in the criminal justice system commit acts that injure others, they may be charged with a violation of either a state or a federal criminal statute. If the offender's actions violate a person's federal civil rights, two criminal statutes may offer that individual redress. These statutes require action by the federal prosecutor and do not permit the victim to sue wrongdoers.[1]

Much confusion surrounds the historical evolution of the present-day civil rights acts. This is not a history textbook; however, understanding the background and evolution of these laws assists professionals in explaining their scope and function to victims. The first law passed by Congress was the Civil Rights Act of 1866.[2] This law declared that all persons born in the United States were citizens regardless of race or prior conditions of servitude. The act made it a crime for any person under color of law to deprive a person of any right secured or protected by the Constitution or by the laws of the United States. This law failed to stop the continuing racial strife in the southern states, and after race riots in Memphis and New Orleans, Congress enacted the Enforcement Act of 1870.[3] This law was intended to guarantee the right to vote without regard to color, race, or previous conditions of servitude. The Enforcement Act made it a crime for a state official to prohibit a person the right to vote. The historical roots of the present-day federal civil rights criminal codes are found in the Civil Rights Act of 1866 (18 U.S.C. 242) and in the Enforcement Act of 1870 (18 U.S.C. 241). In response to continuing violence against blacks, Congress enacted the Ku Klux Klan Act of 1871.[4] This act is best known for its primary civil enforcement mechanism—the ability to file a federal lawsuit for acts under color of law that violate a person's federal civil rights—and was the forerunner of the present-day law allowing such suits (42 U.S.C. 1983). However, when originally enacted, it was viewed as a federal criminal sanction for those who engaged in violence against blacks, specifically members of the Ku Klux Klan.

Title 18 of the U.S. Code Section 241 prohibits conspiracies to deprive a person of his or her civil rights.[5] Section 242 prohibits civil rights violations by persons acting under color of law. The government must prove four elements to establish a violation of Section 242: (1) The victim was an inhabitant of a state, district, or territory of the United States; (2) the defendant acted under color of law; (3) the conduct deprived the victim of a right guaranteed by the U.S. Constitution; and (4) the defendant acted with a specific intent to violate the protected right.[6]

In addition to the criminal sanctions facing those who violate a person's federal civil rights, Congress has provided an additional remedy in the form of civil damages. Title 42 of the U.S. Code Section 1983 provides in part:

> Every person who, under color of any statute, ordinance, regulation, custom, or usage of any State or Territory, subjects, or causes to be subjected, any citizen of the United States or any other person within the jurisdiction thereof to the deprivation of any rights, privileges, or immunities secured by the Constitution and laws, shall be liable to the party injured in an action at law, suit in equity, or other proper proceedings for redress ... .[7]

This quote has been the basis for thousands of lawsuits against those employed in the criminal justice system. It is an important legal tool for victims who have been injured by police officers and by others in positions of authority. As will be discussed in a later section, civil actions filed pursuant to Title 42 have several advantages over the intentional torts already discussed in other chapters.

Requirement of State Action

The U.S. Supreme Court addressed the scope of the Civil Rights Act of 1871 when it interpreted the phrase "under color of state law" in its decision of *United States v. Classic*.[8] The court reversed the dismissal of criminal charges brought against election officials who had engaged in fraudulent activities during a primary election. The court stated that "misuse of power, possessed by virtue of state law and made possible only because the wrongdoer is clothed with the authority of the state, is action taken 'under color' of state law."[9]

The Supreme Court further expanded this definition four years later in 1945 when it decided *Screws v. United States.* The court held that a sheriff's fatal beating of a black prisoner was conduct "under color" of law.[10] Therefore, in criminal cases, conduct **under color of law** involves unauthorized, unlawful conduct of an official when the pretense of authority under which the officer acted furthered or assisted that officer in violating a person's constitutional rights in any way. *Screws* and *Classic* established the availability of criminal actions by persons who were victims of law enforcement misconduct. However, from 1945 until 1961, Section 1983 was virtually ignored by those who were wronged by illegal conduct by agents of the government.

Scope of Liability

The gradual expansion of the due process clause incorporating the Bill of Rights and the growth of the equal protection and due process concepts allowed victims of official misconduct greater latitude in filing of lawsuits. In 1961, the Supreme Court decided *Monroe v. Pape* and established the framework for future use of Section 1983 by those who were victims of illegal governmental activity.[11] In *Monroe,* the plaintiff and his family filed a civil lawsuit instead of criminal action using Section 1983 against thirteen Chicago police officers and the city of Chicago, alleging that the officers broke into their home without a warrant, forced them out of bed, and made them stand naked while the officers searched the house. The police then took the plaintiff to the police station and held him incommunicado for ten hours before releasing him without filing any charges. The plaintiff claimed that the police acted "under color of law" and deprived them of their constitutional protection against unreasonable searches and seizures. The Supreme Court held that color of law had the same meaning in a civil case as it did in a criminal case and concluded that because Section 1983 provided for a civil action, the plaintiffs need not prove that the defendants acted with a specific intent to deprive a person of a federal right. However, the court dismissed the city of Chicago, holding that municipalities were immune from liability under the statute.

In 1978, the law surrounding civil rights violations expanded even further with the Supreme Court decision in *Monell v. Department of Social Services.*[12] In *Monell,* the plaintiffs were a class of female employees who alleged that the board of education of the city of New York and the New York Department of Social Services were forcing pregnant employees to take unpaid leaves of absence before those leaves were medically necessary. The lawsuit sought injunctive relief and back pay for the unlawful forced leaves. The defendants included the mayor, the city of New York, the commissioner of the board of education and the board itself, and the Department of Social Services and its chancellor. In allowing the lawsuit to go forward, the court held that Section 1983 was violated whenever

1. a person was deprived of a right, privilege, or immunity guaranteed under the Constitution and federal laws, and
2. such a deprivation resulted from the official policy or custom of a local governmental entity.

The Supreme Court decision was to have a tremendous impact of the desirability of suing individuals employed by municipalities. Victims of illegal action by agents of municipalities now had a deep pocket that they could reach. It must be stressed that *Monell* addressed the liability of local governmental agencies and not individual states.

Monell also overruled *Monroe* by holding that municipalities were "persons" and therefore not completely immune from suit under Section 1983. However, *Monell* did not address whether local governments, although not entitled to absolute immunity, could claim limited immunity in some situations. This question was answered in *Owens v. City of Independence,* which held that the city was entitled to limited immunity from lawsuit based on the good faith of its officials.[13]

These and other decisions have given victims of illegal local governmental activity an option that should always be considered when local government actions injure them. Using either "due process" or "equal protection," almost any intentional tort committed by a state or local official can be converted into a constitutional violation and thereby made the subject of a Section 1983 action. In addition, if the plaintiff prevails in these actions, that person is entitled to an award of attorney's fees in addition to any equable or money relief.[14] This provision allowing attorney's fees encourages attorneys to take on lawsuits that indicate that they have the potential for success.[15]

SECTION 1983 THEORIES OF LIABILITY

A number of theories of liability under Section 1983 hold individual officials and in many instances their local agency liable for injury to victims. A discussion of these theories is beyond the scope of this textbook; however, several theories of liability should be discussed because of the nature of the acts committed by agents of municipalities.

Denial of Equal Protection

One famous case in the victim's movement involving a denial of equal protection concerned a police department's response to calls for help by a battered spouse. Starting in October 1982 and continuing until June 1983, Tracey Thurman repeatedly contacted the police department in Torrington, Connecticut, begging for protection from her estranged husband, Buck. Tracey signed several sworn complaints against Buck; however, the police department considered the incidents a family matter and did not respond to them in the same manner as they did to "stranger assaults."

On the day of the final beating, Buck stabbed Tracey repeatedly. A police officer arrived and asked Buck for the knife but did not arrest or restrain him in any manner. Buck gave the officer the knife and then proceeded to stomp on Tracey's head in front of the officer. He then went inside the house and returned with their son and cursed and kicked Tracey in the head. This series of blows left her partially paralyzed. Other officers arrived, and they did not arrest Buck until he tried to assault Tracey as she lay on the ambulance stretcher.

Tracey filed suit in federal court against the city of Torrington, its police department, and all twenty-four officers whom she had contacted over the years about Buck's assaultive acts. She alleged that the police department and its officers had been negligent in responding to her, and further, that they had violated her constitutional rights to equal protection under the law by treating her differently than they would persons who were assaulted by strangers.[16]

The jury awarded Tracey $2.3 million in damages, and although the city's insurance company paid the judgment, it indicated that it might not pay any future awards of any police department that refused or failed to educate its officers about domestic violence.[17]

In recent years, victims of family violence have turned to the courts in an attempt to require law enforcement departments to provide effective intervention and protection against intimate partner assault. *Balistreri v. City of Pacifica* involved a spouse who obtained a restraining order against her husband. He violated this order numerous times, and even after serious physical injuries and a firebomb being thrown through her window, the police refused her request to arrest the husband. The federal court dismissed a portion of her complaint but allowed the allegation that the police had violated her equal protection rights in that she had shown that the officers might have treated her differently from other crime victims because she was a battered woman.[18]

Czachorowski v. Degenhart was a New York Superior Court case in which several battered women sued the police department for failing to comply with a state law requiring officers to advise victims of domestic violence of their rights and available services. The case was settled for a change in policy where the police agreed to hand out informational material, train officers in domestic violence, and institute a complaint procedure for victims of intimate partner abuse.[19]

In *Watson v. City of Kansas City,* a federal court ruled that the victim could proceed with her suit against the police department. Nancy Watson was married to a Kansas City police officer who abused her and her son on numerous occasions. When she requested assistance from the police, they refused to help and threatened to take her child away and arrest her. After being raped and battered by her husband, she escaped and he committed suicide. She sued the police department for a denial of equal protection.[20]

As the discussion illustrates, victims of intimate partner abuse have turned to the courts in an attempt to force police departments to arrest the perpetrators of this form of family violence. Increasingly, courts have begun to listen and rule in their favor both on constitutional and tort grounds.

Failure to Act

In certain situations, local agencies may be liable for injuries to citizens that have occurred because of the agencies' failure to act. These failures may involve lack of proper training, lack of proper supervision, or lack of protection on the part of law enforcement officers. It should be stressed that many times plaintiffs will allege a violation of their civil rights based on all these theories.

FAILURE TO TRAIN *Billings v. Vernal City* involved a rookie police officer who had been on the force for less than two weeks when he broke the plaintiff's arm while trying to arrest him.[21] The arrest was illegal because the officer did not have probable cause to place the plaintiff under arrest. The officer was on duty prior to completing the basic training required of all law enforcement officers in the state of Utah. The city argued that such a procedure was proper in that state law allows a police officer to receive formal training "within eighteen months" after beginning duty. The court held that to allow such a police officer on duty for "one minute" was grossly negligent. The plaintiff was awarded $23,500 in damages, $12,000 in court costs, and $25,000 in attorney's fees.

The Supreme Court has held that municipalities can be held liable under Section 1983 for failure to train their police officers if such failure amounts to "deliberate indifference."[22] In *City of Canton v. Harris,* the court stated that deliberate indifference occurs when "in light of the duties assigned to specific officers or employees the need for more or different training is so obvious, and the inadequacy so likely to result in [a] violation of constitutional rights, that the policymakers of the city can reasonably be said to have been deliberately indifferent to the need."[23] The Court stated that the failure to train the officer must be closely related to the ultimate injury.

FAILURE TO SUPERVISE In many private sector situations, supervisors are often sued for actions of their employees based on the common law theory of **respondeat superior**, which is Latin for "let the master answer." Under this doctrine, the master (employer or supervisor) is responsible for the acts or omissions of his servant (employee) toward those to whom the master owes a duty of care. Liability normally attaches if the servant (employee) fails to use due care during the course of employment. This doctrine does not apply to public employment because police chiefs are not the masters of their employees. Both the chief and the officers work for a common master—the city. However, the doctrine applies to sheriffs, because under common law deputies serve at the pleasure of the sheriff and therefore act for the sheriff in the course of employment.

However, in certain situations local police supervisors have been held liable for failure to properly supervise their officers. In *Dewell v. Lawson,* the chief of police was held liable for failing to establish procedures for the diagnosis and treatment of jail inmates.[24] The plaintiff was arrested and detained for public intoxication. He experienced a diabetic reaction that resulted in a coma, stroke, and ultimate death when the jailer failed to recognize the medical condition and therefore did not provide proper medical care. In *Grandstaff v. City of Borger,* the police chief was held liable for acts of his officers when they shot an innocent man during an apprehension of a suspect.[25] The officers opened fire on a pickup driven by the victim when he entered the area to offer assistance after seeing police activity near his house.

In *Parrish v. Luckie,* the city was liable for an officer's sexual assault of a woman, because the city had knowledge of the officer's propensity for violence and failed to take any corrective action.[26] The officer was investigated on two prior occasions for child abuse and criminally charged in one of those incidents. The department had also received complaints from other citizens that the officer had solicited sexual favors from several store clerks. However, the police chief failed to take any action, and investigators discouraged citizens from filing complaints. The jury awarded damages in the amount of $200,000 against both the officer and the chief of police, and because it was alleged that they acted in their official capacity, the city was responsible for paying the judgment.

FAILURE TO PROTECT In other situations, officers will be held liable for failing to follow up on actions they initiated. *Fundiller v. City of Cooper* involved a drug transaction with an undercover officer that resulted in the plaintiff being shot five times.[27] Other officers arrived at the scene and dragged Fundiller from his car and handcuffed him, causing further injury. The appellate court stated that the city and its officials may be liable under Section 1983. The court established the standard for determining liability of agencies and their officers for practices that have become a custom or policy, stating that the custom must be created by an individual who represents the official policy of the agency, and a causal link must exist between the act and the custom. In the area of liability for failure to protect, the court held that supervisors may be liable if a causal link exists between the employee's acts and the acts of the supervisor. The court further ruled that mere presence at the scene of the incident with a failure to act to protect the victim is sufficient for liability.

In *Raucci v. Town of Rotterdam,* a federal court ruled that the municipality owed a battered woman a special duty to protect her from her estranged husband because of actions by the police department that had assured her of protection. In spite of these assurances, the husband killed their six-year-old son and wounded the wife. The court upheld a jury verdict awarding the wife damages.[28]

Smith v. Wade involved a federal civil rights lawsuit by an inmate against a correctional officer who placed inmates with known dangerous propensities in a cell with the victim.[29] The Supreme Court upheld the award of compensatory and punitive damages against the officer, stating that such damages are permitted when the conduct is shown to be motivated by evil intent or when it involves reckless or callous indifference to the federally protected rights of others.

The U.S. Supreme Court may have weakened a victim's recovery in the area of failure to protect when it decided *Castle Rock vs. Gonzales.*[30] This case concerned a local municipality's failure to enforce a valid restraining order. This case is discussed in more detail in the following section dealing with restraining orders.

VIOLENCE AGAINST WOMEN ACT

Background

In August 1994, Congress passed and President Bill Clinton signed the controversial Crime Bill.[31] While this act caused much debate and controversy, one act from the Crime Bill received support from both parties: the Violence Against Women Act (VAWA) of 1994.[32] The VAWA contains one of the Crime Bill's largest crime prevention programs that attempt to respond to the national problem of gender-based violence. It makes crimes committed against women similar to those that are motivated by religious, racial, or political bias.

The act was re-authorized in 2000, and in 2006 President George W. Bush signed the new VAWA of 2005 into law. This law continues to focus on studying and preventing violence against women that the previous laws started. It provides funding and other tools that cities need to combat domestic violence.[33]

The act was again re-authorized in 2013. The renewed act expanded federal protections to gays, lesbians, transgender individuals, Native Americans, and immigrants. The act addresses gender-based violence in many areas. Following is the Table of Contents of the 2013 version of the act. It provides an overview of the topics covered by the act:

TITLE I—ENHANCING JUDICIAL AND LAW ENFORCEMENT TOOLS TO COMBAT VIOLENCE AGAINST WOMEN

Sec. 101. Stop grants.

Sec. 102. Grants to encourage arrest policies and enforcement of protection orders.

Sec. 103. Legal assistance for victims.

Sec. 104. Consolidation of grants to support families in the justice system.

Sec. 105. Sex offender management.

Sec. 106. Court-appointed special advocate program.

Sec. 107. Criminal provision relating to stalking, including cyberstalking.

Sec. 108. Outreach and services to underserved populations grant.

Sec. 109. Culturally specific services grant.

TITLE II—IMPROVING SERVICES FOR VICTIMS OF DOMESTIC VIOLENCE, DATING VIOLENCE, SEXUAL ASSAULT, AND STALKING

Sec. 201. Sexual assault services program.

Sec. 202. Rural domestic violence, dating violence, sexual assault, stalking, and child abuse enforcement assistance.

Sec. 203. Training and services to end violence against women with disabilities grants.

Sec. 204. Enhanced training and services to end abuse in later life.

TITLE III—SERVICES, PROTECTION, AND JUSTICE FOR YOUNG VICTIMS OF VIOLENCE

Sec. 301. Rape prevention and education grant.

Sec. 302. Creating hope through outreach, options, services, and education for children and youth.

Sec. 303. Grants to combat violent crimes on campuses.

Sec. 304. Campus sexual violence, domestic violence, dating violence, and stalking education and prevention.

TITLE IV—VIOLENCE REDUCTION PRACTICES

Sec. 401. Study conducted by the centers for disease control and prevention.

Sec. 402. Saving money and reducing tragedies through prevention grants.

TITLE V—STRENGTHENING THE HEALTHCARE SYSTEM'S RESPONSE TO DOMESTIC VIOLENCE, DATING VIOLENCE, SEXUAL ASSAULT, AND STALKING

Sec. 501. Consolidation of grants to strengthen the healthcare system's response to domestic violence, dating violence, sexual assault, and stalking.

TITLE VI—SAFE HOMES FOR VICTIMS OF DOMESTIC VIOLENCE, DATING VIOLENCE, SEXUAL ASSAULT, AND STALKING

Sec. 601. Housing protections for victims of domestic violence, dating violence, sexual assault, and stalking.

Sec. 602. Transitional housing assistance grants for victims of domestic violence, dating violence, sexual assault, and stalking.

Sec. 603. Addressing the housing needs of victims of domestic violence, dating violence, sexual assault, and stalking.

TITLE VII—ECONOMIC SECURITY FOR VICTIMS OF VIOLENCE

Sec. 701. National Resource Center on Workplace Responses to assist victims of domestic and sexual violence.

TITLE VIII—PROTECTION OF BATTERED IMMIGRANTS

Sec. 801. U nonimmigrant definition.

Sec. 802. Annual report on immigration applications made by victims of abuse.

Sec. 803. Protection for children of VAWA self-petitioners.

Sec. 804. Public charge.

Sec. 805. Requirements applicable to U visas.

Sec. 806. Hardship waivers.

Sec. 807. Protections for a fiancée or fiancé of a citizen.

Sec. 808. Regulation of international marriage brokers.

Sec. 809. Eligibility of crime and trafficking victims in the Commonwealth of the Northern Mariana Islands to adjust status.

Sec. 810. Disclosure of information for national security purposes.

TITLE IX—SAFETY FOR INDIAN WOMEN

Sec. 901. Grants to Indian tribal governments.

Sec. 902. Grants to Indian tribal coalitions.

Sec. 903. Consultation.

Sec. 904. Tribal jurisdiction over crimes of domestic violence.

Sec. 905. Tribal protection orders.

Sec. 906. Amendments to the Federal assault statute.

Sec. 907. Analysis and research on violence against Indian women.

Sec. 908. Effective dates; pilot project.

Sec. 909. Indian law and order commission; Report on the Alaska Rural Justice and Law Enforcement Commission.

Sec. 910. Special rule for the State of Alaska.

TITLE X—SAFER ACT

Sec. 1001. Short title.

Sec. 1002. Debbie Smith grants for auditing sexual assault evidence backlogs.

Sec. 1003. Reports to Congress.

Sec. 1004. Reducing the rape kit backlog.

Sec. 1005. Oversight and accountability.

Sec. 1006. Sunset.

TITLE XI—OTHER MATTERS

Sec. 1101. Sexual abuse in custodial settings.

Sec. 1102. Anonymous online harassment.

Sec. 1103. Stalker database.

Sec. 1104. Federal victim assistants reauthorization.

Sec. 1105. Child abuse training programs for judicial personnel and practitioners reauthorization.

TITLE XII—TRAFFICKING VICTIMS PROTECTION

Subtitle A—Combating International Trafficking in Persons

Sec. 1201. Regional strategies for combating trafficking in persons.

Sec. 1202. Partnerships against significant trafficking in persons.

Sec. 1203. Protection and assistance for victims of trafficking.

Sec. 1204. Minimum standards for the elimination of trafficking.

Sec. 1205. Best practices in trafficking in persons eradication.

Sec. 1206. Protections for domestic workers and other nonimmigrants.

Sec. 1207. Prevention of child marriage.

Sec. 1208. Child soldiers.

Subtitle B—Combating Trafficking in Persons in the United States

Gender-Based Civil Rights

The creation of this federal civil rights law recognizes that gender-based violence against women should be accorded the same dignity as a violation of an individual's constitutional rights. The victim of this type of discrimination may recover compensatory and punitive damages and obtain an injunction to prevent future acts of violence.

Key parts or highlights of the Act include:

- The Act is intended to demonstrate that violence against women cannot be perceived as only a "family" problem, a "private" matter, or a sexual "miscommunication."[34]
- The Act treats gender-motivated violence the same as other bias-motivated attacks.
- Most importantly, the law provides federal remedy for victims of gender-based violence that is not presently available in state courts.
  - The Act declares that every person has the right to be free from crime of violence motivated by gender and that all persons, including those who act under color of any statute, ordinance, regulation, custom, or usage of any state, who commit a gender-motivated crime of violence are liable for compensatory and punitive damages as well as injunction, declaratory relief, and other such relief as a court may deem appropriate.
- It defines a crime of gender-motivated violence as an act or series of acts that would constitute a felony against the person or that would constitute a felony against property if the

conduct presents a serious risk of physical injury to another and that would come within the meaning of state or federal offenses described in Title 18 of the U.S. Code.[35] Such crime of violence is considered to be motivated by gender if it is committed because of the gender or on the basis of gender and is due at least in part to the animus (prejudice, spiteful, or ill will) based on the victim's gender.

• The Act states that nothing in this section entitles a person to relief based on random acts of violence unrelated to gender.

By establishing a civil rights cause of action for gender-based acts of violence, Congress has placed gender at the same level as race and religion. The VAWA and its new civil rights must await interpretation by the courts to determine its full scope and extent; however, there is every reason to believe that it will be accorded the same type of reception that other civil rights laws have received, and therefore in the future female victims of violence will have a new legal weapon at their disposal.

INJUNCTIONS

Injunctions, also known as restraining orders and TROs, are court orders that require somebody involved in a legal action to do something or refrain from doing something. It is a command or order, especially from somebody in a position of authority or an act of ordering somebody: the act of ordering somebody to do or not to do something. Most are restraining orders or protective orders that are court orders that prohibit the offender from having any contact with the victim.[36] They are civil versus criminal in nature and require a judge to rule on sufficient evidence to support the issuance of such an order. These orders are now available in forty-eight states and the District of Columbia. They offer the option of preventing contact such as harassment or threats that might ordinarily lead to an escalation of emotions and future violence.

The state of Massachusetts is one of the leaders in collecting data regarding the effectiveness of restraining orders.[37] In the fall of 1992, efforts by victim services advocacy groups and others resulted in changes to the state justice delivery system. Massachusetts created a Registry of Civil Restraining Orders designed to provide police and the courts with accurate and reliable information necessary to respond appropriately to victims' needs. It was the first statewide database of restraining order information in the nation.

For the program to be effective, a number of criminal justice professionals had to be able to access the database. The Office of the Commissioner of Probation established a statewide users' community (see Figure 14.1). In Massachusetts, the agencies shown have access to the registry.

The program was designed for use on computers. Because of the importance of the data stored in the system, the computer program had to be easy to use and simple to learn. Massachusetts developed the program in COBOL on a Unisys mainframe. At the center of the restraining order program was the data entry screen (see Figure 14.2). This screen is used to enter, display, and update restraining order information. Quality control monitoring was utilized to ensure timeliness, accuracy, and completeness of all information. Since 1992, other states have followed Massachusetts's lead and have adopted statewide restraining order registries. A computerized database is an important goal in responding to victims of crime and specifically to intimate abuse; however, certain geographical areas in the United States still do not use restraining orders. As the following discussion indicates, the debate continues regarding the effectiveness of this unique tool in preventing spousal abuse.

Background and Use of Restraining Orders

In the past, problems with the use of restraining orders stemmed from lack of clarity in the law and many police officers' unfamiliarity with this civil sanction. In 1983, only seventeen states provided protection against abuse from individuals who were living together but not married. However by 1988, twenty-two states had added such protection to their statutes authorizing restraining orders.

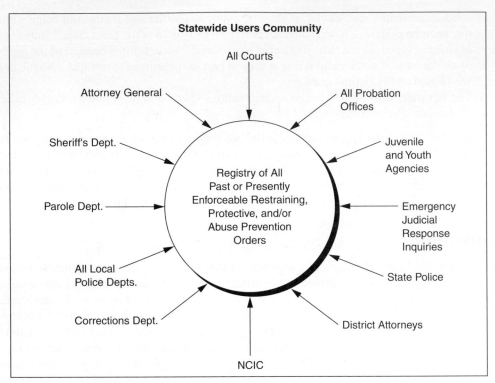

FIGURE 14.1   **State of Massachusetts Accessing Restraining Orders**

The use and nature of restraining orders vary from state to state. Most states now authorize persons who are married, related by blood, or cohabitants to request the issuance of such an order. The six types of behavior that may be prohibited by a restraining order are as follows:

1. Protection against physical assault
2. Threatened physical abuse
3. Attempted physical abuse
4. Sexual assault of an adult
5. Sexual assault of a child
6. Damage to the personal property of the victim

As the list indicates, restraining orders may be issued for a wide variety of acts committed by the offender. However, simply having the order issued does not solve the problem. Due process requires that the offender be served with a copy of the order for it to be effective.

A majority of states provides for the issuance of temporary or emergency restraining orders. These orders are issued by the judge and usually require the threat of immediate injury to the victim. The U.S. Supreme Court upheld the issuance of these ex parte type of orders if (1) the request includes specific facts that justify the relief, (2) the notice and opportunity for a full hearing are given as soon as practicable, and (3) the order is issued by a judge.[38]

In most jurisdictions, police officers or process servers are responsible for serving restraining orders. The five basic methods of service of a temporary or emergency restraining order are (1) personal service, (2) informing the offender of the existence of the order, (3) leaving a copy with the victim so that she or he can serve the offender, (4) posting the notice and order at the residence of the victim, and (5) mailing a copy of the order via certified mail to the offender.

Some police departments have established procedures in which officers can contact judges while they are at the scene of a domestic dispute and have the judge authorize the issuance of

CIVIL RESTRAINING ORDER SCREEN

DEFENDANT		**PROBATION**
PRIMARY NAME: DOE, JOHN	**DOB:** 03/09/65	**CENTRAL FILE #:** 123457CV
	P. O. B.: SOMERVILLE, MA	

SEX: M   **SS#:** 012–22–2222   **MOTHER:** JANE JONES
FATHER: JOHN

ALIAS NAME: MOE, JOHN   6/9/65
DOE, J.W.   3/9/65
LEO, JOHN   3/9/65

PLAINTIFF
NAME: SMITH, JANE
2022 MAIN ST.
ANYTOWN, USA

DOCKET #: _____

TYPE OF
ORDER: MASS GENERAL LAWS: _____ ;   SECTION: _____

ORDER DATE: ___/___/___   **EXPIRATION DATE:** ___/___/___   **STATUS:**
[ ] OPEN
[ ] CLOSED

COURT ORDERS:
[ ] REFRAIN FROM ABUSE
[ ] NO CONTACT
[ ] VACATE/STAY AWAY (RESIDENCE)
[ ] ADDRESS IMPOUNDED
[ ] STAY AWAY (WORKPLACE)
[ ] SURRENDER CUSTODY
[ ] SUPPORT PAYMENTS
[ ] COMPENSATION
[ ] VISITATION RIGHTS: SEE ORDER
[ ] OTHER: SEE ORDER

FIGURE 14.2   State of Massachusetts Computer Screen

such an order via the telephone. The officer then serves the suspect at the scene and requires him to leave the premises. Once a temporary order is issued, it becomes effective immediately and is valid until a formal hearing can be held at which time the abuser has a right to contest the allegations made by the victim. However, the issuance of the temporary order precludes the offender from having any contact with the victim until the formal hearing.

Restraining orders may provide different forms of relief for the victim of intimate partner assault. The traditional and most common form of relief is a no-contact order that prevents the offender from having any form of contact with the victim either at that person's residence, work, or anywhere else. This no-contact order includes telephone, written, and physical contacts. Many orders will set forth specific conditions regarding the visitation of any children that may be involved in the situation. Some will designate certain locations for the visit, and others will require that the offender not consume any alcohol or drugs prior to the visit. A majority of the statutes authorize the court to require counseling for both parties. Even if the counseling does not solve the immediate problem, it is a visible sign of the authority of the court and should serve as a constant reminder to the offender of the power that the court now has over the offender's existence.

In the event the abuser violates the restraining order, many statutes authorize charging the offender with civil contempt, criminal contempt, or a misdemeanor violation of a court order. Although police officers cannot normally arrest a person charged with civil contempt, the court may order that the offender pay a fine and serve a period of incarceration. Criminal contempt, if authorized by the state statute, would allow officers to arrest the offender if they found him or her in violation of the order. Criminal contempt in many jurisdictions is treated as a misdemeanor; however, many restraining order statutes allow officers to make warrantless arrests in these situations. If the violation of the order is considered a misdemeanor, many statutes also authorize the warrantless arrest of the offender. As the next section discusses, the use of this form of sanction still poses many problems.

While many statutes provide for civil contempt, criminal contempt, or even violation of criminal statutes, there is no guarantee that the order will be effective. In *Castle Rock vs. Gonzales*, the U.S. Supreme Court addressed the issue of a municipality's liability for failure to enforce a restraining order.[39] Jessica Gonzales obtained a protective order against her husband as part of divorce proceedings. The order listed the requirements of Colorado law, which mandated that officers use every reasonable means to enforce a restraining order, including the requirement that the officer "shall" arrest a person when there is probable cause to believe he or she has violated the order. The order provided for visitation of the children on alternate weekends.

One afternoon, while the kids were playing outside, Mr. Gonzales kidnapped them. Over the next ten hours, Jessica made repeated requests to the Castle Rock Police Department to enforce her protective order, but they failed to do so. At 3:30 A.M. in the morning after he kidnapped the children, Mr. Gonzales appeared at the police station and opened fire with his weapon. He was killed by officers who returned his fire. Afterward, the officers found the dead bodies of Jessica's three children inside his truck.

Jessica Gonzales sued the city of Castle Rock for failing to enforce her protective order. However, the Supreme Court ruled that despite the mandatory arrest laws in effect in Colorado at that time, Jessica had no personal entitlement requiring the police to enforce the order. It went on to state that the statute simply required police to enforce the order, and the court refused to assume that the statute was meant to benefit victims of domestic violence.

There was a strong reaction by the crime victims' movement to the *Castle Rock* decision. In essence, the decision fails to recognize the dynamics and dangers of domestic violence. Some victim advocates are advising victims and their attorneys to request more specific language in their orders. Others are relying on state tort remedies to hold law enforcement agencies liable. *Castle Rock* has caused us to rethink our traditional responses to restraining orders. Only time will tell what comes from this landmark decision.

Advantages and Disadvantages

Restraining orders provide the victim with another option in lieu of arrest. There are several advantages to the use of restraining orders.[40] Most arrests result in the offender being released in a matter of hours or within a few days at the most. A restraining order can be valid up to a year in most cases.

Arrests may result in the loss of employment, which might increase the tension that already exists in the relationship. Restraining orders do not preclude offenders from continuing with their employment, but at the same time they prevent them from living with their victims.

Restraining orders carry the weight and majesty of a judicial edict, and some offenders may think twice before violating a court order. Although some offenders may have had numerous contacts with the police and even the judicial system, most have not been involved with a direct order from a judge stating that they will not engage in certain conduct. The specter of facing a judge after violating an order may act as a deterrent for some abusers.

Just as there are advantages in this form of protection, so are there serious potential disadvantages in relying solely on the use of restraining orders in this area of family violence. The most obvious and threatening disadvantage is that the offender may simply ignore the order, resulting in injury to the victim. A restraining order is merely a piece of paper that carries only as much force and effect as the offender attaches to it. If the offender chooses to ignore it, there is no protection for the victim unless she or he can contact the police, and they can arrive and intercede before the abuser attacks and harms her or him.

There are additional disadvantages to the use of restraining orders. Many of these weaknesses are written into the very statutes that were enacted to protect the victim. Some statutes require the payment of a filing fee prior to the issuance of a restraining order. Although most jurisdictions allow for the waiver of the fee if the victim cannot afford to pay it, some include the income of the abuser in determining if the fee can be waived. The payment of such fees acts as a deterrent to requesting a restraining order.

Some statutes require court or county clerks to assist the victim in filling out the forms requesting the restraining order. However, no state-provided funds or mandated special training is available for these clerks in this sensitive function. A great majority of intimate partner assault occurs in the evening or on the weekend after the courts are closed. Only twenty-three states provide for the issuance of emergency orders after normal working hours. Thus, during the victim's greatest time of need, there is no alternative available to obtain these orders.

Most states require personal service of the order for them to become effective. However, many offenders are difficult to locate, and therefore the victim is not protected until the abuser has been served. There is a lack of monitoring of the compliance with restraining orders. If the offender can convince or threaten the victim to remain silent, neither law enforcement officers nor the court will be aware that the offender has violated the order.

The *Orange County Register*, a respected Southern California newspaper, conducted an investigation into the use and effectiveness of restraining orders.[41] Key findings from the investigation revealed a system in disarray with conflicting procedures and processes between counties. Even more alarming, one in seven restraining orders issued by a judge were not served on the perpetrator. An order is not effective until served. The *Register* also pointed out that hundreds of restraining orders are not entered into the state database used by law enforcement agencies, and without proof of a valid order, police are powerless to take action.

Although the use of restraining orders presents some serious problems, they do provide some victims of intimate partner assault with an option that may protect them.

DEFENSES

Simply establishing that a person has violated the victim's civil rights does not end the inquiry. The law provides a number of defenses for both individuals and agencies accused of violating another's civil rights. There are two types of defenses: substantive and procedural. *Substantive defenses* are those that claim one of the elements of a civil rights action has not been met. For example, the defendant may argue that no constitutional right was violated by the officer. *Procedural defenses* challenge the validity of the lawsuit based on issues such as the lack of jurisdiction (federal courts have specific jurisdictional requirements that must be satisfied to sue in federal court), statute of limitations, and other procedural requirements.[42]

Two common forms of defense raised in civil rights cases are *absolute immunity* and *qualified immunity*. Both of these defenses are considered "official immunity." At English common law, the concept of sovereign immunity developed based on the assumption that kings were divine and therefore could do no wrong. Thus, the king's subjects could not sue the king. Early American court decisions relied on this rationale to support the position that the United States could not be sued without its permission. As a result, in 1946 Congress passed the Federal Tort Claims

Act that allowed citizens under certain circumstances to sue the government and its agents or employees.[43]

The historical rationale for official immunity is based on the concept that a government can only act through its agents or officials, and official immunity protects those who carry out these actions. Another justification for official immunity was set forth by the Supreme Court when it held:

> The public interest requires decisions and action to enforce laws for the protection of the public....Implicit in the idea that officials have some immunity—absolute or qualified—for their acts, is a recognition that they may err. The concept of immunity assumes this and goes on to assume that it is better to risk some error and possible injury from such error than not to decide or act at all.[44]

The courts have consistently used the common law doctrine of immunity when dealing with Section 1983 cases. As will be discussed, the distinction between absolute and qualified immunity has on occasion become blurred and confusing.

Absolute Immunity

Absolute immunity is a complete shield in a lawsuit and involves a determination that there is no liability for any damages that the victim may have suffered as a result of the actor's conduct. Therefore, when a defendant has absolute immunity, any civil lawsuit will be dismissed by the court without ever considering the plaintiff's claim for damages. However, this defense is not automatic—it must be pled and proved by the defendant before the court will act to dismiss the lawsuit.

The concept of absolute immunity is to encourage a decision-making process without fear of reprisals, no matter how unpopular such a decision may be for a particular person or group of persons. For absolute immunity to apply, persons must be acting within the broad general scope of their duties.[45] In addition, absolute immunity applies even if it is determined that the person acted with malice or other evil intentions. A grant or absolute immunity prevents any civil lawsuits from going forward.

Society has determined that certain individuals and situations should be accorded the shield of absolute immunity. Judges when acting in their judicial capacity are afforded absolute immunity as are witnesses when they are testifying in court. Prosecutors depending on their role and function in the judicial system may have either absolute or qualified immunity.[46] If a prosecutor is acting as an advocate, his or her actions are absolutely immune; however, if the prosecutor is acting in a nonadvocatory role such as investigating cases or administering the office, he or she is afforded only qualified immunity.

Qualified Immunity

Qualified immunity is also known as the *good faith defense*. It is a defense that has grown and evolved during the last 100 years. The present-day defense of qualified immunity has its basis in the U.S. Supreme Court decision of *Anderson v. Creighton*.[47] In *Anderson,* an FBI agent and several local law enforcement officers conducted a warrantless search of the victim's home under the mistaken belief that a bank robbery suspect was in the home. According to the Creightons, the officers brandished shotguns, assaulted their daughter, and knocked Mr. Creighton to the ground. They arrested him and placed him in jail overnight before releasing him without filing any charges. The Creightons filed a Section 1983 action alleging that the officers violated their Fourth Amendment right to be free from unreasonable searches. The officers claimed that they were immune from such lawsuit based on the defense of qualified immunity. The Supreme Court held that individuals would be entitled to qualified immunity if it was determined that the action was the type that a reasonable person could have believed was lawful in light of clearly established law and the information available to that individual at the time of the decision.

The immunity defenses provide those that work in the criminal justice system a shield against meritless lawsuits and at the same time allow a person who has been wronged by those perpetrators to pursue a lawsuit to recover damages for injuries. The laws dealing with the immunity defenses are complex and constantly changing, and therefore it is essential that professionals working with victims refer them to attorneys for a complete explanation of their rights in this area.

Summary

This chapter should not be taken as an indictment of law enforcement officers or others who work in the criminal justice system. The overwhelming majority of personnel in this field are caring professionals who obey the law. However, a small percentage of those in the criminal justice system, because of either negligence or intentional acts, injure private citizens. When this occurs, many victims are hesitant to report such injury because of the mistaken belief that they have no recourse against those in power.

Victim services providers need to understand the history and evolution of the present-day laws that hold those in the criminal justice profession liable for injuries to others. Title 42 U.S. Code Section 1983 is an invaluable tool to use in these situations. It requires that the tortfeasor act under *color of law*. This is a key element in any 1983 action.

The Violence Against Women Act of 1994 has established a new gender-based civil right for women. It provides victims of gender-based crimes with an important legal remedy and states that crimes based on gender will be considered as serious as crimes based on other protected classifications.

Injunctions are a critical aspect of the civil rights of victims of crime. These legal tools are normally used against persons known to the victim, most commonly against former spouses or boyfriends. The effectiveness of injunctions is still being studied. However, some states have automated their records, and now law enforcement agencies can access these records from statewide databases.

Simply knowing that the victim has been injured by someone acting under color of law is only the first step in this process. Victim services providers must be aware of the various types of defenses available to those in the criminal justice system. By understanding these defenses, professionals can better advise victims of their constitutional and civil rights.

Key Terms

Under color of law involves unauthorized, unlawful conduct of an official when the pretense of authority under which the officer acted furthered or assisted them in violating a person's constitutional rights in any way.

Respondeat superior is Latin for "let the master answer." Under this doctrine, the master (employer or supervisor) is responsible for the acts or omissions of his servant (employee) toward those to whom the master owes a duty of care.

Injunctions are restraining orders or protective orders which are court orders that prohibit the offender from having any contact with the victim.

Discussion Questions

1. Does the potential of civil liability affect how police respond to victims of crime?
2. Should local agencies be held liable for failing to train their officers if the officers acted in good faith?
3. Why is the requirement of state action important in 1983 lawsuits?
4. Is a gender-based civil rights law necessary?
5. Are temporary restraining orders a useful tool in responding to domestic violence? List those situations in which you would recommend the issuance of a temporary restraining order and those situations in which it would not be appropriate.
6. Should absolute immunity exist? Why? Why not?

Suggested Readings

Peter Finn & Sarah Colson, *Civil Protection Orders: Legislation, Current Court Practice and Enforcement* (National Institute of Justice, Washington, D.C.) March 1990.

M. D. Dubber, *Victims on the War on Crime: The Use and Abuse of Victims' Rights* (New York University Press) 2006.

The Crime Victim's Right to Be Present (U.S. Department of Justice, Office for Victims of Crime, Washington, D.C.) 2001.

Endnotes

1. See *Powers v. Karen* 768 F. Supp. 46 (E.D. N.Y. 1991).
2. Civil Rights Act (Enforcement Act) of 1866, ch. 31, 14 Stat. 27.
3. Enforcement Act of 1870 (Act of May 31, 1870), ch. 114, 16 Stat. 140, amended by Act of Feb. 28, 1871, ch. 99, 16 Stat. 433.
4. Ku Klux Klan (Anti-lynching) Act, ch. 22, 17 Stat. 13 (1971).
5. 18 U.S.C. Section 241 (1988).
6. 18 U.S.C. Section 242 (1988).
7. 42 U.S.C. Section 1983 (1981, West Supp. 1985).
8. 313 U.S. 299 (1941).
9. 313 U.S. at 326.
10. 325 U.S. 91 (1945).
11. 325 U.S. 167 (1961).
12. 436 U.S. 658 (1978).
13. 455 U.S. 622 (1980).
14. See the Civil Rights Attorneys Fees Awards Act of 1976, 42 U.S.C. Section 1988 (1981, West Supp. 1994).
15. *Hensley v. Eckerhart,* 461 U.S. 423 (1983); and *Farrar v. Hobby,* 113 S. Ct. 566 (1992).
16. *Thurman v. City of Torrington,* 595 F. Supp. 1521 (Conn. 1984).
17. M. Buddy & K. Taylor, "Please Somebody Help Me," 20(20) *News* (January 23, 1986). The judgment was later reduced to $1.9 million.
18. 855 F.2d 1421 (1990).
19. New York Superior Court of Erie County, Case Number 07961 (1988).
20. 520 N.Y.S. 2d 352 (1987).
21. U.S. Dist. Utah, C77-0295 (1982).
22. *City of Canton v. Harris,* 489 U.S. 378 (1989).
23. Ibid.
24. 489 F.2d 877 (10th Cir. 1974).
25. 767 F.2d 161 (5th Cir. 1985).
26. 963 F.2d 201 (8th Cir. 1992).
27. 777 F.2d 1436 (11th Cir. 1985).
28. 902 F.2d 1050 (1990).
29. 103 S. Ct. 1625 (1983).
30. 125 S. Ct. 417 (2005).
31. Pub. L. No. 103-322, 108 Stat. 1796. The Crime Bill contains over $30 billion for punishment and prevention programs.
32. Pub. L. No. 103-322, Title IV, 108 Stat. 1902–1955. Codified in various sections of 8 U.S.C. and 42 U.S.C.
33. "Bush Signs Violence Against Women Act into Law," *Family Violence Prevention Fund*; available online: http://endabuse.org (April 4, 2006).
34. See S. Rep. No. 197, 102d Cong., 1st Session 41 (1991).
35. 18 U.S.C. contains two possible crimes of violence: The first is an offense that has an element of use or attempted use or threatened use of physical force against the person or property of another. The second is any other offense that is a felony and by its nature involves a substantial risk that physical force may be used against the person or property of another in the course of committing the offense.
36. This section has been adapted from Peter Finn & Sarah Colson, *Civil Protection Orders: Legislation, Current Court Practice and Enforcement* (National Institute of Justice, Washington, D.C.) March 1990.
37. Donald Cochran, "Project History of the Massachusetts Statewide Automated Restraining Order Registry," Office of the Commissioner of Probation, Massachusetts Trial Court, Boston (July 1994).
38. *Mitchell v. W.T. Grant Co.,* 416 U.S. 600 (1974).
39. 125 S. Ct. 417 (2005).
40. For an excellent discussion of the advantages to using restraining orders, see Elizabeth Topliffe, "Why Civil Protection Orders Are Effective Remedies for Domestic Violence But Mutual Protective Orders Are Not," 67 *Indiana Law Journal* 1039 (Fall 1992).
41. Monica Rhor, "Orders Often Fail to Restrain Violence," *Orange County Register*; available online: http://www.ocregister.com/ocregister/ (March 20, 2006).
42. There are other technical defenses that are of more interest to lawyers instead of victim services providers. These include collateral estoppel and double jeopardy, laches, and the Younger Doctrine.
43. 28 U.S.C. Section 1346 et al.
44. *Scheuer v. Rhodes,* 416 U.S. 232, 241–242 (1974).
45. See, for example, *Stump v. Sparkman,* 435 U.S. 349 (1978), where the Supreme Court held that a judge who ordered a fifteen-year-old girl sterilized without notice to her and based on a simple request of her mother was absolutely immune from a civil lawsuit even though the judge had no express statutory authority for the acts he did.
46. Brian P. Barrow, "*Buckley v. Fitzsimmons:* Tradition Pays a Price for the Reduction of Prosecutorial Misconduct," 16 *Whittier Law Review,* 301 (1995).
47. 483 U.S. 635 (1987).

15

Compensation and Restitution of Victims

Chapter Outline

LEARNING OBJECTIVES

After reading this chapter, you should be able to:

- Distinguish between compensation and restitution
- Understand the rationale behind the funding of compensation programs
- List the justification for denying benefits to certain types of victims
- Explain the philosophy underlying the concept of restitution
- Distinguish between the various types of restitution available to victims

COMPENSATION

Introduction

Victims often suffer physical injury, emotional and mental trauma, and financial loss as a result of a crime.[1] The financial loss to crime victims can cause additional stress as they worry about hospital and doctor bills being paid, physical recovery from their injuries, and their ability to return to work. Crime victim compensation programs exist to provide financial assistance to crime victims and hopefully reduce some of these stressors. These programs exist in all fifty states, plus the District of Columbia, and many will pay for medical care, mental health counseling, lost wages, and in the case of homicides, funeral costs and loss of support.[2] Although no amount of money can replace the use of an arm or the loss of a loved one, it can help victims preserve their financial stability and dignity and thereby assist in the recovery process.

    In 1984 Congress enacted the Victims of Crime Act (VOCA), which established a Crime Victims Fund, supported by revenues from federal offenders. This revenue was based on fines, penalty assessments, and forfeited appearance bonds. On February 17, 2009, the American Recovery and Reinvestment Act of 2009 was enacted. This

FOCUS
Compensation and Restitution

Victim's Perspectives[3]

"The state paid for both the defense and the prosecution. I had to find a way to pay the $12,000 this crime cost us."

—a victim addressing the issue of compensation

"I think if the criminals who do these things are caught they should have to pay for the damage they do, even if takes them years. My family and I will be trying to recover from this for the rest of our lives."

—a victim addressing the issue of restitution

VOCA also established special assessments for individual crimes that are levied on every conviction. In addition, VOCA has a "Son of Sam" provision that requires royalties from the sale of literary rights or any other profits derived from a crime, to be deposited in the Crime Victims Fund and held for five years to satisfy any civil judgment a victim may obtain. If no judgments are filed, these funds become part of the general Crime Victims Fund.[4] Most states also have their own "Son of Sam" laws that cover state crimes.

Victim assistance programs and services have been discussed in previous chapters. These include organizations that provide a variety of services to victims of state and federal crimes. There are over 8,000 agencies or organizations that provide services to victims and nearly 3,000 of those organizations received some VOCA funding.[5]

Act was designed to make the use of victim compensation funds and to provide for research on victim issues. The Act provides that funds would go to the Office of Justice Programs (OJP) to develop the nation's capacity to prevent and control crime, administer justice, and assist victims.

Some of this money is used to improve the investigation and prosecution of child abuse cases, including those child abuse acts committed against Native Americans. However, most of the money in the fund is used to support state victim compensation and victim assistance service programs. **Victim compensation** is a direct payment to, or on behalf of, a crime victim for crime-related expenses such as unpaid medical bills, mental health counseling, funeral costs, and lost wages.[6] **Victim assistance** includes services such as crisis intervention, counseling, emergency transportation to court, temporary housing, advocacy, and criminal justice support.[7]

The Recovery Act allocated $100 million in funding for victim compensation and assistance. Of that $100 million, $47.5 million in Recovery Act–VOCA Victim Compensation Formula Grants will be distributed among eligible state agencies that administer VOCA-funded crime victim compensation programs to support the provision of crucial financial assistance to victims of crime. An additional $47.5 million in Recovery Act–VOCA Victim Assistance Formula Grants will be distributed among state agencies that administer VOCA-funded crime victim assistance programs to support the provision of services to victims of crime.

Program Operation

California established the first compensation program in 1965, and within three years, five other states created similar programs. California is still the largest program in the nation, with payout at about one-third the total benefits paid by all programs combined.[8] The median annual payout per state is approximately $2 million. (One-half of the states pay less and one-half pay more.)

Every state administers a crime victim compensation program through a central agency. (In two states, Arizona and Colorado, operation of the program has been delegated to counties and districts.[9]) These agencies are organized and funded on a statewide basis with administration, claims investigation, and decision making handled at that statewide headquarters. Debate continues among those in the field regarding centralization versus decentralization of compensation services.[10]

Most victim compensation programs are small agencies employing only a handful of staff. The lack of personnel creates delays in processing claims, prevents training of groups regarding

FOCUS

Son of Sam Laws

From July 1976 to August 1977, David Berkowitz terrorized New York City, killing six people and injuring numerous others. Berkowitz referred to himself as the "Son of Sam," explaining later that the black Labrador retriever owned by his neighbor told him to commit the killings. Once captured, Berkowitz received numerous offers to have his story published.

Son of Sam Laws are statutes designed to keep criminals from profiting from the publicity of their crimes, generally by selling their stories to publishers. The laws differ from asset forfeitures, which are designed to seize assets acquired directly as a result of criminal activity. Where asset forfeiture looks to remove the profitability of crimes by taking away money and assets gained from the crime, Son of Sam laws are designed so that criminals are unable to take advantage of their notoriety. The Son of Sam laws frequently authorize the states to seize monies earned from selling book/movie biographies rights and paid interviews. The monies seized are then used compensate the criminal's victims.

In some cases a Son of Sam law can be extended beyond the criminals themselves to include friends, neighbors, and family members of the lawbreaker who seek to profit by telling publishers and filmmakers of their relationship to the criminal. In other cases, a person may not financially benefit from the sale of a story or any other mementos pertaining to the crime—if the criminal was convicted after the date lawmakers passed the law in the states where the crime was committed.

The first such law was created in New York. Critics of the laws have attacked it arguing that it is a violation of the First Amendment. It is also argued that "Son of Sam" laws take away the financial incentive for criminals to tell their stories, which may of interest to the public. They point out this was the method by which we learned about the Watergate scandal during President Nixon's presidency.

New York's original Son of Sam law was ruled unconstitutional by the U.S. Supreme Court. The Court, however, noted that the laws could be constitutional if written very carefully with regards to First Amendment rights. The current New York State law requires that the victims of crime be notified whenever a convicted criminal receives $10,000 or more from any source. The new law also authorizes a state agency to act on victims' behalf in some circumstances.

In 2007 O. J. Simpson authored *If I Did It*, a hypothetical account of the murders of which he had been acquitted. Later that year, a Florida U.S. Bankruptcy Court awarded the book rights to the Goldmans, allowing the family to auction the rights to help satisfy the civil judgment against Simpson.

Sources: Simon & Schuster v. Crime Victims Board, 502 U.S. 105 (1991); N.Y. Executive Law § 632-a (McKinney 2005); N.Y. Corrections Law § 500-c (McKinney 2006); and "Goldmans awarded rights to O.J. book." Chicago Tribune, July 31, 2007, page A-1.

their right to compensation, and does not allow for specialized services such as bilingual staff. Some agencies are using student interns or volunteers to carry out staff functions.

These programs provide assistance to victims of both federal and state crimes. Although each state compensation program is independently run, most programs have similar eligibility requirements and offer the same types of benefits. The maximum state award generally ranges between $10,000 and $25,000.[11]

Victims applying for compensation must comply with certain requirements, including reporting the crime and filing claims by certain deadlines. In most states, the victim services professional provides compensation applications and information to the victim. The victim then contacts the agency. Thereafter, the program staff mails an application to the victim who fills it out and returns it to the compensation agency. Once the claim form is received, it is processed by an investigator or claims specialist. These employees do not go into the field to obtain their information; rather they collect data using letters, telephone calls, and other techniques. These investigations must verify a variety of information, including the fact that the crime was reported to the proper law enforcement agency, that there is appropriate documentation of medical expenses, that they obtain data regarding funds paid by insurance companies, and that they determine the amount, if any, of lost wages.

Once all pertinent information is gathered, the victim compensation agency will decide whether to make an award and will determine the monetary value of that award to the victim. In most states, victims may appeal a denial of benefits. These appeals are heard by a panel different from the one that made the original determination. Some states require that the appeal be heard by a judge.

The various state compensation programs are represented by the National Association of Crime Victim Compensation Boards (NACVCB). This is a national organization that provides advocacy, training, and communication among the state boards. Occasionally the NACVCB communicates with Congress and federal agencies on all matters affecting the state compensation programs.

Eligibility

Not all victims of every crime are eligible for state compensation. In general, the majority of states limit the compensation to victims who suffered injuries as a result of the criminal conduct of another and to survivors of homicides. In addition, there is a wide disparity between eligibility requirements in these programs with some states mandating that the victim suffer some sort of physical injury and others allowing for physical or mental injuries. Most states allow the parents of deceased victims to collect compensation.

A majority of states disallow some classes of persons from eligibility. Some states preclude firefighters and police officers from victim compensation awards. The rationale for this exclusion is that if their injuries are job related, they are eligible for another state program—workers' compensation program. Some states exclude convicted prisoners from filing claims while they are in jail or prison, or while serving probation or parole. VOCA has required states to provide compensation to nonresidents victimized within a state as well as persons who are subject to federal jurisdiction, such as Native Americans. In addition, state residents who are victimized in another state are eligible in their home state if the state where the crime occurred does not have a victim compensation program to which they can apply. If the claim is denied, the victim usually has no recourse, because the crime did not occur in the state of residence. Only if the state where the crime occurred has no program—or does not extend eligibility to the nonresident—is the victim allowed to file in the state of residence. However, a few states provide that as long as the victims file where the crimes occurred, they may also file in their home states.

Historically, drunk driving was not considered a violent crime that entitled the victim to state-funded compensation. In 1983, only five states classified drunk driving crimes as compensable.[12] As a result of a nationwide public awareness program, as well as successful lobbying by MADD, drunk driving cases are now included as compensable offenses in all states that participate in the VOCA program. Dealing with two or more insurance companies and several lawyers who represent the various parties tends to increase the length of time from filing a claim to receiving an award.[13]

Two key issues are common in drunk driving cases: contributory misconduct and subrogation. Contributory misconduct, discussed in more detail later in this chapter, is an eligibility requirement that applies to all crime victim compensation decisions and takes on special significance in drunk driving cases because of the social environment that accompanies many drinking and driving situations.[14] Many people may go to a bar and have a few drinks and then drive home believing they are fit to accomplish that task. In addition, unlike the majority of crimes, some victims of drunk drivers know the perpetrator and may have been in the same car as the drunk driver when the offense occurred. Some states deny awards if the victim was a willing passenger of a known drunk driver, other states reduce payments if the victim voluntarily rode with a known drunk, and some states do not consider such activity as misconduct. **Subrogation** is the process in which third parties are asked to reimburse the state for compensation payments previously made to the victim. Generally speaking, the state pays any award to which the victim is entitled under the state compensation laws and then attempts to recoup that payment from any insurance companies that are involved in the incident.

In the past, domestic violence victims were summarily denied compensation. Many states denied these claims because of the belief that the victims contributed to their own injuries by staying in the relationship or that any award would benefit the wrongdoer if he/she was still living with the victim. Similar to the change in attitudes toward victims of drunk driving, our perception of domestic violence victims has resulted in a change in policy in all states. All states now include domestic violence as a compensable crime.

Some state compensation programs have very few domestic violence claims. The staff members of these programs believe it is because victims underreport this form of violence. In addition, cultural barriers may prevent certain minority groups from reporting because exposing male offenders to public attention violates cultural norms.

Contributory misconduct occurs when victims participate in the crime or otherwise contribute to their injuries by their own conduct. All states have laws or regulations designed to exclude such parties from receiving compensation. This is one of the most frequent issues facing compensation staff today. The concept of victim participation is a complex and emotional subject that does not have a clear bright line delineating innocent victims from those that caused their own injuries.

In deciding the existence of contributory misconduct, many compensation programs rely on police reports, witness statements, the prosecuting attorney's opinion, the results of any trial, and the oral or written statements of the victim. In most states, if there is an issue of misconduct, the victim is given an opportunity to rebut such a conclusion prior to any final decision resulting in a denial of the claim. Many states do not have hard and fast rules regarding contributory misconduct and end up judging each case on its own merits.

Most states require that the victim promptly report the crime to the police. Generally, states require that a police report be filed within seventy-two hours of the discovery of the crime. In addition, all states require that the victim cooperate in any subsequent investigation or court proceedings, although a number of states can make an exception when the victim's life or safety is at risk. Apprehension or conviction of the perpetrator is not a requirement of receiving compensation.[15]

Eligibility issues pose complex and emotional problems for victims. Victim services professionals should understand the rationale and basis for these requirements so that they can explain them to victims. Being unjustly denied a compensation claim can have severe financial and mental consequences for a victim.

Benefits

Once a victim has qualified for compensation, the next step in the process is determining what types of benefits are available. Many factors are involved in determining the types and amounts of benefits available to victims. Some states have a small deductible amount ($50–$100) that must be reached before they will pay compensation. All states pay for only nonreimbursed expenses. In other words, if a victim has private health insurance that covers the cost of medical treatment, the state compensation award will not pay for those expenses.

Collateral financial sources are any payments received by the victim for costs reimbursed by other sources such as private insurance, workers' compensation, restitution, or disability payments. This policy prevents victims from recovering losses for the same injury twice and thus enriching themselves. Although most states attempt to use subrogation in an attempt to recoup money paid to victims, program staff members have reported frustration with the low amounts recovered.[16]

A majority of states compensate victims for a variety of crime-related costs, including dental care, plastic surgery, vocational rehabilitation (education), home care, and moving expenses. Most states also pay for mental health counseling. However, deciding who is a qualified mental health provider and determining the appropriate forms of treatment are complex issues facing many compensation staff members. Although some states require mental health professionals to be licensed, other states allow "counseling" to be done by a variety of persons, including those without advanced degrees. In addition, the type and extent of the treatment may be difficult to control, because some mental health providers may decide to prolong treatment beyond what is necessary to increase the victim's bill.

A majority of states allow payment for a portion of any attorney's fees incurred by the victim in processing the compensation claim. The amount awarded does not decrease the victim's

PRACTICUM
Contributory Misconduct—Who Is at Fault?[17]

Practicum 1:

The victim was shot by her husband after she had a protection order amended to let him visit their children in her apartment. Did the victim contribute to her injuries?

> Holding: Absent other facts, most programs would find no contributory misconduct on the part of the victim.

Practicum 2:

The victim was robbed and shot after accepting a ride from a stranger on a city street at 3 A.M.

> Holding: Most programs would find no misconduct.

Query: What if the victim was a prostitute and engaged in her work at the time she accepted the ride?

Practicum 3:

The victim was wounded in a drive-by shooting while talking to a third party.

> Holding: Most states would find no misconduct.

> Query: What if the third party was a drug dealer and the defendant was attempting to make a purchase of drugs? What if the shooting was part of an ongoing gang war for control of the city's drug markets?

award; rather it is a separate payment to the attorney. Many compensation staff members feel it is in the victim's best interest to be represented by an attorney when appealing a denial of compensation benefits.

In some states, compensation claims dramatically increased during the period between 1895 and 1992. Several factors contributed to this increase, including higher visibility of compensation programs, more awareness and advocacy on the part of victim services providers, and new laws mandating greater compensation of victims. This increase in claims and awards reflects the fact that victims have an increased awareness that they should receive the financial help they need.

Compensation is only one financial remedy available to victims of crime. Another remedy looks to the offender to make the victim whole. The topic of restitution is discussed in the next section.

RESTITUTION

Introduction

The 1982 *Final Report of the President's Task Force on Victims of Crime* included several key points regarding restitution.[18] The report recommended that legislation be enacted requiring judges to order restitution for property loss and personal injury in all cases unless the judge explicitly finds that restitution is not appropriate. However, the report also stated that although restitution is a proper goal to be pursued, it has limitations. The report noted that restitution cannot be ordered unless the perpetrator is caught and convicted. Even if it is ordered, the offender often has no resources with which to make any payments. Finally, those perpetrators who can make payments may take many years to finally pay off the balance. In the interim, the victim is left to bear the cost of the crime.[19]

As a result of this report and other factors influencing the victims' movement over the last two decades, a number of laws have been enacted addressing the issue of restitution. Hillenbrand reports that one reason these laws may have been enacted is the change in perception regarding restitution. She states that society began to view restitution not as a way to punish or rehabilitate the offender, but as a method of bringing justice to victims.[20] Other authorities argue that laws mandating restitution have been passed as "politically correct" with little or no thought given to their effect. This has resulted in a system that does not deliver its promise of making victims whole. Consequently, victims become more disillusioned with the criminal justice system when they learn that the court order mandating the offender to pay restitution carries no weight or authority.[21]

Even the definition of restitution causes conflict. It represents many things to many people. Whereas the victim may view restitution as a way to regain financial loss and to punish the offender, the court may see it as a method of instilling responsibility in the offender. The agency charged with collecting restitution may view it as simply one more task for an already overburdened department. Traditionally, **restitution** is a court-ordered sanction that involves payment of compensation by the defendant to the victim for injuries suffered as a result of the defendant's criminal act.

As the following Practicum illustrates, the definition of restitution, and who should pay, raises troubling issues. What is fair and just to a victim may seem outlandish to a judge or to the perpetrator. The following sections will examine how we happened to arrive at this juncture in our development of victims' rights. Also, the problems in collecting restitution and some innovative methods that address these issues will also be examined.

History

The concept of making a victim whole is not new.[22] As indicated in Chapter 1, the Code of Hammurabi, created about 1790 B.C., included provisions for payment of money to the victim or the victim's family.[23] In Saxton, England, a legal system was developed that provided for restitution to the victim's family for the injury incurred by the victim and restitution to the king

FOCUS
Compensating the Victims of September 11

On September 11, 2001, the world changed for the United States. Terrorists highjacked four passenger airliners. The first plane was flown into the north tower of the World Trade Center, and just eighteen minutes later, the second plane crashed into the south tower. The third plane hit its target: the Pentagon. The fourth plane crashed in a field in Pennsylvania. The United States' response to the victims of the September 11 tragedy has been both praised and criticized.

The injuries and death toll suffered in the attacks were staggering. The attacks killed 2,551 and seriously injured 215 more. Four hundred twenty-five of those killed or seriously injured were emergency responders. In addition, people suffered emotional trauma, property damage, and loss of business.

Congress responded by establishing the September 11 Victim Compensation Fund of 2001 as part of the Air Transportation Safety and System Stabilization Act. The first part of this act was to protect the financial viability of the airline industry by limiting their liability, and the second portion established a nonfaulty method of compensating victims for their loss.

The act established two options for recovery for victims: (1) They might pursue civil litigation against the airlines with a cap on recovery at the airline's liability coverage, or (2) they could utilize the compensation available from the fund in exchange for a relapse of liability of the airlines.

The fund included calculating an award based on the claimant's age, life expectancy income, marital status, and number and ages of dependents. Contrary to traditional tort law, no punitive damages were available.

The Rand Corporation conducted a study regarding the compensation of the victims of September 11 and found that most of the $38.1 billion in total payouts to individuals and businesses came from insurers ($19.6 billion). The second largest payout was from government programs ($15.8 billion), and the remaining amount came from charitable donations ($2.7 billion).

While many people considered the fund a wonderful and compassionate response by our government, others had questions and criticisms. Some victims' families questioned why the family of a victim who made more money should receive more money than those who made less money. They wondered if one person's life was more valuable than another's. Others questioned why victims of September 11 should receive more compensation than those of the 1995 Oklahoma City bombing.

Discussion questions:
1. Should victims of terrorism receive higher compensation awards than those of other crimes? What about victims of natural disasters?
2. What other issues are raised by this form of compensation?

Sources: Adapted from Josh Romero, "A Victim's Eye View of the September 11th Victim Compensation Fund," 71/I *Defense Counsel Journal* 64(7) (January 2004); and "Compensating the Victims of 9/11," *Research Brief* (Rand Institute for Civil Justice, Santa Monica, Calif.) 2004.

for violating the king's peace. As discussed earlier, this system eventually evolved into one in which the wrong was perpetrated against the state and not the victim. The victim and the victim's rights became secondary to the pursuit of justice.[24]

Modern restitution as we know it today can be traced to the criminal laws that authorized suspended sentences and the use of probation. By the late 1930s, several states had laws that allowed judges to order restitution as a condition of granting probation.[25] This process viewed restitution as part of the correctional process. In the late 1970s and 1980s, the victims' movement began to argue that restitution should be viewed as protecting victims from suffering financial hardship rather than punishing or rehabilitating the offender.

The modern concept of restitution in the criminal justice system serves a variety of purposes in the administration of justice. Restitution attempts to establish a relationship between the perpetrator and the victim in an effort to make the offender aware of the financial consequences suffered by the victim as a result of the offender's acts. Another purpose of restitution is to advance the concept of personal responsibility and accountability to the victim. A third idea regarding restitution holds that although it cannot undo the wrong, it can assist the victim financially and emotionally and at the same time educate the offender. Finally, restitution serves to punish the offender. The funds used to pay restitution must come from the offender's pocketbook and thus have a continuing impact on that offender.[26]

Types of Restitution

Restitution can now be ordered for a variety of criminal acts, including sex crimes, child sexual abuse, telemarketing fraud, and domestic violence.[27] Restitution can also be ordered to pay for lost wages, child care, and other expenses involved in attending court hearings.[28] In addition, there are several different types of restitution.[29]

The most common form of restitution is financial, which requires the offender to make payments directly to the actual victim of the crime. Financial-community restitution requires the offender to make payments to a community agency such as a restitution center, which then pays the victim. Individual service restitution requires the offender to perform a service for the actual victim. For example, the offender might be required to repair or replace property damaged during the commission of the crime. Community service restitution requires the offender to perform some beneficial service to the community. In this type of restitution, society serves as the symbolic victim, sometimes referred to as "symbolic restitution." Finally, some states authorize restitution fines. Restitution fines differ from actual restitution in that they are collected and deposited in the state's crime victim compensation fund. These monies then become part of the fund's operating expenses.

Restitution may be tied to different aspects of a defendant's sentence and is frequently imposed at the earliest possible time in the criminal process. In addition, many plea agreements call for restitution. Imposing payment as a condition of probation is the most common method of collecting restitution. A court order may also follow the defendant to the correctional institution. Many states are now imposing the requirement that inmates work while incarcerated

PRACTICUM

How Much Restitution Should Be Ordered?

The victim is a forty-two-year-old executive who was robbed in New York's Central Park while on a business trip. The offender took the victim's wallet, which contained a picture of his deceased wife, several credit cards, and $400 in cash. The perpetrator also demanded the victim's Rolex watch. The victim explained that the watch was a gift from his deceased wife, but the assailant tore it off his wrist and then proceeded to pistol-whip him.

The perpetrator was caught and convicted, and the court held a hearing to determine the amount of restitution that should be ordered. The defense attorney argued that his client was homeless and had not worked for three years

because of a drinking and drug problem. The prosecutor asked for funds to reimburse the victim for the $400 and the value of the lost Rolex, as well as any medical bills that were not covered either by the state compensation program or the victim's health insurance.

The victim stated that his wife bought him the Rolex twenty-one years ago and it cost her $500; however, today the fair market value of the Rolex was $5,000. The victim wants to replace the watch and is asking for $5,000. He also wants $400 for the lost cash and is asking $10,000 for the lost picture of his wife, stating that he has no other pictures of her. How much restitution should the judge order?

and while working in prison, they normally only receive a minimal amount of money (usually far less than the minimal wage). Several states have passed laws requiring that a portion of that amount, no matter how small, be set aside for payment as restitution to the victim. More states are implementing policies that require restitution to be established as a condition of any parole. In addition, states are passing laws that provide that any restitution order in a criminal case will also be considered as a civil order for remuneration from the defendant to the victim and may be processed in civil courts.

Problems with Restitution

Restitution is a complex process that involves a number of different professionals working in the criminal justice system. Unfortunately, these professionals are usually overworked and underbudgeted. Many of these professionals claim that collecting and disbursing restitution is someone else's job.[30] This leads to poor communication and diminished accountability among agencies inside the criminal justice system. This, in turn, causes poor consultation and communication with victims. Because there may be no agency controlling or coordinating restitution, judges may impose insufficient or excessive restitution orders.

Often victims feel dissatisfied with the restitution process. They may believe that the amount imposed in the court order was insufficient. Other victims feel powerless as they search for answers to their questions, only to be directed from one agency to another.[31]

Occasionally, a crime involves multiple perpetrators against a single victim. If the prosecution grants a perpetrator immunity to testify against the others, the victim will not be able to receive a court order of restitution against that defendant. By the same token, in crimes involving single perpetrators and multiple victims, deciding which victim should receive the limited funds of the perpetrator can create great difficulties.

Another obvious problem with restitution is the socioeconomic status of the perpetrator. In a majority of cases, the offenders are poor and unlikely to earn the funds necessary to make full restitution. In addition, juvenile offenders are often incapable of obtaining or holding jobs that might provide them with the funds necessary to pay the court-ordered restitution.

Methods of Collecting Restitution

Control or monitoring of restitution orders is critical. The American Bar Association (ABA) conducted a survey of restitution directors and recommended that higher compliance rates occur when (1) efforts are made to monitor payments, and (2) consistent action is taken to respond to delinquencies.[32] Respondents in the survey reported that the highest delinquency rates occurred at the time of the first payment and at mid-sentence. They stated that delinquency seldom occurred at the end of the offender's sentence. This study suggests that early and effective responses to delinquency can successfully interrupt a pattern of nonpayment.

The ABA study also suggests that compliance rates were higher in jurisdictions where the judge made an effort to determine if the offender had the ability to pay before the amount of restitution was set. When judges order restitution at a level so high as to be unreachable, it can result in noncompliance because the offender takes the attitude of "why even try to meet this impossible goal?" This noncompliance frustrates both the victim and the official charged with collecting restitution.[33]

Finally, the ABA study suggests the implementation of a policy within the criminal justice system that establishes a priority of collecting and disbursing fines, forfeitures, fees, and other assessments. This policy is necessary because often the offender is not only ordered to pay restitution, but also may have fines and other fees imposed such as repaying the court for the services of the public defender. These competing court-ordered financial obligations may affect the offender's ability to pay restitution to the victim.[34] Other recommendations that may make the restitution process more effective include specializing in the collection of restitution, employing automation, and using other nontraditional methods to collect restitution.

The Los Angeles criminal justice system is a large and sprawling bureaucratic system that seems impervious to change, and the Los Angeles Probation Department is one of the largest in the nation. The adult probation department in Los Angeles tested a process of assigning specialized restitution caseloads to some of their officers. Their sole duty is to monitor and collect the court-ordered restitution. This procedure has proved to be so successful that the department has assigned probation officers to each of its offices in Los Angeles whose primary duty is to collect restitution.[35]

Automation of records and bookkeeping can assist in collecting restitution. An investment in computer systems and software dedicated to the collection and disbursement of restitution sends a message to offenders that this is a high priority. Automation frees staff from performing routine repetitive tasks and can result in allowing them to work more closely with victims. In addition, it can free up time to send letters informing victims of the restitution process by simply typing in their name and address and hitting the print key. Warning letters to offenders who are delinquent can also be generated quickly without much staff time. Finally, computerization gives staff the ability to collect data and develop statistics regarding restitution.[36]

A number of other innovative methods for collecting restitution are in use across the nation. These include filing civil law suits and obtaining judgments based on the restitution order. In states that allow this process, once the default is placed on the judgment, the victim can garnish the offender's wages, file liens on real property, and attach other assets. One department in Phoenix, Arizona, requires offenders to turn over their uncashed paychecks to the department. The department then cashes the check, deducts the amount owed for restitution, and writes the offender another check for the balance. Some states are using restitution centers that house offenders for six months to a year while they work in the community. Their checks are given to the center, which deducts its expenses, other fines, and restitution before paying the balance to the perpetrator.[37] The Office for Victims of Crime continues to fund research in this area by calling for promising practices and policies in the field that address the issue of collection of restitution.

Summary

Crime victim compensation funds can pay for unreimbursed expenses suffered by victims of violent crimes. These state programs are funded by federally imposed fines, forfeitures, and other monies taken from federal offenders. Each state receives a portion of these funds to compensate victims. More victims are filing claims, and although some program managers are concerned over the financial drain caused by these increased claims, most see this as a positive development within the victims' rights movement.

In the last thirty years, restitution has re-emerged within the criminal justice system as a valuable method of assisting victims of crime. Victim advocates continue to call for more efficient methods of monitoring and collecting restitution. As a result, professionals within the criminal justice system are re-evaluating existing programs and policies in an attempt to meet the demand that restitution makes the victim whole. Victim services providers need to be aware of the pros and cons of the restitution process and be prepared to offer suggestions to those who have the power to make necessary changes that will benefit victims of crime.

Key Terms

Victim compensation is a direct payment to, or on behalf of, a crime victim for crime-related expenses such as unpaid medical bills, mental health counseling, funeral costs, and lost wages.

Victim assistance includes services such as crisis intervention, counseling, emergency transportation to court, temporary housing, advocacy, and criminal justice support.

Subrogation is the process in which third parties are asked to reimburse the state for compensation payments previously made to the victim.

Contributory misconduct occurs when victims participate in the crime or otherwise contribute to their injuries by their own conduct.

Restitution is a court-ordered sanction that involves payment of compensation by the defendant to the victim for injuries suffered as a result of the defendant's criminal act.

Discussion Questions

1. Explain how a typical compensation program is funded and operated.
2. List the various eligibility requirements for receiving compensation.
3. List the various benefits victims of crime may receive under a state compensation program.
4. Explain why the historical perspective of restitution is important in understanding today's models.
5. Can you list reasons why an incarcerated prisoner should not have to make restitution to a victim? Assume that you are the prisoner's advocate and must convince a judge of your position.

Suggested Readings

International Terrorism Victim Expense Reimbursement Program, Report to Congress (U.S. Department of Justice, Office of Justice Programs, Washington, D.C.) 2006.

R. E. Hartley, *Alternative Dispute Resolutions in Civil Justice Systems* (LFB Scholarly Publishing, New York) 2002.

M. Hook, *Ethics in Human Services* (Sidran Institute Press, Baltimore, Md.) 2005.

Crime Victim Compensation: A Fact Sheet and Crime Victim Compensation: An Overview (National Association of Crime Victim Compensation Boards, Alexandria, Va.) July 1, 1994.

Dale G. Parent, Barbara Auerbach, & Kenneth E. Carlson, *Compensating Crime Victims: A Summary of Policies and Practices,* Office of Justice Programs (U.S. Department of Justice, Washington, D.C.) January 1992.

Focus on the Future: A Systems Approach to Prosecution and Victim Assistance, National Victim Center, MADD, and American Prosecutors Research Institute (U.S. Department of Justice, Washington, D.C.) no date.

Daniel McGillis & Patricia Smith, *Compensating Victims of Crime: An Analysis of American Programs* (National Institute of Justice, Washington, D.C.) 1983.

A. J. Lurigio, W. G. Skogan, & R. C. Davis, eds., *Victims of Crime: Problems, Policies, and Programs* (Sage, Newbury Park, Calif.) 1990.

B. Gateway & J. Hudson, eds., *Criminal Justice, Restitution, and Reconciliation* (Willow Tree Press, Inc., Monsey, N.Y.) 1990.

National Victim Assistance Academy Text (Office for Victims of Crime, Washington, D.C.) 1996.

A. R. Roberts, *Helping Crime Victims* (Sage, Newbury Park, Calif.) 1990.

Barbara E. Smith, Robert C. Davis, & Susan W. Hillenbrand, *Enforcement of Court-Ordered Restitution: Executive Summary* (American Bar Association, Chicago) 1989.

D. Beatty, L. Frank, A. J. Lurigio, A. Seymour, M. Paparozzi, & B. Macgargle, *A Guide to Enhancing Victim Services Within Probation and Parole* (American Bar Association, Chicago) 1994.

Endnotes

1. NACVCB's, *Crime Victim Compensation: A Fact Sheet and Crime Victim Compensation: An Overview* (National Association of Crime Victim Compensation Boards, Alexandria, Va.) July 1, 1994, hereinafter *Crime Victim Compensation;* Dale G. Parent, Barbara Auerbach, & Kenneth E. Carlson, *Compensating Crime Victims: A Summary of Policies and Practices,* Office of Justice Programs (U.S. Department of Justice) January 1992, hereinafter *Compensating Crime Victims;* and *Focus on the Future: A Systems Approach to Prosecution and Victim Assistance,* National Victim Center, MADD, and American Prosecutors Research Institute (U.S. Department of Justice, Washington, D.C.) no date, hereinafter *Focus on the Future.*
2. *Crime Victim Compensation.*
3. Ibid.
4. *Compensating Crime Victims,* p. 2.
5. Ibid.
6. Ibid.
7. *Final Report, President's Task Force on Victims of Crime* (GPO, Washington, D.C.) December 1982.
8. *Crime Victim Compensation,* p. 2.
9. Ibid.
10. *Compensating Crime Victims,* p. 7.
11. "Victims of Crime Act Crime Victims Fund," *OVC Fact Sheet* (Office for Victims of Crime, Washington, D.C.) no date.
12. Daniel McGillis & Patricia Smith, *Compensating Victims of Crime: An Analysis of American Programs* (National Institute of Justice, Washington, D.C.) 1983.
13. *Compensating Crime Victims,* p. 20.
14. Ibid., p. 21.
15. *Crime Victim Compensation,* p. 3.
16. *Compensating Crime Victims,* p. 30.
17. Adapted from scenarios presented in *Compensating Crime Victims,* pp. 24–25.
18. *Final Report, President's Task Force on Victims of Crime* (GPO, Washington, D.C.) December 1982.
19. Ibid. at 38.
20. Susan Hillenbrand, "Restitution and Victim Rights in the 1980s," in A. J. Lurigio, W. G. Skogan, & R. C. Davis, eds., *Victims of Crime: Problems, Policies, and Programs* (Sage, Newbury Park, Calif.) 1990.
21. Carol Shapiro, "Is Restitution Legislation the Chameleon of the Victims' Movement?" in B. Gateway and J. Hudson, eds., *Criminal Justice, Restitution, and Reconciliation* (Willow Tree Press, Inc., Monsey, N.Y.) 1990.
22. Sterling O'Ran, "Restitution," *National Victim Assistance Academy Text* (Office for Victims of Crime, Washington, D.C.) 1996, hereinafter *National Victim Assistance Academy Text.*
23. See for example, Gordon, *Hammurabi's Code: Quaint or Forward Looking* (Rinehart, New York) 1957; and S. A. Cook, *The Laws of Moses and the Code of Hammurabi* (Adam and Charles Black, London) 1903.
24. Cathryn Jo Rosen & Allen T. Harland, "Restitution to Crime Victims as a Presumptive Requirement in Criminal Cases," in A. R. Roberts, ed., *Helping Crime Victims* (Sage, Newbury Park, Calif.) 1990.
25. L. F. Frank, "The Collection of Restitution: An Overlooked Service to Crime Victims," 8 *St. John's Journal of Legal Commentary,* 107 (1992).
26. *National Victim Assistance Academy Text,* pp. 21–10–5.
27. *Attorney General Guidelines for Victim and Witness Assistance* (U.S. Department of Justice, Washington, D.C.) 1995.
28. 18 U.S.C. Section 3663(b) as amended by Section 40504 of P. L. 103–322 (1994).
29. *National Victim Assistance Academy Text,* pp. 21–10–8 through 11.
30. Michael D. Harris, "No One Wants Responsibility for Restitution," *Los Angeles Daily Transcript,* A-1. (January 6, 1995).
31. *National Victim Assistance Academy Text,* pp. 21–10–7.
32. Barbara E. Smith, Robert C. Davis, & Susan W. Hillenbrand, *Enforcement of Court-Ordered Restitution: Executive Summary* (American Bar Association, Chicago) 1989.
33. Ibid.
34. Ibid.
35. D. Beatty, L. Frank, A. J. Lurigio, A. Seymour, M. Paparozzi, & B. Macgargle, *A Guide to Enhancing Victim Services within Probation and Parole* (American Bar Association, Chicago) 1994.
36. Ibid.
37. Ibid.

16

Victim Impact Statements

Chapter Outline

History of Victim Impact Statements
Purpose
Constitutional Issues
Use of Victim Impact Statements
Law Enforcement
Prosecutors
Judiciary
Effect of Victim Impact Statements
Victim Satisfaction
Sentencing

Victim Impact Panels
Introduction
Procedure
Summary
Key Terms
Discussion Questions
Suggested Readings
Endnotes

LEARNING OBJECTIVES

After reading this chapter, you should be able to:

- Explain the constitutional evolution of victim impact statements
- Understand fundamental fairness and how it relates to victim impact statements
- Distinguish between law enforcement and prosecutorial-based victim assistance programs
- Explain how victims view the affect of victim impact statements and compare this with how judges view this process
- Distinguish between victim impact statements and victim impact panels

HISTORY OF VICTIM IMPACT STATEMENTS

Associate U.S. Supreme Court Justice John Paul Stevens states:

> These two capital cases raise questions concerning the admissibility of so-called "victim impact evidence" during the penalty phase of a capital trial. The term is a misnomer in capital cases because the evidence does not describe the impact of the crime on the victim—his or her death is always an element of the offense itself. Rather, it describes the impact of the victim's death on third parties, usually members of the victim's family. (*Kelly v. California*, 129 S. Ct. 564 [U.S. 2008])

A new series of rights are emerging in our judicial system.[1] These rights confer upon the victim, or the relatives of deceased victims, the opportunity to speak out or be heard during various phases of the criminal justice process.

As with many rights that converge on a single point, an actual or potential conflict results. How we handle this conflict is a reflection of the morals and ethics of our society. This section will review the history of these various rights and examine the rationale behind the current status of the law as it relates to victim impact statements.

Purpose

One controversial "right" bestowed upon victims is known as the **victim impact statement** (VIS). This statement presents the victim's point of view to the sentencing authority. Providing the sentencing authority with all relevant information is not a new phenomenon in the criminal justice system. For many years, courts have accepted information regarding the defendant prior to the imposition of a sentence.

Traditionally, presentence reports have been used by judges to determine the proper punishment for criminal defendants. The report, which is normally prepared by a probation officer, details the defendant's background, education, and prior criminal record. Many of these reports also include information concerning the victim of the crime.[2]

Victim impact evidence is now admitted in sentencing for a variety of criminal acts, including those that fall within the realm of family violence. However, the law on admissibility and use of VISs is based on use of this evidence during death penalty cases. To understand the nature of VISs, it is necessary to review how this evidence is used in the most serious type of criminal case—those involving capital punishment.

The use of victim impact evidence during the sentencing phase of a criminal crime raises serious constitutional issues. The right to confront witnesses comes head-to-head with the right to have all relevant evidence placed before the sentencing authority. Intense feelings have been aroused in the Supreme Court when it has addressed this issue.

Constitutional Issues

In *Booth v. Maryland,* the Supreme Court initially addressed the issue of using VISs in a sentencing jury's determination.[3] In 1983, John Booth and Willie Reed bound and gagged an elderly couple. Believing the couple might be able to identify them, Booth stabbed them numerous times with a kitchen knife. The trial judge in *Booth* allowed the jury to consider a VIS, which detailed the family and community's respect and admiration for the victims as well as the impact of the murders on the victims' family.[4]

The Supreme Court, in reversing the death sentence, held that it was impermissible to allow the jury access to such evidence in the sentencing phase of a death penalty proceeding.[5] The Court listed three factors that precluded the prosecution from introducing evidence of the homicide's impact on the victim's family.

First, in holding that the VIS impermissibly allows the jury to focus on the victim rather than the defendant, the Court stated:

> When the full range of foreseeable consequences of a defendant's actions may be relevant in other criminal and civil contexts, we cannot agree that it is relevant in the unique circumstances of a capital sentencing hearing. In such a case, it is the function of the sentencing jury to "express the conscience of the community on the ultimate question of life or death." When carrying out this task the jury is required to focus on the defendant as a "uniquely individual bein[g]." The focus of a VIS, however, is not on the defendant, but on the character and reputation of the victim and the effect on his family. These factors may be wholly unrelated to the blameworthiness of a particular defendant.[6]

The Court was particularly moved by the fact that the capital defendant does not typically choose his victim and, in fixing the punishment, there should be no correlation between the murder and the grief experienced by the victim's family.

Second, the Court held that the sentence of death should not turn on the characteristics of the victim and the victim's family. Specifically, the Court recognized that the imposition of the death penalty should not be determined on the basis of the ability of the victim's family to articulate their anguish and bereavement, regardless if the victim left behind a family, or on the fact that the victim was a stellar member of the community.[7] These factors focus attention on the victim and away from the central inquiry of whether the defendant's characteristics and background are such that the death sentence is warranted.[8]

Finally, the Court stated that because a VIS contains the subjective perceptions and feelings of family members, the defendant has limited rebuttal opportunity.[9] Furthermore, to the extent the defendant is given an opportunity to rebut such information, "[t]he prospects of a 'mini-trial' on the victim's character is more than simply unappealing, it could well direct the sentencing jury from its constitutionally required task—determining whether the death penalty is appropriate in light of … the crime."[10]

In summing up the Court's holding that introduction of the VIS violates the Eighth Amendment's prohibition against cruel and unusual punishment, Justice Powell commented:

> One can understand the grief and anger of the family caused by the brutal murders in this case, and there is no doubt that jurors generally are aware of these feelings. But the formal presentation of this information by the State can serve no other purpose than to inflame the jury and divert it from deciding the case on the relevant evidence concerning the crimes and the defendant. As we have noted, any decision to impose the death sentence must "be, and appear to be, based on reason rather than caprice or emotion." The admission of these emotionally charged opinions as to what conclusions the jury should draw from the evidence clearly is inconsistent with the reasoned decision making we require in capital cases.[11]

It should be apparent that at the time of the decision in *Booth v. Maryland,* the relevant considerations at the sentencing phase of a murder trial were those aspects of a defendant's background, or character, or those circumstances that extenuate or mitigate the defendant's culpability.

South Carolina v. Gathers followed the rationale of *Booth* and held unconstitutional the imposition of a death penalty based on prosecutorial remarks that were considered inflammatory.[12] Demetrius Gather and three companions sexually assaulted and killed Richard Haynes, a man they encountered in a park. During the incident, the perpetrators ransacked a bag the victim was carrying. The bag contained several articles pertaining to religion, including a religious tract entitled, "Game Guy's Prayer." During the sentencing phase of the trial, the prosecutor's argument included references to Haynes's personal qualities and included a reading of the "Game Guy's Prayer." The Supreme Court reversed the sentence stating that such references to the qualities of the victim were similar to the *Booth* holding, which prohibited VISs. The court determined that such evidence was likely to inflame the jury and thus violate the defendant's Eighth Amendment rights. In a well-reasoned and logical dissent, Justice O'Conner stated, "Nothing in the Eighth Amendment precludes the community from considering its loss in assessing punishment nor requires that the victim remain a faceless stranger at the penalty phase of a capital case." The dissent by Justice O'Conner was a signal that the winds of judicial temperament might be changing.

In *Payne v. Tennessee,* the court completely reversed itself and allowed the imposition of a death sentence to stand, based in part on evidence contained in a VIS. In 1987, Pervis Tyrone Payne entered the apartment of Charisse Christopher and her two children. Payne stabbed Charisse and the two children numerous times with a butcher knife. Charisse and her daughter died; however, three-year-old Nicholas survived.

Payne was caught and convicted for the murders. During the penalty phase, four witnesses testified regarding the defendant's background, reputation, and mental state. These witnesses urged the jury to not impose the death penalty. In rebuttal, the prosecution called the maternal grandmother who was caring for Nicholas. She was allowed to testify, over the defendant's objection, that Nicholas continued to cry out calling for his dead mother and sister. The witness was also allowed to testify regarding her personal grief over the loss of her loved ones.

During the closing argument, the prosecutor hammered on the pain and suffering that Nicholas and his deceased family had endured stating:

> But we do know that Nicholas was alive. And Nicholas was in the same room. Nicholas was still conscious. His eyes were open. He responded to the paramedics. He was able to follow their directions. He was able to hold his intestines in as he was carried to the ambulance. So he knew what happened to his mother and baby sister.
>
> There is nothing you can do to ease the pain of any of the families involved in this case. There is nothing you can do to ease the pain of Bernice or Carl Payne, and that's a tragedy. There is nothing you can do basically to ease the pain of Mr. and Mrs. Zvolanek, and that's a tragedy. They will have to live with it for the rest of their lives. There is obviously nothing you can do for Charisse and Lacie Jo. But there is something you can do for Nicholas.
>
> Somewhere down the road Nicholas is going to grow up, hopefully. He's going to want to know what happened. And he is going to know what happened to his baby sister and his mother. He is going to want to know what kind of justice was done. He is going to want to know what happened. With your verdict, you will provide the answer.[13]

The jury sentenced Payne to death, and the case was appealed to the U.S. Supreme Court. Payne contended that the trial court erred when it allowed the maternal grandmother to testify. Relying on *Booth* and *Gathers,* Payne argued that such evidence was a violation of his Eighth Amendment rights.

After reviewing the principles that have guided criminal sentencing over the ages, the Court stated that the consideration of the harm caused by the crime has been an important factor in the existence of the exercise of judicial discretion. The majority opinion went on to state that neither *Booth* nor *Gathers* even suggested that a defendant, entitled as he is to individualized consideration, is to receive that consideration wholly apart from the crime he has committed.

In setting forth the groundwork for overruling *Booth* and *Gathers,* the Court stated:

> Under our constitutional system, the primary responsibility for defining crimes against state law, fixing punishments for the commission of those crimes, and establishing procedures for criminal trials rests with the States. The state laws respecting crimes, punishments, and criminal procedures are of course subject to the overriding provisions of the United States Constitution. Where the State imposes the death penalty for a particular crime, we have held that the Eight Amendment imposes special limitations upon that process.
>
> The States remain free, in capital cases, as well as others, to devise new procedures and new remedies to meet felt needs. Victim impact evidence is simply another form or method of informing the sentencing authority about the specific harm caused by the crime in question, evidence of a general type long considered by sentencing authorities. We think the *Booth* Court was wrong in stating that this kind of evidence leads to the arbitrary imposition of the death penalty. In the majority of cases, and in this case, victim impact evidence serves entirely legitimate purposes.[14]

Thus the Supreme Court overruled *Booth* and *Gathers* to the extent that they prohibited introduction of evidence or argument regarding the impact of the crime on the victim, families, and the community. In addition, the Court's decision clearly stated that the decision regarding the admission of such evidence was the prerogative of the individual states. The Court ruled that it would not intervene unless the evidence introduced was so unduly prejudicial that it renders the trial fundamentally unfair.[15] If this occurred, the court reasoned, the due process clause of the Fourteenth Amendment provides a mechanism for relief.

The decision was not without heated dissent. In a dissenting opinion, Justices Marshall and Blackmun uttered a quote that will ring in the halls of justice and law school classrooms forever: "Power, not reason, is the new currency of this Court's decision making."[16] Justices Marshall and Blackmun went on to point out that the court was disregarding the accepted judicial principle of stare decisis. In a well-reasoned but emotional conclusion, the justices stated:

> Today's decision charts an unmistakable course. If the majority's radical reconstruction of the rules for overturning this Court's decisions is to be taken at face value—and the majority offers us no reason why it should not—then the overruling of *Booth* and *Gathers* is but a preview of an even broader and more far-reaching assault upon this Court's precedents. Cast aside today are those condemned to face society's ultimate penalty. Tomorrow's victims may be minorities, women, or the indigent. Inevitably, this campaign to resurrect yesterday's "spirited dissents" will squander the authority and the legitimacy of this Court as a protector of the powerless.[17]

The decision also generated controversy in the academic world when a series of articles appeared condemning the court for both allowing victim impact evidence and appearing to repudiate its acceptance of stare decisis.[18] Although the dissent and certain individuals within the academic community may condemn the majority's opinion, it is now clearly the law of the land. In addition, the Supreme Court's decision enhances the victims' rights movement in the United States. It allows individual states to determine what is relevant evidence in the death penalty phase of a capital crime.

Some would argue that the decision in *Payne* leaves prosecutors and defense attorneys scrambling to determine what type of evidence is admissible under the guise of VISs. The answer is simply that evidence that does not result in rendering a trial fundamentally unfair is proper. This concept of fundamental fairness is not a new, untested, or ill-defined doctrine.

There is a long history of defining acts by the state that are classified as fundamentally unfair. The doctrine of fundamental fairness has its roots in two early cases. In *Powell v. Alabama*, several black youths were accused of repeatedly raping two young white girls. They were caught, tried, and convicted. Their conviction was overturned on the ground that the failure of the trial court to appoint counsel until the day of the trial was a violation of the defendants' due process.[19] In *Brown v. Mississippi*, a sheriff hung the defendant from a tree and whipped him until he confessed to the murder of a white man. The Supreme Court held that such actions are revolting to the sense of justice, and the confession was suppressed.[20]

The **doctrine of fundamental fairness** accepts the concept that due process is a generalized command that requires states to provide the defendant with a fair trial. If the admission of the victim impact evidence "revolts the sense of justice" or "shocks the conscience" of the court, such admission would be erroneous under the due process clause.

Victim impact evidence is now an accepted part of the judicial process. The ability of a victim of family violence to inform the court of the impact of the offender's acts on her or his life can only benefit the victim and continue to educate the public regarding the dynamics of violence.

In 2009, Justice Stevens in *Kelly v. California* noted that in the years since *Payne* was decided, the Court has left state and federal courts unguided in their efforts to police the hazy boundaries between permissible victim impact evidence and its impermissible, "unduly prejudicial" forms. According to Stevens, following *Payne*'s model, lower courts throughout the country have largely failed to place clear limits on the scope, quantity, or kind of victim impact evidence capital juries are permitted to consider. Stevens contended that not only have courts allowed capital sentencing juries to hear brief oral or written testimony from close family members regarding victims and the direct impact of their deaths, they have also allowed testimony from friends, neighbors, and coworkers in the form of poems, photographs, hand-crafted items, and—as occurred in these cases—multimedia video presentations (*Kelly v. California*, 129 S. Ct. 564, 567 (U.S. 2008)). In the Kelly case, the Supreme Court refused to review a lower court that had allowed the use of videos as part of the victim's impact statement.

The first known victim impact statement in the United States was in 1976 in the state of California. "It was introduced in Fresno County, California by then Chief Probation Officer James Rowland. At Mr. Rowland's initiation, victim impact statements became a part of all presentence investigation reports conducted in Fresno County." At the time, there was no law in California allowing victim impact statements.

After the 1969 Manson murders, there was a campaign in California to allow victims and their families a say in sentencing and parole hearings. One of the people killed in the Manson Murders was actress Sharon Tate who was pregnant at the time, and it was her mother who spearheaded the campaign as one of her daughter's killers. As a result of this campaign, California law was amended in 1982 to allow crime victims and their families a say in sentencing and parole hearings. Since them, victim impact statements are now allowed in all states. Victim impact statements are also used in other countries like Australia, Finland, and South Africa.

[*Note:* Both authors discussed the history of victim impact statements with James Rowland when he was Director of Corrections for the State of California.]

USE OF VICTIM IMPACT STATEMENTS

Law Enforcement

Law enforcement officers should understand the victim impact process for a number of reasons: (1) Many departmental policy manuals require that they inform victims of this right, (2) the officer can demonstrate concern by explaining the process to the victim, and (3) educating victims about their rights ensures that others within the criminal justice system will understand the impact of crime on the victims.[21] Once any crime has been reported, law enforcement officers should inform the victims of their rights early in the investigation process. They should offer assistance and encourage victims to keep a record or diary of their feelings, emotions, and hardships. This record should also track expenses so that the impact statements accurately reflect the appropriate amount of restitution. After an offender's arrest, victims should be encouraged to talk with the local victim–witness coordinator and the prosecutor regarding their feelings about the crime and any plea bargain.

Law enforcement officers do not stop participating in the process simply because they have arrested the perpetrator, nor should they stop their involvement with the victims of crime. They should "share ownership of the case" by working with and keeping victims informed of their rights. The officer should encourage victims to participate in the process and explain that their information may make a difference. Officers should inform victims of the procedures and policies regarding VISs in their jurisdiction. Do they send a letter to the judge? Do they fill out a form? Where do they get this form? Can they talk with the probation officer? A number of questions need to be answered and law enforcement officers are in the best position to answer these questions for victims.[22]

A particular segment of society believes that victims should not be allowed to speak out at a defendant's sentencing. In February 1995, at the sentencing hearing of Long Island Railroad gunman Colin Ferguson, who shot, wounded, and killed several Long Island commuters, victims spoke out about their anguish and feelings. The *Wall Street Journal,* the *New York Times,* and the *Washington Post* all responded by endorsing the use of victim impact statements.

The *New Republic,* however, argued that the use of such statements might inflame the judge or jury.[23] It stated that one of the most basic requirements of the rule of law is that judges and juries be impartial. Furthermore, the editorial stated that victim impact evidence guarantees "that the trials will degenerate into lawless emotionalism."[24]

The debate continues in the criminal justice profession regarding the extent of law enforcement's role in the VIS process. Supporters of an active role by law enforcement argue that this process provides victims of crime with information about their rights and thus allows them to participate in the justice process almost from the beginning. Supporters also explain that such a process allows victims to begin to document their feelings and financial losses early in the process. Opponents argue that forcing law enforcement officers to give information regarding victims' rights early in the process leads victims to assume that the offender will be identified, arrested, and convicted. Statistically, a number of crimes occur in which the perpetrator is never caught. Opponents also argue that most victims are not familiar with the criminal justice system, and officers will have to spend valuable time educating them about the system when, in fact, the perpetrator may never be caught.[25]

In recent years, many law enforcement agencies have established police-based victim assistance programs. These programs have the ability to provide services to crime victims who might otherwise have been excluded from receiving such services because some of these programs focus on those victims whose cases have formally entered the criminal justice system. For example, a police-based victim assistance program might inform victims of their right to state compensation funds.[26] As the previous chapter explained, these funds are available even if the perpetrator is not apprehended. As these programs gain popularity, victim services providers must be ready to assist law enforcement agencies in setting up their own program and working with these agencies to ensure that victims of crime are informed of their rights.

Prosecutors

The duties of prosecutors and law enforcement officers often overlap within the criminal justice process. Police make arrests, conduct investigations, interrogate suspects, and file cases with the district attorney's office. Many times prosecutors accompany police on raids, sit in on interrogations, and conduct their own follow-up investigations. Just as these two principles in the criminal justice system work together to attain a conviction of the perpetrator, so must they coordinate their efforts in working with victims and their interaction with the criminal justice system. In no place is this more important than during the sentencing phase of any trial.

Our criminal justice system is slowly beginning to recognize that its failure to grant victims an active role in the dispensation of justice is shortsighted because the continued successful functioning of the prosecutor's office depends on the cooperation and assistance of victims. Traditionally, prosecutor's offices have been assigned the role of creating and administrating victim assistance programs. This role was viewed as necessary in that prosecutors have a vested interest in facilitating victim participation in the system.[27]

Placing victim assistance programs in prosecutors' offices provides them with a number of advantages: They have instant access to information about the victim's physical, emotional, and financial status, which can assist in charging or deposition of cases; they will lessen the chances that an adversarial relationship will develop between the victim and the prosecutor; and they can favorably influence the victim's decision regarding any proposed plea bargain.[28]

Prosecutors should establish policies and procedures that assign agency responsibility for the distribution and collection of VISs. These guidelines should address the issue of coordination between the various agencies in the criminal justice system. This coordination is necessary so that victims are not filling out two, three, or more impact forms, and more important, so that victims are not overlooked in the system.

Prosecutors should also ensure that victims are informed of the policies and procedures surrounding the VIS, including the following: the purpose and use of the impact statement; who is eligible to submit a statement; how it should be submitted (written, oral, video, etc.); how the court will use the statement; and how to request assistance with filling out the statement. This information will not only assist the prosecutor in arguing for an appropriate sentence, but will also make the victim feel part of the system. Working with crime victims and helping them to prepare a VIS offer a prosecutor a chance to become more responsive to the needs of victims, and thereby improve the nature of the criminal justice system.

Some prosecutors may resist this active involvement with victims. Some may argue that this infringes on the discretion vested in prosecutors, whereas others will claim that victims do not understand the system, and they as prosecutors do not have the time to explain it to them. Just as some prosecutors resist working with the staffs of rape crisis centers, others may resist this participation by victims of crimes. Victim services providers must be the advocates for these types of change. They are knowledgeable and experienced, and they understand the system and can work with reluctant prosecutors to overcome any fears or concerns about working with victims of crime.

Judiciary

Crime is an extremely personal phenomenon and therefore no two victims will experience the same emotional, physical, or financial impact. It is imperative that judges have access to all pertinent information prior to sentencing so that they can balance society's needs, the defendant's needs, and the victim's needs. One method of balancing these needs is through the use of VISs.

The *President's Task Force on Victims of Crime* addressed the issue of victim participation at sentencing by stating:

> Victims, no less than defendants, are entitled to their day in court. Victims, no less than defendants, are entitled to have their views considered. A judge cannot evaluate the seriousness of a defendant's conduct without knowing how the crime has burdened the victim. A judge cannot reach an informed determination of the danger posed by a defendant without hearing from the person he has victimized.[29]

Judges should participate in this victim impact process by ensuring that victims are made aware of the opportunity to present their views prior to sentencing. This presentation of their position should be facilitated by judges, and victims should be allowed to present victim impact evidence in a variety of methods, including orally, in writing, by video, or via any other method that accurately presents the victim's feelings to the court.

Americans have always believed that the ultimate responsibility for how the judicial system operates rests with judges. Judges should ensure that victims participate at the sentencing hearing, which, with the exception of parole hearings, is the last opportunity that they have to influence the fate of the offender. Allowing victims to be part of this hearing can reaffirm their beliefs in the judicial system.

Under current rules of evidence, trial judges may admit victim impact statements, but it is important to remember that they are not required to admit them in all states. There are still many trial judges who feel that the statements should not be admitted and thus refuse to admit them. In California, under the state constitution, victims have a right to enter victim impact statements.In several other states, the victims have this right and in those states the trial judge may not refuse to admit a valid victim impact statement.

EFFECT OF VICTIM IMPACT STATEMENTS

Victim Satisfaction

The effect of VISs is still being studied and debated. One area being studied carefully is victim satisfaction with VISs. Some authorities believe that impact statements help the victim emotionally deal with the consequences of the crime. Others believe that victims are more satisfied with the criminal justice system if they participate by being allowed to express their feelings in a VIS. This section will briefly examine these and other aspects of victim satisfaction and VISs.

In 1981, a National Institute of Justice study revealed that victims' satisfaction with the criminal justice system increased if they believed that they had influenced the process, regardless of whether they really had. For example, victims who had been able to speak to prosecutors and judges were more satisfied with the system than those who believed they were not able to speak.[30] In 1982, another study indicated that a sense of participation was more critical to victims' satisfaction with the criminal justice process than how severely the defendant was punished.[31] In 1984, another study revealed that victims wanted more information about their case and the opportunity to tell the prosecutor and judge how the case affected them.[32]

In 1989, Dean Kilpatrick reported the results of his research, which indicated that victim participation not only affected potential cooperation within the criminal justice system, but that it was also critical in promoting victims' recovery from the aftermath of crime by helping them to reassert a sense of control over their lives.[33] Kilpatrick stated that a criminal justice system that denies victims a chance to participate fosters a sense of helplessness and lack of control. He pointed out that there is a great danger in promising victims participation in the system and then failing to follow through with that promise, because it results in further victimization.

Robert Wells, another noted authority, stated that VISs may promote the psychological recovery of victims. Just as talking about what happened promotes healing, writing about it may also assist victims to emotionally deal with the crime. Allowing victims to tell how they were affected by the crime sends a supportive message that the criminal justice system cares about what happened.[34]

However, other experts claim the mental and emotional benefits of VISs and victim participation are overrated. In a 1985 study carried out in Brooklyn, Davis compared the outcome of two court experiments in which victims gave impact statements in one court and where no statements were allowed in another court. He found no evidence that victims in the court that mandated impact statements felt a greater sense of participation or increased satisfaction.[35] Davis followed this research with a 1989 study in the Bronx Supreme Court in New York.[36] The study analyzed 293 victims of robbery, nonsexual assault, and burglary. Each victim was assigned to one of three classifications: (1) Some victims were interviewed and a VIS written and distributed, (2) other victims were interviewed, but no impact statement was prepared, and (3) only the name and address of the victim were recorded. A series of interviews was conducted with each victim. The results of this study indicated that VISs are not an effective means of promoting victim satisfaction within the criminal justice system. There were no data to support the theory that VISs led to greater feelings of involvement, greater satisfaction with the criminal justice system, or greater satisfaction with the sentences imposed on the offenders. Davis concluded that more research is necessary regarding the effect of impact statements on victim satisfaction with the system.

As this discussion indicates, controversy continues over the effect of VISs on victim satisfaction. However, there is sufficient individual and anecdotal evidence of victim approval of the use of impact statements that we should continue using them until definitive studies can be conducted. The next section examines whether VISs affect the outcome of sentencing.

FOCUS
Feelings Regarding Victim Impact Statements

"My victim impact statement was the last opportunity I had to let anyone know about my daughter."

—a victim

I want you to go over each victim impact statement.… You have to live with the stupidity of your behavior for the rest of your life, but you also have to understand what these families have to live with as well.…

—Judge to a defendant at time of sentencing[37]

Sentencing

There is limited research on the effect that VISs have on judges. Superficially, it would appear that such evidence can only assist the court in rendering its decision and therefore should be readily accepted and consistently used by the judicial system. However, judges, like every other member of the criminal justice system, are understaffed and overworked. Does additional information really help or does the process simply take more time? Are judges swayed by the emotional appeal of a citizen or are they bound to render impartial justice to the defendant?

Early research indicates that state trial court judges found financial information contained in a VIS useful in determining appropriate sentences and restitution orders.[38] Of those judges interviewed, 70 percent found the information useful and another 20 percent found it useful in regard to restitution orders. Although this research indicates victim impact evidence is useful to judges, this "usefulness" appears limited to the area of restitution and financial issues, and not to other aspects of sentencing the defendant.

In 1990, Erez and Tontodonato produced an important study involving 500 Ohio felony cases and found that the cases in which a VIS was taken were more likely than those without a statement to result in the offender going to prison rather than receiving probation.[39] This research has been cited by a number of VIS proponents as authority for the position that such statements have an effect on sentencing. Although this study was significant, it had several flaws, including a wide disparity in offense seriousness between cases that had impact statements. In addition, the authors acknowledged that further research needed to be conducted in this area.

Davis and Smith also researched the effect of impact statements on sentencing. In the same study that examined victim satisfaction, Davis and his associate evaluated the significance of impact statements on judicial sentencing.[40] They concluded that VISs did not produce sentences that reflect the effects of crime on the victims, nor did they find that sentencing decisions were affected by impact statements once the charge and the defendant's prior record were considered by the court. They did find that the severity of the charges is a high predictor of sentences. Whereas judges professed to be interested in impact statements, prosecutors believed that judges only occasionally considered this information when imposing sentences. Conversely, prosecutors claimed that victims should be consulted on a regular basis, but judges stated that prosecutors rarely related impact evidence to them.

Clearly, more research is also needed in this area. In addition, such research must find a way to get around the "political correctness" of advocating the use of VISs. As Davis's study points out, judges claim they endorse impact statements, but prosecutors do not believe them. On the other hand, the same prosecutors claim that they use impact statements, but the judges do not see them. Realistically, few elected or appointed officials in today's climate within the criminal justice system will admit to anything less than wholehearted endorsement of VISs. What is needed is an in-depth study to determine the impact of such evidence outside the realm of political correctness. Until such research is done, we can only speculate on its real effect.

FOCUS
How to Develop a Victim Impact Statement

Who should submit the statement? If the victim is a child, a parent or family members, such as grandparent, brother, or sister, of the victim can submit the statement to the trial judge. The victim can generally obtain assistance in completing the statement. For example, Mothers Against Drunk Driving (MADD) helps complete VIS statements for victims in driving under the influence (DUI) cases. In cases involving homicide, a close family member is generally permitted to submit a statement.

Rules of evidence. The rules of evidence allow a victim impact statement to be received and considered in any sentencing of defendants who are convicted of crimes of violence.

Content of statement.   The statement should address the personal harm suffered as a direct result of the crime. It should contain accurate information about the harmful consequences; for example, short- and long-term physical, psychological, emotional, mental, and relational consequences. Relevant medical and psychological reports that support the statement may be attached to the victim impact statement. The trial court may accept and consider the statement any time after the conviction and before the sentencing of the defendant.

Formal Requirements of a Victim Impact Statement. In addition to containing details of the personal harm suffered by the victim, the statement should normally contain:

- Identify of the victims.
- The name of the person who wrote the statement.
- It must be signed and dated by person who wrote it.
- Frequently the statutes or regulations require a statement that the victim does not object to the statement being given in court.
- Be in writing and presented in a legible format. It may be either typed or handwritten.
- Most states allow only one victim impact statement for each primary or family victim.

Remember the following points:

- The victim impact statement becomes part of the court case and a public record.
- The defense is entitled to cross-examine the preparer about the contents of the statement. This may happen because the offender does not agree with parts of the statement.
- A victim impact statement may be made available to the offender, the offender's legal representative, or any other person, but in many states the offender will be prevented from retaining copies of the statement.
- The victim impact statement must not contain anything that is offensive, threatening, intimidating, or harassing toward the offender.
- In most states, there is no legal requirement for a victim impact statement to be treated confidentially. There is also no legal requirement to prevent publication.
- Once the victim impact statement has been handed to the court, it becomes a public document, except in relation to children. The media may gain access to the victim impact statement through the court registry and may report on the contents of the statement that are read or referred to in court.

VICTIM IMPACT PANELS

Introduction

Victim impact panels (VIPs) differ significantly from VISs. The VIP is generally a program for offenders of DUI of alcohol or drugs. The panels are a nonconfrontational presentation given by victims of DUI crashes who speak about the impact the DUI crash has had on their lives. However, because they involve victims discussing the impact of the offense on their lives, they are included in this chapter rather than elsewhere in this textbook. MADD established VIPs as a method of dealing with the problem of drunk driving.[41] MADD does not believe that VIPs should replace traditional criminal sanctions for driving under the influence. They are offered to enhance and supplement such sentencing by placing offenders face to face with victims of drunk driving whose lives have been changed by someone who drank and then got behind the wheel of a car.

Procedure

MADD or other victim groups select a panel of three to four victims to speak briefly about the drunk-driving crashes in which they were injured or a loved one was killed, and what the event has meant to them. They do not blame or judge the attendees. A VIP coordinator moderates the panel, and victims are never allowed to speak at groups in which their own offender is present. The attendees are convicted drunk drivers who are required to attend a panel as an element of their sentences. A probation officer or other agent of the court attends each panel to monitor attendance. Any person who fails to appear for a panel is required to return to court for appropriate action.[42]

Victims who have served on these panels find that telling their stories lightens their personal pain and assists in the healing process. Victims also report that they have experienced something positive from a previously devastating event, and they believe that by telling their stories they may be preventing some other family from suffering a similar fate.[43]

The goals of the VIP are to enhance the emotional healing of victims by offering them an opportunity to speak out about the incident. These panels also enable attendees to understand drunk driving from the victim's perspective. Hopefully these stories will curtail the attendees' decisions to drink and drive.

VIPs are different than VISs. However, they both serve to allow victims to express their feelings regarding the consequences of a crime. The opportunity to express feelings regarding the event can be a valuable healing process. Although VIPs are relatively new within the criminal justice system, they offer another sentencing option to judges.

Summary

Victim impact statements are now accepted as a constitutionally firm mechanism that may be used in criminal cases, whether these cases are simple assaults or death penalty cases. The use of these statements is governed by the principle of fundamental fairness, which requires courts to ensure that the defendant receives a fair trial. A properly conducted victim impact statement does not violate this mandate.

To be effective, the victim impact statement must be accepted by all parties within the criminal justice system. Law enforcement officers should be aware of it and be prepared to inform victims of its availability. Prosecutors are the logical choices to coordinate victim impact statements and should take the lead. Judges are looked upon as the final authority within the criminal justice system, and they should demand that the victim have an opportunity to speak at sentencing.

Controversy continues regarding the effectiveness of victim impact statements. More research needs to be conducted on both the issue of victim satisfaction and the effect of impact statements on sentencing. However, victim impact statements should continue to be used, because some evidence supports the fact that victims believe the statements are an important right to which they should be afforded.

Victim impact panels are a new technique that offers victims of drunk driving the opportunity to express their feelings. They are similar to victim impact statements in that victims believe they serve a useful function. We must continue to explore alternative mechanisms that assist victims of crime in overcoming the consequences of the criminal act.

Key Terms

Victim impact panels are often used by MADD as a method to allow victims to express their feelings regarding the consequences of a crime and provide the opportunity for the victim to make a direct statement to the offender. The panels can then provide information to the trial judge and make sentence recommendations.

Victim impact statement presents the victim's point of view to the sentencing authority.

Doctrine of fundamental fairness accepts the concept that due process is a generalized command that requires states to provide the defendant with a fair trial.

Discussion Questions

1. Explain and give concrete examples of fundamental fairness. Can you list ways in which a victim impact statement would violate this constitutional standard?
2. Should law enforcement officers inform the victim of a crime about victim impact statements? Prepare a form that should be given to victims outlining their rights.
3. How are we ever going to determine if victim impact statements serve a valid purpose in the criminal justice system? How would you structure such a study? What are the pitfalls inherent in these types of studies?
4. Should a drunk driver be mandated to attend a victim impact panel? Why? Justify your answer.

Suggested Readings

Robert Wells, "Victim Impact Statements," *Crime Victim and Witness Assistance Training Project* (Federal Law Enforcement Training Center, Glyno, Ga.) 1990.

Ellen K. Alexander & Janice H. Lord, *Impact Statements: A Victim's Right to Speak … A Nation's Responsibility to Listen* (National Victims Center, Arlington, Va.) 1992.

Janice H. Lord, *Victim Impact Panels: A Creative Sentencing Opportunity* (Mothers Against Drunk Driving, Dallas) 1990.

Endnotes

1. This section has been adapted from H. Wallace, *Family Violence: Legal Medical and Social Perspectives* (Allyn & Bacon, Boston) 1996.
2. See Phillip A. Talbert, "The Relevance of Victim Impact Statements to the Criminal Sentencing Decision," 36 *UCLA Law Review,* 199, 202–211 (1988); and Maureen McLeod, "Victim Participation at Sentencing," 22 *Criminal Law Bulletin,* 501, 505–511 (1986).
3. *Booth v. Maryland,* 482 U.S. 496 (1987).
4. Ibid. at 500–01.
5. Ibid. at 509. The Court did, however, carefully note that information typically contained in a victim's statement is generally admissible in noncapital cases and may be considered in capital cases if directly related to the circumstances of the crime. Ibid. at 508 n. 10. For example, the Court noted that the prosecution may produce evidence as to the characteristics of the victim to rebut an argument made by the defendant (e.g., victim's peaceable nature to rebut claim of self-defense). Ibid.
6. Booth v. Maryland, 482 U.S. 496 (1987).
7. Ibid. at 505–07.
8. Ibid. at 507–08.
9. Ibid.
10. Ibid.
11. Booth v. Maryland, 482 U.S. 496 (1987).
12. 490 U.S. 805 (1989).
13. 115 L. Ed. 728–729, U.S. Supreme Court.
14. U.S. Supreme Court.
15. 115 L. Ed. 2d 735.
16. 115 L. Ed. 748.
17. U.S. Supreme Court.
18. See Jimmie O. Clements Jr., "Casenote, Criminal Law—Victim Impact Evidence—The Scope of the Eight Amendment Does Not Include a Per Se Bar to the Use of Victim Impact Evidence in the Sentencing Phase of a Capital Trial *Payne v. Tennessee,*" 23 *St. Mary's Law Journal,* 517 (1991); Aida Alaka, "Note, Victim Impact Evidence, Arbitrariness and the Death Penalty: The Supreme Court Flipflops in *Payne v. Tennessee,*" 23 *Loyola University Chicago Law Journal,* 581 (1992); K. Elizabeth Whitehead, "Case Note, Mourning Becomes Electric: *Payne v.*

Tennessee's Allowance of Victim Impact Statements During Capital Proceedings," 45 *Arkansas Law Review,* 531 (1992).
19. *Powell v. Alabama,* 287 U.S. 45, 53 S. Ct. 55, 77 L. Ed. 158 (1932).
20. 297 U.S. 278, 56 S. Ct. 461, 80 L. Ed. 682 (1936).
21. Robert Wells, "Victim Impact Statements," *Crime Victim and Witness Assistance Training Project* (Federal Law Enforcement Training Center, Glyno, Ga.) 1990, hereinafter *Crime Victim and Witness Assistance.*
22. Ibid.
23. *The New Republic,* p. 9 (April 17, 1995).
24. Ibid.
25. Ellen K. Alexander & Janice H. Lord, *Impact Statements: A Victim's Right to Speak—A Nation's Responsibility to Listen* (National Victim Center, Arlington, Va.) 1992, hereinafter *Impact Statements.*
26. Ibid. at p. 10.
27. Ibid. at p. 14.
28. Ibid.
29. *President's Task Force on Victims of Crime: Final Report* (GPO, Washington, D.C.) 1982, p. 77.
30. Barbara Smith & Susan Hillanbrand, *Non-Stranger Violence: The Criminal Courts Responses* (National Institute of Justice, Washington, D.C.) 1981.
31. Deborah P. Kelly, "Delivering Legal Services to Victims: An Evaluation and Prescription," 9 *Justice System Journal,* 62 (1982).
32. J. Hernon & B. Forst, "The Criminal Justice Response to Victim Harm," *Research Report* (National Institute of Justice, Washington, D.C.) 1984.
33. *Impact Statements,* pp. 10, 17.
34. Robert Wells, "Victim Impact: How Much Consideration Is It Really Given?" *The Police Chief,* p. 44 (February 1991).
35. Robert C. Davis, *First Year Evaluation of the Victim Impact Demonstration Project* (Victim Services Agency, New York) 1985.
36. Robert C. Davis & Barbara E. Smith, "Victim Impact Statements and Victim Satisfaction: An Unfulfilled Promise," 22 *Journal of Criminal Justice,* 1 (1994).
37. Dean Kilpatrick & Randy K. Otto, "Constitutionally Guaranteed Participation in Criminal Proceedings for

Victims: Potential Effects on Psychological Functioning," 34 *The Wayne State Law Review*, 17 (1989).

38. Susan Hillenbrand, *Victim Rights Legislation: An Assessment of Its Impact on the Criminal Justice System* (American Bar Association, Chicago) 1987.

39. E. Erez & P. Tontodonato, "The Effect of Victim Participation in Sentencing on Sentence Outcomes," 28 *Criminology*, 451 (1990).

40. Robert C. Davis & Barbara E. Smith, "The Effects of Victim Impact Statements on Sentencing Decisions: A Test in an Urban Setting," 11(3) *Justice Quarterly*, 453 (September 1994).

41. This section has been adapted from Janice H. Lord, *Victim Impact Panels: A Creative Sentencing Opportunity* (Mothers Against Drunk Driving, Dallas) 1990. Used with permission of MADD.

42. Ibid. at p. 6.

43. Ibid. at p. 10.

17

International Aspects of Victimology

Chapter Outline

LEARNING OBJECTIVES

After reading this chapter, you should be able to:

- Be familiar with the evolution of victimology at the international level
- Discuss the various types of international crime victim surveys
- Explain the globalization of crime and its impact on victims
- Understand the role of the United Nations and its response to victims of crime
- Distinguish between the various types of international crime victims
- Describe the various types of nontraditional international victims

INTRODUCTION

In the United States, we like to think that we are leaders in the many different aspects of victimology. However, as Chapter 1 explained, many of the original concepts regarding victimology came from different countries. It is therefore important that we understand victimology from an international perspective.

There are entire textbooks devoted to international victimology. *Victimology* is an excellent, if somewhat dated, textbook that deals with various aspects of international victimology.[1] In addition, published proceedings of various international conferences offer a global perspective on victimology; a complete analysis of which is beyond the scope of this chapter. However, several key legal, psychological, and social perspectives are briefly analyzed here to provide an overview of international victimology.

HISTORY AND LEADERS IN THE FIELD

Any attempt to research and explain the history of international victimology and to discuss its leaders is a complex and controversial task. To mention some early pioneers and developments is to highlight only a few of the many people who have made international victimology what it is today. Victimology at the international level is viewed by some as a type of criminology and accepted by others as a distinct discipline. To complicate matters further, victimology has not matured at the same rate throughout the world. Some countries have victim assistance legislation; others do not. Crime victimization surveys are conducted in some countries and not in others. Therefore, generalizations and broad statements concerning the discipline should be viewed with caution.[2]

Chapter 1 discussed early leaders in the field, such as Hans von Hentig, Benjamin Mendelsohn, and Stephen Schafer, who argued their case for the discipline of victimology. However, it was not until the 1970s that victimology gained an international perspective. A group of criminologists began meeting in early 1973. The first meeting was in Jerusalem and was followed by a second meeting in Boston, Massachusetts, in 1976. The World Society of Victimology (WSV) was formally established in Munster, Germany, in 1979. The WSV agreed to meet every three years. Also in the 1970s, an American criminologist, Emilio Viano, was instrumental in coordinating a series of meetings and symposia. In 1976, he began publishing a journal entitled *Victimology*.

Many of the early leaders in the field participated in the WSV and continued to debate the direction and goals of the discipline of victimology. For example, Dutch criminologist Willem H. Nagel believed that victimology should remain part of the field of criminology, while Mendelsohn argued for a general multidisciplinary approach that would establish a separate discipline of victimology aimed at reducing human suffering.[3]

The WSV continues to meet every three years at different locations around the world. It holds symposia, offers annual postgraduate courses, and publishes the symposia proceedings. It is actively involved in the implementation of the United Nation's Declaration of Basic Principles of Justice for Victims of Crime and Abuse of Power.[4] Its Web site contains some of the most extensive information about international victimology. The only other organization that has similar information and research is International Victimology. Its Web site is maintained by the Dutch Ministry of Justice, which works with the United Nations Crime Prevention Project in Vienna. This organization works closely with the WSV but serves a wider audience.

As with any new discipline, there have been advances and periods of inactivity, as well as several attempts—some successful—to establish academic journals in international victimology.[5] As mentioned earlier, Emilio Viano was active during the early years of victimology and is credited with publishing its first journal, *Victimology*, in 1976. This journal was very active in the early years but is now defunct. In 1988 in Argentina, *Victimologia* began publication in Spanish and serves many Latin American countries. In 1989, in conjunction with the WSV, the *International Review of Victimology* was published in Great Britain. This journal is considered by many authorities in the field to be the premiere journal in international victimology.[6] In 1990, the Australasian Society of Victimology published a journal for its members. Other societies and countries have published journals as well, including Croatia, Japan, and Serbia. The most recent addition to victimology publications is *International Perspectives in Victimology*, published in 2004 by the Tokiwa International Victimology Institute.

Early leaders in victimology, at both the national and international levels, established a foundation for exploring the process of crime victimization. Current leaders are building on that foundation to develop ways to prevent victimization, to improve the resources available to crime victims, and to shape our thinking in the future. Many students in class as this textbook goes to print will, in the next ten to twenty years, take their place among the early and present-day leaders such as Mendelsohn, von Hentig, Schafer, Viano, Gerd Kirchhoff, Jan van Dijk, John Dussich, and Marlene Young.

CRIME VICTIM SURVEYS

Crime victim surveys have both advocates and detractors. They have flaws in recording and at the same time serve as an invaluable source of information. We are all familiar with crime victim survey in the United States. The major surveys are discussed in Chapter 1. This section discusses surveys conducted by and in other countries.

The International Crime Victimization Survey (ICVS) is the most far-reaching survey of crime in the world.[7] The ICVS was established because of the inadequacy of recorded offenses by law enforcement agencies for purposes of comparing crime in different countries and because there was a notable absence of any other standardized method to record international crimes.

The inadequacy of accurate and comparable reporting can be attributed to a number of cultural differences. Definitions of many crimes vary among nations; for example, some countries do not consider domestic violence a crime, while others recognize it as a serious offense. Recording practices also differ among law enforcement agencies: Some countries may record multiple crimes by the same perpetrator as a single offense; for instance, while another country records each crime individually. Cultural differences also influence a victim's willingness to report a crime. In countries such as Sudan, for example, rape victims are ostracized and associated with deep shame.[8] In other countries, public trust in the police and justice system is lacking, so victims are fearful of any involvement with these institutions.

A number of countries conduct their own national crime victimization surveys. These surveys attempt to rectify the shortcomings of law enforcement crime surveys by asking questions of citizens about their crime experience or victimization. The ICVS uses this same approach. The survey collects social and demographic information from the respondents that allows for analysis of how risks of crime vary for different groups within a wide range of populations. The ICVS answers a growing need for a fully standardized survey in different countries that uses the same methods of sampling selection, survey procedures, and data analysis.

The survey is managed by a working group and, for each surveyed country, assigns a coordinator who is responsible for the actual survey in that country. Data gathered from the survey are integrated and processed by the criminology department at Leiden University in the Netherlands. The survey contacts between 1,000 and 2,000 households in each country. Samples of 1,000 are drawn from the country's largest city, although some countries use several cities, and some nations include rural samples.

To date, five ICVSs have been completed. The first was conducted in 1989. Fifteen countries and several cities participated in the first survey. The second survey was conducted in 1992 and involved eleven countries. The survey was also expanded to include more developing nations. The third survey took place in 1996 and 1997 and was remarkable in its coverage: It included twelve industrial nations, all but one of the counties in central and east Europe, and fifteen developing countries. In 2000, the results of the fourth round of the ICVS were completed. Surveys have been conducted in more than fifty countries since 1989. The fifth round of the ICVS was completed in 2005. It was conducted in fifteen European countries as well as twenty other countries, including the United States, Mexico, New Zealand, and Japan. The International Violence Against Women Survey (IVAWS) is another international survey that provides researchers and countries with information regarding a specific form of victimization: violence against women.[9] The objective of this survey is to assess the level of victimization of women across a number of countries and to promote and implement research on violence against women in countries around the world. It will assist individual countries in implementing their own victimization surveys on violence against women, the results of which would become an important research and policy tool. The project hopes to provide reliable

FOCUS

The United Nations Virtual Knowledge Center to End Violence Against Women and Children

United Nations Declaration on the Elimination of Violence Against Women (1993) defines violence against women as any act of gender-based violence that results in, or is likely to result in, physical, sexual, or psychological harm or suffering to women, including threats of such acts, coercion, or arbitrary deprivation of liberty, whether occurring in public or in private life. The United Nations notes that there are many forms of violence against women, including sexual, physical, or emotional abuse by an intimate partner; physical or sexual abuse by family members or others; sexual harassment and abuse by authority figures (such as teachers, police officers, or employers); trafficking for forced labor or sex; and such traditional practices as forced or child marriages, dowry-related violence and honor killings, when women are murdered in the name of family honor. Systematic sexual abuse in conflict situations is another form of violence against men. The United Nations has created a virtual knowledge center. This center updates the violence against women surveys on a yearly basis. To view the latest data, visit their Web site.

Note: The site keeps data on all types of gender violence.

information as the basis of raising countries' awareness of and response to sexual violence. Developing countries might also benefit from surveys like the IVAWS and perhaps will be encouraged to conduct their own surveys.

The IVAWS is coordinated by a collaboration of two United Nations criminal justice agencies: the United Nations Interregional Crime and Justice Research Institute (UNICRI) and the European Institute for Crime Prevention and Control (HEUNI). The third partner is Statistic Canada. The IVAWS uses the data collected from the ICVS, which was developed by the UNICRI. It also draws upon the expertise of HEUNI in projects aimed at preventing domestic violence and on the expertise of Statistics Canada in developing sensitive surveys for measuring violence against women.

The earliest known discussion of the collection of crime statistics at the international level is considered to have been at the General Statistical Congress held in Brussels in 1853. There was one limited, cross-national crime survey that took place during 1937 through 1946. However, it was not until 1970 that a true international crime survey was conducted: the first United Nations Survey on Crime Trends and Operations of the Criminal Justice Systems.[10]

The United Nations Survey on Crime Trends and Operations of the Criminal Justice Systems is another key international survey. However, it deals with crime and the administration of justice rather than with victimization. Nevertheless, it is important to measure and understand all aspects of international crime victimization, including how data are collected regarding the administration of justice in various countries.

The mission of the United Nations Survey on Crime Trends and the Operations of the Criminal Justice Systems is to collect data on the incidence of reported crime and the operations of the criminal justice systems with a view to improving the analysis and dissemination of that information globally.[11]

Several issues are specific to international crime and victimization surveys: (1) using the same methodology in different cultural and social settings, (2) individual country's differing definition of the term *violence*, (3) interpretation and translation of results, and (4) reaching agreements among the participants. In addition, several ethical concerns specific to victimization surveys include the safety of the respondents and interviewers, emotional trauma resulting from the interview, and interviewer selection and training.

International crime victimization surveys serve a valuable purpose for understanding violence and victimization. We have just started on this process, and much work remains to be done. However, in our rapidly shrinking world, we must continue our efforts to understand the worldwide nature of violence and victimization.

GLOBALIZATION OF CRIME AND VICTIMS

Our world is constantly shrinking, or to phrase it more positively, we are becoming a globalized community. Progress in transportation technologies—from horse and buggy to jet aircraft—has steadily contributed to our faster, easier access to all parts of the world. And the Internet has all but negated the need to even travel by making communication and information transferral nearly instantaneous.

There are a number of different definitions of **globalization.** Social institutions might define it as the process by which social institutions become adopted on a global scale.[12] From a monetary point of view, it has been defined as the integration of economics and society.[13] Perhaps one of the better definitions was set forth by the Rockefeller Brothers Fund, which stated that globalization is the quantitative and qualitative expansion in transborder flows of activities and ideas. This definition includes both financial and cultural flows.[14]

Crime has also become globalized. Nations have become concerned about threats to their security from crime that originates outside their borders. The solutions to this concern involve international cooperation. This condition of international security is intertwined with the fundamental rights of individuals within countries. One of the important forms of international crime is organized crime. Organized crime has been defined as groups of individuals with stable, generally hierarchical organizations that perpetrate illegal actions in order to enrich themselves without regard to international borders. Some of the more well-known organized crime organizations include the Mafia, the Japanese Yakuza, the Colombian drug cartels, and the Chinese Triads.[15]

International crime is always changing and adapting, becoming more diversified each day. It started in traditional fields such as gambling, loan sharking, and prostitution and has evolved into international automobile smuggling, art and archaeological theft, credit card fraud, and other transnational enterprises. Transnational criminal organizations are more concerned about profit than politics, and if they can control the government in various ways, they are content to leave it in power. Corruption of governmental officials is one method by which these organizations accomplish their goals. Corruption undermines the faith citizens have in their government.

A discussion of terrorism and its impact on the victims of terrorism is beyond the scope of this textbook. However, no discussion of international victimology would be complete without a brief mention of terrorism.

Terrorism has existed for many years, but September 11, 2001, brought home the phenomena of international terrorism to millions of Americans and others around the world. Since that date, other countries and their citizens have been victims of terrorist attacks. During 2005, terrorist attacks killed or maimed persons in Italy, England, and Egypt.

The numerous definitions of terrorism vary among countries and among agencies. Terrorism has been defined as the use of force or violence against persons or property to intimidate or coerce a government, the civilian populations, or any segment thereof in furtherance of political or social objective.[16] The Federal Bureau of Investigation further breaks down terrorism into domestic terrorism and international terrorism. Domestic terrorism is the unlawful use, or threatened use, of force or violence by a group or an individual based and operating entirely within the United States or Puerto Rico without foreign direction and whose acts are directed at the U.S. government or its population for the purpose of furthering political or social goals. International terrorism has essentially the same definition, except the acts are committed by a group or by individuals who have some connection to a foreign power or whose activities transcend national boundaries.

As a result of globalization, the threat of terrorism against both Americans and other populations has dramatically increased in the last several years. The use of weapons of mass destruction, such as high-grade explosives and chemical and biological agents, poses significant threats to populations around the world. As a result of these threats, the U.S. Department of Justice, Office for Victims of Crime (OVC), formed the Terrorism and International Victims Unit (TIVU).

This unit is responsible for developing programs and initiatives that will respond to the needs of victims of terrorism, mass violence, and crimes that have transnational effects, such as trafficking of women and children.[17]

The TIVU provides a variety of services to victims of crime. It provides information and benefits to U.S. nationals who are victims of terrorism in other countries. Victims are given assistance in accessing services that may include briefing on the foreign country's criminal justice system. The TIVU makes all the resources of OVC available to victims of terrorism. It serves as the liaison with the U.S. Department of State and other federal agencies responsible for providing assistance to U.S. citizens in other countries.

The TIVU also provides compensation assistance services to U.S. victims in foreign countries. TIVU administers the International Terrorism Victims Compensation Program, which allows U.S. nationals who are victims of terrorism to apply for compensation by filing a claim with a single federal office. This compensation program seeks to address the unique needs of U.S. national international terrorism victims. Many countries are developing or expanding their compensation programs, and TIVU works with the U.S. Department of State to maintain an *International Crime Victim Compensation Program Directory,* which lists the services provided by foreign countries to U.S. nationals who are victims of terrorism while in their country.

The OVC also works with the U.S. Department of State to assist U.S. embassies and consulates around the world. This work is coordinated with the State Department's Office of Overseas Citizens Services, which has established a full-time victim assistance specialist to coordinate these activities and conduct training for departmental personnel who may come into contact with U.S. citizens overseas. The Office of Overseas Citizens Services in the State Department's Bureau of Consular Affairs is responsible for the welfare and whereabouts of U.S. citizens traveling and residing abroad.

The embassy or consulate overseas offers assistance to U.S. citizens who are victims of crime. They can help American victims replace a stolen passport, contact family and friends in the U.S., and obtain appropriate medical care. The officer assigned to assist victims can also give the victim general information about the local criminal justice system and process and can provide information about local resources, including foreign crime victim compensation programs. Some U.S. victim compensation programs may also be available to the victim. Approximately half the states offer benefits to their residents who are victims of violent crime overseas.

THE UNITED NATIONS

Introduction

In 1945, representatives from fifty countries met in San Francisco to draft the United Nations Charter. The concept and charter was ratified by a majority of the other signatories, and the United Nations came into existence on October 24, 1945. The Charter is the controlling document for the United Nations and sets forth the rights and obligations of its member nations and its organization and procedures. As established in the Charter, the mission of the United Nations is to develop friendly relations among nations; to cooperate in solving international economic, social, cultural, and humanitarian problems; to promote respect for human rights and fundamental freedoms; and to be a center for harmonizing the actions of nations in attaining these ends.[18]

There are six principal organizations within the United Nations: the Security Council, the General Assembly, the Economic and Social Council, the Trusteeship Council, the International Court of Justice, and the Secretariat. The United Nations also has fifteen other agencies and several other programs and bodies. These programs, bodies, and funds—such as the U.N. Children's Fund (UNICEF)—have their own governing bodies and budgets.[19]

One of the most important aspects of the United Nations is its creation of a comprehensive body of laws dealing with human rights. For the first time in the history of our planet, we have an international organization that has provided the world with a universal and internationally

Don Emmert/AFP/Getty Images

protected code of human rights. The foundation for these laws is the U.N. Charter and the Universal Declaration of Human Rights, adopted by the General Assembly in 1948.[20] Every organization and agency of the United Nations is involved in some aspect of protecting human rights. Twenty-eight articles establish basic human rights for all people in the Declaration. These include the right to be born free; freedom from discrimination based on race, color, or sex; life liberty and security of person; freedom from slavery and torture; equality before the law; fair and public trails; freedom of movement within the borders of one's state; the right to marriage and a family; and other important rights that allow peoples of this earth to live in happiness and dignity.[21]

Victims and the United Nations

In 1985, the United Nations adopted its Declaration of Basic Principles of Justice for Victims of Crime and Abuse of Power. This is the United Nations' foundational document pertaining to victims. Victims of crime are defined as "persons who, individually or collectively, have suffered harm, including physical or mental injury, emotional suffering, economic loss or substantial impairment of their fundamental rights, through acts or omissions that are in violation of criminal laws operative within Member States, including those laws proscribing criminal abuse of power."[22] Under this Declaration, victims are entitled to access to justice and fair treatment, and the Declaration includes the requirement that victims be treated with compassion and respect for their dignity. They are entitled to be informed of their role in the criminal justice proceeding as well as the scope, timing, and progress of the proceeding. The Declaration urges states to provide victims with financial aid as well as with various victim assistance programs and activities.

The Declaration recommends that offenders or responsible third parties make fair restitution to victims, their families, or when appropriate, their dependents. It urges governments to make restitution part of the criminal codes and argues that when government agents or officials are responsible for the harm or injury, the victim should receive restitution from the nation under whose authority the agents or employees acted.

Compensation is also addressed in the Declaration. It states that when financial support is not available from the offender or other sources, the nations should attempt to provide compensation. It urges nations to establish compensation programs funded by their national treasury.

Victim assistance programs under the Declaration should provide the necessary medical, psychological, and social assistance from either government-based, community-based, or volunteer organizations. Victims should be informed of the availability of these services, and the services should be easily accessible to them.

The Declaration also addresses another form of victimization: victims of abuse of power. This topic is rarely discussed in the United States; it is examined in more detail later in this chapter. Briefly stated, victims of abuse of power are those who suffer harm from acts or omissions that are not criminal in their country but that are considered a violation of international norms relating to human rights.[23]

U.N. Guide for Policymakers on the Implementation of the Declaration of Basic Principles of Justice for Victims of Crime and Abuse of Power

In 1999, the United Nations adopted the Guide for Policymakers on the Implementation of the Declaration of Basic Principles of Justice for Victims of Crime and Abuse of Power. The Guide sets forth "promising practices" that have been used in various jurisdictions to implement the Declaration. The Guide was developed by the United Nations, the Centre for International Crime Prevention, the Office for Drug Control and Crime Prevention, and the OVC.

This Guide sets forth standards that policymakers from various governmental agencies can use to evaluate their own processes and practices. It proposes several ways to improve services to victims of crime. One proposal recommends that a national-level committee, including academic, justice, health, and government officials, be established with the goal of eliminating the barriers faced by victims in the criminal justice system.

U.N. Handbook on Justice for Victims

The *U.N. Handbook on Justice for Victims* was developed with input from forty countries as a tool for implementing victim service programs and developing victim-sensitive policies for those who come into contact with victims. These persons may include law enforcement officers, prosecutors, judges, health care professionals, correctional personnel, and spiritual leaders, among others. The Handbook addresses the issue of organizations that come into contact with victims of crime. These organizations include civil organizations, human rights commissions, and elected officials and bodies.

The Handbook outlines the steps necessary to develop a comprehensive victim assistance program. It also acknowledges that differences in cultures and in legal systems preclude its recommendations being followed by every nation. It points out that financial resources to assist victims will vary dramatically among countries.

The International Court of Justice

The International Court of Justice is the principle judicial body within the United Nations. It is located at the Peace Palace in The Hague (The Netherlands). The Court has two missions: to settle in accordance with international law the legal disputes submitted by member nations and to give advisory opinions on legal questions referred to it by duly authorized bodies and agencies.[24] The Court is composed of fifteen judges elected to nine-year terms of office by the General Assembly and the Security Council. It may not include more than one judge from any country. One-third of the seats are elected every three years, and sitting judges may be re-elected. The members of the Court do not represent their countries but rather act as independent magistrates. Only member nations may appear before the Court. In 2005, there were 191 nations entitled to appear before the Court. Nations must agree to abide by the Court's decision before the case will be heard. The case starts with written pleadings exchanged between the parties. An oral phase is next in which agents address the Court in a public hearing. The Court then goes into private session and returns with a verdict. There is no appeal from the Court's ruling. The Court hears a wide variety of cases, including maritime disputes and other jurisdictional issues.

THE INTERNATIONAL CRIMINAL COURT

In 1998, the Rome Statute of the International Criminal Court established the International Criminal Court (ICC). The ICC is not a part of the United Nations. It is not under its jurisdiction or control. It is an independent international court with its own legal capacity created by an international treaty.[25] The International Court of Justice at The Hague handles only cases between nations. Nations of the world established the court to prosecute and punish *persons* responsible for crimes against humanity, such as genocide and other serious war crimes. The United States signed the Treaty on December 31, 2000.[26]

The Treaty of Rome defines genocide as acts committed with the intent to destroy, in whole or in part, a national, ethnic, or racial or religious group. Genocide includes killing members of a group or preventing births within the group. Crimes against humanity are defined as a widespread or systematic attack directed against any civilian populations. These crimes may include murder, torture, or trafficking in women and children. They also include rape, sexual slavery, and enforced sterilization. War crime is defined as any act that is committed as part of a plan or policy during war. These crimes include conscripting children under the age of fifteen into the armed forces, taking hostages, using poisonous gas, and attacking peacekeeping forces.

The Court is composed of eighteen judges who serve for nine years and may not be re-elected for a second term. The ICC deals with individual responsibility for acts of genocide and other violations of human rights. It does not have automatic jurisdiction over all human rights crimes committed by individuals. The crime must have been committed by a person from a nation that ratified the Rome Treaty, the nation must consent to jurisdiction, or the U.N. Security Council must refer the case to the ICC.[27]

In 2002, the United States withdrew its support from the treaty establishing the ICC. The administration was concerned that the ICC would use the treaty to claim jurisdiction to try U.S. military and government personnel for war crimes. As a result, the United States enters into bilateral treaties with states to ensure that military and government personnel are not subject to the Court's jurisdiction.

INTERNATIONAL VICTIMIZATION

All victims of crime must be treated as individuals with their own special needs. Each classification of crime produces unique categories of victims. All victims are or should be special. We have studied victims of crime from a variety of perspectives: sexual assault victims, child abuse victims, victims of elder abuse, and others. In fact, many of the existing textbooks in the area of victimology devote entire chapters to these victims. However, from an international perspective, there are certain types of individuals whose victimization either crosses national borders or is caused by those in power within the victim's nation. This class of victims may be known as forgotten victims, special victims, or international victims. *Forgotten victims* is not an accurate term, since we as a society are aware of such victims, but many countries or organizations simply do not act to assist them. As mentioned previously, all victims are special. To accept them in any other manner is to dehumanize them and do away with their status. The term *international victims* has gained acceptance, since several international bodies have proposed various actions that address many of these victims. This section briefly analyzes some of these victims.

Trafficking

Trafficking of human beings has existed since early times. In ancient civilizations, people were taken from their own countries and relocated to other countries to be used as slaves for sex or other purposes. In the United States, the practice of invading African nations and abducting blacks from their country to be used as slaves was an accepted part of our culture in many states until the Civil War. Trafficking also occurs within a nation when its citizens are enslaved for cheap labor or other purposes.

There is no simple definition of trafficking that addresses all of its various aspects. Perhaps the most comprehensive definition is contained in the United Nations' Protocol to Prevent, Suppress and Punish Trafficking in Persons, especially Women and Children, which states:

> The recruitment, transportation, transfer, harboring, or receipt of persons by means of threat or use of force or other forms of coercion, of abduction, of fraud, of deception, of the abuse of power or of a position of vulnerability or of the giving or receiving of payments of benefits to achieve the consent of a person having control over another person, for the purpose of exploitation. Exploitation shall include…prostitution of others or other forms of sexual exploitation, forced labor or services, slavery or practices similar to slavery, servitude or the removal of organs.[28]

Some countries mistakenly believe that this definition and its protocol do not apply to internal acts of trafficking in which persons are not transported across national boundaries. It is clear from a reading of the definition as well as its accompanying explanation that it does apply to internal trafficking.

The Protocol sets forth three purposes: (1) to prevent and combat trafficking in persons, (2) to protect and assist victims of trafficking, and (3) to promote cooperation among nations to achieve these goals.[29] Member nations of the protocol agreed that they have an obligation to criminalize trafficking, create penalties that take into account the seriousness of this crime, and investigate traffickers.

Signatories agree that law enforcement and border control activities will be enhanced by the exchange of information between nations. They also agree to protect victims by initiating measures to avoid immediate deportation of the victims.

The United Nations' approach to trafficking by use of the Protocol is a new move toward fighting trafficking. It contains one of the first comprehensive definitions of trafficking. It combines traditional crime control measures used in the past to investigate drug trafficking and other crimes and to prevent trafficking of human beings. Previous efforts to prevent trafficking have focused on the violations of human rights but did not include law enforcement activities to arrest and prosecute offenders.

Generally, trafficking involves a flow of victims from less developed countries to industrialized nations. The largest number of victims is believed to come from South and Southeast Asia. The former Soviet Union may be the newest source for trafficking of persons for prostitution and the sex trade.[30] Traffickers acquire their victims by using a number of different ploys. In some countries, traffickers will purchase a child by paying money to the family and by promising a better life for the child.[31] Sometimes, women are simply kidnapped and forcibly taken to another country. In other cases, victims are lured by false promises of a well-paying position, such as an au pair, maid, dancer, or domestic worker, in a foreign country. Traffickers may advertise these "opportunities" in local papers.[32]

The most common techniques used in trafficking to obtain and retain victims are the use of force or coercion, which can be direct and violent or indirect and more psychological in nature. Psychological force can include threatening to turn a foreign national over to the immigration authorities. Another form of coercion involves the use of bonds or debts to keep a person under control, often referred to as *bonded labor* or *debt bondage*. Many trafficked victims fall prey to bonded labor as they assume an initial debt as part of their terms of employment. They are kept in debt as the amount owed grows, the original terms of service change, and the employer becomes more coercive. Cultures that discourage confrontation, illiteracy, and power differentials make this form of slavery for low-skilled workers almost impossible to eliminate.[33]

It is estimated that between 600,000 and 800,000 persons are victims of international trafficking across borders each year. Approximately 80 percent of these victims are female, and up to 50 percent are children. These figures do not include trafficking within the borders of a country. It is estimated that including this type of trafficking would raise the total number of cases to between two and four million.[34] Estimates for international trafficking brought into the United States vary from a low of 45,000 persons[35] to a high of 87,000 annually.[36]

Asian, South American, and Russian gangs are among the major traffickers of people. Chinese and Vietnamese triads, the Japanese Yukuza, and South American drug cartels interact with local networks to provide transportation, housing, and documentation. Profits from trafficking can be used to fund other criminal activities. Trafficking is a lucrative business for organized crime. These organizations incorporate the knowledge, facilities, and networks used for smuggling drugs and other goods into moving human victims from one location to another.[37]

Trafficking exacts a terrible cost on its victims, inflicting both psychological and physical harm. Many victims of the sex trade suffer from sexually transmitted diseases, including HIV/AIDS. In many cases, the victim of trafficking may be sold and resold. A child may first be sold as forced labor and then resold to a prostitution ring. Trafficking also costs many nations valuable resource that must be used to treat victims of trafficking. Many of these victims, when rescued, suffer from a variety of illnesses that require public health intervention.

The United Nations regards trafficking as different from smuggling of migrants (which is subject to a different protocol, the Protocol against the Smuggling of Migrants by Land, Sea and Air). The smuggling of migrants, while often dangerous and performed under degrading conditions, involves persons who have consented to the smuggling. Trafficking victims, on the other hand, do not consent or their consent is obtained by fraud and deception. Smuggling usually ends when the migrant worker arrives at his or her location, while trafficking victims endure months, years, and even lifetimes of slavery. Finally, smuggling of migrants by definition involves crossing international borders, while trafficking may involve transporting the victim across country borders but can also involve moving the victim from one part of the country to another.[38]

We are making slow progress against human trafficking. Progress was seen in the United States with the passage of the Prosecutorial Remedies and Other Tools to End the Exploitation of Children Today (PROTECT) Act and the Trafficking Victims Protection Reauthorization Act.[39] These acts increase the punishment for U.S. citizens or permanent legal residents who engage in child sex tourism (CST). CST involves people who travel from their own country to another to engage in commercial sex acts with children. These crimes most often occur in developing countries, where perpetrators seek anonymity and the availability of young child prostitutes.[40] This crime exists because of weak law enforcement, poverty, ease of travel, and the Internet. Using PROTECT, if a U.S. citizen is arrested in a foreign country for sexually abusing children, he or she may be extradited to the United States and face trial and possible punishment of up to thirty years in prison. While the United States and other countries are beginning to address this crime, we still have a long way to go toward eradicating it. Education, tougher laws, and remedies for universal poverty are a few of the steps we must take to reduce or eliminate this form of slavery.

Parental Child Abductions

A wide variety of excellent textbooks deal with almost all aspects of child abuse. However, most of them, and almost all of the victimology textbooks, fail to discuss one of the most difficult and frustrating aspects of raising a child—child abduction. Child abduction has been defined as

FOCUS

The Facts about Child Camel Jockeys

The trafficking and exploitation of South Asian and African children as camel jockeys has increased dramatically in the Gulf states, which, after the discovery of oil and the associated surge in wealth, transformed camel racing from a traditional Bedouin sport pastime to a multi-million-dollar activity. Today, thousands of children, some as young as three or four, are trafficked from Asia and Africa and sold into slavery to serve as camel jockeys.

These children live in oppressive environments and endure harsh living conditions. They work long hours, live in unsanitary conditions, and receive little food so that they do not gain weight and increase the load on the camel they are racing. Their handlers and trainers abuse them with beatings, threats, and more. Many of these children are injured or killed by the camels. Once they reach teenage years, they are disposed of because they serve no further use for their masters. Having no skills or education and suffering severe psychological injuries, many of them lead desolate lives and face dim prospects. These victims, like many children who are trafficked, are robbed of their childhood and their future.

Source: Adapted from *Trafficking in Persons Report* (U.S. Department of State, Washington, D.C.) June 2005.

the "taking, retention, or concealment of a child or children by a parent, other family member, or their agent, in derogation of the custody rights, including visitation rights of another family member or their agents."[41]

A parent whose child is abducted to another country faces a daunting task of attempting to regain custody of the child. The parent who abducts the child often has support from family or friends. Some abductors may believe they are rescuing the child from an abusive partner who has placed the child in danger. Others simply feel disenfranchised from American society and want to return to their homeland and take the child with them. Some abductors are victims of intimate partner abuse and take the child to protect him or her, while others take the child as a final act of domination and control over his or her partner.

The most recent national survey examining child abductions was the National Incidence Study on Missing, Abducted, Runaway, and Throwaway Children in America (NISMART).[42] It placed these victims into two broad categories:

Broad Scope Cases: These cases involved a family member who either took the child in violation of a court order or failed to return or release the child at the end of a visit and kept the child at least overnight. In 1988, there were an estimated 354,100 children abducted under this definition.

Policy Focal Cases: These cases fit the broad scope definition but included at least one of the following characteristics: (1) The abductor attempted to conceal the taking or whereabouts of the child and to prevent contact between the child and the other parent, (2) the child was transported out of the state, or (3) there was evidence that the abductor intended to keep the child permanently.

Approximately 46 percent of all abductions (163,200) fell within this definition, and all international abductions are considered policy focal cases.[43]

According to NISMART, abductors and the parent who was left behind usually differed sharply in terms of background, citizenship, and education. Eighty-three percent were of different nationalities, 69 percent were of different ethnicity, and 62 percent were citizens of another country.[44] Both mothers and fathers were equally likely to be the abductors.

The number of children abducted per incident ranged from one to three, but in approximately 70 percent of the cases, only one child was abducted. Abducted children tended to be young, ranging from five months to about twelve and a half years old, with the mean age of five. It may be that the abductor feels he or she has more control over younger children.

Approximately 41 percent of all abducted children were returned to the left-behind parent. In half of all the cases in which the child was recovered, the separation time was less than one year. In general, separations were shorter in abductions to signatories to the Hague Convention. This treaty is discussed in more detail later in this section. In cases in which the child was recovered, nearly all the left-behind parents had to travel to the country where the child had been taken to bring the child back to the United States.[45]

The recovery of abducted children has taken many forms. Some recoveries were the result of court decisions, some involved law enforcement agencies, some occurred when the abductor voluntarily returned the child, and others involved the use of mercenaries.

A number of resources are available to parents of abducted children. The most well-known resource is the National Center for Missing and Exploited Children, which has an extensive Web site with detailed information for parents as well as important links to other Web-based resources dealing with abducted children.[46]

One of the most frustrating and unknown aspects of child abduction is that court orders issued in the United States are not automatically honored in other countries. To solve this problem, the United States, in 1976, began the process of establishing the Hague Convention on the Civil Aspects of International Child Abduction.[47] The Convention became law in the United States on July 1, 1988, and is in force in more than fifty countries around the world. The terms of the Convention apply to wrongful removals or retentions of children in signatory countries.

The Convention is civil in nature and is available to left-behind parents seeking return or visitation of the abducted child. Because it is civil in nature, the parents are the parties to any legal action, not the United States or the government where the abducted child is located.[48] The Convention requires that children who were abducted from one country to another in violation of a valid custody order shall be returned to the country of the left-behind parent who has the custody order. The time within which to petition the country where the child is located is normally one year from the date of the wrongful removal or retention. The left-behind parent may file a petition after the one year, but it is up to the discretion of the court where the child is located whether or not it will act on the petition.

There are a number of exceptions to the mandatory return of the child to the left-behind parent. If the court finds that the child would suffer physical or psychological harm, it may deny return. If the child objects to the return and has reached an age of reason, the court may take his or her desires into consideration. The Convention is silent on the age at which children reach this level of maturity.

Each country establishes a central authority to carry out the duties under the Convention. The central authority in the United States is the Department of State's Office of Children's Issues. The U.S. central authority's role is one of an active facilitator. It seeks to promote cooperation among the parties and various foreign government agencies involved in the case.

Abuse of Power

The Declaration of Basic Principles of Justice for Victims of Crime and Abuse of Power establishes the principle that all persons should be free from **abuse of power.** The concept of abuse of power is multifaceted and is not discussed or analyzed in much if any detail in victimology textbooks in the United States. The United Nations defines abuse of power from the perspective of victims of abuse of power as any person(s), either as an individual or as a group, who suffers harm, including physical, emotional suffering, economic loss, or substantial impairment of their fundamental rights, through acts or omissions that do not yet constitute violations of national criminal laws but are considered violations of internationally recognized norms relating to human rights.[49]

The Declaration states further that countries should consider incorporating into their criminal law codes a prohibition of abuse of power and provide victims of this type of abuse with the same remedies available to victims of crime. It further recommends that countries enter into international treaties regarding abuse of power. Finally, it recommends that countries periodically update their criminal codes to prohibit serious abuses of political or economic power.

One manner of examining the Declaration's definition may be to break it down into subsections for purposes of clarity. A victim may be an individual from any walk of life, including a homeowner, a worker, an outspoken writer or poet who criticizes the government, or a deposed leader of a government; or victims may be groups such as minority or religious groups, or abuse of power may even be based on gender. The harm these victims suffer is very broad and includes physical injuries of all types, such as bullet wounds, sexual assault, and even starvation since it has numerous physical consequences.[50] Mental injuries or emotional suffering may include posttraumatic stress disorder, depression, and other mental illnesses or disorders that result from the abuse of power. Victims may also suffer from economic loss that might occur as a result of forced relocation, loss of businesses or homes, or even death of a loved one who provided economic support.

The final and perhaps the most important aspect of the classification of victims of abuse of power in the Declaration of Basic Principles of Justice for Victims of Crime and Abuse of Power deals with their fundamental rights. The Declaration states that they should not suffer substantial impairment of their (human) rights.

The Declaration defines the prohibited acts as those that are not yet violations of national criminal codes but are substantial violations of internationally recognized norms relating to human rights. For example, a country may not have a law prohibiting trafficking of women or children, but as discussed earlier in this chapter, such a practice not only violates human rights norms, but also in many cases violates treaties between a number of countries.

There is some support for the position that human rights violations can occur under civil law, such as family law dealing with rights of parents or children within the family.[51] Another problem with the Declaration's definition is the use of the term *substantial*. How does one measure a substantial violation versus a minor violation?

The list of possible violations of human rights is long and reflects the suffering of peoples around the world.

Violation of human rights is not a new phenomenon. It has been part of our culture since the beginning of time. It became better known, and nations began to raise international concerns about human rights after World War II. In 1948, the United Nations adopted a Universal Declaration of Human Rights.[52] Some of the more important human rights include political and civil rights; rights for children; economic, social, and cultural rights; freedom of opinion and expression; and freedom of religion and belief.

Another aspect of abuse of power occurs when there is a human rights violation by persons or by organizations, and the government fails to protect those victims.[53] The case of

FOCUS
What Happens if the Protectors Commit Abuse of Power Acts?

One of the most terrifying situations for human rights victims is to be victimized by the persons sent to protect them. In 2001, staff members of the United Nations were asked to investigate reports of sexual abuse of women and children refugees by aid workers in West Africa. As the final report to the United Nations indicates, men, women, and children displaced by conflict or other disasters are among the most vulnerable people in the world. After an extensive investigation, several incidents of sexual abuse were confirmed. It must be noted that interviewing victims in these types of situations is extremely hard, and there is a high percentage of unreported cases because of fear of retaliation or stigmatization, distrust of authority, and other cultural reasons. As a result of the allegations, the United Nations has improved systems of reporting, investigating, and disciplining offenders.

Source: "Investigation into Sexual Exploitation of Refugees by Aid Workers in West Africa," *Report of the Secretary-General on the Activities of the Office of Internal Oversight Services*, United Nations General Assembly, New York, October 11, 2002.

Kaya v. Turkey concerned the disappearance, torture, and death of the victim. The European Court of Human Rights addressed this issue when it held:

> This involves a primary duty of the State to secure [emphasis added] the right to life by putting in place effective criminal-law provisions to deter the commission of offenses against the person backed up by law-enforcement machinery for the prevention, suppression and punishment of breaches of such provisions. It also extends in appropriate circumstances to operational measures to protect an individual or individuals whose life is at risk from the criminal acts of another.[54]

Since the adoption of the Human Rights Declaration in 1948, the U.N. General Assembly has gradually expanded the human rights laws to cover a wide variety of situations. These rights have slowly gained acceptance in the international community. Education campaigns have informed the peoples of the world of their inalienable rights, and various groups and organizations continue to fight to promote these rights and protect the rights of individuals and groups throughout the world.

Victims of Torture

...nor [shall] cruel or unusual punishment be inflicted.

U.S. Constitution, Eighth Amendment (Bill of Rights)

The OVC refers to **torture** victims as the "invisible population of crime victims."[55] Not only is the United States concerned with the issue of victims who are tortured, but the United Nations also has repeatedly addressed this issue. In 1975, it adopted the Declaration on the Protection of All Persons from Being Subjected to Torture and Other Cruel, Inhuman, or Degrading Treatment or Punishment.[56] The United Nations made progress in this area, and in 1984 the General Assembly adopted the Convention Against Torture and Other Cruel, Inhuman, or Degrading Treatment or Punishment, which became effective in 1987.[57]

Torture has been defined as

> any act by which severe pain or suffering, whether physical or mental, is intentionally inflicted on a person for such purposes as obtaining from him or a third person information or a confession, punishing him for an act he or a third person has committed or is suspected of having committed, or intimidating or coercing him or a third person, for any reason based on discrimination of any kind when such pain or suffering is inflicted by or at the instigation of or with the consent or acquiescence of a public official or other person acting in an official capacity. It does not include pain or suffering arising only from, inherent in, or incidental to lawful sanctions.[58]

There are a number of international treaties that prohibit the use of torture. These include the Sixth Amendment to the U.S. Constitution, the U.N. Universal Declaration of Human Rights, and the Geneva Conventions. However, the use of torture continues in many countries. Amnesty International USA conducted an extensive survey regarding the existing use of torture.[59] The survey covered acts of torture from 1997 to 2005. It included 195 countries and territories. It found more than 150 countries still use torture. In more than seventy countries, the use of torture was widespread and accepted by the government. This number is probably a low estimate because torture is conducted in secret, and there is good reason to suspect a large percentage of torture goes unreported.

The OVC estimates that there are 400,000 torture survivors in the United States. It reports that approximately 30 percent of all refugees are torture survivors. These victims are "invisible" since many torturers tell their victims that no one will believe them, and they are concerned that if they openly discuss their experiences, family members remaining in their native country will be tortured.[60]

Many treatment centers across the United States offer a variety of services to victims of torture,[61] including basic needs such as food, clothing, and shelter. In addition, many centers provide psychotherapy, medical services, interpreters, healing groups, case management and other social services, and legal services, including assistance with asylum.

There is a critical need for these types of centers. Survivors of torture exhibit a variety of symptoms, including chronic pain in muscles and joints, severe depression and other mental disorders, nightmares, guilt and self-hatred, impaired memory, the inability to form lasting relationships, and thoughts of suicide. Many of these treatment centers report that some of the following behaviors are common among survivors of torture:

- Sleeping in chairs so they won't dream
- Inability to eat without vomiting
- Panic attacks whenever they hear an automobile backfire
- Inability to turn off lights at night because in the dark they have flashbacks of the torture[62]

The victims of torture come from all walks of life. They include activists for human rights, labor rights, or other causes. They are targeted victims because they are easily recognizable and available for arrest or confinement. Incarcerated persons other than activists may also be tortured. On occasion, ordinary citizens may be tortured if the government is attempting to control the population by creating a climate of fear and repression.

Torture by its very nature seeks to destroy a person's personality by use of pain or other degrading acts. Torture can take many forms, such as beating, sexual assault of both males and females, suspension upside down, submersion in water, denial of medical treatment, and electrical torture on various parts of the body (most often on the genitals of both male and female victims). Torture can also include psychological terror, threats, humiliation, sleep deprivation, mock executions, witnessing torture of others including family members, and being forced to torture others.[63]

The United Nations implements the Convention Against Torture and Other Cruel, Inhuman, or Degrading Treatment or Punishment by a variety of means, including use of the Committee Against Torture. This committee consists of ten international experts who act as a conduit for countries to report to the United Nations on measures they have undertaken to enforce the Convention. The committee also responds to reports or allegations of torture within a country by inviting the country to cooperate in the examination of the information and may, in certain cases, designate one of its members to make a confidential investigation and to report back to the committee.

The Committee Against Torture appoints a Special Rapporteur (expert or scribe appointed to investigate a subject and report on it) to seek information on questions about torture and

FOCUS
Leading the Fight Against Torture

One of the leading private organizations at the forefront of the fight against torture is Amnesty International. It is a worldwide organization based on voluntary memberships, and it consists of sections, structures, international networks, and affiliated groups that campaign for international human rights. Its vision is a world in which every person enjoys all of the human rights enshrined in the Universal Declaration of Human Rights and other international human rights standards. To accomplish its vision, it undertakes research and action focused on the prevention of grave abuses of human rights. It is independent of any government, political perspective, economic interest, or religious ideology. It does not support or oppose any government or any victims. It is concerned only with the protection of human rights.

Source: Amnesty International; http://web.amnesty.org/pages/aboutai-statute-eng

to quickly respond to those questions. The Special Rapporteur has the authority to ask for information and to request responses from any country that is a member of the United Nations, regardless of whether or not it is a signatory to the Convention Against Torture and Other Cruel and Inhuman or Degrading Treatment or Punishment. The Special Rapporteur submits reports to both the Commission on Human Rights and the General Assembly.[64]

Children as Soldiers

The use of children as soldiers is a black mark against humanity.[65] The effects and consequences of children being used as weapons of war last for generations.[66] Almost all civilized nations publicly agree that they should not use **child soldiers.** The great majority of these nations are signatories to various treaties, conventions, and protocols that prohibit or condemn the use of children as soldiers. However, many of them, as well as many nonsignatories, continue to use children as soldiers both in external and internal conflicts. In addition, rebel groups routinely recruit or abduct children for use as soldiers.

The major international standards that prohibit use of children as soldiers are the Convention on the Rights of the Child, the Optional Protocol to the Convention, the Rome Statute of the International Criminal Court, and additional protocols to the four Geneva Conventions.[67]

The Convention to the Rights of the Child contains specific prohibitions that attempt to protect children from serving as soldiers by prohibiting recruitment of children under the age of fifteen. A number of nations decided to build on the principles of the Convention and worked to raise the minimum age for recruitment and participation in the armed forces to eighteen years. The Optional Protocol to the Convention was adopted by the U.N. General Assembly on May 25, 2000, and became effective on February 12, 2002. This Protocol had been signed by 115 countries and ratified by 63 countries. It outlaws compulsory recruitment of children under the age of eighteen by government or nongovernment forces. It raises the age that children may volunteer for the armed forces to sixteen and requires nations to establish methods to prove that the child's acts were in fact voluntary. It further requires that any nation that does accept volunteers under age eighteen ensures that those children do not take part in direct combat operations. Finally, it outlaws the recruitment or participation of any person under the age of eighteen in any insurgency groups or rebel forces under any circumstances.[68] The Rome Statute of the International Criminal Court classifies conscription, enlistment, or use in hostilities of children under age fifteen in internal or external conflicts as a war crime.

Although the United Nations has information that indicates that child soldiers are being used in more than thirty countries, the Security Council actions were limited to six armed conflicts, five of which were in Africa. It appears that members of the Security Council are reluctant to interfere with the actions of other sovereign states or have declined to incur the cost of enforcing sanctions against those nations that violate the various international agreements.[69]

Who are child soldiers? The Treaties, Conventions, and Protocols define them by age. The Coalition to Stop the Use of Child Soldiers defines them as any person under the age of eighteen who is a member of or attached to government forces or any other regular or irregular force or armed group.[70] However, some nations allow young people to join their armed forces with the consent of their parents. In many cases, these are truly voluntary acts by both the parents and the young person. Therefore, it would seem a better definition might be that "a child soldier is any person under the age of sixteen who does not have the voluntary consent of his or her parents and who then becomes a member or is attached to government forces or any regular or irregular force or armed group." In no event shall any person under the age of eighteen be allowed to participate directly or indirectly in armed combat. This definition would undoubtedly raise concern and controversy, but it addresses the realities and practices of modern, industrialized nations, many of which allow sixteen- or seventeen-year-old children to join their armed forces with the consent of their parents. Great Britain and the United States are two examples of nations that allow persons under the age of eighteen to enlist in their armed forces with the consent of their parents.

FOCUS
What Is the Appropriate Age for a Soldier?

The discussion and definition of who is a child soldier raises complex social and cultural issues. In the United States, a person at the age of seventeen may enlist with his or her parent's approval. In the United Kingdom, a person at the age of sixteen may enlist in his or her armed forces.

- What is the appropriate age for a person to become a soldier in his or her armed forces?
- Does it make any difference that a person sixteen years old cannot drive in many states?
- How about the fact that a person who is seventeen years old has only been driving for one year?

- Does your opinion change if the person joining the armed forces is doing so to get out of a ghetto and make a better life for him- or herself?
- Will your opinion change if persons under eighteen were allowed to join the military but were prohibited from directly or indirectly being involved in an armed conflict?
- What about the fact that in many states you may join the armed forces at the age of eighteen but cannot drink in a bar?
- Will your answer be different if instead of joining a formal, recognized military, the person was joining a rebel group?

The true extent of the problem is unknown, since like many other issues addressed in this chapter, in many nations, the actions of recruitment and use of children as soldiers are shrouded in secrecy, and outsiders are barred from examining this issue. However, the Coalition to Stop the Use of Child Soldiers estimates that there are more the 120,000 children under the age of eighteen who are currently participating in armed conflicts in Africa alone. Children are used as solders in other countries, including countries in the Middle East. Some of these children are not more than seven or eight years old.[71] Other estimates state that more than 500,000 children under the age of eighteen have been recruited by state or nonstate armed forces or groups in more than eighty-five countries.[72] A third source, Amnesty International USA, states that approximately 300,000 children under the age of eighteen are participating in armed conflicts in thirty different countries.[73] As can be seen from these figures, well-meaning and dedicated organizations report different facts and figures regarding the extent of the problem of child soldiers. What is clear is that the problem is persistent and that it affects our most valuable resource—children.

Children become soldiers in a variety of ways. Some children are drafted or conscripted, others are kidnapped, and still others are forced to join armed groups to protect their families from retaliation. The kidnapping may occur in a variety of ways: Children may be seized off the street or taken while attending school or living in orphanages. Hunger, poverty, or fear may drive parents to offer their children for service, especially when the armed group offers to pay the child's wages to the family instead of to the child. Sometimes children may "voluntarily" join the armed groups because they may perceive it as the only way to survive.[74]

Children as young as seven years may participate in armed conflict. They may act as porters who carry food or ammunition for the actual fighters. They also act as runners or scouts, sex slaves, cooks, or spies. Girls are especially vulnerable as child soldiers. Many are sexually assaulted, forced to engage in prostitution, or forced to be "wives" of adult combatants. When they reach age ten, their roles may change: They may be given weapons and forced to become soldiers.[75]

Many commanders like using children as soldiers, because they are so young that they view combat as a game or are not afraid of death. They are also viewed as a consumable commodity that should be used in place of the more dependable adult combatants. Since they are considered so expendable, many child soldiers never receive any training and are often massacred during combat. In addition, they are easier to mold into effective fighters. Finally, in some countries, there is a shortage of eligible men, so the combatants widen the recruitment base by accepting or abducting children.

Child soldiers have been witnessed committing atrocities during or after combat. Sometimes, these acts are committed under the influence of drugs or alcohol or at the urging of the adult soldiers. However, drugs or alcohol alone are not responsible for these acts. A more likely cause of the majority of the atrocities is that the children have suffered systematic abuse by adult combatants and have lived in a pervasive culture of killing and violence. This environment, coupled with threats of deadly retaliation if they do not conform to the beliefs of their adult leaders, is probably the major reason that children are involved in acts of mutilations, killings, and rapes. Some of these acts include beheading a captive and playing catch with her head, gouging out victims' eyes, and cutting off their hands and feet.[76]

The consequences of children serving as soldiers have been explored by a number of different authorities. Daya Somasundaram examined the long-term civil war in Sri Lanka and explained that child soldiers suffer brutalization, deprivation, institutionalized violence, and various brutal sociocultural factors. Psychological injuries include somatization, depression, post-traumatic stress disorder, and severe psychosis.[77]

WAR, NATURAL DISASTERS, AND OTHER ACTS OF GOD

Victims of war, natural disasters, and other acts of God are not considered traditional victims. Indeed, they are certainly not classified as crime victims by many organizations. However, they have suffered many of the same consequences as traditional victims. Any chapter dealing with international victimization should briefly discuss these victims for several reasons. Many professionals working with victims of crime may be called upon to assist victims of war, natural disasters, and other acts of God. In addition, understanding different forms of victimization allows professionals to put service to victims of crime in a more centered perspective. Finally, these people are in fact victims, and we should understand the dynamics as well as how to respond to their needs.

The nature of war has changed over the last several decades. In many countries, formalized, uniformed soldiers do not face each other across a delineated battlefield. External conflicts and internal strife have changed the face of war and its casualties. Civilians may become deliberate targets. Combatants and insurgents may live in civilian villages and use civilians, even children, as human shields. Villages that voluntarily or by force provide logistical support for one side in a conflict may face retaliation by the other.[78]

Victims of war include both civilian and military casualties. These casualties include those who are injured and those who are killed during the conflict. The injury may result from hostile fire or actions or from friendly fire or actions. In the long term, it does not matter who caused the injury or death: The consequences of war linger for generations. War casualties include men, women, and children.

Among the most tragic casualties of war are those killed or maimed by landmines. Mines continue to cause injury and death long after the original conflict has ended. Children in more than sixty-five countries live with the threat of more than ten million landmines still buried in the ground awaiting victims.[79] In addition, unexploded ordnance continues to litter the ground of many of these countries. Like landmines, unexploded ordnance does not discriminate against friend or foe, adult or child. Children are at higher risk of injury because some of the ordnance looks like balls or other toys. Clearing landmines is a dangerous, time-consuming, and expensive proposition, and many of these mines and unexploded ordnance are located in the world's poorest countries.[80] In an effort to stop the use of landmines, the Convention on the Prohibition of the Use, Stockpiling, Production, and Transfer of Antipersonnel Mines and Their Destruction was drafted and became effective in 1999. The Treaty has 133 signatories.

One of the modern world's largest natural disasters occurred in December 26, 2004, when a massive undersea earthquake occurred near Indonesia. Measuring 9.0 on the Richter scale, it was one of the strongest earthquakes in the world in forty years. The earthquake caused massive waves, or tsunamis, that devastated several countries. It generated a tsunami that was among the deadliest disasters in modern history.[81] Indonesia, Malaysia, Bangladesh, Somalia, Sri Lanka, India, Thailand, and other countries suffered massive loss of life and destruction of property. Some estimates put the total loss of life at over 250,000.[82]

Countries around the world responded immediately with various forms of assistance. Many nations and organizations sent foreign professionals to work with those who survived the disaster. Others sent funds and resources to search for survivors. The effects of this massive disaster have yet to be determined, but it is a certainty that the victims will suffer physical, financial, and mental hardship for years to come.

There are different types of natural disasters or acts of God that cause death and destruction to millions of people in our society. Earthquakes, droughts, epidemics, famine, floods, and volcanic eruptions are just a few such disasters. The effect on victims of natural disaster is much the same as on victims of crime: physical, financial, and mental trauma to those who survive. As a society, we must be trained and ready to respond to these victims just as we are trying to respond to victims of international or domestic crime.

Summary

The academic and professional discipline of victimology is still a young science. This is especially true at the international level. Some countries continue to make strides forward in serving victims of crime, and others continue their victimization of crime victims as well as entire populations.

Just as there were disagreements about the nature and scope of victimology in the United States, so were there different perspectives on victimology at the international level. One of the most significant achievements was the initiation of the International Crime Victims Survey. While there are criticisms regarding the ICVS, it is the most far-reaching survey of crime in the world. Even though there are different definitions of crime in each country and each country has its own unique culture, the ICVS attempts to account for those differences. The survey is managed by a working group, and each country has its own coordinator. While it is a survey of crime, it also provides us with critical information regarding victims.

Other surveys contribute to the understanding of international victimology. The International Violence Against Women Survey assesses the level of victimization of women across a number of countries, and the United Nations Survey on Crime Trends and Operations of the Criminal Justice Systems, while focused more on crime statistics than on victims, nonetheless provides us with information on how criminal justice agencies in other countries function.

Globalization of our society continues to occur at a rapid pace, opening doors to new ways of communicating, new ways of doing business, and unfortunately, new ways of committing crimes. Commercial use of the Internet allows businesses to access a new population of customers—and criminals to access a new population of victims.

Terrorism has long affected citizens throughout the world, and since September 11, 2001, Americans who once felt insulated from terrorism have realized that they too are potential victims of attack. The United Nations and individual nations are responding to this crisis in a variety of ways. The United States, for example, has increased border security, enforced more stringent identification procedures, established the Department of Homeland Security, and on October 26, 2001, passed the controversial Patriot Act.

The United Nations serves a variety of roles in the world. Its mission is to develop friendly relations among nations; to cooperate in solving international economic, social, cultural, and humanitarian problems and to promote respect for human rights and fundamental freedoms; and to be the center for harmonizing the actions of nations in attaining these goals. One of the most important accomplishments of the United Nations was the creation of a body of laws dealing with human rights. In 1985, it adopted its Declaration of Basic Principles of Justice for Victims of Crime and Abuse of Power. The International Court of Justice is the principle judicial body within the United Nations. It settles international disputes among member nations and gives advisory opinions on certain legal questions.

The International Criminal Court was established by the Rome Treaty of 1998. It is not part of the Untied Nations but an independent judicial body that can prosecute individuals for crimes against humanity.

There are a number of crimes that cross national borders. Trafficking in human beings has existed since the establishment of nations. Trafficking today is a multimillion dollar business that destroys it victims. Generally, trafficking involves moving victims from less developed countries to industrialized nations. Approximately 600,000 to 800,000 victims are trafficked across borders each year. If trafficking within countries is included, the number rises to between two and four million victims.

Child abductions by parents are a problem compounded when the abducting parent leaves the country.

Attempting to regain custody of the child in these situations is extremely difficult. One response to this problem was the adoption of the Hague Convention on the Civil Aspects of International Child Abduction. This Convention is civil in nature and is available to the left-behind parent. That parent may use the Convention to try to obtain the return of the abducted child.

Abuse of power is a topic that needs more research and discussion. It concerns victims who suffer loss of their fundamental rights by acts or by omissions that do not constitute a violation of the country's criminal codes but are considered violations of internationally recognized norms relating to human rights. It may be perpetrated by the government in power, by other groups, or even by individuals.

Victims of torture are sometimes referred to as invisible populations or victims. Torture is prohibited by a number of international treaties; however, it continues to exist. One survey found that more than 150 nations still use torture.

Children as soldiers are another form of international victimization. The effects on our society and the individual victims will last for generations. A number of treaties prohibit using children as soldiers, but like trafficking, abductions, abuse of power, and torture, it continues unabated in our society.

War, natural disasters, and other acts of God sometimes result in mass victimization. While these victims do not meet the traditional definition of crime victims, it is important to understand this form of victimization so that we may better serve all victims worldwide.

International victimology is growing and expanding as an academic discipline. We are continuing to address violations of human rights at the international level. As we gain more knowledge at the international level and as peoples across the world become more aware of the tragedy of victimization, we can begin to solve some of these problems.

Key Terms

Globalization is the quantitative and qualitative expansion in transborder flows of activities and ideas.

Terrorism is the use of force or violence against persons or property to intimidate or coerce a government, the civil populations, or any segment thereof in furtherance of political or social objectives.

Trafficking is the recruitment, transportation, transfer, harboring, or receipt of persons by means of threat or use of force or other forms of coercion, abduction, fraud, or deception; by means of the abuse of power or of a position of vulnerability; or by means of the giving or receiving of benefits to achieve the consent of a person having control over another person for the purpose of exploitation.

Abuse of power is defined in the context of victimization as any person(s), either an individual or as a group, who suffers harm, including physical, emotional suffering, economic loss, or substantial impairment of their fundamental rights, through acts or omissions that do not yet constitute violation of national laws but are considered violations of international norms relating to human rights.

Torture is any act that inflicts pain or suffering on a person for the purposes of obtaining from him or her or a third person information or a confession or punishing him or her for any reason based on discrimination of any kind.

Child soldiers are any persons under age sixteen who do not have the voluntary consent of their parents and who become members of or are attached to government forces or any regular or irregular force or armed group.

Discussion Questions

1. Discuss the impact of international victimization on victim services in the United States. Is there an impact? In what areas?
2. Compare and contrast the National Crime Victimization Survey with the International Crime Victim Survey.
3. Is the United Nations the proper body to address international victimization? In light of the controversies regarding its existence, should the United States continue as a member? What are the alternatives?
4. What is the difference between the International Court of Justice and the International Criminal Court? Do we need two international courts?
5. Compare trafficking with parental child abduction. What are the differences and the similarities?
6. Do we have abuse of power incidents in the United States? Give some examples.
7. What can we do to eliminate torture as a tool of governments or groups?
8. How can we stop nations from using children as soldiers? At what age should a child be able to join the armed forces?

Suggested Readings

Paul Rock, ed., *Victimology* (Dartmouth Publishing, Brookfield, Mass.) 1994.

Stanley Meisier, *United Nations: The First Fifty Years* (Atlantic Monthly Press, London) 1997.

Linda Fasulo, *An Insider's Guide to the UN* (Yale University Press, New Haven, Conn.) 2003.

Basic Facts about the United Nations (Bernan Press, Lanham, Md.) 2004.

Kathryn Farr, *Sex Trafficking: The Global Market in Women and Children* (Worth Publishers, Cranbury, N.J.) 2004.

Craig McGill, *Human Traffic—Sex, Slaves, and Immigration* (Vision Paperbacks, London) 2003.

David Kyle & Rey Koslowski, *Global Human Smuggling* (Johns Hopkins University Press, Baltimore, Md.) 2001.

Kamala Kempadoo, ed., *Trafficking and Prostitution Reconsidered: New Perspectives on Migration, Sex Work, and Human Rights* (Paradigm Publishers, Boulder, Colo.) 2005.

David Rosen, *Armies of the Young: Child Soldiers in War and Terrorism* (Rutgers University Press, Piscataway, N.J.) 2005.

John P. Wilson & Boris Drozdek, eds., *Broken Spirits: The Treatment of Traumatized Asylum Seekers, Refugees, War and Torture Victims* (Brunner-Routledge, London) 2004.

Karen J. Greenberg & Joshua L. Dratel, eds., *The Torture Papers* (Cambridge University Press, New York) 2005.

Andrew Silke, *Terrorists, Victims and Society: Psychological Perspectives on Terrorism and Its Consequences* (John Wiley & Sons, Hoboken, N.J.) 2003.

Donald Hyndman & David Hyndman, *Natural Hazards and Disasters* (Brooks Cole, Florence, Ky.) 2005.

R. J. Terrill, *World Criminal Justice, A Survey*, 2nd ed. (Anderson Publishing, Cincinnati) 1992.

H. R. Dammer & E. Fairchild, *Comparative Criminal Justice Systems*, 3rd ed. (Wadsworth Publishing, Belmont, Calif.) 2005.

J. Donnelly, *International Human Rights* (Westview Press, Boulder, Colo.) 2006.

D. P. Forsythe, *Human Rights in International Relations* (Cambridge University Press, New York) 2006.

Endnotes

1. Paul Rock, ed., *Victimology* (Dartmouth Publishing, Brookfield, Mass.) 1994. A new but promising international journal is *International Perspectives in Victimology*, published by the Tokiwa International Victimology Institute in Mito-shi, Japan.
2. See Ezzat A. Fattah, "Victimology, Past, Present and Future," 33 *Criminologie,* 1 (2000).
3. Jan J. M. van Dijk, "Introducing Victimology"; available online: www.victimology.nl/rechts.htm. This Web site contains the full text of the article, which is based on the foreword by the same author in Van Dijk et al., eds., *Caring for Crime Victims: Selected Proceedings of the 9th International Symposium on Victimology* (Criminal Justice Press, New York) 1999.
4. See *WSV in a Nutshell*; available online: www.world-society-victimology.de/wsv/index
5. Much of the history of the development of journals comes from an excellent article by John Dussich, Ph.D. This editorial is contained in the inaugural publication of *International Perspectives of Victimology*; J. Dussich, "Editorial," 1(1) *International Perspectives of Victimology,* 1–13 (December 2004).
6. Ibid.
7. For an in-depth discussion of the International Crime Victim Survey, please refer to the Leiden University Web site at http://ruljis.lei-denuniv.nl (2005).
8. Emily Wax, "Sudanese Rape Victims Find Justice Blind to Plight," Washington Post Foreign Service (November 8, 2004), p. A01; available online: www.washingtonpost.com/wp-dyn/articles/A32621-2004Nov7.html

9. See, for example, Holly Johnson, "The International Violence Against Women Survey: Challenges and Issues in Developing an International Comparative Research Paper," conference paper presented at Evaluation in Crime and Justice: Trends and Methods, ASB House, Canberra, 24–25 March 2003; accessed from IWS Web site: www.aic.conferences/evalution/johnson.html
10. M. Shaw, J. van Dijk, & W. Rhomberg, "Determining Trends in Global Crime and Justice. An Overview of Results from the United Nations Survey of Crime Trends and Operations of Criminal Justice Systems," 3 *Forum on Crime and Society*, 35 (2003).
11. Ibid.
12. *Encarta Dictionary: English* (North America); available online: www.encarta.msn.com.
13. Available online: www.worldbank.org/economicpolicy/globalization/(August 17, 2006)
14. Ernest J. Wilson III, *Globalization. Information, Technology, and Conflict in the Second and Third Worlds* (Rockefeller Brothers Funds, Inc., New York) 1998.
15. Fulvia Attina, "Globalization and Crime: The Emerging Role of International Institutions," Jean Monnet, *Working Papers in Comparative and International Politics* (February 1997); available online: www.fscpo.unict.it
16. "Terrorism in the United States, 1997," *FBI Bulletin*, Washington, D.C. (1997).
17. *Terrorism and International Victims Unit* (Office for Victims of Crime, U.S. Department of Justice, Washington, D.C.) 2002.
18. Basic Facts about the United Nations; available online: www.un.org/aboutun/basicfacts/unorg.htm (August 17, 2006).

19. Ibid.
20. Ibid.
21. Universal Declaration of Human Rights; available online: www.un.org/overview/rights.html (August 17, 2006).
22. *Declaration of Basic Principles of Justice for Victims of Crime and Abuse of Power*, adopted by General Assembly resolution 40/34 of 29 November, 1985. United Nations, New York; available online: www.ohchr.org/english/law/victims.htm
23. Ibid.
24. International Court of Justice: General Information—The Court at a Glance; available online: www.icj-cij.org/icjwww/igeneral information/ icjgnnot.html (August 17, 2006).
25. AMICC: What Is the ICC—Structure and Basics; available online: www.amicc.org/icc_structure.html (August 17, 2006).
26. U.S. Department of State, Fact Sheet: The International Criminal Court (August 2002); available online: www.state.gov/t/pm/rls/fs/2002/23426.htm (June 8, 2005).
27. What Is the International Criminal Court; available online: www.globalsolutions.org/programs/law_justice/faq_long.pdf (August 17, 2006).
28. Article 3, *United Nations Protocol to Prevent, Suppress and Punish Trafficking in Persons* (November 2000); available online: www.undoc.org/ unodc/en/trafficking_protocol html
29. Ibid.
30. Francis T. Miko, *Trafficking in Persons: The U.S. and International Response*, Congressional Research Service Report to Congress, Washington, D.C. (June 24, 2005).
31. Michael J. Dennis, "Newly Adopted Protocols to the Conventions on the Rights of the Child," 94 *American Journal of International Law*, 789–796 (October 2000).
32. Ibid.
33. *Trafficking in Persons Report* (U.S. Department of State, Washington, D.C.) June 3, 2005.
34. Ibid.
35. "Trafficking in Women and Children a Worldwide Problem," 181(12) *America* 4 (October 23, 1999).
36. "Free the Slaves," 121(19) *The Christian Century*, 6 (September 21, 2001).
37. *Global Programme Against Trafficking in Human Beings*, Centre for International Crime Prevention (Office for Drug Control and Crime Prevention, United Nations at Vienna) February 1999.
38. Available online: www.undoc.org/undoc/en/ trafficking_victims.consents.html; see also "Developments in the Law: The Trafficking Victims Protection Act," 119 *Harvard Law Review*, 2180 (May 2005).
39. See Pub. L. No. 108-193, 117 Stat. 2875 (2003), codified in scattered sections of 8, 18, and 22 USCA.
40. Brenda Platt, "Commercial Sexual Exploitation of Children: A Global Problem Requiring Global Action," 2002 (3) *Sexual Health Exchange*, 10 (Summer 2002).
41. Linda Girdner, Chapter 1: Introduction. In L. Girdner & P. Hoff, eds., *Obstacles to the Recovery and Return of Parentally Abducted Children: Final Report* (U.S. Department of Justice, Office of Justice Programs, Office of Juvenile Justice and Delinquency Prevention, Washington, D.C.), pp. 1–3.
42. See D. Finkelhor, G. Hotaling, & A. Sedlak, *Missing, Abducted, Runaway, and Throwaway Children in America—First Report: Numbers and Characteristics, National Incidence Studies* (U.S. Department of Justice, Office of Justice Programs, Office of Juvenile and Delinquency Prevention, Washington, D.C.) 1990.
43. Janet Chiancone, Linda Girdner, & Patricia Hoff, *Issues in Resolving Cases of International Child Abduction by Parents* (U.S. Department of Justice, Office of Justice Programs, Office of Juvenile and Delinquency Prevention, Washington, D.C.) December 2001.
44. Ibid. at p. 4.
45. Ibid. at p. 4.
46. National Center for Missing and Exploited Children; available online: see www.missing-kids.com (August 17, 2006).
47. Report on Compliance with the Hague Convention on the Civil Aspects of International Child Abduction; available online: http://travel.state.gov/family/abduction/hague_issues/hague_issues_2537.html (August 17, 2006).
48. Ion Hazzikostas, "Note: Federal Court Abstention and the Hague Child Abduction Convention," 79 *New York Law Review*, 421 (April 2004).
49. *Declaration of Basic Principles of Justice for Victims of Crime and Abuse of Power*, adopted by General Assembly resolution 40/34 of November, 29, 1985, United Nations, New York. Available online: www.ohchr.org/ english/law/victims.htm
50. See Rudolph J. Rummel, "Power, Genocide and Mass Murder," 31(1) *Journal of Peace Research*, 1–10 (1994).
51. *Human Rights in the Administration of Justice: A Manual on Human Rights for Judges, Prosecutors, and Lawyers*. Professional Training Series No. 9. Office of the High Commissioner for Human Rights in cooperation with the International Bar Association. Available online: https://webmcdev.oddl.fsu.edu/human-rights/
52. *Universal Declaration of Human Rights*, adopted and proclaimed by General Assembly Resolution 217 A (III) of December 10, 1948.
53. *Human Rights in the Administration of Justice: A Manual on Human Rights for Judges, Prosecutors, and Lawyers*. Professional Training Series No. 9. Office of the High Commissioner for Human Rights in cooperation with the International Bar Association. Available online: https://webmcdev.oddl.fsu.edu/human-rights/
54. Eur. Court HR, *Case of Mahmut Kaya v. Turkey*, judgment of September, 22, 2005 para. 85, of the text of the judgment as published at http://echr.coe.int/
55. Peter Dross, *Survivors of Politically Motivated Torture: A Large, Growing, and Invisible Population of Crime Victims* (Office for Victims of Crime, U.S. Department of Justice, Washington, D.C.) January 2000.
56. *Declaration on the Protection of All Persons from Being Subjected to Torture and Other Cruel, Inhuman or Degrading Treatment or Punishment* (General Assembly, United Nations, New York) 1975.
57. *The Convention Against Torture and Other Cruel, Inhuman, or Degrading Treatment or Punishment* (General Assembly, United Nations, New York) 1984.

58. Amnesty International; http://web.amnesty.org/pages/aboutai-statute-eng.

59. *Denounce Torture*, Amnesty International USA; available online: http://amnestyusa.org/stoptorture/aboutn.html

60. Peter Dross, *Survivors of Politically Motivated Torture: A Large, Growing, and Invisible Population of Crime Victims* (Office for Victims of Crime, U.S. Department of Justice, Washington, D.C.) January 2000.

61. *Survivors of Torture* (International, San Diego, Calif.); available online: www.notorture.org/ links.html.

62. Peter Dross, *Survivors of Politically Motivated Torture: A Large, Growing, and Invisible Population of Crime Victims* (Office for Victims of Crime, U.S. Department of Justice, Washington, D.C.) January 2000, p. 5.

63. *Denounce Torture*, Amnesty International USA; available online: http://amnestyusa. org/stoptorture/aboutn.html

64. *Manual on the Effective Investigation and Documentation of Torture and Other Cruel, Inhuman or Degrading Treatment or Punishment* (Istanbul Protocol), submitted to the United Nations High Commissioner for Human Rights, United Nations Publication, New York (August 9, 1999).

65. Dennis Coday, "Pope Prays for Child Soldiers," 40 (23) *National Catholic Reporter*, 7 (April 9, 2004).

66. "The Hidden Health Trauma of Child Soldiers," 363 (9412) *The Lancet* 831 (March 13, 2004).

67. International Standards [Coalition to Stop the Use of Child Soldiers]; available online: www.child-soldiers.org/resources/international-standards (August 17, 2006).

68. IRIN Web special on Child Soldiers; available online: http://irinnews.org/webspecials/ childsoldiers/print/intro.asp (August 17, 2006).

69. *Child Soldiers Global Report 2004*, Coalition to Stop the Use of Child Soldiers, London (2004).

70. Ibid.; www.child-soldiers.org/resources/global-reports

71. Ibid.; www.child-soldiers.org

72. IRIN Web special on Child Soldiers; available online: http://irinnews.org/webspecials/ childsoldiers/print/intro.asp

73. Amnesty International USA; available online: www.amnestyusa.org/child_soldiers/index.do (August 17, 2006).

74. Child Soldiers: An Affront to Humanity; available online: www.un.org/rights/concerns.htm (August 17, 2006).

75. "Tens of Thousands of Girls Fighting on the Front Lines," 1 *Women in Action*, 6 (April 2004).

76. The Use of Children as Soldiers in Africa; available online: www.reliefweb.int/library/ documents/chilsold.htm (August 17, 2006).

77. Daya Somasundaram, "Child Soldiers: Understanding the Context," 324 *British Medical Journal*, 1268–1271 (May 25, 2002).

78. Supra, fn. 76.

79. Landmine Monitor Deport 2005: Toward a Mine-Fire world; available online: www.icbi.org/lm2005/

80. Ibid.

81. Platform for the Promotion of Early Warning; available online: www.unisdr.org/ppew/tsunami/what-is-tsunami:/backinfor-historical.htm

82. Ibid.

EPILOGUE

There are many challenges in the field of victimology. In the previous edition, a series of emerging topics was listed: campus crime, stalking, workplace violence, and others. Some, such as gang violence, are looked at a bit more closely in this edition than in the first edition, but all of them are still in need of further study. However, rather than listing specific areas for study, this epilogue discusses broad themes that need to be researched and acted upon.

UPDATE

The victims' rights movement has been more successful at the state level in securing legal protections as constitutional amendments. All 50 states have some statutory rights and provisions addressing crime victims and 33 states have amended their constitutions to guarantee victims' rights and services. Typically, these rights and services include the following:

- The right to information about victims' rights, assistance, and services;
- The right to notification of all court proceedings related to the offense;
- The right to be reasonably protected from the accused offender;
- The right to make victim impact statements;
- The right to information about the conviction, sentencing, imprisonment, and release of the offender;
- The right to an order of restitution from the convicted offender;
- The right to crime victims' compensation; and
- The right to enforce these rights.

LACK OF RESEARCH

There are so many areas within the discipline of victimology that cry out for research. Some research has already been done and has raised additional questions, while other areas need initial or groundbreaking study. As with any new discipline, areas for new research are limited only by the imagination.

We need to preserve our history. Many of the outstanding leaders in victimology are growing older. Some of the early leaders have already passed away. There are a number of excellent articles dealing with the history of victimology. However, unlike other significant historical events, no one has yet established an oral history of victimology. A number of professionals, advocates, and academics have lived through the various phases of the discipline of victimology. All of their recollections, sometimes conflicting in nature, need to be preserved for those who follow after us.

We do not yet understand the causes of either crime or its enduring impact on victims. More research is needed in the area of family violence, effectiveness of restraining orders and victim impact statements, and social and psychological effects on victims of crime, just to list a few areas. Simply select a chapter in this textbook and review the literature or lack thereof on any academic search engine, and you will find noticeable gaps in knowledge and application.

When the first edition of this textbook was published in 1998, there were very few academic or professional journals that discussed various aspects of victimology. However, with the passage of time and the increased awareness of this discipline both within the general public and academe, we have seen an increase in journals at both the national and international levels. While there are a number of criminal justice, profiling, and cop shows on television, victimology and victim services have not yet captured the public's interest. This is regrettable because the human drama and emotions encountered in victim advocacy are as intense—and sometimes even more intense—as that in any of the existing crime dramas on television today.

THE CONTINUED CHANGE FROM A MOVEMENT TO A DISCIPLINE

Many persons in victim services still refer to it as a movement. We must progress and change that thinking to embrace the concept that victimology and victim services are a discipline. A movement is defined as an organized effort to promote or attain a specific end. For example, we think of the efforts to bring equality to our society as the civil rights movement. To most people, a movement connotes a passionate and zealous attempt to reach broad goals. A discipline, by contrast, is defined as a subject that is taught or a training that corrects, molds, or perfects the mental faculties or moral character.[1] Disciplines are thought of as learned professions. It may be that victimology continues to be both a movement and a discipline. Being a movement that encompasses passion and zeal while relying on education and training is perhaps what victimology should be.

BROADENING HORIZONS TO EMBRACE INTERNATIONAL VICTIMOLOGY

As discussed in Chapter 17, international victimology continues to gain recognition and respect within the United States. Our world is shrinking, and what happens to victims of a tsunami in the Far East affects our thinking and feelings in the United States. We can also learn from other countries' efforts in the field of victimology.

International conferences and organizations continue to gain members from the United States. These memberships allow for the informal and formal transmission of knowledge. More important, a network of advocates, professionals, and academics is developing that allows for the instantaneous exchange of promising practices and emerging trends.

PROFESSIONALISM IN VICTIMOLOGY AND VICTIM SERVICES

Victimology is a relatively new academic discipline. Increasingly, universities are offering courses in victimology through various departments: criminology or criminal justice, sociology, social work, psychology, and women studies departments, to mention just a few. Only a few universities offer degrees specifically related to victimology. With the passage of time, it is clear that victimology as an academic discipline will gain wider acceptance, and academic degrees will become more available to those who wish to study this profession. Victimology degrees involve a combination of disciplines, including victimology, victim services, law, counseling, psychology, and public policy, to name a few.

Similar to many other new occupations, there are barriers to changing the status of victim services from merely an occupation to a profession. Traditionally, victim advocates were victims who had suffered pain and hardship as a result of some crime or had been revictimized in the criminal justice system. They became advocates to help others and to prevent them from suffering the types of abuse they had endured. Many of these advocates relied on word-of-mouth training or utilized their own experiences or learned on the job. A great number of these early advocates provided outstanding support to victims of crime. However, with time, there came an acknowledgment that more training and education was necessary to fully prepare advocates who serve victims of crime. It was hoped that this additional training and education would lead toward professionalism within the field of victim advocacy.

There were and are several obstacles that face this move toward professionalism. The first obstacle is defining what a profession is, the second deals with the authority or credentials necessary to perform the duties of the position, the third concerns the type of skills required to perform various functions within the field, and the fourth concerns establishing a standard of ethics for service providers.

Victim Advocacy as a Profession

Perhaps one of the earliest calls for professionalism within the field occurred with the publication of Marlene A. Young's 1993 textbook, *Victim Assistance: Frontiers and Fundamentals,*[2] in which Young sets forth the nature of professions, discusses the process of professionalization in victim services, and proposes a code of ethics. Experts such as Thomas Underwood and Melissa Hook have also discussed professionalism within the context of victim advocacy. They attempt to define it in the form of certain characteristics. Thomas Underwood states that the concept of professionalism involves a dynamic process that allows for consideration of the extent of professionalization that an occupation has achieved based on various characteristics.[3] Melissa Hook analyzes ethics as they relate to victim service professionals.[4] She uses as a basis for this analysis the research conducted by the OVC-funded National Victim Assistance Standards Consortium, whose goal was to create a model for competency and ethics for victim services providers.

The evolution of victim advocacy as a profession in many ways resembles the transformation of law enforcement from an occupation to a profession. The move toward professionalism in law enforcement started in the 1800s and continues today. Law enforcement has moved from the layperson simply pinning on a badge and acting as an officer to one who requires formal training in state or federal academies prior to being sworn in as a peace officer.[5] More and more programs require or list as a preference some sort of formal training in victim advocacy before allowing individuals the opportunity to work in the field.

Credentials or Authority to Perform the Duties of the Profession

What authority or credentials should a victim advocate possess in order to perform his or her duties? At present, a person may be employed without any formal training in many victim advocate programs. Some of these programs have internal training, and others rely on university-based education. Some states have mandatory state training that prospective victim advocates must undergo. Some argue for a national set of standards that all victim advocates should possess. Others feel that state licensure should be required to practice as a victim advocate. However, at this stage of our evolution as a profession, there is not one accepted standard that all agencies adhere to.

Skills Required for Various Functions within the Field

Several prominent researchers, including Thomas Underwood and Steven Walker, have addressed the skills required of a victim advocate. A review of their work indicates that victim advocates need at least three types of skills: legal, management, and personal.

1. Legal skills include public policy knowledge. Advocates need knowledge of victim's rights, the criminal and civil justice systems, public policy and implementation, and research ability, to name just a few of the skills any professional working as an advocate should possess.
2. Management skills include budgeting and personnel experience. Victim advocacy is more than simply offering services to victims of crime. It requires that budgets be maintained, grants written, and programs administered. The victim advocate of today is by all definitions a corporate executive in everything but name.
3. Personal skills include responding to the needs of victims and their families. This is considered the most important aspect of victim advocacy; however, it cannot be accomplished effectively without the use of legal and management skills. Responding to the needs of victims includes not only offering advice and support but also having a practical knowledge of counseling and intervention skills, death notification protocols, stress management, and so on.

Ethical Standards for Victim Services Providers

Victim advocates deal with persons who are vulnerable, who lack knowledge about the system, and who are in desperate need of assistance. In the past, there have been isolated incidents in which advocates have taken advantage of victims or violated their trust. Furthermore, almost all acknowledged professions have a standard of ethical behavior. Hook suggests that ethical issues in this profession include duel relationships and boundaries (friend vs. client), the issue of confidentiality, and legal responsibilities and liabilities. Young sets forth classifications based on relationships with victims, relationships with colleagues and other professionals, and public and professional conduct. Both Young's treatise and Hook's textbook offer detailed analyses of some of the ethical dilemmas faced by victim advocates.

Evolution as a profession continues with each encounter with a victim. The same zeal and passion that motivated early leaders to form what are now national organizations should be focused on attaining professional status for the victim services occupation. We hope that, within the next few years, our avocation will become a discipline and a profession.

Endnotes

1. *Webster's Ninth New Collegiate Dictionary* (1981).
2. Marlene Young, *Victim Assistance: Frontiers and Fundamentals* (NOVA, Washington, D.C.) 1993.
3. Thomas Underwood, "Professionalizing the Discipline of Victim Services," *National Victim Assistance Text* (Office for Victims of Crime, U.S. Department of Justice, Washington, D.C.) 2003.
4. Melissa Hook, *Ethics in Victim Services* (Sidran Institute Press, Baltimore, Md.) 2005.
5. H. Wallace, C. Roberson, and C. Steckler, *Fundamentals of Police Administration* (Prentice Hall, Englewood Cliffs, N.J.) 1995.

APPENDIX

Critical Dates in the Victims' Rights Movement

1972

- The first three victim assistance programs are created:
  —Aid for Victims of Crime in St. Louis, Missouri;
  —Bay Area Women Against Rape in San Francisco, California; and
  —Rape Crisis Center in Washington, D.C.

1974

- The Federal Law Enforcement Assistance Administration (LEAA) funds the first victim–witness programs in the Brooklyn and Milwaukee District Attorneys' offices, plus seven others through a grant to the National District Attorneys Association, to create model programs of assistance for victims, encourage victim cooperation, and improve prosecution.
- The first law enforcement-based victim assistance programs are established in Fort Lauderdale, Florida, and Indianapolis, Indiana.
- The U.S. Congress passes the Child Abuse Prevention and Treatment Act, which establishes the National Center on Child Abuse and Neglect (NCCAN). The new Center creates an information clearinghouse and provides technical assistance and model programs.

1975

- The first "Victims' Rights Week" is organized by the Philadelphia District Attorney.
- Citizen activists from across the country unite to expand victim services and increase recognition of victims' rights through the formation of the National Organization for Victim Assistance (NOVA).

1976

- The National Organization for Women forms a task force to examine the problem of battering. It demands research into the problem, along with money for battered women's shelters.
- Nebraska becomes the first state to abolish the marital rape exemption.
- The first national conference on battered women is sponsored by the Milwaukee Task Force on Women in Milwaukee, Wisconsin.
- In Fresno County, California, Chief Probation Officer James Rowland creates the first victim impact statement to provide the judiciary with an objective inventory of victim injuries and losses prior to sentencing.
- Women's advocates in St. Paul, Minnesota, starts the first hotline for battered women. Women's advocates and Haven House in Pasadena, California, establish the first shelters for battered women.
- *Victimology: An International Journal* is the first scholarly journal on victims published by Emilio Viano.

1977

- Oregon becomes the first state to enact mandatory arrest in domestic violence cases.

1978

- The National Coalition Against Sexual Assault (NCASA) is formed to combat sexual violence and promote services for rape victims.
- The National Coalition Against Domestic Violence (NCADV) is organized as a voice for the battered women's movement on a national level. NCADV initiates the introduction of the Family Violence Prevention and Services Act in the U.S. Congress.
- Parents of Murdered Children (POMC), a self-help support group, is founded in Cincinnati, Ohio.
- Minnesota becomes the first state to allow probable cause (warrantless) arrest in cases of domestic assault, regardless of whether a protection order had been issued.

1979

- Frank G. Carrington, considered by many to be "the father of the victims' rights movement," founds the Crime Victims' Legal Advocacy Institute, Inc., to promote the rights of crime victims in the civil and criminal justice systems. The nonprofit organization was renamed VALOR, the Victims' Assistance Legal Organization, Inc., in 1981.
- The Office on Domestic Violence is established in the U.S. Department of Health and Human Services, but is later closed in 1981.
- The U.S. Congress fails to enact the Federal Law Enforcement Assistance Administration (LEAA), and federal funding for victims' programs is phased out. Many grassroots and "system-based" programs close.

1980

- Mothers Against Drunk Driving (MADD) is founded after the death of thirteen-year-old Cari Lightner, who was killed by a repeat offender drunk driver. The first two MADD chapters are created in Sacramento, California, and Annapolis, Maryland.
- The U.S. Congress passes the Parental Kidnapping Prevention Act of 1980.
- Wisconsin passes the first "Crime Victims' Bill of Rights."
- The First National Day of Unity in October is established by NCADV to mourn battered women who have died, celebrate women who have survived the violence, and honor all who have worked to defeat domestic violence. This day becomes Domestic Violence Awareness Week and, in 1987, expands to a month of awareness activities each October.
- NCADV holds its first national conference in Washington, D.C., which gains federal recognition of critical issues facing battered women, and sees the birth of several state coalitions.
- The first Victim Impact Panel is sponsored by Remove Intoxicated Drivers (RID) in Oswego County, New York.

1981

- Ronald Reagan becomes the first president to proclaim "Crime Victims' Rights Week" in April.
- The disappearance and murder of missing child Adam Walsh prompts a national campaign to raise public awareness about child abduction and enact laws to better protect children.
- The Attorney General's Task Force on Violent Crime recommends that a separate Task Force be created to consider victims' issues.

1982

- In a Rose Garden ceremony, President Reagan appoints the Task Force on Victims of Crime, which holds public hearings in six cities across the nation to create a greatly needed national focus on the needs of crime victims. The Task Force *Final Report* offers 68 recommendations that become the framework for the advancement of new programs and policies.

- The Federal Victim and Witness Protection Act of 1982 brings "fair treatment standards" to victims and witnesses in the federal criminal justice system.
- California voters overwhelmingly pass Proposition 8, which guarantees restitution and other statutory reforms to crime victims.
- The passage of the Missing Children's Act of 1982 helps parents guarantee that identifying information of their missing child is promptly entered into the FBI National Crime Information Center (NCIC) computer system.
- The first Victim Impact Panel sponsored by MADD, which educates drunk drivers about the devastating impact of their criminal acts, is organized in Rutland, Massachusetts.

1983

- The Office for Victims of Crime (OVC) is created by the U.S. Department of Justice within the Office of Justice Programs to implement recommendations from the President's Task Force on Victims of Crime.
- The U.S. Attorney General establishes a Task Force on Family Violence, which holds six public hearings across the United States.
- The U.S. Attorney General issues guidelines for federal victim and witness assistance.
- In April, President Reagan honors crime victims in a White House Rose Garden ceremony.
- The First National Conference of the Judiciary on Victims of Crime is held at the National Judicial College in Reno, Nevada.
- President Reagan proclaims the first National Missing Children's Day in observance of the disappearance of missing child Etan Patz.
- The International Association of Chiefs of Police Board of Governors adopts a Crime Victims' Bill of Rights and establishes a victims' rights committee to bring about renewed emphasis on the needs of crime victims by law enforcement officials nationwide.

1984

- The passage of the Victims of Crime Act (VOCA) establishes the Crime Victims Fund, made up of federal criminal fines, penalties and bond forfeitures, to support state victim compensation and local victim service programs.
- President Reagan signs the Justice Assistance Act, which establishes a financial assistance program for state and local government and funds 200 new victim services programs.
- The National Minimum Drinking Age Act of 1984 is enacted, providing strong incentives to states without "21" laws to raise the minimum age for drinking, saving thousands of young lives in years to come.
- The National Center for Missing and Exploited Children (NCMEC) is created as the national resource for missing children. Passage of the Missing Children's Assistance Act provides a Congressional mandate for the Center.
- The Spiritual Dimension in Victim Services is founded to involve the religious community in violence prevention and victim assistance.
- The U.S. Congress passes the Family Violence Prevention and Services Act, which earmarks federal funding for programs serving victims of domestic violence.
- Concerns of Police Survivors (COPS) is organized at the first police survivors' seminar held in Washington, D.C., by 100 relatives of officers killed in the line of duty.
- The first National Symposium on Sexual Assault is co-sponsored by the Office of Justice Programs and the Federal Bureau of Investigation.
- A victim–witness notification system is established within the Federal Bureau of Prisons.

- The Office for Victims of Crime hosts the first national symposium on child molestation.
- Victim–Witness Coordinator positions are established in the U.S. Attorneys' offices within the U.S. Department of Justice.
- California State University, Fresno, initiates the first Victim Services Certificate Program offered for academic credit by a university.
- Remove Intoxicated Drivers (RID) calls for a comprehensive Sane National Alcohol Policy (SNAP) to curb aggressive promotions aimed at youth.

1985

- The Federal Crime Victims' Fund deposits total $68 million.
- The National Victim Center is founded in honor of Sunny von Bulow to promote the rights and needs of crime victims and to educate Americans about the devastating effect of crime on our society.
- The United Nations General Assembly passes the International Declaration on the United Nations Declaration of Basic Principles of Justice for Victims of Crime and Abuse of Power.
- President Reagan announces a Child Safety Partnership with twenty-six members. Its mission is to enhance private sector efforts to promote child safety, to clarify information about child victimization, and to increase public awareness of child abuse.
- The U.S. Surgeon General issues a report identifying domestic violence as a major public health problem.

1986

- The Office for Victims of Crime awards the first grants to support state victim compensation and assistance programs.
- Rhode Island passes a constitutional amendment granting victims the right to restitution, to submit victim impact statements, and to be treated with dignity and respect.
- MADD's "Red Ribbon Campaign" enlists motorists to display a red ribbon on their automobiles, pledging to drive safe and sober during the holidays. This national public awareness effort has since become an annual campaign.

1987

- The Victims' Constitutional Amendment Network (VCAN) and Steering Committee is formed at a meeting hosted by the National Victim Center.
- Security on Campus, Inc. (SOC) is established by Howard and Connie Clery, following the tragic robbery, rape, and murder of their daughter Jeanne at Lehigh University in Pennsylvania. SOC raises national awareness about the hidden epidemic of violence on our nation's campuses.
- The American Correctional Association establishes a Task Force on Victims of Crime.
- NCADV establishes the first national toll-free domestic violence hotline.

1988

- The National Aging Resource Center on Elder Abuse (NARCEA) is established in a cooperative agreement among the American Public Welfare Association, the National Association of State Units on Aging, and the University of Delaware. Renamed the National Center on Elder Abuse, it continues to provide information and statistics.
- *State v. Ciskie* is the first case to allow the use of expert testimony to explain the behavior and mental state of an adult rape victim. The testimony is used to show why a victim of repeated physical and sexual assaults by her intimate partner would not immediately call the police or take action. The jury convicts the defendant on four counts of rape.

- The Federal Drunk Driving Prevention Act is passed, and states raise the minimum drinking age to 21.
- Constitutional amendments are introduced in Arizona, California, Connecticut, Delaware, Michigan, South Carolina, and Washington. Florida's amendment is placed on the November ballot, where it passes with 90 percent of the vote. Michigan's constitutional amendment passes with over 80 percent of the vote.
- The first "Indian Nations: Justice for Victims of Crime" conference is sponsored by the Office for Victims of Crime in Rapid City, South Dakota.
- VOCA amendments legislatively establish the Office for Victims of Crime, elevate the position of Director by making Senate confirmation necessary for appointment, and induce state compensation programs to cover victims of homicide and drunk driving.

1989

- The legislatures in Texas and Washington pass their respective constitutional amendments, which are both ratified by voters in November.

1990

- The Federal Crime Victims' Fund deposits total over $146 million.
- The U.S. Congress passes the Hate Crime Statistics Act requiring the U.S. Attorney General to collect data of incidence of certain crimes motivated by prejudice based on race, religion, sexual orientation, or ethnicity.
- The Student Right-to-Know and Campus Security Act, requiring institutions of higher education to disclose murder, rape, robbery, and other crimes on campus, is signed into law by President George H. W. Bush.
- The Child Protection Act of 1990, which features reforms to make the federal criminal justice system less traumatic for child victims and witnesses, is passed by the U.S. Congress.
- The first National Incidence Study on Missing, Abducted, Runaway, and Throwaway Children in America shows that more than one million children fall victim to abduction annually.
- The National Child Search Assistance Act requires law enforcement to enter reports of missing children and unidentified persons in the NCIC computer.

1991

- U.S. Representative Ilena Ros-Lehtinen (R-FL) files the first Congressional Joint Resolution to place victims' rights in the U.S. Constitution.
- The Violence Against Women Act of 1991 is considered by the U.S. Congress.
- California State University, Fresno, approves the first Bachelors Degree Program in Victimology in the nation.
- The Campus Sexual Assault Victims' Bill of Rights Act is introduced in the U.S. Congress.
- The results of the first national public opinion poll to examine citizens' attitudes about violence and victimization, *America Speaks Out,* are released by the National Victim Center during National Crime Victims' Rights Week.
- The U.S. Attorney General issues new comprehensive guidelines that establish procedures for the federal criminal justice system to respond to the needs of crime victims.
- The first national conference that addresses crime victims' rights and needs in corrections is sponsored by the Office for Victims of Crime in California.
- The first International Conference on Campus Sexual Assault is held in Orlando, Florida.
- The American Probation and Parole Association (APPA) establishes a Victim Issues Committee to examine victims' issues and concerns related to community corrections.

- The International Parental Child Kidnapping Act makes the act of unlawfully removing a child outside the United States a federal felony.
- The Spiritual Dimension in Victim Services facilitates a conference of leaders of thirteen religious denominations to plan ways in which these large religious bodies can increase awareness of crime victims' needs and provide appropriate services.
- The New Jersey legislature passes a victims' rights constitutional amendment, which is ratified by voters in November.
- Colorado legislators introduce a constitutional amendment on the first day of National Crime Victims' Rights Week. Fifteen days later, the bill is unanimously passed by both Houses to be placed on the ballot in 1992.
- In an 8–0 decision, the U.S. Supreme Court ruled in *Simon & Schuster v. New York Crime Victims Board* that New York's notoriety-for-profit statute was overly broad and, in the final analysis, unconstitutional.

1992

- *Rape in America: A Report to the Nation* clarifies the scope and devastating effect of rape in this nation, including the fact that 683,000 women are raped annually in the United States.
- The Association of Paroling Authorities International establishes a Victim Issues Committee to examine victims' needs, rights, and services in parole processes.
- The U.S. Congress reauthorizes the Higher Education Bill, which includes the Campus Sexual Assault Victims' Bill of Rights.
- The Battered Women's Testimony Act, which urges states to accept expert testimony in criminal cases involving battered women, is passed by Congress and signed into law by President George H. W. Bush.
- In a unanimous decision, the U.S. Supreme Court—in *R.A.V. v. City of St. Paul*—struck down a local hate crimes ordinance in Minnesota.
- Five states—Colorado, Kansas, Illinois, Missouri, and New Mexico—ratify constitutional amendments for victims' rights.
- Twenty-eight states pass antistalking legislation.
- Massachusetts passes a landmark bill creating a statewide computerized domestic violence registry and requires judges to check the registry when handling such cases.

1993

- Wisconsin ratifies its constitutional amendment for victims' rights, bringing the total number of states with these amendments to fourteen.
- President Bill Clinton signs the "Brady Bill" requiring a waiting period for the purchase of handguns.
- Congress passes the Child Sexual Abuse Registry Act establishing a national repository for information on child sex offenders.
- Twenty-two states pass stalking statutes, bringing the total number of states with stalking laws to fifty, plus the District of Columbia.

1994

- The American Correctional Association Victims Committee publishes the landmark *Report and Recommendations on Victims of Juvenile Crime,* which offers guidelines for improving victims' rights and services when the offender is a juvenile.
- Six additional states pass constitutional amendments for victims' rights—the largest number ever in a single year—bringing the total number of states with amendments to twenty. States with new amendments include Alabama, Alaska, Idaho, Maryland, Ohio, and Utah.

- President Bill Clinton signs a comprehensive package of federal victims' rights legislation as part of the Violent Crime Control and Law Enforcement Act. The Act includes the following:
  — Violence Against Women Act, which authorizes more than $1 billion in funding for programs to combat violence against women.
  — Enhanced VOCA funding provisions.
  — Establishment of a National Child Sex Offender Registry.
  — Enhanced sentences for drunk drivers with child passengers.

1995

- The Federal Crime Victims' Fund deposits total $233,907,256.
- The Crime Victims' Rights Act of 1995 is introduced in the U.S. Congress.
- Legislatures in three states—Indiana, Nebraska, and North Carolina—pass constitutional amendments, which will be placed on the ballot in 1996.
- The National Victims' Constitutional Amendment Network proposes the first draft of language for a federal constitutional amendment for victims' rights.
- The U.S. Department of Justice convenes a national conference to encourage the implementation of the Violence Against Women Act.
- The first class graduates from the National Victim Assistance Academy in Washington, D.C. The academy is supported by the Office for Victims of Crime, the university-based academy provides an academically credited 45-hour curriculum on victimology, victims' rights, and a myriad of other topics.

1996

- Federal Victims' Rights Constitutional Amendments are introduced in both houses of Congress with bipartisan support.
- Both presidential candidates and the attorney general endorse the concept of a Victims' Rights Constitutional Amendment.
- The Federal Crime Victims' Fund reaches a historic high with deposits totaling over $500 million.
- Eight states ratify the passage of constitutional amendments for victims' rights—raising the total number of state constitutional amendments to 29 nationwide.
- The Community Notification Act, known as "Megan's Law," provides for notifying communities of the location of convicted sex offenders by amendment to the national Child Sexual Abuse Registry legislation.
- President Bill Clinton signs the Antiterrorism Act providing one million dollars in funding to strengthen antiterrorism efforts, making restitution mandatory in violent crime cases, and expanding the compensation and assistance services for victims of terrorism both at home and abroad, including victims in the military.
- The National Domestic Violence Hotline is established to provide crisis intervention information and referrals to victims of domestic violence and their friends and family.
- To fully recognize the sovereignty of Indian Nations, OVC for the first time provides all grants in Indian Country directly to the tribes.
- OVC launches a number of international crime victim initiatives, including working to foster worldwide implementation of a United Nations declaration on victims' rights and working to better assist Americans who are victimized abroad.
- The VOCA definition of "crime victim" is expanded to include victims of financial crime, allowing this group to receive counseling, advocacy, and support services.
- The Church Arson Prevention Act is signed into law in response to an increasing number of acts of arson against religious institutions around the country.

1997

- The Federal Crime Victims Fund deposits total $363 million.
- Congress passes the Victims' Rights Clarification Act of 1997 to clarify existing federal law allowing victims to attend a trial and give victim impact statements during sentencing both in capital and noncapital cases.
- Congress enacts a federal antistalking law.
- OVC officially launches it Web homepage allowing Internet access to its comprehensive services.
- *New Directions from the Field: Victims' Rights and Services for the twenty-first Century* is published by OVC.

1998

- Congress enacts the Child Protection and Sexual Predator Punishment Act providing for numerous sentencing enhancements and other initiatives addressing sex crimes against children.
- Congress passes the Crime Victims with Disabilities Act, which represents the first effort to gather information about the extent of victimization of individuals with disabilities.
- The Identity Theft and Deterrence Act is signed into law, which outlaws identity theft.
- OVC provides funding to the U.S. Department of State to support a Victim Assistance Specialist to improve the coordination of services provided to U.S. citizens who become victimized abroad.

1999

- The Violence Against Women Act II is introduced in Congress.
- The fifth National Victim Assistance Academy (NVAA) is held in June at five university locations across the United States.
- OVC issues the first grants to create the State Victim Assistance Academy.
- The National Crime Victim Bar Association is formed to promote justice for victims of crime.

2000

- Congress passes a new national drunk driving limit of 0.08 blood alcohol concentration.
- President Bill Clinton signs into law the Violence Against Women Act of 2000, extending the current law until 2005.
- The Internet Fraud Complaint Center Web site is created by the federal government to combat Internet fraud.
- Congress passes the Trafficking Victims Protection Act to combat trafficking of humans.
- In November, the National Victim Assistance Academy (NVAA) launches its Advanced Topic Series.

2001

- There were 3,047 victims killed in the terrorist attacks on American soil on September 11.
- Congress responds to the attacks with a series of laws protecting the financial health of the airline industry, tax relief for victims, a special compensation fund, and other protections.
- The USA Patriot Act is passed.

2002

- The National Association of VOCA Assistance Administrators is created to provide technical assistance and training to state VOCA administrators.

- OVC sponsors a National Public Awareness and Education Campaign in conjunction with Justice Solutions, Parents of Murdered Children, and the Victims' Assistance Legal Organization to promote the scope and availability of victims' rights and services nationwide.
- Congress appropriates approximately $20 million to fund services to trafficking victims.
- All fifty states, the District of Columbia, U.S. Virgin Islands, Puerto Rico, and Guam have established crime victim compensation programs.

2003

- OVC celebrates its twentieth anniversary of service to crime victims and those who assist them.
- Congress passes the PROTECT Act—also known as the "Amber Alert" law— which creates a national network of AMBER (America's Missing: Broadcast Emergency Response) to facilitate rapid law enforcement and community response to kidnapped or abducted children.
- The American Society of Victimology (ASV) is established in Kansas City, Kansas.
- Congress passes the Prison Rape Elimination Act designed to track and address the issue of rape in correctional institutions.
- The U.S. Postal Service releases the Stop Family Violence postage stamp to raise money for domestic violence prevention programs.
- Congress appropriates $22 million to be used for awareness, intervention, and prevention of domestic violence in the military.

2004

- Congress passes legislation defining aggravated identity theft and establishing penalty enhancements for the crime.
- October 12 marks the twentieth anniversary of the enactment of the Victims of Crime Act, which has collected $6 billion for services to crime victims.
- Congress enacts the Justice for All Act, which provides substantive rights for crime victims.

2005

- The U.S. Department of Justice established an online national sex offender registry that provides real-time access to public sex offender data nationwide.
- Congress establishes the Victims' Rights Caucus, whose mission is to elevate crime victim issues in Congress without infringing on the rights of the accused.
- The American Bar Association releases *Elder Abuse Fatality Review Teams: A Replication Manual*, which provides guidance for communities that want to establish Elder Abuse Fatality Review Teams.

Source: Adapted and modified from material compiled by the National Victim Center and U.S. Department of Justice Office for Victims of Crime, Victims' Assistance Legal Organization, Inc. (VALOR), and many national, state, and local victim services providers who offered documentation of their key victims' rights landmark activities.

2009

American Recovery Act of 2009 founded, which allowed monies for victim compensation funds and research on victim issues.

2013

Violence Against Women Act re-enacted, which expanded rights for both genders and Native Americans living on reservations.

Victimology-Related Web Sites

Federal Agencies/Resources

Bureau of Justice Assistance	www.ojp.usdoj.gov/BJA
Bureau of Justice Statistics	www.ojp.usdoj.gov/bjs
Center for Substance Abuse Prevention	http://prevention.samhsa.gov
Center for Substance Abuse Treatment	http://csat.samhsa.gov
Centers for Disease Control and Prevention	www.cdc.gov
Federal Bureau of Investigation	www.fbi.gov
Uniform Crime Reports	www.fbi.gov/ucr/ucr.htm
Federal Judicial Center	www.fjc.gov
FirstGov	www.firstgov.gov
International Victimology	www.victimology.nl
National Archive of Criminal Justice Data	www.icpsr.umich.edu/NACJD/index.html
National Clearinghouse for Alcohol and Drug Information	www.ncadi.samhsa.gov
National Criminal Justice Reference Service	www.ncjrs.org
National Domestic Violence Fatality Review Initiative	www.ndvfri.org
National Highway Traffic Safety Administration	www.nhtsa.dot.gov
National Institute of Corrections	www.nicic.org
National Institute of Justice	www.ojp.usdoj.gov/nij
National Institute on Alcohol Abuse and Alcoholism	www.niaaa.nih.gov
National Institute on Drug Abuse	www.drugabuse.gov
National Sex Offender Registry	http://www.nsopr.gov/
Office for Victims of Crime	www.ovc.gov
Office of Community Oriented Policing Services	www.cops.usdoj.gov
Office for Justice Programs	www.ojp.usdoj.gov
Office of Juvenile Justice and Delinquency Prevention	www.ojjdp.ncjrs.org
Office of National Drug Control Policy	www.whitehousedrugpolicy.gov
Office on Violence Against Women	www.usdoj.gov/ovw/
Supreme Court of the United States	www.supremecourtus.gov
THOMAS: Federal Legislation	http://thomas.loc.gov
The United Nations Virtual Knowledge Center to End Violence Against Women and Children	http://www.endvawnow.org/
U.S. Department of Education, Higher Education Center for Alcohol and Other Drug Prevention	www.edc.org/hec
U.S. Department of Education Office of Safe and Drug-Free Schools	www.ed.gov/about/offices/list/osdfs
U.S. Department of Health and Human Services Grantsnet	www.hhs.gov/grants.net
U.S. Department of Health and Human Services: Grants Information	www.hhs.gov/grants/index.shtml
U.S. Department of Health and Human Services, HRSA Funding Opportunities	www.hrsa.gov/grants/default.htm
U.S. Department of Justice	www.usdoj.gov
U.S. Department of State, Bureau of Consular Affairs, Overseas Citizens Services Victim Assistance	http://travel.state.gov/travel/tips/emergencies/emergencies_1748.html

U.S. Department of Veterans Affairs National Center on PTSD	www.ncptsd.org
U.S. House of Representatives Victim's Rights Caucus	www.house.gov/poe/vrc/index.htm
U.S. Parole Commission	www.usdoj.gov/uspc

National Victim-Related Organizations

American Bar Association	
Center on Children and the Law	www.abanet.org/child
Commission on Domestic Violence	www.abanet.org/domviol
Commission on Law and Aging	www.abanet.org/aging
American Humane Association	www.americanhumane.org
American Professional Society on the Abuse of Children	www.apsac.org
Anti-Defamation League	www.adl.org
Asian Task Force Against Domestic Violence	www.atask.org
Battered Women's Justice Project	www.bwjp.org
Child Abuse Prevention Network	http://child-abuse.com
Childhelp USA	www.childhelpusa.org
Child Quest International	www.childquest.org
Child Welfare League of America	www.cwla.org
Concerns of Police Survivors	www.nationalcops.org
Family Violence & Sexual Assault Institute	www.fvsai.org
Family Violence Prevention Fund	http://endabuse.org
Institution on Domestic Violence in the African American Community	www.dvinstitute.org
Justice Solutions	www.justicesolutions.org
Long-Term Care Ombudsman	www.ltcombudsman.org/static_pages/help.cfm
Mothers Against Drunk Driving	www.madd.org
National Alliance to End Sexual Violence	www.naesv.org
National Association of Crime Victim Compensation Boards	www.nacvcb.org
National Association of Social Workers	www.naswdc.org
National Association of VOCA Assistance Administrators	www.navaa.org
National Center for Missing & Exploited Children	www.missingkids.com
National Center for Victims of Crime	www.ncvc.org
National Center on Elder Abuse	www.elderabusecenter.org
National Center on Elder Abuse (Title II)	http://www.nlrc.aoa.gov/Legal_Issues/Elder_Abuse
National Children's Alliance	www.nca-online.org
National Clearinghouse on Child Abuse and Neglect Information	http://nccanch.acf.hhs.gov
National Coalition Against Domestic Violence	www.ncadv.org
National Coalition of Homicide Survivors	www.mivictims.org/nchs
National Court Appointed Special Advocates Association	www.nationalcasa.org

(continued)

National Victim-Related Organizations (*Continued*)

National Crime Victim Law Institute	www.lclark.edu/org/ncvli/
National Crime Victims Research and Treatment Center	www.musc.edu/cvc
National Fraud Information Center	www.fraud.org
National Insurance Crime Bureau	www.nicb.org
National Multicultural Institute	www.nmci.org
National Network to End Domestic Violence	www.nnedv.org
National Organization Against Male Sexual Victimization	www.malesurvivor.org
National Organization for Victim Assistance	www.trynova.org
National Organization of Parents of Murdered Children, Inc.	www.pomc.com
National Resource Center on Domestic Violence	www.nrcdv.org
National School Safety Center	www.nssc1.org
National Sexual Violence Resource Center	www.nsvrc.org
National Victim Assistance Academy (OVC)	www.ojp.usdoj.gov/ovc/assist/vaa.htm
National Victim Assistance Academy (VALOR)	www.nvaa.org
National Victims' Rights Constitutional Amendment Network	www.nvcan.org
National Violence Against Women Prevention Research Center	www.vawprevention.org
Office of Crime Victims Advocacy	www.commerce.wa.gov/Programs/ PublicSafety/OCVA
Parents for Megan's Law	www.parentsformeganslaw.com
Prevent Child Abuse America	www.preventchildabuse.org
Rape, Abuse & Incest National Network	www.rainn.org
Safe Campuses Now	www.safecampusesnow.org
Safe NOW Project, Inc.	http://safenowcproject.org
Security on Campus, Inc.	www.securityoncampus.org
Stalking Resource Center	www.ncvc.org/src
Victims' Assistance Legal Organization (VALOR)	www.valor-national.org
Victims of Violence	www.victimsofviolence.on.ca
Voices for America's Children	www.childadvocacy.org
Witness Justice	www.witnessjustice.org

National Criminal and Juvenile Justice- and Public Policy-Related Associations

Amber Alert	www.amberalert.gov
American Center for Law and Justice	www.aclj.org
American Correctional Association	www.aca.org
American Correctional Health Services Association	www.corrections.com/achsa
American Council for Drug Education	www.acde.org
American Jail Association	www.corrections.com/aja
American Judges Association	http://aja.ncsc.dni.us

American Probation and Parole Association	www.appa-net.org
American Youth Policy Forum	www.aypf.org
Association for Conflict Resolution	www.acrnet.org
Association of Paroling Authorities International	www.apaintl.org
Association of State Correctional Administrators	www.asca.net
Balanced and Restorative Justice Project	www.barjproject.org
Center for Restorative Justice & Peacemaking	http://ssw.che.umn.edu/rip
Center for Sex Offender Management	www.csom.org
Center on Juvenile & Criminal Justice	www.cjcj.org
Coalition for Juvenile Justice	www.juvjustice.org
Community Anti-Drug Coalition Institute	http://cadca.org
Community Justice Exchange	www.communityjustice.org
Community Policing Consortium	www.communitypolicing.org
Correctional Educational Association	www.ceanational.org
Council of State Governments	www.csg.org
Governors Highway Safety Association	www.ghsa.org
Higher Education Center for Alcohol and Other Drug Prevention	www.edu.org/hec
Institute for Law and Justice	www.ilj.org
International Association of Campus Law Enforcement Administrators	www.iaclea.org
International Association of Chiefs of Police	www.theiacp.org
International Association of Reentry	www.reentry.cc/
Join Together	www.jointogether.org
National Association for Community Mediation	www.nafcm.org
National Association for Native American Children of Alcoholics	www.whitebison.org/nanacoa
National Association of Attorneys General	www.naag.org
National Association of Counties	www.naco.org
National Association of Court Management	www.nacmnet.org
National Association of Drug Court Professionals	www.nadcp.org
National Association of Police Organizations	www.napo.org
National Association of State Alcohol & Drug Abuse Directors	www.nasadad.org
National Association of State Judicial Educators	http://nasje.umn.edu
National Association of Women Judges	www.nawj.org
National Center on Addiction and Substance Abuse	www.casacolumbia.org
National Center for Neighborhood Enterprise	www.ncne.com
National Center for State Courts	www.ncsconline.org
National Conference of State Legislatures	www.ncsl.org
National Consortium for Justice Information and Statistics	www.search.org
National Council of Juvenile and Family Court Judges	www.ncjfcj.org
National Criminal Justice Association	www.ncja.com
National District Attorneys Association	www.ndaa-apri.org

(*continued*)

National Criminal and Juvenile Justice- and Public Policy-Related Associations (*Continued*)

National Governors Association	www.nga.com
National Indian Justice Center	www.nijc.indian.com
National Judicial College	www.judges.com
National Juvenile Detention Association	www.njda.com
National Law Enforcement and Corrections Technology Center	www.nlectc.org
National League of Cities	www.nlc.org
National Mental Health Association	www.nmha.org
National Organization of Black Law Enforcement Executives	www.noblenatl.org
National Sheriffs' Association	www.sheriffs.org
Partnership for a Drug-Free America	www.drugfreeamerica.org
Police Executive Research Forum	www.policeforum.org
Police Foundation	www.policefoundation.org
This Power and Control Wheel	http://www.theduluthmodel.org/stop-violence/index.htmls
Restorative Justice Online	www.restorativejustice.org
Restorative Justice Project	www.fresno.edu/pacs/rjp
Southern Poverty Law Center	www.splcenter.org
State Justice Institute	www.statejustice.org
Victims of Crime and Abuse of Power	www.world-society-victimology.de
Victim Offender Mediation Association	www.voma.org

Source: OVC Victims' Rights Week Resource Guide (2006).

INDEX